'The *Routledge Handbook of Asian Demography* is a much needed compendium of data and analysis on the causes and consequences of the population changes underway in Asia. A lineup of superstar contributors carefully examines the commonalities and the diversity of Asia's demographic transitions. The volume will be indispensable not only for students and scholars but also for policy makers, program managers, journalists and others interested in the evolution of population and Asia's development in the twenty-first century.'

Peter J. Donaldson, *President Emeritus, Population Council*

Routledge Handbook of Asian Demography

Home to close to 60 per cent of the world's population, Asia is the largest and by far the most populous continent. It is also extremely diverse, physically and culturally. Asian countries and regions have their own distinctive histories, cultural traditions, religious beliefs and political systems, and they have often pursued different routes to development. Asian populations also present a striking array of demographic characteristics and stages of demographic transition.

This handbook is the first to provide a comprehensive study of population change across the whole of Asia. Comprising 28 chapters by more than 40 international experts this handbook examines demographic transitions on the continent, their considerable variations, their causes and consequences, and their relationships with a wide range of social, economic, political and cultural processes. Major topics covered include: population studies and sources of demographic data; historical demography; family planning and fertility decline; sex preferences; mortality changes; causes of death; HIV/AIDS; population distribution and migration; urbanization; marriage and family; human capital and labour force; population ageing; demographic dividends; political demography; population and environment; and Asia's demographic future.

This handbook provides an authoritative and comprehensive reference for researchers, policymakers, academics, students and anyone who is interested in population change in Asia and the world.

Zhongwei Zhao is a graduate of Peking University and the University of Cambridge. He now works at the Australian National University (ANU). His research interests are broad and he has published widely on historical demography, computer microsimulation, family and kinship, mortality, fertility, famine and environmental impacts on population health.

Adrian C. Hayes was educated in the UK and the US and has combined an active academic career with extensive development experience in Asia. He has taught at major universities in the United States, Canada, China and Nepal, and has worked with the United Nations, the World Bank and other bilateral and international agencies. He is currently based at the ANU.

Editorial Board

Editors

Adrian C. Hayes
Australian National University

Zhongwei Zhao
Australian National University

Editorial Advisors

Monica Das Gupta
University of Maryland

Tim Dyson
London School of Economics

Marwan Khawaja
United Nations Economic and Social Commission for Western Asia

Peter McDonald
University of Melbourne

Geoffrey McNicoll
Population Council

S. Philip Morgan
University of North Carolina at Chapel Hill

Noriko Tsuya
Keio University

Jacques Véron
Institut National d'Études Démographiques

Routledge Handbook of Asian Demography

Edited by Zhongwei Zhao and Adrian C. Hayes

LONDON AND NEW YORK

First published 2018
by Routledge
2 Park Square, Milton Park, Abingdon, Oxon OX14 4RN

and by Routledge
711 Third Avenue, New York, NY 10017

Routledge is an imprint of the Taylor & Francis Group, an informa business

© 2018 selection and editorial matter, Zhongwei Zhao and Adrian C. Hayes; individual chapters, the contributors

The right of Zhongwei Zhao and Adrian C. Hayes to be identified as authors of the editorial material, and of the authors for their individual chapters, has been asserted in accordance with sections 77 and 78 of the Copyright, Designs and Patents Act 1988.

All rights reserved. No part of this book may be reprinted or reproduced or utilised in any form or by any electronic, mechanical, or other means, now known or hereafter invented, including photocopying and recording, or in any information storage or retrieval system, without permission in writing from the publishers.

Trademark notice: Product or corporate names may be trademarks or registered trademarks, and are used only for identification and explanation without intent to infringe.

British Library Cataloguing in Publication Data
A catalogue record for this book is available from the British Library

Library of Congress Cataloging in Publication Data
Names: Zhao, Zhongwei (Professor), editor. | Hayes, Adrian C., editor. |
Container of (work): Goodkind, Daniel. Asia's major demographic data sources.
Title: Routledge handbook of Asian demography / selection and editorial matter, Zhongwei Zhao and Adrian C. Hayes.
Description: New York : Routledge, 2018. | Includes bibliographical references and index.
Identifiers: LCCN 2017032014 | ISBN 9780415659901 (hardback) | ISBN 9781315148458 (ebook)
Subjects: LCSH: Asia–Population. | Demography–Asia.
Classification: LCC HB3633.A3 R68 2018 | DDC 304.6095–dc23
LC record available at https://lccn.loc.gov/2017032014

ISBN: 978-0-415-65990-1 (hbk)
ISBN: 978-1-315-14845-8 (ebk)

Typeset in Bembo
by Out of House Publishing

Contents

List of figures		xiv
List of maps		xix
List of tables		xx
List of contributors		xxv
Preface		xxix

1	Introduction	1
	Zhongwei Zhao and Adrian C. Hayes	
	Historical population change in Asia and the world	1
	Preliminary matters	4
	Demographic transition	5
	Fertility decline	5
	Mortality decline	7
	Migration and population distribution	8
	Family and household formation and the individual life course	10
	Population and development	11

2	Asia's major demographic data sources	15
	Daniel Goodkind	
	Introduction	15
	Censuses	17
	Civil registration	21
	Surveys and surveillance systems	22
	Secondary sources of Asian demographic data	23
	Evaluation of data quality	24
	Conclusion	29

3	The development of population research institutions in Asia	32
	Peter McDonald	
	Background: the development of population research institutions prior to the 1960s	32
	The establishment of population institutions in Asia in the 1960s and 1970s	36

Contents

	Population institutions in Asia from the 1980s onwards	39
	The development of population research in China in the 1980s	41
	The Asian Population Association	41
	The future of population research and training institutions	42
4	Asian historical demography	45
	Cameron Campbell and Satomi Kurosu	
	Introduction	45
	Topics	46
	Demographic behaviours and outcomes	49
	Sources	53
	Conclusion	57
5	Fertility decline	64
	Stuart Gietel-Basten	
	Asia's heterogeneous fertility experience	64
	Exploring the types of fertility decline	72
	Conclusions and the future of fertility in the region	80
6	Family planning policies and programmes	87
	Adrian C. Hayes	
	The family planning revolution in Asia	87
	Programme maturation	93
	Critical issues	95
	Family planning policies and programmes in Asia since the 1994 Cairo conference	99
	The future of family planning in Asia	102
7	Family planning, contraceptive use and abortion	109
	Yan Che and Baochang Gu	
	Introduction	109
	Use of contraception	109
	Abortion	121
	Conclusions and practical implications	128
8	Reproductive health and maternal mortality	131
	Terence H. Hull and Meimanat Hosseini-Chavoshi	
	Introduction	131
	Maternal mortality as the central indicator of reproductive health	131
	Problems of measurement	132
	Rise in skilled birth attendance	136
	The rise in caesarean deliveries	138

	Burdens of reproductive disease	142
	Conclusion	148
9	Son preference, sex ratios and 'missing girls' in Asia	151
	Monica Das Gupta, Doo-Sub Kim, Shuzhuo Li and Rohini Prabha Pande	
	Underlying causes of son preference	152
	Patterns and mechanisms of sex selection and factors associated with increases in selection	156
	The consequences of high child sex ratios: men and women in the marriage market	158
	Factors that help reduce son preference and its manifestations	160
10	Child mortality	168
	Danzhen You, Lucia Hug and Kenneth Hill	
	Introduction	168
	Data sources	169
	Levels and trends in child mortality	170
	Gender gaps in child mortality	175
	Mortality disparities by social-economic status	178
	Risk factors of child mortality	178
	Leading causes of child deaths	180
	Successes and challenges	182
11	Changes in old-age mortality since 1950	190
	Danan Gu, Patrick Gerland, Kirill Andreev, Nan Li, Thomas Spoorenberg, Gerhard Heilig and Francois Pelletier	
	Introduction	190
	Trends in life experience at age 65	190
	Declines in age-specific death rates and their contribution to rising e_{65}	197
	Socioeconomic development and e_{65}	200
	Future prospects	202
	Concluding remarks	203
12	Age patterns and sex differentials in mortality	209
	Yan Yu and Zhongwei Zhao	
	Introduction	209
	Data and their limitations	210
	Mortality trends 1950–2015 and variations across Asia	211
	Age patterns of mortality change	214
	Age patterns of fast or slow mortality change	219
	Sex differentials in mortality change	221
	Discussion	224

Contents

13	Trends in causes of death and burden of diseases	228
	Colin D. Mathers	
	Introduction	228
	Asian data on mortality and causes of death	229
	Trends in disease and injury causes of death	231
	Causes of disability and lost health	236
	Burden of disease	237
	Risk factors and determinants of health	239
	Projections of causes of death to 2050	242
	Conclusions	244
14	HIV/AIDS in Asia	247
	Binod Nepal	
	Background	247
	Data collection developments and limitations	248
	Emergence of HIV in Asia	251
	Cross-national patterns and trends	251
	Affected populations and population groups	255
	Major forces shaping the epidemics	258
	Major efforts in controlling the epidemics	260
	Hopes and challenges	261
15	Population distribution	268
	Christophe Z. Guilmoto and Sébastien Oliveau	
	The changing share of Asia's population in the world	268
	Population densities	273
	The distribution of population across Asia	278
	Conclusion	280
16	The urbanization of low- and middle-income Asia	285
	Mark R. Montgomery and Deborah Balk	
	The demography of urbanization and settlement growth	287
	New and under-studied developments	297
	Climate change and extreme-event risks in urban Asia	301
	Estimates of risk exposure in urban Asia	303
	Conclusions	305
17	Asia's international migration	310
	Graeme Hugo	
	Introduction	310
	Trends in international migration	311
	Feminization of Asian migration	318
	Undocumented migration in Asia	319

Contents

	Migration and development	319
	Policy implications	324
	Conclusion	326
18	Forced and refugee migration in Asia	331
	Mohammad Jalal Abbasi-Shavazi and Ellen Percy Kraly	
	Introduction	331
	Who are forced migrants and refugees?	331
	Studies of forced and refugee migration	334
	Data sources on forced and refugee migration	335
	Levels and trends of forced migration: Asia within a global context	337
	Demographic characteristics of forced and refugee migrants in Asia	340
	Drivers of forced and refugee migration	345
	Summary and conclusions	346
19	Changing marriage patterns in Asia	351
	Gavin W. Jones	
	Kinship systems and marriage arrangement	351
	Trends towards later and less marriage	353
	Issues arising from rising singlehood	358
	Consanguineous marriage	359
	Problems of continued early marriage	361
	Divorce trends	363
	Conclusions	365
20	Family and household composition in Asia	370
	Albert Esteve and Chia Liu	
	Introduction	370
	Background	371
	Data	373
	Household perspective	374
	The individual perspective	376
	Conclusion	384
21	Asia's demographic transition: variations and major determinants	394
	Minja Kim Choe	
	Mortality transition in Asia and its variations	395
	Fertility transition in Asia and its variations	399
	Cultural, political, economic and social conditions of Asian countries	401
	Effects of cultural, political, economic and social conditions on mortality and fertility	403
	Illustrative examples of mortality and fertility transition	408
	Summary and discussion	409

xi

Contents

22	Human capital formation in Asia 1970–2010	412
	Samir KC and Wolfgang Lutz	
	Introduction	412
	Changes in educational attainment 1970–2010	413
	Gender differences	423
	Labour force participation	425
	Conclusion	428
23	The process of population ageing and its challenges	431
	Heather Booth	
	Introduction	431
	Population ageing in Asia: a historical perspective	433
	The challenges of population ageing	443
24	Demographic dividends	456
	Tomoko Kinugasa	
	Introduction	456
	The first demographic dividend in Asia	458
	Capital accumulation, human capital and the second demographic dividend	460
	The second demographic dividend in Asia	463
	Policy implications	466
25	Population and environment in Asia	472
	Adrian C. Hayes	
	Theoretical perspectives on population and environment	473
	Population change, consumption and the environment	474
	Rapid urbanization and the rise of the middle class in Asia	479
	Trends in resource use and environmental indicators	485
	Population change and sustainable development	492
26	Population, the state and security in Asia	499
	Geoffrey McNicoll	
	Scale and statehood	500
	Political counterparts of demographic transition	501
	Relativities and regionalization	503
	Population and international conflict	506
	'Game-changers'	508
	Political demography of Asia's century	510
27	The demographic future of Asia	514
	Wolfgang Lutz and Samir KC	
	Projecting future population size and structure	514

History of population projections for Asian countries and analysis of past errors	515
Defining the assumptions for projecting twenty-first century population trends in Asia	517
Projection results for all of Asia and individual countries	520
Conclusions	527
28 Conclusion	**532**
Zhongwei Zhao and Adrian C. Hayes	
Major demographic trends in Asia in the first half of the twenty-first century	532
Demographic trends and sustainable development in Asia	536
Index	*540*

Figures

2.1	Estimates of under-five mortality (deaths under age five per 1,000 live births) in Kazakhstan by year from various sources	26
5.1	Patterns of fertility in four major world regions, 1920–2010	65
5.2	Rural and urban TFRs for 20 countries, derived from latest Demographic and Health Surveys	67
5.3	Total fertility rates in India and 15 of its major states, 1900–2008	75
6.1	Contraceptive prevalence rate (per cent, left-axis), and total fertility rate (live births, right-axis), Turkey, China, Indonesia and India, 1970–1975 to 2010–2015	92
6.2	Contraceptive prevalence rate (per cent, left-axis), and unmet need (per cent, right-axis), Turkey, China, Indonesia and India, 1970–1975 to 2010–2015	103
7.1	Prevalence of any contraceptive method and modern method in Asian countries/territories	111
7.2	Relationship between contraceptive prevalence rate and total fertility rate in Asia	113
7.3	Contraceptive prevalence rate and total fertility rate in South Korea and Japan, 1990–2010	114
7.4	Contraceptive prevalence rate and total fertility rate in China and India, 1990–2010	114
7.5	Relationship between unmet contraceptive need and total fertility rate in Asia, c.2009	120
7.6	Relationship between country's family planning effort and contraceptive prevalence in Asia, 2009	121
7.7	Association between abortion rate (/1,000 women aged 15–44 in relationship), contraceptive prevalence (/100 women of reproductive age in relationship) and total fertility rate (TFR) in selected Asian countries, 2010–2015	125
7.8	Methods of abortion	126
9.1	Excess female child mortality, China, 1920–1995	153
9.2	Trends in child (<5 year) sex ratios, China, India and South Korea, 1950–2010	154
9.3	Trends in sex ratio at birth, South and West Asia, 1980–2010	154

9.4	Trends in sex ratio at birth, East Asia, 1980–2010	155
10.1	Under-five mortality rates, 1970–2015	171
10.2	Distribution of under-five mortality rate in Asia, 1970, 1990 and 2015	172
10.3	Annual rate of decline in under-five mortality rate and annual rate of change in GDP per capita (per cent) in 1990–2000 and 2000–2015 by countries in Asia	173
10.4	Average annual rate of reduction (per cent) in the neonatal mortality rate, and in the mortality rate from 1 to 59 months, by Asian regions, 1990–2015	175
10.5	Expected female and estimated female and male under-five mortality in Japan and India, 1990–2015	176
10.6	Excess female mortality and ratio of estimated to expected female mortality for countries in Asia with outlying sex ratios and higher female mortality than expected, 1990 and 2015	177
10.7	Under-five mortality rate by wealth quintile, mother's education and residence for countries in Asia, 2005–2013	178
10.8	Under-five mortality rate by birth interval, birth order and age of mother for countries in Asia, 2005–2013	179
10.9	Neonatal mortality rate by birth size for countries in Asia, 2005–2013	179
10.10	Distribution of deaths among children under five in Asia, by cause, 2000 and 2015	181
11.1	e_{65} (both sexes combined) in 1950–1955 and gains from 1950–1955 to 2010–2015 by region and subregion	191
11.2	e_{65} for subregions in Asia and selected regions, 1950–2015	192
11.3	e_{65} (both sexes combined) in Asia by country, 1950–2015	193
11.4	Association between e_{65} and e_0 (both sexes combined) in Asia	194
11.5	Gender difference in e_{65} (years) for subregions in Asia and selected regions	195
11.6	Gender difference in e_{65} (years) in Asia by country, 1950–1955 to 2010–2015	196
11.7	Projected e_{65} from 2015–2020 to 2095–2100 for regions and subregions in Asia	202
12.1	Change in e_0 vs. initial e_0, by time period, females, Asia	212
12.2	Change in e_0 vs. initial e_0, by time period, males, Asia	213
12.3	Change in age-specific death probabilities (% decline), Asian countries grouped by e_0	216
12.4	Contribution of age-specific mortality change to the gain in e_0 (in years), Asian countries grouped by e_0	218
12.5	Sex differences in e_0 (years of life), by female e_0, Asia	222
13.1	Cause-specific death rates, Asian subregions, 2000 and 2012	232
13.2	Age-standardized death rates for major causes, Asian countries, 2012	233
13.3	Leading causes of death, Asia, 2000–2012	234
13.4	Progression through the epidemiological transition in Asia	236

List of figures

13.5	Ten leading causes of years lost due to disability (YLD) in Asia, 2000–2012	237
13.6	YLL and YLD contributions to total DALY rates, Asian subregions, 2000 and 2012	238
13.7	Major cause contributions to DALY rates, Asian subregions, 2012	239
13.8	Projected deaths in Asia from selected causes, 2010–2050	243
13.9	Decomposition of projected changes in annual numbers of deaths in Asia from selected cause groups, 2010–2030	244
14.1	HIV prevalence among adults aged 15–49 years, selected countries of Asia	254
14.2	Adult HIV incidence, selected countries of Asia	254
15.1	Annual population growth per region, 1950–2100	269
15.2	Lorenz Curve of population concentration in four different continents, 2010	280
16.1	Urban percentage of subregional population, low- and middle-income Asian countries, 1950–2050	290
16.2	Urban population growth less rural growth in previous five years, by subregion of Asia, 1950–2050	290
16.3	Urban population growth rates in previous five years, by subregion of Asia	291
16.4	Percentages of India's population, and that of Kerala state, living in census towns, statutory towns and rural villages, according to the census of 2011	297
16.5	Percentage share of de facto and de jure urban residents in China's population, 1970–2010	301
16.6	Urban populations in low-elevation coastal zone (LECZ), inland flood zones and drylands, expressed in terms of total urban residents and in percentages of subregional urban population	304
18.1	Age and sex composition of populations of concern to UNHCR in Syria, Iraq and Pakistan, end of 2015	342
20.1	Average household size by country, Asia 1980–2010	375
20.2	Household composition by age groups, selected Asian countries	375
20.3	Distribution of households by number of members, selected Asian countries	376
20.4	Parental, spousal and filial coresidence by age and sex, India 2004	377
20.5	Age-specific, between-country variability in living alone by sex, selected Asian countries	378
20.6	Age-specific, between-country variability in living with at least one parent by sex, selected Asian countries	379
20.7	Age-specific, between-country variability in living with spouse by sex, selected Asian countries	381
20.8	Age-specific, between-country variability in living with children by sex, selected Asian countries	382
21.1	Trends in life expectancy at birth: world and regions in Asia	396

List of figures

21.2	Distribution of countries in Asia according to the life expectancy at birth for both sexes, selected years between 1950 and 2010	397
21.3	Age-standardized DALYs by three major causes of death and disability in three groups of countries classified by their level of mortality	398
21.4	Distribution of age-adjusted DALYs (per 100,000 population) by three broad categories of causes among Asian countries grouped by level of mortality (High, Medium, Low), 2007	399
21.5	Trends in period total fertility rates: world and regions in Asia	400
21.6	Distribution of countries in Asia according to the total fertility rate, selected years between 1950 and 2010	401
22.1	Changes in the stock of human capital in Asia, as described by the number of persons age 15 and over in six different education categories	414
22.2	Population distribution by age, sex and educational attainment level in Asia, 1970 and 2010	415
22.3	Trends in the proportion of the population aged 15 years and above with no formal education, 43 Asian countries, 1970–2010	416
22.4	Trends in the proportion of the population aged 20–24 years with at least completed lower secondary education	419
22.5	Trends in the proportion of the population aged 25–29 with at least completed upper secondary education	421
22.6	Trends in the proportion of the population aged 30–34 years with tertiary/post-secondary education	422
22.7	Labour force participation rates by age and sex in India in 1971 and 2001	425
22.8	Labour force participation rates by age and sex in Singapore in 1970 and 2008	426
22.9	Labour force participation rates by age and sex in South Korea in 1971 and 2010	427
22.10	Labour force participation rates by age and sex in Indonesia in 1971 and 2010	427
22.11	Labour force participation rates among men and women aged 30–34 years for countries in Asia (latest available year)	428
23.1	Population aged 65+ as a percentage of total population, world regions, 1950–2050	434
23.2	Age-sex structures for selected Asian countries, 2010	435
23.3	Indicators of ageing in Asia and Asian regions, 1950–2010	437
23.4	Percentage aged 65+, populations within Asian regions, 1950–2010	438
23.5	Old-age share of total dependency, by population, 1950 and 2010	442
23.6	Relationship between degree of ageing in 1950 and 2010, old-age share of total dependency and OADR	443
24.1	The first demographic dividend in Asia	459
24.2	Average years of education in Asia	462
24.3	The second demographic dividend in Asia	465
25.1	Social-ecological systems	474

List of figures

25.2	GDP (billion US 2005 dollars, PPP), 20 Asian countries, 1975–2010	476
25.3	Attribution of average annual rate of growth of GDP to average annual rate of growth of population (rPop) and of GDP per capita (rGDP/Pop), Turkey, China, Indonesia and India, 1970s–2000s	478
25.4	Percentage of population residing in urban areas, estimates and projections, 20 Asian countries, 1950–2050	480
25.5	Expenditure classes by per cent of total population and by per cent of total aggregate annual expenditure, Malaysia, China, Indonesia and India, *c.*2005	484
25.6	Total primary energy supply (petajoules), 20 Asian countries, 1975–2010	488
25.7	CO_2 emissions (million tonnes of CO_2), 20 Asian countries, 1975–2010	490
25.8	CO_2 emissions and the Kaya decomposition of 'drivers', Turkey, China, Indonesia and India, 1975–2010	491
27.1	Trends in total population size of Asia 2010 to 2100 according to three shared socioeconomic pathways (SSP) scenarios	521
27.2	Age and education pyramids for the entire Asian continent in 2010 and projected to 2060 under the medium scenario	522
27.3	Projected changes in the percentages above age 65 under the different SSP scenarios in Asia	526
27.4	Projected trends in the percentage of the population above the age of 65 (squares) and above the age when the remaining life expectancy is less than 15 years (circles) for all of Asia over the twenty-first century	527

Maps

5.1	Countries by typology	69
10.1	Under-five mortality and under-five deaths in countries in Asia in 2015	172
15.1	Population density in Asia, 2015	274
16.1	Urban agglomerations of 300,000 population and above in developing Asia, in 2015. Size of circle indicates estimated population (in thousands)	293
16.2	Urbanized areas in the Greater Jakarta region, as indicated by VIIRS night-time lights	295
16.3	India's low-elevation coastal zone and arid regions, with locations of cities indicated in night-time lights imagery	302
17.1	International migration by country of destination, 2013	312
17.2	International migration by country of origin, 2013	313
23.1	Countries of Asia showing change in the median age, 1950–2010	441
23.2	Countries of Asia showing old-age share of total dependency (per cent), Asia, 2010	444
23.3	Countries of Asia showing old-age dependency ratio per 100, 2010	445

Tables

1.1	Regions, countries and territories of Asia, their surface area and population size, 1950, 2015	3
2.1	Estimated population 2015 and projected population 2050, world regions, according to UN Population Division and US Census Bureau	17
2.2	2010 round censuses and vital registration completeness in Asia	19
2.3	Estimated per cent of children under-reported in the 2000 census round of Asia	28
5.1	TFRs of Asian countries and other territories, 1950–2010	70
6.1	Total fertility rate (mean number of live births per woman), major regions of Asia, 1950–1955, 1975–1980 and 2000–2005	88
6.2	Summary statistics describing trends in CPR, 46 countries of Asia, 1970–2015	90
6.3	'Programme effort' (measured as percentage of maximum score possible for each dimension) in government FP programmes, selected countries, 1982 and 1989	96
6.4	Summary statistics describing trends in unmet need for FP, 46 countries of Asia, 1970–2015	101
7.1	Percentage distribution of contraceptive methods by subregions in Asia	116
7.2	Cumulative 12-month discontinuation probabilities per 100 episodes (single decrement life table) for all discontinuation reasons in five Asian countries, by methods	117
7.3	Status at three months after discontinuing any method for method-related reason for five Asian countries (%)	118
7.4	Reasons for non-use among women with unmet need for modern contraception (%) in South Central and South-Eastern Asia	119
7.5	Percentage distribution of grounds on which abortion is permitted (% of countries) in 2009	123
7.6	Estimated number of induced abortions (in millions), abortion rate (per 1,000 women aged 15–44) and percentage of unsafe abortion worldwide, in Asia and by Asian subregion, 1995–2008	124
8.1	Trends in WHO estimates of maternal mortality ratio (MMR, maternal deaths per 100,000 live births), in Asia by region and country, 1990–2015	133

8.2	Trends and differences in estimates of percentage of deliveries attended by 'skilled' personnel in Asia	137
8.3	Trends in estimates of caesarean section deliveries in Asia	139
8.4	Distribution of deliveries by mode of delivery for selected Asian countries derived from a survey conducted in 2007–2008	141
8.5	Number (millions) and rates (per 1,000) of incidence and prevalence for selected STDs in WHO defined regions, 2008	144
8.6	Estimates of average age-standardized death rates (number of deaths per 100,000 persons) for major reproductive cancers, in Asia by region and country, 2011–2015	146
9.1	Child sex ratios (males/females <5 years) for selected regions and countries, 2010	152
9.2	Percentage of men and women age 60+ coresiding with children, by gender of married children, Philippines 1984, Taiwan 1989 and South Korea 1990	155
10.1	Estimated under-five mortality rate and under-five deaths (in thousands) by continent, 1970, 1990 and 2015	170
10.2	Ten countries in Asia with highest proportion (%) of estimated under-five deaths caused by pneumonia, diarrhoea or injury, 2015	182
Appendix Table 10.1	Estimated under-five mortality rate, neonatal mortality rate and annual rate of reduction, 1970, 1990 and 2015	184
Appendix Table 10.2	Sex ratio in under-five mortality, estimated male and female under-five mortality and expected female under-five mortality, 1990 and 2015	186
11.1	Age-specific death rates in 2010–2015 and percentage reduction compared with 1950–1955 by region and subregion of Asia (both sexes combined)	198
11.2	Years gained in e_{65} from 1950–1955 to 2010–2015 and the percentage contribution by age-specific mortality by sex and region and subregion	199
12.1	List of Asian countries and territories by life expectancy (e_0)	217
13.1	Fifteen leading causes of deaths in each of the Asian subregions, 2012	234
13.2	Fifteen leading causes of burden of disease, Asian subregions, 2012	240
13.3	Ten leading risk factors for attributable deaths, Asian subregions, 2012	241
14.1	Total population, number of people living with HIV and HIV prevalence among people who inject drugs and female sex workers, Asia	252
14.2	Differentials in HIV prevalence among women and men aged 15–49 years	257
14.3	Estimated per cent of adults with HIV in need of antiretroviral therapy receiving the treatment (based on WHO 2010 Guidelines), selected countries of Asia, 2012	262
15.1	Various population estimates for Asia during the Holocene	270
15.2	Population, urbanization, growth rates and density: Asian countries	271

List of tables

16.1	Total urban and rural population, low- and middle-income Asian countries, 1950–2050 by subregion	289
16.2	Largest urban agglomerations in 2015, by subregion of developing Asia	294
17.1	International migration in Asia, 1990–2013	312
17.2	Australia, USA, Canada and New Zealand: growth (in thousands) of the Asia-Pacific-born population, 1971–2011	314
17.3	Asian tertiary education international students and their main destinations, 2010	316
17.4	Selected Asian out-migration economies: proportion of international labour migrants who are women	318
17.5	Emigration rates of tertiary-educated by country of origin, c.2000	320
17.6	Main Asian labour exporting countries: workers' remittances relative to exports and imports in US$ million, 1980–2012	322
17.7	Views and policies of Asian governments regarding immigration, 1976–2011	324
17.8	Views and policies of Asian governments regarding emigration, 1976–2011	325
18.1	Persons of concern to UNHCR	333
18.2	Persons of concern to UNHCR by region of asylum, end of 2015	338
18.3	Persons of concern to UNHCR by major region of origin, end of 2015	338
18.4	Persons of concern to UNHCR for top ten countries of asylum in Asia, end of 2015	339
18.5	Persons of concern to UNHCR for top ten countries of origin in Asia, end of 2015	340
18.6	Sex ratio, by age group, of populations of concern to UNHCR for top ten countries of asylum in Asia, end of 2015	342
18.7	Refugees and people in refugee-like situations by top ten Asian countries of origin by major countries of asylum, end of 2015	343
19.1	Trends in singulate mean age at marriage, various Asian countries, 1970–2010	354
19.2	Per cent never married at ages 30–34, various Asian countries, 1970–2010	356
19.3	South Korea, China and Singapore: per cent still single women and men, by age and education, 2010	357
19.4	Teenage marriage: per cent of females ever married at ages 15–19, various countries, 1960–2010	361
19.5	Indonesia and Bangladesh: per cent of women married by exact ages 15, 18 and 20, from 2007 Demographic and Health Surveys	363
19.6	General divorce rates (number of divorces per 1,000 population aged 15+), various countries and regions, 1980–2010	364
20.1	Percentage of children aged 25–29 living with at least one parent, by sex and marital status, selected countries	380

List of tables

20.2	Percentage of persons aged 65+ by sex, living with children, selected Asian countries	383
20.3	Percentage of persons aged 65+, living with married sons or married daughters, selected Asian countries	384
Appendix Table 20.1	Average household size by country, Asia 1980–2010	387
Appendix Table 20.2	Percentage of population residing alone, with at least one parent, with spouse and with at least one child by sex and five-year age group	387
21.1	Asian countries classified by the mortality level in 2005–2010	398
21.2	Cultural, political, economic and social characteristics of the countries in five regions of Asia	402
21.3	Correlation between indicators of mortality and socioeconomic conditions, *c.*2007	405
21.4	Correlation between indicators of fertility and socioeconomic conditions, *c.*2007	405
22.1	Definition of educational attainment categories used in this study	414
22.2	Percentage of population with at least lower secondary education for men and women in the age group 20–39, for Asian countries in 1970, 1990 and 2010	424
23.1	Regions and subregions of Asia and constituent populations	436
25.1	Attribution of average annual rate of growth of GDP to average annual rate of growth of population and of GDP per capita, 20 Asian countries, 1970s–2000s	477
25.2	Expenditure classes by per cent of total population and by per cent of total aggregate annual expenditure, selected developing countries of Asia, *c.*2005	483
25.3	Water resources and water security estimates, 20 Asian countries, *c.*2005	486
26.1	Country population relativities in major world regions, 2014: population size as per cent of population of largest country in region, for the six most populous countries in each region	504
26.2	Population aged 20–40 years in major Asian countries and world regions, estimates and projections (millions), 2010–2050	506
27.1	Baseline errors and projection errors of the 1978 and 1982 UN population projections for six South-East Asian countries	516
27.2	Medium TFR assumptions for China, India and Indonesia according to the 2014 Wittgenstein Centre and the UN 2012 assessment	519
27.3	Projections of total population size (in millions) for world and major regions to 2100 under the medium scenario, SSP2	520
27.4	Trends in total population size (in millions) for individual Asian countries under the most likely medium scenario (SSP2) as well as the rapid development scenario (SSP1) and the stalled development scenario (SSP3)	523

List of tables

27.5 Percentages of women aged 20–39 with at least lower secondary education for all Asian countries for which consistent education data were available for the base year — 525

27.6 Projected trends in the percentages of the population above the age of 65, and above the age when the remaining life expectancy is less than 15 years, Asian countries over the twenty-first century — 528

Contributors

Mohammad Jalal Abbasi-Shavazi, University of Tehran and National Institute of Population Research, Iran

Kirill Andreev, United Nations

Deborah Balk, City University of New York, USA

Heather Booth, Australian National University

Cameron Campbell, Hong Kong University of Science and Technology

Yan Che, Shanghai Institute of Planned Parenthood Research, China

Minja Kim Choe, The East-West Center, USA

Monica Das Gupta, University of Maryland, USA

Albert Esteve, Centre d'Estudis Demogràfics, CERCA, Spain

Patrick Gerland, United Nations

Stuart Gietel-Basten, University of Oxford, UK

Daniel Goodkind, Independent researcher, USA

Baochang Gu, Renmin University of China

Danan Gu, United Nations

Christophe Z. Guilmoto, Institut de Recherche pour le Développement, France

Adrian C. Hayes, Australian National University

Gerhard Heilig, United Nations

List of contributors

Kenneth Hill, Johns Hopkins University, USA

Meimanat Hosseini-Chavoshi, University of Melbourne, Australia

Lucia Hug, United Nations Children's Fund

Graeme Hugo, Formerly University of Adelaide, Australia

Terence H. Hull, Australian National University

Gavin W. Jones, Australian National University and Murdoch University, Australia

Samir KC, Shanghai University, China and Wittgenstein Centre for Demography and Global Human Capital (IIASA, VID/ÖAW, WU), Austria

Doo-Sub Kim, Hanyang University, South Korea

Tomoko Kinugasa, Kobe University, Japan

Ellen Percy Kraly, Colgate University, USA

Satomi Kurosu, Reitaku University, Japan

Nan Li, United Nations

Shuzhuo Li, Xi'an Jiaotong University, China

Chia Liu, Centre d'Estudis Demogràfics, CERCA, Spain

Wolfgang Lutz, Wittgenstein Centre for Demography and Global Human Capital (IIASA, VID/ÖAW, WU), Austria

Colin D. Mathers, World Health Organization

Peter McDonald, University of Melbourne, Australia

Geoffrey McNicoll, Population Council, USA

Mark R. Montgomery, Population Council, USA

Binod Nepal, Independent researcher, Australia

Sébastien Oliveau, Aix-Marseille University, France

Rohini Prabha Pande, Independent consultant, USA

Francois Pelletier, United Nations

Thomas Spoorenberg, United Nations

Danzhen You, United Nations Children's Fund

Yan Yu, University of Canberra, Australia

Zhongwei Zhao, Australian National University

Preface

Asia currently has four-and-a-half billion people living in 51 countries and territories. It has been experiencing an astonishing demographic transition since the mid-twentieth century and is now re-emerging as a global centre of economic and political power. Asian demography has long captivated researchers worldwide. But, among numerous scholarly handbooks published in recent years, none has focused specifically on population change across the whole of Asia. This may be partly due to the considerable difficulties facing anyone who attempts to summarize and compare research findings about such a vast and diverse continent. Asia's populations are highly heterogeneous culturally, religiously, socially, politically and economically, and the availability and comprehensiveness of data about the region's 51 countries and territories are very uneven. Some years ago, however, the editors agreed with Routledge representatives that these challenges are not insuperable and the idea of producing the *Routledge Handbook of Asian Demography* was born.

This undertaking has taken several years to complete, and we want to thank all those who contributed and helped bring the project to completion. First, we want to thank members of the Editorial Board who since the earliest stages of the project have provided sound advice and encouragement. Second, we want to thank all the authors who contributed chapters. We thank them for the hard work they have put into their chapters: many were not only willing to write about those parts of Asia with which they were already well acquainted, but were also prepared to undertake further research so that they could include other parts of Asia with which they were less familiar in their analyses. Furthermore, not only did they write their own chapters, but most of them in addition reviewed and provided comments on other chapters 'neighbouring' their own in the handbook.

Third, we want to acknowledge the contribution of many colleagues who agreed to review individual chapters and provide critical feedback. Peer review is an indispensable element of science and scholarship, and we are grateful to those who generously gave their time to review chapters: Susana Adamo, Sin Yin Alice Chow, Youssef Courbage, Valerie Hull, Jack Goldstone, Helen James, Leiwen Jiang, Siew-Ean Khoo, Christopher Manning, Andrew Mason, Peter Xenos and the editorial board members and authors. We are also grateful to the editorial staff at Routledge, especially Leanne Hinves, Stephanie Rogers, Alexandra Buckley, Helena Hurd, Lucy McClune, Rebecca Lawrence and Georgina Bishop, as well as the copy editor, Goretti Cowley. We thank them for their enthusiastic support for the project, and their patience.

In Canberra, we thank Barbara Edgar, Kim Xu and Qing Guan for research assistance and help with copy-editing and formatting. We also want to thank the School of Demography at The Australian National University for providing financial support and a congenial and supportive environment for the editors as they worked on this handbook over several years.

Preface

Sadly one of our contributors, Graeme Hugo, passed away soon after he submitted a draft version of his chapter. Graeme was an outstanding scholar as well as a good friend and colleague. We are pleased that we are able to include Graeme's chapter in his memory, and we thank Siew-Ean Khoo, one of Graeme's close collaborators, for revising and finalizing his chapter.

Zhongwei Zhao and Adrian C. Hayes

1
Introduction

Zhongwei Zhao and Adrian C. Hayes

Among the countless scholarly handbooks published in recent years this is the first on the demography of Asia. The chapters in this handbook focus on the four-and-a-half-billion people who live in Asia today and their ancestors – especially the extraordinary demographic transition they have experienced since the middle of the last century, the variations in the underlying demographic trends that contribute to their national and subregional differences, and their demographic history. The chapters also include analyses of the causes and consequences of these trends, and population projections describing what the demographic future of Asia might look like. The aim of the handbook is to provide an authoritative and comprehensive reference for researchers, policymakers, students and general readers who are interested in population change in Asia and the world. The purpose of this introductory chapter is to introduce the subject matter and the book. We do not attempt to summarize individual chapters but try to show where they fit into the broader picture as we see it.

Historical population change in Asia and the world

First, what do we mean by 'Asia'? By convention Asia is often defined geographically as a 'major region' or 'continent' which comprises that part of the Eurasian landmass (and adjacent islands) located to the east of an imaginary line drawn through the Black Sea, the Caucasus, the Caspian Sea and north along the Ural Mountains to the Arctic Ocean. This historical construction, dating from the eighteenth century (with precursors going back to the ancient Greeks), is Eurocentric in the residual way it classifies 'Asia' as everything that is not part of Europe.

The United Nations Statistical Division (UNSD) and the United Nations Population Division (UNPD), use a different classification of 'major areas and regions of the world'. Table 1.1 lists the countries and territories of Asia according to this geoscheme and groups them in five regions: Eastern, Southern, Central, South-Eastern and Western Asia, respectively (UNSD 1999). The vast stretch of Russia east of the Urals (otherwise known as 'Northern Asia') is not included as part of Asia in this scheme. In general the present volume follows this UN classification, although different ways of grouping countries and territories are occasionally used due to constraints imposed by data sources, since different sources, including autonomous agencies within the UN system, define Asia differently. Using this UN definition, Asia is still the largest 'major area' of the world in terms of total land area and population size: its surface land area (32 million sq. km) is slightly larger than the second largest (Africa, with 30 million sq. km), and its population (4.4 billion in 2015) is much larger than the second largest (again Africa, with 1.2 billion). Asia accounts for about 23 per cent of the world's total land area. It is estimated that this area accounted for 60 per cent of the world's population in 2015 (UNPD 2015), and about 35 per cent of global GDP (estimated using exchange rates) or 41 per cent (using purchasing power parities) (World Bank 2017).

Asia's share of world population and the global economy have varied considerably through the centuries. According to the detailed historical estimates made by Angus Maddison (2003), in the year AD 1 Asia accounted for 75 per cent of world population and 76 per cent of the global economy, compared to Western Europe's shares of 11 and 11 per cent, respectively (Western Europe here includes Western, Northern and Southern Europe according to Maddison's classification). In AD 1000 the proportions had changed only modestly: Asia's share of world population was 68 per cent and of the global economy 70 per cent; the corresponding proportions for Western Europe were 10 and 9 per cent, respectively. The end of the first millennium was a low point for Europe, and evidence suggests a decline in average living standards in the West. By 1820, however, the picture looks significantly different: Asia still accounts for 68 per cent of world population but only 59 per cent of the global economy, while Western Europe (and its 'Western Offshoots' in North America and Oceania) now account for 14 per cent of world population and 25 per cent of the global economy. The West had pulled ahead, and average living standards in the West were now appreciably higher than in Asia.

Even so it is *after* 1820 that populations and economies around the world change at accelerating rates and living standards between the West and the Rest diverge considerably. During 1820–1950, Asia's share of the global economy shrinks from 59 to 18 per cent, while Western Europe and its offshoots ('the West') increases from 25 to 57 per cent (Maddison 2010). At the same time, Asia's share of world population declines from 68 to 55 per cent, while the West's increases from 14 to 19 per cent. Development in the West had surged ahead, in many ways at the expense of Asia (and other parts of the world) and many Asian countries became colonies of Western powers.

The mid-twentieth century constitutes another turning point in world history, however, and the last 60 years have seen the re-emergence of Asia. With the end of World War II a new international order was established (the 'Pax Americana') that promoted peace, world trade and international collaboration. The post-war period also saw the rise of the Cold War and many regional conflicts, but the new order generally prevailed. Western empires, built up over many centuries and consolidated in the period before World War I, were drastically weakened by the cost and violence of World War II and they were quickly dismantled thereafter. Many previously colonized Asian countries became independent states, especially in the third quarter of the century, and fashioned new paths to development. As a result many experienced, or have begun to experience, unprecedented economic growth and rise in living standards. By 2005, Maddison (2010) estimates Asia accounts for 42 per cent of the global economy (compared to the West's 41 per cent), and 59 per cent of the world's population (compared to the West's 12 per cent). Asia has re-emerged and is now widely regarded as the most dynamic area of the world (ADB 2011; Kupchan 2012; Shie and Meer 2010). It is within this historical and global context that many Asian countries commenced what demographers call their 'demographic transition'.

The main focus of the handbook is on population change in Asia since the mid-twentieth century, especially the years 1950–2015. The authors of different chapters approach their respective topics using different approaches and different scales, and have had to adjust their coverage depending on the availability of reliable data. At the same time, the heterogeneity of Asia is a

Table 1.1 Regions, countries and territories of Asia, their surface area and population size, 1950, 2015

Region, country or territory	Surface area (000 km²)	Population (thousands) 1950	Population (thousands) 2015	Population multiplier, 1950–2015
Asia	31,915	1,394,018	4,393,296	3.2
Eastern Asia		666,586	1,612,287	2.4
China	9,597	544,113	1,376,049	2.5
China, Hong Kong SAR	1.1	1,974	7,288	3.7
China, Macao SAR	<0.1	196	588	3.0
China, Taiwan Province		7,562	23,381	3.1
Japan	378	82,199	126,573	1.5
Mongolia	1,564	780	2,959	3.8
North Korea	121	10,549	25,155	2.4
South Korea	100	19,211	50,293	2.6
South-Eastern Asia		164,900	633,490	3.8
Brunei	5.8	48	423	8.8
Cambodia	181	4,433	15,578	3.5
Indonesia	1,911	69,543	257,564	3.7
Laos	237	1,683	6,802	4.0
Malaysia	330	6,110	30,331	5.0
Myanmar	677	17,527	53,897	3.1
Philippines	300	18,580	100,699	5.4
Singapore	0.7	1,022	5,604	5.5
Thailand	513	20,710	67,959	3.3
Timor-Leste	15	433	1,185	2.7
Vietnam	331	24,810	93,448	3.8
Southern Asia		493,443	1,822,974	3.7
Afghanistan	653	7,752	32,527	4.2
Bangladesh	148	37,895	160,996	4.2
Bhutan	38	177	775	4.4
India	3,287	376,325	1,311,051	3.5
Iran	1,629	17,119	79,109	4.6
Maldives	0.3	74	364	4.9
Nepal	147	8,483	28,514	3.4
Pakistan	796	37,542	188,925	5.0
Sri Lanka	66	8,076	20,715	2.6
Central Asia		18,131	67,314	3.7
Kazakhstan	2,725	6,703	17,625	2.6
Kyrgyzstan	200	1,740	5,940	3.4
Tajikistan	143	1,532	8,482	5.5
Turkmenistan	488	1,211	5,374	4.4
Uzbekistan	447	6,945	29,893	4.3
Western Asia		50,957	257,231	5.0
Armenia	30	1,354	3,018	2.2
Azerbaijan	87	2,896	9,754	3.4
Bahrain	0.8	116	1,377	11.9
Cyprus	9	494	1,165	2.4

(continued)

Table 1.1 (Cont.)

Region, country or territory	Surface area (000 km²)	Population (thousands) 1950	Population (thousands) 2015	Population multiplier, 1950–2015
Georgia	70	3,527	4,000	1.1
Iraq	435	5,719	36,423	6.4
Israel	22	1,258	8,064	6.4
Jordan	89	449	7,595	17.0
Kuwait	18	152	3,892	25.6
Lebanon	11	1,335	5,851	4.4
Oman	310	456	4,491	9.8
Palestine	6	932	4,668	5.0
Qatar	12	25	2,235	89.4
Saudi Arabia	2,207	3,121	31,540	10.1
Syria	185	3,413	18,502	5.4
Turkey	784	21,238	78,666	3.6
U. Arab Emirates	84	70	9,157	130.8
Yemen	528	4,402	26,832	6.1

Sources: UNPD (2015) and UNSD (2016).

constant challenge for the analyst. Several chapters commence at the highest scale comparing Asia with other main areas or regions of the world, then look more closely at variations among the main regions of Asia, and finally discuss the variations among different countries and territories. Depending on the particular characteristic or variable being examined, there is often far more variation within the units being compared than there is between them. Most chapters stress that Asia is not only vast, but is also enormously diverse and heterogeneous.

Preliminary matters

Following this chapter there are three more dealing with preliminary matters. Demographic analysis depends on quantitative measurement of populations and their properties. Chapter 2 on demographic data by Daniel Goodkind reviews where these data come from and the relative strengths and weaknesses of the different sources, especially population censuses and household surveys. Data quality is a major concern for demographers, although it is often ignored in popular accounts of population trends. One recent positive development is the greater accessibility of large quantities of data to researchers and the public accompanying the introduction of digital technology.

Generating, compiling and analysing reliable data requires technical skills and other resources. The scientific study of Asia's population would never have reached the level of maturity that it has if a range of population research and training centres had not emerged, as well as governments and philanthropic organizations prepared to fund them. Peter McDonald, in Chapter 3, describes how this came about. A plethora of relevant institutions and capabilities were developed in Asia after World War II, with many preconditions fashioned before the war. McDonald discusses the contributions of Western and international agencies to this effort.

Although the handbook focuses on the period since the mid-twentieth century, recent population trends cannot be fully understood without some appreciation of how Asia's population changed in earlier centuries. The chapter by Cameron Campbell and Satomi Kurosu provides such an account, at least for parts of Eastern, South-Eastern and Southern Asia where lineage genealogies and other needed historical records are available. Historical demography, as a discipline, has flourished since the 1950s, and researchers have uncovered fascinating findings that prompt further questions. For example, why (as appears to be the case) was marital fertility lower in China than in Europe for many centuries? If, as Campbell and Kurosu argue, this reflects deliberate behaviour on the part of Asian couples, does this then suggest that they were 'predisposed' to the rapid fertility decline that occurred in the second half of the twentieth century?

Demographic transition

The central concept used by demographers to understand the broad contours of population change in modern times is that of 'demographic transition'. The term refers to 'the decline in mortality and fertility from the high rates characteristic of premodern and low-income societies to the low rates characteristic of modern and high-income societies' (Casterline 2003: 210). The transition first started in Western and Northern Europe around AD 1800 and spread gradually to other areas. The transition accelerated in the twentieth century and took place throughout the world (Lee 2003; Levi-Bacci 2007; Notestein 1945). As a result life expectancy at birth for the world population more than doubled from less than 30 to about 70 years during the twentieth century, and the average number of births a woman can expect during her lifetime (total fertility rate, or TFR) fell from 5.7 to 2.4 births per woman (UNPD 2015). Because of these unprecedented population changes and their profound implications, the twentieth century has been tagged the 'demographic century' (Caldwell 1999; see also Dyson 2010). Already by the middle of the century the transition was largely completed in the developed countries of Europe, Northern America and Oceania, and life expectancies at birth had reached 67 years or higher, and TFRs had fallen to less than 3.4 births per woman. In contrast, in the countries of Asia the long-term mortality and fertility declines had only just begun.

In Chapter 21 Minja Choe shows how the timing and speed of the demographic transition vary greatly across the regions and countries of Asia in the second half of the twentieth century. The overall decline of mortality has been 'spectacular', with average life expectancy increasing by more than 28 years (from 42 to 70) during 1950–2010; the decline in fertility has been 'even more spectacular', with the TFR declining by 3.6 births, from 5.8 births in 1950–1955 to 2.2 births in 2005–2010. While Asia's demographic transition started late relative to the West's, it caught up rapidly. In recent years many of the lowest fertility rates in the world have been recorded in Eastern Asia, and by 2005–2010, 20 out of 51 Asian countries and territories had TFRs below replacement level (of 2.1 births); seven of those recorded TFRs below 1.5 births. At the same time, TFR remained above four births in five countries. Choe shows how these remarkable trends and cross-country variations can be understood by examining how they are interrelated with economic development, urbanization, public health programmes, the status of women, cultural factors and income.

Fertility decline

All the Asian populations listed in Table 1.1 have grown significantly during 1950–2015. In most cases this is due mainly to the fact that each year there are more births than deaths. How many more depends on the relative timing and pace of the decline in mortality and fertility respectively. With more countries reaching ultra-low fertility the pattern is beginning to change: Japan now has more deaths than births each year and its population growth rate is already negative. It is important to study and understand the declines in vital rates in some depth. Chapters 5 through 9 examine different aspects of fertility decline, and Chapters 10 through 14 examine mortality decline.

Stuart Gietel-Basten, in Chapter 5, outlines the basic dimensions of fertility decline in Asia, and examines the underlying dynamics by identifying different groups of countries with different patterns in the timing and speed of their declines. The different groups, therefore, represent different 'types of fertility transition', including 'demographic forerunners', 'slow fallers', 'rapid fallers still in transition' and 'laggards'. Gietel-Basten shows how this typology is fruitful in the way it encourages us to think of different clusters of factors being important for analysing different types of fertility decline rather than attempting to apply the same set of explanatory variables to all cases.

One of the distinctive features of post-World War II fertility declines in Asia compared with earlier declines in the West is the role of governments and national family planning programmes. This aspect is examined in Chapters 6 and 7. In Chapter 6, Adrian Hayes reviews the policies and programmes that were adopted in many Asian countries, and how these policies and programmes evolved over several decades in responses to successes and failures, and to growing public criticism. Yan Che and Baochang Gu focus on the behavioural aspects of birth control in Chapter 7, and on abortion. They discuss the relationship between contraceptive prevalence and fertility level in a population, although other factors such as age at marriage and breastfeeding practices can also affect the birth rate. Demographers have developed sophisticated models for estimating the relative influence of different 'proximate determinants'. Che and Gu also examine which contraceptive methods are commonly used across Asia.

Over the past 60 years there has been a major shift in emphasis in many quarters regarding public support for national family planning programmes. In the 1960s and 1970s, a lot of the motivation was couched in terms of reducing the population growth rate. By the 1980s and 1990s, more emphasis was placed once again on the health benefits for women and children (as had been the case with the early pioneers of family planning, like Margaret Sanger in the early decades of the twentieth century). The 1994 UN Conference on Population and Development codified this shift in emphasis in its *Programme of Action*. Terence Hull and Meimanat Hosseini-Chavoshi examine trends in various indicators of reproductive and sexual health since the early 1990s. They focus on maternal mortality, whether mothers giving birth are assisted by trained birth attendants, the use of caesarean section, and sexually transmitted diseases, as well as several other conditions associated with reproductive health. Studying maternal health brings home the point that the vital events of birth and death are often intimately interconnected. The lack of reliable data for many countries makes systematic comparison difficult, but it is clear that although the sexual and childbearing lives of women are on average improving in Asia there are still serious shortcomings in the provision and quality of reproductive health services.

Another issue relating to both fertility decline and reproductive health is the recent increase in sex ratio at birth in some Asian populations. The last chapter in this cluster by Monica Das Gupta, Doo-Sub Kim, Shuzhuo Li and Rohini Prabha Pande examines this issue. It arises in parts of Asia where there is not only son preference but where it is 'strong enough to result in substantial levels of prenatal/postnatal sex selection'. The underlying causes are shown to be primarily cultural constructs, not economic. In areas where there is such a strong son preference, the issue is exacerbated by a rapid decline in fertility, and the result is an unusually high sex ratio (males to females) at birth. The authors examine both the causes and the consequences of this phenomenon. Longer-term effects include a 'marriage squeeze' where men cannot find brides, which in turn leads to an increase in marriage migration. They also point out that other social transformations underway in Asia (urbanization, increasing education) tend to undermine son preference, as appears to have happened in South Korea.

Mortality decline

Mortality decline, like fertility decline, takes place at different times, at different speeds and sometimes in different patterns across the populations of Asia. When mortality declines it does not do so evenly across all ages at the same time. The first chapter on mortality, Chapter 10, by Danzhen You, Lucia Hug and Kenneth Hill, examines the decline in mortality during the first five years of life. The Millennium Development Goal (MDG) number 4 called for reducing under-five mortality by two-thirds between 1990 and 2015. Although under-five mortality declined in all regions of Asia only Eastern Asia reached the goal (with a decline of 80 per cent), largely as a result of improvements in China. Interestingly, for Asia as a whole the decline accelerated during 2000–2015. The risk of dying is highest in the neonatal period (first 28 days); as under-five mortality declines the proportion of neonatal deaths rises, and although children in Asia on average still face a higher risk of dying than those in the West, the proportion of under-five deaths that occur in the neonatal period is now virtually the same as in Europe (around 55 per cent). The authors uncover a range of variations in the pattern of mortality decline across the regions and countries of Asia, and examine their association with household characteristics and risk factors (including age of mother, birth intervals, etc.). The evidence confirms the vital role played by government programmes and a strong health sector in instances of rapid mortality decline.

In Chapter 11, Danan Gu, Patrick Gerland, Kirill Andreev, Nan Li, Thomas Spoorenberg, Gerhard Heilig and Francois Pelletier discuss mortality decline at older ages by examining changes in the expectation of life at age 65. In early stages of mortality decline, most of the gains in life expectancy are due to reduced mortality among infants and children. In advanced stages, additional increases in life expectancy at birth will be due to reduced mortality at old ages. An Asian who lived to be 65 years old in the early 1950s could expect to live on average another 9.7 years; someone who survived to age 65 in 2010–2015 can expect to live another 16.7 years. Gu et al. analyse this change in depth and show how this average gain in longevity in Asia compares with similar gains in other major regions of the world, and how it varies across the regions and individual countries within Asia itself. In general the principle holds: the higher the life expectancy at age 65 at the beginning of a period of long-term mortality decline, the larger the proportion of any gain during that period that can be attributed to reductions in age-specific mortality rates at the ages 75 and above, and the lower the proportion attributable to reduced mortality at ages 65–74.

Yan Yu and Zhongwei Zhao examine age patterns and sex differentials in mortality for all age groups in Chapter 12. Studying how mortality decline is distributed across different age categories for different populations, and how these patterns differ by sex, provides a useful diagnostic tool for deepening our understanding. Yu and Zhao identify three clusters of countries in terms of common patterns of mortality decline over the last 60 years (which they divide into two 30-year periods) defined relative to the central tendency. The 'vanguard' countries and territories (including Japan, Hong Kong, Israel, Macao, Singapore, South Korea, Taiwan and Lebanon) have faster than expected improvements; a second cluster comprises the eight former Soviet republics (in Central Asia and the Caucasus) which in the 1950s had advanced mortality levels similar to the first cluster but which have not subsequently made the expected gains; and the third cluster of 'laggards' comprises countries mostly in Southern and South-Eastern Asia where improvements have been slow. The authors conclude that 'the persistence over time and geo-clustering of disadvantages point to environmental and systemic socioeconomic factors that hinder mortality improvement'.

Colin Mathers extends the analysis of mortality decline in Chapter 13 by looking at trends in the causes of death, and in the changing 'burden of disease' across Asia's regions and countries.

Overall during the last 60 years mortality rates from infectious diseases have declined and more deaths are now due to non-communicable diseases (NCD), but as we have already seen the long-term decline in mortality (and the accompanying 'epidemiological transition') is at different stages in different populations of Asia. Thus while the five leading causes of death in 2012 in Eastern Asia are stroke, ischaemic heart disease, chronic obstructive pulmonary disease (COPD), lung cancer and liver cancer, in Southern Asia they are ischaemic heart disease, COPD, stroke, lower respiratory infections and diarrhoeal diseases. Using data from the 2010 Global Burden of Disease study as well as other sources, Mathers also identifies the leading causes of the 'burden of disease'. Knowing not only the age- and sex-specific death rates for a population but also the causes and underlying risk factors is obviously vital information for the policymaker, and as Mathers notes there is increasing stress on the NCDs of adulthood and injuries in the post-2015 development agenda in Asia. However, infectious diseases are still a problem and cannot be ignored.

In Chapter 14, Binod Nepal looks at the special case of HIV/AIDS. Although the aetiology, prevention and treatment of this disease are much better understood today than when it was first identified in the 1980s, the rate of new infections in the first decade of the present century was still increasing in Bangladesh, Indonesia, Kazakhstan, Kyrgyzstan, the Philippines and Sri Lanka. As Nepal explains, infection levels are generally low in national populations in Asia but can be very high among certain population groups such as people who inject drugs, female sex workers, men who buy sex and men who have sex with men. An emerging feature of epidemics in Asia is a narrowing of the gender gap.

Migration and population distribution

The third and final factor which, in addition to fertility and mortality, determines the size of populations is migration. The UN estimates that there were 244 million international migrants (defined as people who are living in a country other than their country of birth) in the world in 2015, up from 173 million in 2000, and 76 million of them lived in Europe, 75 million in Asia and 54 million in Northern America (UNPD 2016). However during 2000–2015, Asia added more international migrants (26 million) than any other major area. The extraordinary growth of some of the small oil-producing countries in Western Asia in Table 1.1 (last column) is due to net immigration. International migrants comprise 58 per cent of the population of Kuwait, 75 per cent of Qatar and 88 per cent of United Arab Emirates. Of major areas in the world Asia is also by far the largest source of international migrants: 104 million in 2015, up from 68 million in 2000; Europe is the next largest, accounting for 62 million in 2015.

Within Asia, over the eleven five-year periods from 1950–1955 to 2010–2015, negative net migration rates (more people moving out of the country than in) are recorded for at least ten periods in Bangladesh, Indonesia, Nepal, the Philippines, Sri Lanka, Syria and Turkey; China, Iraq, State of Palestine and Yemen each have nine. For the same 11 periods, positive net migration rates are recorded for at least ten periods in Bhutan, Brunei Darussalam, Israel, Kuwait, Qatar, Saudi Arabia and United Arab Emirates; countries and territories with nine include Japan, Singapore, Bahrain, Hong Kong and Macao.

Chapters 15–18 examine various aspects of population movement and spatial distribution. Humans have been moving across the landscape for millennia. In modern times the population growth accompanying the demographic transition has stimulated migration on a far larger scale. In Chapter 15, Christophe Guilmoto and Sébastien Oliveau describe the broad features of the resulting spatial distribution of population in Asia. For centuries Asia has had not only the largest population among major areas of the world but also the most densely populated. By 1800, its population density was around 17 persons per sq. km, and by 2000 (around the time when Asia's share of world population peaked) it reached 130 or more.

In ancient times Asia's population concentrated along the major river basins, especially the Tigris and Euphrates in West Asia, the Ganges and Brahmaputra Rivers on the Indian subcontinent and along the Yellow River (Huang He) in China. The availability of fresh water and fertile soils allowed these regions to support large and dense populations and to become 'cradles of civilization': it is noteworthy that all the major 'world religions' originate in Asia. These densely-settled populations along major rivers are still a key feature of Asia's population distribution today, but Guilmoto and Oliveau identify two more of increasing significance in recent decades. One is the *desakota* characteristic of many high-density areas in Asia, where it is virtually impossible to describe them as either 'rural' or 'urban' because so many of the common urban and rural functions are mixed together. Population concentration in Asia cannot be fully understood in terms of a conventional Western understanding of urbanization. The other is the growing concentration of population along the coast, especially in China and Vietnam, due to migration to these areas to support export-oriented industry. This is a major concern since many of these areas are highly vulnerable to climate change.

The most prominent kind of migration in Asia since 1950 is rural–urban. In 1950 the level of urbanization in Asia was low: the urban population of 245 million accounted for only 18 per cent of the total population, significantly lower than the world average of 30 per cent (UNPD 2014). Since then, Asia's urban population has increased to 2.11 billion (in 2015), or 48 per cent of total population. This growth is faster than that for all other major areas except Africa. There has also been an increase in the number of large urban agglomerations. In 1950, among the 30 largest urban agglomerations in the world 17 were in Europe and Northern America, and only eight in Asia (and only two of those had populations of more than five million); in 2015, 17 of the world's 30 largest urban agglomerations were in Asia, and all of them had more than 10 million people. Asia's rapid urbanization is a major factor in the region's rapid development, but at the same time there is considerable variation in the level, pace and form. Urbanization rates are very high (80 per cent and over) in Bahrain, Hong Kong, Israel, Japan, Lebanon, Kuwait, Macao, Qatar, Saudi Arabia, Singapore, South Korea and United Arab Emirates; meanwhile Afghanistan, Cambodia, Nepal, Sri Lanka and Tajikistan are still very rural, with urban populations below 30 per cent.

Mark Montgomery and Deborah Balk illustrate the complexity of urbanization in Asia in Chapter 16 and describe some of the obstacles researchers face due to lack of standardization in official definitions of 'urban' among countries, and to low access to the disaggregated census data needed to study residents' involvement in urban structures across administrative units, both horizontally and vertically. More importantly, they demonstrate the analytical power that comes with exploiting new sources of data such as LANDSAT and other satellite imagery to identify built structures and land use in order to map the form of urban agglomerations. Since the rapid pace of urbanization is expected to continue for several decades, it is important to develop a richer understanding of urbanization and test common assumptions. One common view, for example, is that urbanization in Asia is dominated by the growth of megacities; this may be true in some cases, but Montgomery and Balk remind us that for Asia's urban population as a whole (in 2015) only 11.9 per cent live in megacities while 41.1 per cent live in small cities and towns below 300,000.

Graeme Hugo gives a comprehensive account of international migration in Chapter 17, covering trends in permanent migration, South-North migration, temporary labour migration, student migration, North-South and South-South migration and marriage migration. Reasons for migration at the individual level often do not fit into a single category, but the different types of migration flows do show distinct patterns. The scale and diversity of migration has increased over the last 60 years and Hugo points to the increasing involvement of governments seeking to influence the patterns (including regarding return migration). He also reviews the role of migration in development and the growing awareness that a diaspora can contribute to development of the sending country in ways extending beyond remittances.

Mohammad Jalal Abbasi-Shavazi and Ellen Percy Kraly discuss the special cases of forced and refugee migration in Chapter 18. According to the UN High Commissioner for Refugees (UNHCR), there were 64 million 'persons of concern' in the world at the end of 2015, 29 million of whom were from Asia and about 10 million of whom were officially designated as refugees or people in refugee-like situations. Refugees are by definition international migrants. The category growing the fastest in the early twenty-first century is internally displaced persons (IDPs), up from 4 million in 2003 to 38 million in 2015. Data reported by the UNHCR can be particularly problematic, however, since both data collection on the ground and subsequent reporting are often poorly coordinated. Abbasi-Shavazi and Kraly discuss the data limitations. Countries in Asia with the most persons of concern are Syria, Iraq, Pakistan, Yemen and Turkey, but the numbers involved are very fluid and changeable. Overall Afghanistan appears to have generated the largest number of refugees in recent decades, with flows beginning in 1979: in 2012 one out of every four refugees in the world was from Afghanistan, most of whom were located in Pakistan and Iran. More recently the war in Syria has meant that that country by the end of 2015 presents the most persons of concern, with the UNHCR recording more than 11 million.

Family and household formation and the individual life course

So far we have focused on population change at the aggregate level. These processes also have profound effects on the life courses of individuals, and on the shared experiences of the families and households in which they live. The average woman in a pre-transition population, for example, has a higher risk of experiencing the death of her parents while she is still a child than her modern post-transition counterpart, and also a lower chance of sharing time with her grandparents. Furthermore, because of the high fertility regimes of pre-transition populations she will most likely devote many more years of her life to childbearing and childrearing than her modern counterpart, and a proportion of this time will be in a sense 'wasted' since some of her children will die in childhood (Reher 1995). A smaller part of her life will be spent in activities unrelated to human reproduction.

Gavin Jones, in Chapter 19, examines how marriage patterns have changed in Asia since the middle of the last century. The overall trends are towards later and less marriage, and towards more divorce, but as always it is only when we examine carefully the full range of variation in the levels and rates of change across regions and countries that we can fully appreciate the complexity of factors affecting these trends. Arranged marriage systems in Southern Asia have proved far more durable than was the case in Eastern and South-Eastern Asia, for example, and in some parts of Pakistan consanguineous marriage appears to be on the rise. The convergence towards the nuclear family pattern hypothesized by modernization theorists in the 1950s and 1960s has not been confirmed. A new theory will need to take into account many factors, including what Jones calls 'the many existential dilemmas facing increasingly educated women in East Asia'.

Albert Esteve and Chia Liu discuss changes in family composition and household structure in Chapter 20. Living arrangements are determined by demographic, economic and cultural factors. Using census microdata, Esteve and Liu track individuals' living arrangements throughout their life courses. They find that intergenerational coresidence is relatively stable during 1980–2010 and remains a distinctive feature of Asian family life, even though the average household size is declining due to lower fertility. From an individual perspective, sex differentials are (as expected) striking in some countries and not in others: nearly 60 per cent of married men in patriarchal India, for example, live with their parents and only 1 per cent of married women; such differentials are far less pronounced, or absent altogether, in bilateral countries of South-Eastern Asia. The main new dynamic noted by Esteve and Liu is that living arrangements are increasingly 'shaped by the desires and needs of both the older and younger generations' rather than by cultural filial obligations alone.

Population and development

The historical record shows that a number of societal changes invariably accompany the demographic transition, either as cause or effect or both. Demographers and other population scientists have long been interested in these interrelationships (Birdsall et al. 2001; Dyson 2010; McNicoll 2003; World Bank Group 2016). The interrelationships between the demographic transition and urbanization, mentioned above, are a good example. While towns and cities emerged in pre-demographic transition societies the level of urbanization was low, and it is only in concert with demographic transition that high levels of urbanization emerge. The two processes reinforce one another in multiple ways and there are no empirical cases of countries with high levels of urbanization without significant progress through the demographic transition, and similarly there are no cases of countries that have passed through the demographic transition without also reaching a high level of urbanization. Nevertheless, the shape these relationships assume in specific cases varies depending on a range of exogenous factors. Another prominent example is the way the demographic transition transforms the age structure of the population, and this has a major impact on family and other social institutions, including the economy (Bloom and Williamson 1998; Bloom et al. 2000; World Bank Group 2016).

Following Chapter 21, on the demographic transition (already mentioned), the remaining chapters (22–28) in the handbook explore the implications of the transition for broader social and environmental systems. Chapter 22 by Samir KC and Wolfgang Lutz analyses population change and human capital formation. One implication of fertility decline is that parents, and society at large, can invest more in the human capital development of each child: there is a trade-off of 'quantity' for 'quality' (Becker 1960; Becker and Lewis 1973; Blake 1981). Developed countries spend a lot on average on each child's upbringing and formal education, and the rapidly developing countries of Asia have started to do the same. Lutz, KC and colleagues have developed a powerful methodology (using multidimensional demographic back projections) to estimate the stocks and flows of human capital in a population, using years of completed schooling as a simple yet robust indicator (Lutz et al. 2014). They have also used this method to construct mutually consistent time series data sets for most countries in the world. In Chapter 22, KC and Lutz discuss their findings for Asia for the period 1970–2010. In their approach, the change in stock of human capital is viewed as the result of changes in the flows represented by cohorts moving up the age pyramid. This captures conceptually the nexus between 'demographic transition' and 'education transition' and allows systematic comparison of the sequencing of educational expansion among different countries. Comparing India and China, for example, or Pakistan and Iran, highlights the different outcomes that can be achieved through implementing different education policies. There is a synergy between the two transitions in that education (especially of girls) tends to reduce fertility, and at the same time lower fertility facilitates higher educational investment per child. While the population of Asia doubled during the 40-year period, the increase in human capital is even more dramatic, and the differences between countries are striking.

In a closed population, changes in mortality and fertility will have a determinate effect on the population age structure, and this in turn impacts on social and economic institutions. These are discussed in the next two chapters. Heather Booth explains in Chapter 23 how the underlying population dynamics of the demographic transition produces 'population ageing' in the form of a 'structural transformation from a youthful population with a large proportion in childhood or young adulthood to a mature population with increased proportions at middle and older ages'. In 2010, the proportion of Asia's population 65 or older was still only 7 per cent (compared to 17 per cent in Europe), but those Asian countries that experienced rapid fertility decline 30 or 40 years ago are now experiencing rapid population ageing. Booth examines population ageing across regions and countries using four different indicators, and discusses the implications for families, governments and the elderly. Evidence suggests that the system of filial obligations in Eastern Asia (where population ageing is most advanced) is 'adapting' to changing circumstances, but public policy will need to change to, and soon. The working generation is increasingly 'squeezed' between their financial obligations towards their parents (who are living longer) and their children (who are increasingly expensive).

Tomoko Kinugasa examines the impact of changing age structure on the economy in Chapter 24. Growth in GDP per capita can be decomposed into growth in the economic support ratio (ratio of producers to consumers) and productivity per producer (GDP per worker). As a population goes through the demographic transition, there will be a period when the proportion in the working ages is unusually high, and this, other things being equal, is conducive to growth of the first component: this constitutes the so-called 'first demographic dividend'. Eventually the population ages further and the proportion of elderly increases to unprecedented levels (as discussed by Booth). If this stimulates people to save for their old age and their savings are invested in physical and human capital, this will then improve productivity. This constitutes a 'second demographic dividend', due to changing age structure impacting the savings ratio. Kinugasa explains the theory and presents estimates of the magnitude and timing of both dividends for most countries of Asia.

In Chapter 25, Adrian Hayes examines how population change in Asia is impacting the natural environment and basic life support systems. Asian populations are making accelerating demands on natural resources partly because they are growing, and partly because with rapid development (especially in the early stages) the demand per capita is increasing rapidly too. This dynamic is clarified by looking at the environmental impact of urbanization and the 'rise of the middle class'. The environmental pollution produced by this dynamic threatens population health, and more broadly the viability of Asia's long-term development, unless policies and practices are changed so as to be better aligned with principles of sustainability. There are welcome examples of this happening (notably in China), but recent reports on climate change stress the increasing urgency of shifting to sustainable development paths.

Geoffrey McNicoll examines how population change can affect the security and governance of states. Internally, for example, a change in age structure that presents a 'youth bulge' can either produce a demographic dividend that turbo-charges the economy, or angry demonstrations of unemployed young people that bring down the government, depending on circumstances. Another view common in some quarters is that the rise of the middle class will foster more liberalization in Asian countries. McNicoll checks such views on population change and the exercise of state power against the available evidence; the questions raised warrant more thorough research. One central question is, as populations grow larger which state governance functions are easily scalable and which are not? Internationally, different rates of growth of national populations implies a change in the ranking of countries by demographic weight, and when factored in with economic growth this will impact on international strategic relationships within Asia and its subregions.

Chapter 27, by Wolfgang Lutz and Samir KC, discusses how the demography of Asia might change over the rest of the twenty-first century. This is not so speculative as it may at first seem to some readers. Many population trends are long term and they change course relatively slowly; we already have some information on the 85 and over population in 2100, for instance, since they are already born (in 2015 and before). Lutz and KC use 'expert opinion' to set some of the parameters in their projections, so their results (as they explain) vary from those presented by the UN Population Division. Moreover their projections are 'three dimensional': they include level of educational attainment, as well as age and sex. Their projections of total population size for individual countries and for Asia as a whole tend to be slightly lower than those of the UN, in part because of the way they have taken into account the effect of increasing education on fertility. Their conclusion is 'there is little doubt that Asia as a whole will experience an end to population growth over the course of the twenty-first century'.

Taken as a complete set, the chapters in this book make a strong case for the argument that demographic change will play a central role in the continuing rise and development of Asia. Even so, more analysis and better data are needed in order to take full advantage of this insight. It is our sincere hope that a deeper understanding of the interrelationships between population change and development will be forthcoming, and that this understanding will be used to help fashion a more prosperous and sustainable future for all the people of Asia.

References

Asian Development Bank (ADB) (2011) *Asia 2050: Realizing the Asian Century*. Manila: ADB.
Becker G. S. (1960) 'An economic analysis of fertility'. In Universities-National Bureau (ed) *Demographic and Economic Change in Developed Countries*. New York: Columbia University Press. Pp. 209–240.
Becker, G. S. and H. G. Lewis (1973) 'On the interaction between the quantity and quality of children'. *Journal of Political Economy*, 81(2): S279–S288.
Birdsall, N., A. C. Kelley and S. Sinding (eds.) (2001) *Population Matters: Demographic Change, Economic Growth and Poverty in the Developing World*. New York: Oxford University Press.
Blake, J. (1981) 'Family size and the quality of children'. *Demography*, 18(4): 421–442.
Bloom, D. E., D. Canning and P. N. Malaney (2000) 'Demographic change and economic growth in Asia'. In C. Chu and R. Lee (eds.) *Population and Economic Change in East Asia. Population and Development Review*, Supplement, 26: 257–290.
Bloom, D. E. and J. G. Williamson (1998) 'Demographic transitions and economic miracles in emerging Asia'. *World Bank Economic Review*, 12: 419–455.
Caldwell, J. C. (1999) 'Population: explosion or implosion?' *Australian Quarterly*, (July–August): 28–31.
Casterline, J. (2003) 'Demographic transition'. In P. Demeny and G. McNicoll (eds.) *Encyclopedia of Population*. New York: MacMillan Reference USA. Pp. 210–216.
Dyson, T. (2010) *Population and Development: The Demographic Transition*. London: Zed Books.
Kupchan, C. A. (2012) *No One's World: The West, the Rising Rest and the Coming Global Turn*. Oxford: Oxford University Press.
Lee, R. (2003) 'The demographic transition: three centuries of fundamental change'. *Journal of Economic Perspectives*, 17(4): 167–190.
Levi-Bacci, M. (2007) *A Concise History of World Population*, Fourth Edition. Oxford: Blackwell Publishing.
Lutz, W., W. P. Butz and S. KC (eds.) (2014) *World Population and Human Capital in the Twenty-First Century*. Oxford: Oxford University Press.
Maddison, A. (2003) *The World Economy: A Millennial Perspective*. Paris: OECD.
Maddison, A. (2010) 'Statistics on world population, GDP and per capita GDP, 1–2008 AD'. Available from: www.ggdc.net/maddison/oriindex.htm.
McNicoll, G. (2003) 'Population and development'. In P. Demeny and G. McNicoll (eds.) *Encyclopedia of Population*. New York: MacMillan Reference USA. Pp. 226–234.

Notestein, F. W. (1945) 'Population: the long view'. In T. W. Schultz (ed.) *Food for the World*. Chicago: University of Chicago Press.
Reher, D. (1995) 'Wasted investments: some economic implications of childhood mortality patterns'. *Population Studies*, 49(3): 519–536.
Shie V. H. and C. D. Meer (2010) 'Is this the Asian Century? China, India, South Korea and Taiwan in the age of intellectual capitalism'. *Journal of Contemporary Asia*, 40(1): 1–21.
United Nations, Department of Economic and Social Affairs, Population Division (UNPD) (2014) *World Urbanization Prospects: The 2014 Revision*. CD-ROM Edition.
United Nations, Department of Economic and Social Affairs, Population Division (UNPD) (2015) *World Population Prospects: The 2015 Revision*. Available from: https://esa.un.org/unpd/wpp/DataQuery/.
United Nations, Department of Economic and Social Affairs, Population Division (UNPD) (2016) *International Migration Report 2015*. New York: UN.
United Nations Statistics Division (UNSD) (1999) 'Standard country or area codes for statistical use (M49)'. Available from: https://unstats.un.org/unsd/methodology/m49/.
United Nations Statistics Division (UNSD) (2016) *Statistical Yearbook*. New York: UN.
World Bank Group (2016) *Global Monitoring Report 2015/2016: Development Goals in an Era of Demographic Change*. Washington, DC: World Bank.
The World Bank (2017) 'World Development Indicators'. Available from: http://data.worldbank.org/data-catalog/GDP-ranking-table.

2
Asia's major demographic data sources

Daniel Goodkind

Introduction

Over the past several decades, most countries in Asia have reported profound changes in population size, structure and geographic distribution. These changes are said to have had fundamental implications for every aspect of everyday family life and social organization. They have also affected patterns of public and private spending.

Yet how do we know that such changes have actually occurred? What data exist that might confirm them? How easy is it to identify, locate and obtain such data? And do different sources of data all point to similar conclusions? These may seem like dull questions, but they are fundamental for researchers and other observers, underpinning our understanding of changes in the populations of Asian nations.

This chapter attempts an overview of major sources of Asian demographic data. Two broad data types are distinguished. The first are the primary data provided by those who actually collect them (Shryock and Siegel 1976). The collection of such primary data can be very expensive (Bryan 2004). Providers of primary data may be government agencies, non-governmental organizations and many others. The most comprehensive sources of primary data on human populations are typically national censuses. In addition to censuses, demographic data are often provided through continuous vital registration systems, surveys and surveillance systems, as well as a variety of smaller-scaled collection efforts. The socioeconomic diversity of the Asian region is mirrored by the differing availability of such primary data for each country.

In addition to primary data, the other major category is secondary data, which includes compilations of primary data or derived estimates based on primary data and/or other sources of information. Although this chapter notes some key compilations of primary data, the discussion of secondary data focuses on major sources of derived estimates. Such derivations often entail adjustments to primary data. The process of making such adjustments is often tricky and is typically preceded by an assessment of the quality, completeness and representativeness of the data in question. Such assessments are often one of the most challenging tasks faced by a provider of statistics.

This chapter also reviews a variety of methods for evaluating the quality of demographic data sources. These include consistency checks, indirect estimation techniques and the demographic balancing equation – a simple accounting system requiring that population change equal births minus deaths plus net migration. Cohort component projection methods (to be discussed below), which are based on the balancing equation, are valuable not only for providing future demographic profiles of a society, but also for providing a tool for demographic analysis of the past and present. The chapter concludes by considering issues of access. Although some sources of demographic data in Asia have been available for many decades in paper format, access to many newer sources has been vastly improved through digital technology. This access offers unprecedented opportunities to researchers.

A couple of important qualifications delimit the scope of this chapter. Given that the sources of demographic data available for the Asian region can differ markedly from place to place, the discussion makes no attempt to provide an encyclopedic reference of data sources specific to every country or territory. Nor will it attempt to identify sources relevant to all topics that may be of interest to all subfields of demography. The discussion and references focus on the major data sources related to the demographic variables of the balancing equation (population, births, deaths and migration), with some reference to other substantive topical areas, such as education, ethnicity and labour force.

The reference section includes a list of online sources to help readers access many of the major Asian data sources described in the following pages. The links cover multiple Asian societies and include official data collected by government authorities, data collected by non-governmental agencies and research groups, estimates of demographic parameters based on analysis of or adjustments to primary sources and compilations of the above.

The Asian region is home to some of the world's oldest demographic record taking. In ancient times, official population counts were undertaken in regions ranging from China and Japan in Eastern Asia to ancient Babylon and Israel in Western Asia. Such official population counts were often taken to ensure the stability and survival of the ruling establishment and provide records relevant for taxation, military recruitment or controlling unrest. The present-day collection of statistics is obviously more comprehensive and technologically sophisticated, yet it still often reflects both cultural patterns and concerns of the ancients. For instance, China's *hukou* system of household registration is designed to both enumerate, monitor and control population movements (Chan and Buckingham 2008), not unlike systems of centuries ago. Although many official records of ages past have been lost, researchers have been extremely resourceful in identifying sources from which demographic data might be recreated to bring the past back to life. (Chapter 4 reviews some of these historical sources and related techniques of analysis.)

As we fast forward to the present day, perhaps the most basic question to begin with is about data sources for estimating Asia's population size. Censuses attempt a complete accounting of country populations, and a simple compilation of Asia's census counts might provide a starting point for estimating its population. However, despite their comprehensive scope, reported census counts provide at best an estimate of what an actual population is. The quality and accuracy of each census count requires careful demographic analysis based on prior censuses and other available sources of data. Moreover, not all countries conduct censuses regularly, and even those that do may enumerate in different years. Thus, a simple compilation of reported census counts, while providing a ballpark figure of Asia's population, may not be accurate.

In recent decades, only two organizations have regularly conducted and updated detailed demographic analyses on a country-by-country basis – the Population Division of the United Nations and the Population Division of the US Census Bureau. Table 2.1 shows 2015 population estimates by each organization for the major geographic regions of the world. All in all, these two independent sources provide remarkably similar estimates – in 2015, the world population

Table 2.1 Estimated population 2015 and projected population 2050, world regions, according to UN Population Division and US Census Bureau

World region	Estimated population, 2015 (billions)	Projected population, 2050 (billions)
Asia	4.385	5.164
Africa	1.166	2.393
Europe	0.743	0.709
Oceania	0.039	0.057
North America	0.361	0.446
Latin America and the Caribbean	0.631	0.782
World Total	**7.325**	**9.551**

Source: United Nations (2012).

World region	Estimated population, 2015 (billions)	Projected population, 2050 (billions)
Asia	4.348	5.190
Africa	1.151	2.242
Europe	0.744	0.708
Oceania	0.037	0.049
North America	0.357	0.441
Latin America and the Caribbean	0.617	0.747
World Total	**7.253**	**9.376**

Source: US Census Bureau (n.d.) *International Database*. Available from: www.census.gov/population/international/data/idb/informationGateway.php (accessed February 2015).

is estimated at 7.3 billion, while Asia's population is estimated to be 4.3–4.4 billion. Population estimates by other organizations and the popular media often quote statistics from one of these two sources.

We will shortly provide more details about demographic analysis and the cohort component methodologies that underlie the estimates in Table 2.1. First we turn to the primary data sources in Asia that provide the foundation of demographic research. As we do, it is useful to keep in mind a key difference in the statistics provided by different areas of the United Nations. The UN Statistical Division compiles primary data from official demographic statistics, while the UN Population Division provides estimates based on demographic analysis; these estimates may not match official statistics.

Censuses

Most countries in Asia take periodic censuses that attempt to count the entire population. In many countries, the interval between censuses is 10 years, but that interval may vary, as does the year within the decade in which censuses are conducted. The 2010 census round is reckoned to include censuses taken from 2005–2014. Of the 50 countries and territories that the United Nations lists within the Asian region, 43 had taken a census in the 2010 round as of August 2014 (Table 2.2). Prior to the 2010 census round, the United Nations Economic and Social Commission for Asia and the Pacific (ESCAP) organized regional meetings to help statistical agencies plan and develop their censuses.

Among Asian countries with 50 million people or more, the only one not to conduct a census was Pakistan. Of the 4.3 billion people estimated to reside in Asia, roughly 95 per cent were recorded in a census from the 2010 round. Six countries, for various reasons, did not conduct a census (Afghanistan, Iraq, Lebanon, Pakistan, Syria and Uzbekistan), even though some had planned to do so.

Table 2.2 indicates the date at which the 2010 round censuses were conducted. Among some notable regional patterns, many countries in Southern Asia take censuses in years ending in a one (Bangladesh, India, Iran, Nepal and Sri Lanka), perhaps mirroring a long-standing tradition dating back to 1881 – the date of India's first complete census (ORG 2010–2011). In contrast, almost half of countries in South-East Asia take the census in years ending in zero (Malaysia, Indonesia, Thailand, Singapore and Timor-Leste). Table 2.2 also indicates whether the census was officially designed as de jure or de facto. A de facto census counts all people present in the country at the time of the census, both usual residents and visitors. A de jure approach counts all usual residents, whether or not they are present in the country at the time of the census. In countries with substantial migration, de facto and de jure approaches may produce quite different results. Most subregions of Asia exhibit a mixture of these two approaches, although the de facto approach tends to be more common in Central and Western Asia.

The method through which the population is enumerated also varies. In India, for instance, the census interviews were all face-to-face, with mostly local teachers serving as enumerators. That approach was chosen in part due to the relatively high rate of illiteracy, which prevents many respondents from filling out the census questionnaire on their own. In Thailand, most of the census enumeration was also based on face-to-face interviews, although there were also options to respond by phone, the Internet or by mailing the census form back by standard post. In Singapore, the 2010 census was compiled largely from administrative records, which contain basic information about the age and sex of residents. Among those selected to be surveyed for additional information about social and economic characteristics, almost 38 per cent responded via the Internet, as opposed to those responding by telephone (46 per cent) or through a personal visit (16 per cent; Wei 2011).

Evaluation of census data completeness generally takes one of two forms. One involves a post-enumeration survey (PES), which is a re-enumeration of a sample of the census population by a select group of highly trained and experienced enumerators and a matching of such sampled individuals to information from the original census enumeration (United Nations 2010a). The advantage of this method is that it can provide details about types of 'coverage error' (undercounts, overcounts and the net error) as well as 'content error' (erroneous responses to particular questions) and can do so at lower geographic levels. The disadvantage of a PES is its substantial cost as well as the planning and technical resources needed if it is to be implemented successfully. Among the limited number of countries in Eastern, Southern and South-East Asia taking a PES and reporting the results, net coverage error in the 2000 census round was no higher than 6.7 per cent in the Philippines and 5.3 per cent in Nepal (United Nations 2010b). In the 2010 census round, it was no higher than 4.0 per cent in Thailand and 3.6 per cent in Indonesia (United Nations 2014).

The second basic form of census evaluation is demographic analysis, which provides a comparative standard based on other available information. The limitations of demographic analysis of a census are that it typically only addresses national counts (sometimes splayed across broad social categories), can only indicate net errors, and, since it typically involves population projections, it is not appropriate for all questions asked in a census (e.g. those related to housing). The great advantage of demographic analysis is that it is far cheaper to implement than a PES.

The United Nations (2008) provides a list of guidelines for the key topics and questions that should be addressed in a census. Although questions about the age and sex of the population are

Table 2.2 2010 round censuses and vital registration completeness in Asia

Region country/territory	2010 round censuses per region, date/type of each census*	Vital registration completeness*
ASIA (50)	44	29 C, 9 U, 10 other, 2 n.a.
Central Asia (5)	4	4 C, 1 U
Kazakhstan	25 Feb – 6 Mar 2009 f	C
Kyrgyzstan	24 Mar – 3 Apr 2009 f	C
Tajikistan	21–30 Sept 2010 f	U
Turkmenistan	15–26 Dec 2012 f	C
Uzbekistan	n.a.	C
Eastern Asia (7)	7	5 C, 2 I
China	1 Nov 2010 j	I
China, Hong Kong, SAR	30 Jun – 2 Aug 2011 j	C
China, Macao, SAR	12–26 Aug 2011 f	C
Democratic PR Korea	1–15 Oct 2008 j	I
Japan	1 October 2005 j	C
Mongolia	11–17 Nov 2010 f	C
Republic of Korea	1–14 Nov 2005 j	C
Southern Asia (9)	7	3 C, 1 U, 3 I, 2 n.a.
Afghanistan	n.a.	n.a.
Bangladesh	15 Mar 2011 f	U
Bhutan	30–31 May 2005 f	I
India	9–28 Feb 2011 f	n.a.
Iran	24 Oct – 13 Nov 2011 j	C
Maldives	21–28 Mar 2006 f	C
Nepal	22 June 2011 j	I
Pakistan	n.a.	I
Sri Lanka	27 Feb – 21 Mar 2011 j	C
South-Eastern Asia (11)	11	5 C, 3 U, 3 n.a.
Brunei	20 Jun – 3 Jul 2011 f	C
Cambodia	3 Mar 2008 f	U
Indonesia	1–31 May 2010 j	n.a.
Lao PDR	1–7 Mar 2005 j	n.a.
Malaysia	6 Jul – 22 Aug 2010 j	C
Myanmar	1 April 2014 f	U
Philippines	1 Aug 2007 j	C
Singapore	30 Jun 2010 j	C
Thailand	1 Sep – 31 Oct 2010 j	U
Timor-Leste	11–25 Jul 2010 f	n.a.
Vietnam	1–15 Apr 2009 j	C
Western Asia (18)	15	9 C, 4 U, 3 mix of C/U, 2 n.a.
Armenia	12–21 Oct 2011 f	C
Azerbaijan	13–22 Apr 2009 j	C
Bahrain	27 Apr 2010 j	C
Cyprus	1 Oct 2011 j	C
Georgia	Planned 5–19 Nov 2014 f	C
Iraq	n.a.	U
Israel	1 Oct 2005 f	C

(continued)

Table 2.2 (Cont.)

Region country/territory	2010 round censuses per region, date/type of each census*	Vital registration completeness*
Jordan	30 Nov – 10 Dec 2015 f	C (births) U (deaths)
Kuwait	21 Apr – 31 May 2011 f	C
Lebanon	n.a.	C
Oman	12 Dec 2010 f	U
Qatar	21 Apr – 5 May 2010 f	C
Saudi Arabia	28 Apr – 12 May 2010 f	n.a.
State of Palestine	1–16 Dec 2007 f	C (births) U (deaths)
Syrian Arab Republic	n.a.	U
Turkey	3 Oct – 30 Nov 2011 j	C (births) U (deaths)
United Arab Emirates	5–6 Dec 2005 f	n.a.
Yemen	Planned 7–17 Dec 2014 f	U

Notes: *For censuses, an 'f' indicates de facto and 'j' indicates de jure. For vital registration, 'C' indicates estimates of 90 per cent or more complete, 'U' indicates less than 90 per cent complete, 'I' indicates that the estimates are considered reliable based on other sources of information; 'n.a.' indicates information not available.
Sources: Census information from United Nations Statistics Division, available from: http://unstats.un.org/unsd/demographic/sources/census/censusdates.htm. Vital registration estimates from United Nations (2014).

universal in population censuses, other questions that go beyond these primary demographic identifiers show considerable diversity throughout the world. Censuses may ask about each individual's marital status, occupation, education, ethnicity, language, religion and other characteristics, in addition to questions that may pertain to the household itself (physical structure of the residence, whether they own or rent, availability of running water, etc.).

As an example of the diversity of such questions, consider ethnicity, which provides a measure of social identification. In a review of international questionnaires, Morning (2008) found that roughly two-thirds of countries in Asia asked a question about such social identification in their 2000 census rounds. Among those that did, 'ethnicity' was the term most often used in the question that was asked. The second most common term was 'nationality'. In contrast, while the terms 'race' or 'indigenous/tribe' were not used in any of the Asian censuses reviewed, all other regions of the world had at least some countries that used those terms.

There is even some diversity in the universal questions about age and sex, albeit more limited. In regard to age, some countries ask only about age itself, some ask only about birth dates (which are used to calculate age), while others ask about both. The questions and categories for sex tend to be more uniform (either male or female), although the most recent round of Asian censuses exhibited a notable expansion of the sex category. India in its 2011 census became the first country in the world to allow a third 'other' category for individuals who did not wish to be recorded as either male or female, and Nepal's 2011 census followed suit by allowing a third sex in its listing of household members.

The amount of data released from population censuses varies from society to society and across the census rounds. Typically, data releases may include a basic report as well as summary profiles of key topics and basic statistics – distribution of the population by age and sex, education levels, ethnic composition and regional patterns. Census results may be published through reports or compilations of statistical tables. These are sometimes available in both paper and electronic format, the latter through websites of the statistical agency conducting the census. Some of the data in these reports come in a fixed format, while others permit users some flexibility to extract data organized in a specific way. Those seeking key tabulations from censuses (e.g. populations broken down by age and sex) without adjustment may also turn to the United Nations Demographic Yearbook (published every year by the UN Statistics Division), which is available online. Note that population estimates available from the United Nations Population Division are typically derived from demographic analysis and thus may not match the official estimates.

Some countries take samples from their censuses to permit advanced statistical analysis. These individual-level or 'microdata' sources are sometimes made available for public use. For those interested in obtaining such data (or comparing different microdata sources), a convenient resource is the Integrated Public Use Microdata Series (IPUMS). The catalogue in this series currently lists 18 Asian societies for which at least one census microdata sample is available.

Civil registration

Civil registration, the results of which are also referred to as vital registration, provides an ongoing record of basic demographic events, such as births, deaths and marriages. According to the United Nations Statistical Division,

> Civil registration is defined as the continuous, permanent, compulsory and universal recording of the occurrence and characteristics of vital events pertaining to the population as provided through decree or regulation in accordance with the legal requirements of a country. Civil registration is carried out primarily for the purpose of establishing the legal documents provided by the law. These records are also a main source of vital statistics. Complete coverage, accuracy and timeliness of civil registration are essential for quality vital statistics.
> *(United Nations Statistics Division, n.d.)*

The government ministries bearing legal responsibility for civil registration vary from country to country. Within Asia, the ministries typically bearing that responsibility are (in descending order of frequency) the Ministries of Interior, Justice and Health (IIVRS 1995). Once created for the mentioned legal purposes, such records are sometimes compiled into vital statistics by a different agency – the most common in Asia being the Ministries of Health, Planning and Interior. Vital statistics provide critical snapshots of social and health characteristics as well as the factors contributing to population change and family formation. In some countries, vital registration may only cover a portion of the population, bounded by a particular geographic space. In others, vital registration covers a specific sampling of areas.

To what extent do the events recorded by vital statistics systems cover the number of such events that actually occur? The United Nations provides an assessment of the completeness of coverage of vital statistics on a country-by-country basis in its periodic Population and Vital Statistics reports. A summary of that assessment for the Asian region is provided in Table 2.2 (right-hand column). Sometimes country authorities themselves provide such assessments of completeness at the time that they submit such statistics for inclusion in the United Nations Demographic Yearbook. Assessments may be based on a variety of comparative methods and demographic analysis. For vital registration estimates that are not derived from civil registration itself, but rather 'official estimates from censuses, sample surveys or demographic analysis' (United Nations 2014), an 'I' is used to indicate when those estimates are considered to be reliable.

Based on such assessments, of the 50 countries in Asia, vital registration is considered 'C' (complete) in 26 of them (and in another three in the case of births but not deaths). The proportion of those estimated to have complete vital registration is highest in Eastern Asia, where there were no instances of 'U', and Central Asia, where four out of five recorded a 'C'. Completeness is lower in Southern, South-East and Western Asia.

Surveys and surveillance systems

Demographic and Health Surveys (DHS)

Demographic and Health Surveys (DHS) have been conducted since the 1980s under the auspices of the US Agency for International Development (USAID), with additional contributions from other donors and participating countries. The goal of such surveys has been to provide data on population, health and nutrition to better monitor conditions and evaluate the effect of programme interventions. These surveys typically include five to ten thousand households, although some samples can be much larger. Standard question modules typically address fertility, child mortality, knowledge and practice of family planning, and nutrition.

In some countries, such as Bangladesh, a DHS has been taken every three to four years, but they have been less frequent in most other countries. DHS efforts have been undertaken in 19 countries in Central, Southern and South-East Asia. Some countries have adapted standard questionnaires or included other modules depending on their specific needs. Other surveys have focused on a particular thematic topic, such as HIV/AIDS indicators, health services or maternal mortality. Thematic reports of each survey are publicly available, as are the underlying data.

One of the strengths of the DHS approach is that it can provide data that are nationally representative in a compact time frame. Yet at lower geographic and administrative levels (two or more levels below the nation), results may not be available or statistically representative.

Multiple Indicator Cluster Surveys (MICS)

Multiple Indicator Cluster Surveys (MICS) have been organized by the United Nations Children's Fund (UNICEF) since the mid-1990s. Successive rounds have been taken about every five years since 1995, with about 50 or 60 countries included in each round. About 20 countries in Asia have been included in at least one round.

MICS typically cover such topics as health, education, child protection, vaccination and disease prevalence. Modules and questions are often chosen to complement other data collection efforts, such as the DHS. Specialized questionnaires have been developed for households, women and children, with recent additions developed for men. Some results of the fourth round of 2009–2010 are available. MICS organizers are interested to increase the frequency to every three years.

As is the case for DHS, an advantage of the MICS surveys is that they can fill gaps in knowledge left unaddressed by other large surveys and can produce quality estimates. Interpretation of results can be challenging due to the varying contents of questionnaires and sample representativeness.

Health and demographic surveillance systems (HDSS)

Health and demographic surveillance systems (HDSS) are designed to monitor households and individuals over time within a specific geographic subarea. Several dozen sites exist, primarily in Africa and Asia, under a global network known as INDEPTH (International Network for the Demographic Evaluation of Populations and Their Health). Some prominent examples of HDSS sites in Asia include Matlab (Bangladesh), Filabavi (Vietnam), Kanchanaburi (Thailand) and Vadu

(India). HDSS sites typically begin by taking a census of all the individuals within that area with basic characteristics (age, sex, marital status, access to health and sanitation systems, etc.).

Following this initial census, data on births, deaths and migration are recorded in subsequent rounds of data collection to monitor basic demographic changes in the area. Other information related to marital events, pregnancy and employment may also be collected. The frequency of monitoring varies widely from system to system. The advantage of HDSS over other survey systems is that the same group of individuals is monitored over time. Such 'longitudinal' data on individuals and individual households may yield more robust findings than periodic randomized surveys, even if the results may not be fully representative of national conditions.

Sample Vital Registration with Verbal Autopsy (SAVVY)

Another approach that provides detailed information on causes of death in developing areas is Sample Vital Registration with Verbal Autopsy (SAVVY). This approach relies on a structured interview with surviving family members of a deceased which asks about the symptoms and circumstances of the events preceding the death. Separate questionnaires are typically used for different broad age groups, where causes of death may differ substantially (e.g. infants and children, maternal deaths, etc.). Medical experts then assess each 'verbal autopsy' to determine the cause of death in line with guidelines from the World Health Organization. The design of SAVVY systems varies based on resources and local circumstances. They can provide one-off estimates at a particular point in time (e.g. as a survey rider attached to a national census) or yield estimates over time in a specified area where there is ongoing registration (see references). The latter approach has been applied in several Asian societies – SAVVY tools are part of the routine data collection for mortality statistics in sample registration systems in India, China and rural Iran. Such systems help to improve understanding of mortality risks and to better target health interventions.

Other data collection efforts by institutions and individuals

In addition to the many sources of data noted above, an ever-expanding variety of primary data sources may be available from non-governmental organizations, academic institutions and individual researchers. One prominent category includes longitudinal surveys, such as Family Life Surveys in Malaysia and Indonesia, the China Longitudinal Healthy Longevity Survey, and the China Health and Retirement Longitudinal Study. Another category includes collected thematic reports from the research community, such as the growing sex ratio imbalances in Asia (e.g. Attané and Guilmoto 2007). Of course, the results of smaller-scale data collection efforts and fieldwork also dot the literature published in academic journals and the popular media.

Secondary sources of Asian demographic data

As noted earlier, secondary data are data presented or analysed by someone other than the person collecting them. Many of the sources just discussed are primary data, but such data are often disseminated by other users in broader compilations or reports, which are technically considered secondary sources. Some of the key compiled demographic data sources for Asia have already been identified above and/or are listed in the references. Examples include much of the data provided by the United Nations Statistical Division, which focuses on disseminating, without adjustment, the primary data collected by national statistical organizations.

It is not uncommon, however, to find secondary sources in which primary data have been adjusted, reprocessed, reorganized, extrapolated or otherwise re-mixed to meet the specific interests of the secondary observer. Examples can be found throughout the academic literature, the popular press and in the publications of both public and private organizations (including sometimes in the reports of primary data producers). There are also secondary data sources that blend both primary and secondary data and/or estimates. For instance, the demographic data available from the Population Reference Bureau's World Population Data Sheet comes from many of the primary data sources listed earlier (vital statistics, censuses, official statistical yearbooks, etc.), but also from derived estimates provided by such organizations as the United Nations Population Division and the US Census Bureau, which often differ from official estimates (to be further described below). Similarly, ESCAP's Statistical Yearbook for Asia and the Pacific (2013) is compiled from a variety of sources including other United Nations agencies, the World Bank, the World Health Organization, the Asian Development Bank and others.

In the evaluation of data quality, which will be discussed further in the next section, the issues one faces are often the same whether one is using primary or secondary data. However, a special challenge in the evaluation of secondary data concerns citation and documentation of sources (Stewart and Kamins 2012). In addition to the (already) substantial slate of questions that one should think through regarding primary data sources, users of secondary data should consider the extent to which primary data may have been altered. Further, whenever a secondary source draws from another secondary source, this requires another evaluative link in the chain leading back to the primary source. Unfortunately, the documentation of this chain is not always complete. For example, a secondary researcher may cite the exact source from which they find a demographic statistic (e.g. an article, expert or a report), yet that source may actually be drawing the statistic from another source.

Evaluation of data quality

As should be clear from above, primary and secondary sources of demographic data for Asia are increasingly plentiful and, with modern technologies, many of them can be easily accessed from the comfort of one's home or office. Stewart and Kamins (2012) recommend asking six questions about each source: (1) What was the purpose of the data collection? (2) Who collected the data? (3) What data were collected? (4) When were the data collected? (5) How were the data collected? (6) How consistent were the data with other sources?

It is useful to keep such general questions in mind amidst the expanding mass of accessible sources. In particular, when estimates of the same demographic parameter differ from one source to another – as they often do – how can one decide which estimate (and underlying source) is most reliable? This section considers the evaluation of demographic data quality. Three broad categories of evaluative techniques are considered – consistency checks, indirect estimation and the demographic balancing equation (including cohort component projections). These methods are illustrated using examples from the Asian region.

Consistency checks

When estimates of a demographic parameter (e.g. population size, births, rate of change, etc.) differ from one source to the next, perhaps the first question to ask is whether the assembled estimates all compare 'apples to apples' (the exact same parameter, in the same geographic unit, during the same time period, etc.). Next, a key step in assessing the consistency of such estimates is to plot them on a graph. Such plots provide a simple tool for visualizing consistency, which is a critical element of data quality analysis all by itself.

A helpful illustration of consistency checks is provided by the United Nations Interagency Group for Child Mortality Estimation (IGME), a consortium of the United Nations Children's Fund, the World Health Organization, the United Nations Population Division and the World Bank. The UN IGME's child mortality estimation database provides country estimates of neonatal, infant and under-five mortality from household surveys, population censuses and vital registration systems. The estimates are then plotted, with historical time on the x-axis (Figure 2.1). The result is referred to as a 'spaghetti graph' where each source is represented by a separate strand that may cover multiple years. The graphed estimates sometimes reveal considerable diversity due to errors, lack of representativeness or under-reporting in certain sources. For instance, Figure 2.1 shows estimates over time of the under-five mortality rate for Kazakhstan, obtained from the UN IGME database. Around 1990, reported estimates range from below 40 to more than 60 child deaths per 1,000 live births. Low estimates often come from vital registration systems that are incomplete. Conclusions about levels and trends of child mortality in Kazakhstan will be rather different depending on the source of data one accepts as correct.

Given such variation, IGME provides its own best estimate. A simple average of all available estimates for each year might seem like a democratic approach, yet this would give too much weight to sources that may be the least reliable or complete. After assessing the data quality of each source (and making adjustments, if needed), IGME applies a statistical model to generate a smooth trend curve and extrapolate the model to a target year. The IGME also generates statistical uncertainty bounds around its preferred estimates (the lightly shaded area on Figure 2.1).

Indirect estimation

In countries where sources or quality of demographic data are limited, a variety of indirect techniques are available to estimate demographic indicators. A demographic estimate is indirect if it is based on information other than the data needed to calculate it. For example, direct estimates of birth rates require data on births and population size, both at a particular point in time. When such data are unavailable or lacking in quality, a creative array of indirect methods has been developed to estimate birth rates based on other information, such as population structure (by age and sex) or survey questions about the total number of children ever born, and other information.

Indirect estimation methods rely on the application of mathematical formulas (United Nations 1983), and computer software packages are now available for some of the best known methods. Example include MORTPAK from the United Nations, Population Analysis Spreadsheets (PASEX) from the US Census Bureau, and Tools for Demographic Estimation from the International Union for the Scientific Study of Population. Indirect methods typically rely on simplifying assumptions of one kind or another, such as no international migration, constant population growth, complete reporting or unchanged completeness of reporting over time. In general, the more reliable indirect methods make fewer of these simplifying assumptions, yet estimates from the least restrictive models may be particularly sensitive to reporting errors. Ideally, at least two methods should be considered before accepting the results from a single indirect method. The spaghetti graph of child mortality in Figure 2.1 contains estimates derived from direct and indirect methods, both of which are often derivable from the same data source (such as the various Kazakhstan DHS surveys).

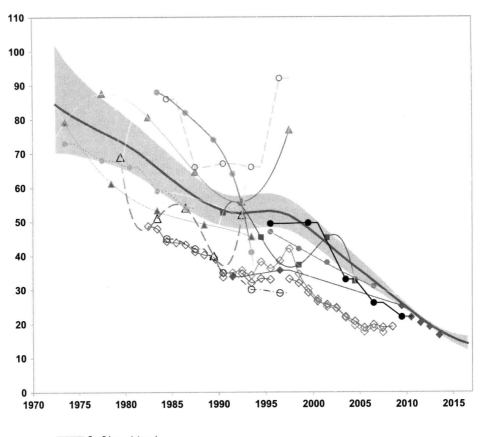

Figure 2.1 Estimates of under-five mortality (deaths under age five per 1,000 live births) in Kazakhstan by year from various sources

Notes: Observations from the same data series are joined by lines. The shaded area denotes statistical uncertainty bounds around the preferred estimates.

Source: United Nations Inter-agency Group for Child Mortality Estimation (UN IGME) (2015).

Indirect methods also encompass a variety of comparative standards, sometimes based on historical observations. For example, regional model life tables provide templates of age patterns of mortality rates. Thus, if one has a single piece of information about mortality at a particular age (e.g. infant mortality) and knowledge about which regional model is most appropriate for a particular country, one can map out the entire mortality picture at all ages. When no information is available at all, an even more basic comparative method is to borrow estimates from other countries with similar characteristics. Data from other countries may also provide clues about demographic conditions in the country of interest. For instance, studies of migration may benefit from 'mirror statistics' – that is, population outflows from Country A, where data may be lacking in quality, might be inferred by population inflows from A recorded in Country B.

The balancing equation and residual methods

A major advantage of working with core demographic data is that there is a simple accounting system available to evaluate its quality. Basic population change results from just three components – births, deaths and net migration (immigration minus emigration). These formulaic components of population and population change are like pieces of a puzzle that must fit together perfectly. Ideally, the pieces of demographic data collected in each country that relate to population change should also fit together perfectly.

Consider, for instance, two successive census counts of a population distributed by age and sex. If demographic events (birth, deaths, net migration) can be correctly estimated for each age and sex component of the population during the intervening years between the two censuses, then a projection of individuals from the first census based on such events (a 'cohort component' projection undertaken for each age and sex component of the population) should in theory match those counted in the second census. In practice, however, this never happens. The reasons include either mismeasured components of change (fertility, mortality or net migration) or errors in one or both censuses. Assessments can be made by back projecting the second census population to the date of the first census, or projecting forward the first census population to the date of the second census. Yet the proper identification of the parameters that account for any misfit can be tricky, as multiple 'solutions' to the puzzle are possible. If all but one demographic component can be estimated with confidence, the remaining component can be estimated as a residual.

As noted earlier, in recent decades only two organizations have regularly engaged in demographic analysis to provide estimates of the demographic past and projections into the future – the Population Division of the United Nations and the Population Division (International Programs Centre for Demographic and Economic Studies) of the US Census Bureau. Estimates from both organizations will not always match official primary data sources (or official estimates) because they are generated from cohort component projections. As a result, by definition, the demographic estimates of these organizations are each fully consistent with the demographic balancing equation. That said, modest differences in the country-by-country estimates of these two organizations remind us that not all estimated components of the underlying projections may be entirely accurate.

Cohort component projections serve two critical purposes. First, they provide a guide to future patterns of population size as well as its distribution by age and sex (and sometimes other characteristics, such as labour force or education). Such information is important for any number of planning purposes. How many children will be in need of immunizations? What will be the available pool of young people for military conscription? What kinds of products will societies be most likely to buy? How many older persons may require social assistance?

Daniel Goodkind

Table 2.3 Estimated per cent of children under-reported in the 2000 census round of Asia

Area of Asia	Census year	Ages 0–4	Ages 5–9
Cambodia	1998	11.4	3.9
China, estimate #1	2000	19.1	11.9
China, estimate #2	2000	17.2	4.4
China, estimate #3	2000	26.2	12.1
Indonesia	2000	13.4	7.0
Japan	2000	2.3	1.2
Macau	2001	3.9	–1.1
Philippines	1995	7.9	3.6
South Korea	2000	3.6	3.3
Sri Lanka	2001	7.6	5.3
Taiwan	2000	0.3	–0.3
Thailand	2000	5.3	2.1
Vietnam	1999	10.1	0.1

Notes: Estimates derived from demographic analysis (comparison of census counts to cohort component projections of those counts from prior census to the time of the 2000 round census). Estimates indicate net coverage error; negatives imply net overcounts.
Source: Based on Goodkind (2011: Table 1).

The second purpose of cohort component projections is to improve demographic analysis itself. How do we know that a census is accurate? In addition to post-enumeration surveys (PES), demographic analysis allows one to assess the consistency of census data at aggregate levels. Cohort component projections provide a comparative standard against which a census can be evaluated. When that standard is based upon a previous census, a cohort component projection to the time of any future census provides a relative standard of comparison. When there is a discrepancy between the two, the question is whether that is due to flaws in the census or in the comparative standard itself. The answer often requires familiarity with the data and country context in question, and opinions may differ, even among country experts.

Table 2.3 shows estimates of net errors in Asian censuses – in this case, for children under age ten – from such intercensal analyses. In each area, models began with a population by age and sex based on a previous census, some with adjustments derived from demographic analysis. Then, estimates of fertility, mortality and net migration at each age group were used in cohort component projections to the time of each census taken during the 2000 round. All in all, the results suggest that child under-reporting (net census error) is less severe in those areas with higher incomes (Japan, Macau, South Korea and Taiwan), while those with lower incomes showed more under-reporting (Cambodia, Indonesia, Sri Lanka and Vietnam). Of course, given that children under age ten were not born at the time of the earlier census, the reliability of the comparative standard from each projection is heavily dependent on the accuracy of fertility estimates. In China, where fertility levels between the 1990 and 2000 censuses are uncertain, a range of estimates based on different fertility assumptions is provided.

The estimates for China provide a good example of the challenges one can face in demographic analysis. The estimate (#1) that 19 per cent of young children in China went unrecorded in its 2000 census is reckoned against a comparative projection from the 1990 census that uses a consensus assumption among scholars that China's total fertility rate (TFR) fell below 1.6 births per woman by 2000 (Zhao and Chen 2011), not much different from what is implied by adjusted estimates from China's National Bureau of Statistics (Goodkind 2011).

Some observers remain sceptical that children in China's 2000 census could have been under-counted to a much greater extent than elsewhere in Asia and more than double that estimated in China's prior censuses. However, an implicit consensus regarding exceptional child under-reporting in China's 2000 census already exists – the recorded TFR (1.2) is about 20 per cent below what most observers believe was the true TFR (1.5–1.6). China's strict birth quotas provide a good reason to expect deliberate under-reporting. Such quotas began in the 1970s, and after 1991 punitive penalties increased against both parents who did not comply with the quotas and local officials who did not enforce them (Scharping 2003). Thereafter, reported fertility fell quickly in line with required quotas. If such under-reporting is indeed systematic, even consistent estimates of fertility levels reported across multiple data sources may not provide sufficient evidence that such levels are correct.

Conclusion

To conclude this overview of Asia's major demographic data sources, it might be useful to reflect briefly on the difference between sources and access. Some of the demographic sources described herein have existed for a long time. For instance, complete population censuses in India have been taken since the late nineteenth century. What has changed recently has been the improved access to such sources afforded by digital technology. In decades past, a researcher might have needed days or weeks to locate and obtain demographic data, paper records of which might require a trip to a major library or statistical office. As should be clear from the web links provided at the end of this chapter, it may now require only minutes to obtain the same data. For observers raised in the Internet age, sources that are not instantly searchable and available on the Internet may be easily overlooked.

Given the proliferation of compilations of secondary data on the Internet, it might also be useful to reiterate some concerns about the gentle art of referencing and citation. Ideally, those who make use of primary data should give credit to the collector of the original data. Yet when such data are recompiled and recycled, it is not uncommon to find references to the re-compiler rather than the original collector. Although such flaws in referencing hardly began with the digital era, their implications are now magnified. As secondary data are ever more easily redistributed, the original source of the quoted statistics may be more easily lost or obscured. In addition, as modifications to the original data can occur as they are recycled, assessment of the quality of recycled data becomes increasingly difficult.

Along with the increased dissemination of tabulated data, Ruggles (2014) notes that 'the quantity of microdata available to demographic research is exploding'. Microdata sources may help to distinguish causal patterns and trends across societies, including those in Asia, that were heretofore difficult to see. Yet we should also be cautious about the challenges and limitations of 'big data', as well the conclusions drawn from them. As observers grow further and further distant from the data collection efforts they analyse, their ability to assess the reliability of the data, as well as pay attention to commonplace human errors of transposition, coding, missing data, and the like, may be increasingly compromised.

References

Attané, I. and C. Guilmoto (2007) *Watering the Neighbour's Garden: The Growing Demographic Female Deficit in Asia*. Paris: Committee for International Cooperation in National Research in Demography (CICRED).

Bryan, T. (2004) 'Basic sources of stastics'. In J. S. Siegel and D. A. Swanson (eds.) *The Methods and Materials of Demography*, Second Edition. San Diego: Academic Press.

Chan, K. W. and W. Buckingham (2008) 'Is China abolishing the *Hukou* system?' *The China Quarterly*, 195(1): 582–606.
Goodkind, D. (2011) 'Child underreporting, fertility and sex ratio imbalance in China'. *Demography*, 48(1): 291–316.
International Institute for Vital Registration and Statistics (IIVRS) (1995) 'Organization of national civil registration and vital statistics systems: an update'. *Technical Papers 63*. Bethesda, MD: IIVRS.
Morning, A. (2008) 'Ethnic classification in global perspective: a cross-national survey of the 2000 census round'. *Population Research and Policy Review*, 27(2): 239–272.
Office of the Registrar General and Census Commissioner (ORG) (2010–2011) 'History of Indian census – introduction'. New Delhi: Government of India, Ministry of Home Affairs.
Ruggles, S. (2014) 'Big microdata for population research'. *Demography*, 51(1): 287–297.
Scharping, T. (2003) *Birth Control in China, 1949–2000: Population Policy and Demographic Development*. London and New York: RoutledgeCurzon.
Shryock, H. S. and J. S. Siegel (1976) *The Methods and Materials of Demography*. San Diego: Academic Press.
Stewart, D. W. and M. A. Kamins (2012) 'Evaluating secondary sources'. In J. Goodwin (ed.) *Secondary Data Analysis*. New York: Sage Publications.
United Nations (1983) *Manual X: Indirect Techniques for Demographic Estimation*. New York: UN Population Division.
United Nations (2008) *Principles and Recommendations for Population and Housing Censuses. Revision 2*. New York: UN Statistics Division.
United Nations (2010a) *Post Enumeration Surveys. Operational Guidelines*. New York: UN Statistics Division.
United Nations (2010b) *United Nations Regional Workshop on the 2010 World Programme on Population and Housing Censuses: Census Evaluation and Post-Enumeration Surveys*. New York: UN Statistics Division.
United Nations (2012) *World Population Prospects: The 2012 Revision*. New York: UN Population Division. Available from: http://esa.un.org/wpp/unpp/panel_population.htm.
United Nations (2014) *Population and Vital Statistics Report*. New York: UN Statistics Division. Available from: http://unstats.un.org/unsd/demographic/products/vitstats/.
United Nations Economic and Social Commission for Asia and the Pacific (ESCAP) (2013) *Statistical Yearbook for Asia and the Pacific*. Bangkok: ESCAP.
United Nations Inter-agency Group for Child Mortality Estimation (UN IGME) (9 September 2015). Available from: www.childmortality.org/.
United Nations Statistics Division (n.d.) *Civil Registration Systems*. Available from http://unstats.un.org/unsd/demographic/sources/civilreg/.
US Census Bureau (2009) 'China's population to peak at 1.4 billion around 2026: Census Bureau projects India to become most populous country in 2025'. Newsroom.
Wei, C. H. (2011) 'Census of population 2010 – increased use of Internet in census submission'. *Statistics Singapore Newsletter* (March). Singapore Department of Statistics.
Zhao, Z. W. and W. Chen (2011) 'China's far below-replacement fertility and its long-term impact: comments on the preliminary results of the 2010 census'. *Demographic Research*, 25(26): 819–836.

Online sources

The web links listed below were operable as of August 2014. Additional compilations of demographic data for Asia can also be found on the websites of the Asian Development Bank; Child Mortality Estimation Group (IGME); International Labour Organization; Population Reference Bureau; United Nations Educational, Scientific and Cultural Organization (UNESCO); United Nations Global Migration Database; United Nations Population Division; United Nations Statistics Division; World Bank; World Health Organization.

Censuses

International Census Questionnaires and Census Dates
Available from: http://unstats.un.org/unsd/demographic/sources/census/.
List of National Statistical Offices and Their Websites
Available from: http://unstats.un.org/unsd/methods/inter-natlinks/sd_natstat.asp.

Asia's major demographic data sources

United Nations Demographic Yearbook
Available from: http://unstats.un.org/unsd/demographic/products/dyb/dyb2.htm.
Integrated Public Use Microdata Series (IPUMS)
Available from: https://international.ipums.org/international/.

Vital registration

United Nations Demographic Yearbook
Available from: http://unstats.un.org/unsd/demographic/products/dyb/dyb2.htm.
United Nations Population and Vital Statistics Report
Available from: http://unstats.un.org/unsd/demographic/products/vitstats/.

Surveys and surveillance

Demographic and Health Surveys (DHS)
Available from: http://dhsprogram.com/.
Multiple Indicator Cluster Surveys (MICS)
Available from: www.unicef.org/statistics/index_24302.html.
Health and Demographic Surveillance Systems (HDSS)
Available from: www.indepth-network.org/.
Sample Vital Registration with Verbal Autopsy (SAVVY)
Available from: http://pdf.usaid.gov/pdf_docs/PNADI525.pdf and www.cpc.unc.edu/measure/publications/cl-07-03.

Derived estimates from cohort component projections

United Nations Population Division
Available from: http://esa.un.org/wpp/unpp/panel_population.htm.
US Census Bureau
Available from: www.census.gov/population/international/data/idb/informationGateway.php.

3
The development of population research institutions in Asia

Peter McDonald

Background: the development of population research institutions prior to the 1960s

In this chapter, the terminology, population research institutions, is used broadly to include any institution in which population research is conducted including universities, statistical and other government agencies and, rarely in the case of Asia, private organizations. The first formal associations and institutions in the field of population studies date from the 1920s. While the history of the discipline itself lies in academic studies in Europe, the history of the discipline's institutions lies initially in the United States and the main driving forces were philanthropists and advocates rather than scientists.

The Scripps Foundation for Research in Population Problems which can claim to be the first institution in the field of demography was founded in 1922, interestingly with research on the demography of East Asia as its rationale. Warren Thompson was appointed as its director and it was located at Miami University in Ohio. Thompson was soon joined by Pascal Whelpton and the two worked together for over 30 years. The philanthropist Edward Scripps was a successful media magnate who was concerned about the effects that population pressure might have upon the countries of the Far East (Zunz 2012). Consistent with Scripps's view, in his 1929 book, *Danger Spots in World Population*, Thompson argued that the effects of population pressures in East Asia, the Indian Ocean and Central Europe (including Italy and Germany) would be 'certain to make trouble in the not distant future' (Thompson 1929; Notestein 1981). Thompson took the neo-Malthusian position that vigorous family planning programmes were the solution to these population pressures.

Mainly at the instigation of American philanthropists and the family planning advocate, Margaret Sanger, a World Population Conference was convened in Geneva in September 1927. The conference resolved 'that a permanent international organization be created for the object of studying population problems in a strictly scientific spirit'. Professor Kiyo Sue Inui, as Japan's representative at the conference, was co-opted to serve on the committee set up to define the constitution as its only Asian member. At the time, he was lecturing at Waseda and Tokyo universities but he was a graduate of the University of Michigan and had had a previous appointment at the University of Southern California. The constitutional committee met on

4 July 1928 in Paris as the First General Assembly of the International Union for the Scientific Investigation of Population Problems (IUSIPP). No Asians including Professor Inui were present.[1] The International Union was created as a union of national committees, not of individuals and, at the first assembly, it was agreed that 21 countries could set up national committees. The only Asian nation to be allocated a national committee was Japan. This was partly because Asian countries that were colonies were considered to be part of the colonial power rather than entities in themselves. While national committees were set up in the United States and several European countries, I have found no evidence that a national committee of the International Union was ever established in Japan or in any other Asian country. However, within the Japanese bureaucracy, the Institute of Population Problems (now the National Institute of Population and Social Security Research) was set up in 1939.

The new Union was constituted with a very long list of statutes and regulations. One particular sub-statute provided a vehement and eccentrically-worded rejection of the activists and philanthropists who had organized the financial support that had helped to create the Union. Statute 1(e) reads:

> The Union confines itself solely to scientific investigation in the strict sense, and refuses either to enter upon religious, moral, or political discussion, or as a Union to support a policy regarding population, of any sort whatever, particularly in the direction either of increased or diminished birth rates.
>
> *(IUSSP 1985: 35)*

In October 1928, a national committee was established in Britain known as the British Population Society. Its membership included such luminaries as Julian Huxley, Lord Beveridge and John Maynard Keynes (IUSSP 1985). By the time of the Second General Assembly in London in June 1931, only 14 national associations had been created. Notably, in the land of the Union's President, Raymond Pearl, the American National Committee of IUSIPP was not formed until 4 February 1931, almost three years after the creation of the Union. Pearl's term as president of the Union was marked by vilification by his peers in the field of biology because he had questioned the science of eugenics. Louis Dublin, a statistician at the Metropolitan Life Insurance Company who, at the time, was strongly opposed to birth control was the first head of the American National Committee. He also took a very strong stance that science should not be contaminated by advocacy. Parallel to the American National Committee of IUSIPP and with essentially the same membership, the Population Association of America (PAA) was established on 7 May 1931. In the United Kingdom also, a parallel organization to the British Population Society, the Population Investigation Committee (PIC), was set up in 1936. It seems that the national associations were attempting to avoid the politics and strictures of the International Union especially, at least in the case of the PAA, in relation to policy advocacy and family planning. The PAA was slow to get moving but received major impetus through the establishment of the Office of Population Research (OPR) at Princeton University in 1935, with Frank Notestein as its first director.

Through the 1930s, the International Union was plagued by political differences related to fascism. In 1931, two competing international conferences of the Union were held, one in London and one in Rome. In 1935, the Berlin meeting of the Union was boycotted by the American National Committee and by individuals from other countries. Despite its troubled history, the International Union staged a very successful conference in Paris in 1937. At the 1937 meeting, Adolphe Landry, an economic historian and member of the French Parliament (for Corsica), was elected as president of the Union. In 1932, as French Minister for Labour and

Social Welfare, Landry had instigated the France-wide system of cash support for families with children as a pronatalist policy placing him firmly on one side of the pronatalist–antinatalist debate that had bedevilled the International Union, but, as evidenced later when he successfully defended a takeover of the Union by the wartime German administration, Landry was vehemently anti-fascist.

Activities of the International Union essentially ceased during the Second World War. Most national committees ceased to function while others had become embroiled in wartime propagandist activities (Population Index, published by the Office of Population Research, 1947: 284). Landry had remained president of the Union throughout the war years and, in 1947, he was instrumental in the reorganization of the old International Union as the International Union for the Scientific Study of Population (IUSSP). He became the first president of the IUSSP, now reconstituted as an association of individuals rather than of national committees. This took place in the context of the mushrooming of major new population institutions immediately after the war.

In 1946, the United Nations Population Division was created with Frank Notestein as its head. The UN Population Commission was set up and held its first meeting. The French Institute for Demographic Studies, INED, was also opened in 1946. In the United Kingdom, the British Population Society was wound up and the Population Investigation Committee took on its role. The PIC, led by David Glass, was located at the London School of Economics, which in 1947 opened a new Department of Demography. Also in 1947, the Australian Government, in creating the new Australian National University (ANU) specified demography as one of the four disciplines that the new university must include and a demographer, W. D. Borrie, was appointed as the university's first appointment in social sciences. A Department of Demography was set up at ANU in 1952.

In the 1950s, many new centres of population studies opened in universities in the United States, mainly with funding from the Ford Foundation (Caldwell and Caldwell 1986); and the United Nations created regional training centres in demography in Bombay, now Mumbai (Asia-Pacific), Santiago (Latin America and the Caribbean) and Cairo (Africa). The aim of the UN centres was to produce local demographic expertise in developing countries to address issues of rapid population growth and urbanization. In 1953, the Population Council opened its doors with funding from John D. Rockefeller III and he then served as its first president.

The demography of Asia was a major issue of interest to the newly emerging centres of population research in the United States. In this context, in the 1950s, Princeton University's OPR produced a series of influential books on the issue of population in Asian countries including *The Population of India and Pakistan* (Davis 1951), *Population Growth in Malaya* (Smith 1952), *Colonial Development and Population in Taiwan* (Barclay 1954), *The Population of Japan* (Taeuber 1958), and *Population Growth and Economic Development in Low-Income Countries* (Coale and Hoover 1958).

The last of these books argued that economic development in Asian countries was constrained by high levels of fertility because available capital at both the national and the household level needed to be devoted in large measure to the care and nurture of the 40 per cent of the population aged less than 15 years. Fewer children, they argued, would provide the opportunity for more productive investment of capital and enable a stronger focus on developing the human capital of the next generation of workers, both essential features of economic development. In more recent times, this argument of Coale and Hoover has become known as the 'demographic dividend' whereby, with a fall in fertility and the number of children, the population concentrates in the working ages thus providing a 'dividend' to the economy (see Chapter 24).

Interestingly, two senior American demographers who were strong proponents of this approach, Warren Thompson and Frank Lorimer, worked with the MacArthur administration in early post-war Japan, not surprisingly advocating a decline in Japan's birth rate (Hodgson 2003). In 1948, a Rockefeller Foundation delegation including demographers, Frank Notestein and Irene Taeuber, visited China, Japan, Korea, Taiwan, the Philippines and Indonesia to obtain a perspective on issues of population growth. Notestein allegedly became convinced during this mission that fertility control could be implemented prior to economic development (counter to his own demographic transition theory) and that, in reverse, population control was a desirable strategy to promote economic development and to counter the spread of communism (Balfour 1950; Hodgson 1983; Caldwell and Caldwell 1986; Szreter 1993; Williams 2011). Caldwell (2005) argues that, in the late 1940s, Notestein and the OPR at Princeton were not quite as strategic in their thinking as this implies. While this is probably correct, with the communist victory in China, the motivation for fertility control programmes became even stronger and the OPR had established an intellectual base for action. By the early 1950s, both Japan and India had policies in place to lower the level of fertility. While the idea of development through fertility control was conceptualized as a support to development through capitalism, later it was also a central rationale of China's one-child policy (Potts 2006) along with, ironically, the Club of Rome arguments about limits to growth (Greenhalgh 2003).

Thus, the development of population institutions prior to the 1960s was associated with the 'big politics' of liberal democracies, fascism, capitalism and communism, and with the advocacy or otherwise of family planning as a means of dealing with rapid population growth. In these debates, population growth in Asian countries figured prominently from the 1920s onwards but, by 1960, there were very few population institutions in the Asian countries. India was the main exception to this. As already mentioned, the UN set up the Demographic Training and Research Centre in Mumbai in 1956 to train people in the region in the science of demography. The Centre, now the International Institute for Population Sciences (IIPS), a deemed university, has, for 50 years, maintained its place as the leading population research and training centre in Asia. Early in the 1950s, the Ford Foundation was involved in the creation of the National Institute of Family Planning and the National Institute for Health Administration and Education in India (Minkler 1977). Also in the early 1950s, the Khanna study was commenced in the State of Rajasthan to demonstrate (unsuccessfully as it turned out) that family planning programmes could be effective in poor populations (Williams 2011). A similar study, the United Nation's Mysore study, was carried out in 1951–1952 (United Nations 1961). In relation to foreign engagement in the development of population institutions in India, Rao has written:

> It is not possible to understand the Indian family-planning programme without reference to the international actors who set the agenda, primarily in the United States (US). Indeed it has been argued that 'a small group of men and women' in the US many of them bankrolled by the Rockefeller Foundation, gave shape to the global population movement (Connelly 2003: 128).[2] The post-war population control movement comprised a closely-knit group of public and private organisations including the Rockefeller Foundation, the Population Council, the Ford Foundation and the USAID, along with its counterparts in other Western countries.
>
> *(Rao 2004: 27)*

Of course, prior to the 1960s, national statistical agencies in many Asian countries (often supported by experts from the United Nations Statistical Division) provided basic population data and these agencies often provided research that was important in population and development planning, but the raison d'être of these organizations was not population. The relative deficit of population institutions in Asia at the end of the 1950s became an abundance in the following 20 years. The early post-war years were the beginning of the end of the colonial era and, one by one, developing countries gained independence. In the context of the Cold War and the approach to population issues developed in the United States in the 1950s, it could be seen as inevitable that population institutions would emerge in the newly independent countries of Asia.

The establishment of population institutions in Asia in the 1960s and 1970s

Much has been written about the emergence of family planning programmes in Asian countries from the 1960s onwards. In this literature, a central controversy is the extent to which the observed outcomes were the product of American institutions, notably USAID, the Ford Foundation, the Population Council and the Rockefeller Foundation for the most part acting in concert and backed by a small number of centres in American universities notably Princeton, Chicago, Michigan and North Carolina (Reed 1976; Minkler 1977; Hodgson 1983; Caldwell and Caldwell 1986; Harkavy 1985; Rao 2004; van der Tak 2005a, 2005b and 2005c; Caldwell 2005; Connelly 2008). While not attempting to address the broader aspects of this controversy, there is little question that these American institutions were heavily involved in the development of population institutions in Asia from 1960 onwards.

An early example of the engagement of the Population Council (with Notestein as its president) in institutional development in Asia is recounted by Ronald Freedman:

> In 1960, the Population Council subverted me by sending me to the Third World for the first time. They sent me to India for two months and on the way back I stopped in Thailand, Hong Kong, Japan, and I became interested in what was going on there. The Population Council then asked me if I wanted to be involved in the Taiwan work.
>
> *(van der Tak 2005c: 73)*

Soon afterwards, the Ford Foundation funded the creation of the Population Studies Center in the University of Michigan on the basis that it would be involved in family planning research in Asia and in the training of Asians in population research. The Taiwan Population Studies Center was then established within the Provincial Health Department of Taiwan in 1961. Freedman, with advice from Bernard Berelson of the Population Council, was instrumental in the conduct of the Taichung study that became a model for family planning programme development in Asia (Freedman and Takeshita 1969; Caldwell and Caldwell 1986; van der Tak 2005c). The Taichung study was conducted by the Taiwan Population Studies Center with financial support from the Ford Foundation and the Population Council (Freedman et al. 1964). John Takeshita, a Michigan graduate, was the in-country advisor.

As a result of the success of the Taiwan model, Freedman went with Marshall Balfour of the Rockefeller Foundation to the Republic of Korea. In December 1961, the Korean Government adopted a family planning programme as part of its public health services. Supported by the Population Council, a study similar to the Taichung study began in Koyang in 1962 led by Sook Bang, a Michigan graduate, at Yonsei University College of Medicine (Sook et al. 1963). Freedman refers to John Ross (also a Michigan graduate) in the Korea research context as 'an important figure over the years in fertility and family planning research' (van der Tak 2005b). Michigan was joined as a player in this endeavour in 1963 when the Ford Foundation provided support to the Community and Family Study Center in the University of Chicago led by Donald Bogue (Caldwell and Caldwell 1986). Bogue recounts:

> In the early days of the family planning program in South Korea, we offered two workshops on family planning communication there and that helped result in a steady stream of people from Korea coming to the University of Chicago for training at the master's and Ph.D. level. Many of the leaders of the present Korean family planning movement are from there. The same could be said for India. We trained a large number of people from India at the master's and Ph.D. level.
>
> *(van der Tak 2005c: 46)*

The interconnectedness of people and institutions is indicated by the fact that Bogue had been a foreign adviser at the UN's Demographic Training and Research Centre in Bombay in the 1950s and returned to the University of Chicago to create a centre focused upon family planning research (van der Tak 2005c; Caldwell and Caldwell 1986). Then, in the early 1970s, Haryono Suyono, having completed his PhD at Chicago, returned to Indonesia via Korea to study the family planning programme in that country. Back in Indonesia, Haryono then played a fundamental role in the implementation of the Indonesian family planning programme (van der Tak 2005c).

Despite these apparent successes, there was only so much that the American foundations could do within their funding constraints and in the face of powerful voices in the United States and elsewhere that were opposed to government-sponsored family planning, but the funding situation changed with the appointment in 1965 of Reimert Ravenholt to the position of Director of the Office of Population of USAID. Ravenholt began a major, vigorous and often controversial programme to support the provision and distribution of contraceptives in developing countries, and the nationals of these countries were provided with scholarships to be trained in a small number of United States universities to return to their countries as academic demographers and government planners or to run family planning programmes (Gillespie 2000). Based on the success of the Mysore study in India (UN 1961), the Taichung study in Taiwan and the Indianapolis study in the US, USAID and/or the Foundations also provided financial support for the gathering of data that would assess the progress of family planning in these countries. One such example was the 1973 Indonesian Fertility-Mortality Survey (McDonald et al. 1976). Later, the major international comparative fertility survey, the World Fertility Survey, was funded largely by USAID as was subsequently and until today, its successor, the Demographic and Health Surveys. The Ford Foundation and the Population Council (with funding from USAID) supported the development of population centres in universities and government agencies in developing countries and foreign experts to assist in the process (Harkavy 1985; Caldwell and Caldwell 1986). Typically, a new population centre would be headed by a national who was a recent US-trained graduate and who had been selected specifically for that purpose. This person would then recruit a cadre of young people from among local university students. Finally, foreigners would be brought in to provide expertise and support.

As it was essential to have high-level, political backing for this policy direction, it was necessary to gain the support of the leaders of the countries involved. In 1967, 30 heads of governments in developing countries signed a Declaration on Population strikingly worded as follows:

> As Heads of Governments actively concerned with the population problem, we share these convictions: We believe that the population problem must be recognised as a principal element in long-range national planning if governments are to achieve their economic

goals and fulfill the aspirations of their people. We believe that the great majority of parents desire to have the knowledge and the means to plan their families; that the opportunity to decide the number and spacing of children is a basic human right. We believe that lasting and meaningful peace will depend to a considerable measure upon how the challenge of population growth is met. We believe the objective of family planning is the enrichment of human life, not its restriction; that family planning, by assuring greater opportunity to each person, frees man to attain his individual dignity and reach his full potential.

(Ayala and Caradon 1968: 3)

Among the Asian countries, this statement was signed by the leaders of India, Indonesia, Iran, Japan, Jordan, Republic of Korea, Malaysia, Nepal, Pakistan, the Philippines, Singapore and Thailand. The statement was endorsed by the Secretary-General of the United Nations but much of the effort in obtaining the signatures was made by John D. Rockefeller III and the Population Council.

The Taiwan model of the establishment of an in-country population research institute with an adviser linked to an American or other international university with funding from an American or international agency (e.g. United Nations Fund for Population Activities, UNFPA) was soon replicated in many other Asian countries. Examples were the University of the Philippines Population Institute (1964), the Demographic Institute of the University of Indonesia (1964), the Population Research Center of Seoul National University (1965), the Population Research and Training Center of Chulalongkorn University (1966), the Department of Demography of the University of Tehran (1970), the Institute for Population and Social Research of Mahidol University (1971), the Office of Population Studies of the University of San Carlos (1971), the Mindanao Center for Population Studies (1971), the Demographic Training and Research Unit (later the Department of Demography) of the University of Colombo (1973), the Center for Population Research and Training of Gadjah Mada University (1973), the Center of Demographic Studies of Shiraz University (1974), the Population Studies Center of the National Taiwan University (1974) and the Population Studies Department at the University of Jordan (1979). The study of demography also became prominent in this period in the Department of Sociology and Anthropology of the Hebrew University of Jerusalem. In Japan, the Nihon University Population Research Institute (NUPRI) was created in 1979 and has continued to be a strong, university-based centre until today.

Outside of universities, important also was the creation in 1963 of the world's longest-running demographic surveillance site at Matlab, in what was then East Pakistan but is now Bangladesh. The Matlab field site has been run by the International Centre for Diarrhoeal Disease Research, Bangladesh (ICDDR,B) which, as an international centre, has made Matlab a focal point for a great deal of innovative population research over 50 years. Other non-university centres of note established in this period are the demographic groups in the Pakistan Institute of Development Studies and the Indonesian Institute of Social Sciences (LIPI).

Caldwell and Caldwell (1986) have detailed the story of the establishment of the first of these institutes, the University of the Philippines Population Institute (UPPI). UPPI emerged as the result of a Ford Foundation mission in late 1962 to investigate the possibility of setting up population research and training programmes in South-East Asia. The model that they recommended was one where the developing country centre would have the backing of leading universities in developed countries and be staffed by nationals returning from graduate training in the United States or other developed countries. Mercedes Concepcion, completing her PhD at the University of Chicago, was the only person that met this criterion at that time. The plan that the Foundation would support a programme at the University of the Philippines led by Concepcion was discussed with the university and it came to fruition in 1964. Also in 1964, Nathanael Iskandar was appointed to lead the newly-created Demographic Institute in the Faculty of Economics of the University of Indonesia, from which position he went to complete a PhD degree at the OPR in Princeton. When he returned in 1968, a major programme of support was initiated involving the Ford Foundation, the Population Council and USAID.

Like Concepcion and Iskandar, most of the early heads of these new centres had been trained outside the country in which the centre was located, often in the United States and most had in-country, foreign consultants in the early years of their establishment. Most received financial support from American funding agencies. Most were also engaged in research on the levels and trends of fertility and the impact of new family planning programmes with international funding backing the research. Often, these centres provided short-course training to their fellow nationals working in government agencies or in regional universities. A prominent example of this was the training course provided in the early 1970s by the Demographic Institute of the University of Indonesia (Iskandar and Jones 1974).

While the discussion above has emphasized the role of American organizations in the development of population research institutions in Asia, some non-American organizations also played prominent roles. The United Nations Population Fund (UNFPA) became active in the field after its creation in 1969 and by the end of the 1970s had become the most prominent funder of population research in Asia. It was to take on an even larger role in the 1980s. Universities like the Australian National University and the London School of Hygiene and Tropical Medicine also played significant roles. Probably most significantly, the International Institute for Population Studies (IIPS) in Mumbai trained very large numbers of students from the Asian region in demography and spawned a large number of demographic research centres in India itself.

At the end of the 1970s, the institutional structure for population research was strong across most of Asia. Research strength was focused upon fertility and family planning reflecting the interests of the international funding agencies and, to some extent, the countries themselves. However, attention was also given to demographic estimates underpinning population projections required for planning purposes and to such areas as urbanization, internal migration and mortality. The solid foundation established in the 1960s and 1970s, however, was not sustained in later years.

Population institutions in Asia from the 1980s onwards

Ravenholt was removed from his USAID position in 1979 and a more conservative tide of politics in the US brought an end to the Ford Foundation support of population programmes. Most Ford population posts were terminated by 1981 (Caldwell and Caldwell 1986). While from 1980 onwards, this left room for other American foundations such as Mellon, Hewlett, Packard and MacArthur to move into the field, their support was mainly project-based rather than institutional and was never particularly oriented towards Asia. Reflecting levels of development, these foundations have been much more active in supporting population research in sub-Saharan Africa.

Strong support for population institutions in Asia in the 1980s was provided by UNFPA and by World Bank country agreements in which matching funds were provided by the national government. The Australian Government also provided support through its Association of South-East Asian Nations (ASEAN) Population Programme, initially funded by UNFPA. UNFPA also funded the International Population Dynamics Program at the Australian National University, which worked with population institutions in Asia in the 1980s to assist them in their research and training activities. Most of this support in the 1980s went to the centres that had been created through the 1960s and 1970s with the support of US institutions, although such support was no longer available for the countries that had become wealthier by this time. By the 1990s, these external funding sources had also dwindled and population research centres were left to find their own support. This was done more successfully in some countries than in others.

Indonesia provides an example of this progression that is at the less successful end. In the 1980s, World Bank funding through the Indonesian State Ministry of Population and Environment was used very much in the same way as Ford-USAID support had been used in the 1970s – a few strong centres were identified as leaders and they then provided training and assistance with research to smaller centres spread across the archipelago (Utomo 2015). Funding was also available from UNFPA and from the Australian Government. However, when the Ministry of Population and Environment was closed in 1993, World Bank funding was transferred to the National Family Planning Coordinating Board (BKKBN) which was more interested in the delivery of family planning services than in training and research. Since that time, population centres in Indonesia have languished having to rely upon contract income often not in areas related to mainstream demographic issues. The 2011–2015 8th Country Programme between the Government of Indonesia and UNFPA contains the following planned outcome:

> Strengthened capacity of national and subnational institutions to analyse and use data on population and development on the MDGs and ICPD-related issues for policy formulations.
> *(UNFPA Indonesia 2011: Table 2)*

Leaving aside the references to MDGs and ICPD, this was the agenda of the American funding in the late 1960s, almost 50 years earlier, suggesting that the earlier strength of the Indonesian population research centres had fallen away. The university study of population also declined in the Republic of Korea as the original leaders such as Tai Hwan Kwon of Seoul National University retired.

With a history of the development of population institutions roughly similar to that of Indonesia, Thailand has had more success in maintaining the strength of population institutions as international funds dwindled. The centres in Mahidol and Chulalongkorn universities remain strong. Mahidol provides a successful training programme in demography in English for students from other countries. Another example of continued strength is the Department of Demography at the University of Tehran. This department was able to absorb the sudden shock of relative international isolation resulting from the Islamic revolution and re-emerged very strongly to have a major influence on the direction of population policy in the mid-1980s. It has subsequently built on that strength to be a highly viable organization today. More commonly, however, as the nature of funded research changed, the population institutions in most Asian countries struggled to maintain their existence, with the majority diverting their focus to other areas of research.

In Japan, continued strength in the field of demography has been due mainly to the work of NUPRI and individuals such as Noriko Tsuya, who led research on Japan's rapidly ageing population. In more recent times, two government agencies, the National Institute of Population and Social Security Research in Japan and the Korean Institute for Health and Social Affairs (KIHASA) in Korea have been prominent in demographic research.

Whether population research and training institutions have floundered or flourished in Asian universities seems to be related to the extent to which external funding has been replaced by mainstream support through the country's higher education system. Another factor is the extent to which the institution has been able to generalize its activities or to act independently rather than engaging only with the latest political interests of either national governments or international agencies (Jones 2005). India is the classic example of success in this regard. There are numerous successful population institutes that engage in training and research related to population and development issues in India. The Indian Ministry of Health and Family Welfare provides 100 per cent funding to a network of 18 population research centres spread across India mainly located in major state universities (see http://mohfw.nic.in/about-us/research-institutions), with IIPS Mumbai playing a coordinating role. The Indian approach is similar to that used by the National Institute of Child Health and Development to fund population research centres in American universities.

The development of population research in China in the 1980s

So far, there has been no mention of China because it has its own story. In China, population research was essentially off the agenda until the emergence of planned control of population growth at the end of the 1970s. Of this time, Susan Greenhalgh writes:

> Population experts were needed to help the party define and then reach its (planned population) goals. In the late 1970s and early 1980s, China was home to one of the most rapid institutionalizations of a field of population studies in history ... the mission the new field was assigned was not to build population science for science's sake. It was to develop population science to assist the state in solving the country's population problems.
>
> *(Greenhalgh 2003: 167)*

In 1980, Ansley Coale provided an intensive series of lectures at the People's University to around 60 people from 12 Chinese universities and various government agencies. He found a keen desire to learn and to gather the necessary demographic data. This was then realized in the 1982 census and the 1982 Fertility Survey (Coale 2000). Also in the 1980s, UNFPA, with Aprodicio Laquian as its representative in Beijing, played an important role in supporting selected university population centres in China through research funding and international training of staff.

Like India, strong government support for population institutions in China has led to the development of a large number of well-established centres today. Notable among these are the following universities: Renmin, Peking, Fudan, Xi'an Jiaotong, Wuhan, Zhejiangin, Fujian Normal and, most recently, Shanghai. Population research is also prominent in the Institute of Population and Labour Economics and the Institute of Sociology in the Chinese Academy of Social Sciences and the government agency, the China Population and Development Research Center. Today, population research is strong in China but it lacks an international perspective because it has tended to eschew international engagement. In the past, this may have been due to sensitivities surrounding the one-child policy, but it may also have been caused by a sense among Chinese demographers that China was enough – we don't need to know about the rest of the world. As China grapples with its low fertility rate and rapid ageing of its population, it might be predicted that Chinese demographers will be more likely to draw on the experiences of other countries.

The Asian Population Association

The Asian region was the last region in the world to create a regional population association. The association was set up in 2008 and held its first conference in 2010 in New Delhi. Subsequent conferences have been held in Bangkok in 2012 and Kuala Lumpur in 2015. The association is particularly important in providing a means for relatively isolated population researchers to present their results in an international forum. Given the poor state of population research institutions in many countries in Asia, this is an important means through which improvement can occur. The number and quality of papers presented by young Asian demographers at the 2015 conference is an indication that the future of population research may be brighter than in the recent past.

The future of population research and training institutions

Demography is a small discipline and it will never attract mass numbers of students. As such, it is difficult to justify the discipline to academic administrators who are motivated first and foremost by student numbers. At the same time, in order to maintain its quality and its relevance, it is important that the discipline is based in university settings where it can contribute to and learn from theoretical developments in cognate disciplines. Outside of academia, demography is about numbers and methods. As indicated by experience in India and China (and in the United States), the discipline can flourish in universities if governments recognize that the discipline has national significance that requires government support.

With the success of family planning programmes in many countries in Asia, funding levels fell for university-based population institutes. Often this led to the demise or decline of institutions that had flourished in the past. Countries that have allowed this situation to occur now find themselves devoid of good population researchers at a time when new demographic issues have emerged. The new priorities for research include low fertility, population ageing, the growth and management of megacities, internal and international migration and associated labour market issues, changes in family functioning and population and environment. In selected countries, the issue of rapid population growth remains important. In addressing these important areas of research, countries need a core of highly qualified demographers who are able to interact with economists, sociologists, environmentalists and other disciplines. Increasing fertility from low levels is proving to be a much more intractable issue than lowering it from high levels. The incessant movement of people to the largest cities also presents unprecedented challenges for planners. Countries are looking around for local demographic expertise often to find that it is not there.

Notes

1 Inui wrote *Quantitative Phases of the Japanese Population Problem*, published in 1929 by the League of Nations Association of Japan. *Volume 17 of Documents of the Third Conference, Institute of Pacific Relations, Kyoto, Japan, 1929*, Institute of Pacific Relations Conference (Kyoto).
2 Connelly was in fact arguing against this proposition and for the greater significance of actors in the countries themselves. From my perspective as an observer of family planning programmes in Asia, there is no doubt that the spectacular successes of the programmes in Taiwan, South Korea, Singapore, Indonesia, Thailand and Iran were driven by the nationals of those countries, albeit many of them having been trained in the United States.

References

Ayala, T. and L. Caradon (1968) 'Declaration on population: the world leaders' statement'. *Studies in Family Planning*, 1(26): 1–3.
Balfour, M. (1950) *Public Health and Demography in the Far East: Report of a Survey Trip, September 13–December 13, 1948*. New York: The Rockefeller Foundation.
Barclay, G.W. (1954) *Colonial Development and Population in Taiwan*. Princeton, NJ: Princeton University Press.
Caldwell, J. (2005) 'Demographers' involvement in twentieth-century population policy: continuity or discontinuity?' *Population Research and Policy Review*, 24(4): 359–385.

Caldwell, J. and P. Caldwell (1986) *Limiting Population Growth and the Ford Foundation Contribution*. London and Dover, NH: Frances Pinter.

Coale, A. J. (2000) 'Ansley J. Coale: an autobiography'. *Memoirs of the American Philosophical Society*, 236. Philadelphia: American Philosophical Society.

Coale, A. J. and E. M. Hoover (1958) *Population Growth and Economic Development in Low-Income Countries*. Princeton, NJ: Princeton University Press.

Connelly, M. (2003) 'Population control is history: new perspectives on the international campaign to limit population growth'. *Comparative Study of History and Society*, 45(1): 122–147.

Connelly, M. (2008) *Fatal Misconception: The Struggle to Control World Population*. Cambridge, MA: Belknap Press.

Davis, K. (1951) *The Population of India and Pakistan*. Princeton, NJ: Princeton University Press.

Freedman, R. and J. Takeshita (1969) *Family Planning in Taiwan: An Experiment in Social Change*. Princeton, NJ: Princeton University Press.

Freedman, R., J. Takeshita and T. H. Sun (1964) Fertility and family planning in Taiwan: a case study of the demographic transition'. *American Journal of Sociology*, 70(1): 16–27.

Gillespie, D. (2000) 'Reimert T. Ravenholt, USAID's Population Program Stalwart'. *Population Reference Bureau Article*. Available from: www.prb.org/Publications/Articles/2000/ReimertTRavenholtUSAIDsPopulationProgramStalwart.aspx.

Greenhalgh, S. (2003) 'Science, modernity and the making of China's one-child policy'. *Population and Development Review*, 29(2): 163–196.

Harkavy, O. (1985) *The Ford Foundation's Work in Population*. New York: The Ford Foundation.

Hodgson, D. (1983) 'Demography as social science and policy science'. *Population and Development Review*, 9(1): 1–34.

Hodgson, D. (2003) 'Thompson, Warren S.'. In P. Demeny and G. McNicoll (eds.) *Encyclopedia of Population*. New York: Thomson-Gale. Pp. 939–940.

International Union for the Scientific Study of Population (IUSSP) (1985) *The IUSSP in History*. Liège: IUSSP.

Iskandar, N. and G. Jones (1974) 'The building of demographic competence in Indonesia'. *Studies in Family Planning*, 5(9): 289–293.

Jones, G. (2005) 'Why are population and development issues not given priority?' *Asia-Pacific Population Journal*, 20(1): 5–9.

McDonald, P., M. Yasin and G. Jones (1976) *Levels and Trends in Fertility and Childhood Mortality in Indonesia*. Monograph No. 1. Indonesian Fertility-Mortality Survey 1973. Jakarta: Demographic Institute, University of Indonesia.

Minkler, M. (1977) 'Consultants or colleagues: the role of US population advisors in India'. *Population and Development Review*, 3(4): 403–419.

Notestein, F. (1981) 'The PAA at age 50: memories of the early years of the association'. *Population Index*, 47(3): 484–488.

Office of Population Research (OPR) (1947) *Population Index*, 13(4): 274–348.

Potts, M. (2006) 'China's one child policy'. *British Medical Journal*, 333: 361–362.

Rao, M. (2004) *From Population Control to Reproductive Health: Malthusian Arithmetic*. New Delhi: Sage.

Reed, J. (1976) *The Birth Control Movement and American Society: From Private Vice to Public Virtue*. Princeton: Princeton University Press.

Smith, T. E. (1952) *Population Growth in Malaya: An Analysis of Recent Trends*. London: Royal Institute of International Affairs.

Sook, B., M. Lee and J. Yang (1963) 'A survey of fertility and attitudes toward family planning in rural Korea'. *Yonsei Medical Journal*, 4: 77–102.

Szreter, S. (1993) 'The idea of demographic transition and the study of fertility change: a critical intellectual history'. *Population and Development Review*, 19(4): 659–701.

Taeuber, I. B. (1958) *The Population of Japan*. Princeton: Princeton University Press.

Thompson, W. S. (1929) *Danger Spots in World Population*. New York: A. A. Knopf.

UNFPA Indonesia (2011) *UNFPA-GOI 8th Country Programme 2011–2015*. Jakarta: UNFPA.

United Nations (1961) *The Mysore Population Study*. Population Studies Series No. 34. New York: UN.

Utomo, I. (2015) Interview conducted by the author.

van der Tak, J. (2005a) 'Demographic destinies: interviews with presidents and secretary-treasurers of the Population Association of America. Interview with Frank Notestein'. *PAA Oral History Project Vol 1*. Washington, DC: Population Association of America.

van der Tak, J. (2005b) 'Demographic destinies: interviews with presidents and secretary-treasurers of the Population Association of America. Interview with Ronald Freedman'. *PAA Oral History Project Vol 2*. Washington, DC: Population Association of America.

van der Tak, J. (2005c) 'Demographic destinies: interviews with presidents and secretary-treasurers of the Population Association of America. Interview with Donald Bogue'. *PAA Oral History Project Vol 2*. Washington, DC: Population Association of America.

Williams, R. (2011) 'Rockefeller Foundation support to the Khanna study: population policy and the construction of demographic knowledge, 1945–1953'. University of Warwick: Department of History.

Zunz, O. (2012) *Philanthrophy in America: A History*. Princeton, NJ: Princeton University Press.

4
Asian historical demography

Cameron Campbell and Satomi Kurosu

Introduction

Historical demography as an academic discipline was established in the 1950s, and has made significant progress since then. Asian historical demography originally focused on estimation and interpretation of spatial and temporal trends and patterns in mortality and fertility. Key areas of substantive interest included the role of Malthusian processes in accounting for relationships between population and resources in the more distant past, the impact of colonialism, public health measures and other changes in the nineteenth and twentieth centuries. While most studies relied on aggregate estimates of population size or basic demographic rates from official sources, some made use of individual-level data from genealogies, population registers or other sources. *Asian Population History* edited by Liu, Lee, Reher, Saito and Wang (2001) provides a comprehensive survey of relevant findings on these classic topics for East, South-East and South Asia.

This chapter focuses on East, South-East and South Asia. East Asia receives disproportionate attention because the relative abundance of relevant sources and widespread interest in comparison between East and West has facilitated research. Temporally, we focus on the period up to and including the early twentieth century. We emphasize topics that received less attention in Liu, Lee, Reher, Saito and Wang (2001), most notably developments in the field since the publication of that volume.

Historical demography has recently expanded to consider outcomes other than birth and death, and make use of new sources and methods. Especially in China, Japan and Korea, analysis of individual-level data from population registers and genealogies has transformed the study of population in past times. These studies focus on reconstruction and comparison of patterns of social, economic and family contextual differences in adoption, fertility, marriage, mortality, migration and other demographic behaviour. Household and kinship organization have also emerged as major concerns. Elsewhere in Asia, research continues to focus on classic topics such as estimation and interpretation of trends and patterns in population size and demographic rates, and the relationship of these trends and patterns to local economic, social and political context.

The chapter is divided into three parts. It begins with an examination of two major areas of concern in Asian historical demography: the role of Malthusian processes in population dynamics, and household and family organization. It then moves on to research on specific demographic behaviours and outcomes, including marriage, reproduction, mortality and migration.

The chapter concludes by reviewing the most important sources for the study of Asian historical demography. As much as possible, we have organized the chapter topically, drawing attention to commonalities in sources, findings and debates across the region.

Through this chapter, we demonstrate that Asian historical demography has emerged as a distinct area of inquiry, with substantive concerns different from the ones that dominated European historical demography. Topics that distinguish Asian historical demography include the role of kinship networks in shaping individual outcomes, the diversity of marriage forms, the availability of adoption and other alternatives to biological reproduction, and in some societies, the use of infanticide. We suggest that the time is now right for research in Asia to emphasize comparisons within the continent, and move away from the monographic studies of single countries or regions and broad comparisons between Asia and the West that have dominated work so far.

Topics

Population dynamics in historical Asian populations

The broad outlines of long-term trends in population in East Asia, especially China, have been known for quite some time (Durand 1960; Ho 1959) and much work has focused on assessment of the role of Malthus's preventive and positive checks in population dynamics. From Malthus onward, the received wisdom has been that in pre-industrial Asia, the mortality-based positive check dominated population dynamics. The fertility-based preventive check was unimportant because women all married at early ages, and married couples did nothing to regulate their reproduction. Invocations of the positive check are especially common in interpretations of Chinese population dynamics (Chuang, Engelen and Wolf 2006; Wolf 2001). In this view, the famines and other disasters that beset China during the nineteenth century were a Malthusian response to the rapid growth in population that had taken place since the seventeenth century. In Japan, historians initially attributed population stagnation in the eighteenth century to a mortality-based Malthusian positive check (Saito 1992). In Korea, apparent stagnation in the nineteenth century was commonly attributed to economic and political crises (Ho, Lewis and Kang 2008).

Revisionist accounts, however, suggest that the fertility-based preventive check also played a role in many parts of Asia (Das Gupta 1995; Lee and Wang 1999). In this view, families adjusted their reproduction according to their circumstances. Revisionist arguments have been made most forcefully for Japan and China. They suggest that increased population growth in Japan in the nineteenth century and in China starting from the seventeenth century may have been the result of higher fertility, not lower death rates. Disasters in China in the nineteenth century may have been exogenous climatic or political shocks, not systematic responses to resource pressure. While population dynamics in South and South-East Asia are generally assumed to be Malthusian with a primary role for the positive check, there has been some recent recognition of a possible role for the preventive check. As we will discuss later, there is evidence that marital fertility in South and South-East Asia was moderate, and this at least partially reflected deliberate control for South Asia (Das Gupta 1995).

For South Asia, work continues to focus on reconstructing historical trends. Overall, total population appears to have grown slowly before the nineteenth century (Guha 2001a; Visaria and Visaria 1983). Available population estimates for the period before the nineteenth century are mostly indirect, and rely heavily on extrapolation from fragmentary evidence. Nevertheless, results suggest four distinct phases between the seventeenth century and mid-twentieth century. Growth appears to have been fastest in the first phase, the seventeenth century, one of the high points of the Mughal reign (Dyson 2004: 17). Growth was slower in the second phase, the eighteenth century. In the late eighteenth century, when Mughal rule collapsed and there were foreign incursions, there may have been no growth at all, or even decline (Dyson 1989: 8). This was also a period of multiple famines and other disasters (Guha 2001b: 35).

Population growth in India resumed in the third phase, the nineteenth century, reaching 283.4 million by 1900, and then accelerated dramatically in the 1920s. Much more data are available for the nineteenth century because the officials of the British East India Company began collecting information on the population under their control, and colonial authorities collected even more data starting in the late nineteenth century. Dyson (2004: 19) suggests that population growth in the nineteenth century may have been driven by modest reductions in mortality associated with increased social and economic stability. The acceleration in the early twentieth century was due to a further reduction in mortality. There were substantial regional variations in growth rates, with the clearest differences between north and south (Guha 2001b; Guha 2001a: 37–60). There were also some massive famines and other disasters in the late nineteenth century and early twentieth century.

Reconstructing temporal trends and spatial patterns in population growth has also been a central concern in studies of South-East Asia. Echoing arguments regarding East and South Asia, Reid (1987) has suggested that population growth rates were low overall, and that this reflected moderate levels of both mortality and fertility before the spread of wet-field rice cultivation, and Islam and Christianity. Population growth in South-East Asia appears to have occurred in three different phases. In the sixteenth and early seventeenth centuries, population growth rates varied by region, reflecting local circumstances. Some locations were characterized by economic expansion and increasing urbanization consistent with population growth. At the same time, other locations experienced warfare, famine and disease that may have reduced population, and marital fertility may have been lower (Reid 2001).

From the seventeenth century to the middle of the eighteenth century, the population grew very slowly or in some cases declined (Reid 1987, 2001). It is unclear whether this reflected a systematic Malthusian response to population pressure on resources, or the influence of exogenous factors. Economic stagnation, interaction with colonial powers, warfare and climate shocks have been suggested as possible reasons for stagnation or decline (Boomgaard 2001). In north Vietnam, famine and war substantially reduced the population, and helped drive the settlement of south Vietnam (Li 1998). While these may have been systematic responses to changes in the balance between population and resources, they also may have been the result of exogenous shocks that had nothing to do with population pressure.

In the third phase, the nineteenth century, the population of South-East Asia grew rapidly. Studies have largely discounted earlier concerns that the apparent growth was an artefact of bad data, and credible estimates now put growth rates in many locations at above two per cent per annum (Hirschman and Bonaparte 2012: 18–19). Suggested causes for the rapid increase include a reduction in warfare as a result of colonial rule, and higher fertility in frontier regions (Owen 1987b; Reid 1987). The spread of wet-rice agriculture to frontier areas in South-East Asia during the late nineteenth century and early twentieth century also contributed to this rapid population growth.

Household and family

Recognition of differences in family and household between Europe and Asia goes back at least to Malthus. Empirical research carried out in the second half of the twentieth century has refined our understanding of family and household in Asia, especially in East Asia. This research has not challenged the broad outlines of key differences between European and Asian families described by Hajnal (1965, 1982), but it has uncovered important differences between and within societies. Evidence confirms that female marriage was early and universal, and that at least in South and East Asia, newly married couples joined existing households, new households formed through the division of existing ones, and households were more likely to include additional kin than were households in Europe. Nevertheless, there was substantial diversity in household structure, processes of household formation and headship succession, and organization of kin networks. Families seeking to ensure continuity also had a diverse variety of options for sustaining themselves, most notably adoption and variant forms of marriage discussed later.

In China and North India, the joint family household was the ideal, and networks of kin outside the household played an important role. Parents, sons, their wives and their children were supposed to live together, and kin networks such as lineages were key units of social organization. Low life expectancy and other constraints, however, meant that at most stages of their life course, the proportion of Chinese who could have lived in households with three or more generations was not very large (Zhao 2000). Large, complex households also appear to have been rare in India (Guha 2001a: 95–109). Nevertheless, Wolf (1985) showed that in Taiwan, the three-generation household was an important part of the domestic cycle, in that many individuals did experience life with their parents and grandparents when they were children. Larger, more complex joint households consisting of married brothers, cousins or still more distant kin may have been common elsewhere in China (Lee and Campbell 1997).

Elsewhere in Asia, other systems prevailed. In Japan, the stem family became the ideal family form and the most common one for commoners from the seventeenth century. The stem family was also prevalent in Korea (Park and Cho 1995). Comparative studies have contrasted the stem family in Asia with its European counterpart (Saito 1998). In other parts of South-East Asia, bilateral kinship systems prevailed, with close ties to both maternal and paternal relatives, flexible living arrangements and less rigidly defined gender roles compared to East and South Asia (Hirschman and Teerawichitchainan 2003).

Perhaps the most important recent substantive development in our understanding of the role of the family in Asian society is the realization that extended families not only facilitated the marriage and reproduction of junior members by providing resources, but in some cases constrained them (Das Gupta 1999). Malthus and his intellectual heirs assumed resources available through the extended family underpinned the high fertility of married couples by insulating them against the cost of their childbearing. For China, however, Lee and Wang (1999) have argued that extended families exercised collective control over the fertility and other behaviour of their members. Das Gupta (1995) has made a similar argument for India. This is an important theoretical advance in that it resolves an obvious but unacknowledged conundrum: in the absence of collective control by the extended family over the resource use of individual members, families should have faced a 'tragedy of the commons'.

Inspired by this growing appreciation of the complexity of family contextual influences on behaviour, recent comparative projects have moved beyond description of differences in household formation and marriage, to examination of how household and family context influenced individual demographic and social outcomes. Participants in the Eurasia Project in Population and Family History (EAP) used household register data from eighteenth and nineteenth century communities in Europe and Asia and the same or similar statistical models to examine the relationship between mortality, fertility, and marriage outcomes and characteristics of the community, the household and the individual (Bengtsson, Campbell, Lee et al. 2004; Tsuya, Wang, Alter, Lee et al. 2010; Lundh, Kurosu et al. 2014). Similarly, the 'Life at the Extremes' project used early twentieth century Taiwanese and nineteenth century Dutch household register data to compare family influences on demographic behaviour in Europe and Asia (Chuang, Engelen and Wolf 2006; Engelen and Hsieh 2007; Engelen, Shepherd and Yang 2011; Engelen and Wolf 2005). More recently, researchers working with Japanese, Korean and Chinese historical register data have formed a network to share expertise and develop plans for coordination and comparison (Campbell 2013; Dong, Campbell, Kurosu, Yang and Lee 2015).

For South-East Asia, quantitative evidence on household structure and family organization is limited. Researchers are more dependent on accounts of travellers and colonial officials, and fragmentary records and anthropological observations from the early twentieth century. In Java, Indonesia, it appears that households typically consisted of parents and their children (Boomgaard 1989: 150–151). Sometimes a daughter-in-law or son-in-law would coreside with the parents. Coresidence of more distant kin was uncommon.

Demographic behaviours and outcomes

Mortality

There was substantial variation in mortality levels within Asia, but in contrast with the predictions of a Malthusian interpretation of Asian population dynamics, there has been little to suggest that mortality levels in historical Asia were systematically higher than in pre-industrial Europe. For example, comprehensive reviews of available mortality estimates for different locations and time periods in China reveal substantial internal variation reflecting differences in population density, ecology and local disease regime, but not much evidence that mortality was systematically higher than in Europe (Lavely and Wong 1998; Bengtsson, Campbell, Lee et al. 2004). Early surveys of mortality in Tokugawa Japan based on analysis of Tokugawa household registers have suggested that death rates were broadly comparable to those in historical Europe (Hanley 1974) or lower (Hanley and Yamamura 1977).

Analysis of individual-level data has revealed distinctive features of mortality patterns by age, sex and other characteristics in at least some Asian populations. In the small number of pre-twentieth century Chinese populations for which reliable estimates of female mortality are available, female death rates were higher than male death rates from infancy into early adulthood (Campbell 1997; Lee and Campbell 1997). Male mortality in late middle age and old age was higher in China and other parts of the Far East than in model life tables with comparable levels of mortality at earlier ages (Goldman 1980). It has been suggested, however, that this pattern was not unique to the Far East (Zhao 2003). Mortality chances in China and Japan were also influenced by community, household and individual context (Bengtsson, Campbell, Lee et al. 2004; Engelen, Shepherd and Yang 2011). Household context was a more important determinant of mortality in East Asia than in Western Europe, where socioeconomic status was more influential (Bengtsson, Campbell, Lee et al. 2004).

Famines, warfare, epidemics and other mortality crises have been major foci in Asian historical demography. Apparent associations between population pressure and the frequency of crises were frequently cited as evidence of a Malthusian positive check in Asia, especially in late nineteenth century China. Newer studies make use of more detailed demographic data to map the mortality of famine, epidemics and other disasters by age, sex, region, and in some cases, individual or household characteristics. Late nineteenth century and early twentieth century Indian famines in particular have been the subject of detailed studies using census and vital registration data (Dyson 2002; Guz 1989; Maharatna 2002). Jannetta (1987) has argued that Japan's geography and isolation limited epidemics and helped keep mortality rates lower than in Europe. Recent analysis of microdata has also shed new light on the mortality impact of crises in East

Asia, and especially on variations by age, sex and other individual and household characteristics (Campbell and Lee 2010a; Tsuya and Kurosu 2010). Boomgaard (2001) has examined the frequency of various types of crises in Indonesia, and has suggested that they may have contributed more to mortality than previously thought.

Recent studies have illuminated mortality trends and patterns in the late nineteenth and early twentieth centuries, especially in South and South-East Asia. Bhat (1989) has shown that mortality rates in India were lower than previously thought, and comparable to those in rural China. The unusual and widely noted phenomenon of lower male than female mortality in India, meanwhile, did not emerge until the 1950s. Ortega Osona (2001) examined changes in the pattern of mortality fluctuations in Punjab and Bengal in the late nineteenth century. Dyson and Das Gupta (2001) examined time trends in demographic rates in the Punjab. Owen (1987a, 1998) and Xenos and Ng (1998) examined time trends and spatial variation in mortality in the Philippines in the nineteenth century. Vital statistics collected and published by Japanese colonial authorities in Taiwan in the first half of the twentieth century are of exceptionally high quality, and have been used extensively to study mortality trends and patterns there (Barclay 1954; Liu and Liu 2001; Shepherd 2011a, 2011b).

Studies of morbidity and cause-specific mortality have helped clarify the role of public health efforts, medical innovations, and other factors in shaping mortality trends before the worldwide decline in death rates that started in the 1950s. Trends in disease and mortality in Taiwan in the early twentieth century are especially well documented because of the availability of rich, detailed data (Engelen, Shepherd and Yang 2011; Liu and Liu 2001). For mainland China, Campbell (1997) used early twentieth century data from Beijing to examine the impact of early public health interventions. Boomgaard (1987) and Gardiner and Oey (1987) used colonial reports from Java to study mortality and morbidity there during the nineteenth and early twentieth centuries. Cholera and influenza mortality in India have been subjected to study (Dyson 1989), as have disease patterns in the British Army in India (Guha 2001a: 110–139).

Reproduction

There is now agreement that total fertility rates in Europe and East Asia were similar and that marital fertility in historical East Asia was lower than in Europe, but disagreement about whether low marital fertility was the result of deliberate behaviour (Campbell and Lee 2010b; Cornell 1996; Hanley 1974; Tsuya, Wang, Alter, Lee et al. 2010). While many scholars argue that low marital fertility was the result of deliberate behaviour on the part of families (Lee and Wang 1999), others regard it as an unintended byproduct of other factors (Wolf 2001; Chuang, Engelen and Wolf 2006). Even if low marital fertility was common in East Asian societies, the reasons for it may have varied. Cultural and social institutions that influence marriage and reproduction deserve further examination. These factors include spousal separation after marriage (Cornell 1996), arranged marriage, breastfeeding, coital frequency, poverty and malnutrition (Lavely 2007; Engelen and Hsieh 2007).

Revisionist accounts of population dynamics have been most influential for China and Japan. Japanese historical demographers have reinterpreted available evidence to emphasize a fertility-based preventive check in which low population growth reflected 'rational' behaviour on the part of Japanese peasants who were seeking to maintain or improve their standard of living (Smith 1977; Hanley and Yamamura 1977). Similarly, some historical demographers argue that in China, extended families influenced the fertility of the couples who depended on them for resources (Lee and Wang 1999; Wang, Lee and Campbell 1995; Zhao 1997). Deliberate fertility control, infanticide and other behaviours would have had profound implications for the Chinese demographic regime (Lavely and Wong 1998).

Claims that low marital fertility in China, Japan and India reflected deliberate behaviours are based on evidence that families exercised preferences for the number and sex composition of children. In China and Japan, they deliberately adjusted their reproductive behaviour according to the sex composition of their surviving children and their goals for the overall sex composition of their family. Chinese couples generally practiced son preference (Campbell and Lee 2010b), while couples in Japan were more likely to seek a sex-balanced and possibly sex-ordered (daughter first) offspring set (Smith 1977; Tsuya, Wang, Alter, Lee et al. 2010). There is substantial evidence that families in both countries used infanticide to achieve goals for family size and sex composition (Drixler 2013; Lee, Wang and Campbell 1994). Female infanticide was also common in India (Guha 2001a: 9). Though Korea was heavily influenced by the Confucian family norms that underpinned son preference in China, we are not aware of any historical studies suggesting that son preference led to infanticide.

Elsewhere in Asia, marital fertility may also have been lower than previously thought, and perhaps even subject to deliberate control. Analysis of Indian census data suggests moderate levels of marital fertility before the fertility decline (Bhat 1989). A recent study of Dutch population registers from Sri Lanka in the mid-eighteenth century also claims evidence of fertility limitation (Drixler and Kok 2016). In South-East Asia, marital fertility may actually have been relatively low before the spread of wet-field rice cultivation and arrival of Islam and Christianity changed marriage patterns and reproductive behaviour (Hull 2001; Reid 1987, 2001). In particular, travellers' reports suggest that in populations in these regions that had not yet converted to Islam or Christianity, birth rates were low. Although women began childbearing at a relatively early age, they may have had their births at a slow pace and ceased childbearing early. Conversion to Christianity or Islam and/or shifts to wet-rice cultivation may have increased birth rates by encouraging a domestic role for wives and reducing spousal separation.

Adoption played a key role in reproduction everywhere in East Asia. Indeed, it may have helped make low marital fertility sustainable by providing another option for attaining goals for the number or sex of children. Practices varied in terms of timing, with some adoptions taking place in childhood, but others taking place in adulthood. Studies have focused on understanding adoption in the context of childlessness, need for old age care or household labour, and the desire to secure an heir or otherwise secure family continuity (Kurosu 2013; Lee and Wang 1999: 108; Wolf and Huang 1980; Wang and Lee 1998; Kim and Park 2010).

If low marital fertility in the past reflected deliberate behaviour on the part of couples, at least some parts of Asia may have been predisposed to rapid fertility decline. While this has been argued most forcefully for East Asia (Lee and Wang 1999), it has also been suggested for South Asia (Das Gupta 1995). Lee and Wang (1999) suggested that this culture of control over reproduction set the stage for rapid fertility decline in East Asia: since fertility limitation was already within couples' 'calculus of conscious choice' (Coale 1973), decline only required a change in family size preferences and new technology to facilitate attainment of those goals, not a fundamental transition in couples' mindset. This may also account for the rapid fertility declines in South-East Asian settings such as Thailand and Vietnam where families retained traditional ways of thinking about reproduction.

Marriage

Marriage patterns in Asia had some common elements. In East Asia, South Asia and at least some parts of South-East Asia (Boomgaard 1989: 140–141; Reid 1987: 38), female marriage was early and universal. In China, Korea and South Asia, marriages were arranged. While arranged marriage was also common among high status families in Japan, its prevalence among lower status families is less clear. All over Asia, couples tended to join the household of the husband's or wife's parents instead of forming their own household. In East and South Asia couples usually joined the husband's existing household (Hajnal 1982; Skinner 1997). South-East Asian societies, however, were almost universally bilateral and newly married couples often joined the wife's family (Hirschman and Teerawichitchainan 2003).

Comparative studies have delineated the role of family and household characteristics in shaping marriage chances in Asia, and contrasted patterns there with the ones in Europe (Lundh, Kurosu et al. 2014; Engelen and Wolf 2005). Using individual-level data, these studies reveal that apparent aggregate differences in timing and prevalence of marriage in Asia and Europe conceal numerous similarities in the patterns of influence of household and kin characteristics on marriage chances. For example, in both Europe and Asia, the presence of parents and siblings was as important as socioeconomic status and other factors in shaping marriage chances.

Depending on community norms and family circumstances, variant forms of marriage occurred. In some cases, a new couple joined the wife's household. In Japan, the husband might be adopted as a son by the wife's parents. In parts of China where this was an option, the husband would retain his name, but any son he fathered would take his wife's family name. Child betrothal was also common in many regions in Asia. In China, a daughter might be adopted to help take care of a young son when he was a child, and then become his wife when he was older (Wolf and Huang 1980).

Divorce was rare, except in Japan and some parts of South-East Asia. In Tokugawa Japan, the divorce rate was very high. Divorce took place within the first few years after marriage (Kurosu 2011). Divorce rates only fell after the Meiji restoration, when the government restricted it and promoted a 'traditional' model of marriage (Fuess 2004). Divorce rates were also relatively high before modernization and industrialization in Malaysia, parts of Indonesia such as Java, and Taiwan (Boomgaard 1989: 145; Goode 1993). The contexts in which divorce rates were high had some common features including early marriage, wife's active role in agriculture, wife's parents' support, and ease of remarriage (Hirschman and Teerawichitchainan 2003; Kurosu 2011).

The most detailed studies of remarriage are for East Asia. Remarriage was least common in China, and more common in Japan (Lundh, Kurosu et al. 2014). Remarriage was more common among men than women, and more common among younger widows than older ones (Chen, Campbell and Lee 2014). In China and Japan, individual likelihood of remarriage was affected by socioeconomic status and presence of kin (Kurosu 2007). Remarriage most commonly followed widowhood, but in Japan and some parts of South-East Asia, it also took place after divorce.

Migration

Studies of migration in Asia originally focused on large, long-term population movements associated with the settlement or resettlement of underpopulated regions. The settlement or repopulation of regions in China has been an especially common topic, with numerous historical studies focused on population movements from North to South China, into South-West China, and more recently, into North-East China. These studies focused on the political, economic and institutional causes and consequences of these population movements. Major population movements that are widely known but perhaps not studied in as much detail include the settlement of south Vietnam in the seventeenth and eighteenth centuries (Li 1998), the movement from hills to valley floors in Indonesia and other parts of South-East Asia in connection with the development of wet-rice cultivation, and the movement from rural areas to cities.

Attention has now turned to the more routine forms of migration, including the circulation of individuals and families within regions, or between the countryside and the city, because individual-level data allow researchers to characterize migrants and relate the probability of migration to individual, household and community circumstances (Campbell 2013). Results so far suggest that individuals were anything but sedentary. For two villages in north-eastern Japan during the Tokugawa era, Tsuya and Kurosu (2013) show that there were differences by social class and family context in the likelihood of out-migration for service, marriage/adoption and other reasons. For early twentieth century Korea, Kye and Park (2013) have studied the characteristics of migrants in Seoul, and Son and Lee (2013) have studied origins, destinations and family characteristics in a rural township. Doeppers (1998a, 1998b) used parish and civil registration data to examine the characteristics of urban migrants in the Philippines in the nineteenth century.

Sources

Genealogies

Lineage genealogies are one of the most commonly used sources of individual-level data for Chinese and Korean historical demography. They may also be available among ethnic Chinese populations in South-East Asia, but we are not aware of any published demographic studies that have used them. Lineage genealogies vary tremendously in terms of their completeness and level of detail. They are compiled for use in ancestor worship, and to define relationships among living members of a lineage. Typically they are retrospective, updated at regular intervals by surviving family members. The most common Chinese genealogies consist solely of the names of the male descendants of a lineage founder, organized by generation, with each male linked to their father (Telford 1986). Some genealogies include dates of birth and death, allowing for estimation of fertility and mortality. The most detailed but least common Chinese genealogies include information about social status, marriage and daughters. While many Chinese genealogies only span five to fifteen generations and record only a few hundred individuals, the largest Chinese genealogies span 20 or more generations and record thousands of individuals.

Korean lineage genealogies resemble the largest and most detailed Chinese genealogies (Park and Lee 2008). They often include details not available in Chinese genealogies. Information on social status is especially plentiful. Early in the Chosun dynasty (1392–1895), genealogies not only recorded daughters, but their husbands and children. They also recorded information about the natal families of wives. Early Korean genealogies have proven most useful for studies of marriage, adoption and succession (Lee and Park 2008; Kim and Park 2010). Later in the Chosun, especially after the seventeenth century, Korean genealogies came to resemble Chinese ones. They no longer recorded information on the families of wives and daughters, but recorded dates of birth and death for males, making them useful for demographic studies.

The first published demographic study to use an Asian family genealogy was Yuan's (1931) study of trends in life expectancy in southern China from the fourteenth to the nineteenth centuries. Later, Liu transcribed and analysed lineage genealogies from Zhejiang, Fujian, and other provinces in China to produce the first contemporary estimates of long-term trends in mortality and fertility during the Ming (1368–1644) and Qing (1644–1911) dynasties (Liu 1985, 1995a, 1995b). Zhao (1997) used a lineage genealogy to reconstruct mortality trends over a 1,000 year period. English-language studies using Korean genealogies are more recent, for example Lee and Park (2008) and Lee and Son (2010). In Japan, available genealogies mostly record Samurai families, the elite bureaucrats and administrators during the Tokugawa era. Studies focus on patterns of succession via marriage and adoption, and social mobility as well as estimates of fertility, mortality and reproduction (e.g. Yamamura 1974). Genealogies should be available for Vietnam, but we have not yet located relevant studies.

Chinese and Korean lineage genealogies have limitations relevant to their use in demographic studies. The most well-known limitation of lineage genealogies is that they omit sons who died in infancy and childhood, and almost all daughters, so that fertility based on recorded births is underestimated, and mortality is only estimated for males who survive to adolescence (Lee and Son 2010; Harrell 1987; Zhao 2001). The most prominent Chinese exception is the Qing Imperial Lineage genealogy, which records almost all sons and daughters, and provides dates of death for sons, and dates of death or out-marriage for daughters (Lee, Campbell and Wang 1993). Korean genealogies are more likely than Chinese genealogies to include daughters and wives, but may not provide the marriage or death dates normally needed for demographic analysis. To compensate for omitted births, fertility estimates typically adjust rates based on an assumed level of under-recording.

Selectivity in the lineages that maintained genealogies and in the members who are recorded suggests additional caution (Harrell 1987; Zhao 2001; Campbell and Lee 2002; Lee 2010). Demographically successful lineages and lineage branches were more likely to be recorded in a genealogy, since they had descendants who could maintain it. High status lineage members were especially likely to be included in Chinese (Campbell and Lee 2002; Harrell 1987) and Korean (Lee 2010) genealogies. Chinese genealogies were more likely to record men if they had more sons (Campbell and Lee 2002), raising the possibility that fertility estimates from genealogies are upwardly biased (Campbell and Lee 2002).

Household registers

Household registers have become an increasingly important source for the study of historical demography in China, Japan and Korea. Registers record on a prospective basis the demographic events, household context, socioeconomic status and other characteristics of the individuals in a community. The resulting databases resemble contemporary panel survey data, and may be analysed using the same quantitative methods, most notably event-history analysis. These methods allow for examination of how community, household and individual characteristics influence demographic outcomes such as marriage, migration, fertility and mortality. Registers differ in format according to when they were produced. Before the twentieth century, they recorded the population either annually or triennially. They allow for longitudinal linkage of observations of the same individual or household across successive registers, and for reconstruction of life and family histories. The data may also be left unlinked, and analysed cross-sectionally, as in Drixler (2013). Registers compiled by Japanese colonial authorities in Taiwan and Korea in the early twentieth century were produced differently. Each household had an entry that was initiated at a specific point in time, and then annotated as individuals left or joined the household, or experienced other changes.

The earliest demographic studies using household registers were by Akira Hayami, who began to collect and analyse Tokugawa (1600–1868) Japanese population registers in the late 1960s. He produced estimates of marriage, fertility and mortality (Hayami 1986, 1987), and measurements of household size, structure and domestic cycle (Hayami 1972). In the 1970s, Wolf and his collaborators began to use registers compiled by Japanese colonial authorities to study family organization and demographic behaviour in Taiwan in the first half of the twentieth century (Wolf and Huang 1980). In the 1980s, Lee and collaborators began their analysis of household registers from eighteenth and nineteenth century North-East China (Lee and Campbell 1997).

Researchers have begun to analyse Korean registers from the Chosun dynasty (Kim, Park and Jo 2013). For South Asia, one recent study makes use of population registers compiled by Dutch authorities in Sri Lanka in the eighteenth century (Drixler and Kok 2016).

Tokugawa Japanese registers come in two forms. *Shūmon aratame cho* (hereafter SAC) have been the principal source of data in Japanese historical demography (Cornell and Hayami 1986). SAC are annual registers of religious affiliation compiled by local headmen. They were initiated in 1638 by the Tokugawa government as a measure to prevent the entry and spread of Christianity. The SAC were typically de jure records of the legally domiciled residents of a community. *Ninbetsu aratame cho* (NAC) emerged from the SAC. Most NAC recorded the de facto population of the community, and did not include information on religious affiliation of individual villagers. Surviving NAC and SAC are mainly from the late Tokugawa period, that is the mid-eighteenth century to 1870. The more detailed listings include name, age, relationship to household head, and household landholding and social status. Sex may be inferred from relationship to household head. Information on migrants may include their origin or destination, and reasons for their movements such as marriage, adoption or service. The compilation of SAC ceased when the current Japanese household register, *Koseki*, was initiated in 1872. Although *Koseki* data are not accessible, pilot registers compiled in 1870 are available.

The most commonly used Chinese registers are those compiled in North-East China during the Qing (1644–1911) dynasty (Lee and Campbell 1997; Ding, Guo, Li (Lee) and Kang (Campbell) 2004). These registers recorded populations with a hereditary affiliation with the Eight Banners, a civil and military organization that the Qing state used to govern China. Distinguishing features of these sources include complete recording of married women and widows, detail on household relationship and generally excellent recording of mortality. Sons who died in infancy or childhood were often omitted, along with most daughters. Databases constructed from registers from Liaoning and Shuangcheng, Heilongjiang have been publicly released as the China Multi-Generational Panel Dataset (CMGPD), Liaoning and Shuangcheng (Lee and Campbell 2010; Lee, Campbell and Chen 2010). The Liaoning registers cover the period 1749 to 1909, while the Shuangcheng registers cover the period from 1866 to 1914. Similar registers covering populations in and around Beijing survive, but have yet to be exploited for demographic analysis. Household registers compiled in the Tang dynasty (AD 618–907) are the oldest available records of this kind and have been analysed in Liao (2001, 2004), but are fragmentary, limiting the scope of analysis and requiring advanced methods to account for their limitations.

Korean registers produced during the Chosun dynasty are also emerging as a source for studying family, population and society in the past (Park and Lee 2008). These household registers were triennial, and organized by household. Indeed, many aspects of the format are remarkably similar. There was a much higher turnover between registers than in the CMGPD, making reconstruction of life and family histories via longitudinal linkage much more difficult (Kim, Park and Jo 2013). Household relationship was not recorded in as much precision, making it more difficult to reconstruct families and trace descent lines. Relative to the CMGPD, however, the Korean registers provide much more detail on social status and the natal families of wives. Thus far, registers for three locations have been transcribed: Danseong, Daegu and Chaeju.

The most complete and detailed East Asian registers are from the late nineteenth and early twentieth centuries, and were compiled by colonial authorities. Taiwanese registers compiled by Japanese colonial authorities have been subject to analysis since at least the 1970s, and have been shown to be of extremely high quality. They are especially well-suited to the calculation of mortality and fertility rates. In contrast with almost every other historical Chinese population source, the registers not only recorded sons who died in infancy and childhood, but all daughters. The registers are amenable to the study of a variety of other topics, including household organization, marriage, adoption and migration (Wolf and Huang 1980). Demographic analysis of data in Korean registers from the Japanese colonial era has just begun, but initial results suggest the potential of these data to illuminate population and family processes in early twentieth century Korea (Kim and Park 2009; Son and Lee 2013). Annual civil registers (*vecindario*) from some locations in the Philippines exist for the late nineteenth century and have at least some features in common with household registers (Doeppers 1998a, 1998b).

Church and temple records

Parish registers of baptisms, marriages and burials have been an important source for the study of the demographic history of the Philippines, and Goa, India, where the Catholic Church dominated. These registers are useful not only because they offer counts of key demographic events, but also because they may be used in family reconstitution studies. By the nineteenth century, registration of baptisms, marriages and burials was common in the Philippines and became a major source of population statistics compiled by the Church and later the Spanish colonial bureaucracy (Cullinane 1998). These records have been the basis of studies of the demographic history of the Philippines such as Owen (1987a, 1998) and Xenos and Ng (1998). Parish registers from Goa were used in some early demographic studies that demonstrate their potential (Srivastava 1976, 1987), but we have not yet located any recent studies. Presumably, parish registers were also compiled in French colonies in South-East Asia such as Vietnam, but we have yet to locate any published studies.

In Japan, Buddhist temples in some locations maintained death registers (*kakochō*) that recorded the deaths of members of the local population affiliated with the temple. In some cases, they recorded the age and sex of the deceased, their village of residence and even the cause of death. In contrast with many other Asian historical sources, at least some of them recorded the deaths of infants, and even stillbirths (Jannetta and Preston 1991). Like parish registers, the temple death registers only recorded events, and did not provide a denominator. The assumptions required to estimate the size and age composition of the total population are sometimes controversial (Saito 1992).

Censuses

Asian states have a long tradition of producing population counts, but none of these resembled modern censuses, and the individual-level data do not survive. National or regional counts were typically produced by adding together totals for local areas reported by officials, not by a complete count directly managed by the central government. Counts often focused on specific segments of the population, for example, adult males, taxpayers, tribute payers or household heads. Criteria and geographic coverage for these early population counts might vary from one count to another, leading to wildly varying figures.

China is well known for the state's efforts at various points in time to count subjects (Ho 1959; Durand 1960). While counts date back at least to the Zhou dynasty (1046 BC–256 BC), the first count that is treated as reliable is from the Han dynasty (206 BC–AD 226), in the year AD 2. Such counts have been used to produce estimates of the total size of China's population at different points in time, and assess the role of long-term Malthusian homeostatic processes. Tax and household registers from the Chinese-inspired *ritsuryo* system in ancient Japan survive, and have been used to estimate long-term population dynamics (Kito 1983; Farris 1985).

Detailed population and household counts are only available for a few locations and time periods in Asia before the nineteenth century. Ecclesiastical authorities produced counts of tribute payers in the Philippines in 1591, and on numerous occasions afterward. In Vietnam, counts of households or taxpayers were produced as early as the ninth century AD (Li 1998). Colonial authorities in Indonesia produced population estimates and other demographic statistics beginning in 1820 (Boomgaard 1989, 1987). In Japan, the Tokugawa government conducted surveys every six years between 1721 and 1846 (Hayami 1986). A tabulation of populations and households from 1886 has also been used in demographic studies (Feeney and Hamano 1990; Hayami 1987).

Especially in South Asia, modern censuses have been an important source for the study of family and demographic change during the late nineteenth and early twentieth centuries. The first modern census in Asia was in India in 1871. Bhat (1989) and other studies in Dyson (1989) used Indian census data to examine changes in mortality and fertility. Visaria and Visaria (1983) used census data to reconstruct trends in population size and distribution in India. Caldwell (2001) also used late nineteenth century and early twentieth century census data to study changes in marriage patterns in Sri Lanka.

Vital registration

Vital registration was carried out in some locations in Asia starting in the middle or late nineteenth century, or the beginning of the twentieth. The resulting vital statistics have been especially important in illuminating trends and patterns in demographic behaviour in India. In Punjab, death registration began in 1868, and birth registration began in 1880. The resulting data from Punjab and Bengal have been used in studies of trends in mortality, and appear to be of high quality (Dyson and Das Gupta 2001; Ortega Osona 2001). Other studies, of Indian famines, rely heavily on vital registration data (Dyson 2002; Maharatna 2002). Published vital statistics in Taiwan in the early twentieth century are also of extraordinarily high quality (Barclay 1954). Vital statistics were compiled in a small number of major cities elsewhere in China in the early twentieth century (Campbell 1997). Vital statistics data are also available for Sri Lanka (Langford 2001), Japan and other locations beginning in the late nineteenth or early twentieth century. For Tokugawa Japan, pregnancy registers (*Kainin kakiage cho*) that tracked pregnancies and their outcomes to prevent abortion and infanticide (Drixler 2013) share some of the features of vital event registers, as do the previously mentioned temple registers.

Conclusion

Asian historical demography is developing rapidly as a result of the availability of new data and new methods. From an initial concern with the role of Malthusian processes in population dynamics and East/West comparisons of family and household organization, at least for East Asia the field is now moving towards a focus on the role of community, household and individual characteristics in shaping specific demographic behaviours. This development has been driven largely by the creation and analysis of longitudinal individual- and household-level datasets, some spanning many generations. Results from these micro-level studies have clarified how household and family outcomes shaped the life outcomes of individuals. The configuration of kin around the individual, including the presence or absence of specific relatives, has emerged as a factor of considerable importance. For South and South-East Asia, work continues on reconstructing geographic and temporal patterns of population variation, and relating them to social, political, economic and ecological context.

Data to support further household- and individual-level analysis of the determinants of demographic behaviour are most abundant for East Asia, but prospects also exist for additional, more detailed studies using micro-level data in some other parts of Asia. Researchers working with East Asian household registers continue to expand their datasets by adding new communities, and in some cases linking to other sources of data. As the number of sites available for each country increases, we can look forward to more within-country comparisons to complement existing between-country comparisons. Parish registers and other individual-level data for the nineteenth century Philippines seems relatively abundant and accessible (Doeppers and Xenos 1998), and they also exist for at least some parts of India (Srivastava 1976, 1987).

Prospects for detailed comparisons within Asia, especially within East Asia, are good. As more results on trends and patterns in population accumulate for South and South-East Asia, we can look forward to pan-Asian comparisons. Within East Asia, household registers available for some parts of China, Japan and Korea before the twentieth century are similar enough in format and content to raise the possibility of fine-grained comparisons between settings that are similar in terms of broad cultural context, but differ in terms of specifics (Campbell 2013; Dong, Campbell, Kurosu, Yang and Lee 2015). Such comparison between settings with broadly similar contexts may turn out to be more productive than the East/West comparisons that have been the preoccupation of researchers for decades. It should be easier to link demographic behaviour to particular features of economic, social or cultural context. By contrast, East and West differ on many dimensions, thus explaining any difference in demographic outcomes by ascribing it to a single or small number of dimensions is nearly impossible.

Acknowledgements

The authors are grateful to Dwight Davis, Hao Dong, James Lee, Xi Song, three anonymous referees and the volume editors for their comments and feedback on early versions of this chapter.

References

Barclay, G.W. (1954) *Colonial Development and Population in Taiwan*. Princeton, NJ: Princeton University Press.
Bengtsson, T., C. Campbell, J. Lee et al. (2004) *Life Under Pressure: Mortality and Living Standards in Europe and Asia, 1700–1900*. Cambridge, MA and London, England: MIT Press.
Bhat, P. N. M. (1989) 'Mortality and fertility in India, 1881–1961: a reassessment'. In T. Dyson (ed.) *India's Historical Demography: Studies in Famine, Disease and Society*. London: Curzon Press. Pp. 73–118.
Boomgaard, P. (1987) 'Morbidity and mortality in Java, 1820–1880: changing patterns of disease and death'. In G. O. Norman (ed.) *Death and Disease in Southeast Asia: Explorations in Social, Medical and Demographic History*. Singapore, Oxford and New York: Oxford University Press. Pp. 33–47.
Boomgaard, P. (1989) *Children of the Colonial State: Population Growth and Economic Development in Java, 1795–1880*. Amsterdam: Free University Press.
Boomgaard, P. (2001) 'Crisis mortality in seventeenth-century Indonesia'. In T. J. Liu, J. Lee, D. S. Reher, O. Saito and F. Wang (eds.) *Asian Population History*. Oxford: Oxford University Press. Pp. 191–220.
Caldwell, B. (2001) 'Marriage patterns and demographic change in Sri Lanka: a long-term perspective'. In T. J. Liu, J. Lee, D. S. Reher, O. Saito and F. Wang (eds.) *Asian Population History*. Oxford: Oxford University Press. Pp. 416–440.
Campbell, C. (1997) 'Public health efforts in China before 1949 and their effects on mortality: the case of Beijing'. *Social Science History*, 21(2): 179–218.
Campbell, C. (2013) 'Migration in historical East Asia: new sources and new methods'. *The History of the Family*, 18(4): 371–377.
Campbell, C. and J. Lee (2002) 'State views and local views of population: linking and comparing genealogies and household registers in Liaoning, 1749–1909'. *History and Computing*, 14(1+2): 9–29.
Campbell, C. and J. Lee (2010a) 'Demographic impacts of climatic fluctuations in Northeast China, 1749–1909'. In S. Kurosu, T. Bengtsson and C. Campbell (eds.) *Demographic Responses to Economic and Environmental Crises*. Kashiwa: Reitaku University Press. Pp. 107–132.

Campbell, C. and J. Lee (2010b) 'Fertility control in historical China revisited: new methods for an old debate'. *The History of the Family*, 15(4): 370–385.

Chen, S., C. Campbell and J. Lee (2014) 'Categorical inequality and gender difference: marriage and remarriage in Northeast China, 1749–1913'. Chapter 11 in L. Christer, S. Kurosu et al. *Similarity in Difference: Marriage in Europe and Asia, 1700–1900*. MIT Press. Pp. 393–438.

Chuang, Y. C., T. Engelen and A. P. Wolf (eds.) (2006) *Positive or Preventive? Reproduction in Taiwan and the Netherlands, 1850–1940*. Amsterdam: Aksant Academic Publishers.

Coale, A. J. (1973) 'The demographic transition reconsidered'. In *Proceedings of the International Population Conference, Volume 1*. Liège, Belgium: International Union for the Scientific Study of Population. Pp. 53–72.

Cornell, L. L. (1996) 'Infanticide in early modern Japan? Demography, culture and population growth'. *The Journal of Asian Studies*, 55(1): 22–50.

Cornell, L. L. and A. Hayami (1986) 'The shūmon aratame cho: Japan's population registers'. *Journal of Family History*, 11(4): 311–328.

Cullinane, M. (1998) 'Accounting for souls: Ecclesiastical sources for the study of Philippine demographic history'. In D. F. Doeppers and P. Xenos (eds.) *Population and History: The Demographic Origins of the Modern Philippines*. Madison, WI: Center for Southeast Asian Studies, University of Wisconsin. Pp. 281–346.

Das Gupta, M. (1995) 'Fertility decline in Punjab, India: parallels with historical Europe'. *Population Studies*, 49(3): 481–500.

Das Gupta, M. (1999) 'Lifeboat versus corporate ethic: social and demographic implications of stem and joint families'. *Social Science and Medicine*, 49(2): 173–184.

Ding, Y. Z., S. Y. Guo, Z. Q. Li (J. Lee) and W. L. Kang (C. Campbell) (2004) *Liaodong yimin zhong de qiren shehui (Banner Society and the Settlement of Eastern Liaodong)*. Shanghai: Shanghai shehui kexue chubanshe (Shanghai Social Science Publisher).

Doeppers, D. F. (1998a) 'Civil records as sources for Philippine historical demography'. In D. F. Doeppers and P. Xenos (eds.) *Population and History: The Demographic Origins of the Modern Philippines*. Madison, WI: Center for Southeast Asian Studies, University of Wisconsin. Pp. 347–363.

Doeppers, D. F. (1998b) 'Migrants in urban labor markets: the social stratification of Tondo and Sampaloc in the 1890s'. In D. F. Doeppers and P. Xenos (eds.) *Population and History: The Demographic Origins of the Modern Philippines*. Madison, WI: Center for Southeast Asian Studies, University of Wisconsin. Pp. 253–264.

Doeppers, D. F. and P. Xenos (eds.) (1998) *Population and History: The Demographic Origins of the Modern Philippines*. Madison, WI: Center for Southeast Asian Studies, University of Wisconsin (published in cooperation with Ateneo de Manila University Press).

Dong, H., C. Campbell, S. Kurosu, W. S. Yang and J. Lee (2015) 'New sources for comparative social science: historical population panel data from East Asia'. *Demography*, 52(3): 1061–1088.

Drixler, F. (2013) *Mabiki: Infanticide and Population Growth in Eastern Japan, 1660–1950*. Berkeley: University of California Press.

Drixler, F. and J. Kok (2016) 'A lost family-planning regime in eighteenth-century Ceylon'. *Population Studies*, 70(1): 93–114.

Durand, J. D. (1960) 'The population statistics of China, AD 2–1953'. *Population Studies*, 13(3): 209–256.

Dyson, T. (ed.) (1989) *India's Historical Demography: Studies in Famine, Disease and Society*. London: Curzon Press.

Dyson, T. (2002) 'Famine in Berar, 1896–7 and 1899–1900: echoes and chain reactions'. In T. Dyson and C. Ó Gráda (eds.) *Famine Demography: Perspectives from the Past and Present*. Oxford: Oxford University Press. Pp. 93–112.

Dyson, T. (2004) 'India's population – the past'. In T. Dyson, R. Cassen and L. Visaria (eds.) *Twenty-First Century India: Population, Economy, Human Development and the Environment*. Oxford: Oxford University Press.

Dyson, T. and M. Das Gupta (2001) 'Demographic trends in Ludhiana District, Punjab, 1881–1981: an exploration of vital registration data in colonial India'. In T. J. Liu, J. Lee, D. S. Reher, O. Saito and F. Wang (eds.) *Asian Population History*. Oxford: Oxford University Press. Pp. 79–104.

Engelen, T. and Y. H. Hsieh (eds.) (2007) *Two Cities, One Life: The Demography of Lugang and Nijmegen, 1850–1945*. Amsterdam: Aksant Academic Publishers.

Engelen, T., J. R. Shepherd and W. S. Yang (eds.) (2011) *Death at the Opposite Ends of the Eurasian Continents: Mortality Trends in Taiwan and the Netherlands 1840–1945*. Amsterdam: Aksant Academic Publishers.

Engelen, T. and A. P. Wolf (eds.) (2005) *Marriage and the Family in Eurasia: Perspectives on the Hajnal Hypothesis.* Amsterdam: Aksant Academic Publishers.

Farris, W. W. (1985) *Population, Disease, and Land in Early Japan, 645–900.* Cambridge, MA and London, England: the Council on East Asian Studies, Harvard University Press and the Havard-Yenching Institute.

Feeney, G. and K. Hamano (1990) 'Rice price fluctuations and fertility in late Tokugawa Japan'. *Journal of Japanese Studies*, 16(1): 1–30.

Fuess, H. (2004) *Divorce in Japan: Family, Gender and the State 1600–2000.* California: Stanford University Press.

Gardiner, P. and M. Oey (1987) 'Morbidity and mortality in Java, 1880–1940: the evidence of the colonial reports'. In O. G. Norman (ed.) *Death and Disease in Southeast Asia: Explorations in Social, Medical and Demographic History, Singapore.* Oxford and New York: Oxford University Press. Pp. 48–69.

Goldman, N. (1980) 'Far Eastern patterns of mortality'. *Population Studies*, 34(1): 5–19.

Goode, W. J. (1993) *World Changes in Divorce Patterns.* New Haven: Yale University Press.

Guha, S. (2001a) *Health and Population in South Asia: From Earliest Time to the Present.* London: Hurst and Company.

Guha, S. (2001b) 'The population history of South Asia from the seventeenth to the twentieth centuries: an exploration'. In T. J. Liu, J. Lee, D. S. Reher, O. Saito and F. Wang (eds.) *Asian Population History.* Oxford: Oxford University Press. Pp. 63–78.

Guz, D. (1989) 'Population dynamics of famine in nineteenth century Punjab, 1896–7 and 1899–1900'. In T. Dyson (ed.) *India's Historical Demography: Studies in Famine, Disease and Society.* London: Curzon Press. Pp. 197–221.

Hajnal, J. (1965) 'European marriage patterns in perspective'. In D. V. Glass and D. E. C. Eversley (eds.) *Population in History: Essays in Historical Demography, Volume I: General and Great Britain.* Chicago, IL: Publishing Company. Pp. 101–143.

Hajnal, J. (1982) 'Two kinds of preindustrial household formation system'. *Population and Development Review*, 8(3): 449–494.

Hanley, S. B. (1974) 'Fertility, mortality and life expectancy in pre-modern Japan'. *Population Studies*, 28(1): 127–142.

Hanley, S. B. and K. Yamamura (1977) *Economic and Demographic Change in Preindustrial Japan 1600–1868.* Princeton, NJ: Princeton University Press.

Harrell, S. (1987) 'On the holes in Chinese genealogies'. *Late Imperial China*, 8(2): 53–79.

Hayami, A. (1972) 'Size of household in a Japanese county throughout the Tokugawa era'. In P. Laslett with the assistance of R. Wall (eds.) *Household and Family in Past-time: Comparative Studies in the Size and Structure of the Domestic Group over the Last Three Centuries in England, France, Serbia, Japan and Colonial North America, with Further Materials from Western Europe.* Cambridge: Cambridge University Press. Pp. 473–515.

Hayami, A. (1986) 'Population changes'. In M. B. Jansen and G. Rozman (eds.) *Japan in Transition: From Tokugawa to Meiji.* Princeton, NJ: Princeton University Press. Pp. 280–317.

Hayami, A. (1987) 'Another Fossa Magna: proportion marrying and age at marriage in late nineteenth-century Japan'. *Journal of Family History*, 12(1–3): 57–72.

Hirschman, C. and S. Bonaparte (2012) 'Population and society in Southeast Asia: a historical perspective'. In L. Williams and M. P. Guest (eds.) *Demographic Change in Southeast Asia: Recent Histories and Future Directions.* Ithaca, NY: Cornell Southeast Asia Program Publications. Pp. 1–37.

Hirschman, C. and B. Teerawichitchainan (2003) 'Cultural and socioeconomic influences on divorce during modernization: Southeast Asia, 1940s to 1960s'. *Population and Development Review*, 29: 215–253.

Ho, J. S., J. B. Lewis and H. R. Kang (2008) 'Korean expansion and decline from the seventeenth century to the nineteenth century: a view suggested by Adam Smith'. *Journal of Economic History*, 68(1): 244–282.

Ho, P. T. (1959) *Studies on the Population of China, 1368–1953.* Cambridge, MA: Harvard University Press.

Hull, T. H. (2001) 'Indonesian fertility behaviour before the transition: searching for hints in the historical record'. In T. J. Liu, J. Lee, D. S. Reher, O. Saito and F. Wang (eds.) *Asian Population History.* Oxford: Oxford University Press. Pp. 152–175.

Jannetta, A. B. (1987) *Epidemics and Mortality in Early Modern Japan.* Princeton, NJ: Princeton University Press.

Jannetta, A. B. and S. H. Preston (1991) 'Two centuries of mortality change in central Japan: the evidence from a temple death register'. *Population Studies*, 45(3): 417–436.

Kim, K. and H. Park (2009) 'Landholding and fertility in Korea: 1914–1925'. *Journal of Family History*, 34(3): 275–291.

Kim, K. and H. Park (2010) 'Family succession through adoption in the Chosun dynasty'. *The History of the Family*, 15(4): 443–452.

Kim, K., H. Park and H. Jo (2013) 'Tracking individuals and households: longitudinal features of Danseong household register data'. *The History of the Family*, 18(4): 378–397.

Kito, H. (1983) *Nihon Nisen-nen no Jinkoshi (Population History of Japan's Two Thousand Years)*. Tokyo: PHP Kenkyujo.

Kurosu, S. (2007) 'Remarriage in a stem family system in early modern Japan'. *Continuity and Change*, 22(3): 429–458.

Kurosu, S. (2011) 'Divorce in early modern rural Japan: household and individual life course in northeastern villages, 1716–1870'. *Journal of Family History*, 36: 118–141.

Kurosu, S. (2013) 'Adoption and family reproduction in early modern Japan'. *The Economic Review*, 64(1): 1–12.

Kye, B. and H. Park (2013) 'Age patterns of migration among Korean adults in early 20th-century Seoul'. *The History of the Family*, 18(4): 398–421.

Langford, C. M. (2001) 'Trends and fluctuations in fertility in Sri Lanka during the first half of the twentieth century'. In T. J. Liu, J. Lee, D. S. Reher, O. Saito and F. Wang (eds.) *Asian Population History*. Oxford: Oxford University Press. Pp. 176–188.

Lavely, W. (2007) 'Sex, breastfeeding and marital fertility in pre-transition China'. *Population and Development Review*, 33(2): 289–320.

Lavely, W. and R. B. Wong (1998) 'Revising the Malthusian narrative: the comparative study of population dynamics in late imperial China'. *The Journal of Asian Studies*, 57(3): 714–748.

Lee, J. and C. Campbell (1997) *Fate and Fortune in Rural China: Social Organization and Population Behavior in Liaoning, 1774–1873*. Cambridge: Cambridge University Press.

Lee, J. and C. Campbell (2010) *China Multi-Generational Panel Dataset, Liaoning (CMGPD-LN), 1749–1909 [Computer file], ICPSR27063-v2*. Ann Arbor, MI: Inter-university Consortium for Political and Social Research [distributor], 2010-08-17.

Lee, J., C. Campbell and S. Chen (2010) *China Multi-Generational Panel Dataset, Liaoning (CMGPD-LN) 1749–1909: User Guide*. Ann Arbor, MI: Inter-university Consortium for Political and Social Research.

Lee, J., C. Campbell and F. Wang (1993) 'The last emperors: an introduction to the demography of the Qing (1644–1911) imperial lineage'. In D. S. Reher and R. Schofield (eds.) *Old and New Methods in Historical Demography*. Oxford: Oxford University Press. Pp. 361–382.

Lee, J. and F. Wang (1999) *One-Quarter of Humanity: Malthusian Mythology and Chinese Reality 1700–2000*. Cambridge, MA: Harvard University Press.

Lee, J., F. Wang and C. Campbell (1994) 'Infant and child mortality among the Qing nobility: implications for two types of positive check'. *Population Studies*, 48(3): 395–411.

Lee, S. (2010) 'The impacts of birth order and social status on the genealogy register in thirteenth- to fifteenth-century Korea'. *Journal of Family History*, 35(2): 115–127.

Lee, S. and H. Park (2008) 'Marriage, social status, and family succession in medieval Korea (thirteenth-fifteenth centuries)'. *Journal of Family History*, 33(2): 123–138.

Lee, S. and B. G. Son (2010) 'Long-term patterns of seasonality of mortality in Korea from the seventeenth to the twentieth century'. *Journal of Family History*, 37(3): 270–283.

Li, T. (1998) *Nguyễn Cochinchina: southern Vietnam in the seventeenth and eighteenth centuries*. Ithaca, NY: Cornell University Southeast Asia Program Publications.

Liao, T. F. (2001) 'Were past Chinese families complex? Household structures during the Tang Dynasty, 618–907 AD'. *Continuity and Change*, 16(3): 331–355.

Liao, T. F. (2004) 'Estimating household structure in ancient China by using historical data: a latent class analysis of partially missing patterns'. *Journal of the Royal Statistics Society A*, 167(1): 125–139.

Liu, T. J. (1985) 'The demography of two Chinese clans in Hsiao-shan, Chekiang, 1650–1850'. In S. B. Hanley and A. P. Wolf (eds.) *Family and Population in East Asian History*. Stanford: Stanford University Press. Pp. 13–61.

Liu, T. J. (1995a) 'A comparison of lineage populations in South China, ca. 1300–1900'. In S. Harrell (ed.) *Chinese Historical Microdemography*. Berkeley, LA and London: University of California Press. Pp. 94–120.

Liu, T. J. (1995b) 'Demographic constraint and family structure in traditional Chinese lineages, ca. 1200–1900'. In S. Harrell (ed.) *Chinese Historical Microdemography*. Berkeley, LA and London: University of California Press. Pp. 121–140.

Liu, T. J., J. Lee, D. S. Reher, O. Saito and F. Wang (eds.) (2001) *Asian Population History*. Oxford: Oxford University Press.

Liu, T. J. and S. Y. Liu (2001) 'Disease and mortality in the history of Taiwan'. In T. J. Liu, J. Lee, D. S. Reher, O. Saito and F. Wang (eds.) *Asian Population History*. Oxford: Oxford University Press. Pp. 248–269.

Lundh, C., S. Kurosu et al. (2014) *Similarity in Difference: Marriage in Europe and Asia, 1700–1900.* Cambridge, MA: MIT Press.

Maharatna, A. (2002) 'Famines and epidemics: an Indian historical perspective'. In T. Dyson and C. Ó Gráda (eds.) *Famine Demography: Perspectives from the Past and Present.* Oxford: Oxford University Press. Pp. 113–142.

Ortega Osona, J. A. (2001) 'The attenuation of mortality fluctuations in British Punjab and Bengal, 1870–1947'. In T. J. Liu, J. Lee, D. S. Reher, O. Saito and F. Wang (eds.) *Asian Population History.* Oxford: Oxford University Press. Pp. 306–349.

Owen, N. G. (1987a) 'Measuring mortality in the 19th century Philippines'. In N. G. Owen (ed.) *Death and Disease in Southeast Asia: Explorations in Social, Medical and Demographic History.* Singapore, Oxford and New York: Oxford University Press. Pp. 91–114.

Owen, N. G. (1987b) 'The paradox of nineteenth-century population growth in Southeast Asia: evidence from Java and the Philippines'. *Journal of Southeast Asian Studies*, 18(1): 45–57.

Owen, N. G. (1998) 'Life, death and the sacraments in a nineteenth-century Bikol parish'. In D. F. Doeppers and P. Xenos (eds.) *Population and History: The Demographic Origins of the Modern Philippines.* Madison, WI: Center for Southeast Asian Studies, University of Wisconsin. Pp. 225–252.

Park, H. and S. Lee (2008) 'A survey of data sources for studies of family and population in Korean history'. *The History of the Family*, 13(3): 258–267.

Park, I. H. and L. J. Cho (1995) 'Confucianism and the Korean family'. *Journal of Comparative Family Studies*, 26(1): 117–135.

Reid, A. (1987) 'Low population growth and its causes in pre-colonial Southeast Asia'. In N. G. Owen (ed.) *Death and Disease in Southeast Asia: Explorations in Social, Medical and Demographic History.* Singapore, Oxford and New York: Oxford University Press. Pp. 33–47.

Reid, A. (2001) 'South-East Asian population history and the colonial impact'. In T. J. Liu, J. Lee, D. S. Reher, O. Saito and F. Wang (eds.) *Asian Population History.* Oxford: Oxford University Press. Pp. 45–62.

Saito, O. (1992) 'Infanticide, fertility and "population stagnation": the state of Tokugawa historical demography'. *Japan Forum*, 4(2): 369–381.

Saito, O. (1998) 'Two kinds of stem family system? Japan and Europe compared'. *Continuity and Change*, 13(1): 167–186.

Shepherd, J. R. (2011a) 'Regional and ethnic variation in mortality in Japanese colonial period Taiwan'. In T. Engelen, J. R. Shepherd, W. S. Yang (eds.) *Death at the Opposite Ends of the Eurasian Continent: Mortality Trends in Taiwan and the Netherlands, 1850–1945.* Amsterdam: Aksant Academic Publishers. Pp. 99–150.

Shepherd, J. R. (2011b) 'Trends in mortality and causes of death in Japanese colonial period Taiwan'. In T. Engelen, J. R. Shepherd, W. S. Yang (eds.) *Death at the Opposite Ends of the Eurasian Continent: Mortality Trends in Taiwan and the Netherlands, 1850–1945.* Amsterdam: Aksant Academic Publishers. Pp. 45–79.

Skinner, G. W. (1997) 'Family systems and demographic process'. In D. I. Kertzer and T. Fricke (eds.) *Anthropological Demography: Towards a New Synthesis.* Chicago, IL: The University of Chicago Press. Pp. 53–59.

Smith, T. C. with R. Y. Eng and R. T. Lundy (1977) *Nakahara: Family Farming and Population in a Japanese Village, 1717–1830.* Stanford, CA: Stanford University Press.

Son, B. and S. Lee (2013) 'Rural migration in Korea: a transition to the modern era'. *The History of the Family*, 18(4): 422–433.

Srivastava, H. C. (1976) 'Selection by place of baptism and age at marriage of spouses in a Goan parish'. *Canadian Studies in Population*, 3: 87–95.

Srivastava, H. C. (1987) *Demographic Profile of North East India.* Delhi: Mittal Publications.

Telford, T. A. (1986) 'Survey of demographic data in Chinese genealogies'. *Late Imperial China*, 7(2): 118–148.

Tsuya, N. O. and S. Kurosu (2010) 'To die or to leave: demographic responses to famines in rural northeastern Japan, 1716–1870'. In S. Kurosu, T. Bengtsson and C. Campbell (eds.) *Demographic Responses to Economic and Environmental Crises.* Kashiwa: Reitaku University Press. Pp. 79–106.

Tsuya, N. O. and S. Kurosu (2013) 'Social class and migration in two northeastern Japanese villages, 1716–1870'. *The History of the Family*, 18(3): 1–22.

Tsuya, N. O., F. Wang, G. Alter, J. Lee et al. (2010) *Prudence and Pressure: Reproduction and Human Agency in Europe and Asia, 1700–1900.* Cambridge, MA and London, England: MIT Press.

Visaria, L. and P. Visaria (1983) 'Population (1757–1947)'. In D. Kumar with the editorial assistance of M. Desai (eds.) *The Cambridge Economic History of India, Volume 2, c. 1757–c. 1970.* Cambridge: Cambridge University Press. Pp. 463–532.

Wang, F. and J. Lee (1998) 'Adoption among the Qing nobility and its implications for Chinese demographic behavior'. *The History of the Family*, 3(4): 411–427.

Wang, F., J. Lee and C. Campbell (1995) 'Marital fertility control among the Qing nobility: implications for two types of preventive check'. *Population Studies*, 49(3): 383–400.

Wolf, A. P. (1985) 'Chinese family size: a myth revitalized'. In J. C. Hsieh and Y. C. Chang (eds.) *The Chinese Family and Its Ritual Behavior*. Taipei: Academia Sinica Institute of Ethnology. Pp. 30–49.

Wolf, A. P. (2001) 'Is there evidence of birth control in late imperial China?' *Population and Development Review*, 27(1): 133–154.

Wolf, A. P. and C. S. Huang (1980) *Marriage and Adoption in China, 1845–1945*. Stanford, CA: Stanford University Press.

Xenos, P. and S. M. Ng (1998) 'Nagcarlan, Laguna: a nineteenth-century parish demography'. In D. F. Doeppers and P. Xenos (eds.) *Population and History: The Demographic Origins of the Modern Philippines*. Madison, WI: Center for Southeast Asian Studies, University of Wisconsin. Pp. 183–223.

Yamamura, K. (1974) *A Study of Samurai Income and Entrepreneurship: Quantitative Analyses of Economic and Social Aspects of the Samurai in Tokugawa and Meiji Japan*. Cambridge, MA: Harvard University Press.

Yuan, I. C. (1931) 'Life tables for a southern Chinese family from 1365 to 1849'. *Human Biology*, 3(2): 57–79.

Zhao, Z. (1997) 'Deliberate birth control under a high-fertility regime: reproductive behavior in China before 1970'. *Population and Development Review*, 23(4): 729–767.

Zhao, Z. (2000) 'Coresidential patterns in historical China: a simulation study'. *Population and Development Review*, 26(2): 263–293.

Zhao, Z. (2001) 'Chinese genealogies as a source for demographic research: a further assessment of their reliability and biases'. *Population Studies*, 55(2): 181–193.

Zhao, Z. (2003) 'On the Far Eastern pattern of mortality'. *Population Studies*, 57(2): 131–147.

5
Fertility decline

Stuart Gietel-Basten

Fifty years ago when Asia had a population of 1.6 billion, only one country, Japan, had sub-replacement fertility accounting for just 90 million people. At that time 43 out of the 50 countries had total fertility rates (TFRs) of greater than 5.0.[1] In Europe, meanwhile, there was only one country, Albania, with a TFR of greater than 5.0. Today, around 3.4 billion people across the world live in countries characterized by below-replacement fertility. Of these, 2.1 billion – almost two-thirds – live in Asia. If we were to subdivide India into its constituent states we would add another almost half a billion. Over the second half of the twentieth century, therefore, Asia has become the predominant world centre of below-replacement fertility; but it is also home to some of the highest fertility rates in the world. As such, the story of Asia's fertility decline is a complex and multifaceted one.

This chapter will outline some of the key themes and features of Asia's fertility decline from 1950 to the present day. Given the expanse of the continent and the heterogeneity of experience, the discussion of individual countries will be necessarily limited. In addition, reliable demographic data on historical and, in some cases, contemporary Asian settings is often found wanting. Despite these limitations, the chapter will paint a general descriptive picture of the characteristics of fertility decline in Asia over the past century, and lead the reader to further, deeper analyses found either in other chapters in this volume or elsewhere.

Asia's heterogeneous fertility experience

The contours of fertility decline in Asia

While low TFRs were certainly present in Asia from the 1950s, the decline in the mean number of live births per woman from more than 5.0 in the late 1970s to a little over 2.0 within 30 years is certainly spectacular.[2] Yet, as the world's most populous continent, Asia should perhaps be expected to show a wide variety of demographic regimes and patterns of fertility transition. Figure 5.1 demonstrates the true extent to which the heterogeneity of both the Asian experience and the present situation in the continent can be gauged in comparison to other major world regions. In 1920, total fertility rates in Europe, North America, Australia and New Zealand sat in a range of about 2.5 to 5.0. Fertility at or below replacement levels was not uncommon in

Fertility decline

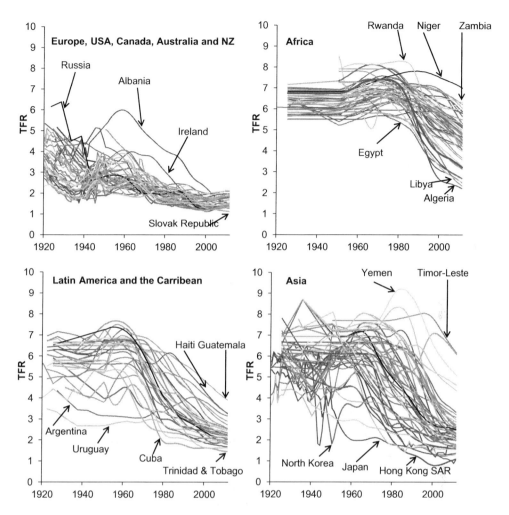

Figure 5.1 Patterns of fertility in four major world regions, 1920–2010
Source: UNPD (2013).

the years between World Wars I and II (van Bavel 2010). Apart from a handful of outliers such as Russia, Albania and Ireland, fertility in this most economically developed region took the form of a relatively orderly transition – aside from the mid-century 'baby boom' that occurred in many countries – towards a convergence at, or more generally below, replacement level (Reher 2007; Wilson 2011). In this group only a handful of countries (including Ireland, Iceland and New Zealand) reported TFRs above 2.0 in the early 2010s.

Africa's fertility decline is marked by a number of distinct characteristics. First, the almost complete dearth of evidence for the first half of the century, and indeed for much of the second half, means that estimates translate into deceptively smoother lines than would otherwise be the case. Second, as is common in the first stage of the fertility transition, fertility rates appear to have risen from around 5.5–7.0 to around 6.0–7.5. Third, there is a heterogeneous fertility transition ranging from a relatively rapid decline in North Africa to the 'stalled' and (so far) stubbornly high rates seen in Niger, Zambia and other settings. Generally, however, the pattern is of a transition

65

from high fertility rates to a very wide range. In Latin America and the Caribbean, there has been a general movement from TFRs of 5.0–6.0 in the early twentieth century towards a broad convergence around 1.5–3.0 (although a few outliers such as Argentina and Uruguay reported lower fertility rates early on).

Asia produces, by some distance, the 'messiest' graph. While the pattern of a slight increase from pre-transitional rates of 5.0–7.0, followed by a general decline, is in evidence, the transitions seem peculiarly erratic with extremes at both the high and low ends. The continent is currently home to some of the highest and the lowest fertility rates in the world, ranging from Afghanistan and Timor-Leste where TFRs are around 6.0, down to the ultra-low fertility rates of the Special Administrative Region of Hong Kong (hereafter Hong Kong SAR), Taiwan and Singapore where TFRs are around 1.0–1.3.

Some of the largest areas of very low fertility in Asia are found within the Chinese mainland. While the Chinese national fertility rate is disputed (Basten et al. 2014), there is no doubt that fertility rates much lower than 1.0 can be found in many populous regions across that huge country. Indeed, a 2005 PhD thesis famously 'discovered' an urban district in China's Heilongjiang province with a TFR of just 0.41 (Terrell 2005). If the states of India as well as China's provinces were included in the Asia plot, the heterogeneity of the continent would be even more marked. The Indian states, many of which are larger in population than most European countries, return fertility rates ranging from 1.7 in Punjab and Tamil Nadu up to 3.5 in Bihar and 3.3 in Uttar Pradesh (e.g. Säävälä 2010). It should be noted that the population of Bihar and Uttar Pradesh combined is over 300 million, roughly the same as the United States of America.

Some general characteristics of fertility decline in Asia

What are the general features of fertility decline that can be applied to most territories in the continent? First, regarding the proximate determinants of fertility across the continent, there has been a general shift towards later marriage (Chapter 19), declines in infant and child mortality (Chapter 10), and improved access to family planning (Chapters 6, 7 and 8). More broadly, there has been improved education particularly for females (Chapter 22), and a marked degree of economic and political development over the continent which has impacted upon family and household structures (Chapter 20), female participation in the labour force, and on the ability of state systems to shape fertility rates. There has also been massive migration, determined through both international movements (Chapter 17) and urbanization (Chapter 16). Elements of all of these changes can be found in almost all countries across the Asian continent, but clearly to greater or lesser degrees in particular places and for particular social groups. On a qualitative level, all of the above apply to almost all countries in Asia. However, the degree to which these countries share quantitative similarities in either the input or output of these determinants clearly varies.

As indicated earlier, a second feature that is common across most countries of Asia is the persistent difference between fertility *within* countries, especially between rural and urban areas, and then within types of urban areas themselves, as well as by region or ethnicity. Figure 5.2 shows the relative TFRs reported in the latest Demographic and Health Surveys (pre-1995 surveys excluded) for rural and urban settings for 20 countries across Asia. Across the sample, the mean difference between rural and urban TFRs is 0.86 live births (standard deviation 0.45). Economic development in rural areas, as well as the ongoing process of urbanization and peri-urbanization, is affecting these rates and their relative contribution to national fertility rates across the continent.

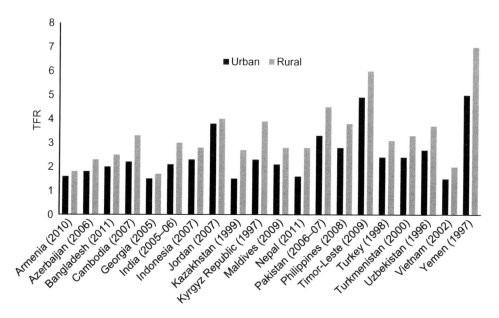

Figure 5.2 Rural and urban TFRs for 20 countries, derived from latest Demographic and Health Surveys
Source: NIPS and ICF International (2013).

A further transition common to many Asian settings is a profound shift in childbearing desires and intentions. This process occurs concomitantly with the broader process of fertility transition (Bongaarts 1975). In areas characterized by higher rates of fertility and in the early stages of fertility transition, fertility desires are usually *lower* than actual fertility outcomes. The gap between desires and outcomes might be a result of an unmet need for family planning or other prevailing factors which lead a couple to 'overshoot' their reproductive target. Meanwhile, in advanced economies characterized by low fertility, fertility desires are usually *higher* than actual outcomes. This feature of European and, increasingly, East Asian societies such as Hong Kong SAR and Taiwan, can be translated into an unmet need for children where higher rates of childlessness and curtailed fertility contribute to an 'undershooting' of fertility (Basten 2013).

According to Demographic and Health Surveys, the positive gap between ideals and actual fertility outcomes has closed in a number of settings. Only a handful of countries, however, have reported a complete transition to a negative gap (Basten 2013). In East Asia, and in China in particular, growing evidence suggests that there may now have been a significant deviation from the two-child norm prevalent in Europe and North America. In China, national data from 2001 suggests the mean desired number of children among married women aged 20–29 is 1.50 for urban areas and 1.75 for rural women (Zhang 2004). In Taiwan and Hong Kong SAR, surveys of young people indicate similar levels to China, of around 1.5–1.7 (Basten 2013). On the flip side, according to the latest Demographic and Health Surveys in South Asia the mean ideal number of children is lower than the actual number in India and Nepal, roughly the same in Pakistan and Bangladesh and higher than the actual number in the Maldives. In Pakistan the mean ideal number of children is 4.1 (NIPS and ICF International 2013). This indicates that while diffusion of small family norms is certainly spreading, there is a lingering unmet need for family planning in numerous Asian contexts.

Stuart Gietel-Basten

A final feature common to many, if not most, Asian experiences of fertility transition is that just before a recorded decline in fertility occurs, fertility in fact increases (Dyson and Murphy 1985). This increase may be due to improved nutrition and health linked to greater longevity of husbands, declining maternal mortality, as well as changes in traditional patterns of breastfeeding. As Lutz and Scherbov (1993: 27) observe, 'these fertility-increasing aspects of modernization are then soon outweighed by decreases in desired family size and the spread of family-size limitation'.

Types of fertility decline

Because of the tremendous heterogeneity in not just demographic experience, but also in population size, economic performance, institutional systems, religions, cultures, labour markets, welfare systems, etc., providing a quantitative overview of fertility decline in Asia is difficult. Whichever approach one takes, a significant compromise has to be made. If the primary level of analysis is the UN-defined *region* then, for example, when considering South-East Asia we would have to examine fertility decline in Singapore and Timor-Leste – settings at polar opposites in terms of development and fertility rates – in the same breath. A simple answer would be simply to group countries by their current TFR. In this scenario Singapore and Timor-Leste would, indeed, be considered quite separately. However, if we took, for example, quartiles of contemporary TFR as the unit of analysis, we would be considering Hong Kong SAR, Armenia, China, Turkey and the UAE in the same batch – something which, again, is far from ideal considering their highly divergent paths to below-replacement fertility. An alternative pragmatic choice is to take a *thematic* approach. While some themes clearly come to the fore – territories characterized by high levels of internal conflict, or rapid North-East Asian industrializers – the reality is that such themes are highly subjective and using them will inevitably gloss over many localized trajectories.

In order to present an alternative approach to breaking down, and rebuilding, the presentation of fertility decline in Asia represented in Figure 5.1, this chapter uses a novel approach to distinguish 'types of fertility transition'. (See Palloni 1990 for a comparable example studying population change in Latin America.) These 'types' are based not only on current fertility levels, but also take into account the pace of transition over the past 60 years. While this approach could be considered highly positivist, it allows for the potential to consider a hybrid of approaching fertility transition in Asia from either a *spatial* or a *thematic* perspective – both of which, as already indicated, have significant shortcomings when used separately given the high levels of heterogeneity inherent in both forms of categorization. Within each of the types, certain 'storylines' emerge that bind particular countries together in some ways but, critically, not in others. The 'type' approach allows for a very loose grouping by a particular characteristic followed by an exploration of intra-group similarities. The countries included in each type are shown in Map 5.1. The types employed here are distinguished in terms of two key characteristics: (i) the time of onset of fertility decline (early or late); and (ii) the pace of fertility decline (fast or slow).

The first group of countries is characterized by a rapid transition from very high fertility rates to contemporary TFRs around, or well below, replacement level. It would be inaccurate to term these *rapid industrializers* as not all are characterized by such a pattern of economic development. While many have, indeed, been characterized by rapid economic growth, the falls in other territories are more closely linked to highly effective family planning programmes (FPPs) or large-scale social and cultural changes. As such, they can simply be termed *early rapid fallers*, or *demographic forerunners*. These countries are formally characterized as settings in Asia that are

Fertility decline

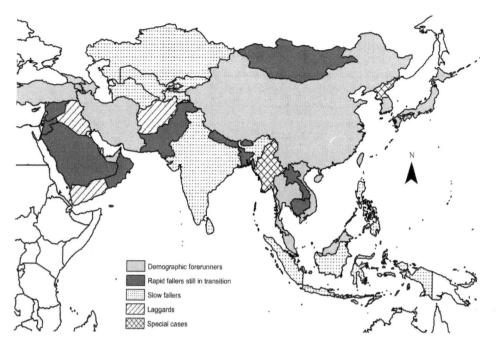

Map 5.1 Countries by typology
Source: Based on author's own typology.

currently at, or below, a TFR of 2.1 and can generally be considered to be at the forefront of fertility transition in the continent. (Despite the fact Japan's fertility decline began well in advance of almost any other country in the continent, the speed of its decline in the 1950s places it in this category.)

A second group is characterized by a steady and lethargic decline, where fertility declines from high rates to rates still above 2.5 have occurred, but those declines have taken the best part of the post-World War II era to achieve. These countries might be termed *slow fallers*. These are countries that are formally characterized by above replacement rate fertility but below 4.0, and where declines since 1980 have frequently been to less than 3.0 children per woman.

A third group can be characterized by a rapid rate of decline similar to that experienced by the first group of countries but, owing to the time of onset, still report fertility rates above 2.1, despite indications that fertility decline is either continuing or is stabilizing at around this level. These might be characterized as *rapid fallers still in transition*. This group is formally characterized as countries that have seen a fertility decline of more than 3.0 children per woman since 1980, but still have above replacement rate fertility.

Fourth, there are some countries that are still in the early stages of fertility transition, with high or stalled rates for fertility. This fourth category might be considered as being in the early stages of transition or *laggards* and have TFRs of above 4.0.

Finally, there is a small group of countries that, because of their very particular recent histories and the way in which those histories relate to fertility decline, require individual analysis in their own right as *special cases*.

The fertility decline seen in these five types is shown in Table 5.1, utilizing figures from the 2012 round of the UN's *World Population Prospects*. Table 5.1 has been designed as a quasi-heat

69

Table 5.1 TFRs of Asian countries and other territories, 1950–2010

	1950	1960	1970	1980	1990	2000	2010
Demographic forerunners							
Armenia	4.5	4.5	3.0	2.4	2.4	1.7	1.7
Azerbaijan	5.5	5.6	4.3	3.0	2.9	2.0	1.9
Bahrain	7.0	7.2	5.9	4.6	3.4	2.7	2.1
Brunei	7.0	6.6	5.9	3.9	3.3	2.3	2.1
China	6.1	6.1	4.8	2.7	2.1	1.6	1.7
Georgia	3.0	3.0	2.6	2.3	2.1	1.6	1.8
Hong Kong SAR	4.4	5.3	3.3	1.7	1.2	1.0	1.1
Iran	6.9	6.9	6.2	6.5	4.0	2.0	1.9
Japan	3.0	2.0	2.1	1.8	1.5	1.3	1.4
Lebanon	5.7	5.7	4.7	3.7	2.8	2.0	1.5
Macao SAR	4.4	4.4	1.8	2.0	1.4	0.8	1.1
Malaysia	6.2	6.0	4.6	3.7	3.4	2.5	2.0
Qatar	7.0	7.0	6.8	5.5	3.7	3.0	2.1
Rep of Korea	5.1	5.6	4.3	2.2	1.7	1.2	1.3
Singapore	6.6	5.1	2.8	1.7	1.7	1.3	1.3
Taiwan*	5.9	5.3	3.4	2.2	1.8	1.4	1.2
Thailand	6.1	6.1	5.1	2.9	2.0	1.6	1.4
Turkey	6.6	6.1	5.3	4.1	2.9	2.3	2.1
UAE	7.0	6.9	6.4	5.2	3.9	2.4	1.8
Vietnam	5.4	6.4	6.3	4.6	3.2	1.9	1.8
Slow fallers							
India	5.9	5.8	5.3	4.5	3.7	3.0	2.5
Indonesia	5.5	5.6	5.3	4.1	2.9	2.5	2.3
Kazakhstan	4.4	4.4	3.5	3.0	2.6	2.0	2.4
Kuwait	7.2	7.3	6.9	5.0	2.0	2.6	2.6
Kyrgyzstan	4.5	5.4	4.7	4.1	3.6	2.5	3.1
Philippines	7.4	7.0	6.0	4.9	4.1	3.7	3.1
Sri Lanka	5.8	5.2	4.0	3.2	2.4	2.3	2.4
Tajikistan	6.0	6.3	6.8	5.5	4.9	3.7	3.9
Turkmenistan	6.0	6.8	6.2	4.8	4.0	2.8	2.3
Uzbekistan	6.0	6.8	6.3	4.7	3.9	2.6	2.3
Rapid fallers still in transition							
Bangladesh	6.4	6.8	6.9	6.0	4.1	2.9	2.2
Bhutan	6.7	6.7	6.7	6.4	5.1	3.1	2.3
Cambodia	6.9	6.9	6.2	6.2	5.1	3.5	2.9
Jordan	7.4	8.0	7.8	7.0	5.1	3.9	3.3
Lao PDR	5.9	6.0	6.0	6.4	5.9	3.7	3.0
Maldives	6.0	7.1	7.2	7.3	5.2	2.8	2.3
Mongolia	5.6	7.5	7.5	5.8	3.3	2.1	2.4
Nepal	6.0	6.0	5.9	5.7	5.0	3.7	2.3
Oman	7.3	7.3	7.4	8.3	6.3	3.2	2.9
Pakistan	6.6	6.6	6.6	6.4	5.7	4.0	3.2
Saudi Arabia	7.2	7.3	7.3	7.0	5.4	3.5	2.7
Syria	7.2	7.5	7.5	6.8	4.8	3.7	3.0

Fertility decline

Table 5.1 (Cont.)

	1950	1960	1970	1980	1990	2000	2010
Laggards							
Afghanistan	7.7	7.7	7.7	7.7	7.7	7.4	5.0
Iraq	7.3	6.6	7.2	6.4	5.6	4.8	4.1
Palestine	7.4	8.0	7.7	7.0	6.6	5.0	4.1
Timor-Leste	6.4	6.4	5.5	5.4	5.7	7.0	5.9
Yemen	7.3	7.3	7.7	9.2	8.2	5.9	4.1
Special cases							
DPR Korea	3.5	3.9	4.0	2.8	2.3	2.0	2.0
Israel	4.3	3.8	3.8	3.1	2.9	2.9	2.9
Myanmar	6.0	6.1	5.7	4.7	3.1	2.2	2.0

Notes: The shade of grey indicates the magnitude of TFR; dates are quinquennial beginning in the year given.
* Specified in the UN projections as 'Other non-specified areas'.
Source: UNPD (2013).

map, with high fertility represented as dark grey with a transition to lowest fertility as light grey to white. It allows the reader to identify both the patterns of fertility decline within and between each type, but also serves as a reference for the precise TFRs of the different countries of Asia. As such, the quasi-heat map attempts to combine the presentation of precise information that is the advantage of a table, with the ability to clearly visualize change over time, an advantage of the graph.

It should be noted, however, that these groupings are very much open to interpretation. As Goodkind points out in Chapter 2 of this volume, data issues lie at the heart of any demographic analysis of Asia. The vast range of economic development visible in the continent is reflected in the capacity for scholars to access high-quality information from which to both evaluate interventions and measure vital rates (Cleland 1996). A patchwork of systems for estimating fertility rates exists across Asia, ranging from using multi- and single-round instruments such as the Demographic and Health Surveys through to highly efficient census and vital registration systems. As such, some countries might be misclassified because of mismeasurement by the UN – hardly surprising given that the accuracy of fertility measurement across the region varies from 'near perfect' to 'anyone's guess'.

Furthermore, the 'types' are very time-dependent in terms of trends. Thailand, for example, would have been in a different group just a few years ago; while others, in turn, are likely to be transferred to a new group in the near future. Closely related to this is one of the problems of utilizing the TFR, namely, that being a *period* measurement often taken to be a measure of *quantum*, it is too sensitive to changes in the *tempo* of childbearing. In Europe, for example, much of the widely reported 'baby bust' of the late 1990s and early 2000s was, in fact, an artefact of the TFR not adequately reflecting the disproportionate postponement of births (Sobotka 2004). While the relatively low rates of fertility at higher ages (over 40) in East Asia suggest that this might not be such a major methodological headache as in Europe currently (Frejka, Jones and Sardon 2010), the very recent nature of the postponement transition in many territories means that the true impact of the *tempo effect* may be hard to gauge, throwing further doubt onto the validity of our measurements and, hence, the allocation of 'types'.

In the following section we explore each type in turn, trying to draw out similarities between countries within the types as well as observing, and attempting to explain, the particular trajectories of certain countries. Of course, it is recognized that as with any artificial dividing line, units of analysis with strong similarities in experience can fall either side of the synthetic dividing line (in this case fertility rates). However, it was still felt that countries should be kept strictly grouped together to avoid confusion.

Exploring the types of fertility decline

The 'early rapid fallers' or 'demographic forerunners'

This group consists of countries characterized today by below-replacement rate fertility and relatively sustained development, namely Armenia, Azerbaijan, Bahrain, Brunei Darussalam, China, Georgia, Hong Kong SAR, Iran, Japan, Lebanon, Macao SAR, Malaysia, Qatar, Republic of Korea, Singapore, Taiwan, Thailand, Turkey, the UAE and Vietnam. Together, these countries have a total population of 1.93 billion (or 556 million without China). Given that this group is, in itself, very heterogeneous in nature, we first consider those territories that reached below-replacement fertility before the 1990s, then go on to examine the later 'early rapid fallers'.

In some ways, some Asian sites of ultra-low fertility have come to symbolize fertility across the whole continent. These territories, characterized by fertility of well below replacement levels, include the highly developed Pacific Asian states of the Republic of Korea, Japan, Taiwan, Hong Kong SAR, Macao SAR and Singapore (for a review, see Basten et al. 2014: 55–56). Each of these territories, which now report some of the lowest fertility rates in the world, are characterized by rapid economic growth, limited welfare states that are geared towards maximizing production rather than social protection or family support, and the implementation of highly effective FPPs. Each of these territories (apart from Japan, which began its fertility decline much earlier) had persistently high fertility rates (TFRs of around 5–6) until the 1970s followed by extremely rapid declines to well below replacement rates. TFRs in these territories are within the 1.0–1.4 boundary and can be generally characterized as being 'lowest-low' (Billari and Kohler 2004).

Rapid economic development, increasing levels of education among women (leading to increasing participation in the labour force), and effective national FPPs initiated in the 1960s are considered to have been major forces behind the rapid fertility decline in the Republic of Korea, Hong Kong SAR and Taiwan (Chang 2003; Sun 2012; Song, Chang and Sylvian 2013; Lin and Yang 2009). Fertility declines in recent decades are mostly due to delayed onset of childbearing, resulting in part from increasing age at first marriage combined with still low levels of non-marital births (Frejka, Jones and Sardon 2010). Persistent gender inequality marked by limited involvement of men in household tasks and childrearing, as well as the often precarious employment situation of mothers, have contributed to these trends.

Educational differentials between couples notwithstanding, fertility decline proceeded almost simultaneously in most social groups. Especially in South Korea, there was a remarkable convergence in fertility by education level, indicating that rising education levels contributed only a little to the observed fertility decline (Choe and Park 2006). At the same time, Lee (2005) argued that under competitive conditions typical for East Asia, the desire of parents to provide their children with high quality education makes children very costly in terms of both time and money, and this 'education fever' constitutes an important force behind the very low fertility in the region.

China occupies something of a liminal space in Pacific Asian fertility, reporting fertility rates similar to those of many of its neighbours, but often considered separately. While a notable fertility reduction had already been observed in a number of urban Chinese centres in the 1950s and 1960s (Zhao 2001), national fertility decline in China did not begin until the early 1970s, when its TFR fell from about 6 to around 2.5 children per woman by 1980. Following the enactment of more proscriptive family planning regulations, the TFR fluctuated between 2.3 and 2.9, falling to below-replacement levels in the early 1990s. Although there is much debate regarding the actual TFR of contemporary China, there is some consensus that it lies between 1.4 and 1.6 (Basten et al. 2014; Zhao and Zhang 2010; Zhao and Chen 2011; Cai 2008).

China's unique history of family planning regulations has undoubtedly impacted upon its recent demographic history. The 'later, longer, fewer' family planning programme played an important role in shaping fertility decline in the 1970s. Recently, however, many scholars have argued that the macro-level effect of the famous one-child policy introduced in 1978 may have been overstated, with much of the further decline seen from the 1980s being primarily driven by economic development and urbanization shaping proximate determinants (Basten and Jiang 2014; Wang, Cai and Gu 2013). There is some scepticism as to whether the recent shift to a national two-child policy will have any major effect on China's TFR, given the apparent internalization of a one-child norm and the challenges of raising a family in contemporary China (Basten and Jiang 2015).

Adding to these 'usual suspects' of very low fertility are some South-East Asian countries that have seen significant rates of economic growth in recent years. With a current TFR of 1.4, falling from about 6.0 in the late 1960s, Thailand has clearly joined the 'club' of Asian states characterized by very low fertility. However, fertility decline in neighbouring Vietnam has been equally sharp, if not more so, falling from a TFR of around 5.0 at the start of the 1990s down to just 1.75 today. As Hull (2012) notes, 'observers in the 1960s could never have imagined that Vietnam, a country engaged in civil war, and increasingly hammered by international military interventions, could recover to promote a unitary government with a strong policy of fertility control … yet this is precisely what happened starting in 1975' (Hull 2012: 48). Elsewhere in South-East Asia, sub-replacement fertility rates can be seen in Brunei Darussalam, Malaysia, and, of course, within a number of Indonesian provinces. In each of these cases, rapid social and economic change caused couples to increasingly view large numbers of children as an economic burden, all within the context of highly effective FPPs. Some countries, such as Thailand, are at a significant crossroads regarding population policy and the potential move towards pronatalism (UNFPA 2011).

The remainder of the 'early rapid fallers' can be found scattered across Western and Central Asia. In 1950, the total fertility rate in Western Asia stood at 7.0, higher than in other world regions including sub-Saharan Africa. Yet today, Iran (1.9), Bahrain (2.1), Lebanon (1.5), Turkey (2.1) and the UAE (1.8) each report fertility rates at or below replacement. Iran's fertility transition is remarkable for being one of the most rapid recorded in human history. In the early 1980s, Iran's TFR stood at 6.53. By 2000–2005, the country reported a sub-replacement fertility rate of just 1.97. This was driven by a wide-ranging family planning policy embraced by religious authorities in tandem with government policies such as the extension of public education, particularly for girls, the establishment of a healthcare system, and the increase in access to electricity and safe water, transport and communication in remote areas of Iran (Abbasi-Shavazi et al. 2009).

The decline of fertility among these Middle Eastern countries in recent decades appears to be closely linked to urbanization, advancement of women's education (Torabi et al. 2013; Abbasi-Shavazi and McDonald 2006), and rising aspirations for women who seek employment, as well as access to media, changing family ideals, decline of infant mortality and the introduction of effective contraception. Finally, there are indications that universality of marriage is also being questioned (Rashad, Osman and Roudi-Fahimi 2005), with divorce rising in most countries (Singerman 2004).

The final group of 'early rapid fallers' consists of some of the former states of the Soviet Union (for a comprehensive review for the period up to 1991, see Anichkin and Vishnevsky

1993; for the post-Soviet period, see Spoorenberg 2013a and Billingsley 2010). We are able to observe that fertility among Asian former Soviet states since 1950 has followed a number of tracks. Georgia has followed a generally 'European' system of steady decline to 1.8 today; Armenia (TFR=1.7) had seen significant decreases from the inter-war period and continued its decrease to converge with Georgia by the mid-1970s. In Azerbaijan (TFR=1.9) secular decline in fertility was observed among both the European and ethnic Azeri populations (Agadjanian et al. 2013). Jones and Grupp (1987) argued that it was the decline of fertility among these ethnic Azeris that drove the overall pace of fertility decline there. At present, fertility in all bar one of the republics examined here is below 2.6. Recent minor increases have been observed in Armenia, while rates appear to be stabilizing at or just above replacement rate in Azerbaijan. However, it is important to note that the fertility transition in these former Soviet states has been prompted by a quite different set of drivers from those seen in East Asia and most of the other 'early rapid fallers'. In common with other former Soviet states in Europe, the general pattern of fertility decline in these countries was driven more by universal education and employment, a rhetorical attachment to egalitarian ideology, diminishing importance of private property lowering barriers to marriage, rapid secularization, high rates of women's participation in the labour force, and high divorce rates.

'Slow fallers'

The second group of countries can be characterized by generally slow, lethargic falls in fertility over the course of the 1950–2010 period. These countries include India, Indonesia, Kazakhstan, Kuwait, Kyrgyzstan, the Philippines, Sri Lanka, Tajikistan, Turkmenistan and Uzbekistan, with a combined population of 1.67 billion (or 431 million without India).

Former Soviet states in Central Asia tend to congregate in this category, with Uzbekistan (TFR=2.3), Turkmenistan (TFR=2.3), Kazakhstan (TFR=2.4), Kyrgyzstan (TFR=3.1) and Tajikistan (TFR=3.9), a state that is something of an outlier, all featuring in this group. These states saw a somewhat different fertility decline from those in the more 'European USSR' (discussed above) in terms of their temporal development (Spoorenberg 2013a; Jones and Grupp 1987). The main outlier in the group appears to be Tajikistan, where fertility decline had been steady but is now the only republic where fertility is substantially above three children per woman. The two main causes of Tajikistan's growth pattern have been the high value placed by society on large families and the virtual absence of birth control, especially in rural areas where the majority of the population live (Clifford, Falkingham and Hinde 2010; Haub 1994). Fertility rates in Turkmenistan appear to be continuing their spectacular downward trajectory from 6.7 in 1960 to just over replacement rate today. As in Azerbaijan, fertility decline in Kazakhstan has been seen in both the European and ethnic Kazakh populations, but with the lion's share of total decline arguably being driven by ethnic Kazakhs (Jones and Grupp 1987). Minor increases have been observed in recent years in Kazakhstan, while a stabilization of TFR around replacement rate appears to be occurring in Uzbekistan.

In South Asia, fertility transition in Sri Lanka is notable for the much earlier onset of fertility decline in the late 1950s, when fertility fell from a steady rate of around 6.0 down to 4.0 by the early 1970s, and to around replacement level today. This decline has been driven by a constant move towards later marriage and to rising use of contraception, leading to declines in marital fertility as well as rising household incomes (Wright 1968; Caldwell 1996; Weerasinghe and Parr 2002). Caldwell (1996) also observed the critical importance of the Sri Lankan conjugal family system which, unlike the agnatic family system prevalent in other parts of South Asia, generally lends women a stronger position in society and a stronger say in health and fertility behaviour – a

Fertility decline

feature further reinforced by improved educational opportunities for women. However, a recent increase in fertility has been observed in Sri Lanka, possibly attributable to a decline in the age of marriage, marked declines in the use of contraception and the unavailability of abortion services (Silva 2013).

The most significant country in this category is almost certainly India. In India the demographic transition started during the third decade of the twentieth century. In the early expanding stage, infant and child mortality declined as a result of improved public health interventions related to water and sanitation, and medical interventions such as vaccine coverage and use of antibiotics. In this stage, fertility decline was minimal. In the early 1950s, however, India introduced what is arguably the world's first holistic population policy, along with the development and expansion of family planning services. The late-expanding stage of transition, where both fertility and mortality start declining, occurred around 1970. The pace of fertility decline in India has been much slower than that of mortality decline. From the 1970s, fertility has declined dramatically (James 2011). However, as Figure 5.3 demonstrates, this fertility decline has not been uniform across the country: lower fertility is found in the south and very north of the country, while noticeably higher fertility is found in the so-called 'Hindi Belt' of North-Central India (Säävälä 2010).

Data from the National Family Health Survey (IIPS and Macro International 2007) show that 18 out of India's 29 states have TFRs lower than the national TFR (2.7) and most of them have achieved replacement level or are at below-replacement level. Furthermore, most of the states that have not reached overall replacement fertility return urban fertility rates of below-replacement level. The latest estimates of TFR show that urban India reached below-replacement

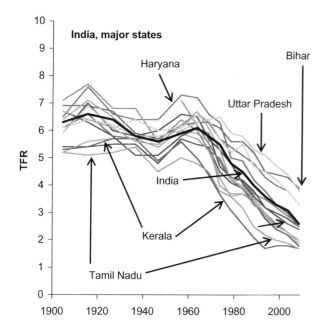

Figure 5.3 Total fertility rates in India and 15 of its major states, 1900–2008
Sources: Ram and Ram (2009); Rele (1987); and various Sample Registration Reports published by the Office of the Registrar General of India.

75

fertility of 2.0 in 2007. Nine out of 17 states have reached below-replacement fertility and in urban areas 13 out of 17 states have fertility of 2.1 or less.

Economic theories do not account for the variation in fertility declines between Indian states. As Tenhuna and Säävälä (2012) observe, the southern states, which are characterized by the lowest fertility rates, return only average rates of economic growth compared to, for example, Punjab. Other studies have emphasized the role of women's relatively better social and economic position in the south which, in tandem with generally better social welfare systems, educational levels, more equitable economic development and enhanced female labour force participation, as well as higher prevalence of cousin marriage, may have contributed to disproportionately lower fertility (Pande, Malhotra and Namy 2012; Dyson and Moore 1983).

The two 'slow fallers' in South-East Asia are both demographic 'big hitters', namely Indonesia and the Philippines. The significant decline seen in Indonesia, from more than 5.0 in the 1970s to 2.4 in 2010–2015, while indicative of the successful FPPs in the country, masks the inevitable high levels of heterogeneity in the experience of fertility decline in the country (Molyneaux and Gertler 2014). Bali, Yogyakarta and Jakarta, for example, report sub-replacement level fertility rates while other provinces such as West Nusa Tenggara and south-east Sulawesi have significantly higher rates of well over three children per woman. Recent data suggest a possible slowing of the pace of fertility decline across Indonesia; however, the proximate determinants of delayed marriage and use of contraception appear to be strong despite quite dramatic economic decline following the Asian Financial Crisis. Finally, as Hull (2002: 409) observes, 'the rising cohorts of women of childbearing age continue to show higher levels of education, increasing involvement in both the formal and informal workforces, and firm resolution to control their fertility at comparatively low levels' (see also Kim 2010). Meanwhile, the experience of the Philippines as an outlier with higher fertility than other countries in the region is the subject of much discussion (Mapa et al. 2012). While the role of the Catholic Church in deterring access to contraception and abortion is one of the most widely cited reasons, Hull (2012: 47–48) suggests that other contributing factors have hindered FPPs such as 'macho cultures, huge disparities in income, the politics of elite conflict' and the 'persistent idea of a large and growing population producing a huge diaspora' being a matter of pride (see also Herrin 2007).

Kuwait is the only Western Asian country in this group. The ups and downs of the country's fertility decline are largely shaped by the impact of the oil crisis, pronatalist ideologies and the fact that, as Courbage (2012) observes, high levels of female labour force participation (as in Bahrain) are compatible with high fertility as highly paid working women are able to shift the burden of childcare onto hired domestic staff. However, by the mid-1990s an ever-increasing number of women were practising modern contraceptive methods (Shah, Shah and Radovanovic 1998).

'Rapid fallers still in transition'

This third type can be characterized by a rapid rate of decline but, owing to the time of onset, report fertility rates still above 2.1 despite the indications suggesting that fertility decline is continuing or stabilizing at around this level. As such, it is useful to consider these countries separately from those 'early rapid fallers' outlined above that have achieved below-replacement level, because there is no guarantee of the direction of their future trajectories. The group of countries characterized by this type is a mixed bag. The majority are characterized by a pronounced drive towards extensive FPPs in recent years and large-scale changes in education, employment and female empowerment. This group consists of Bangladesh, Bhutan, Cambodia, Jordan, Laos, the Maldives, Mongolia, Nepal, Oman, Pakistan, Saudi Arabia and Syria. Together, these countries have a combined contemporary population of 444 million. In the early 1980s, each country was characterized by high fertility levels bounded by Nepal (TFR=5.7) and Oman (TFR=8.3), with an unweighted average of 6.6. By 2010–2015, this same group of countries was bounded by Bangladesh (TFR=2.2) and Jordan (TFR=3.3) with an unweighted average of just 2.7.

In South Asia, Pakistan, Nepal, the Maldives, Bangladesh and Bhutan can be characterized by persistently high fertility rates until the 1970s, followed by notable declines. Bangladesh and Nepal saw fertility transition begin in 1980–1985, while the other countries saw the onset in 1985–1990. Fertility decline over the entire period in many of these countries has been strongly dependent on the development of robust FPPs (as described in Chapters 6 and 7) but the relationship has not been simple. In Pakistan, for example, despite the fact that FPPs were introduced in the mid-1960s, little impact on fertility was felt until the late 1980s – and even then, it is held that these modest declines were almost entirely due to increases in age at first marriage (Soomro 2000; Sathar and Casterline 1998). Pakistan's fertility decline has been halting and selective. Indeed, it is crucial to realize that the success of such programmes has gone hand in hand with other important drivers, namely through the proximate determinants of childbearing and the declining demand for children, often mediated through improved education and female empowerment. In Bangladesh, for example, FPPs were developed at a time of rapid social and economic change (Caldwell et al. 1999) with a distinct emphasis on reaching the rural poor and women, as well as through the active role of NGOs (Amin and Lloyd 2002). Relating to this latter point, certain studies have examined the role played by microcredit schemes in shaping approaches to childbearing in both Bangladesh (Kuchler 2012) and elsewhere (Li, Gan and Hu 2011), with mixed results. Either way, Bangladesh saw a dramatic fall in fertility from 6.9 in 1970–1975 to 2.2 today, or almost five children per woman within four decades.

Turning to South-East Asia, the role of conflict cannot be ignored in shaping fertility decline in the two 'rapid fallers in transition', namely Cambodia and Laos. In Cambodia, for example, fertility and marriage rates were very low under the Khmer Rouge within a context of excess mortality, forced relocation and violence (de Walque 2004). Similarly, the post-war era in Laos was characterized by civil conflict and insurgent action. However, in the last 10–15 years, as stability has increased, access to education and family planning has improved and economic opportunities have grown, fertility has fallen to around 3.0 in both countries.[3] Despite this, lower contraceptive prevalence rates and higher fertility rates are still very much present in rural areas of Laos (World Bank 2011).

The only East Asian state in this group is Mongolia, and the twists and turns in its fertility transition require special attention. A strongly pronatalist policy was in evidence in Mongolia for much of the third quarter of the twentieth century, when TFR reached a peak of almost eight children per woman. During this period, women with more than four children were awarded medals of honour, additional child allowances, subsidized leave and early retirement at age 50. On the flip side, special taxes were imposed upon the childless and unmarried, the importation, distribution and use of modern contraceptives was prohibited, and strict regulations were imposed upon abortion (Aassve and Altankhuyag 2001). From 1976, however, in a *volte face*, the government began to provide some family planning provision, expanding this in 1988. By 1990 all restrictions on the use and importation of modern contraceptives had been lifted and abortion was fully legalized (Neupert 1996). The demise of these pronatalist policies, in conjunction with net falls in income levels, increased uncertainty in job prospects and reduced public transfers brought about by the collapse of the socialist system and economic crisis of the 1990s, saw TFR decline dramatically to replacement rate in 2000. In recent years, however, Mongolia has seen an increase in fertility rates, reaching almost 2.7 by 2009. This increase has coincided with a shift in policy back towards encouraging population growth and boosting household incomes through direct cash transfers (Enkhtsetseg and Spoorenberg 2012).

The remainder of the 'rapid fallers in transition' are found in Western Asia. Fertility transition in Syria and Jordan has been a rather disjointed affair, with falls from very high levels (Jordan's TFR exceeded 8.5 in the 1970s) commencing from the 1970s to converge at around 2.9 today (Courbage 2012; Augustin 2012). A critical element in shaping fertility decline, especially in Lebanon, is tension in the marriage market owing to the large-scale emigration of men, coupled with women now generally having a higher level of education than men (Engelen and Puschmann 2011; Keysar 2009). A second critical factor is the role played by the generally depressed economic situation, to which the political insecurity arising from the Arab-Israeli conflict has undoubtedly made a major contribution. Despite these overall declines, a number of studies have identified stalls in this decline for both Jordan and Syria in recent years (Courbage and Todd 2011). Jordanian fertility has remained relatively constant at above 3.5 children per woman for more than a decade (Cetorelli and Leone 2012). It will remain to be seen what effect the present-day civil conflict in Syria will have on fertility rates in that country. In Saudi Arabia, meanwhile, fertility decline began in earnest in the 1980s, despite governmental opposition to family planning. Khraif found that age at first marriage and women's education levels were the most important determinants of fertility decline (Khraif 2002). Finally, Oman saw an extremely rapid fertility decline from almost 8.0 in the late 1980s down to around 2.9 today, driven largely by a shift towards later childbearing coupled with a move to almost no childbearing in the teenage years (Islam, Dorvlo and Al-Qasmi 2012). Furthermore, Oman has the most robust FPP of all the Gulf Arab States, with 77 per cent of Omani women (in a 1997 survey) practising modern family planning methods compared to, for example, 13 per cent of Yemeni women (Eltigani 2001).

'Laggards'

The fourth group of Asian countries can be characterized as being only at the very first stages of fertility transition, or even experiencing reversing fertility declines.[4] These are Afghanistan, Iraq, Palestine, Timor-Leste and Yemen, which together have a combined population of 91 million. Each of these countries has a contemporary TFR of more than 4.0. Afghanistan is a clear outlier in South Asia with one of the highest fertility rates in Asia (TFR=5.0) (Spoorenberg 2013b). In South-East Asia, meanwhile, the clear outlier is Timor-Leste with a TFR of 5.9, up from 4.3 in the early 1990s. While the fertility decline in Yemen has been relatively steep, despite some slowing in recent years, the extremely high levels of fertility prior to, and in the first stages of, transition mean that the current reported TFR in Yemen is still 5.5 (Eltigani 2001; Augustin 2012). Elsewhere in Western Asia, fertility decline in both Iraq and the Palestinian Territories has been extremely slow and is currently around 4.0. While these two sites could easily be included in the previous group of 'slow fallers', the current geopolitical uncertainty of these two areas, and their higher mortality rates (especially in the Gaza Strip), means that we consider them within the type we call 'laggards'.

From a demographic perspective, the high fertility rates observed in these societies are clearly linked to universal and early marriage, childbearing at a relatively early age, and the achievement of high parities relatively quickly (Eltigani 2001). Contraceptive prevalence rates are often very low, with such rates for Afghanistan in 2012 estimated to be just 5 per cent (Shaikh, Azmat and Mazhar 2013). Abortion is often highly stigmatized and dangerous. Inhabitants of countries such as Timor-Leste often have very poor knowledge of reproductive health and little access to primary care services (Belton et al. 2009; Wild et al. 2010), the latter point exacerbated by the withdrawal of the Indonesian FPP upon independence.

Beyond this, each of these countries has suffered decades of warfare, invasion, uncertainty, fanaticism and oppression that have devastated infrastructure, not least relating to health. The role of conflict must not be underestimated, nor that of the inheritance of strongly pronatalist ideologies. According to Khawaja, Assaf and Jarallah (2009) pronatalist ideologies and discourses in the Palestinian territories conceived of children as 'weapons against occupation' (see also Hansson et al. 2013; Khawaja and Randall 2006). In the 1980s the Iraqi government provided cash bonuses and salary increases upon childbirth, monthly payments to mothers of large families and 10 weeks' maternity leave on full pay as part of the pronatalist agenda. Much of this was driven by regional conflict. In a 1986 speech Saddam Hussein famously expressed his intention to penalize those families that have fewer than four children (Faour 1989). As well as 'conflict fertility' during the course of hostilities, dealing with the aftermath is clearly an important issue. As Belton, Whittaker and Barclay (2009: 20) note in their explanation of the very high fertility rates in Timor-Leste, 'the Timorese people have experienced enormous loss of family and friends due to the conflict and are now enjoying a post-war baby boom'. Beyond conflict and political uncertainty/instability, low levels of investment in education, limited formal employment opportunities and low levels of female empowerment play a critical role in shaping high fertility (Khawaja, Assaf and Jarallah 2009; Faour 1989).

Despite an environment hostile to women's empowerment in many of these countries, they now appear to be undergoing the first steps in fertility transition – even in the face of inadequate family planning systems and extremely high maternal mortality (Huber, Saeedi and Samadi 2010).

The 'special cases'

The final group of countries are special cases that have almost nothing in common with each other. However, their recent histories prevent them from being categorized in any other type and they are therefore considered separately. This group is made up of Israel, the Democratic People's Republic of Korea and Myanmar, with a combined population of 85 million.

The first special case is Israel. Despite having some of the highest measures on the Human Development Index in the world, Israeli fertility has been characterized by only a modest fall from 3.8 in the mid-1950s to around 2.9 today. Crucially, since its formation the State of Israel has been characterized by quite different internal fertility declines. For the late 1990s, for example, Friedlander (2002) observed that while Israel's overall TFR was 2.9, this masked differences between the Jewish 'non-religious' group (67–70 per cent of total population) with a TFR of 2.0–2.2, the Arab Christian population (2 per cent) with a TFR of 2.6, Arab Muslims and Druze (16 per cent) with a TFR of 4.0, and the Jewish Ultra-Orthodox and the National Orthodox (12–15 per cent) with a TFR of between 6.0 and 7.0. The reasons for this disparity are rooted in a multiplicity of causes such as sociocultural norms among Ultra-Orthodox groups and a large gap in the opportunity structure between Jews and Muslims (not least in the quality of educational provision and discrimination in the labour market). It appears that fertility decline among Muslims in Israel has stalled in recent years (Nahmias and Stecklov 2007). Furthermore, while total fertility rates among the Bedouin groups have declined dramatically from over 10.0 in the 1990s, they are still more than twice the national average at around 5.5 (Abu-Srihan 2013). Despite these internal differences, other important elements such as economic opportunities for women (Ekert-Jaffe and Stier 2009) should not be forgotten.

The Democratic People's Republic of Korea (DPRK) is a special case because of the relative dearth of reliable demographic data concerning the state (Spoorenberg and Schwekendiek 2012). The territory of DPRK saw a dramatic collapse in fertility rates to well below 2.0 during World War II, the Soviet Occupation and the War with the South, followed by something of a rebound after partition in 1953. After returning to a level of around 3.5 by the late 1950s, North

Korea embarked upon a pronatalist campaign. According to Ness (1985) this was driven by the hostile relations with South Korea, with its significantly larger population, setting the context for a political will for demographic growth. Despite this, local authorities did make available contraceptive information and access to family planning (Eberstadt and Banister 1992). A prolonged decline ensued from the mid-1970s, driven by the usual motors of later marriage and urbanization. Limited housing space and extremely high female labour force participation rates also contributed. As in similar 'traditional-socialist' countries where gender inequality is high and childcare facilities are limited, this can result in an overburdening of responsibilities on females in both the private and public spheres, which can limit fertility (Goodkind 1999).

Myanmar is also considered separately because of the lack of reliable recent data, with much of the twentieth century appearing as a 'demographic black hole' (Spoorenberg 2013c). However, it appears fertility began to decline during the 1970s and reached a level of around 4.5–5.0 in the early 1980s. Its subsequent transition to below-replacement fertility rates (TFR=2.0) is quite difficult to explain. The country is a good example, along with North Korea and Saudi Arabia, of a setting where fertility has fallen in spite of the government being hostile to the mass provision of contraception (Cleland 2001). As a number of studies have observed, the fertility decline in Myanmar during the 1970s took place in the context of limited official access to reproductive health services, well before the expansion of public-sector contraception services in the 1990s (Ba-Thike 1997; Panitchpakdi et al. 1993; Ross and Mauldin 1996). As Spoorenberg (2013c) observes, 'the social and economic factors that contributed to the country's fertility decline clearly deserve further attention in their own right'. The transition towards a new governmental system and the running of the 2014 census will likely allow for further reconstruction of the demographic past of this important, populous country.

Conclusions and the future of fertility in the region

This chapter has sought to present the main trends in fertility decline across Asia. The continent has been home to a wide variety of experiences, which can be grouped together in a number of types. These types attempt to capture both the ultimate level of fertility in countries across Asia and their transition to that rate over the past six decades, while providing a cluster of countries in which similarities and differences can be explored. The first type consists of 20 territories currently characterized by below-replacement level fertility that include both highly developed settings such as Singapore and Hong Kong SAR, as well as new sites of low fertility in South-East Asia and the Middle East. The second group, including India, Indonesia, the Philippines and Sri Lanka, is characterized by slow but steady falls in fertility from around 5.0–7.0 in the 1950s down to roughly between replacement rate and a TFR of 3.0. The third group has seen a much more rapid rate of fertility decline than the second group, with TFRs of around 5.0 persisting into the 1990s, then falling to between replacement and around 3.0 today. The fourth group, including Afghanistan, Iraq and Timor-Leste, is still characterized by higher rates of fertility (above 4.0). The final group is considered to be special cases that are, for very particular reasons, extremely difficult to categorize with any other groups. It includes DPRK, Israel and Myanmar.

There are clearly a number of factors that are relevant to many of the countries analysed here in relation to their particular patterns of fertility decline – postponement of marriage and age of first birth, increased educational attainment, changing attitudes towards the value of children, economic development and the introduction of FPPs, for example. Each of these factors played a greater, or lesser, role in the decline of fertility in countries across the continent throughout this period, although the timing and the pace has differed enormously. We have also tried to identify some of the broader themes and potential drivers that have played a role in shaping the experience in fertility decline across the continent over the past century, such as rapid economic growth, education, changing gender roles and social conflict. Given the heterogeneity of the continent and of the experience of fertility decline among its constituent countries, the chapter has necessarily taken only a broad overview of the patterns and drivers of fertility decline.

The final point is to consider briefly the possible future of fertility in Asia. Of course, assumptions of future fertility changes are integral to the method by which forecasts are made. According to the medium fertility scenario in the 2012 *Revision* of the UN's *World Population Prospects*, all countries in Asia will see fertility below the replacement rate by 2050, apart from Timor-Leste (TFR=2.7), Iraq (2.6), Tajikistan (2.5), State of Palestine (2.5), Israel (2.2), Kyrgyzstan (2.2), Kuwait (2.2) and the Philippines (2.1) (UNPD 2013). Taking these data, it is important to distinguish between countries where fertility is generally assumed to increase and those where it is likely to continue decreasing.

In terms of countries where it is assumed that a general decrease will occur, the evidence presented in this chapter – both in terms of the trajectories of fertility decline over recent decades as well as the underlying reasons – suggests that such a scenario is indeed likely in many, if not most, settings. A recent survey of population experts has also concluded that further decline would be a feature of higher fertility Asian countries such as India, Pakistan, Nepal, Bangladesh, the Philippines and Indonesia (Fuchs and Goujon 2014). This should be tempered by the possibility that declines in many of these countries could be erratic and entail either stalls, or possibly even (temporary) increases, in the wake of major policy shifts. In this sense, therefore, population experts and UN forecasts are somewhat in accord – among the 'slow fallers', 'rapid fallers still in transition' and 'laggards' referred to in this chapter, further fertility decline appears likely. What is less certain, however, is where this fertility decline will stop. Will we see more countries becoming characterized by the very low fertility rates seen in parts of East and South-East Asia? In other words, we can be confident in anticipating further general decline, but given the heterogeneity of the continent, not counting the heterogeneity of individual countries, determining where fertility decline will stop is much more uncertain.

What is also uncertain is how fertility levels will develop in some of the 'demographic forerunners' that are currently characterized by very low TFRs. The medium fertility trajectory of the 2012 *World Population Prospects* generally assumes a steady increase to mid-century in Macao SAR, Hong Kong SAR, Taiwan, DPRK, Japan and Thailand, with each of these territories characterized by a TFR of between 1.6 and 1.7 (up from 1.1–1.4 in 2010). China's fertility rate is forecast to increase modestly from 1.7 to 1.8 mid-century, though, as mentioned earlier, the validity of this reported current fertility rate is questionable. Finally, under this scenario only Singapore is assumed to have a fertility rate below 1.5 mid-century, seeing only modest increases from a current TFR of 1.3 to 1.4 by mid-century.

This view is not, however, universal. Local statistical offices in Hong Kong SAR, Taiwan, Singapore, Japan and DPRK, for example, assume only very modest increases or even stagnation in future fertility rates (Basten 2013). Similarly, a recent survey of population experts has concluded that general stagnation or even further decreases could be likely in China and Japan (Basten et al. 2014). The notion that these countries may have fallen into a trap where self-reinforcing social, economic, cultural and demographic mechanisms serve to perpetuate low fertility, especially in the context of relatively weak policy frameworks, is a widely held one (Lutz et al. 2006; Lutz 2008). Again, however, the very recent nature of the fertility transition in many of these parts of Pacific Asia, as well as the potential role of the *tempo effect*, means that any future assumptions must be couched in more than the usual caveats of uncertainty.

Acknowledgements

The author is very grateful for the advice of the editors, two anonymous reviewers, David Coleman and Danny Dorling for their helpful reviews of this chapter, as well as to Kei Takahashi and Yulia Shenderovich who assisted in formatting and data gathering respectively.

Notes

1. The primary unit of measurement we employ in this chapter is the total fertility rate (TFR). This represents the number of children that would be born to a woman if she were to live to the end of her childbearing years and bear children in accordance with current age-specific fertility rates. While unlike measurements such as the Crude Birth Rate (CBR), the TFR is not affected by the age structure of the population, this synthetic unit of measurement is far from perfect (Sobotka and Lutz 2011).
2. In this chapter, unless noted otherwise, we employ fertility data derived from the 2012 *Revision* of the UN's *World Population Prospects* (UNPD 2013).
3. A further consequence of the genocide in Cambodia was that the shortage of eligible males meant that the age difference between partners tended to reduce the age and schooling differences between couples, which may have led to increased bargaining within the household by women.
4. It should be noted that smaller-scale conflicts and rebellions – such as in Aceh, Papua, Southern Thailand, Myanmar and Mindanao – as well as natural disasters would have disrupted development activities and contributed to temporary changes in fertility decline that may not show up at the national level.

References

Aassve, A. and G. Altankhuyag (2001) *Changing Pattern of Fertility Behaviour in a Time of Social and Economic Change: Evidence from Mongolia*. Max Planck Institute for Demographic Research. MPIDR Working Papers. Rostock: MPIDR.

Abbasi-Shavazi, M. J. (2001) 'The fertility revolution in Iran'. *Population et Sociétés*, 373: 1–4.

Abbasi-Shavazi, M. J. and P. McDonald (2006) 'Fertility decline in the Islamic Republic of Iran: 1972–2000'. *Asian Population Studies*, 2(3): 217–237.

Abbasi-Shavazi, M. J., P. McDonald and M. Hosseini-Chavoshi (2009) *The Fertility Transition in Iran: Revolution and Reproduction*. Dordrecht: Springer.

Abu-Srihan, N. (2013) 'Bedouin fertility in the Israeli Negev'. Paper presented at ESRC Seminar on Fertiltiy Transition, Oxford, July 2013.

Agadjanian, V., P. Dommaraju and L. Nedoluzhko (2013) 'Economic fortunes, ethnic divides, and marriage and fertility in Central Asia: Kazakhstan and Kyrgyzstan compared'. *Journal of Population Research*, 30(3): 197–211.

Amin, S. and B. C. Lloyd (2002) 'Women's lives and rapid fertility decline: some lessons from Bangladesh and Egypt'. *Population Research and Policy Review*, 21(4): 275–317.

Anichkin, A. and A. Vishnevsky (1993) 'Three types of fertility behavior in the USSR'. In W. Lutz, S. Scherbov and A. Volkov (eds.) *Demographic Trends and Patterns in the Soviet Union Before 1991*. Abingdon: Routledge.

Augustin, E. (2012) 'Demographic transition and gender systems: the case of Jordan and Yemen'. In H. Groth and A. Sousa-Poza (eds.) *Population Dynamics in Muslim Countries*. Berlin, Heidelberg: Springer.

Basten, S. (2013) *Re-Examining the Fertility Assumptions for Pacific Asia in the UN's 2010 World Population Prospects*. Barnett Papers in Social Research 2013/1, Oxford: Department of Social Policy and Intervention, University of Oxford.

Basten, S. and Q. Jiang (2014) 'China's family planning policies: recent reforms and future prospects'. *Studies in Family Planning*, 45(4):493–509.

Basten, S. and Q. Jiang (2015) 'Fertility in China: an uncertain future'. *Population Studies*, 69(suppl.1): s97–s105.

Basten, S., T. Sobotka and K. Zeman (2014) 'Future fertility in low fertility countries'. In W. Lutz, W. P. Butz and S. KC (eds.) *World Population and Human Capital in the Twenty-First Century*. Oxford: Oxford University Press.

Ba-Thike, K. (1997) 'Abortion: a public health problem in Myanmar'. *Reproductive Health Matters*, 5(9): 94–100.

Belton, S., A. Whittaker and L. Barclay (2009) *Maternal Mortality, Unplanned Pregnancy and Unsafe Abortion in Timor-Leste: A Situational Analysis*. Dili: ALOLA/UNFPA.

Belton, S., A. Whittaker, Z. Fonseca, T. Wells-Brown and P. Pais (2009) 'Attitudes towards the legal context of unsafe abortion in Timor-Leste'. *Reproductive Health Matters*, 17(34): 55–64.

Billari, F. C. and H. P. Kohler (2004) 'Patterns of low and lowest-low fertility in Europe'. *Population Studies*, 58(2): 161–176.

Billingsley, S. (2010) 'The post-communist fertility puzzle'. *Population Research and Policy Review*, 29(2): 193–231.

Bongaarts, J. (1975) 'Why high birth rates are so low'. *Population and Development Review*, 1(2): 289–296.

Cai, Y. (2008) 'An assessment of China's fertility level using the variable-r method'. *Demography*, 45(2): 271–281.

Caldwell, B. (1996) 'The family and demographic change in Sri Lanka'. *Health Transition Review*, 6(suppl.): 45–60.

Caldwell, J. C., B. Caldwell, I. Pieris and P. Caldwell (1999) 'The Bangladesh fertility decline: an interpretation'. *Population and Development Review*, 25(1): 67–84.

Cetorelli, V. and T. Leone (2012) 'Is fertility stalling in Jordan?' *Demographic Research*, 26(13): 293–318.

Chang, K. S. (2003) 'The state and families in South Korea's compressed fertility transition: a time for policy reversal?' *Journal of Population and Social Security*, 6(21): 596–610.

Choe, M. K. and K. A. Park (2006) 'Fertility decline in South Korea: forty years of policy-behavior dialogue'. *Korea Journal of Population Studies*, 29(2): 1–26.

Cleland, J. (1996) 'Demographic data collection in less developed countries 1946–1996'. *Population Studies*, 50(3): 433–450.

Cleland, J. (2001) 'Potatoes and pills: an overview of innovation-diffusion contributions to explanations of fertility decline'. In National Academic Press (ed.) *Diffusion Processes and Fertility Transition: Selected Perspectives*. Washington, DC: National Academies Press.

Clifford, D., J. Falkingham and A. Hinde (2010) 'Through civil war, food crisis and drought: trends in fertility and nuptiality in post-Soviet Tajikistan'. *European Journal of Population / Revue Européenne de Démographie*, 26(3): 325–350.

Courbage, Y. (2012) *Issues in Fertility Transition in the Middle East and North Africa*. Economic Research Forum Working Papers 9103. Cairo: Economic Research Forum.

Courbage, Y. and E. Todd (2011) *A Convergence of Civilizations*. New York: Columbia University Press.

de Walque, D. (2004) *The Long-term Legacy of the Khmer Rouge Period in Cambodia*. World Bank Policy Research Working Paper 3446. New York, NY: The World Bank.

Dyson, T. and M. Moore (1983) 'On kinship structure female autonomy and demographic behaviour in India'. *Population and Development Review*, 9(1): 35–60.

Dyson, T. and M. Murphy (1985) 'The onset of fertility transition'. *Population and Development Review*, 11(3): 399–440.

Eberstadt, N. and J. Banister (1992) *The Population of North Korea*. Berkeley: University of California Institute of East Asian Studies, Center for Korean Studies.

Ekert-Jaffe, O. and H. Stier (2009) 'Normative or economic behavior? Fertility and women's employment in Israel'. *Social Science Research*, 38(3): 644–655.

Eltigani, E. (2001) 'Levels and trends of fertility in Oman and Yemen'. Paper presented at Workshop on Prospects for Fertility Decline in High Fertility Countries at Department of Economic and Social Affairs Population Division, UN, New York, July 2001.

Engelen, T. and P. Puschmann (2011) 'How unique is the western European marriage pattern? A comparison of nuptiality in historical Europe and the contemporary Arab world'. *The History of the Family*, 16(4): 387–400.

Enkhtsetseg, B. and T. Spoorenberg (2012) 'Social policy and recent fertility increase in Mongolia'. Paper presented in International Union for Scientific Study of Population Seminar on Patterns of Economic Development, Social Change, and Fertility Decline in Comparative Perspective: Analysis and Policy Implications, Shanghai, May 2012.

Faour, M. (1989) 'Fertility policy and family planning in the Arab countries'. *Studies in Family Planning*, 20(5): 254–263.

Frejka, T., G. V. Jones and J. P. Sardon (2010) 'East Asian childbearing patterns and policy developments'. *Population and Development Review*, 36(3): 579–606.

Friedlander, D. (2002) 'Fertility in Israel: is the transition to replacement level in sight?' Paper presented at the Expert Group Meeting on Completing the Fertility Transition, New York, 11–14 March 2002.
Fuchs, R. and A. Goujon (2014) 'Future fertility in high fertility countries'. In W. Lutz, W. P. Butz and S. KC (eds.) *World Population and Human Capital in the Twenty-First Century*. Oxford: Oxford University Press.
Gapminder Foundation (2010) 'Children per woman (total fertility rate) for countries and territories'. *Gapminder Documentation 008, version 5*. Stockholm: Gapminder Foundation. Available from: www.gapminder.org/data/documentation/gd008/#.U7f3-I1dV3o (accessed 2 July 2014).
Goodkind, D. (1999) 'Do parents prefer sons in North Korea?' *Studies in Family Planning*, 30(3): 212–218.
Hansson, L. N., S. Tellier, B. L. Segal and M. Bseiso (2013) 'Political fertility in the Occupied Palestinian Territory: an ethnographic study'. *Lancet*, 382: S17.
Haub, C. (1994) 'Population change in the former Soviet Republics'. *Population Bulletin*, 49(4): 1–52.
Herrin, A. N. (2007) 'Development of the Philippines' family planning program: the early years, 1967–80'. In W. C. Robbinson and J. A. Ross (eds.) *The Global Family Planning Revolution: The Decades of Population Policies and Programs*. Washington, DC: World Bank Publications.
Huber, D., N. Saeedi and A. K. Samadi (2010) 'Achieving success with family planning in rural Afghanistan'. *Bulletin of the World Health Organization*, 88(3): 227–231.
Hull, T. H. (2002) 'Caught in transit: questions about the future of Indonesian fertility'. *Population Bulletin of the United Nations: Completing the Fertility Transition*, Special Issue no. 48–49. New York: UNDESA.
Hull, T. H. (2012) 'Fertility in Southeast Asia'. In L. Williams and P. M. Guest (eds.) *Demographic Change in Southeast Asia: Recent Histories and Future Directions*. Ithaca: Cornell SEAP.
International Institute for Population Sciences (IIPS) and Macro International (2007) *National Family Health Survey (NFHS-3), Volume 1, 2005–2006*. Mumbai, India: IIPS.
Islam, M. M., A. S. S. Dorvlo and A. M. Al-Qasmi (2012) 'Proximate determinants of declining fertility in Oman in the 1990s'. *Canadian Studies in Population*, 38(3–4): 133–152.
James, K. S. (2011) 'India's demographic change: opportunities and challenges'. *Science*, 333(6042): 576–580.
Jones, E. and F. W. Grupp (1987) *Modernization, Value Change and Fertility in the Soviet Union*. Cambridge: Cambridge University Press.
Keysar, A. (2009) 'Women and demography in the meditterranean world'. In B. A. Kosmin and A. Keysar (eds.) *Secularism, Women & the State: The Mediterranean World in the 21st Century*. Hartford: ISSC.
Khawaja, M., S. Assaf and Y. Jarallah (2009) 'The transition to lower fertility in the West Bank and Gaza Strip: evidence from recent surveys'. *Journal of Population Research*, 26(2): 153–174.
Khawaja, M. and S. Randall (2006) 'Intifada, Palestinian fertility and women's education'. *Genus*, 63(1): 21–51.
Khraif, R. (2002) 'Fertility in Saudi Arabia'. *Al-Darah*, 28(2): 9–84 (in Arabic).
Kim, J. (2010) 'Women's education and fertility: an analysis of the relationship between education and birth spacing in Indonesia'. *Economic Development and Cultural Change*, 58(4): 739–774.
Kuchler, A. (2012) 'Do microfinance programs change fertility? Evidence using panel data from Bangladesh'. *The Journal of Developing Areas*, 46(2): 297–313.
Lee, C. J. (2005) 'Korean education fever and private tutoring'. *KEDI Journal of Educational Policy*, 2(1): 99–107.
Li, X., C. Gan and B. Hu (2011) 'The impact of microcredit on women's empowerment: evidence from China'. *Journal of Chinese Economic and Business Studies*, 9(3): 239–261.
Lin, W.-I. and S. Y. Yang (2009) 'From successful family planning to the lowest of low fertility levels: Taiwan's dilemma'. *Asian Social Work and Policy Review*, 3(2): 95–112.
Lutz, W. (2008) 'Has Korea's fertility reached the bottom? The hypothesis of a "low fertility trap" in parts of Europe and East Asia'. *Asian Population Studies*, 4(1): 1–4.
Lutz, W. and S. Scherbov (1993) 'Survey of fertility trends in the Republics of the Soviet Union'. In W. Lutz, S. Scherbov and A. Volkov (eds.) *Demographic Trends and Patterns in the Soviet Union Before 1991*. Abingdon: Routledge.
Lutz, W., V. Skirbekk and M. R. Testa (2006) 'The low-fertility trap hypothesis: forces that may lead to further postponement and fewer births in Europe'. *Vienna Yearbook of Population Research 2006*, 4: 167–192.
Mapa, D. S., M. Lucagbo, A. M. Balisacan, J. R. T. Corpuz and C. L. S. Ignacio (2012) *Is Income Growth Enough to Reduce Total Fertility Rate in the Philippines? Empirical Evidence from Regional Panel Data*, Munich RePEc Working Papers no. 40750. Munich: MPRA.
Molyneaux, J. W. and P. J. Gertler (2014) 'The impact of targeted family planning programs in Indonesia'. *Population and Development Review*, 26(suppl.): 61–85.
Nahmias, P. and G. Stecklov (2007) 'The dynamics of fertility amongst Palestinians in Israel from 1980 to 2007'. *European Journal of Population / Revue Européenne de Démographie*, 23(1): 71–99.

National Institute of Population Studies (NIPS) [Pakistan] and ICF International (2013) *Pakistan Demographic and Health Survey 2012–2013*. Islamabad, Pakistan and Calverton, Maryland, USA: NIPS and ICF International.

Ness, G. D. (1985) 'Managing not-so-small numbers'. *International Journal of Comparative Sociology*, 1–2(26): 1–13.

Neupert, R. F. (1996) *Population Policies, Socioeconomic Development and Population Dynamics in Mongolia*. Canberra: National Capital Printing.

Palloni, A. (1990) 'Fertility and mortality decline in Latin America'. *The Annals of the American Academy of Political and Social Science*, 510(1): 126–144.

Pande, R. P., A. Malhotra and S. Namy (2012) *Fertility Decline and Changes in Women's Lives and Gender Equality in Tamil Nadu, India*. Fertility and Empowerment Network Working Paper Series 007-2012-ICRW-FE. Washington, DC: Fertility and Empowerment Network.

Panitchpakdi, P., A. Podhipak, U. K. Sein and B. Kywe (1993) 'Family planning: knowledge, attitudes and practice survey in Zigone, Myanmar'. *The Southeast Asian Journal of Tropical Medicine and Public Health*, 24(4): 636–646.

Ram, U. and F. Ram (2009) 'Fertility in India: policy issues and program challenges'. In K. K. Singh, R. C. Yadava and A. Pandey (eds.) *Population, Poverty and Health: Analytical Approaches*. New Delhi, India: Hindustan Publishing Company.

Rashad, H., M. Osman and F. Roudi-Fahimi (2005) *Marriage in the Arab World*. Washington, DC: Population Reference Bureau.

Reher, D. S. (2007) 'Towards long-term population decline: a discussion of relevant issues'. *European Journal of Population / Revue Européenne de Démographie*, 23(2): 189–207.

Rele, J. R. (1987) 'Fertility levels and trends in India, 1951-1981'. *Population and Development Review*, 13(3): 513–530.

Ross, J. A. and W. P. Mauldin (1996) 'Family planning programs: efforts and results, 1972–94'. *Studies in Family Planning*, 27(3): 137–147.

Säävälä, M. (2010) 'Below replacement-level fertility in conditions of slow social and economic development: a review of the evidence from South India'. *Finnish Yearbook of Population Research*, 45: 45–66.

Sathar, Z. and J. Casterline (1998) 'The onset of fertility transition in Pakistan'. *Population and Development Review*, 24(4): 773–796.

Shah, N. M., M. A. Shah and Z. Radovanovic (1998) 'Patterns of desired fertility and contraceptive use in Kuwait'. *International Family Planning Perspectives*, 24(3): 133–138.

Shaikh, B. T., S. K. Azmat and A. Mazhar (2013) 'Family planning and contraception in Islamic countries: a critical review of the literature'. *Journal of Pakistan Medical Association*, 63(4): s67–s72.

Silva, W. I. D. (2013) 'Seizing the opportunity: demographic dividend and economic growth in Sri Lanka'. *Asian Population Studies*, 8(3): 249–250.

Singerman, D. (2004) *The Economic Imperatives of Marriage: Emerging Practices and Identities among Youth in the Middle East*. The Middle East Youth Initiative Working Papers no. 6. Dubai: Middle East Youth Initiative.

Sobotka, T. (2004) 'Is lowest-low fertility in Europe explained by the postponement of childbearing?' *Population and Development Review*, 30(2): 195–220.

Sobotka, T. and W. Lutz (2011) 'Misleading policy messages derived from the period TFR: should we stop using it?' *Comparative Population Studies*, 35(3): 637–644.

Song, Y. J., K. S. Chang and G. Sylvian (2013) 'Why are developmental citizens reluctant to procreate? Analytical insights from Shirley Sun's Population Policy and Reproduction in Singapore and Takeda Hiroko's The Political Economy of Reproduction in Japan'. *Inter-Asia Cultural Studies*, 1–12.

Soomro, G. Y. (2000) 'A re-examination of fertility transition in Pakistan'. *The Pakistan Development Review*, 39(3): 247–261.

Spoorenberg, T. (2013a) 'Fertility changes in central Asia since 1980'. *Asian Population Studies*, 9(1): 37–41.

Spoorenberg, T. (2013b) 'An evaluation of the recent fertility changes in Afghanistan: a parity-specific analysis'. *Journal of Population Research*, 30(2): 133–149.

Spoorenberg, T. (2013c) 'Demographic changes in Myanmar since 1983: an examination of official data'. *Population and Development Review*, 39(2): 309–324.

Spoorenberg, T. and D. Schwekendiek (2012) 'Demographic changes in North Korea: 1993–2008'. *Population and Development Review*, 38(1): 133–158.

Sun, S. H. L. (2012) *Population Policy and Reproduction in Singapore: Making Future Citizens*. Abingdon: Routledge.

Tenhuna, S. and M. Säävälä (2012) *An Introduction to Changing India: Culture, Politics and Development*. London: Anthem Press.

Terrell, H. K. M. (2005) 'Fertility in China in 2000: a county level analysis'. Unpublished thesis, Texas A&M University.

Torabi, F., A. Baschieri, L. Clarke, and M. J. Abbasi-Shavazi (2013) 'Marriage postponement in Iran: accounting for socio-economic and cultural change in time and space'. *Population, Space and Place*, 19(3): 258–274.

United Nations Population Division (UNPD) (2013) *World Population Prospects: The 2012 Revision*. New York: UNPD.

United Nations Population Fund (UNFPA) (2011) *Impact of Demographic Change in Thailand*. Bangkok: UNFPA.

van Bavel, J. (2010) 'Subreplacement fertility in the West before the baby boom: past and current perspectives'. *Population Studies*, 64(1): 1–18.

Wang, F., Y. Cai and B. Gu (2013) 'Population, policy, and politics: how will history judge China's one-child policy?' *Population and Development Review*, 38: 115–129.

Weerasinghe, D. P. and N. J. Parr (2002) 'Effect of wealth on marital fertility in Sri Lanka'. *Journal of Health, Population and Nutrition*, 20(2):112–119.

Wild, K., L. Barclay, P. Kelly and N. Martins (2010) 'Birth choices in Timor-Leste: a framework for understanding the use of maternal health services in low resource settings'. *Social Science and Medicine*, 71(11): 2038–2045.

Wilson, C. (2011) 'Understanding global demographic convergence since 1950'. *Population and Development Review*, 37(2): 375–388.

World Bank (2011) *Reproductive Health at a Glance: Lao PDR*. New York: World Bank. Available from: http://siteresources.worldbank.org/INTPRH/Resources/376374-1303736328719/LAOhealth41811web.pdf.

Wright, N. H. (1968) 'Recent fertility change in Ceylon and prospects for the National Family Planning Program'. *Demography*, 5(2): 745.

Zhang, G. (2004) 'Does the family planning program affect fertility preferences? The case of China'. Paper presented at 12th biennial on Population and Society: Issues, Research, Policy, Canberra. Canberra: Australian Population Association, 15–17 September 2004.

Zhao, Z. (2001) 'Low fertility in urban China'. Paper presented at International Union for Scientific Study of Population Low Fertility Working Group Seminar on International Perspectives on Low Fertility: Trends, Theories and Policies, Tokyo, 21–23 September 2001. Paris: IUSSP.

Zhao, Z. and W. Chen (2011) 'China's far below replacement fertility and its long-term impact: comments on the preliminary results of the 2010 Census'. *Demographic Research*, 25(26): 819–836.

Zhao, Z. and X. Zhang (2010) 'China's recent fertility decline: evidence from reconstructed fertility statistics'. *Population*, 65(3): 451–478.

6
Family planning policies and programmes

Adrian C. Hayes

Births rates declined across Asia in the second half of the twentieth century (see Chapter 5). From a historical point of view the speed and scale on which this occurred were unprecedented. In the early 1950s the average number of live births a woman in Asia could expect during her lifetime (total fertility rate or TFR) was 5.8; 50 years later (2000–2005) it was 2.4 (Table 6.1). The decline was especially striking in Eastern Asia, but even in Western and South-Central Asia, where fertility was highest, the TFR had almost halved by the end of the century. Similar declines had already occurred in much of Europe, North America and Australia, but in those areas they occurred over much longer time periods and followed in the wake of long-term trends in improved living conditions. In Asia the fertility decline was faster and often appeared to be in the vanguard of socioeconomic development. How did this happen? What accounts for the distinctive trends in Asia? A crucial part of the answer involves government interventions and the introduction of population policies and programmes that at the time were regarded by many as revolutionary.

In what follows, we adopt the following definitions: by 'population policy' we mean 'deliberately constructed or modified institutional arrangements and/or specific programs through which governments influence, directly or indirectly, demographic change' (Demeny 2003: 752); by 'family planning programs' we mean 'organized outreach activities, often under government auspices, that distribute information, services, and supplies for modern means of fertility regulation' (Sinding 2003: 363). In this chapter, the terms 'family planning' (FP) and 'birth control' are used interchangeably.

The family planning revolution in Asia

The setting

The defeat of the Axis powers in World War II ushered in a period of profound political and demographic change in Asia. The war's aftermath saw the rise of independence movements in many parts of the region, especially in countries of Eastern and South-Eastern Asia that had been colonized by Western powers and then occupied by the Japanese. A large wave of countries and

Adrian C. Hayes

Table 6.1 Total fertility rate (mean number of live births per woman), major regions of Asia, 1950–1955, 1975–1980 and 2000–2005

	1950–1955	*1975–1980*	*2000–2005*	*Percentage decline 1950–1955 to 2000–2005*
Asia	5.82	4.10	2.39	58.9
Western Asia	6.32	5.33	3.21	49.2
Eastern Asia	5.60	2.86	1.48	73.6
South-Eastern Asia	5.92	4.80	2.51	57.6
South-Central Asia	6.00	5.26	3.17	47.2

Source: UNPD (2015).

territories were decolonized during 1945–1960, including North Korea (1945), South Korea (1945), Taiwan (1945), Vietnam (1945), Philippines (1946), Jordan (1946), India (1947), Pakistan (1947), Palestine (1948), Israel (1948), Ceylon (1948), Burma (1948), Cambodia (1953), Laos (1953), Malaya (1957) and Cyprus (1960). All were involved in a drama of achieving national consolidation and economic development as quickly as possible (Myrdal 1968). The significance of these political developments for the future of Asia and its role in international relations was of great interest to world leaders, especially as the Cold War became entrenched. The issue of rapid population growth came to be perceived as pivotal.

As one American observer noted,

> When I first went to China in 1939, and later to India in 1942, I recall my first impression of the masses of humanity who filled the cities and extended throughout the hundreds of thousands of villages. To one who was devoting his career to the prevention of disease and illness it was sobering to think how success in disease control would increase the number of people ... In 1948 I took part in a survey or reconnaissance of Japan, China, Taiwan, the Philippines and Indonesia. The report of that survey concluded with a warning about the problem of population growth, but I doubt that any of us foresaw the dramatic decline in death rates that was to occur during the next ten years. By 1958 the mortality statistics of all the countries under consideration had shown reductions of 25 to 50 per cent ... As a result the rates of population growth in Asian countries increased from averages of 1 to 1.5 per cent to growth rates of 2 up to 3.5 or even 4 per cent per year.
>
> (Balfour 1961: 102–103)[1]

The view that rapid population growth is detrimental to economic development gradually gained acceptance during the 1950s and 1960s. A classic study focusing on India published in 1958 raised the specific question: 'What difference would it make in economic terms if the birth rate, instead of remaining unchanged, should be cut drastically in this generation?' The authors concluded (Coale and Hoover 1958: v, 333):

> [I]t is clear that a reduction of fertility from high levels has immediate economic advantages. The pace of economic development depends on the diversion of resources from consumption to uses that raise future output. A population with a high ratio of dependents to producers consumes more of a given output and devotes less to investment. Thus high fertility, which produces a high level of dependency, promotes consumption at the expense of investment.

Family planning policies and programmes

Nonetheless FP was still a highly sensitive issue in most countries at the time. The United Nations was officially barred from direct involvement, and when the Population Commission of the Economic and Social Council started work in 1946 it began with non-controversial technical matters. In 1952 John Rockefeller established the Population Council, and for a time this was the only organization in the world which countries could turn to for technical assistance for FP; India and Pakistan were among the first to do so. As the facts of rapid population growth, and their meaning for economic development, became apparent to more and more governments, the UN progressively broadened its involvement in population issues. In 1969, the United Nations Fund for Population Activities (UNFPA)[2] was established with terms of reference covering 'the entire range of population activities, including advice in the formulation of population policies, assistance in demographic studies, in applied basic research, in education and training and support for family planning projects' (quoted in Johnson 1987: 54). Slowly at first, then at an accelerating rate during the 1960s, more and more countries in Asia introduced national FP programmes, with the understanding that this would limit their population growth and thereby increase their economic development. India was the first in 1952, followed by Hong Kong in 1955, South Korea in 1962, Thailand in 1964, Malaysia and Singapore in 1966, Indonesia in 1967, and the Philippines in 1968 (Robinson and Ross 2007a).[3] By 1976, 25 Asian countries (out of 37 surveyed) considered their population growth rates too high and therefore provided direct government support for FP; by 1996 there were 32 such countries (out of 45 surveyed) (UNPD 2016b).

The practice of family planning and its effects

Table 6.2 presents summary statistics on the CPR for 46 Asian countries and territories. The CPR is the percentage of married or in-union women of reproductive age (here taken to be 15–49 years of age) who are practising birth control using modern methods of contraception (see Chapter 7). If we label the change from a small to a large proportion of married couples who are using modern contraception as the 'family planning transition', then the data display wide variation in the timing and speed of this transition among regions and countries. Japan had already gone through this transition before 1970; Singapore was already far along by 1970; and China, Hong Kong and South Korea passed through the largest part of their transitions during 1970–1990. Thailand and Indonesia also went through a large part of their transitions during 1970–1990 but their transitions continued after 1990 as well; Vietnam's transition is spread more evenly between the two time periods. Cambodia and Nepal start their transitions later and they accelerate during 1990–2010. Meanwhile the transition is progressing slowly but steadily in most of the Arab countries of Western Asia.[4]

The effects of these FP programmes were multiple and variable. Many had the desired effect of increasing the use of modern contraception among married couples and reducing fertility where it had been high.[5] Figure 6.1 shows the trends in the CPR for the largest country in each of the four major regions of Asia, i.e. China (Eastern Asia), Indonesia (South-Eastern), India (South-Central) and Turkey (Western Asia). In Indonesia, for example, the average CPR during 1970–1975 was below 10 per cent; 20 years later it had passed 50 per cent. India introduced a FP programme before Indonesia but to begin with it was not very successful; the CPR was a little over 10 per cent during 1970–1975 and still only a little over 40 per cent 20 years later, although in such a large and diverse country this still represents a major shift in reproductive behaviour. China introduced a robust FP programme in the early 1970s, which was pursued so vigorously that the average CPR during 1970–1975 already reached over 50 per cent; with the addition of the one-child policy in 1979, the CPR reached over 80 per cent by early 1990s. Figure 6.1 also shows the statistical association between rising CPR and declining TFR.

89

Table 6.2 Summary statistics describing trends in CPR, 46 countries of Asia, 1970–2015

	CPR			Percentage point change		
	1970	*1990*	*2010*	*1970–1990*	*1990–2010*	*1970–2015*
Eastern Asia						
China	44.3	77.3	83.5	33.0	6.2	38.2
Hong Kong	39.8	77.6	73.7	37.8	−3.9	32.3
Japan	52.8	53.7	48.1	0.9	−5.6	−2.5
Mongolia	21.0	40.2	50.3	19.2	10.1	36.2
South Korea	18.5	67.1	68.8	48.6	1.7	50.2
South-Eastern Asia						
Cambodia	0.4	5.3	35.0	4.9	29.7	40.3
Indonesia	5.3	46.7	59.1	41.4	12.4	53.9
Laos	1.5	12.0	42.5	10.5	30.5	46.5
Malaysia	12.4	31.8	34.4	19.4	2.6	23.1
Myanmar	1.8	13.0	42.7	11.2	29.7	46.2
Philippines	10.9	23.6	35.9	12.7	12.3	28.4
Singapore	45.5	51.8	56.8	6.3	5.0	12.1
Thailand	18.3	67.1	77.2	48.8	10.1	58.3
Timor-Leste	6.1	19.2	21.0	13.1	1.8	20.0
Vietnam	10.8	40.6	67.0	29.8	26.4	54.2
South Asia						
Afghanistan	1.1	3.9	18.4	2.8	14.5	22.8
Bangladesh	2.8	27.9	51.4	25.1	23.5	52.4
Bhutan	1.8	12.9	59.1	11.1	46.2	61.5
India	7.8	36.1	49.6	28.3	13.5	44.4
Iran	15.5	36.4	57.9	20.9	21.5	43.9
Maldives	6.0	18.7	29.4	12.7	10.7	28.3
Nepal	1.3	17.7	44.4	16.4	26.7	47.1
Pakistan	3.0	9.1	23.2	6.1	14.1	25.3
Sri Lanka	16.2	43.9	54.6	27.7	10.7	39.6
Central Asia						
Kazakhstan	20.7	42.2	51.6	21.5	9.4	32.9
Kyrgyzstan	22.2	42.7	38.2	20.5	−4.5	16.6
Tajikistan	12.2	24.8	28.8	12.6	4.0	17.8
Turkmenistan	22.5	44.4	52.1	21.9	7.7	31.5
Uzbekistan	23.4	46.8	62.7	23.4	15.9	39.8
Western Asia						
Armenia	13.8	24.5	26.2	10.7	1.7	16.5
Azerbaijan	9.9	16.3	18.4	6.4	2.1	13.1
Bahrain	16.2	31.6	41.9	15.4	10.8	26.0
Georgia	8.5	17.8	34.5	9.3	16.7	29.0
Iraq	9.9	15.2	38.7	5.3	23.5	31.4
Israel	25.5	48.0	53.1	22.5	5.1	28.5
Jordan	15.4	27.4	42.2	12.0	14.9	28.9
Kuwait	16.4	34.6	42.9	18.2	8.3	29.3
Lebanon	23.1	37.6	43.3	14.5	5.7	21.7
Oman	2.7	10.3	18.0	7.6	9.7	18.6
Palestine	12.1	26.3	42.7	14.2	16.4	33.1

Table 6.2 (Cont.)

	CPR			Percentage point change		
	1970	1990	2010	1970–1990	1990–2010	1970–2015
Qatar	14.4	30.3	36.7	15.9	6.4	24.6
Saudi Arabia	9.2	21.0	25.7	11.8	4.7	20.7
Syria	12.4	26.3	38.2	13.9	11.9	28.5
Turkey	11.1	32.6	46.5	21.5	13.9	37.1
U. Arab Emirates	7.7	19.6	35.7	11.9	16.1	31.3
Yemen	0.7	5.4	25.3	4.7	19.9	30.7

Note: The contraceptive prevalence rate (CPR) is here defined as the percentage of married or in-union women aged 15 to 49 years using any modern method of contraception.
Source: UNPD (2016a).

Facilitating circumstances

Regardless of the differences in the FP transition trajectories the fact that hundreds of millions of couples adopted modern contraception in Asia since the 1960s is remarkable, especially since many of the countries involved were relatively poor at the time, most areas were still rural and mainly agricultural, and the prevailing family values across the entire region were predominantly pronatalist. What accounts for the degree of success enjoyed by the national FP policies and programmes introduced in much of Asia? How did they facilitate such a revolution in reproductive behaviour on such a scale? There is not enough space here to answer these questions comprehensively but three favourable initial conditions should be noted.

First, governments wanting to introduce FP programmes but lacking sufficient expertise and other resources to do so were offered substantial amounts of technical, material and financial international assistance. Growing international concern about population growth gradually transformed groups and organizations interested in FP into a genuine 'worldwide social movement' by the end of the 1960s (Donaldson and Tsui 1990: 4). The International Planned Parenthood Federation (IPPF) was founded in 1952 at the Third International Conference on Planned Parenthood in Bombay.[6] Around the same time other American philanthropic groups followed the example of the Rockefeller Foundation and became interested in the population concerns of developing countries. Smaller non-profit organizations that had previously been providing FP services in the UK, the US and elsewhere broadened their horizons. The trust fund for UNFPA was set up in 1967. The 'Teheran Proclamation' stating that 'Parents have a basic human right to determine freely and responsibly the number and spacing of their children' was issued by the UN International Conference on Human Rights in 1968, and in the same year the US Congress for the first time allocated foreign aid funds for FP. Many of these movements coalesced and cooperated with one another. This meant that when governments in Asia were interested in developing national FP policies and programmes, international support was available if needed to assist with the practicalities of design and implementation.

Meanwhile, a number of international conferences sponsored by the United Nations helped develop the emerging consensus around the importance of population-development interactions. Jointly with the International Union for the Scientific Study of Population (IUSSP), the UN sponsored world conferences on population in Rome in 1954 and in Belgrade in 1965. The first official UN conference for *governments* was the World Population Conference in Bucharest in 1974. Its purpose was to consider 'basic demographic problems, their relationship with economic and social development and population policies and action programmes

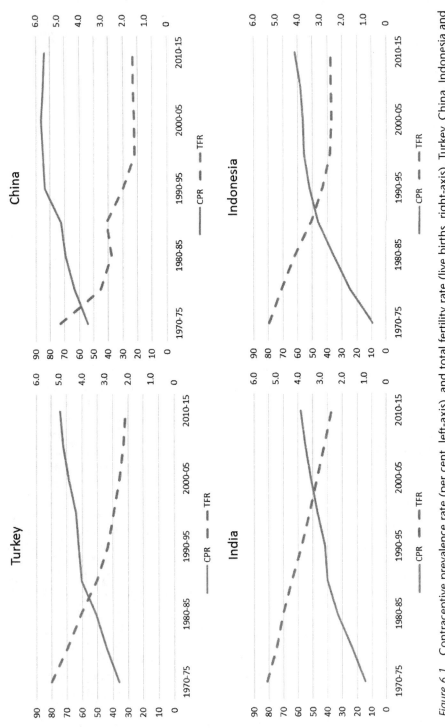

Figure 6.1 Contraceptive prevalence rate (per cent, left-axis), and total fertility rate (live births, right-axis), Turkey, China, Indonesia and India, 1970–1975 to 2010–2015

Note: CPR is here defined as the percentage of married or in-union women aged 15 to 49 years using any method of contraception.

Sources: TFR data from UNPD (2015); CPR data from UNPD (2016a).

needed to promote welfare and development' (quoted in Johnson 1987: 80). The Plan of Action, adopted at the conference by acclamation, was presented as an 'instrument of the international community' (UN 1974: para 1) and it affirmed FP as a basic human right. It also recommended integrating population into development planning:

> Population measures and programmes should be integrated into comprehensive social and economic plans and programmes and this integration should be reflected in the goals, instrumentalities and organizations for planning within countries. In general, it is suggested that a unit dealing with population aspects be created and placed at a high level of the national administrative structure and that such a unit be staffed with qualified persons from the relevant disciplines.
> *(UN 1974: para 95)*

Second, the outreach activities of the new government FP programmes – modelled to a large extent on earlier successful public health interventions – proved invaluable in recruiting new FP acceptors and overcoming lingering community resistance to practising birth control. The details would vary according to country and local needs, but typically scores of fieldworkers and volunteers would be recruited and trained (in addition to existing corps of doctors, nurses and paramedics) to take promotional activities and some FP services out of health clinics and into villages and hamlets (Hull et al. 1977; Kamal and Sloggett 1996). Additional 'beyond family planning' activities were also often organized to further integrate FP into everyday life (Berelson 1969). The fact that many private doctors and progressive activists had long been advocating birth control for health and family welfare reasons, and that these people were now often championing the new government interventions, helped legitimate them.

Third, the times were also propitious for promoting FP in terms of medical-technological advances. The development of new contraceptive technologies in the 1960s meant that the programmes had a range of new products to offer, which on the whole were more effective, more convenient and safer than what had been available before (Potts 2003; Zorea 2012). Improved birth control methods undoubtedly contributed to the success of many programmes.

Programme maturation

The success of FP programmes in Asia also depended to a large extent on learning from doing and trial-and-error. Although programmes developed differently in different countries depending on local challenges and conditions, many approached common problems in similar ways and adopted similar features in their 'institutional design'. Some of these common features are described below, with illustrations taken mostly from the 12 country studies included in Robinson and Ross (2007a): Hong Kong, India, Indonesia, Malaysia, Nepal, Pakistan/Bangladesh, the Philippines, Singapore, South Korea, Sri Lanka, Thailand and Turkey.[7]

The first design feature of note is that a number of programmes in their first two or three decades were incorporated into national development plans (typically for five years). This was true for India, Indonesia, Malaysia, Nepal, Pakistan/Bangladesh, the Philippines, South Korea, Sri Lanka and Thailand for at least some of the time during the period 1960–1980. Development plans are normal practice in many Asian countries and represent the standard way public funds are allocated for specific purposes. India's first attempt at a FP programme, for instance, would probably have failed even if a number of other factors had been more favourable simply because the funds allocated in the five-year development plan were insufficient (Srinivasan 1993).

A second feature is the role played by voluntary FP associations (FPAs). These often predate the launching of national programmes, initially serving small urban elites, then offering

Adrian C. Hayes

technical and moral support (and international contacts) when the government programmes begin. FPAs were established in India (in 1949), Hong Kong (1950), Malaysia (1953), Indonesia (1957), South Korea (1961) and the Philippines (1965). FPAs were often discretely advocating the merits of birth control (primarily in terms of the benefits for health and family well-being) long before governments were interested in population control. This was certainly the case in India and Indonesia (Harkavy and Roy 2007; Hull 2007). Once national programmes were up and running, FPAs often continued to provide constructive criticism, or services that might not be included in the governments' programmes such as services for unmarried couples or abortion.

A third institutional feature adopted is the de-medicalization of some contraceptive service delivery. Thailand pioneered the use of non-medical health workers to provide clinical methods such as IUDs and injectable contraceptives in rural areas.

> After a thorough review of the medical issues involved, a pilot study was initiated in 1969 to test the ability of auxiliary midwives to safely prescribe the pill. In four provinces used as experiments, auxiliary midwives were trained to use a specially developed checklist, which included a simple medical history and examination, to screen for women for whom use of the pill was contraindicated. ... The number of women accepting the pill in the experiment provinces quadrupled during the first six months of the study ... The incidence of side effects did not increase for women who received the pill from an auxiliary midwife. In mid-1970, the Ministry of Public Health reviewed the evidence and ruled that all auxiliary midwives could prescribe the pill, a pivotal decision that coincided with the cabinet's announcement of an official population policy.
>
> *(Rosenfield and Min 2007: 225)*

Similarly, the livelihoods of many private midwives in Indonesia depend on their being allowed to provide injectable contraceptives to clients on a regular basis.

A fourth very common feature is outreach to special populations, such as rural and remote communities (to inform and deliver services), or special groups such as religious leaders (to 'win-over') or adolescents (to educate). Telling teenagers or unmarrieds about birth control is still sensitive in many parts of Asia, allegedly because it could encourage promiscuity; only Hong Kong and the Philippines, among the 12 countries highlighted in this section, appear to have trialled such programmes before the end of the 1980s. In Hong Kong it was the FPA that took the lead in 1967, using the less controversial title, 'Family Life Education (FLE)'; as a result FLE was introduced into both primary and secondary schools during the following decade.

A fifth feature concerns contraceptive method mix and whether a programme is designed to give clients a meaningful choice so that everyone can choose a method that is well-suited to their personal circumstances (see Chapter 7). A number of programmes promoted a single method when they first started but gradually expanded the selection over the years. It sounds simple to provide a choice of methods, but the medical, ethical, cultural and logistical issues involved were not easy to solve when FP programmes were first introduced. Warren Robinson (2007: 328) writes of the Pakistan experience:

> Let us recall what family planning meant in 1965. The important new developments in contraceptive technology – the pill and the intrauterine device (IUD) – were new and more than a little controversial. There was much talk at the time about the cafeteria approach to family planning, meaning that the client would have a choice of several methods of birth control, and five methods were listed as officially available: (a) surgical contraception (or sterilization), both female and male; (b) the IUD; (c) the pill; (d) female barrier and

spermicidal methods; and (e) the condom. The first two were considered in Pakistan and elsewhere to be clinical methods requiring an appropriate medical setting for proper use, and their availability was generally limited to clinics in urban areas. The IUD was, moreover, still a relatively new method. In 1965, responsible medical opinion in Pakistan and elsewhere was opposed to using paramedics or fieldworkers to insert IUDs, even had such workers been available. The pill was still first generation, and side effects were common. The minidosage varieties had not yet been developed, and many trained medical people were extremely suspicious of this powerful, new, hormonal intervention. The traditional barrier methods had proven difficult for village women, who lacked privacy and a sound knowledge of their own anatomy, to use effectively, and hence were never very popular. This situation meant that in 1965, the Pakistan program offered most rural couples the condom. Strongly motivated couples could obtain an IUD or the pill, but follow-up for complications or resupply was unreliable. Surgical contraception required an even greater effort by the client and involved genuine health risks for many.

A sixth design feature seen in many programmes as they mature is that they develop more sophisticated systems for collecting and analysing data in order to monitor progress and to inform decision-making. Some countries developed specialized centres for research, such as the Korean Institute for Family Planning, the National Institute for Health and Family Welfare in India, and the Population Institute at the University of the Philippines.

The final feature included here concerns the administrative location of the programme in the governmental apparatus. One of the earliest programmes, that of South Korea, was 'placed well down within the structure of the Ministry of Health and Social Affairs as an activity within the new Maternal and Child Health Section. This was judged to be a better approach than a highly visible new bureau that would hamper cooperation within the ministry and with other ministries and increase public embarrassment if the new program failed or caused a major scandal'. At the same time, 'The country's top leaders were engaged, including the president, the prime minister and other leading figures, who publicly endorsed and privately supported the new viewpoints' (Kim and Ross 2007: 180, 183). Some of the more effective programmes launched a little later were set up as free-standing vertical structures, reporting directly to the president or prime minister. Malaysia established a National Family Planning Board under the Prime Minister's Department in 1966, and Indonesia established its National Family Planning Coordinating Board (best known by its Indonesian acronym, BKKBN) in 1970, reporting directly to President Suharto. Tsui (2012: 46) notes that a common pattern in such cases is that, 'Over time, the maturation of the family planning programme saw many of their functions absorbed into ministries of health and social affairs'; this indeed happened in Malaysia, where FP was de-emphasized after Dr Mahathir Mohamad became prime minister in 1981 and where (what was by then called) the National Population and Family Development Board was moved from the PM's Department in 1989 (Tey 2007), but such a move was resisted in Indonesia by BKKBN, even after the governmental apparatus was largely decentralized in 2001 (Hayes 2012a). The Asian experience shows that a high-level FP board or commission does not guarantee success, nor is it an essential prerequisite for success, as is shown, for example, by the revitalization of FP in Iran in the late 1980s (Hoodfar and Assadpour 2000).

Critical issues

The new FP programmes were not uniformly successful, of course, but the international nature of the FP movement meant that lessons learned in one country could often be applied in another, and late-comers increasingly had a lot of the world's 'best practice' to draw on. India's first attempt at a government-supported FP programme in 1952, for example, did not succeed and not only because of being allocated insufficient funds. While a bold FP policy was integrated into the country's First Five-Year Plan (1952–1957) with the full support of Prime Minister Nehru, the minister of health who was expected to implement the FP programme was herself a loyal disciple of the late Mahatma Gandhi who preached the virtues of abstinence and firmly opposed 'artificial' methods of contraception. The compromise was to rely on 'natural' methods, supplemented by coloured necklaces custom-designed to help illiterate women keep track of their fertile periods. The result was widely seen as a fiasco (Harkavy and Roy 2007; Visaria and Chari 1998). Nevertheless, within a few years other programmes in Taiwan and elsewhere were having better success (Berelson and Freedman 1964), and experts began cataloguing the successes and failures to look for whatever underlying factors might determine the difference (Nortman 1985).

One frequently used methodology was to compare programmes in terms of their 'programme effort' on component dimensions such as policy and stage setting, services and service delivery, record keeping and evaluation, and the availability and accessibility of contraceptives (Ross, Mauldin and Miller 1993; Ross and Mauldin 1997).[8] Compendia of 'lessons learned' by comparing the results from programmes around the world were also produced (Ross and Frankenberg 1993; Sadik 1991). Table 6.3 gives summary statistics for programmes in 16 countries in 1982

Table 6.3 'Programme effort' (measured as percentage of maximum score possible for each dimension) in government FP programmes, selected countries, 1982 and 1989

Country	Policy '82	Policy '89	Services '82	Services '89	Records '82	Records '89	Availability '82	Availability '89	Total '82	Total '89	CPR 1990
Strong											
China	97	95	78	80	57	67	96	100	84	87	75
South Korea	73	69	72	79	88	94	98	100	79	81	76
Taiwan	63	64	74	84	96	86	100	100	79	81	78
Sri Lanka	67	69	68	82	59	87	70	84	67	80	66
Indonesia	77	81	78	83	93	83	57	69	75	80	52
Bangladesh	58	73	55	73	43	56	68	78	57	72	33
India	81	81	62	63	60	58	58	87	66	72	45
Moderate											
Malaysia	59	71	35	53	73	82	63	79	51	66	57
Singapore	67	52	76	49	83	76	98	100	79	63	74
Nepal	55	65	30	62	42	58	27	45	37	59	18
Iran	13	51	9	58	17	56	10	64	11	57	31
Philippines	57	51	52	48	47	39	67	57	56	49	49
Pakistan	59	58	28	49	53	54	37	28	40	48	15
Weak											
Turkey	60	40	16	43	29	48	17	58	29	46	66
Syria	17	28	8	55	13	58	8	37	11	44	11
Afghanistan	15	49	13	38	4	32	8	15	11	36	2

Note: 'Policy' = 'Policy and stage setting'; 'Services' = 'Service and service-related'; 'Records' = 'Record keeping and evaluation'; and 'Availability' = 'Availability and accessibility'.
Source: Data from Ross et al. (1993: 68–69).

and 1989, displaying whether they were assessed as 'strong', 'moderate' or 'weak'. Data like these were not always reliable but they did stimulate reflection among many programme managers and planners, and improvements in programme effort were tracked in many Asian countries. Research findings suggested that 'success' depended on strong effort across multiple dimensions, and impressed on policymakers that good policies and good services located in urban clinics are not enough to effect behavioural change in traditional rural areas. Table 6.3 also illustrates how 'effort' in the 1980s was already trailing off in one or two countries like Singapore, where programmes were implemented relatively early and a growing majority of couples no longer needed the support of a government programme to practice FP. National FP programmes were introduced to facilitate the FP transition and can be largely disbanded when the practice of birth control is the 'new norm'.

Voluntarism and quality of care

Specific policies and programmes were frequently criticized, within country and internationally, because of documented or alleged shortcomings, or for political and ideological reasons. Those in the FP movement viewed the principal functions of FP programmes as providing 'services, information, persuasion, and legitimation' (Ross and Frankenberg 1993: 13); countries varied in the relative emphases they gave to these functions and in the way they performed them, and virtually all aspects were scrutinized and criticized at one time or another. The quantity and quality of public discussion and criticism varied considerably by time and place. In the Philippines, the Catholic Church challenged the legitimacy of the national FP programme on religious grounds (Dixon-Mueller and Germain 1994; Herrin 2007). Religious leaders in other parts of Asia similarly argued that the practice of birth control is immoral on occasion, but more impressive was the extent to which the majority of religious leaders in Asia accepted, and often actively supported, FP (see, for example, Faour 1989).

More important critical questions raised during the 1970s and 1980s had to do with whether the programmes were 'voluntary', the quality of the services they provided, and the soundness of the underlying developmental rationale. These criticisms played a constructive role in the evolution of 'mature' FP programmes in Asia, despite a fair amount of rhetoric and posturing by stakeholders. Proponents of FP, with few exceptions, always argued that these programmes should be 'voluntary'. In the words of the Plan of Action adopted in 1974 at the UN Conference on Population:

> All couples and individuals have the basic right to decide freely and responsibly the number and spacing of their children and to have the information, education and means to do so; the responsibility of couples and individuals in the exercise of this right takes into account the needs of their living and future children, and their responsibilities towards the community.
>
> (UN 1974: paragraph 14f)

Some programmes were criticized for abrogating this basic right by pressuring or coercing couples to practice birth control.[9] One extreme case was in India during the 1975–1977 'Emergency', when the prime minister's son, Sanjay Gandhi, launched a mass-sterilization campaign; the programme counted more than 8 million sterilizations in a 12-month period, most of them vasectomies 'forced' (through harassment, imposition of fines for non-compliance with targets, and other means) on low-level civil servants and poor villagers (Gwatkin 1979). In the 1977 elections, Mrs Gandhi's Congress Party suffered a massive defeat and both she and her son lost their seats in parliament, and ever since the Government of India has gone to great lengths to stress the voluntary nature of the nation's FP programmes.

Meanwhile, criticism of China's one-child policy has been more prolonged and widespread (e.g. Aird 1990; Scharping 2003). Critics argued that the Chinese programme relied on coercive practices, including 'forced abortions'. The Family Planning Commission of China responded, however, by pointing out on occasion that using various incentives and penalties (such as promotions for cadres who met targets, or fines for peasant farmers who exceeded official birth quotas) is no more than what governments do everywhere to achieve compliance and implement policies, that coercion is not part of official policy, and that restricting the number of births a couple can have, far from violating human rights actually enhances them by encouraging couples to act 'responsibly', in light of the 'externalities' and negative consequences for society as a whole attributed to rapid population growth.[10] Many political leaders in Asia, not just in China, feel Western-styled statements of universal rights put too much stress on individual liberties and need to balance these with similar emphasis on collective rights (like the collective right to development).[11]

Other criticisms can be seen as addressing different aspects of 'quality of care'. One well-known framework (Bruce 1990) distinguishes six key aspects of FP services relating to client satisfaction: choice of contraceptive methods offered; information given to clients about the pros and cons of different methods and their side effects; technical competence of service providers; interpersonal relations between providers and client; follow-up procedures and mechanisms; and appropriateness of the constellation of services (in relation to local needs and culture). With limited resources it was inevitable that any FP programme in developing Asia would have room for improvement in all these dimensions, but, as a result of carefully monitoring and learning more from clients about their needs and preferences, many programmes were able to improve the quality of their services by introducing more choice of methods, training staff to be more respectful of clients (especially the poor and illiterate), and by making sure clients were invited to give their 'informed consent' before being signed up as 'acceptors' (Jain et al. 1992; see also Chapters 7 and 8).

Underlying rationale

A different kind of criticism concerns the underlying rationale of FP programmes. As more data became available, analysis for the 1960s and 1970s showed 'a general lack of correlation between the growth rates of population and per capita income' (Kelley and Schmidt 1994: 18). Although it is well known that such simple correlations are fraught with difficulties, and further research has shown there are multiple pathways operating on different time scales connecting population change and development (see, for example, NAS 1971; NRC 1986; and Chapter 24), the lack of a simple, clear-cut formulation meant the original rationale needed to be revisited. Many governments of developing countries in Asia (and other parts of the world) remained convinced of the importance of reducing population growth, however, and many were shocked when, at the World Population Conference in 1984 in Mexico City, the United States delegation announced it was shifting its position from affirming the importance of reducing population growth to a position of 'neutrality' regarding population growth. (It also announced its categorical opposition to abortion.) As a former senior USAID official and Director of IPPF assessed the situation some years later:

> The U.S. announcement came as a shock to delegations accustomed to the United States urging them to take more vigorous action to curb high fertility. Crafted by the Reagan

administration to deliver a campaign promise to the religious right in the United States, this 'Mexico City policy', as it came to be called, ushered in 12 years of U.S. exceptionalism in international population affairs and foreshadowed an even deeper antipathy toward international cooperation in relation to population with the advent of the George W. Bush administration in 2001.

(Sinding 2007: 9)

The immediate impact of the US Mexico City policy on FP programmes in Asia was slight. Most programmes relied little, if at all, on international assistance by the 1980s let alone bilateral aid. The stance of the Reagan administration was, however, as Sinding suggests, a harbinger of things to come.

Family planning policies and programmes in Asia since the 1994 Cairo conference

A number of burgeoning arguments critical of FP or advocating programme reform coalesced around the time of the next World Population Conference held in Cairo in 1994, with the official title, 'The International Conference on Population and Development' (ICPD). Preparation for this conference was far more extensive on the part of UN organizers who wanted to avoid the kind of 'surprises' that occurred in the earlier conferences in 1974 and 1984, which could jeopardize the chances of reaching a firm consensus (McIntosh and Finkle 1995). They consulted a number of organizations and NGOs leading up to the conference, a number of which argued that existing programmes often relied on the 'instrumental use of women's bodies' for political ends. The final outcome of ICPD was a new consensus document, *World Population Programme of Action* (United Nations 1994), generally seen as reflecting 'the agenda advanced by a coalition of women's organizations and Western governments' (McIntosh and Finkle 1995: 225). In the eyes of many stakeholders it represents a 'paradigm shift' from the earlier 1974 *Plan of Action*, although there is no clear agreement about the relative merits of this. According to Sinding (2007: 10):

> At the Cairo conference, the combination of a lack of macro-level urgency on the question of population growth and an intense micro-level concern with reproductive health and rights led to what became an almost complete reformulation of global population policies and strategies. The International Conference on Population and Development Program of Action explicitly called for dropping demographic and family planning targets in favor of a broader policy agenda that included a range of reproductive health measures, including family planning that would cater to women's overall reproductive health needs, as well as a series of social and economic policy measures designed to empower women and to strengthen their rights. While population issues were mentioned, they were not a prominent part of the Cairo agenda and were almost entirely forgotten once the conference was over. Family planning became an almost forgotten term after Cairo. Indeed, the main chapter of the Program of Action on service delivery programs, which had been entitled 'Family Planning and Reproductive Rights and Health' in preconference documents, was simply called 'Reproductive Rights and Reproductive Health' in the final version adopted by the more than 180 delegations present.

The new emphases on reproductive rights and on 'bundling' FP as an integral part of reproductive health services are important for correcting the excesses associated with treating birth control as primarily a means for maximizing material prosperity, but a significant price was paid for these gains in downplaying any parallel emphasis on the important role of population policy in addressing urgent matters of nation building and macro-level development. FP itself brings with it many benefits, some individual and others social. In 1974, the emphasis was on the social-economic public benefits; in 1994, it was on individual private welfare. The collective benefits are still mentioned in the later document, but the passion and energy are in the emphasis on human rights, especially women's rights and the rights of girls. One might hope for a more reasoned balance between individual and society in future programmes of action addressing population and development issues.

Broader questions about reproductive health are discussed in Chapter 8. This chapter concludes with some observations about FP in Asia in the post-ICPD era. Some programmes had already given up demographic targets long before 1994 (e.g. Sri Lanka in 1972) and absorbed their FP programmes into existing health programmes (again Sri Lanka in 1972). Others moved in this direction, but not necessarily because of Cairo. Still others argued that their policies were fully consistent with Cairo, when clearly in certain respects they were not (Hayes 2006). Meanwhile the newest nation in Asia, Timor-Leste, cites the ICPD *Programme* verbatim in its 2004 National Family Planning Policy (Hayes 2012b). Regardless, a widespread sense emerged after Cairo that things were not going as well as expected. 'Although ICPD was emphatic in its support to family planning, many feel that in the decade that followed, and beyond, family planning has suffered and stalled because it did not receive the priority that it should have received. Political, programmatic and financial commitments are said to be waning' (Horibe and Zaman 2012).

All agree that a major ICPD goal is to reduce the unmet need for FP (Zaman et al. 2012). This is a measure of the number or proportion of women who are currently married or in a union and are fecund, and who desire either to terminate or to postpone childbearing but are not currently using a modern contraceptive method; it is a measure that focuses on women's reproductive preferences, rather than on contraceptive prevalence or fertility rates per se.[12] Table 6.4 gives estimates for the same 46 countries included in Table 6.2. As with CPR, the data exhibit wide variation in the levels and trends of unmet need. Only Japan has an estimated unmet need below 20 per cent in 1970, but by 1990 China, Hong Kong, South Korea, Indonesia and Thailand have reached this threshold, and by 2010 we can add Vietnam, Bhutan, Kazakhstan, Turkmenistan and Uzbekistan. Countries that made their largest gains in CPR during one time period also often reduced their unmet need at the same time; this is true of China, Hong Kong, South Korea, Indonesia, Malaysia and Thailand during 1970–1990, and of Cambodia, Laos, Myanmar and Bhutan during 1990–2010. However, unmet need for FP does not always decrease linearly as contraceptive prevalence increases, because improvements in FP programmes can increase demand for contraception and lead to a situation where supply is unable to keep up with demand, at least temporarily. Also, some countries can have high unmet demand for FP and yet have low fertility because they rely significantly on induced abortion; Japan is a case in point (Sato 2006).

Figure 6.2 shows the association of unmet need with CPR for the same four countries included in Figure 6.1. The decline in unmet need over the 45-year period is most dramatic in China, from around 50 per cent of married or in-union women in 1970–1975 to less than 5 per cent by 1990–1995. The unmet need is halved in Indonesia, from 28 to 14 per cent. The decline is more modest for India, from 31 to 21 per cent. Turkey starts with an estimated unmet need of 50 per cent during 1970–1975 and is still 33 per cent in 2010–2015, but it needs to be recognized that in some Arab countries many couples are using traditional methods of birth control; if unmet need is measured 'for any method'[13] in Turkey, then the trend is from 26 per cent in 1970–1975 to 6 per cent in 2010–2015. Roughly one-fifth of couples rely on non-modern

Table 6.4 Summary statistics describing trends in unmet need for FP, 46 countries of Asia, 1970–2015

	Unmet need for FP			Percentage point decline		
	1970	1990	2010	1970–1990	1990–2010	1970–2015
Eastern Asia						
China	22.2	6.5	4.3	15.7	2.2	17.9
Hong Kong	27.2	10.3	9.9	16.9	0.4	16.8
Japan	18.1	19.8	22.9	−1.7	−3.1	−3.3
Mongolia	32.8	29.2	20.9	3.6	8.3	11.9
South Korea	33.2	16.3	15.7	16.9	0.6	17.8
South-Eastern Asia						
Cambodia	29.8	35.0	32.3	−5.2	2.7	0.2
Indonesia	27.6	19.4	14.3	8.2	5.1	13.8
Laos	31.5	34.5	26.9	−3.0	7.6	7.2
Malaysia	34.8	37.9	35.4	−3.1	2.5	0
Myanmar	27.2	28.6	21.3	−1.4	7.3	7.7
Philippines	44.6	46.1	35.6	−1.5	10.5	11.4
Singapore	25.7	24.9	19.7	0.8	5.2	6.5
Thailand	29.7	11.5	7.4	18.2	4.1	22.3
Timor-Leste	25.4	21.8	30.8	3.6	−9.0	−3.5
Vietnam	38.2	33.4	17.2	4.8	16.2	19.9
South Asia						
Afghanistan	29.8	31.1	32.2	−1.3	−1.1	−1.1
Bangladesh	31.6	33.1	22.5	−1.5	10.6	12.0
Bhutan	29.7	30.2	15.2	−0.5	15.0	16.5
India	31.4	25.4	21.4	6.0	4.0	11.0
Iran	36.6	35.5	25.3	1.1	10.2	13.0
Maldives	36.1	39.0	34.8	1.5	4.2	3.8
Nepal	33.6	35.1	30.5	−1.5	4.6	6.0
Pakistan	30.1	32.4	31.9	−2.3	0.5	0.2
Sri Lanka	38.5	32.3	23.6	6.2	8.7	15.8
Central Asia						
Kazakhstan	37.5	29.8	18.4	7.7	11.4	19.9
Kyrgyzstan	32.3	24.3	20.3	8.0	4.0	12.2
Tajikistan	32.4	29.3	25.5	3.1	3.8	7.5
Turkmenistan	33.8	25.1	18.7	8.7	6.4	16.0
Uzbekistan	30.5	21.2	13.7	9.3	7.5	16.9
Western Asia						
Armenia	43.5	47.6	44.7	−4.1	2.9	1.6
Azerbaijan	39.5	46.6	49.9	−7.1	−3.3	−7.3
Bahrain	39.9	39.6	34.1	0.3	5.5	7.5
Georgia	36.1	38.7	31.8	−2.6	6.9	5.2
Iraq	29.4	30.6	29.0	−1.2	1.6	1.3
Israel	37.3	29.1	25.7	8.2	3.4	12.2
Jordan	38.6	38.4	30.1	0.2	8.3	9.4
Kuwait	32.4	27.7	27.7	4.7	0	5.8
Lebanon	45.9	37.7	30.2	8.2	7.5	16.6
Oman	34.6	37.3	44.8	−2.7	−7.5	−8.7
Palestine	35.8	35.2	27.0	0.6	8.2	9.2
Qatar	31.6	27.9	24.7	3.7	3.2	7.6

(continued)

Table 6.4 (Cont.)

	Unmet need for FP			Percentage point decline		
	1970	1990	2010	1970–1990	1990–2010	1970–2015
Saudi Arabia	33.8	32.2	31.2	1.6	1.0	3.7
Syria	35.8	35.1	32.8	0.7	2.3	4.6
Turkey	48.2	43.8	33.7	4.4	10.1	16.1
U. Arab Emirates	33.5	33.0	29.0	0.5	4.0	5.5
Yemen	35.2	42.5	36.3	–7.3	6.2	2.0

Note: Unmet need for family planning is here defined as the percentage of married or in-union women aged 15 to 49 years in need of any modern method of contraception.
Source: Data from UNPD (2016a).

methods of birth control in Turkey, whereas the proportion is only one or two percentage points in China and Indonesia (in 2010–2015) and about 6 per cent in India.

Overall, the data confirm that while the practice of birth control has increased hugely across Asia since the end of World War II there is still a considerable unmet need for FP information and services. This need is estimated to be of the order of 12.9 million women in China (or 10.3 million if unmet need is measured for any method), 6.9 million in Indonesia (or 6.3 million for any method), 51.0 million in India (or 33.2 million for any method) and 4.3 million in Turkey (or 0.8 million for any method) (UNPD 2016a).

The future of family planning in Asia

Asia's astonishing decline in fertility during the second half of the twentieth century – historically unprecedented in its speed and scale – has played an indispensable role in the region's economic and political 're-emergence'. Revolutionary population policies and innovative FP programmes positioned in the vanguard of development are, to a large extent, what made this possible. The tying of FP by governments and other stakeholders to the urgent need for economic and social development helped mobilize the resources needed for national FP programmes on a mass scale.

Experts agree that the FP challenge now lies in achieving universal access to quality FP services, along with meeting all the other reproductive health needs that people present (see Chapter 8). Given the scale of the remaining unmet need for FP some talk about the need for 'revitalizing' family planning programmes. Our account in this chapter suggests a more significant shift in perspective might be needed. With the advantage of hindsight, it is becoming increasingly clear to many commentators that the post-World War II era (through to the early 1970s) was special and in many ways was a global 'golden age' (Hobsbawm 1995) characterized by unprecedented economic growth in the developed countries and by unprecedented waves of decolonization and political transformation in the developing world. We may never see the same energizing consensus around FP, individual well-being and nation building again. Moreover, the broad population and development issues facing Asian countries today are quite different and arguably more diverse than they were in the post-World War II era, with 46 per cent of the region's population during 2010–2015 already living in countries with below-replacement fertility, and the proportion is rising (Chapter 5; UNPD 2015). From a developmental perspective the emphasis now is on increasing the quality of human resources that a population represents (Chapter 22; Greenhalgh 2010).

With the advent and spread of neo-liberalism through the 1980s and beyond, governments everywhere have become leaner and meaner.[14] The accomplishments of FP policies and

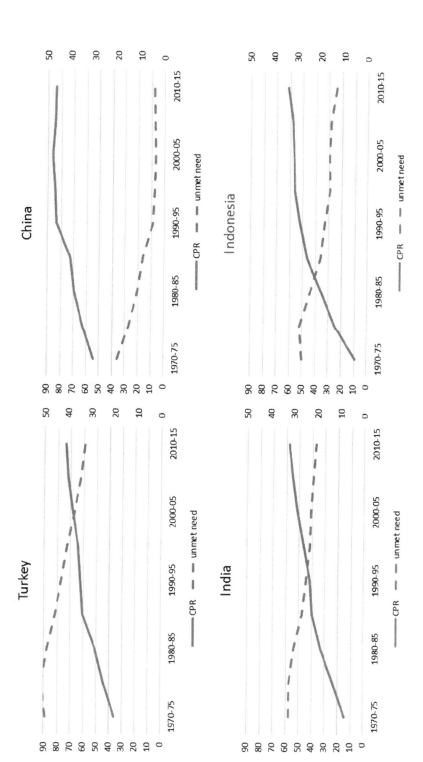

Figure 6.2 Contraceptive prevalence rate (per cent, left-axis), and unmet need (per cent, right-axis), Turkey, China, Indonesia and India, 1970–1975 to 2010–2015

Notes: CPR is here defined as the percentage of married or in-union women aged 15 to 49 years using any method of contraception. Unmet need for family planning is here defined as the percentage of married or in-union women aged 15 to 49 years in need of any modern method of contraception.

Source: Data from UNPD (2016a).

programmes in Asia in the last half of the twentieth century remain a testament to what governments can do, when they have the will, to address national and transnational population issues using enlightened public policy (Robinson and Ross 2007b; Tsui 2001). The region's political and civil society leaders need to fashion more innovative approaches if they are to mobilize the political will and public support needed to achieve universal access to quality family planning services in Asia in the twenty-first century.

Notes

1. The 1948 survey mentioned was instigated by John D. Rockefeller and the reconnaissance team was headed by Frank Notestein.
2. Now called the United Nations Population Fund, but the organization still uses the old acronym UNFPA.
3. Public policy is a process not an event. Consequently it is not always easy to determine when a national FP programme begins, especially since policies can often be announced long before there is action on the ground. Applying the following criteria to countries and territories – 'Official policy to reduce the population growth rate. In addition to supporting family planning to implement this policy, countries in this category support family planning for reasons of health and as a human right' (Nortman 1985: 34) – the Population Council identified the years in which the position was adopted as follows: Bangladesh (1971), China (1962), Hong Kong (1973), India (1952), Iran (1967; reversed in 1979), Malaysia (1966), Nepal (1966), Pakistan (1960), Singapore (1965), South Korea (1961), Sri Lanka (1965), Taiwan (1968), Thailand (1970), Turkey (1965), Vietnam (1977).
4. Data on family planning practices have been collected by Demographic and Health Surveys (and other similar survey instruments) going back to the 1970s, but these surveys do not cover all countries of Asia, are not always representative of the complete relevant national population, and are only conducted at irregular time intervals. In this chapter we make use of the data in UNPD (2016a). These data represent annual time series estimates of CPR and unmet need for family planning going back to 1970 for 194 countries; the estimates (with confidence intervals) are based on all available data using a Bayesian hierarchical statistical model. The methodology is described in Alkema et al. (2013).
5. There is a long-standing debate about the extent to which increases in the CPR are due to organized FP programmes and how much they might be due to other developments (and might have occurred therefore even without programme interventions). See, for example, Bongaarts et al. (1990). Furthermore, fertility will also be affected by changes in the average age of first marriage, or in the average length of breastfeeding or postpartum sexual abstinence, as well as in the practice of birth control. Induced abortion practices are also a major factor, and they are not included as a method of birth control when calculating CPR (see Chapter 7).
6. Founding members were the family planning associations from Hong Kong, India and Singapore, as well as Germany, the Netherlands, Sweden, UK and USA.
7. This section builds on a brief account of 'patterns of programme development' by Amy Tsui (2012: 43–46). China is not included in the Robinson and Ross (2007a) volume, and is in any case something of a special case because its FP programme was so autochthonous. For an account of the early FP programme in China in the 1970s (the 'later-longer-fewer' period) see Tien (1980), for an account of the overall trajectory of China's population policy see Greenhalgh (2005), for an analysis of the origins of the one-child policy see Greenhalgh (2008), and for a reflection on the later relaxation of that policy see Wang et al. (2016). Taiwan is also not included in Robinson and Ross (2007a). Taiwan was actually a pioneer in developing a model FP programme in East Asia. See Berelson and Freedman (1964) and Freedman (1998).
8. A limitation of this approach is that it tends to suggest that 'effort' is an attribute of those working in or for the programme, whereas in fact a lot of the success of such programmes may result from broader properties of the society such as the quality of human resources and governance structures. According to Hull and Hull (1997: 392, 384), 'the most dramatic achievement of the New Order government [in Indonesia] of the period 1966–1990 was the major construction of state and civil institutional structures in ways that enhanced central government control while promoting decentralized responsibilities'. It was the government's ability to use this political-administrative apparatus which, in combination with a highly patrimonial ideology, was responsible for the success of 'a wide variety of popular government programmes including primary schooling, health service delivery and family planning'. See also Entwistle (1989).

9 For a clarification of different interpretations of what it might mean to decide 'freely and responsibly' see Freedman and Isaacs (1993).
10 For a brief attempt to clarify the ethical issues involved with using incentives and disincentives in FP programmes see Isaacs (1995) and Hardee et al. (2014).
11 UN declarations on human rights invariably include the so-called 'liberty rights' (or 'civil liberties') such as the right to life, liberty, freedom of expressions, and equality before the law; and often they also include 'social entitlements' (or 'welfare rights'), such as the right to a decent standard of living, access to education, employment opportunities, and other aspects of (or preconditions for) well-being. Western democracies tend to give precedence to individual liberties, but the governments of some developing countries in Asia have sometimes argued that the obligation to provide basic entitlements is more fundamental. This latter argument can be grounded in local morality or a theory of justice, but in practice it can sometimes be a pretext used by ruling groups to limit or suppress civil liberties (Hayes 1995).
12 Although data on unmet need have been collected by the Demographic and Health Surveys (and similar surveys) for decades it is difficult to obtain precise estimates, partly because it is difficult to estimate accurately all the women at risk of pregnancy and screen out all the 'infecund women' in the numerator (including, for example, those who are postpartum amenorrheic) (Cleland, Harbison and Shah 2014). The operational definition of unmet need for family planning was revised in 2012, resulting in slightly higher estimates, but which can nonetheless be applied consistently across countries and to measure more reliably trends over time (UNPD 2014).
13 That is to say, if those who are practising traditional ('non-modern') methods of FP are considered to be practising FP and therefore *not* to have an unmet need, then the number of cases of those women in need of FP in the numerator when calculating the per cent with unmet need will be smaller.
14 For a sample of views about the future of voluntary family planning programmes see Bongaarts et al. (2012), Caldwell et al. (2002), Jain (1998), Jones and Leete (2002), McIntosh and Finkle (1994) and Robinson and Ross (2007a).

References

Aird, J. S. (1990) *Slaughter of the Innocents: Coercive Birth Control in China*. Washington, DC: American Enterprise Institute for Public Policy.
Akin, A. (2007) 'Emergence of the family planning program in Turkey'. In W. C. Robinson and J. A. Ross (eds.) *The Global Family Planning Revolution: Three Decades of Population Policies and Programs*. Washington, DC: World Bank. Pp. 85–102.
Alkema, L., V. Kantorova, C. Menozzi and A. Biddlecom (2013) 'National, regional and global rates and trends in contraceptive prevalence and unmet need for family planning between 1990 and 2015: a systematic and comprehensive analysis'. *Lancet*, 381: 1642–1652.
Balfour, M. C. (1961) 'Family planning in Asia'. *Population Studies*, 15(2): 102–109.
Berelson, B. (1969) 'Beyond family planning'. *Science*, 163(3867): 533–543.
Berelson, B. and R. Freedman (1964) 'A study in fertility control'. *Scientific American*, 21(5): 29–37.
Bongaarts, J., J. Cleland, J. W. Townsend, J. T. Bertrand and M. Das Gupta (2012) *Family Planning Programs for the 21st Century: Rationale and Design*. New York: Population Council.
Bongaarts, J., W. P. Mauldin and J. Phillips (1990) 'The demographic impact of family planning programs'. *Studies in Family Planning*, 21(6): 299–310.
Bruce, J. (1990) 'Fundamental elements of quality of care: a simple framework'. *Studies in Family Planning*, 21(2): 61091.
Caldwell, J. C., J. F. Phillips and Barkat-e-Kuda (2002) 'Family planning programs in the twenty-first century'. *Studies in Family Planning*, 33(1): 1–23.
Cleland, J., S. Harbison and I. H. Shah (2014) 'Unmet need for contraception: issues and challenges'. *Studies in Family Planning*, 45(2): 105–122.
Coale, A. J. and E. M. Hoover (1958) *Population Growth and Economic Development in Low-Income Countries*. Princeton, NJ: Princeton University Press.
Demeny, P. (2003) 'Population policy'. In P. Demeny and G. McNicoll (eds.) *Encyclopedia of Population*. New York: Macmillan Reference. Pp. 752–763.
Dixon-Mueller, R. and A. Germain (1994) 'Population policy and feminist political action in three developing countries'. In J. L. Finkle and C. A. McIntosh (eds.) *The New Politics of Population: Conflict and Consensus in Family Planning*. New York: Oxford University Press. Pp. 197–219.

Donaldson, P. J. and A. O. Tsui (1990) 'The international family planning movement'. *Population Bulletin*, 45(3):1–46.
Entwistle, B. (1989) 'Measuring the components of family planning programs in the twenty-first century'. *Demography*, 26(1): 53–76.
Fan, S. (2007) 'Hong Kong: evolution of the family planning program'. In Robinson and Ross (eds.) *The Global Family Planning Revolution: Three Decades of Population Policies and Programs*. Washington, DC: World Bank. Pp. 193–200.
Faour, M. (1989) 'Fertility policy and family planning in Arab countries'. *Studies in Family Planning*, 20(5): 254–263.
Finkle, J. A. and C. A. McIntosh (eds.) (1994) *The New Politics of Population: Conflict and Consensus in Family Planning. Population and Development Review*, Supplement to Vol. 20. Oxford: Oxford University Press.
Freedman, L. P. and S. L. Isaacs (1993) 'Human rights and reproductive choice'. *Studies in Family Planning*, 24(1): 18–30.
Freedman, R. (1998) 'Operations and other types of research in Taiwan's family planning history'. In J. R. Foreit and T. Frejka (eds.) *Family Planning Operations Research: A Book of Readings*. New York: Population Council. Pp. 35–45.
Greenhalgh, S. (2005) *Governing China's Population: From Leninist to Neoliberal Biopolitics*. Stanford, CA: Stanford University Press.
Greenhalgh, S. (2008) *Just One Child: Science and Policy in Deng's China*. Berkeley, CA: University of California Press.
Greenhalgh, S. (2010) *Cultivating Global Citizens*. Cambridge, MA and London, UK: Harvard University Press.
Gwatkin, D. R. (1979) 'Political will and family planning: the implications of India's emergency experience'. *Population and Development Review*, 5(1): 29–59.
Hardee, K., S. Harris, M. Rodriguez, J. Kumar, L. Bakamjian, K. Newman and W. Brown (2014) 'Achieving the goal of the London Summit on Family Planning by adhering to voluntary, rights-based family planning: what can we learn from past experiences with coercion?' *International Perspectives on Sexual and Reproductive Health*, 40(4): 206–214.
Harkavy, O. and K. Roy (2007) 'Emergence of the Indian National Family Planning Program'. In Robinson and Ross (eds.) *The Global Family Planning Revolution: Three Decades of Population Policies and Programs*. Washington, DC: World Bank. Pp. 301–323.
Hayes, A. C. (1995) 'Cairo and the changing definition of population and development issues'. *Journal of the Australian Population Association*, 12(1): 15–23.
Hayes, A. C. (2006) 'Towards a policy agenda for population and family planning in Indonesia, 2004–2015'. *Jurnal Kependudukan Indonesia*, 1(1): 1–11.
Hayes, A. C. (2012a) 'The status of family planning and reproductive health in Indonesia: a story of success and fragmentation'. In Zaman et al. (eds.) *Family Planning in Asia and the Pacific: Addressing the Challenges*. Selangor, Malaysia: International Council on Management of Population Programmes (ICOMP). Pp. 225–241.
Hayes, A. C. (2012b) 'The status of family planning and reproductive health in Timor-Leste: an ICPD success story in the making'. In Zaman et al. (eds.) *Family Planning in Asia and the Pacific: Addressing the Challenges*. Selangor, Malaysia: International Council on Management of Population Programmes (ICOMP). Pp. 335–344.
Herrin, A. N. (2007) 'Development of the Philippines' family planning program: the early years, 1967–80'. In Robinson and Ross (eds.) *The Global Family Planning Revolution: Three Decades of Population Policies and Programs*. Washington, DC: World Bank. Pp. 277–297.
Hobsbawm, E. (1995) *The Age of Extremes: 1914–1991*. London: Little, Brown.
Hoodfar, H. and S. Assadpour (2000) 'The politics of population policy in the Islamic Republic of Iran'. *Studies in Family Planning*, 31(1): 19–34.
Horibe, N. and W. Zaman (2012) 'Foreword'. In Zaman et al. (eds.) *Family Planning in Asia and the Pacific: Addressing the Challenges*. Selangor, Malaysia: International Council on Management of Population Programmes (ICOMP). Pp. vii–viii.
Hull, T. H. (2007) 'Formative years of family planning in Indonesia'. In Robinson and Ross (eds.) *The Global Family Planning Revolution: Three Decades of Population Policies and Programs*. Washington, DC: World Bank. Pp. 235–256.
Hull, T. H. and V. J. Hull (1997) 'Culture, politics and family planning in Indonesia'. In G. W. Jones, R. Douglas, J. C. Caldwell and R. D'Souza (eds.) *The Continuing Demographic Transition*. Oxford: Oxford University Press. Pp. 383–421.
Hull, T. H., V. J. Hull and M. Singarimbun (1977) 'Indonesia's family planning story: success and challenge'. *Population Bulletin*, 32(6): 1–52.

Isaacs, S. L. (1995) 'Incentives, population policy, and reproductive rights: ethical issues'. *Studies in Family Planning*, 26(6): 363–367.

Jain, A. (1998) 'The future of population policies'. In A. Jain (ed.) *Do Population Policies Matter?* New York: Population Council. Pp. 193–202.

Jain, A., J. Bruce and B. Mensch (1992) 'Setting standards of quality in family planning programs'. *Studies in Family Planning*, 23(6): 392–395.

Johnson, S. P. (1987) *World Population and the United Nations: Challenge and Response*. Cambridge, UK and New York, US: Cambridge University Press.

Jones, G. and R. Leete (2002) 'Asia's family planning programs as low fertility is attained'. *Studies in Family Planning*, 33(1): 114–126.

Kamal, N. and A. Sloggett (1996) 'The effect of female family planning workers on the use of modern contraception in Bangladesh'. *Asia-Pacific Population Journal*, 11(3): 15–26.

Keeley, C. B. (1994) 'Limits to papal power: Vatican inaction after Humanae Vitae'. In Finkle and McIntosh (eds.) *The New Politics of Population: Conflict and Consensus in Family Planning*. *Population and Development Review*, Supplement to Vol. 20. Oxford: Oxford University Press. Pp. 220–240.

Kelley, A. C. and R. M. Schmidt (1994) 'Population growth and economic development'. In D. A. Ahlburg (ed.) *Population and Economic Development: A Report to the Government of the Commonwealth of Australia*. Pp. 13–24.

Kim, T. I. and J. A. Ross (2007) 'The Korean breakthrough'. In Robinson and Ross (eds.) *The Global Family Planning Revolution: Three Decades of Population Policies and Programs*. Washington, DC: World Bank. Pp. 177–192.

Leete, R. and I. Alam (eds.) (1993) *The Revolution in Asian Fertility: Dimensions, Causes and Implications*. Oxford: Clarendon Press.

McIntosh, C. A. and J. L. Finkle (1994) 'The politics of family planning: issues for the future'. In Finkle and McIntosh (eds.) *The New Politics of Population: Conflict and Consensus in Family Planning*. *Population and Development Review*, Supplement to Vol. 20. Oxford: Oxford University Press. Pp. 265–275.

McIntosh, C. A. and J. L. Finkle (1995) 'The Cairo Conference on Population and Development: a new paradigm?' *Population and Development Review*, 21(2): 223–260.

Myrdal, G. (1968) *Asian Drama: An Inquiry into the Poverty of Nations*. London: Allen Lane, The Penguin Press.

National Academy of Sciences (NAS, US) (1971) *Rapid Population Growth: Consequences and Policy Implications*. (2 vols.) Baltimore: Johns Hopkins University Press for the NAS.

National Research Council (NRC, US) (1986) *Population Growth and Economic Development: Policy Questions*. Washington, DC: National Academy Press.

Nortman, D. (1985) *Population and Family Planning Programs: A Compendium of Data through 1983*. New York: Population Council.

Potts, M. (2003) 'History of birth control'. In P. Demeny and G. McNicoll (eds.) *Encyclopedia of Population*. New York: Macmillan Reference. Pp. 93–98.

Robinson, W. C. (2007) 'Family planning programs and policies in Bangladesh and Pakistan'. In Robinson and Ross (eds.) *The Global Family Planning Revolution: Three Decades of Population Policies and Programs*. Washington, DC: World Bank. Pp. 301–323.

Robinson, W. C. and J. A. Ross (eds.) (2007a) *The Global Family Planning Revolution: Three Decades of Population Policies and Programs*. Washington, DC: World Bank.

Robinson, W. C. and J. A. Ross (2007b) 'Family planning: the quiet revolution'. In Robinson and Ross (eds.) *The Global Family Planning Revolution: Three Decades of Population Policies and Programs*. Washington, DC: World Bank. Pp. 421–449.

Rosenfield, A. G. and C. J. Min (2007) 'The emergence of Thailand's National Family Planning Program'. In Robinson and Ross (eds.) *The Global Family Planning Revolution: Three Decades of Population Policies and Programs*. Washington, DC: World Bank. Pp. 221–234.

Ross, J. A. and E. Frankenberg (1993) *Findings from Two Decades of Family Planning Research*. New York: The Population Council.

Ross, J. A. and W. P. Mauldin (1997) *Measuring the Strength of Family Planning Programs*. Washington, DC: Futures Group International.

Ross, J. A., W. P. Mauldin and V. C. Miller (1993) *Family Planning and Population: A Compendium of International Statistics*. New York: Population Council.

Ross, J. A., J. Stover and A. Willard (1999) *Profiles for Family Planning and Reproductive Health Programs: 116 Countries*. Glastonbury, CT: Futures Group International.

Sadik, N. (ed.) (1991) *Population Policies and Programmes: Lessons Learned from Two Decades of Experience*. New York: New York University Press.

Sato, R. (2006) 'Contraceptive use and induced abortion in Japan: how is it so unique among the developed countries?' *Japanese Journal of Population*, 4(1): 33–54.

Scharping, T. (2003) *Birth Control in China: Population Policy and Demographic Development*. London and New York: RoutledgeCurzon.

Sinding, S. W. (2003) 'Family planning programs'. In P. Demeny and G. McNicoll (eds.) *Encyclopedia of Population*. New York: Macmillan Reference. Pp. 361–371.

Sinding, S. W. (2007) 'Overview and perspective'. In Robinson and Ross (eds.) *The Global Family Planning Revolution: Three Decades of Population Policies and Programs*. Washington, DC: World Bank. Pp. 1–12.

Srinivasan, K. (1993) *Regulating Reproduction in India's Population: Efforts, Results and Recommendations*. New Delhi, and Thousand Oaks, CA: Sage.

Teng, Y. M. (2007) 'Singapore: population policies and programs'. In Robinson and Ross (eds.) *The Global Family Planning Revolution: Three Decades of Population Policies and Programs*. Washington, DC: World Bank. Pp. 201–220.

Tey, N. P. (2007) 'The family planning program in Peninsular Malaysia'. In Robinson and Ross (eds.) *The Global Family Planning Revolution: Three Decades of Population Policies and Programs*. Washington, DC: World Bank. Pp. 257–276.

Tien, H.Y. (1980) 'Wan, Xi, Shao: how China meets its population problem'. *International Family Planning Perspectives*, 6(2): 65–70.

Tsui, A. O. (2001) 'Population policies, family planning programs, and fertility: the record'. *Population and Development Review*, 27(suppl.): 184–204.

Tsui, A. O. (2012) 'Family planning programmes in Asia and the Pacific and achieving Millennium Development Goal 5'. In Zaman et al. (eds.) *Family Planning in Asia and the Pacific: Addressing the Challenges*. Selangor, Malaysia: International Council on Management of Population Programmes (ICOMP). Pp. 39–60.

Tuladhar, J. (2007) 'Emergence and development of Nepal's family planning program'. In Robinson and Ross (eds.) *The Global Family Planning Revolution: Three Decades of Population Policies and Programs*. Washington, DC: World Bank. Pp. 363–376.

United Nations (1974) *World Population Plan of Action*, adopted at the World Population Conference, Bucharest. Available from: www.un.org/popin/icpd/conference/bkg/wppa.html.

United Nations (1994) *World Population Programme of Action*, adopted at the International Conference on Population and Development, Cairo. Available from: www.un.org/popin/icpd/conference/offeng/poa.html.

United Nations Population Division (UNPD) (2014) *World Contraceptive Use 2014*. New York: UN.

United Nations Population Division (UNPD) (2015) *World Population Prospects: The 2015 Revision*, DVD Edition.

United Nations Population Division (UNPD) (2016a) *Model-based Estimates and Projections of Family Planning Indicators 2016*. New York: UN.

United Nations Population Division (UNPD) (2016b) *World Population Database*. Available from: http://esa.un.org/PopPolicy/about_database.aspx.

Visaria, P. and V. Chari (1998) 'India's population policy and family planning program: yesterday, today and tomorrow'. In A. Jain (ed.) *Do Population Policies Matter?* New York: Population Council. Pp. 53–112.

Wang, F., B. Gu and Y. Cai (2016) 'The end of China's one-child policy'. *Studies in Family Planning*, 47(1): 83–86.

Wright, N. H. (2007) 'Early family planning efforts in Sri Lanka'. In Robinson and Ross (eds.) *The Global Family Planning Revolution: Three Decades of Population Policies and Programs*. Washington, DC: World Bank. Pp. 341–362.

Zaman, W., H. Masnin and J. Loftus (eds.) (2012) *Family Planning in Asia and the Pacific: Addressing the Challenges*. Selangor, Malaysia: International Council on Management of Population Programmes (ICOMP).

Zorea, A. W. (2012) *Birth Control*. Santa Barbara, CA: Greenwood.

7

Family planning, contraceptive use and abortion

Yan Che and Baochang Gu

Introduction

The concept of contraception has been with human kind almost as long as human history (Taylor 1976). Nevertheless the use of modern contraceptives has been associated with family planning, which refers to practices which help individuals/couples to avoid unintended pregnancy in order to attain their desired number of children, and the desired spacing and timing of their births. As a response to rapid population growth, many countries of the world set up national family planning programmes in the second half of the twentieth century. One of the crucial components of such programmes is promoting contraceptive use among couples of reproductive age. This has been particularly true across Asian countries. The contraceptive prevalence rate, measured by the percentage of women aged 15–49 or their partners who use a contraceptive method, has increased in Asia from 28.3 per cent in 1970 to 66.8 per cent in 2010. This compares with increases from 39.6 to 75.7 per cent in South America and from 8.2 to 30.3 per cent in Africa over the same period (UN 2013a). Closely related to this change, Asia's total fertility fell from 5.8 to 2.3 children per woman, and its population growth rate declined from 2.1 to 1.1 per cent over the period from 1960–1965 to 2005–2010 (UN 2013b).

This chapter reviews contraceptive use in Asia in terms of its prevalence and relationship with fertility decline, patterns of using contraception, choices of different methods and method switching, unmet need for contraception and determinants of contraceptive use. While abortion is not a contraceptive, it plays a role as a method of birth control and has an important impact on fertility. The chapter also examines abortion policies, safe and unsafe abortion practices, the relationship between abortion rate and contraceptive prevalence, techniques for safe abortion and post-abortion care in Asian countries.

Use of contraception

Use of contraception refers to the use of any contraceptive method to prevent unintended pregnancy, including condoms, natural methods (periodic abstinence or withdrawal), intrauterine devices (IUDs), oral contraceptive pills, male and female sterilization, injections, implants, diaphragms, spermicides, etc. Sexually active couples who do not use any method of contraception have an approximately 85 per cent chance of experiencing a pregnancy over the course of a year (WHO 2004). Technological advances during the past 50 years have provided couples with an increasingly wide range of highly effective and safe contraceptive options that have enabled women to avoid unintended pregnancies, and this has helped to improve the health of children and mothers. Since high population growth has been perceived as being unfavourable to socio-economic development, contraceptive use has been promoted widely in developing countries, including many in Asia.

Contraceptive prevalence and trends in Asia

Soon after independence, the Indian Government recognized the dangers posed by increasing population pressure on its natural resources. The world's first national family planning programme was launched in the country in 1951 (Harkavy and Roy 2007). While China's top leaders were warned that a growing population was detrimental to national development and population control was discussed in the late 1950s and 1960s, nationwide family planning did not start until the early 1970s, when the government developed a stringent population policy and made modern contraception widely available to the population. Throughout the 1960s and 1970s, many other Asian countries, including Pakistan, Republic of Korea, Singapore, Sri Lanka, Indonesia, the Philippines, Thailand, Vietnam and Nepal, also responded to perceived high fertility and population growth rates by providing direct support for contraceptive use. Since then, contraceptive prevalence has risen steadily in Asia, from 48 per cent in 1980 to 57 per cent in 1990, 61 per cent in 2000 and 67 per cent in 2010 (UN 2013a) which is 2 to 4 percentage points higher than the world average.

According to the United Nations (2012), there has been considerable variation in contraceptive prevalence across countries. Among 47 countries/territories with at least two demographic surveys since 1965, most showed a monotonic increase in contraceptive prevalence, though some countries had several small fluctuations (UN 2012). Around 2010, contraceptive prevalence was highest in China (85 per cent) and lowest in Afghanistan (22 per cent). China's very high level of contraceptive use is attributable to its stringent family planning policy since 1979 and its well-developed contraceptive service delivery network all over the country. India was a pioneer in setting up its national family planning programme, but in 2005–2006 only 56 per cent of women of reproductive age and in a sexual union had adopted any contraceptive method. Low female literacy and the lack of choice of contraceptive methods has hampered the use of contraception in India, although this has also been related to lack of coordination between the central government and governments at lower levels (Harkavy and Roy 2007). A family planning programme in Pakistan was included in the government's third Five-Year Plan (1965–1970). Although thousands of family planning clinics were created across the country, they appear to have been ineffectual, and only 3 in 10 married women of reproductive age reported using any method of contraception in 2007–2008. Japan is the only developed country among the ten most populous nations in Asia. Unlike other countries, its fertility has fallen to a very low level without a government family planning programme, and slightly more than half of married women have adopted contraceptive methods in Japan today. The use of contraceptives in several poor countries is extremely low. For instance, the prevalence was 19 per cent in Afghanistan (2006), 22 per cent in Timor-Leste (2009–2010), 27 per cent in Pakistan (2007–2008) and 28 per cent in Yemen (2006), as shown in Figure 7.1.

There has been a significant increase in the use of modern contraceptive methods, such as cervical caps, diaphragms, oral pills, male or female condoms, injectable contraceptives, implants, IUDs and male or female sterilization, in Asia, from 53 per cent in 1990 to 61 per cent in 2012.

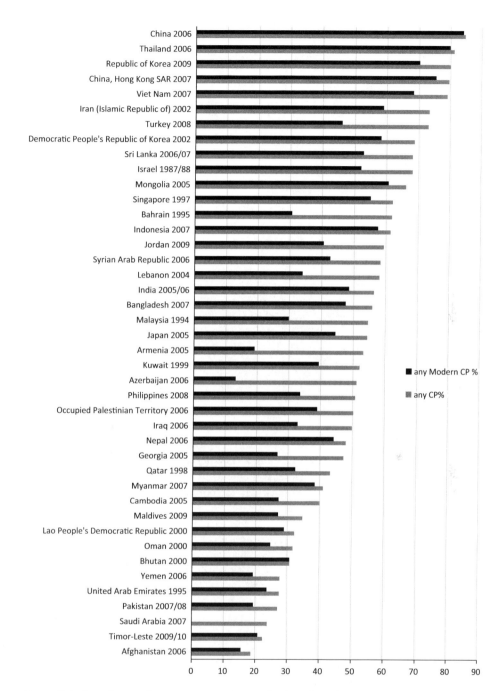

Figure 7.1 Prevalence of any contraceptive method and modern method in Asian countries/territories
Source: United Nations (2012).

In Bhutan, China, Kazakhstan and Kyrgyzstan, over 95 per cent of married contraceptive users have adopted modern methods. Greater reliance on modern contraceptives carries well-known benefits for women and their families, because they are very effective in lowering the risk of unintended pregnancy, unsafe abortion and maternal and child morbidity and mortality, as well as slowing population growth. In Azerbaijan, Armenia and Bahrain, however, more than 50 per cent of married contraceptive users still rely on traditional methods such as periodic abstinence and coitus interruptus to prevent unintended pregnancy.

Relationship between contraceptive prevalence and fertility level

Bongaarts published a proximate determinants model in 1978 showing that the fertility level in a society depends mainly on contraception, marriage, induced abortion and postpartum infecundability. Their relationship can be expressed as

$$TFR = TF \times Cm \times Ci \times Ca \times Cc$$

where TFR=total fertility rate, TF=total fecundity rate, Cm=index of marriage, Ci=index of postpartum infecundability, Ca=index of abortion and Cc=index of contraception.

The index of marriage is intended to show the reduction in fertility caused by women not being sexually active throughout their entire reproductive period, and is often approximated by the proportion of women aged 15–49 who are married. The index of postpartum infecundability is intended to measure the effects on fertility of postpartum infecundability or postpartum insusceptibility, due to postpartum amenorrhea and postpartum abstinence. The index of contraception indicates the fertility-inhibiting effects of contraceptive use, and varies inversely with contraception prevalence and effectiveness. The index of abortion measures the inhibiting effect of induced abortion.

Using data from 41 developed and developing countries, Bongaarts and Potter (1983) observed that 96 per cent of the variation in TFR could be explained by the factors in the model. However, the proximate determinants model is a simplification of reality. It is not intended to produce an accurate estimate of TFR; rather, it is intended to aid the explanation of fertility differentials, by focusing interest on the links between each of the proximate fertility variables and various socioeconomic and cultural 'background' factors.

Through analysing data collected by the UN for Asian countries, we have found an inverse relationship between levels of TFR and contraceptive use. The least-squares regression line in Figure 7.2a suggests that an increase of 8.4 percentage points in contraceptive use may reduce fertility by an average of one birth during a woman's life time. Even when the four extreme cases (Afghanistan, Iraq, Timor-Leste and Yemen) are removed, an increase of 11.8 percentage points in contraceptive use may reduce fertility by one birth, as shown in Figure 7.2b.

Variations in TFR may also be explained by various socioeconomic and cultural 'background' factors. However, empirical studies from individual countries have revealed different patterns. As plotted in Figure 7.3, contraceptive prevalence in Republic of Korea was fairly stable during 1990–2010, around 80 per cent, while its TFR declined rapidly from 1.70 to 1.22 children per woman. The relationship differs slightly in Japan where the contraceptive prevalence fell from 62 per cent in 1990–1995 to 53 per cent in 2005–2010 and the TFR also declined from 1.48 to 1.34.

China and India are the two most populous countries in Asia and the world. From 1990–1995 to 2005–2010, contraceptive prevalence in China was high and stable, ranging from 83 to 86 per cent, while contraceptive prevalence in India increased from 42 to 55 per cent. During the same period, China's TFR declined from 2.01 to 1.64, while TFR in India declined by one child from 3.72 to 2.73 (see Figure 7.4).

Contraceptive use and abortion

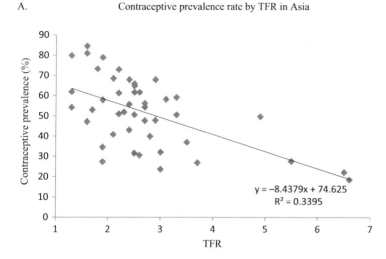

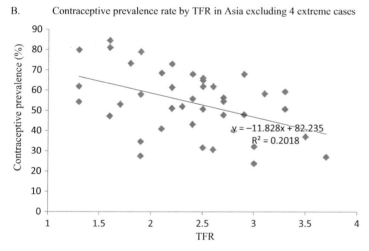

Figure 7.2 Relationship between contraceptive prevalence rate and total fertility rate in Asia
Source: United Nations (2011a).

The fertility level is strongly influenced by couples' intended family sizes. The fertility transitions in Republic of Korea and Japan were achieved mainly through voluntary family planning programmes, while in China and India there was strong government intervention. Fertility trends are also closely related to changes in patterns of marriage in some Asian countries.

Contraceptive methods and patterns of use

A wide variety of contraceptive options are available in many countries. Couples can either use traditional methods such as periodic abstinence or adopt modern contraception such as oral pills, male or female condoms, IUDs and male or female sterilization. Modern contraceptive methods are in general much more effective than traditional methods. For instance, the failure rate of sterilization is less than 1 per cent, compared to 25 per cent for periodic abstinence.

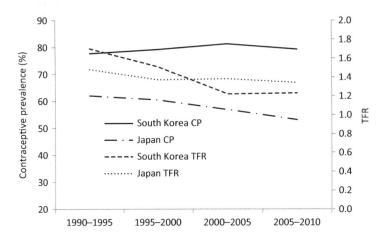

Figure 7.3 Contraceptive prevalence rate and total fertility rate in South Korea and Japan, 1990–2010
Sources: United Nations (2011a, 2012).

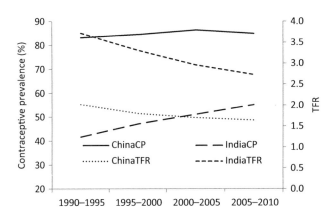

Figure 7.4 Contraceptive prevalence rate and total fertility rate in China and India, 1990–2010
Sources: United Nations (2011a, 2012).

Overall, the most commonly used contraceptive method in Asia is female sterilization, with 34 per cent of women of reproductive age in a sexual union employing this method in 1980–1984, increasing to around 42–43 per cent for the period 1985–2005. However, there are sharp subregional variations. In 2011, female sterilization rates were 32 per cent and 54 per cent among married contraceptive users in Eastern Asia and Southern Asia, respectively (see Table 7.1). This is mainly attributable to the large number of sterilizations undertaken in China and India. In the early 1970s, India implemented a forced sterilization programme. Men with two or more children had to submit to sterilization. Women were offered cash or material incentives to undergo tubal ligation. Such policies provoked social and political unrest, and a popular joke at the time suggested that coercive family planning was more likely to bring down the government than the birth rate (Harkavy and Roy 2007).

Similarly, for many years Chinese women were told to use an IUD after their first birth and to undergo sterilization after the second. Many county-level family planning officials took extreme actions against women who had unapproved pregnancies, sometimes asking them to have abortions or pay fines. This was particularly the case until 'informed choice' was introduced to the family planning programme in the mid-1990s (Gu 2000).

In Asia, the proportion of contraceptive users relying on vasectomies was 9 per cent in 1990–1994, and had dropped to 3 per cent by 2009 (Seiber, Bertrand and Sullivan 2007; UN 2011a). Three Asian countries which once had relatively high vasectomy rates have reported declines – from 9 per cent of contraceptive users in 1993 to 2 per cent in 2005 in India, from 31 per cent in 1991 to 16 per cent in 2011 in Nepal, and from 8 per cent in 1987 to 1 per cent in 2006–2007 in Sri Lanka (UN 2012).

With 140 million users, accounting for 18 per cent of married women of reproductive age, IUDs are the second most popular contraceptive method in Asia. In Central Asia, 26 to 50 per cent of married women aged 15–49 use IUDs, which represent 63 to 77 per cent of the sub-region's married contraceptive users. The IUD is also very popular in Eastern Asian countries like North Korea, China and Mongolia, where 44 to 62 per cent of married contraceptive users choose this method. Much of the IUD's popularity stems from its effectiveness and long-lasting nature. Its failure rate is less than 1 per cent over the first year and about 2 per cent over ten years of use. Its use involves only one action and is reversible. However, the method is much less popular in Southern Asia. In India only about 2 per cent of women using contraception rely on IUDs. The low rate of use is largely attributable to the inadequate training of personnel and lack of facilities to handle side effects, as well as the absence of efficient follow-up services. This situation partially reflects the Indian Government's preference for irreversible contraceptive methods as a way to control the country's rapid population growth. Since IUD insertion and removal both require medical involvement, difficulty in accessing medical services may also be an important reason for low usage in poor Asian countries like Afghanistan.

Condoms are the third most popular contraceptive method in Asia, but are only used by 54 million Asian couples, or 10 per cent of contraceptive users. The low prevalence of condom use in many Asian countries may result in part from a cultural bias against male methods of contraception. However, the method is particularly favoured in three more-developed Asian countries – Japan, Republic of Korea and Singapore – where condom use ranges from 22 to 41 per cent of those using contraception. The history of condom use in Japan goes back to 1872 when condoms of thin leather were imported to Japan from England and France (Uchida 1981). The government has distributed condoms to prevent STIs since World War II, while low-dosage oral pills and copper-bearing IUDs were not officially approved until 1999 (JICA 2005). Condoms were thus the only available modern contraceptive method in Japan for a long time.

Hormonal contraceptives, including oral pills, injectables and implants, are used by 15 per cent of married contraceptive users in Asia. The oral pill alone accounts for 9 per cent, but its use varies across the region, ranging from about 2 per cent in Eastern Asia to 25 per cent in South-Eastern Asia (Table 7.1). Oral pills are very popular in Kuwait, Thailand and Bangladesh, accounting for, respectively, 45 per cent, 45 per cent and 51 per cent of married contraceptive users (UN 2011a). Although the oral pill is one of the safest contraceptive drugs, ill-informed concerns about side effects and the inconvenience of having to take it regularly have prevented more widespread acceptance in Asia. In particular, of all contraceptive methods the share of oral pills has not exceeded 2 per cent in countries in Eastern Asia, with the exception of Mongolia (17 per cent).

Injectables have a 5 per cent share of the method mix. Notably, the share in South-Eastern Asia is 28 per cent (Table 7.1), ranging from 1 per cent in Vietnam to 52 per cent in Indonesia. The

Table 7.1 Percentage distribution of contraceptive methods by subregions in Asia

Subregion	Modern methods %									Traditional methods %		
	FS	MS	Pill	Injection	Implant	IUD	Condom	Barrier	Other	Rhythm	Withdrawal	Other
ASIA	35	3	9	5	1	27	10	0	0	4	4	1
Central Asia	2	0	6	3	0	73	5	0	0	2	2	5
Eastern Asia	32	6	2	0	0	46	13	0	0	1	1	0
Southern Asia	54	2	13	3	0	4	9	0	0	8	6	1
South-Eastern Asia	12	0	25	28	2	16	5	0	0	5	5	1
Western Asia	8	0	16	2	0	26	12	0	0	4	26	5

Note: FS: Female Sterilization; MS: Male Sterilization.
Source: United Nations (2011a).

proportion of married contraceptive users relying on injectables in Central Asia and Southern Asia is close to 3 per cent, ranging from 1 per cent in Kazakhstan to 4 per cent in Uzbekistan in Central Asia and from 0.2 per cent in India to 29 per cent in Afghanistan. Injectables are less common in Western Asia, except Oman where 25 per cent of married contraceptive users adopt them. This method is least popular in Eastern Asia, e.g. less than 0.1 per cent of married contraceptive users in China and in Democratic People's Republic of Korea. Mongolia is an exception with 17 per cent of married contraceptive users using injectables.

Emergency contraception (also known as the morning after pill) can stop ovulation within three to five days after ingestion. WHO deemed emergency contraception to be safe and effective in the mid-1990s. Among Asian countries, emergency contraception has been gaining popularity in China, India and Thailand. In 2009, the Indian market for emergency contraceptive pills grew 47 per cent. This method is now also available in Bangladesh, Japan, Iraq, Israel, Malaysia, Pakistan, Saudi Arabia, Republic of Korea and Sri Lanka (Office of Population Research at Princeton University 2016). Previous studies have shown emergency contraception to be more popular among unmarried young people because this group are more likely to have unplanned sex and to have only limited, or no, contraceptive knowledge and experience. Since this method is not recommended for use on a regular basis, WHO has recommended that good counselling be provided to these novices (WHO 2011a).

Traditional methods are reported to be the primary method of family planning by 6 per cent of married women aged 15–49 in Asia (UN 2011a), though it is likely that many more women use some form of abstinence from time to time. The proportion of pregnancy prevention attributed to traditional methods varies widely by subregion. These methods are most popular in Western Asia where between 10 and 30 per cent of married women of reproductive age use traditional methods, which may partly be due to religious reasons. The proportion using traditional methods is also relatively high (17 per cent) in Japan, and this may largely be due to the limited choice of modern methods other than condoms (UN 2011a).

Since no contraceptive method is perfect, women need to consider the trade-offs of different methods and to have access to a range of methods. The choice of contraceptive method may therefore represent a choice of the least unpleasant of a set of alternatives. Such choices can be influenced by users' characteristics such as age, nature of union and medical conditions. No ideal method mix has been recognized, but increasingly contraceptives which provide protection against unwanted pregnancies and the acquisition of HIV and other STIs, will be an important part of any method mix.

While most Asian countries have been moving towards offering a wide range of methods and letting couples decide which method to use, a few countries have a very skewed method mix, in which a single method accounts for more than half of contraceptive use. For example, despite a 1996 national population policy that eliminated the use of targets and called for the promotion of a wider variety of contraceptive choices, female sterilization continues to dominate India's method mix (Harkavy and Roy 2007). In keeping with family planning policy, Chinese women with one child tend to use IUDs, while those with two or more children mostly rely on female sterilization, which leads to disproportionate use of IUDs and female sterilization in the country (Winckler 2002). Although there is no compulsory family planning programme, over 90 per cent of married users of modern contraceptives in Japan rely on male condoms (UN 2011a). Another example is the recent rise of injectables in Indonesia due to major declines in the promotion of longer acting implants and IUDs, and the failure of the programme to support surgical sterilization for people wishing to have a permanent end to childbearing (Hull and Mosley 2009). Generally speaking, a mature family planning programme should have a balanced distribution of methods so that the proportion of any single method would not be too high, i.e. comprise more than half of contraceptive use in a society. Thus, to further improve the well-being and autonomy of women, considerable efforts in this area should be made in Asia, even among countries with a high prevalence of contraceptive use.

Contraceptive discontinuation and switching

Finding an appropriate method is often a process of trial and error. Even if a method is enthusiastically adopted by a woman, it may be discontinued for a number of reasons, i.e. method failure, desire for pregnancy, side effects or health concerns. Method failure and side effects are often the reasons for contraceptive switching. Other reasons include inconvenience in use, ideal family size being reached, desire to use another method, fears or health concerns, method no longer medically advised, change in breastfeeding status and method no longer available or accessible, etc.

Table 7.2 shows cumulative 12-month discontinuation rates per 100 episodes (an episode is a period between the start and end of continuously using a particular contraceptive method) in five Asian countries (Ali, Cleland and Shah 2012). The rate for all methods for all reasons was highest in Bangladesh (50 per cent) and lowest in Vietnam (25 per cent). With respect to specific methods, 38 to 71 per cent of condom users discontinued within one year of use; the 12-month

Table 7.2 Cumulative 12-month discontinuation probabilities per 100 episodes (single decrement life table) for all discontinuation reasons in five Asian countries, by methods

Country	All methods	Pills	IUDs	Injection	Condoms	Rhythm	Withdrawal
Bangladesh (2004)	49.9	46.1	32.9	47.8	71.0	41.1	58.9
Indonesia (2007)	25.9	38.7	9.1	22.4	38.0	24.6	23.3
Jordan (2009)	45.1	51.9	14.6	65.4	50.8	46.3	40.5
Philippines (2003)	37.7	38.6	13.8	52.7	55.9	31.2	42.0
Vietnam (2002)	25.3	36.4	12.5	–	38.5	33.2	30.5

Source: Based on data from Ali, Cleland and Shah (2012: Tables B.1.1–B.1.7).

Table 7.3 Status at three months after discontinuing any method for method-related reason for five Asian countries (%)

Country	At risk*	Became pregnant	IUDs	Pills	Injections	Barrier	Sterilization	Traditional methods
Bangladesh (2004)	21.6	5.9	0.9	25.7	18.5	11.7	0.4	15.3
Indonesia (2007)	27.1	6.1	2.9	35.7	21.5	2.1	0.2	4.4
Jordan (2009)	22.8	8.0	17.5	15.1	2.6	9.1	0.1	24.7
Philippines (2003)	34.0	11.7	2.5	19.4	8.5	5.5	0.4	18.0
Vietnam (2002)	12.2	9.8	25.2	12.3	0.9	13.7	2.8	23.2

Note: *At risk of becoming pregnant.
Source: Based on data from Ali, Cleland and Shah (2012: Table 4).

discontinuation rate of pills ranged from 36 to 52 per 100 episodes; the rate for injectables ranged from 22 to 65 per 100 episodes; and the rate for IUDs ranged from 9 to 33 per 100 episodes. The discontinuation rate for the two traditional methods ranged from 25 to 46 per 100 episodes for rhythm, and from 23 to 59 per 100 episodes for withdrawal. Overall, short-term methods are more likely to be discontinued than long-term methods. Reasons for discontinuing modern methods were dominated by side effects and concerns of adverse effects on women's health. Discontinuations of traditional methods were mainly due to unintended pregnancy or a desire to switch to a more effective method.

Contraceptive switching often implies dissatisfaction with a previously used method. Table 7.3 shows medical status three months after discontinuation for five Asian countries as recorded by recent surveys. Couples who discontinued contraception but did not switch to another method were classified as either being pregnant or at risk of becoming so. The proportion switching to another modern method ranged from 36 per cent in the Philippines to 62 per cent in Indonesia. In most cases in Bangladesh, Indonesia and the Philippines, the next contraceptive choice was pills. In Jordan and Vietnam, many switched to IUDs or traditional methods. Injectables were also favoured in Indonesia and Bangladesh. The proportion switching to sterilization was very low.

Contraceptive discontinuation or switching does not necessarily mean a failure of the family planning programme. However, they are important indicators of how well programmes are meeting the family planning needs of women and couples. A high rate of discontinuation points to a need to improve service quality, particularly counselling, so that women can make informed choices by being forewarned about side effects and reassured about health concerns. Facilitating method switching and increasing the availability of the full range of methods are designed to improve consumer satisfaction and increase contraceptive prevalence rates.

Discontinuation probabilities are particularly high in Bangladesh and Jordan, implying the necessity of enhancing counselling capacity among service providers. Studies of contraceptive discontinuation and switching in Asia are still limited. There is an urgent need to improve studies in this area to better inform policymakers and family planning programme managers concerned with contraceptive prevalence.

Unmet need for contraception

Women with unmet needs for contraception are those who are fecund, sexually active and want to delay or stop childbearing but are not using any method of contraception. Globally, 222 million women in developing countries do not use any contraceptive method but do not want to become pregnant (WHO 2013). Sub-Saharan Africa has the highest percentage of women with unmet need – approximately one-quarter of women of reproductive age in the region or about 47 million women. Although Asia has a lower proportion of women with unmet need, its total population is the largest of any region so the size of the population with unmet need (140 million) is also greatest in absolute terms. In South-Eastern Asia and Southern and Central Asia, more than 100 million women have an unmet need for contraception (Guttmacher Institute 2012a).

As contraceptive prevalence has increased, the level of unmet need in Asia has declined four percentage points, from 15 per cent in 1990 to 11 per cent in 2010. Southern Asia has contributed most to the reduction, with a decline from 22 to 15 per cent, while the reduction in Eastern Asia was the smallest, from 6 to 4 per cent. These results are expected because contraceptive prevalence was lowest in Southern Asia and highest in Eastern Asia. Unmet need in Central Asia, South-Eastern Asia and Western Asia has been moderate, ranging from 13 to 17 per cent in 2010, about 5 per cent lower than in 1990 (Alkema et al. 2013).

In six Asian countries – Cambodia, Maldives, Nepal, Pakistan, Laos and Timor-Leste – more than a quarter of women of reproductive age in union have lacked access to contraception (Alkema et al. 2013). Unmet need in the countries of Eastern Asia has been relatively low. For example, it was 4 per cent in China and 5.5 per cent in the Republic of Korea, but slightly higher in Mongolia (13.2 per cent) and Japan (17.2 per cent) (Alkema et al. 2013).

Difficulties in accessing contraceptives can result from an inability to obtain or afford contraceptives, or from having to travel too far to get them. However, many other reasons can also lead to women not using any contraceptive method, including limited choice of methods, fear or experience of side effects, personal, cultural or religious opposition, health concerns and poor quality of available services. In South-Central Asia and South-Eastern Asia, the top two reasons for unmet need were reported to be woman's (or partner's) personal opposition and infrequent sex, as shown in Table 7.4 (Darroch, Sedgh and Ball 2011). Substantial proportions of women with unmet need reported health concerns or side effects, and no access or high cost, as barriers to contraceptive use. Only a small segment reported unawareness of methods or perceived subfecundity.

Unmet need is also associated with variations in the norms of reproduction and ideal family size. In countries where many women prefer large families and do not want to space or limit births, both unmet need and contraceptive use can be low. In other countries that are in transition to smaller family sizes, unmet need will probably increase until information, supplies and services are improved to meet the increasing demand for contraception. Therefore, high levels

Table 7.4 Reasons for non-use among women with unmet need for modern contraception (%) in South Central and South-Eastern Asia

	South-Central Asia	South-Eastern Asia
Woman/partner opposed	32	10
Infrequent sex	22	25
Postpartum/breastfeeding	19	11
Health/side effects	18	39
No access/high cost	6	11
Unaware of methods	2	1
Perceived subfecund	1	3

Source: Based on data from Darroch, Sedgh and Ball (2011: Table 5).

Yan Che & Baochang Gu

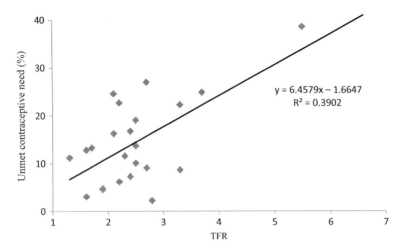

Figure 7.5 Relationship between unmet contraceptive need and total fertility rate in Asia, c.2009
Source: United Nations (2011b).

of unmet need do not necessarily reflect limitations of the family planning programme, but may reflect a growing demand for contraception.

Figure 7.5 shows a regression line indicating the relationship between level of unmet need and TFR among 45 Asian countries. It shows that the level of unmet need increases along with TFR, suggesting that a reduction of 6.45 per cent of unmet need may reduce fertility by one child on average during an Asian woman's life course. Moreover, Figure 7.5 may also imply that the desire for smaller families has been outpacing the availability and use of contraception in Asia, which may have led to unwanted births and high rates of abortion in some countries. Strengthening family planning services should therefore be given a high priority in countries with a high level of unmet need.

Determinants of contraceptive use

The choice of contraceptive method can depend upon a variety of factors. In deciding which method to use, women or couples are often influenced by a number of factors such as age, gender, education, parity, contraceptive needs, reproductive intentions, frequency of intercourse, lactation status, health profile, expectations and experiences of using contraception, tolerance of side effects, the convenience of a method, the influence of others, women's socioeconomic status and the relationship with one's partner, etc.

Contraceptive choice is also, in part, dependent on how effective the method is, and continuation rates are generally higher with more effective methods. Many factors influence patterns of contraceptive use, and variations in such patterns are often related to and reflect differences in social structures, cultural contexts and the development of family planning policies. While much of the increase in contraceptive use reflects a transition from high to low desired family size, it also reflects the continuing efforts of national and international family planning organizations and a wider availability of contraceptive choices.

Government can play an important part in promoting contraceptive use. A recent UN report summarized data from 26 countries across Asia, which are presented in Figure 7.6. According to this figure, government sponsored family planning effort can greatly increase contraceptive use,

Contraceptive use and abortion

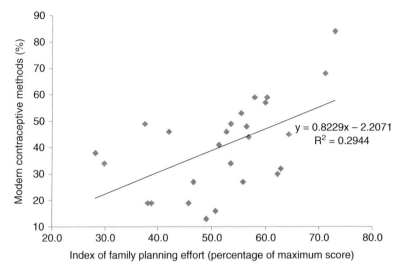

Figure 7.6 Relationship between country's family planning effort and contraceptive prevalence in Asia, 2009
Source: United Nations (2011a).

particularly the use of modern contraceptive methods, in the country (UN 2011a). As family planning is one of the most important and successful governmental interventions during last five decades in Asia, increasing investment in family planning is recommended especially for countries where unmet need is high.

Abortion

Abortion is the termination of an established pregnancy, either spontaneously or as a deliberate action. Induced abortion can be a response to an unintended pregnancy or a decision to terminate a planned pregnancy for economic or health-related reasons. Unintended pregnancy is currently the most common reason for abortion. The two main factors contributing to unintended pregnancy have been contraceptive failure and non-use of contraception. Since no contraceptive method is 100 per cent effective, women need to consider trade-offs among different methods. Many social and personal factors also hinder individuals' effective contraceptive use. Moreover, a number of interrelated causes of unintended pregnancy can lead to an abortion, including increasingly liberal attitudes towards sex alongside lack of knowledge or education related to contraception, as well as apprehension about the safety of contraceptive methods. In many nations, the presence of these factors has combined with a growing acceptance of safe medical abortion. As a result, it is almost impossible to eliminate abortion even in places where it is vigorously discouraged by law or religion. Moreover, rape or incest can result in an unwanted pregnancy. Consequently, the need for abortion will always be present.

Globally, there were an estimated 45.6 million abortions in 1995. This declined to 41.6 million in 2003, but rose to 43.8 million in 2008, accounting for about one-fifth of the world's annual total pregnancies. Estimates of abortions in Asia were 26.8 million, 25.9 million and 27.3 million in 1995, 2003 and 2008, respectively, which accounted for 59–62 per cent of all abortions in the world (Sedgh et al. 2012).

Abortion in a modern medical setting is a safe procedure and poses little risk to a woman's health when it is done by well-trained practitioners under hygienic conditions in a nation where it is legal, or where any legal sanctions are unlikely to be applied to the woman or the provider. However, abortion can be unsafe if the procedure is done by people lacking the necessary skills or in an environment that does not conform to minimum medical standards, or both. If fear of prosecution is high, the safety of the procedure can also be affected.

Abortion may have a series of adverse consequences even in settings where the procedure is legal. A good example is China where abortion is allowed on broad grounds. A nationwide intervention study to improve post-abortion care was initiated in China in 2013. The study showed that both the women who experienced abortion and their service providers perceived a range of potential physical consequences after abortion, including immediate pain, discomfort, bleeding, complications leading to damage to the reproductive organs, and a range of reproductive and sexual health issues with potential long-term impacts on future fertility (especially in the case of repeat abortion) (INPAC Consortium 2013). Adverse psychological consequences were also mentioned, such as distress and anxiety related to the abortion and future sexual activity, and potential effects on future relationships. Women with untreated complications often experience long-term health consequences, including anaemia, chronic pain, inflammation of the reproductive tract, pelvic inflammatory disease and infertility (INPAC Consortium 2013).

Unsafe abortion has been recognized as a major global public health problem and a human rights imperative. Almost all unsafe abortions (98 per cent) occur in settings with limited resources (WHO 2011b). Approximately half of the global unsafe abortion procedures are performed in Asia each year. Abortions in countries that restrict abortion are very likely to be unsafe. Below, we review abortion laws, levels and trends of abortion, and its association with contraceptive use. Some technical issues and post-abortion care are also discussed.

Overview of abortion policies

Abortion raises fundamental questions about human existence, such as when life begins, and what it is that makes us human. Abortion is at the heart of such contentious issues as the right of women to control their own bodies, the nature of the state's duty to protect the unborn child, the tension between secular and religious views of human life and the individual and society, the rights of spouses and parents to be involved in the abortion decision and the conflicting rights of the mother and the fetus (United Nations 2001).

Even though abortion is commonly practiced throughout most countries, as in the words above, it is a subject that arouses passion and controversy.

Today, among the 195 members of the United Nations, the majority (97 per cent) allow the procedure to save a woman's life. About two-thirds of these nations allow it to preserve a woman's physical and mental health. Less than half (49 per cent) allow it in cases of rape or incest. One-third or less allow it for economic or social reasons or on request (WHO 2012).

In all countries in Asia, the law permits abortion to be performed in order to save a woman's life. Slightly over 60 per cent of these countries allow the procedure to preserve a woman's physical or mental health. In about half the countries, abortion is permitted in cases of rape, incest or fetal impairment. Forty per cent of countries allow it on economic or social grounds, and about one-third of countries allow abortion on request (WHO 2012).

As shown in Table 7.5, three-quarters of countries in Eastern Asia allow abortion on the woman's request, compared with 27 per cent in South-Eastern Asia, 29 per cent in Western Asia and 43 per cent in South-Central Asia. The variation in abortion laws across Asia in large part reflects diverse historical, political and religious roots in this region.

Contraceptive use and abortion

Table 7.5 Percentage distribution of grounds on which abortion is permitted (% of countries) in 2009

Country or area	To save the woman's life	To preserve physical health	To preserve mental health	Rape or incest	Fetal impairment	Economic or social reasons	On request
All countries	97	67	63	49	47	34	29
Asia	**100**	**63**	**61**	**50**	**54**	**39**	**37**
Eastern Asia	100	100	100	100	100	75	75
South-Central Asia	100	64	64	57	50	50	43
South-Eastern Asia	100	55	45	36	36	27	27
Western Asia	100	59	59	41	59	29	29

Source: WHO (2012).

It is evident that legislative change does not automatically lead to universal access to safe abortion services within the bounds of the law. International studies have identified a number of obstacles to the provision and accessibility of safe abortion services in countries where the law permits abortion on broad grounds. Some countries limit the procedure to the early stage of pregnancy and to a limited number of providers or personnel. Some other countries require medical approval/authorization for an abortion, or spouse/partner/parental authorization. In some developed countries, abortion laws demand a pregnant woman be given counselling before having an abortion and/or after a mandatory waiting period. Objection on religious or moral grounds and penalties for illegal abortion are often seen in regions where Islam or Catholicism has a strong influence (IPPF 2008).

Abortions that occur outside of the law are usually clandestine and unsafe because the procedures are performed by unskilled providers or under unhygienic conditions. Sometimes they are induced by the pregnant woman herself. In these settings, abortions contribute substantially to maternal illness and death. In addition to endangering women, unsafe abortion and its consequences place a costly burden on health systems.

Safe and unsafe abortion: level, trend and reasons

Detailed data on abortion levels and trends can help identify gaps between women's contraceptive demands and the provision of family planning services in a country, and inform policymakers and international agencies of the need for action to improve women's reproductive health.

Globally, the estimated abortion rate decreased from 35 abortions per 1,000 women aged 15–44 in 1995 to 29 per 1,000 in 2003 and further to 28 per 1,000 in 2008. Asia shared a similar trend: the annual abortion rate was 33 per 1,000 in 1995, and declined to 29 and 28 per 1,000 in 2003 and 2008, respectively. Abortion rates were highest in South-Eastern Asia, ranging from 36 to 40 abortions per 1,000 women between 1995 and 2008. This is partly due to the high abortion incidence in Vietnam, which has 15 per cent of the population in the subregion. Abortion rates declined faster in Eastern Asia than in other subregions, decreasing from 36 abortions per 1,000 women in 1995 to 28 per 1,000 women in 2008. In South-Central Asia the decline during the same period was only two abortions per 1,000 women. Unlike other areas, the abortion rate in Western Asia increased slightly from 24 per 1,000 women in 2003 to 26 per 1,000 women in 2008, suggesting the desire for smaller families outpaced the reduction in unmet need in this area (WHO 2011b).

In countries which allow abortion on request, the rate varies between 5.3 per 1,000 women in Nepal to 32 per 1,000 women in Kazakhstan, indicating a weak association between the frequency of abortion and its legal grounds. In countries where abortion is permitted only to save a woman's life, the reported abortion rate tends to be low (i.e. 1.3 per 1,000 women aged 15–44 in Qatar) or the data are not available (UN 2011b).

Recent data show that the number of abortions in Asia increased slightly from 26.9 million in 1995 to 27.3 million in 2008. Though the number of abortions declined slightly in Eastern Asia, from 12.5 million in 1995 to 10.2 million in 2008, it increased considerably in South-Central Asia, from 8.4 million in 1995 to 10.5 million in 2008. The volume of abortions in South-Eastern Asia (about 5 million a year) and Western Asia (ranging from 1.2 to 1.4 million a year) did not change very much over this period.

Each year, 21.6 million women undergo unsafe abortions which terminate one in ten pregnancies worldwide. Approximately half of the global unsafe abortion procedures are performed in Asia. Among the 47,000 women who die each year from complications due to unsafe abortion, 17,000 or more than one-third are in Asia (WHO 2011b; Sedgh et al. 2012; Shah and Ahman 2010; Guttmacher Institute 2010). In addition, 2.3 million women in Asia are hospitalized annually for treatment of complications from unsafe abortion.

South-Central Asia has reported the highest level of unsafe abortions. In 1995, nearly 80 per cent of abortions in this subregion were recognized to be unsafe. This proportion declined to 65 per cent in 2008, partly because of liberalization of abortion laws in Nepal and India as well as the widespread availability of menstrual regulation services in Bangladesh. Nonetheless, many procedures are still performed in substandard conditions. For instance, in India abortion has been legal on broad grounds since 1971, but substandard conditions are often found in public health facilities and high fees are charged by private facilities. More than 5.5 million of the 6.5 million abortions that take place annually in India are conducted by uncertified providers or in unregistered facilities (Guttmacher Institute 2012b). Although changes in abortion numbers in Western Asia were small, the proportion of unsafe procedures increased from 42 per cent in 1995 to 60 per cent in 2008, as shown in Table 7.6. Better measurement of unsafe abortion and a steady decline in abortion in countries where abortion is legal and safe are reported to be the main reasons for this change.

Where abortion is permitted on broad legal grounds, it is generally safe; and where it is highly restricted, it is typically unsafe. Nevertheless, a liberal abortion law alone does not ensure the safety of abortions. International studies indicate the following interventions are essential for successfully implementing a liberal abortion law (Guttmacher Institute 2012c). They include: disseminating information about the new law to government agencies, public and private health care providers, and the general public; publishing and disseminating regulations, guidelines and

Table 7.6 Estimated number of induced abortions (in millions), abortion rate (per 1,000 women aged 15–44) and percentage of unsafe abortion worldwide, in Asia and by Asian subregion, 1995–2008

	2008			2003			1995		
	Number	Rate	%Unsafe	Number	Rate	%Unsafe	Number	Rate	%Unsafe
World	43.8	28	49	41.6	29	47	45.6	35	44
Asia	27.3	28	40	25.9	29	38	26.8	33	37
Eastern Asia	10.2	28	<0.5	10	28	<0.5	12.5	36	<0.5
South-Central Asia	10.5	26	65	9.6	27	66	8.4	28	78
South-Eastern Asia	5.1	36	61	5.2	39	59	4.7	40	60
Western Asia	1.4	26	60	1.2	24	34	1.2	32	42

Source: Based on data from Sedgh et al. (2012: Tables 1 and 2).

Contraceptive use and abortion

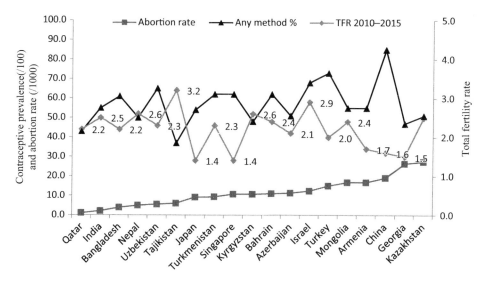

Figure 7.7 Association between abortion rate (/1,000 women aged 15–44 in relationship), contraceptive prevalence (/100 women of reproductive age in relationship) and total fertility rate (TFR) in selected Asian countries, 2010–2015
Sources: United Nations (2011a, 2012).

protocols for providing safe abortion services; training health workers to perform safe abortions, and providing supplies and equipment for safe abortion at authorized facilities; and monitoring and evaluating the incidence of safe and unsafe abortion and the health impact of new abortion services.

Relationship between abortion rate and contraceptive prevalence

Abortion is often used as a back-up method to terminate pregnancy in case of contraceptive failure. Thus, one would expect that a rise in contraceptive prevalence would lead to a decline in induced abortion and vice versa. Nevertheless, in many circumstances, the relationship between abortion rate and contraceptive prevalence does not follow this pattern without considering other factors. Figure 7.7 plots abortion rates, contraceptive prevalence and TFR for 19 Asian countries, and shows that the relationship among contraceptive prevalence, abortion rate and total fertility rate may vary from one country to another. For example, in China, the abortion rate and contraceptive prevalence are both high while TFR is far below replacement. In Tajikistan, both abortion rate and contraceptive prevalence are low while the TFR exceeds 3. In contrast, in Kazakhstan, the abortion rate is high, contraceptive prevalence is moderate and the TFR is 2.5. It appears that a low TFR tends to be associated with high contraceptive prevalence and abortion rates, and a high TFR is related to low rates of contraceptive use and abortion. Nevertheless, this is not always the case, for example, this pattern is not shown in Singapore and Turkmenistan. These two countries have very similar levels of contraceptive use (62 per cent) and abortion (9 per 1,000 women aged 15–44), but TFR in Turkmenistan is 2.3, compared with 1.4 in Singapore.

Bongaarts and Westoff reported in 2000 that at a given TFR, a rise in contraceptive use or effectiveness leads to a decline in induced abortion (Bongaarts and Westoff 2000). However, in countries where fertility is falling rapidly, contraceptive prevalence and abortion rates can rise in parallel because increased contraceptive use alone is unable to meet the growing need for fertility regulation. Singapore and Republic of Korea are two examples. In Singapore, a rise in both abortion and contraceptive use occurred under conditions of fertility decline (1970–1985), followed by a decline in abortion rates during 1985–1997. In Republic of Korea, contraceptive prevalence and abortion rates increased in parallel before the late 1970s. Subsequently, however, the abortion rate fell whereas contraceptive prevalence continued to rise. During the 1970s and 1980s, Republic of Korea underwent a fertility transition – desired family sizes became smaller and the TFR declined (Marston and Cleland 2003).

Techniques for safe abortion: vacuum aspiration and medical abortion

A variety of techniques may be used to induce abortion safely. The choice of an appropriate technique will depend largely on the length of time a woman has been pregnant. Figure 7.8 summarizes methods of abortion that are most appropriate at different stages of pregnancy. The methods recommended by WHO to terminate pregnancy up to 12–14 weeks of gestation are vacuum aspiration (VA) and medical methods using a combination of mifepristone followed by misoprostol (WHO 2012).

VA involves the evacuation of the contents of the uterus through a plastic or metal cannula attached to a vacuum source. Electric VA employs an electric vacuum pump. With manual VA, the vacuum is created using a hand-held, hand-activated aspirator. Efficacy of VA is reported to be over 95 per cent. Electric and manual VA equipment is inexpensive and easy to operate and maintain. Most women can leave the service facility after a 30-minute observation period. Hence VA is easier, less likely to involve complications and more cost-effective than dilation and surgical curettage under general anesthesia.

Medical abortion (MA) – also called medication abortion or the abortion pill – is a method of using prescription drugs to end a pregnancy. Like VA, MA is also very safe and effective. The unique advantages of MA are that it is noninvasive and women can use it in a range of settings, including their own homes.

Mifepristone with misoprostol or gemeprost has been the most widely accepted MA method and has proved to be highly effective (up to 98 per cent) and safe for abortion in the first three months of pregnancy. The procedure of MA is similar between different regimens. Typically,

Completed weeks since last menstrual period		
4 5 6 7 8 9 10 11 12	13 14 15 16 17 18 19 20 21 22	
Preferred methods		
Vacuum aspiration (manual/electric)	• • • By specially trained providers	
	Dilatation and evacuation	
Mifepristone + misoprostol/gemeprost	Mifepristone and repeated doses of misoprostol or gemeprost	
Other methods		
Dilatation and curettage	Hypertonic solutions	
	Intra/extra-amniotic prostaglandins	

Figure 7.8 Methods of abortion
Source: Based on discussion in WHO (2012).

women take mifepristone under clinical supervision, with a second visit to the health facility two days later to take the prostaglandin (misoprostol or gemeprost). About 2 to 5 per cent of women treated with MA will require surgical intervention due to an incomplete abortion, to terminate a continuing pregnancy or to control bleeding (WHO 2012).

Short-term side effects of typical MA regimens include strong cramps, bleeding, nausea, vomiting, fever and chills. In most cases, side effects can be managed with appropriate counselling and symptomatic treatments, such as oral analgesics for pain. There is no evidence of long-term risks with mifepristone when used for MA and no long-term effects have been associated with misoprostol.

The availability of manual VA and MA is uneven across Asia. Manual VA was invented and first used in China in the 1950s. In Nepal, manual VA was not available until March 2004 and MA was introduced in 2009, although abortion was legalized in 2002 (Basnett et al. 2011). In Indonesia, 38 per cent of women who had obtained an abortion at a clinic reported that they used VA to terminate the unwanted pregnancy, while VA was virtually never used in Pakistan (Guttmacher Institute 2009). In the Philippines, less than one-quarter of abortions were performed by VA, while 22 per cent of poor Filipino women used a catheter or heavy abdominal pressure in an abortion attempt (Guttmacher Institute 2013).

In Bangladesh, induced abortion is illegal except when performed to save a woman's life. However, menstrual regulation – a procedure that uses manual VA to safely establish non-pregnancy after a missed period – is legal, but many women don't know about this service, lack access to the procedure or don't understand the difference between menstrual regulation and unsafe abortion (Guttmacher Institute 2012b).

Cost remains an important barrier to providing mifepristone medical abortion, although Asian manufacturers have significantly reduced the price of the medication. Because of the limited indications for use of mifepristone, it is only registered and available in a small number of Asian countries, including Azerbaijan, China, Georgia, India, Mongolia, Uzbekistan and Vietnam though it can be found in the black market elsewhere.

Post-abortion care

Access to safe abortion is a key sexual health and reproductive right. Induced abortion, especially repeat abortion and unsafe abortion, is associated with a high risk of injury or long-term physical and psychological morbidity. Most women hospitalized for abortion-related complications do not receive any counselling about the need to use contraceptives once they are discharged. Treatment of complications and provision of family planning services to prevent future unwanted pregnancies are key components of post-abortion care (PAC).

Originated by Ipas in the early 1990s, PAC is an approach for reducing deaths and injuries from incomplete and unsafe abortions, their related complications and repeated abortions. A global PAC Consortium was formed over a decade ago to sound an alarm within the reproductive health community about the need to effectively treat complications of miscarriage and incomplete abortion in order to reduce maternal mortality worldwide, and to promote PAC as an effective strategy for addressing this global problem (www.pac-consortium.org/). The PAC Consortium supports a comprehensive public health model of Five Essential Elements of post-abortion care. These elements include: treatment of incomplete and unsafe abortion and complications; counselling to identify and respond to women's emotional and physical health needs; contraceptive and family planning services to help women prevent future unwanted pregnancies and abortions; reproductive and other health services that are preferably provided on-site or via referral to other accessible facilities; and community and service-provider partnerships to prevent unwanted pregnancies and unsafe abortions, to mobilize resources to ensure timely care for abortion complications, and to make sure health services meet community expectations and needs.

In many Asian countries, the quality of PAC services is not optimal. Common shortcomings include inadequate access, delays in providing treatment, shortages of trained health workers and medical supplies, use of inappropriate methods, and high costs imposed on patients (Guttmacher Institute 2012b). For instance, one study (Karki and Regmi 2007) showed that in Nepal, an estimated 165,000 abortions took place annually but a vast majority of PAC clients (87 per cent) were diagnosed as having had incomplete abortion. One in six PAC clients were vulnerable adolescents aged 15–19 years. The coverage of PAC was low and the unmet need for it was about 90 per cent. In Cambodia, first-trimester abortion has been allowed upon request since 1997, but safe abortion care has remained out of reach for most Cambodian women for years. In 2005, more than 30,000 women sought PAC in public health facilities alone, with evidence suggesting that more than 40 per cent of complications resulted from unsafe abortions (Ipas 2010). In India, unsafe abortion accounts for 8 per cent of all maternal deaths. In Pakistan, approximately 890,000 abortions are conducted annually and about 197,000 women are treated for post-abortion complications (Guttmacher Institute 2009).

Some countries have launched national PAC intervention programmes in recent years. For example, such a programme was launched in Cambodia in 2006. Five years later in 2010, significant changes were evident in service provision, abortion-related morbidity and provider attitudes, including: wider availability of safe abortion in public-sector facilities, large improvement in PAC services, increasing use of appropriate abortion technologies, reduction in abortion morbidity and better-known abortion law among service providers (Ipas 2010).

Following legal reform, Nepal initiated a National Safe Abortion Program in 2003 establishing services across the country and training public and private service providers. The PAC training curriculum has provided trainees with a wide range of knowledge and skills, such as initial assessment of clients, family planning/history/counselling, initial infection prevention, physical examination, client information, manual VA preparation, manual VA procedure, evacuation examination, post-procedure care and post-procedure family planning.

In Bangladesh, a countrywide programme was launched in 2011 to strengthen PAC services and menstrual regulation services in order to reduce mortality and morbidity from unsafe abortion (Ipas 2011). In China, abortions are performed by trained service providers under hygienic conditions. However, repeated abortion is becoming a public health problem, particularly among unmarried young women. A nationwide PAC practical guide was issued in 2011 and a national campaign to improve the quality of PAC was launched in 2012. To date, more than 50 hospitals across the country are recognized as model units providing PAC service with good quality care (CWDF 2014).

Conclusions and practical implications

Despite the lack of standardized data in some countries, it is possible to conclude that contraceptive use has increased and unmet need has declined in Asia during recent decades. However, rising contraceptive practice has not brought a significant fall in abortion rates in this region, particularly in South-Central Asia. Theoretical and empirical studies suggest that when the fertility level in a country is falling, both contraceptive use and abortion tend to increase simultaneously. Asia as a whole is currently in a transition from high to low fertility. The above results indicate that, in Asia, the desire for smaller families continues to outpace the availability and use of contraception.

The data and discussion presented above also reveal considerable variations in contraceptive use and abortion among the countries in Asia. Programmes and policies that improve women's and men's knowledge of, access to, and use of contraceptive methods should be established and strengthened in countries with a high level of unmet need. Moreover, to reduce the number of clandestine procedures, the grounds for legal abortion should be broadened, especially in countries where this procedure is restricted. Access to safe abortion services should be improved for women who meet legal criteria. The analysis has identified that improvement of contraceptive and abortion services is urgent, particularly in South-Central Asia and South-Eastern Asia.

References

Ali, M. M., J. Cleland and I. H. Shah (2012) *Causes and Consequences of Contraceptive Discontinuation: Evidence from 60 Demographic and Health Surveys*. Geneva: World Health Organization.

Alkema, L., V. Kantorova, C. Menozzi and A. Biddlecom (2013) 'National, regional and global rates and trends in contraceptive prevalence and unmet need for family planning between 1990 and 2015: a systematic and comprehensive analysis'. *Lancet*, 381(9878): 1642–1652. Available from: http://dx.doi.org/10.1016/s0140-6736(12)62204-1.

Basnett, I., K. Andersen, S. Neupane, K. KrennHrubec and V. Acre (2011) 'Pathways to safe abortion in Nepal'. *Research Brief*. Ipas, NC, 29 March.

Bongaarts, J. (1978) 'A framework for analyzing the proximate determinants of fertility'. *Population and Development Review*, 4(1):105–132.

Bongaarts J. and R. G. Potter (1983) *Fertility, Biology and Behaviour: An Analysis of Proximate Determinants*. New York: Academic Press.

Bongaarts J. and C. F. Westoff (2000) 'The potential role of contraception in reducing abortion'. *Studies in Family Planning*, 31(3):193–202.

China Women's Development Foundation (CWDF) (2014) Summary report of the national workshop on promotion of PAC in 2014. Available from: www.cwdf.org.cn/News_tendency_info.asp?id=2363 (accessed 6 September 2014).

Darroch, J. E., G. Sedgh and H. Ball (2011) *Contraceptive Technologies: Responding to Women's Needs*. New York: Guttmacher Institute.

Gu, B. (2000) 'Reorienting China's family planning program: an experiment on quality of care since 1995'. Paper presented at the annual meetings of the Population Association of America. Los Angeles, CA. 23–25 March.

Guttmacher Institute (2009) *In Brief: Abortion in Pakistan*. New York: Guttmacher Institute, No. 2.

Guttmacher Institute (2010) *Facts on Investing in Family Planning and Maternal and Newborn Health* – updated November 2010 using new maternal and neonatal mortality data. New York: Guttmacher Institute.

Guttmacher Institute (2012a) *Adding It Up: Costs and Benefits of Contraceptive Services – Estimates for 2012*. New York: Guttmacher Institute, June 2012.

Guttmacher Institute (2012b) *In Brief – Facts on Abortion in Asia*. New York: Guttmacher Institute, January 2012.

Guttmacher Institute (2012c) *Making Abortion Services Accessible in the Wake of Legal Reforms*. New York: Guttmacher Institute, April 2012.

Guttmacher Institute (2013) *Fact Sheet – Unintended Pregnancy and Unsafe Abortion in the Philippines*. New York: Guttmacher Institute, July 2013.

Harkavy, O. and K. Roy (2007) 'Emergence of the Indian National Family Planning Program'. In W. C. Robinson and J. A. Ross (eds.) *The Global Family Planning Revolution: Three Decades of Population Policies and Programs*. Washington, DC: The World Bank. Pp. 301–323.

Hull, T. H. and H. Mosley (2009) *Revitalization of Family Planning in Indonesia*. The Government of Indonesia and United Nations Population Fund.

INPAC Consortium (2013) *Report on Situation Analysis*. Deliverable 3.1. European Commission FP7 INPAC project 'Integrating Post-Abortion Family Planning Services into China's Existing Abortion Services in Hospital Settings'.

International Planned Parenthood Research (IPPF) (2008) *Access to Safe Abortion: A Tool for Assessing Legal and Other Obstacles*. London: International Planned Parenthood Research, June.

Ipas (2010) *Expanded Safe Abortion Services Making Difference in Cambodia.* www.ipas.org/en/News/2010/September/Expanded-safe- abortion-services-making- difference -in-Cambodia.aspx (accessed 15 August 2013).

Ipas (2011) *Ipas Launches Country Program in Bangladesh.* www.ipas.org/en/News/2011/August/Ipas-launches-country- program- in-Bangladesh.Aspx (accessed 19 August 2013).

Japan International Cooperation Agency (JICA) Research Institute (2005) Chapter 4: Family Planning. In *Japan's Experiences in Public Health and Medical Systems.* Tokyo: JICA.

Karki,Y. B. and K. Regmi (2007) 'Document of post-abortion care program process in Nepal'. *Nepal Family Health Program.* Sanepa Lalipur, 14 April 2007.

Marston, C. and J. Cleland (2003) 'Relationships between contraception and abortion: a review of the evidence'. *International Family Planning Perspectives,* 29(1): 6–13.

Office of Population Research at Princeton University. Emergency Contraception: Emergency Contraceptives Pills Worldwide. http://ec.princeton.edu/questions/dedicated.html (accessed 14 January 2016).

Robinson, W. C. and J. A. Ross (eds.) (2007) *The Global Family Planning Revolution: Three Decades of Population Policies and Programs.*Washington, DC: The World Bank.

Sedgh G., S. Singh, I. H. Shah, E. Ahman, S. K. Henshaw and A. Bankole (2012) 'Induced abortion: incidence and trends worldwide from 1995 to 2008'. *Lancet,* 379 (9816): 625–632. Available from: http://dx.doi.org/10.1016/S0140-6736(11)61786-8.

Seiber, E. E., J.T. Bertrand and T. M. Sullivan (2007) 'Changes in contraceptive method mix in developing countries'. *International Family Planning Perspectives,* 33(3): 117–123.

Shah, I. and E. Ahman (2010) 'Unsafe abortion in 2008: global and regional levels and trends'. *Reproductive Health Matters,* 18(36): 90–101. Available from: http://dx.doi.org/10.1016/S0968-8080(10)36537-2.

Taylor, H. C. (1976) *Human Reproduction: Physiology, Population and Family Planning.* Cambridge, Mass: MIT Press.

Uchida,Y. (1981) 'Male acceptance of condoms in Japan'. *Concern (Anaheim),* 20: 3–5.

United Nations (2001) *Abortion Policies: A Global Review.* Department of Economic and Social Development. New York: United Nations.

United Nations (2011a) *World Contraceptive Use 2011.* Department of Economic and Social Affairs, Population Division. New York: United Nations.

United Nations (2011b) *World Fertility Policies 2011.* Department of Economic and Social Affairs, Population Division. Available from: www.unpopulation.org (accessed 8 January 2013).

United Nations (2012) *World Contraceptive Use 2012.* Department of Economic and Social Affairs, Population Division (POP/DB/CP/Rev2012). New York: United Nations.

United Nations (2013a) *Model-Based Estimates and Projections of Family Planning Indicators: 2013 Revision.* Department of Economic and Social Affairs, Population Division. New York: United Nations.

United Nations (2013b) *World Population Prospects: The 2012 Revision,* DVD Edition. Department of Economic and Social Affairs, Population Division. New York: United Nations.

Winckler, E. A. (2002) 'Chinese reproductive policy at the turn of the Millennium: dynamic stability'. *Population and Development Review,* 28(3): 379–418.

World Health Organization (WHO) (1992) *The Prevention and Management of Unsafe Abortion.* Report of a technical working group. Geneva: World Health Organization (WHO/MSM/92.5).

World Health Organization (WHO), Department of Reproductive Health and Research (2004) *Selected Practice Recommendations for Contraceptive Use,* Second Edition. Geneva: World Health Organization.

World Health Organization (WHO) and Johns Hopkins Bloomberg School of Public Health/Center for Communication Programs (JHU–CCP) (2011a) 'Emergency contraceptive pills'. In *Family Planning: A Global Handbook for Providers.* Geneva: World Health Organization.

World Health Organization (WHO) (2011b) *Unsafe Abortion: Global and Regional Estimates of the Incidence of Unsafe Abortion and Associated Mortality in 2008,* Sixth Edition. Geneva: World Health Organization.

World Health Organization (WHO) (2012) *Safe Abortion: Technical and Policy Guidance for Health Systems.* Geneva: World Health Organization.

World Health Organization (WHO) (2013) *Family Planning Fact Sheet N 351,* updated May 2013. Geneva: World Health Organization.

8
Reproductive health and maternal mortality

Terence H. Hull and Meimanat Hosseini-Chavoshi

Introduction

Of the three pillars of demography – fertility, mortality and migration – fertility encompasses some of the most complex and sensitive behavioural issues for social research. Much of the literature on fertility focuses on family planning, contraception, abortion and marriage, each covered by other chapters in this volume. What these topics do not cover is what might be broadly called sexual and reproductive health. This chapter looks into the complex notion that the lifelong health of sexual organs and childbearing behaviour is important because of the way it touches on every individual life either directly or as a matter of risk. As Ruth Dixon-Mueller (1993) argues, a sexual and reproductive health perspective is not only a matter of biology, it is a central issue of human rights. This is a fact recognized by the United Nations in the various formulations of the Millennium Development Goals (MDGs) and the recently adopted Sustainable Development Goals (SDGs) but never fully formulated to go beyond the central goal of eliminating maternal mortality and to recognize the need for a rational, non-moralistic approach to the management of sexually transmitted infections and cancers of the reproductive organs. Sexual and reproductive health and rights are regarded by many governments as sensitive issues, too difficult to meld into educational, health or social welfare programmes. As such, much of the data reviewed here are underfunded and of questionable validity and reliability. Government hesitance should not undermine the need for careful consideration of important dimensions of human welfare, so we will attempt to draw valid meaning out of the questionable data on reproductive health.

Maternal mortality as the central indicator of reproductive health

Few deaths cause as much social or individual angst as the loss of a woman in the act of giving birth. Motherhood is revered across the globe, and is a key defining element of feminine gender roles. Death in childbirth is embedded in myth and history across Asia. Maya of Sakya, the birth mother of Gautama Buddha, the sage-founder of the Buddhist religion, died within seven days of giving birth to him. The stories written into the religious texts tell of her spiritual interventions to help her son. The Taj Mahal, one of the architectural wonders of the world, was built by Shah Jahan in remembrance of his favourite wife, Mumtaz Mahal (née Arjumand Banu) who died in 1631 giving birth to the fourteenth child produced during their nineteen-year marriage. Only seven of her children survived infancy. The grief embodied in the Taj Mahal has today become a monument to love and loss. Less than four decades later in 1674 Chinese Empress Xiaochengren died at the age of 20, shortly after giving birth to her second child. Late in the nineteenth century, Javanese Raden Ajeng Kartini obeyed the practices of her culture and her father to become the wife of a high ranking official who was attracted to her because of her success in establishing a school. He wanted her to care for the offspring left by his first wife who had died in childbirth. Although she was in poor health throughout her short marriage (less than one year), Kartini cared for the children, and maintained a prolific correspondence with friends across the globe. Her pregnancy left her weak, and when she died a few days after the birth of a son her parents and husband tried unsuccessfully to explain the causes of her demise to the many Javanese and foreign friends who wrote to enquire. Today Kartini is lauded as a national hero for education, learning and enterprise, but few Indonesians recognize that she was also a martyr to motherhood, all before the age of 25. These four women are only the tip of the vast numbers of Asian women who have succumbed to the risks of childbirth over the ages. The other anonymous deaths are even less understood.

Thankfully over the last century we have seen the growth of systems of care and treatment to prevent maternal death. Modern medicines to prevent or treat infections, to assist difficult deliveries and to anticipate and overcome challenges of high blood pressure are now available even in distant villages. National governments are increasingly committed to the equitable accessibility of health services, as exemplified by the world leaders' commitments to the Millennium Development Goal number 5 to prevent maternal death. For most countries of Asia, this goal was translated into a promise to cut the indicator of the maternal mortality ratio (MMR) by three-quarters between 1990 and 2015. In this chapter their efforts will be reviewed, and an assessment will be made to determine the trends and differences of maternal death indicators across the whole of Asia, but with particular attention to some of the most populous and rapidly changing cultural zones.

Problems of measurement

While maternal mortality is declared a major policy issue in all Asian countries, it is a demographically rare event, and is thus very difficult to measure or monitor in any setting, but particularly in poor, less-developed countries. Major efforts to improve estimates have been made by both United Nations agencies (WHO 2010, 2012a, 2014a) and autonomous groups such as the Institute for Health Metrics and Evaluation (GBD 2015 Maternal Mortality Collaborators 2016) at the University of Washington. Recognizing the difficulties of directly recording and reporting deaths when systems of governance are either weak or disorganized, recent efforts have concentrated on the use of statistical techniques to convert underlying data that are presumed to be accurate into more robust indirect estimates of maternal mortality ratios or rates. While not perfect, these approaches have been successful in providing programmes of advocacy with information to raise public awareness and foster legislative support for health interventions.

National and regional maternal mortality data compilations for all 48 countries and five regions of Asia are available from the WHO (2015) and are set out in Table 8.1. The numbers given in Table 8.1 are point estimates and are the most common measures used in government discussions of mortality levels and trends. The four time points in the table, 1990, 2000, 2010 and 2015 cover the reference period of the targets for the Millennium Development Goals, set at the turn of the century by world leaders. The MDG global target for maternal mortality was to reduce MMR in each nation and region by at least 75 per cent between

Table 8.1 Trends in WHO estimates of maternal mortality ratio (MMR, maternal deaths per 100,000 live births), in Asia by region and country, 1990–2015

Region / Country	MMR 1990	2000	2010	2015	% change between 1990 and 2015
Asia	341	259	154	123	−64.0
Central Asia	69	50	37	33	−52.0
Kazakhstan	78	65	20	12	−84.6
Kyrgyzstan	80	74	84	76	−5.0
Tajikistan	107	68	35	32	−70.1
Turkmenistan	82	59	46	42	−48.8
Uzbekistan	54	34	39	36	−33.3
Western Asia	160	122	96	91	−43.0
Armenia	58	40	33	25	−56.9
Azerbaijan	64	48	27	25	−60.9
Bahrain	26	21	16	15	−42.3
Cyprus	16	15	8	7	−56.3
Georgia	34	37	40	36	−5.9
Iraq	107	63	51	50	−53.3
Israel	11	8	6	5	−54.5
Jordan	110	77	59	58	−47.3
Kuwait	7	7	5	4	−42.9
Lebanon	74	42	19	15	−79.7
Oman	30	20	18	17	−43.2
State of Palestine	118	72	54	45	−61.9
Qatar	29	24	16	13	−55.2
Saudi Arabia	46	23	14	12	−73.9
Syria	123	73	49	68	−44.7
Turkey	97	79	23	16	−83.5
UAE	17	8	6	6	−64.7
Yemen	547	440	416	385	−29.6
Southern Asia (excluding India)	495	384	235	180	−64.0
Afghanistan	1,340	1,100	584	396	−70.4
Bangladesh	569	399	242	176	−69.1
Bhutan	945	423	204	148	−84.3
India	556	374	215	174	−68.7
Iran	123	51	27	25	−79.7
Maldives	677	163	87	68	−90.0
Nepal	901	548	349	258	−71.4
Pakistan	431	306	211	178	−58.7
Sri Lanka	75	57	35	30	−60.0
South-Eastern Asia	320	201	136	110	−66.0
Brunei	35	31	27	23	−34.3
Cambodia	1,020	484	202	161	−84.2
Indonesia	446	265	165	126	−71.7
Laos	905	546	294	197	−78.2
Malaysia	79	58	48	40	−49.4

(continued)

Table 8.1 (Cont.)

Region Country	MMR 1990	2000	2010	2015	% change between 1990 and 2015
Myanmar	453	308	205	178	−60.7
Philippines	152	124	129	114	−25.0
Singapore	12	18	11	10	−16.7
Thailand	40	25	23	20	−50.0
Timor-Leste	1,080	694	317	215	−80.1
Vietnam	139	81	58	54	−61.2
Eastern Asia (excluding China)	51	68	52	43	−16.0
China	97	58	35	27	−72.2
Japan	14	10	6	5	−64.3
Mongolia	186	161	63	44	−76.3
North Korea	75	128	97	82	−9.3
South Korea	21	16	15	11	−47.6

Note: Estimates have been computed to ensure comparability across countries, thus they are not the same as official statistics of the countries, which may use alternative data sources and methods of estimation.
Source: WHO (2015).

1990 and 2015. Table 8.1 shows that such reductions were seldom met across the countries of Asia, although some nations appeared to do remarkably well (Kazakhstan, Tajikistan, Lebanon, Turkey, Bhutan, Iran, Maldives, Nepal, Cambodia, Indonesia, Laos, Timor-Leste, China and Mongolia), while a few hardly moved the indicator at all (Kyrgyzstan, Georgia and North Korea).

The higher MMR was in 1990, the greater was the potential for large reductions, in part because of the so-called soft-rock versus hard-rock concept of difficulties faced in mortality reductions. It is argued that it should be easier for governments to reduce very high mortality causes of death with simple, inexpensive medical interventions and preventive measures. The spread of skilled birth attendants, the accessibility of antibiotics and other medications, and the assurance of good nutrition in pregnancy can quickly reduce MMR from over 1,000 per 100,000 births to less than 200, as was seen in the cases of Cambodia and Timor-Leste. In both those nations the cessation of civil hostilities fostered major social improvements. Similarly, Afghanistan's MMR fell from over 1,300 to under 400, but ongoing social violence continues to inhibit greater medical improvements. Researchers refer to these changes as drilling into the soft rock, but for the governments and communities, such a metaphor underestimates the severity of their challenges. Even simple interventions are costly when required to reach across difficult terrain to serve poor villagers.

Success in negotiating the 'soft rock' brings governments to the remaining causes of death at lower levels of MMR, the hard rock requiring higher levels of organization and more complex technologies. By 2015 most Asian nations, and the majority of the Asian population, were facing increasing challenges of hard rock. There are still some important countries with MMR over 100 including Yemen, Afghanistan, Bhutan, Cambodia, Indonesia, India, Laos, Myanmar, Timor-Leste, Nepal, Pakistan, Bangladesh and the Philippines. Conflicts and poverty conspire to prevent access to reproductive health services among their poorer citizens so the MMR remains stubbornly high. The bulk of the population across the Asian continent today struggles with the hard rock issues requiring access to medications, technologies and complex skills that are both expensive and difficult to organize.

At the lowest levels of MMR, countries face ever more expensive and complex medical interventions to address rare and difficult genetic, chronic or congenital conditions. By 1990 Israel, Kuwait, Singapore and Japan had already reached levels of MMR that were regarded as low by international standards. In the first two countries, relatively small population sizes meant that a difference of even one or two maternal deaths could change the MMR significantly so practices of recording and reporting deaths as pregnancy- or delivery-related could have an impact on the MMR. Japan, though more populous, had very low fertility, and very highly developed medical systems so even at the 'hard-rock' of MMR of 14 deaths per 100,000 births in 1990, it was possible to drill further down to MMRs well below ten in the twenty-first century. At this stage it is unlikely that there will be much more improvement because some deaths, though preventable in theory, may not be prevented in the context of rare and unexpected conditions.

The statistical vagaries of civil registration and population sizes mean that the calculation of MMR at the regional, national and local level are subject to considerable standard errors, as measured through confidence intervals. There is a great contrast between Eastern and Southern Asia both in terms of the level and reliability of MMR estimates. Essentially the MMR figures are indicators of many social, cultural and economic differences. Inequality, gender inequity and contrasting adequacy of health services explain some of the gaps, but not all. History has heavy hands in each region, whether in terms of persistent caste village structures across South Asia or the deep institutions of patriarchy that disadvantage women in many societies. By contrast the revolutionary socialist investments in universal health services in Central and Eastern Asia ensured survival of poor women through simple effective interventions, pushing down maternal mortality rates.

Table 8.1 sets alarm bells ringing concerning India and the surrounding South Asian countries which have high average MMR levels. It makes sense that high mortality levels prevail in countries where systems of research and measurement are weak, but this also leads us to have a lack of confidence in estimates. Sinic countries of Eastern Asia in contrast, tend to have lower MMR while South-Eastern and Western Asia sit somewhere in between. The ex-Soviet countries of the Caucasus and Central Asia are all below MMR of 50 except Kyrgyzstan, a notable laggard. We are more confident about lower MMRs, but not overly confident in countries like Indonesia, Cambodia and Laos where birthing services are still poorly developed, particularly in rural areas.

The levels and trends of measured MMR represent both a statistical conundrum and an epidemiological challenge. The indirect methods we rely on to estimate the national maternal death rates for most of the poorer countries of Asia utilize statistical regressions that may be unreliable. Regressions are equations that link reliable national data on MMR (usually from developed countries) with a number of social or economic variables to calculate parameters to predict MMR in countries with poor MMR data. So long as countries with no or unreliable civil registration of maternal deaths can produce good quality social or economic estimates from survey or census data those variables can be used as regression parameters. Information on women's age, education, fertility levels and access to skilled birth attendants are commonly used to generate estimates of MMR. These results are very attractive to international agencies wanting to generate comprehensive league tables of all countries rather than patchy lists limited to the few countries with good maternal death monitoring systems. The regressions possess the strength of a standard methodology but the weakness of potential inconsistency among meanings and reliability of the co-variate measures. While this conundrum may be of concern to the statisticians, for epidemiologists it focuses attention on the nature of the covariates, and particularly the link between a variable like proportion of births attended by a skilled birth attendant and the likelihood that a relatively simple cause of death will be prevented. There is strong logic behind the idea that midwives or doctors with modern medical training will save the lives of many women who might previously have died from eclampsia, bleeding or obstructed labour.

It would be a mistake, however, to assume that reproductive health personnel and services are homogeneous in the level of their skills across Asia, as seems to be implied in the parameters used in the regression methods of estimation of mortality levels. It is important to examine two key indicators of health, the proportion of births attended by a skilled attendant, and the proportion of births delivered through surgical interventions involving caesarean section. These are the issues to which we now turn.

Rise in skilled birth attendance

While it may seem like common sense to assume that women in childbirth will benefit from the skills of modern medically trained personnel, the realities they face are far more nuanced than the simple notion of calling a midwife or doctor. There are many questions swirling around the terms 'skill', 'trained', and 'personnel' and these are hidden in common survey questions showing international differences in access to birth attendants.

Table 8.2 shows that over half the countries of Asia report universal access to skilled birthing assistance for their populations, particularly in the regions of Central, Western and Eastern Asia. However, the surveys and health system records that report the nature of birthing practices in different countries can vary enormously. Without greater standardization and validation of the levels of skill attained by the doctors and midwives helping women in the community or in formal health facilities there is little point in calling all such attendants 'skilled'. The Indonesian midwife with less than a year's training cannot be assumed to have the skills of a nurse-midwife of four year's training in Japan, much less a person who is required to have university education followed by graduate level midwifery before being certified to practice. Thus, while it is encouraging to see so many births in Table 8.2 assisted by people said to be skilled, interpretation of the national differences needs to be tempered. Certainly Yemen, Nepal, Afghanistan, Timor-Leste, Laos and other countries with less than universal skilled birth assistance are likely to have high risks facing their women in motherhood. At the same time, the persistent high MMRs in Western and Southern Asian countries pose questions about the capabilities of personnel charged with handling the complex challenges of prenatal, postnatal and delivery care.

While there is no doubt that well-trained and fully-resourced health personnel will save maternal and infant lives, the data in Table 8.2 do not inspire confidence. The table relies on two of the most important international databases available on skilled birth attendants. The first is the United Nations official database for indicators of the Millennium Development Goals that gathered baseline data around 1990 at the outset of the MDGs. The second is the UNICEF database for *Monitoring the Situation of Children and Women 2017* that provides the most recent comprehensive statement on proportions of births delivered by a skilled attendant. Many countries have blank entries, and some countries like the State of Palestine and Israel are either missing from the database, or show no data. United Nations agencies often face difficulties obtaining valid and reliable data from smaller, poorer countries due to the lack of funding for national data collection. Even richer countries may ignore requests for data, preferring to concentrate on their national needs instead of participation in international efforts to monitor maternal and infant welfare.

Table 8.2 Trends and differences in estimates of percentage of deliveries attended by 'skilled' personnel in Asia

Region / Country	Per cent of births with skilled attendant			
	First year	Per cent	Recent year	Per cent
World	1990	61.0	2015	75.0
Central Asia				
Kazakhstan	1990	99.0	2012	99.9
Kyrgyzstan	1990	98.9	2014	98.4
Tajikistan	1991	90.3	2012	87.4
Turkmenistan	–	–	2006	99.5
Uzbekistan	–	–	2006	99.9
Western Asia				
Armenia	1990	99.7	2010	99.5
Azerbaijan	1990	97.3	2012	97.2
Bahrain	–	–	2013	99.8
Cyprus	–	–	–	–
Georgia	1990	96.6	2014	99.9
Iraq	–	–	2011	90.9
Israel	n.a.	n.a.	–	–
Jordan	1990	87.2	2012	99.6
Kuwait	–	–	2007	100.0
Lebanon	–	–	2004	98.2
Oman	–	–	2014	99.1
State of Palestine	–	–	2014	99.6
Qatar	1998	–	2012	100.0
Saudi Arabia	–	–	2012	98.0
Syria	–	–	2009	96.2
Turkey	1993	75.9	2013	97.4
United Arab Emirates	–	–	2010	100.0
Yemen	1992	15.9*	2013	44.7
Southern Asia				
Afghanistan	–	–	2014	45.2
Bangladesh	1994	9.5	2014	42.1
Bhutan	–	–	2012	74.6
India	1993	34.2	2008	52.3
Iran	–	–	2010	96.4
Maldives	1994	90.0	2012	95.5
Nepal	1991	7.4	2014	55.6
Pakistan	1991	18.8	2013	52.1
Sri Lanka	1993	94.1	2007	98.6
South–Eastern Asia				
Brunei	1994	98.0	2013	99.7
Cambodia	–	–	2014	89.0
Indonesia	1991	31.7	2013	87.4
Laos	–	–	2012	41.5
Malaysia	1990	92.8	2014	99.0
Myanmar	1991	46.3	2010	70.6

(continued)

Table 8.2 (Cont.)

Region	Per cent of births with skilled attendant			
Country	First year	Per cent	Recent year	Per cent
Philippines	1993	52.8	2013	72.8
Singapore	–	–	–	–
Thailand	–	–	2012	99.6
Timor-Leste	–	–	2010	29.3
Vietnam	–	–	2014	93.8
Eastern Asia				
China	1990	94.0	2014	99.9
Japan	1990	100.0	–	–
Mongolia	–	–	2014	98.9
North Korea	–	–	2009	100.0
South Korea	1990	98.0	–	–

Note: '–' indicates no data in the database; '*' indicates questionable validity; 'n.a.' indicates information not available.
Sources: First year estimate from MDG Indicators (2017). Latest year estimate from UNICEF (2017).

More concerning is the meaning of the term 'skilled birth attendant' when used as a parameter for estimating MMR indirectly. Depending on the country and data source, the skill could refer to a highly trained specialist medical practitioner, or a minimally trained midwife placed in remote settings with little by way of technical back-up. Even assuming an increase in the training of personnel in recent years, it is not sensible to assume that quality reaches common standards across the steppes, deserts, cityscapes and scattered islands of the continent. Variation in quality necessarily implies variation in birthing outcomes.

This is not to begrudge the value of the data in Table 8.2 in pointing out problem areas in Asia. Even though more than half the countries have over 95 per cent of births attended by a skilled person of some sort, there are still many countries and large numbers of women lacking skilled assistance. India stands out with barely half of births being delivered by trained medical personnel. Western Asia overall has good institutional coverage of trained attendants, Southern Asia lags behind, and South-Eastern Asia ranges from the very low rate of 29.3 per cent in Timor-Leste, to the remarkable levels of 99 per cent in Thailand, Malaysia and Brunei. The national comparisons between 1990 and 2015 show some remarkable, and some very slow improvements, but there is no sign of regress anywhere. The important goal for all countries is to raise the quality of care while ensuring that all women giving birth have access to the best care appropriate for their condition.

The rise in caesarean deliveries

Caesarean section is one of the most common obstetric operations performed, with rates continuing to rise, particularly in Latin America and Asia. While the operation is intended to protect mother and baby when the birth is obstructed, caesarean section itself is not without health risks. The rate of caesareans should not exceed 10 to 15 per cent of deliveries and research indicates no improvement in mortality when the rate goes beyond 15 per cent. Beyond that rate, risks of complications following surgery may even increase.

Table 8.3 gives estimates of caesarean section rates for 48 Asian countries during the period 1990–2014, showing the rates increasing in all cases. The rates have reached especially high levels in Iran (47.6 per cent of all births in 2009), Turkey (47.5 per cent in 2011), Maldives (41.1 per cent in 2011), China (36.2 per cent in 2011), Georgia (36.7 in 2012) and South Korea

Table 8.3 Trends in estimates of caesarean section deliveries in Asia

Region	Caesarean section as per cent of all births				Ratio of estimates from most recent to first year
Country	First year	Rate	Recent year	Rate	
World	1990	6.7	2014	18.6	2.8
Asia	1990	4.4	2014	19.5	4.4
Central Asia	–	–	–	–	–
Kazakhstan	1990	4.6	2012	15.2	3.3
Kyrgyzstan	1990	3.1	2014	7.4	2.4
Tajikistan	1990	1.9	2012	4.6	2.4
Turkmenistan	1991	3.0	2012	6.6	2.2
Uzbekistan	1995	1.9	2012	10.5	5.5
Western Asia	–	–	2014	26.8	–
Armenia	1990	3.4	2012	22.5	6.6
Azerbaijan	1990	1.4	2012	16.7	11.9
Bahrain	1995	16.0	2012	26.0	1.6
Cyprus	2005	6.9	2010	11.4	1.7
Georgia	1990	3.8	2012	36.7	9.7
Iraq	–	–	2011	22.2	–
Israel	1989	9.9	2011	19.8	2.0
Jordan	1990	5.7	2012	28.0	4.9
Kuwait	–	–	–	–	–
Lebanon	1995	15.1	2004	23.2	1.5
Oman	1995	6.6	2011	17.0	2.6
State of Palestine	–	–	–	–	–
Qatar	1998	15.9	2012	19.5	1.2
Saudi Arabia	1996	8.1	2012	22.3	2.8
Syria	–	–	–	–	–
Turkey	1993	8.0	2011	47.5	5.9
United Arab Emirates	1995	15.8	2013	23.9	1.5
Yemen	1997	1.4	2013	4.8	3.4
Southern Asia	1990	4.0	2014	11.4	2.9
Afghanistan	–	–	2011	3.6	–
Bangladesh	1999	2.4	2013	19.1	8.0
Bhutan	–	–	2010	12.4	–
India	1992	2.5	2008	8.2	3.3
Iran	2000	35.0	2009	47.9	1.4
Maldives	–	–	2011	41.1	–
Nepal	1996	1.0	2011	4.6	4.6
Pakistan	1991	2.7	2012	14.1	5.2
Sri Lanka	2003	20.0	2012	30.5	1.5
South–Eastern Asia	1990	4.1	2014	14.8	3.6
Brunei	–	–	–	–	–
Cambodia	2000	0.8	2010	3.0	3.8
Indonesia	1991	1.3	2012	12.3	9.5

(continued)

Table 8.3 (Cont.)

Region	Caesarean section as per cent of all births				Ratio of estimates from most recent to first year
Country	First year	Rate	Recent year	Rate	
Laos	–	–	2012	3.7	–
Malaysia	–	–	2006	15.7	–
Myanmar	–	–	–	–	–
Philippines	1993	5.9	2014	9.3	1.6
Singapore	1968	20.0	2003	31.0	1.6
Thailand	1990	15.2	2012	32.0	2.1
Timor–Leste	–	–	2009	1.7	–
Vietnam	1997	3.4	2014	27.5	8.0
Eastern Asia	–	–	2014	34.8	–
China	1990	4.4	2011	36.2	8.2
Japan	1990	10.0	2011	19.2	1.9
Mongolia	1998	5.1	2013	23.4	4.6
North Korea	–	–	2009	12.5	–
South Korea	1991	17.3	2009	36.6	2.1

Sources: Most of Asia: Betrán et al. (2016); Singapore: Ganesan (2004: 2).

(36.6 per cent in 2009). There is a likely association between the rate of caesareans and the rate of birth attendance by trained health personnel. Where the proportion of births attended by health personnel is low, the chance of caesarean section is also very low, and indeed the maternal mortality rate is higher in those cases. For example, the Betrán Report shows a caesarean section rate of below 5 per cent for Yemen, Tajikistan, Timor-Leste, Cambodia, Laos, Afghanistan and Nepal. Less than 50 per cent of births in these places were attended by health personnel. However, it is not only a matter of skilled health personnel but more importantly the availability of specialist gynaecologists that determines the potential for caesareans, particularly in nations with large portions of the medical profession engaged in private practice.

Regarding China, in August 2014 the media website *Asian Scientist* posed the question of whether a caesarean rate of 50 per cent for China was dangerously high. Indeed, China's health system has the highest national number of caesareans in the world – an estimated 8 million C-section deliveries in 2010. According to official estimates, the rate of caesarean section rose from 3.4 per cent in 1988 to 39.3 per cent in 2008. While the increase has occurred across all regions, a substantial increase has occurred among urban women (64 per cent). One of the factors pushing up the caesarean rate was the national One Child Policy that aimed at one perfect delivery per woman over the three and a half decades of the restrictive government intervention. Mothers and doctors pressed for medical technologies to guarantee safe and easy deliveries and despite the lack of scientific evidence caesareans seemed to promise efficiency. In fact, the perception that caesarean delivery improves infant and maternal safety is one factor which has increased the rate of caesarean section globally, reaching epidemic proportions in most middle-income countries.

As part of the *2004–2008 WHO Global Survey on Maternal and Perinatal Health*, Souza and colleagues (2010), looking at nine Asian countries, analysed caesarean procedures in terms of decision-making before delivery (antepartum) and at the time of delivery (intrapartum) (see Table 8.4). China is exceptional in terms of the proportion of antepartum caesareans performed

Table 8.4 Distribution of deliveries by mode of delivery for selected Asian countries derived from a survey conducted in 2007–2008

Country	Vaginal delivery			Caesarean section				All
	Spontaneous	Operative	Overall	Without indications		With indications		
				Antepartum	Intrapartum	Antepartum	Intrapartum	
Cambodia	77.6	7.7	85.3	0.0	0.2	2.6	11.8	14.7
China	52.6	1.2	53.8	9.3	2.4	19.6	14.9	46.2
India	79.3	2.9	82.2	0.1	0.2	3.6	13.9	17.8
Japan	74.1	6.1	80.2	0.1	0.0	13.9	5.9	19.8
Nepal	75.9	3.8	79.7	0.0	0.1	6.2	14.0	20.3
Philippines	78.4	2.8	81.2	0.0	0.1	8.0	10.6	18.8
Sri Lanka	65.9	3.5	69.4	0.6	0.2	20.1	9.8	30.6
Thailand	61.6	4.3	65.9	0.3	0.2	13.4	20.1	34.1
Vietnam	62.2	2.2	64.4	0.2	0.8	4.3	30.2	35.6
Total	69.5	3.2	72.7	1.4	0.5	10.1	15.3	27.3

Source: Souza et al. (2010).

without and with medical indications (28.9 per cent of all births). Hellerstein et al. (2015) speculate that the causes of such high rates are related to both the very low fertility rates making the procedures unusually safe, and the system of payment of medical personnel offering strong incentives for surgical interventions. If fertility rises, and publicity about inordinately high C-section rates changes women's preferences for delivery, the authors anticipate the rates could fall. Sri Lanka, Japan and Thailand also stand out for antepartum caesareans based on anticipated problems with the birth, and it is possible that medical remuneration systems may have an influence on such judgements. The high level of decisions by health professionals to perform caesarean sections at the time of delivery in response to medical indications (30 per cent in Vietnam, 20 per cent in Thailand) far exceeds the WHO recommended standard of 10–15 per cent. Among Asian countries, Japan can boast universal delivery by trained birth attendants, and caesareans are conducted solely in response to medical indications. Almost one-fifth of deliveries are through caesarean section, of which 14 per cent are antepartum due to medical indications, and 6 per cent are performed in response to medical indications at the time of delivery.

A recent study by Neuman et al. (2014) shows that in Bangladesh women's education level is associated with higher rates of caesarean, while in urban India economic capacity to utilize private facilities has a direct association with caesareans. In Bangladesh, there is a higher probability of caesarean being performed in private health facilities compared with public hospitals and caesarean is common in the absence of serious medical indications either antepartum or intrapartum. Across South Asia it appears that caesareans are being performed for reasons other than medical need. The authors concluded that while the rate of intervention in Bangladesh and in India is below the ideal rate of 10–15 per cent, the private sector is a driving force behind the higher rates of caesarean section for non-medical purposes.

Countries in Central Asia are exceptional; Kyrgyzstan, Tajikistan, Turkmenistan and Uzbekistan show almost universal rates of attendance by trained personnel but low rates of caesarean – below 10 per cent. Caesarean sections are confined to extreme medical situations.

WHO has introduced a 'secure delivery' programme aimed at reducing the high rate of caesarean section in some countries in Asia (including Iran). The programme educates pregnant women about ways to lower their risk of medical problems and the safety of natural delivery. This programme includes provision of psychological health education, addressing the fears that many young women have concerning natural delivery. It seems clear that many nations of Asia need to adopt such programmes to prevent inappropriate medical interventions at the same time they work to expand high quality medical services for all their citizens.

Burdens of reproductive disease

The adjective 'reproductive' may direct attention to childbearing, as suggested by the policy concentration on maternal mortality and conditions of delivery discussed above, but it should also suggest consideration of key issues of health and well-being associated with female and male reproductive organs. Genitals and associated glands and tissues are susceptible to a number of serious ailments, irrespective of individual experience of pregnancy or childbirth. Those risks can rightly be regarded as universal challenges. Medical literature consolidates a wide range of congenital, infectious and acquired conditions and dysfunctions affecting individuals, most of which are either rare or benign in their impact. Across the nations of Asia, the two main reproductive organ problems affecting large numbers of people in the community are sexually transmitted infections and cancers.

Reproductive health and maternal mortality

Sexually transmitted infections

While the deaths of women in childbirth and cancers are the most dramatic and socially affecting dimensions of individual reproductive health, infections and chronic diseases of the reproductive system pose risks that threaten the well-being of the whole community over the life-cycle. Fungal, bacterial and viral infections are widespread, but in most countries of Asia they are not routinely the subject of effective epidemiological monitoring or mass public health campaigns. The exceptions are sexually transmitted diseases that attract community concern due to both the seriousness of sequelae and association with problematic moral issues. The most notable of these are gonorrhoea, chlamydia and syphilis, all of which affect both women and men and are spread largely through sexual contact.

Many countries withhold data on sexually sensitive health issues, so it is very difficult to generate comparable indicators on STIs by small regions or nations. Instead, the World Health Organization draws on their regional staff to obtain best estimates of infections based on surveys, research projects and health facility reports and compiles these in large regions to give rough comparisons across the globe. Asia straddles three WHO regions. The Eastern Mediterranean region includes most Arab countries, Iran, Pakistan and Israel, but also extends across many Muslim countries of North Africa. The South-East Asian region links India, Nepal, Sri Lanka, Bangladesh, Myanmar, Thailand, Indonesia and Brunei. The Western Pacific has China, Japan, South Korea, Vietnam and Cambodia, but includes Australia and Papua New Guinea. Given the impact of large Asian populations in each region it is not likely that the estimates published here will be greatly biased by the slippery borders at the edges of Asia. These groupings of nations are odd, to say the least, but they were defined at a time when local conflicts demanded divisions between enemies. Many of those divisions have been made redundant by subsequent peacemaking but the WHO has not redefined its administrative groupings to better reflect geographic or cultural patterns of relevance to health.

Table 8.5 presents data on sex differentials in the incidence and prevalence for selected STDs per 1,000 people in the population. This measure of incidence reflects an annual infection rate. In the contemporary medical world of antibiotics and effective antiviral medications the annual incidence does not show the current number of people suffering from the diseases. To determine that you would need to measure the prevalence as a number of people infected at any given time. In situations where treatment is quick, effective and sustainable the incidence could be high but the prevalence low. If treatment is ineffective the incidence could accumulate over time, and a large pool of people could carry the infection for years on end. Table 8.5 shows the contrast between the incidence and prevalence for females and males for the three serious STIs plus the more commonly contracted problem of the parasite causing Trichomonas vaginalis.

The patterns, such as they are, imply large differences from countries in the Asian west, to the east. The Western Pacific countries have higher numbers and higher rates of chlamydia and gonorrhoea than the South-East Asia and Eastern Mediterranean regions, perhaps because of the huge population and high quality health system of China which likely has better data quality. Syphilis prevalence is high in South-East Asia both in comparison with the region's incidence rate, and in contrast to the other two regions. One explanation would be a difference in the efficacy of diagnosis and treatment in India, Indonesia, Bangladesh, Thailand and Nepal where commercial sex industries are entrenched and marginalized.

Women are much more likely to have persistent prevalence of the Trichomonas protozoan pathogen than their male counterparts even though both sexes are nearly equally likely to contract the infection. This is explained in part because women are more likely to display

Table 8.5 Number (millions) and rates (per 1,000) of incidence and prevalence for selected STDs in WHO defined regions, 2008

Asia region

Selected STDs	Female Incidence N	Rate	Female Prevalence N	Rate	Male Incidence N	Rate	Male Prevalence N	Rate
Eastern Mediterranean								
Chlamydia trachomatis	1.5	9.8	1.6	11.0	1.7	10.9	1.4	9.0
Neisseria gonorrhoea	1.2	8.1	0.5	3.0	1.9	11.6	0.5	3.0
Syphilis	0.3	2.1	0.8	5.0	0.3	2.1	0.8	5.0
Trichomonas vaginalis	9.7	64.4	12.0	80.0	10.6	66.1	13.0	8.0
South-East Asia								
Chlamydia trachomatis	4.2	9.2	5.0	11.0	3.0	6.2	3.0	6.0
Neisseria gonorrhoea	7.5	16.2	3.4	8.0	18.0	37.0	5.9	12.0
Syphilis	1.5	3.2	6.1	13.0	1.5	3.1	6.3	13.0
Trichomonas vaginalis	18.5	40.3	25.7	56.0	24.3	50.1	3.0	6.0
Western Pacific Asia								
Chlamydia trachomatis	18.4	38.4	20.5	43.0	21.5	42.5	17.3	34.0
Neisseria gonorrhoea	16.8	34.9	6.9	15.0	25.3	49.9	6.3	13.0
Syphilis	0.3	0.5	0.6	1.0	0.3	0.5	0.6	1.0
Trichomonas vaginalis	21.9	45.6	27.2	57.0	23.8	47.0	2.9	6.0

Source: WHO (2014c).

discomforting symptoms, in part because the protozoa adhere to vaginal and cervical epithelial cells causing irritation. Males can carry the infection with no or very few symptoms.

The transmissions of sexual infections depend in part on the practice of any forms of sexual intercourse, either heterosexual or homosexual. Clinical advice dispensed worldwide is to use condoms to prevent skin to skin contact, and to delay the timing of sexual debut until physical and psychological maturity is attained. In the cultures of Asia there are many injunctions calling for protection against multiple partner contacts, but sometimes these are paired with teachings that condoms are dangerous or immoral. The social debates over propriety can themselves put young people at risk, and the gender disparities on sexual behaviour can frame barriers for women to have protected sex. At the same time cultures of male dominance often promote premarital and extramarital sexual relations for men, consequently putting chaste wives in danger of infections brought home to the marital bed. As mentioned above, the secrecy of sexual health issues makes it difficult for many political cultures to develop effective policies for diagnosis and treatment of STIs. The challenge is not so much the development of drugs and prophylactics as it is a matter of community awareness and open societies.

Cancers

Human beings undergo constant cell renewal over the course of their lives. Cancer occurs when new cells grow abnormally. Sometimes this means they grow into tumours which spread to other parts of the body in a process called metastasis. Often the cancer develops into a lump that does not grow or spread, in which case it is called benign. The nature of the cancer depends on the type of host cell and the potential for the tumour to spread to other organs. The reproductive systems of females and males are notable for soft tissue, often with hormonal involvement that facilitates cancerous growths. While both women and men can develop cancers of the breast and the various components of sexual organs, women tend to have both greater risk of reproductive cancers, and greater mortality from the spread of the disease. The key sites of female reproductive cancer are breast, cervix, uterus and ovary, while the key sites in males are the prostate gland and testes, both of which are involved in the production of sperm. Prostate cancer is the more common and dangerous of the two.

Statistics on cancer incidence are hard to come by in less developed countries, and even many developed countries struggle to produce valid estimates of mortality related to key reproductive cancers. Researchers have attempted to overcome these deficiencies by applying the experiences of countries with good data to adjust the estimates for data-deficient nations. Table 8.6 compiles data from the Institute for Health Metrics and Evaluation's 2015 Global Burden of Disease to give a snapshot of recent reproductive cancer mortality rate estimates for 48 countries of Asia.

Across Asia breast cancer stands out as the highest level of reproductive cancer mortality risk, followed by prostate cancer. Both are notable for the variety of manifestations and complications that can occur after initial presentation, and both have been associated with genetic, dietary and environmental conditions. The majority of breast cancers occur in women, though men can rarely develop breast cancer either as a primary or secondary site of a tumour. Overwhelmingly anatomical males have prostates and prostate cancer, though aberrations of the sex organs can produce a true prostate in a person who otherwise presents as a woman. More important is the so-called female prostate, the Skene's or paraurethral gland, which is homologous to the male prostate, having a similar structure but different function. Public health professionals stress the need for regular medical checks for lumps in the breast tissue using self-examination and mammograms to detect breast cancer. If lumps are found they can be surgically examined for active cancer cells. Prostate cancer can be identified by doctors through digital rectal exams (DRE) or prostate-specific antigen blood tests (PSA), but neither procedure is highly reliable, and in many settings therapeutic treatments are outside the financial reach of the patients and the technical capacity of local health services. Naturally, it would be expected that mortality risks for both breast and prostate cancers would vary substantially across the heterogeneous social and geographic environments in Asia, since both genetic and environmental factors are known to affect cancer incidence. Table 8.6 does show great variation in mortality, but the reliance on indirect methods of estimating mortality, and the lack of systematic studies of cancer epidemiology in most countries, undermines confidence in the comparisons of figures between nations and regions.

Roughly speaking nations with high estimates of breast cancer mortality also have high prostate cancer death rates. Unusually high rates of breast cancer deaths are seen in Myanmar, Pakistan, Afghanistan and other countries of Western Asia, and elevated prostate cancer deaths follow similar patterns. By contrast Tajikistan, Saudi Arabia, Oman and Syria have lower rates. Whether this is a function of real environmental differences, or contrasts in the identification and measurement of disease is the question we must ask, but the answers will require much more detailed local research that countries will struggle to fund and organize.

South-Eastern Asia and Western Asia have a number of remarkably high cervical cancer mortality countries, with Myanmar standing out again with levels multiple times Asian averages. The most populous countries of China, India and Indonesia indicate moderate or low levels of cervical cancer estimates by global comparison, but Cambodia, Thailand, Mongolia,

Table 8.6 Estimates of average age-standardized death rates (number of deaths per 100,000 persons) for major reproductive cancers, in Asia by region and country, 2011–2015

Region	Types of cancers				
	Female breast cancer	Cervical cancer	Uterine cancer	Ovarian cancer	Male prostate cancer
World	**14.70**	**6.81**	**2.63**	**4.56**	**14.21**
Asia[a]	**11.00**	**5.72**	**2.07**	**3.19**	**8.09**
Central Asia					
Kazakhstan	18.96	10.47	3.45	7.19	10.80
Kyrgyzstan	12.40	10.12	2.83	4.70	7.10
Tajikistan	8.54	2.68	1.70	3.50	6.92
Turkmenistan	12.82	7.86	1.32	3.42	6.66
Uzbekistan	11.13	5.50	1.43	2.01	6.17
Western Asia					
Armenia	26.73	8.79	2.79	5.97	12.84
Azerbaijan	12.58	5.16	1.98	3.53	9.64
Bahrain	17.84	1.96	1.82	4.11	10.86
Cyprus	17.49	2.37	2.24	5.37	20.12
Georgia	21.64	8.42	5.27	5.65	13.27
Iraq	26.98	3.19	3.84	3.89	9.78
Israel	24.72	3.00	2.47	6.83	13.05
Jordan	13.67	1.65	2.15	2.97	9.39
Kuwait	16.86	2.12	3.29	3.67	7.38
Lebanon	22.74	2.63	3.43	7.62	21.57
Oman	8.72	3.50	1.40	3.11	8.06
State of Palestine	16.55	1.25	3.02	2.13	9.36
Qatar	20.22	2.18	2.07	4.80	8.46
Saudi Arabia	7.59	1.23	1.17	1.98	6.42
Syria	9.33	1.50	1.55	2.09	10.87
Turkey	9.57	1.71	2.04	3.66	14.74
UAE	19.94	5.61	1.88	4.09	12.41
Yemen	18.00	5.68	4.19	3.44	10.90
Southern Asia					
Afghanistan	29.34	13.61	8.49	4.12	15.98
Bangladesh	10.23	6.37	1.49	2.24	4.83
Bhutan	9.75	6.01	1.50	2.72	5.64
India	9.83	8.23	1.83	3.21	7.42
Iran	8.61	2.14	0.94	2.16	12.22
Maldives	7.05	2.45	0.95	2.25	6.73
Nepal	9.94	8.36	1.88	2.81	5.64
Pakistan	32.40	3.83	6.67	4.72	7.74
Sri Lanka	10.13	3.18	1.56	2.86	6.84
South-Eastern Asia					
Brunei	15.49	7.72	1.78	6.08	13.74
Cambodia	16.24	11.51	3.42	4.79	13.42
Indonesia	13.71	8.92	2.77	4.75	12.32
Laos	16.72	12.33	3.61	4.68	12.48

Table 8.6 (Cont.)

Region	Types of cancers				
	Female breast cancer	Cervical cancer	Uterine cancer	Ovarian cancer	Male prostate cancer
Malaysia	15.93	5.96	1.54	5.07	8.24
Myanmar	36.31	23.32	7.28	9.63	13.87
Philippines	20.93	6.96	3.01	5.15	18.13
Singapore	16.35	3.97	2.29	5.10	8.02
Thailand	14.59	10.67	1.54	4.73	11.13
Timor-Leste	12.37	10.89	3.21	4.40	8.71
Vietnam	9.51	4.81	1.57	4.33	7.84
Eastern Asia					
China	8.45	4.61	2.01	2.21	6.74
Japan	10.90	3.07	2.03	4.14	8.59
Mongolia	8.48	12.86	2.09	3.87	5.22
North Korea	10.96	5.65	2.71	3.17	8.32
South Korea	8.11	3.36	1.13	2.90	7.92

Note: [a] Data for Asia are for the year 2015.
Source: Global Burden of Disease Study (2015).

Afghanistan and Laos are very high by comparison. While we may be justifiably cautious in accepting the exact estimates of these mortality rates, that does not mean that we should disbelieve the implication that many Asian countries are suffering from serious epidemics of reproductive mortalities requiring government interventions and targeted health service improvements.

The three central columns of Table 8.6 are of greatest importance in considering public health interventions that might reduce reproductive mortality in Asia. Cancers of the cervix, uterus and ovaries are often difficult to monitor at the population level, and they are rarer than breast or prostate cancers. At the same time there is an important new preventive vaccination measure that promises to greatly reduce the incidence of these three cancers for a fraction of the cost of identification and treatment of the malignancies.

In the last two decades cervical and uterine cancers have turned out to be susceptible to relatively inexpensive and highly effective preventive measures. The Human Papilloma Virus (HPV) has been identified as one of the most common sexually transmitted infections with around 100 variations of the virus, 40 of which are associated with both genital warts and a variety of cancer presentations. Most importantly HPV causes cervical cancer but is also implicated in vaginal, uterine and ovarian cancers. The most dangerous forms of HPV can be prevented through the mass immunization of pre-pubescent girls and boys, though guidelines imply the vaccinations can still be effective through the mid-20s since the transmission of infection depends to some extent on the conditions of sexual debut, variety of sexual behaviours, and number of sexual partners.

Bruni et al. (2016), in a comprehensive international review of mass HPV immunization, have shown that Asia in 2014 had the lowest rate of coverage of all continents. Only 1.1 per cent of 10 to 20-year-old females were vaccinated, compared with 1.2 per cent in Africa, 19 per cent in Latin America, and over 30 per cent in Europe, North America and Oceania. Even so, many cervical cancer death rates given in Table 8.6 are low compared to the world average of 6.81, especially among West and East Asian countries; but it has to be asked whether the estimates are true reflections of reality, or artefacts of measurement. In any case, the rates in all countries would pose a challenge for health systems. Should the cancer risks of future generations be accepted as inevitable, or should the pubescent vaccination of all boys and girls be guaranteed in an effort to prevent most reproductive cancers that are caused by the major dangerous strains of HPV? Health systems with high rates of coverage of infant and child vaccinations for diphtheria, pertussis and tetanus (DPT), measles, polio and other 'childhood' illnesses are certainly technologically equipped to mount routine programmes in schools for pre-teen students, and in communities for other children who have dropped out of school at young ages. It is important to reach both boys and girls before they have begun to engage in sexual behaviours that expose them to the transmission of the virus. Since the vast majority of Asian children are now attending school to at least the junior high school level, a vaccination programme for HPV integrated with school health lessons between the ages of 10 and 14 would be effective. Recently a WHO group urged consideration of an even earlier introduction: 'If a two-dose schedule could be used or vaccination could be given at an earlier age when other vaccines are given (e.g. school-entry or even infancy), vaccine delivery could be greatly facilitated, and evaluation of these options is urgently required' (Cutts et al. 2007: 723).

A world without HPV requires health systems with efficient organization of this simple intervention. Unfortunately, in some countries economic cost-benefit analyses sometimes produce results claiming that premature cancer deaths are so far in the future that their prevention does not benefit the nation as much as saving the immediate costs of immunization of entire cohorts of children. This is an artefact of cost-benefit logic. Rare events decades in the future appear inexpensive, but if they are not as rare as assumed, and not as inexpensive as presumed, the balance would be different. Certainly parents would likely prefer their children to be immunized against HPV irrespective of the epidemiological rarity of the risk or the problematic excuse of a high cost-benefit ratio.

Conclusion

The vast continent of Asia is a mosaic of nations, and the largest nations of China, India, Pakistan, Indonesia, the Philippines and Vietnam are themselves mosaics of districts encompassing hundreds of socio-ethnic groups, each reflecting different reproductive cultures. In this chapter, using a broad brush and a limited number of indicators, we have seen how the sexual health and childbearing lives of women have been improving, though the health care conditions are still far from adequate for most Asian people. The numbers of trained birth attendants are growing, but the quality of training needs vast improvements to catch up to the levels of survival found in developed nations of the West. Medicalization of birth delivery is a double-edged sword, saving many lives, but unnecessarily exposing women to risks when drugs, treatments and timeliness of interventions fail to meet international standards. Similarly, when the institutions of reproductive and sexual health are inhibited by inadequate budgets, inadequately trained health workers or overly moralistic policymakers, citizens continue to suffer from infections and non-communicable diseases that are amenable to preventive or curative care elsewhere in the world. That being said, no generalization about Asia stands up when comparisons are made between Singapore, Japan and megacities of China on the one hand, and the poverty stricken and under-resourced regions of Eastern Indonesia, Laos and Afghanistan on the other. Maternal mortality will continue to fall everywhere, but the huge inequities of women's sexual health and rights appear to be wilfully persistent in the face of religious and cultural institutions disadvantaging women.

References

Betrán A. P., J. Ye, A. B. Moller, J. Zhang, A. M. Gülmezoglu and M. R. Torloni (2016) 'The increasing trend in caesarean section rates: global, regional and national estimates: 1990–2014'. *PLoS ONE*, 11(2): e0148343.

Bruni, L., M. Diaz, L. Barrionuevo-Rosas, R. Herrero, F. Bray, F. X. Bosch, S. de Sanjosé and X. Castellsagué (2016) 'Global estimates of human papillomavirus vaccination coverage by region and income level: a pooled analysis'. *The Lancet Global Health*, 4(7): e453–e463.

Cutts, F. T., S. Franceschi, S. Goldie, X. Castellsagué, S. de Sanjosé, G. Garnett, W. J. Edmunds, P. Claeys, K. L. Goldenthal, D. M. Harper and L. Markowitz (2007) 'Human papillomavirus and HPV vaccines: a review'. *Bulletin of the World Health Organization*, 85(9): 719–726.

Dixon-Mueller, R. (1993) 'The sexuality connection in reproductive health'. *Studies in Family Planning*, 24(5): 269–282.

Ganesan, G. (2004) *Deliveries in Singapore: Volume and Resources*. MOH Information Paper: 2004/2006. Available from: www.moh.gov.sg/content/dam/moh_web/Publications/Information%20Papers/2004/Deliveries_in_Singapore_Paper.pdf.

Global Burden of Disease Study (GBD 2015 Maternal Mortality Collaborators) (2016) 'Global, regional and national levels of maternal mortality, 1990–2015: a systematic analysis for the Global Burden of Disease Study 2015'. *Lancet*, 388: 1775–1812.

Hellerstein, S., S. Feldman and T. Duan (2015) 'China's 50% caesarean delivery rate: is it too high?' *British Journal of Obstetrics and Gynaecology (BJOG)*, 122: 160–165.

Hogan M. C. et al. (2010) 'Maternal mortality for 181 countries, 1980–2008: a systematic analysis of progress towards Millennium Development Goal 5'. *Lancet*, 375(9726): 1609–1623.

Lumbiganon, P., M. Laopaiboon, A. M. Gülmezoglu, J. P. Souza, S. Taneepanichskul, P. Ruyan, D. E. Attygalle, N. Shrestha, R. Mori, N. D. Hinh and H. T. Bang (2010) 'Method of delivery and pregnancy outcomes in Asia: the WHO global survey on maternal and perinatal health 2007–08'. *Lancet*, 375(9713): 490–499.

Millennium Development Goals Indicators: The Official United Nations Site for the MDG Indicators (2017) *Indicator 5.2 Proportion of Births Attended by Skilled Personnel, Percentage*. Available from: https://mdgs.un.org/unsd/mdg/SeriesDetail.aspx?srid=570 (accessed 16 April 2017).

National Research Council (2013) *Reducing Maternal and Neonatal Mortality in Indonesia: Saving Lives, Saving the Future*. Washington, DC: The National Academies Press. Available from: www.nap.edu/openbook.php?record_id=18437.

Neuman M., G. Alcock, K. Azad et al. (2014) 'Prevalence and determinants of caesarean section in private and public health facilities in underserved South Asian communities: cross-sectional analysis of data from Bangladesh, India and Nepal'. *BMJ Open*, 4(12): e005982. Available from: http://dx.doi.org/10.1136/bmjopen-2014-005982.

Souza J. P., A. M. Gülmezoglu, P. Lumbiganon, M. Laopaiboon, G. Carroli, B. Fawole, P. Ruyan and the WHO Global Survey on Maternal and Perinatal Health Research Group (2010) 'Caesarean section without medical indications is associated with an increased risk of adverse short-term maternal outcomes'. The 2004–2008 WHO Global Survey on Maternal and Perinatal Health. Available from: http://bmcmedicine.biomedcentral.com/articles/10.1186/1741-7015-8-71.

Sukumar, V., H. Reddy, A. Gupta, A. Chandran, J. Fledderjohann and D. Stuckler (2017) 'A qualitative study of factors impacting accessing of institutional delivery care in the context of India's cash incentive program'. *Social Science Medicine*, 178: 55–65.

UNICEF Data: Monitoring the Situation of Children and Women (2017) *Delivery Care to December 2016*. Available from: https://data.unicef.org/topic/maternal-health/delivery-care/ (accessed 16 April 2017).

World Health Organization (WHO) (2010) *Trends in Maternal Mortality 1990–2008: WHO, UNICEF, UNFPA and the World Bank Estimates*. Geneva: World Health Organization. Available from: www.who.int/reproductivehealth/publications/monitoring/9789241500265/en/index.html (accessed 15 August 2014).

World Health Organization (WHO) (2012a) *Trends in Maternal Mortality: 1990 to 2010: WHO, UNICEF, UNFPA and the World Bank Estimates*. Geneva: World Health Organization. Available from: http://whqlibdoc.who.int/publications/2012/9789241503631_eng.pdf (accessed 15 August 2014).

World Health Organization (WHO) (2012b) *Global Incidence and Prevalence of Selected Curable Sexually Transmitted Infections – 2008*. Geneva: World Health Organization. Available from: http://apps.who.int/iris/bitstream/10665/75181/1/9789241503839_eng.pdf?ua=1.

World Health Organization (WHO) (2014a) *Trends in Maternal Mortality: 1990 to 2013: Estimates by WHO, UNICEF, UNFPA, the World Bank and the United Nations Population Division*. Geneva: World Health Organization. Available from: http://apps.who.int/iris/bitstream/10665/112682/2/9789241507226_eng.pdf?ua=1 (accessed 3 April 2017).

World Health Organization (WHO) (2014b) *Clinical Practice Handbook for Safe Abortion*. Geneva: World Health Organization. Available from: http://apps.who.int/iris/bitstream/10665/97415/1/9789241548717_eng.pdf (accessed 15 August 2014).

World Health Organization (WHO) (2014c) *Report on Global Sexually Transmitted Infection Surveillance 2013*. Geneva: World Health Organization. Available from: http://apps.who.int/iris/bitstream/10665/112922/1/9789241507400_eng.pdf.

World Health Organization (WHO) (2015) *Trends in Maternal Mortality: 1990 to 2015. Estimates by WHO, UNICEF, UNFPA, the World Bank and the United Nations Population Division*. Geneva: World Health Organization. Available from: http://apps.who.int/iris/bitstream/10665/194254/1/9789241565141_eng.pdf?ua=1 (accessed 3 April 2017).

9
Son preference, sex ratios and 'missing girls' in Asia

Monica Das Gupta, Doo-Sub Kim, Shuzhuo Li and Rohini Prabha Pande

Most societies show some degree of preference for sons over daughters, though mostly so slight as to be virtually undetectable (Williamson 1976). However, son preference strong enough to result in substantial levels of prenatal/postnatal sex selection – as manifested in high child sex ratios (an excess of boys over girls under five years of age)[1] – is evident only in parts of Asia and the Balkans (Table 9.1).

The discussion of sex selection is often dominated by prenatal sex selection, which became possible when new technology became widely available after the early 1980s. It is important to note that sex selection also takes place postnatally, and accounts for the high child sex ratios that have been documented in China and Northern India since the early twentieth century (Figures 9.1 and 9.2; Visaria 1971). Moreover, since parents giving birth at home are unlikely to report female infanticide unless probed in special surveys (Li et al. 2004; Ren 1995), this will show in the statistics as prenatal sex selection. For these reasons we use the term 'sex selection' to refer to both prenatal and postnatal periods.

Sex selection and subsequent skewed sex ratios are closely related to son preference and 'missing girls'. It is the underlying preference for sons that triggers prenatal or postnatal sex selection as the means to realize son preference. A consequence of sex selection is 'missing girls', as manifested by skewed sex ratios from birth to age five years.

Sex selection has been documented in large parts of East and South Asia, including China, South Korea, Taiwan, India, Pakistan and Bangladesh. It has also begun to be noted recently in Vietnam and Nepal.[2] In West Asia it manifested itself starkly in the South Caucasus countries of Georgia, Armenia and Azerbaijan in the 1990s (Figure 9.3), probably due to severe economic and other disruptions following the dissolution of the Soviet Union. Outside Asia it has been noted in the Balkans, especially in Albania since the 1970s (Gjonça 2011). It is notably absent in South-East Asian populations (Table 9.1), where ethnographic studies show no underlying cause for son preference (Das Gupta 2010).

The trends in sex ratios at birth from 1980 onwards in different regions of Asia are shown in Figures 9.3 and 9.4. Given that sex selection can take place both before and after birth, the data in Table 9.1 refers to the sex ratios of children aged below five and incorporates both pre- and postnatal selection. Levels of sex selection are now declining in several countries, starting with South Korea.

Table 9.1 Child sex ratios (males/females <5 years) for selected regions and countries, 2010

World	1.07
More developed regions	1.05
Less developed regions (excluding China)	1.06
Latin America & Caribbean	1.04
Sub-Saharan Africa	1.02
North Africa	1.04
Asia	1.10
South-Eastern Asia	1.05
Central Asia	1.04
Western Asia	1.05
Armenia	1.34*
Azerbaijan	1.15
Georgia	1.11
Eastern Asia	1.16
China	1.17
China, Hong Kong SAR	1.08
Vietnam	1.10
Southern Asia	1.10
India	1.11
Pakistan	1.08
Europe	1.05
Albania	1.10
Montenegro	1.10

Notes: Individual countries in each region are shown only if their child sex ratios are above 1.06.
*The data for Armenia seem to be a considerable overestimate. The 2009 census of Armenia reports a child sex ratio of 1.14, close to the 1.15 estimated for the year 2010 in the UN 2010 Revision.
Source: United Nations (2013).

The first section of this chapter discusses the underlying causes of son preference. The second discusses the patterns and mechanisms of sex selection and the factors associated with increases in selection. The consequences of high child sex ratios for men and women in the marriage market are discussed in the third section, and the factors that help reduce son preference are discussed in the fourth.

Underlying causes of son preference

The literature posits several possible explanations for son preference, including cultural, economic, biological and technological factors. The cultural explanation hinges on variation between pre-industrial family systems in their rules of inheritance and rules of residence. In some societies, inheritance is through the male line (patrilineal), and post-marital residence is with the husband's father (patrilocal). More rigid forms of this system exclude girls from contributing to the parental home. Only sons can remain in the parental home to cultivate the land and care for their parents in their old age and eventually inherit the land. In such cultures, a woman's productivity belongs to her husband's family. Thus, daughters are perceived by parents to be of little or no economic value to their parents, while sons are of high value. In sharp contrast, societies with

Son preference and 'missing girls' in Asia

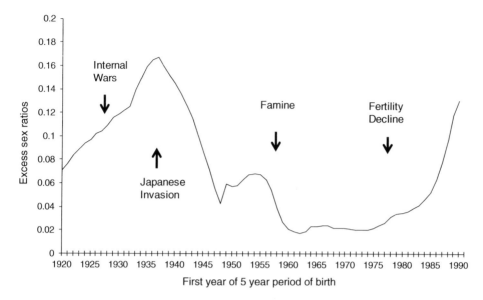

Figure 9.1 Excess female child mortality, China, 1920–1995

Notes: Calculations based on the method developed by Ansley Coale and Judith Banister (1994), using the same data-sets as they did, but adding the 1995 sample census data that were not available at the time of their writing.
Years indicate first year of five-year birth cohort. These estimates are possible because of the high level of accuracy of age-reporting in East Asia, where people know their animal year of birth in the 60-year cycle of animal-element years. The excess ratios peak among cohorts born just before a war or famine, because those who were young girls at the time of the crisis experienced the maximum excess mortality.
Source: Das Gupta and Li (1999), based on data from the 1953, 1964, 1982 and 1990 population censuses of China and the 1995 National One Per cent Sample Survey.

bilateral kinship systems – prevalent for example across much of South-East Asia – permit both sons and daughters to inherit and to have their old parents live with them. These societies have normal child sex ratios (Table 9.1).

There is a striking correspondence between the ethnographic data on the rigidity of patrilineal family systems and the demographic data on levels of sex selection (Das Gupta 2010). This is illustrated in Table 9.2, which shows very different patterns of coresidence with married children in the neighbouring islands of Taiwan and the Philippines, as well as South Korea. In South Korea and Taiwan, parents coresided with married sons, but only rarely with married daughters. By contrast, parents in the Philippines were equally likely to coreside with married children of either gender. Correspondingly, sex selection was found in South Korea and Taiwan, but not in the Philippines. Cultural constructs can thus generate economic incentives for parents to value sons more than daughters.

Pre-industrial family structures that sharply reduce the value of daughters relative to sons are also documented in China, Northern India, South Korea, Vietnam, Albania and the South Caucasus countries.[3]

Countries can show considerable heterogeneity in family structures. For example, several minority populations in China show little or no sex selection, and the same is true of the Southern and Eastern regions of India.[4] Vietnam spans South-East Asia in the south and central regions to East Asia in the north, and the historical cultural affinities differ accordingly (Coedes 1966). Despite much population mobility within the country, these differences are still evident

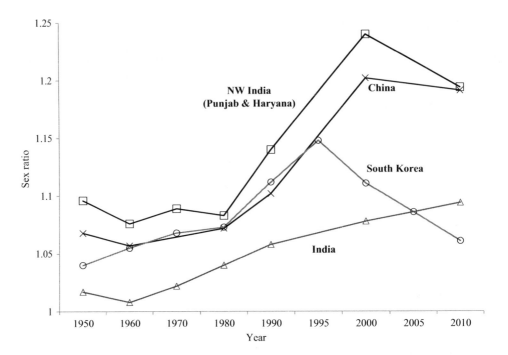

Figure 9.2 Trends in child (<5 year) sex ratios, China, India and South Korea, 1950–2010
Note: The sex ratios (males/females) for China and South Korea are for children aged 0–4 years, and for India for children aged 0–6 years.
Sources: Guo et al. (2016), based on census data (only complete censuses, not sample censuses). For South Korea: Population and Housing Census of Korea, 1950, 1960, 1970, 1980, 1990, 1995, 2000, 2005 and 2010; for China: Population Census of China 1953, 1964, 1982, 1990, 2000 and 2010; for India: Census of India, 1951, 1961, 1971, 1981, 1991, 2001 and 2011.

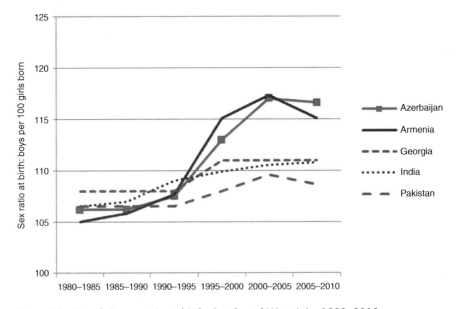

Figure 9.3 Trends in sex ratio at birth, South and West Asia, 1980–2010
Notes: The UN estimates are used for countries whose trend estimates of the sex ratio at birth are uncertain. The vital registration system in the Caucasus suffered for some years following the dissolution of the Soviet Union (Duthé et al. 2012). In India, the Sample Registration System began publishing the sex ratio at birth in 2000 (Kulkarni 2007).
Source: UN (2013).

Son preference and 'missing girls' in Asia

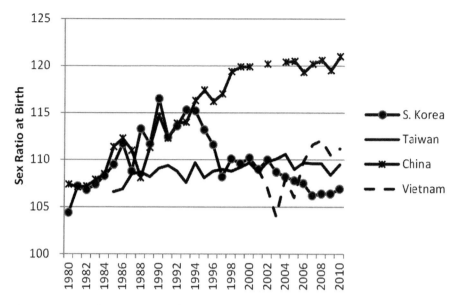

Figure 9.4 Trends in sex ratio at birth, East Asia, 1980–2010
Sources: South Korea: Korean Statistical Information Service, Statistics Korea; Taiwan: National Statistics, Republic of China (Taiwan); China: 1980–2007 from Das Gupta, Chung and Li (2009), 2008–2009 from the National Bureau of Statistics of China (2009 and 2010), and 2010 from the 2010 census; Vietnam: Government of Vietnam (2011: Table 5.8).

Table 9.2 Percentage of men and women age 60+ coresiding with children, by gender of married children, Philippines 1984, Taiwan 1989 and South Korea 1990

Sex of the elderly	Living with married son	Living with married daughter
Philippines 1984		
Male	29	24
Female	28	34
Taiwan 1989		
Male	55	5
Female	63	7
South Korea 1990 (Age 65+)		
Male	36	2
Female	54	7

Sources: The data for Taiwan and the Philippines are from Casterline et al. (1993). The figures for South Korea are estimates of the authors, based on data from the 1990 population census of South Korea.

in the lower prevalence of coresidence with married daughters and higher sex selection in the North than in the South (Khuat and Gammeltoft 2011; Guilmoto 2012a).

People from cultures with a strong son preference continue to sex select even when they move to countries with normal child sex ratios. This has been found, for example, among Indians in the United Kingdom and among Chinese, Koreans and Indians in the United States.[5] Interestingly, Abrevaya (2009) finds that in the United States the sex selection is especially high if the father is from the same race, while Asian women from countries with strong son

155

preference who marry men from other ethnicities exhibit less need to bear sons to continue their husband's family line.

Other patrilineal cultures offer greater opportunity for adult daughters to contribute to their parental homes. These cultures show much more muted levels of sex selection, for example in the Middle East (Kandiyoti 1991; Yount 2001). Historically, in parts of Europe, sons were favoured as heirs but there was scope for unmarried adult daughters to remain with their parents and care for them (Sieder and Mitterauer 1983). In a study of historical Germany, Klasen (1994) found sex selection but at low levels.

Family systems can leave residual traces that do not show in routine demographic indices. This is shown in studies of census and survey data from the United States over the period 1960–2000, which find that having sons significantly reduces the probability of divorce (Morgan et al. 1988; Dahl and Moretti 2008). They argue that for fathers, family obligations and attachments are greater if they have sons, and that this has serious negative income and educational consequences for the affected children.

Besides those deriving from cultural constructs, other economic reasons are sometimes put forward for son preference. One is that males are more productive in agricultural work, but this does not explain the fact that only some societies manifest son preference. A dowry system is also mentioned as an economic incentive to disfavour girls, but this is at most an additional contributing factor – child sex ratios are high even when a bride price has been the norm, as has been historically the norm in China and South Korea and in north-west India in the early twentieth century. In fact, bride price is consonant with the shortage of brides generated by discrimination against daughters.[6]

Biological factors can contribute to gender differentials in mortality (Waldron 1983, 1998), but this does not account for prenatal sex selection and postnatal discrimination in seeking healthcare for girls.[7] Offering an alternative biological explanation of high sex ratios at birth, Oster (2005) argued that parental infection with the hepatitis B virus (HBV) accounts for much of the high child sex ratios attributed to sex selection. However, Lin and Luoh (2008) showed conclusively that this made only a marginal difference with regard to levels of sex selection. Oster herself also subsequently retracted her theory.[8]

Sex selection has also been attributed to advances in prenatal diagnostic techniques, but this is not an underlying cause. Although the use of such techniques is widespread across the world, it is used for sex selection only in settings with strong son preference. However, the new technologies reduce the physical and emotional costs of sex selection, which can combine with fertility reduction to increase child sex ratios.

Patterns and mechanisms of sex selection and factors associated with increases in selection

Mechanisms and patterns of prenatal and postnatal sex selection

There is a very clear pattern of sex selection by birth order, clearly seen in data from many countries.[9] Whether or not females 'go missing' – before or after birth – is determined by the existing sex composition of the family into which they are conceived. Girls conceived in families which have no son and already have a daughter experience steeply higher probabilities of being aborted or of dying in early childhood. Studies in China, India and Bangladesh also find that boys born into families that already have one or more boys have slightly elevated mortality compared to the firstborn boy, but this effect is small compared with that for girls. A related pattern revealing son preference is a shorter birth interval following the birth of a girl, as parents hope to have a boy.[10]

Sex selection can take place at the time of conception, during pregnancy, shortly after birth through infanticide or abandonment, and in early childhood through differential care. Postnatal sex selection was obviously the only method used in the past, but is now used largely by people who lack the physical and financial access to prenatal sex selection technologies. The primary mode of 'neglect' in early childhood is discussed in the next section.

In analysing the statistics on sex ratio at birth, it is important to note that these may include cases of infanticide/abandonment, as few parents are likely to report such cases, especially if they gave birth at home. Probing births in a survey, Li et al. (2004) report that in the Shaanxi province of China, most of the excess female deaths occurred among those who died at home, and about two-thirds of the excess female deaths took place within the first 24 hours of birth. Similarly, Ren (1995) found in three provinces in China that the odds of dying are far higher for girls among children born at home.

The spread of sex selective technology has made it much easier for parents to avoid having unwanted daughters. The rise in sex selection since the spread of the technology may indicate that access to the easier method increases the levels. However, very high child sex ratios have been reached in the past through postnatal selection, as evidenced, for example, in China during the first half of the twentieth century (Figure 9.1).

Goodkind (1996) pointed out that there is a substitution effect, with parents shifting from postnatal to prenatal selection. This is evidenced, for example, in Taiwan, where Lin et al. (2014) found that an increase in sex ratio at birth was associated with lower excess female neonatal mortality (which includes the traditional practice of female infanticide). Goodkind (1996) notes that this substitution effect suggests that 'a ban on the use of prenatal sex selection ... could result in an increase in postnatal parental discrimination against daughters'.

Mechanisms of neglect of unwanted girls

Life-threatening neglect can take the form of under-feeding and/or withholding medical care for girls, relative to boys. However, a high selection bias needs to be borne in mind when interpreting findings from studies of neglect. Documenting discrimination against living girls accurately is difficult, since many of those girls who are the most unwanted and neglected are likely to have died and therefore not included in any study sample.

Studies that actually measure gender differentials in food intake and health care find that there is little or no difference in food intake, but a clear difference in expenditure on medical care. This was found, for example, in studies in Bangladesh, North India, Pakistan and the Shaanxi province of China.[11] Reviews of the literature have found much more evidence of gender differences in health care than in food intake.[12] Other studies rely on gender differentials in anthropometric measurements as indicators of undernutrition (Marcoux 2002). However, poor anthropometric measures can result from either inadequate food intake or the stress of responding to infection, so are affected by differentials in health care.

Differences in health care can be in the use of preventive services such as immunization, or in the use of medical treatment when a child is ill. Discrimination in immunization is found in India and China (Pande 2003; Li et al. 2004). Data from several countries show clear gender differentials in the use of medical care. For example, data from Pakistan show sharp differences in the probability of consulting a doctor in the case of illness, and in medical expenditure if the child is taken for treatment (World Bank 2005). Similar results were found for Pakistan by

Hazarika (2000), and for Nepal (Pokhrel et al. 2005). Li et al. (2004: 19) found from their survey in the Shaanxi province of China that:

> The main mechanism of excess female child mortality is lack of use and effectiveness of curative health care, rather than preventive health care or nutrient deficiency. When children became ill, parents tended to consider illness of boys more serious than that of girls, and were more likely to seek medical treatment for boys than for girls. Further, once parents decided to seek medical treatment for their children, there were significant sex differences in the effectiveness of treatment, as reflected in expenses on medical treatment and times of hospital transfer.

Several of these studies indicate that higher birth order girls are especially neglected in medical care. Li et al. (2004) found this in the Shaanxi province in China, and Asfaw et al. (2008) found this in India.

Factors associated with increases in levels of prenatal and postnatal sex selection

In societies with a strong son preference, levels of sex selection rise when parents are under additional pressure to make hard choices about which children to raise (Figure 9.1). This can be due, for example, to severe economic stresses, as evidenced by the rise in sex selection during the wars in China in the 1930s and the economic meltdown in the former Soviet republics following the breakup of the Soviet Union. Sex selection can also increase with fertility decline, as parents want sons but within the constraint of a small family, giving them fewer 'tosses of the coin' to achieve a son. Bongaarts (2013) shows that in several countries which still have high fertility, the desired sex ratio of children is much higher than the actual sex ratio. As fertility declines, actual sex ratios could rise unless son preference is reduced by a range of factors (summarized in the fourth section below).

Economic stress and/or fertility decline heighten sex selection because the most crucial requirement in these contexts is to have at least one surviving son. However, such stresses increase the proportions of 'missing girls' only in cultures with a strong son preference. While economic disruption took place across much of the former-USSR region, only the Caucasus countries showed a rise in sex ratios at birth. This is in line with the observation that the spread of sex selective technology helped raise sex ratios at birth only in settings with a strong son preference.

The consequences of high child sex ratios: men and women in the marriage market

There is a growing literature on the consequences of masculine sex ratios for men, women and societies overall. The sex selection and neglect of girls that underlie the masculine sex ratios have immediate implications for gender equality. Longer-term effects include the availability of marriage partners (the 'marriage squeeze'), influence on crime and safety, the availability of household care for ageing populations in the future, and social consequences such as violence against women. In this section, we focus on the marriage squeeze (on which the research literature has largely focused).

The marriage squeeze is tightening in China, South Korea and India, and will continue to do so for some time, given the high levels of sex selection in the preceding decades. This is exacerbated by rapid fertility decline, which reduces the size of each successive cohort into which men can marry. In response to this, the age gap between spouses at marriage has shrunk. China presents the starkest scenario, with the *People's Daily* (2010) citing a China Academy of Social Sciences report predicting that by 2020, one in five men will be unable to find a bride.

This has many ramifications for both men and women, but the ramifications differ for higher and lower socioeconomic groups. Economically advantaged men are able to attract wives, while poorer men and their households face an uphill task to find a bride. Studies indicate that in China, poorer households in areas with high sex ratios have higher savings rates – and are more prepared to take on higher-risk activities in the hope of higher returns – in an effort to improve their son's chances in the marriage market (Wei and Zhang 2011a, 2011b). Consistent with this, Edlund et al. (2013) found that in China, households in regions with higher sex ratios invest more in their sons' educations, perhaps to enhance their prospects in the marriage market. Similar findings are reported from Taiwan, when the large influx of male soldiers from mainland China sought to find brides (Chang and Zhang 2012).

A growing literature suggests that, at least in some countries, the marriage squeeze can increase the bargaining power of women. For instance, where marriage market sex ratios are higher in China, women exercise greater bargaining power within a marriage (Porter 2009a, 2009b; Edlund et al. 2013). A study in Taiwan found that with the sudden shortage of brides caused by the influx of the Nationalist army and government from the mainland in 1949, bride prices rose, and women's bargaining power within the household increased (Francis 2011).

Women can also benefit by marrying men who can offer them higher living standards. In China, women from poorer areas migrate to marry men in wealthier areas (Fan and Huang 1998; Sharygin et al. 2013). Marriage migration shows a clear pattern, one in which poor women marry men who live in wealthier locations (whether within the country or in a wealthier country) and can therefore offer them a better life financially. At the same time, however, these men are typically socioeconomically disadvantaged in their own setting, which is why they were unable to attract a local wife. This is evident in studies from China, South Korea and India.[13]

Other literature suggests that the growing trend of men marrying women from poorer countries or different ethnic/linguistic groups within the same country can disadvantage women in many ways. They face problems in assimilation, not knowing the local language and customs, having limited social networks in their new setting, and being viewed as outsiders by the people among whom they marry. Many such marriages are to men who live in rural areas, as local women prefer to marry upwards.

The literature points to the difficulties these women face in adjusting to their new situation, and to the inadequate effort by the receiving countries to help the women adjust.[14] These difficulties can go beyond social isolation and cultural misunderstandings. In Taiwan, marriage migration is viewed as a risk factor in domestic violence (Williams and Yu 2006). In South Korea, Kim (2010) found a greater likelihood of divorce among such marriages. Lee (2012) found that marriage migrants play an important role in caring for the elderly and handicapped in their marital household, perhaps because men who have extra responsibilities are especially unlikely to attract local wives.

Nguyen and Tran (2010) studied marriage migration from Vietnam to Taiwan, and found that brides are overwhelmingly from poor families. The selection process can be humiliating, with the women required to show their bodies. The women marry out to escape poverty and to help their families financially. While most of the brides report that they are happy because they are able to help their natal families, some report serious problems. Some are humiliated by their husbands and in-laws for their poverty, some report domestic violence, some report being made to work like a slave. The authors report some cases of women being forced to engage in paid sex with other men.

A similar situation exists in India, where the bride shortage is concentrated in the relatively prosperous north-western region, whose men seek brides from poor families in the East and South regions (Kaur 2004, 2008). Chowdhry (2005: 5195) describes the difficulties these women face, not only because the local culture and language is completely alien to them, but also because they are treated as second-class citizens:

> Most of these purchased women do not even know the language or participate in any of the cultural activities of this region. With severely limited or even non-existing communication, these women are isolated and experience an extreme sense of alienation from the families they are supposed to belong ... The other women of the family who have come through a proper ritual wedding and a dowry, refuse to give them any recognition.

Some have also suggested that high levels of enforced bachelorhood may raise levels of crime and violence. There are reports of abduction and forced marriage of some women in the Chinese media[15] that is increasingly reported in studies.[16] Edlund et al. (2013) have examined province-level variations in sex ratios in China. They found that higher sex ratios among males aged 16–25 can account for one-seventh of the rise in crime. Drèze and Khera (2000) also found that 'the strongest correlate of the murder rate is the female-male ratio: districts with higher female-male ratios have lower murder rates'. In both studies, the findings could result partly from a composition effect; that is, since men are more likely to commit crimes, a higher proportion of men in a population may raise the crime rate even without tumultuous social processes. Drèze and Khera (2000) also caution that both outcomes may be driven by the same underlying factor of differences in regional cultures, with cultures that emphasize masculinity and violence being associated both with sex selection and with higher murder rates.

Factors that help reduce son preference and its manifestations

A variety of factors help reduce son preference. First, most countries have for several decades implemented policies that help increase gender equity – for example in schooling, in the workplace, access to credit and other legal changes such as promoting women's rights to inheritance. They also include universal franchise, and sometimes affirmative action to increase female political representation.[17] These measures are not intended directly to reduce son preference, but they can help do so. For example, increasing women's schooling and access to income gives them a better bargaining position in the household and encourages the understanding that females and males can be equally valuable. Qian (2008) showed that increasing female income improves the survival rate of girls, while the reverse worsens their survival rates. Sex selection has also declined in Bangladesh (Alam et al. 2007), where a similar argument to that made by Qian has been used to explain the decline (Kabeer 2014).[18]

This erosion of son preference can be accelerated by exposure to the media, as indicated by two studies in India: one using a 'natural experiment' generated by different timing of the introduction of cable television (Jensen and Oster 2009), and the other cross-sectional survey data (Pande and Astone 2007). Jensen and Oster argue that this has much to do with the fact that audiences are exposed to new values and ideas, for example, with female characters in popular soap operas working outside the home and participating actively in public life.

More direct measures to reduce sex selection include bans on the use of sex selection technology that were put into place in several countries, and financial incentives to raise girls that were put into place in India and China, in the latter case under the Care for Girls policy. There is little rigorous evaluation of the impact of these measures, however. The few assessments of financial incentive programmes in India do not suggest much impact.[19] Evaluations of India's ban on sex selection indicate implementation problems, which also make it difficult to evaluate programme impact (Jaising et al 2007; Nandi and Deolalikar 2013[20]). A vigorous effort in China to implement the ban since 2006 (under the Care for Girls policy) did not reduce the overall sex ratio at birth between the censuses of 2000 and 2010 (Guo et al. 2016), nor the trend in the sex ratio at birth before and after the intervention (Figure 9.4).[21]

Urbanization and socioeconomic development erode the traditional cultural constructs underlying son preference, for example by making it equally likely that a daughter and a son will live and work in the same city as the parents. Yet the effect of these factors is not linear (Bhat and Zavier 2003): they can first exacerbate selection through reducing desired family size (heightening pressure for sex selection) and facilitating access to new technologies for sex selection. Over time, the shifts in social norms associated with urbanization and development erode son preference, as was the case in South Korea (Chung and Das Gupta 2007). And if access to pensions and social protection systems increases, the need to depend on sons for old age support decreases.

Over time, these social and economic transformations can erode son preference permanently, as appears to have happened in South Korea. This happened also in the past in Germany: Brockmann (2001) found that women born before 1910 in Germany had a shorter waiting time to the next birth if their first child was a girl, but this pattern disappeared in later-born cohorts of women. Residual traces of son preference may remain, as indicated by the studies on the United States cited above.

A similar logic can be found in the relationship between maternal education and sex selection such that higher education is not always associated with lower sex selection. In fact, several studies have found that more educated women sex select more heavily, both because they reduce their fertility earlier than the less educated, and also because they are better placed in terms of information and access to services to remove unwanted daughters. This was noted for example in studies in north-west India and Bangladesh.[22] It is shown clearly by Chun (2009) who used successive rounds of surveys from South Korea to show that educated women were more likely to sex select in the earlier surveys, but in later surveys their pattern normalized, while less educated women increased their sex selection.[23] However, the forces of social change caught up quickly with all groups of women in South Korea, and levels of sex selection dropped sharply nationwide regardless of educational level and socioeconomic status.

The relationship between socioeconomic development and levels of sex selection is not linear, as shown by the South Korean data. This can help explain why the 2011 census data for India show that sex selection is rising in a few (large) northern states that are developing gradually, while declining in other states such as Gujarat, Punjab and Haryana which have experienced much more rapid development for some decades.

Studies indicate that son preference is declining. Bongaarts (2013: 202–203) points out that 'in nearly all DHS countries and in states of India, the desired sex ratio at birth has either remained constant or has declined between the two most recent surveys. In a separate study of trends in son preference in Korea, Chung and Das Gupta (2007) found that the proportion of women reporting "must have a son" declined from nearly 50 per cent in 1985 to less than 20 per cent in 2003'. Using data from successive surveys in Taiwan, Tin-Chi Lin (2009: Table 9.2) found a similar societal shift: the proportion of women reporting that they would try to have more children in order to have at least one son regardless of the number of additional pregnancies dropped from 36 per cent in 1973 to 5 per cent in 1986.

The data from South Korea, Taiwan, and north-west India show that there is a lag between a decline in reported son preference and a decline in levels of sex selection.[24] Levels of sex selection are now declining in several countries, with juvenile sex ratios almost normalized in South

Korea, plateauing in China between 2000 and 2010, and increasing at a much slower pace in India during 2001–2011 than in previous decades (Figure 9.2).[25] In India, child sex ratios are becoming less masculine in regions that have a long history of high sex ratios (Figure 9.2), and a similar pattern appears in China (Guo et al. 2016). It is possible that sex selection will continue to recede at an accelerating pace.

Notes

1. Note that in South Asia, sex ratios are calculated in reverse, as girls divided by boys.
2. This is a large literature, but see for example Choe (1987), Park and Cho (1995), Kim (2004), Lin and Luoh (2008), Visaria (1971), Kishor (1993), Sathar (1987), Bhuiya and Streatfield (1991), Khuat and Gammeltoft (2011), and Puri and Adhikari (2007).
3. See, for example, Das Gupta et al. (2003) on China, India and South Korea; Li et al. (2007) on China; Kim (2004) on South Korea; Khuat and Gammeltoft (2011) and Guilmoto (2012a) on Vietnam; Gjonça (2011) and Whitaker (1976) on Albania; and Ishkanian (2003), Heyat (2002) and Dragadze (1988) on the South Caucasus. There is a large literature on family structures in Europe, Asia and the Middle East, and some of this is reviewed in Das Gupta (2010).
4. See Guo et al. (2016) on minority populations in China, and regional differences in child sex ratios in India. The Indian pattern continues to bear out the thesis of Dyson and Moore (1983).
5. Dubuc and Coleman (2007) on the UK; Almond and Edlund (2008) and Abrevaya (2009) on the US.
6. Studies indicate that the surge in dowry payments in India during the mid-twentieth century was due to an unusual configuration of demographic forces, making for a surplus of women relative to men (Rao 1993). Since then, a combination of fertility decline and sex selection has generated a surplus of grooms.
7. Differences between the genders in genetic make-up and in behavioural patterns cause differential morbidity and mortality among adults (Waldron 1983; Vlassoff and Bonilla 1994; Vlassoff 2007). For children this is evident in higher neonatal mortality among boys in populations that do not practice female infanticide. Waldron (1998) concludes that in the absence of discrimination gender differentials in childhood, mortality from infectious diseases are highly variable while boys have much higher accident mortality.
8. See http://faculty.chicagobooth.edu/emily.oster/papers/hbvnotecon.pdf.
9. This is a large literature, but see for example on Korea Choe (1987), Park and Cho (1995) and Kim (2004, 2011); on Northern India Das Gupta (1987) and Pebley and Amin (1991); on China Zeng et al. (1993) and Li et al. (2004); on Bangladesh Muhuri and Preston (1991); on the Caucasus countries Duthé et al. (2012); and on rural Germany in the eighteenth and nineteenth centuries Klasen (1994).
10. See, for example, Choe et al. (1992) on China, Larsen et al. (1998) on South Korea, and Brockmann (2001) on German women born before 1910.
11. See, for example, Chen et al. (1981) on Bangladesh, Das Gupta (1987) on north-west India, Li et al. (2004) on China, and Hazarika (2000) on Pakistan.
12. See, for example, Basu (1989) and DeRose et al. (2000).
13. See, for example, Fan and Huang (1998) on China; Kaur (2004, 2008) and Chowdhry (2005) on India; and Kim (2010) and Lee (2012) on South Korea.
14. See, for example, Williams and Yu (2006) on Taiwan; and Lee (2012) on South Korea.
15. See, for example, the article in the *China Daily* reporting on a study by the Chinese Academy of Social Sciences, and relating the skewed sex ratio to abduction and trafficking of women and infants (http://bbs.chinadaily.com.cn/viewthread.php?gid=2&tid=657774).
16. See, for example, Banister (2004), and Chao (2005). Dyson (2012) summarizes the growing literature on this.
17. For a summary of some of these policies in China, India and South Korea, see Das Gupta et al. (2004).
18. However, levels of sex selection in Bangladesh were very low compared to those of East Asia and Northern India.
19. See for example, Sinha and Joong (2009) and Holla et al. (2007) on financial incentives.
20. Nandi and Deolalikar (2013) evaluated the PCPNDT Act in Maharashtra state, India, and argued that the ban may have helped to avert rises in sex selection. However, they are unable to establish that the bans in neighbouring states were implemented equally well.

21 While banning prenatal sex selection, Chinese law also states 'Discrimination against, maltreatment and abandonment of baby girls are prohibited' (Li 2007: Appendix Table 1).
22 See, for example, Pebley and Amin (1991) and Das Gupta (1987) on north-west India, and Bhuiya and Streatfield (1991) on Bangladesh.
23 Pockets of South Korea where sex selection persisted longer than in other areas show a pattern consistent with both this pattern as well as the effect of easier access to sex-selective technology. In the Youngnam region in 2009, sex selection was higher among those of low socioeconomic status in metropolitan areas, while in rural areas higher sex ratios at birth were found among those with high socioeconomic status and thus easier access to medical facilities (Kim 2011).
24 This is evidenced by the findings of Lin (2009) on Taiwan; Chung and Das Gupta (2007) on South Korea; and Guo et al. (2016) on India.
25 See Guo et al. (2016) for China, India and South Korea; and Alam et al. (2007) for Bangladesh.

References

Abrevaya, J. (2009) 'Are there missing girls in the United States? Evidence on gender preference and gender selection'. *American Economic Journal: Applied Economics*, 1(2): 1–34.
Alam, N., J. van Ginneken and A. Bosch (2007) 'Decreases in male and female mortality and missing women in Bangladesh'. In I. Attané and C. Z. Guilmoto (eds.) *Watering the Neighbour's Garden*. Paris: CICRED. Pp. 161–182.
Almond, D. and L. Edlund (2008) 'Son-biased sex ratios in the 2000 United States Census'. *Proceedings of the National Academy of Sciences*, 105(15): 5681–5682.
Asfaw, A., S. Klasen and F. Lamanna (2008) 'Intra-household gender disparities in children's medical care before death in India'. Proceedings of the German Development Economics Conference, Zürich.
Banister, J. (2004) 'Shortage of girls in China today'. *Journal of Population Research*, 21(1): 19–45.
Basu, A. M. (1989) 'Is discrimination in food really necessary for explaining sex differentials in childhood mortality?' *Population Studies*, 43(2): 193–210.
Bhat, P. N. M. and A. J. F. Zavier (2003) 'Fertility decline and gender bias in Northern India'. *Demography*, 40(4): 637–657.
Bhuiya, A. and K. Streatfield (1991) 'Mothers' education and survival of female children in a rural area of Bangladesh'. *Population Studies*, 45(2): 253–264.
Bongaarts, J. (2013) 'The implementation of preferences for male offspring'. *Population and Development Review*, 39(2): 185–208.
Brockmann, H. (2001) 'Girls preferred? Changing patterns of sex preferences in the two German states'. *European Sociological Review*, 17(2): 189–202.
Casterline, J., M. C. Chang and L. Domingo (1993) 'Which children co-reside with elderly parents? A comparative analysis of the Philippines and Taiwan'. Paper presented at the annual meeting of the Gerontological Society of America, 19–23 November, New Orleans.
Chahnazarian, A. (1988) 'Determinants of the sex ratio at birth: review of recent literature'. *Social Biology*, 35(3–4): 214–235.
Chang, S. and X. Zhang (2012) 'The economic consequences of excess men: evidence from a natural experiment in Taiwan'. Paper presented at the Northeast Universities Development Consortium Conference, Dartmouth College, 3–4 November.
Chao, E. (2005) 'Cautionary tales: marriage strategies, state discourse and women's agency in a Naxi village in southwestern China'. In N. Constable (ed.) *Cross Border Marriages and Gender and Mobility in Transnational Asia*. Philadelphia: University of Pennsylvania Press.
Chen, L. C., E. Huq and S. D'Souza (1981) 'Sex bias in the family allocation of food and health care in rural Bangladesh'. *Population and Development Review*, 7(1): 55–70.
Choe, M. K. (1987) 'Sex differentials in infant and child mortality in Korea'. *Social Biology*, 34: 12–25.
Choe, M. K., F. Guo, J. Wu and R. Zhang (1992) 'Progression to second and third births in China: patterns and covariates in six provinces'. *International Family Planning Perspectives*, 18(4): 130–136.
Chowdhry, P. (2005) 'Crisis of masculinity in Haryana: the unmarried, the unemployed and the aged'. *Economic and Political Weekly*, 40(49): 5189–5198.
Chun, H. (2009) 'Trends in sex ratio at birth according to parental social positions: results from vital statistics birth, 1981–2004 in Korea'. *Journal of Preventive Medicine and Public Health*, 42(2): 143–150 (in Korean, with English abstract).

Chung, W. and M. Das Gupta (2007) 'The decline of son preference in South Korea: the roles of development and public policy'. *Population and Development Review*, 33(4): 757–783.
Coale, A. and J. Banister (1994) 'Five decades of missing females in China'. *Demography*, 31(3): 459–480.
Coedes, G. (1966) *The Making of South East Asia*. Berkeley: University of California Press.
Dahl, G. B. and E. Moretti (2008) 'The demand for sons'. *Review of Economic Studies*, 75: 1085–1120.
Das Gupta, M. (1987) 'Selective discrimination against female children in rural Punjab, India'. *Population and Development Review*, 13(1): 77–100.
Das Gupta, M. (2010) 'Family systems, political systems, and Asia's "missing girls": the construction of son preference and its unravelling'. *Asian Population Studies*, 6(2): 123–152.
Das Gupta, M., W. Chung and S. Li (2009) 'Evidence for an incipient decline in numbers of missing girls in China and India'. *Population and Development Review*, 35(2): 401–416.
Das Gupta, M., Z. Jiang, Z. Xie, B. Li, C. Woojin and H. O. Bae (2003) 'Why is son preference so persistent in East and South Asia? A cross-country study of China, India and the Republic of Korea'. *Journal of Development Studies*, 40(2): 153–187.
Das Gupta, M., S. Lee, P. Uberoi, D. Wang, L. Wang and X. Zhang (2004) 'State policies and women's agency in China, the Republic of Korea and India 1950–2000: lessons from contrasting experiences'. In V. Rao and M. Walton (eds.) *Culture and Public Action: A Cross-Disciplinary Dialogue on Development Policy*. Stanford, CA: Stanford University Press.
Das Gupta, M. and S. Z. Li (1999) 'Gender bias in China, South Korea and India 1920–1990: the effects of war, famine and fertility decline'. *Development and Change*, 30(3): 619–652.
DeRose, L. F., M. Das and S. R. Millman (2000) 'Does female disadvantage mean lower access to food?' *Population and Development Review*, 26(3): 517–547.
Dragadze, T. (1988) *Rural Families in Soviet Georgia: A Case Study in Ratcha Province*. London: Routledge.
Drèze, J. and R. Khera (2000) 'Crime, gender, and society in India: insights from homicide data'. *Population and Development Review*, 26(2): 335–352.
Dubuc, S. and D. Coleman (2007) 'An increase in the sex ratio of births to India-born mothers in England and Wales: evidence for sex-selective abortion'. *Population and Development Review*, 33(2): 383–400.
Duthé, G., F. Meslé, J. Vallin, I. Badurashvili and K. Kuyumjyan (2012) 'High sex ratios at birth in the Caucasus: modern technology to satisfy old desires'. *Population and Development Review*, 38(3): 487–501.
Dyson, T. (2012) 'Causes and consequences of skewed sex ratios'. *Annual Review of Sociology*, 38: 443–461.
Dyson, T. and M. Moore (1983) 'On kinship structure, female autonomy and demographic behavior in India'. *Population and Development Review*, 9(1): 35–60.
Edlund, L., H. Li, J. Yi and J. Zhang (2013) 'Sex ratios and crime: evidence from China'. *Review of Economics and Statistics*, 95(5): 1520–1534.
Fan, C. C. and Y. Huang (1998) 'Waves of rural brides: female marriage migration in China'. *Annals of Association of American Geographers*, 88(2): 227–251.
Francis, A. M. (2011) 'Sex ratios and the red dragon: using the Chinese Communist Revolution to explore the effect of the sex ratio on women and children in Taiwan'. *Journal of Population Economics*, 24(3): 813–837.
Ganatra, B. (2008) 'Maintaining access to safe abortion and reducing sex ratio imbalances in Asia'. *Reproductive Health Matters*, 16(suppl. 31): 90–98.
Gjonça, A. (2011) 'Sex imbalances in Albania: a demographic historical perspective'. Paper presented at 'Sex selection: from Asia to Europe', CEPED, Paris, 2 December.
Goodkind, D. (1996) 'On substituting sex preference strategies in East Asia: does prenatal sex selection reduce postnatal discrimination?' *Population and Development Review*, 22(1): 111–125.
Government of Vietnam (2011) *The 1/4/2011 Population Change and Family Planning Survey: Major Findings*. Hanoi: Ministry of Planning and Investment, General Statistics Office.
Guilmoto, C. Z. (2012a) 'Son preference, sex selection and kinship in Vietnam'. *Population and Development Review*, 38(1): 31–54.
Guilmoto, C. Z. (2012b) 'Gender imbalances at birth, trends, differentials and policy implications'. Report prepared for United Nations Population Fund. Bangkok: UNFPA.
Guo, Z., M. Das Gupta and S. Z. Li (2016) '"Missing girls" in China and India: trends and policy challenges'. *Asian Population Studies*, 12(2): 135–155.
Hazarika, G. (2000) 'Gender differences in children's nutrition and access to health care in Pakistan'. *Journal of Development Studies*, 37(1): 73–92.
Heyat, F. (2002) *Azeri Women in Transition: Women in Soviet and post-Soviet Azerbaijan*. London: Routledge Curzon.

Holla, A., R. Jensen and E. Oster (2007) 'Daughters as wealth? The effect of cash incentives on sex ratios'. Working Paper, Brown University.

Ishkanian, A. (2003) 'Women in Armenia'. In L. Walter (ed.) *The Greenwood Encyclopedia of Women's Issues Worldwide: Europe.* Westport, CT: Greenwood Publishing Group.

Jaising, I., C. Sathyamala and A. Basu (2007) *From the Abnormal to the Normal: Preventing Sex Selective Abortions through the Law.* New Delhi: Lawyers Collective (Women's Rights Initiative).

Jensen, R. and E. Oster (2009) 'The power of TV: cable television and women's status in India' (with Robert Jensen). *Quarterly Journal of Economics*, 124(3): 1057–1094.

Johnson, K., B. Huang and L. Wang (1998) 'Infant abandonment and adoption in China'. *Population and Development Review*, 24(3): 469–510.

Kabeer, N. (2014) 'Diverging stories of "missing women" in South Asia: is son preference declining in Bangladesh?' *Feminist Economics*, 20(4): 138–163.

Kabeer, N. (forthcoming) 'Diverging stories of "missing women" in South Asia: is son preference declining in Bangladesh?' *Feminist Economics*.

Kandiyoti, D. (1991) 'Islam and patriarchy: a comparative perspective'. In N. R. Keddie and B. Baron (eds.) *Women in Middle Eastern History.* New Haven: Yale University Press.

Kaur, R. (2004) 'Across-region marriages: poverty, female migration and the sex ratio'. *Economic and Political Weekly*, 39(25): 2595–2603.

Kaur, R. (2008) 'Dispensable daughters and bachelor sons: sex discrimination in North India'. *Economic and Political Weekly*, 43(30): 109–114.

Khuat, T. H. and T. Gammeltoft (2011) *Son Preference in Vietnam.* Hanoi: UNFPA.

Kim, D. S. (2004) 'Missing girls in South Korea: trends, levels and regional variations'. *Population*, (English edition) 59(6): 865–878.

Kim, D. S. (2010) 'The rise of cross-border marriage and divorce in contemporary Korea'. In W. S. Yang and M. C. W. Lu (eds.) *Asian Cross-Border Marriage Migration: Demographic Patterns and Social Issues.* Amsterdam: Amsterdam University Press.

Kim, D. S. (2011) 'Recent changes in sex ratio at birth and simulations on sex-selective reproductive behavior: with a special focus on Youngnam Region'. *Korea Journal of Population Studies*, 34(1): 159–178 (in Korean, with English abstract).

Kishor, S. (1993) 'May God give sons to all: gender and child mortality in India'. *American Sociological Review*, 58(2): 247–265.

Klasen, S. (1994) 'Family composition, gender preference, and parental "investment": excess female mortality among infants and children during early German development'. Harvard University, Mimeographed.

Kulkarni, P. M. (2007) *Estimation of Missing Girls at Birth and Juvenile Ages in India.* New Delhi: UNFPA.

Larsen, U., W. Chung and M. Das Gupta (1998) 'Fertility and son preference in Korea'. *Population Studies*, 52(3): 317–325.

Lee, H. (2012) 'Political economy of cross-border marriage: economic development and social reproduction in Korea'. *Feminist Economics*, 18(2): 177–200.

Li, S. Z. (2007) 'Imbalanced sex ratio at birth and comprehensive intervention in China'. Paper prepared for the 4th Asia Pacific Conference on Reproductive and Sexual Health and Rights, Hyderabad, India.

Li, S. Z., Y. Wei, Q. Jiang and M. W. Feldman (2007) 'Imbalanced sex ratio at birth and female child survival in China: issues and prospects'. In I. Attané and C. Z. Guilmoto (eds.) *Watering the Neighbour's Garden.* Paris: CICRED.

Li, S. Z., C. Zhu and M. W. Feldman (2004) 'Gender differences in child survival in contemporary rural China: a county study'. *Journal of Biosocial Sciences*, 36(1): 83–109.

Lin, T. C. (2009) 'The Decline of son preference and rise of gender indifference in Taiwan since 1990'. *Demographic Research*, 20: 377–402.

Lin, M. J., J. T. Liu and N. Qian (2014) 'More missing women, fewer dying girls: the impact of sex selective abortion on sex at birth and relative female mortality in Taiwan'. *Journal of the European Economic Association*, 12(4): 889–926.

Lin, M. J. and M. C. Luoh (2008) 'Can hepatitis B mothers account for the number of missing women? Evidence from three million newborns in Taiwan'. *American Economic Review*, 98(5): 2259–2273.

Marcoux, A. (2002) 'Sex differentials in undernutrition: a look at survey evidence'. *Population and Development Review*, 28(2): 275–284.

Morgan, S. P., D. N. Lye and G. A. Condran (1988) 'Sons, daughters and the risk of marital disruption'. *American Journal of Sociology*, 94(1): 110–129.

Muhuri, P. K. and S. H. Preston (1991) 'Effects of family composition on mortality differentials by sex among children in Matlab, Bangladesh'. *Population and Development Review*, 17(3): 415–434.

Nandi, A. and A. B. Deolalikar (2013) 'The Impact of a ban on sex-selective abortion on the juvenile sex ratio in India: evidence from a policy change'. *Journal of Development Economics*, 103: 216–228.

National Bureau of Statistics of China (2009) *Statistical Bulletin for National Economic and Social Development*. Beijing: China Statistics Press.

National Bureau of Statistics of China (2010) *Statistical Bulletin for National Economic and Social Development*. Beijing: China Statistics Press.

Nguyen, X. and X. Tran (2010) 'Vietnamese-Taiwanese marriages'. In W. S. Yang and M. C. W. Lu (eds.) *Asian Cross-Border Marriage Migration: Demographic Patterns and Social Issues*. Amsterdam: Amsterdam University Press.

Oster, E. (2005) 'Hepatitis B and the case of the missing women'. *Journal of Political Economy*, 113(6): 1163–1216.

Pande, R. (2003) 'Selective gender differences in childhood nutrition and immunization in rural India: the role of siblings'. *Demography*, 40(3): 395–418.

Pande, R. P. and N. M. Astone (2007) 'Explaining son preference in rural India: the independent role of structural versus individual factors'. *Population Research and Policy Review*, 26(3): 1–29.

Park, C. B. and N. H. Cho (1995) 'Consequences of son preferences in a low-fertility society: imbalance of the sex ratio at birth in Korea'. *Population and Development Review*, 21(1): 59–84.

Pebley, A. R. and S. Amin (1991) 'The impact of a public health intervention on sex differentials in childhood mortality in rural Punjab, India'. *Health Transition Review*, 1(2): 143–169.

People's Daily (2010) '1 in 5 marriage age Chinese men to remain bachelors within 10 years' (13 January). Available from: http://english.peopledaily.com.cn/90001/90782/90872/6867770.html (accessed 13 February 2014).

Pokhrel, S., R. Snow, H. Dong, B. Hidayat, S. Flessa and R. Sauerborn (2005) 'Gender role and child health care utilization in Nepal'. *Health Policy*, 74: 100–109.

Porter, M. (2009a) 'The effects of sex ratio imbalance in China on marriage and household decisions'. University of Chicago Department of Economics.

Porter, M. (2009b) 'How marriage market conditions in China influence intergenerational transfers'. University of Chicago Department of Economics.

Puri, M. and R. Adhikari (2007) *A Rapid Assessment on Sex Ratio at Birth with Special Reference to Sex Selective Abortion and Infanticides*. Report prepared for the United Nations Population Fund. Kathmandu: UNFPA.

Qian, N. (2008) 'Missing women and the price of tea in China: the effect of sex-specific earnings on sex imbalance'. *The Quarterly Journal of Economics*, 123(3): 1251–1285.

Rao, V. (1993) 'Dowry "inflation" in rural India: a statistical investigation'. *Population Studies*, 47(2): 283–293.

Ren, X. S. (1994) 'Infant and child survival in Shaanxi, China'. *Social Science and Medicine*, 38(4): 609–621.

Ren, X. S. (1995) 'Sex differences in infant and child mortality in three provinces in China'. *Social Science and Medicine*, 40(9): 1259–1269.

Sathar, Z. (1987) 'Sex differentials in mortality: a corollary of son preference?' *Pakistan Development Review*, 26(4): 555–568.

Sharygin, E., A. Ebenstein and M. Das Gupta (2013) 'Implications of China's future bride shortage for the geographical distribution and social protection needs of never-married men'. *Population Studies*, 67(1): 39–59.

Sieder, R. and M. Mitterauer (1983) 'The reconstruction of the family life course: theoretical problems and empirical results'. In R. Wall, J. Robin, and P. Laslett (eds.) *Family Forms in Historic Europe*. Cambridge: Cambridge University Press. Pp. 309–346.

Sinha, N. and J. Yoong (2009) 'Long-term financial incentives and investment in daughters: evidence from conditional cash transfers in North India'. Policy Research Working Paper #4860. Washington, DC: The World Bank.

Statistics Korea (2013) *Marriage and Divorce Statistics, 2012*. Daejeon, Korea: Statistics Korea.

United Nations (2013) *World Population Prospects: The 2012 Revision*. New York: United Nations.

United Nations Secretariat (1998) 'Levels of trends of sex differences in infant, child and under-five mortality'. Chapter 4 in *Too Young to Die: Genes or Gender?* New York: United Nations.

Visaria, P. (1971) *The Sex Ratio of the Population of India, Census of India 1961, Vol. 1*. Monograph No. 10. New Delhi: Ministry of Home Affairs, Office of the Registrar General.

Vlassoff, C. (2007) 'Gender differences in determinants and consequences of health and illness'. *Journal of Health Population and Nutrition*, 25(1): 47–61.

Vlassoff, C. and E. Bonilla (1994) 'Gender-related differences in the impact of tropical diseases on women: what do we know?' *Journal of Biosocial Sciences*, 26: 37–53.

Waldron, I. (1983) 'Sex differences in human mortality: the role of genetic factors'. *Social Science and Medicine*, 17(6): 321–333.

Waldron, I. (1998) 'Sex differences in infant and early childhood mortality: major causes of death and possible biological causes'. In *Too Young to Die: Genes or Gender?* New York: United Nations. Pp. 64–83.

Wei, S. J. and X. Zhang (2011a) 'The competitive saving motive: evidence from rising sex ratios and savings rates in China'. *Journal of Political Economy*, 119(3): 511–564.

Wei, S. J. and X. Zhang (2011b) 'Sex ratios, entrepreneurship and economic growth in the People's Republic of China'. Working Paper #16800. Cambridge, MA: National Bureau of Economic Research.

Whitaker, I. (1976) 'Familial roles in the extended patrilineal kin-groups in Northern Albania'. In G. Peristiany (ed.) *Mediterranean Family Structures*. Cambridge: Cambridge University Press.

Williams, L. and M. K. Yu (2006) 'Domestic violence in cross-border marriage – a case study from Taiwan'. *International Journal of Migration, Health and Social Care*, 2(3/4): 58–69.

Williamson, N. E. (1976) *Sons or Daughters? A Cross-Cultural Survey of Parental Preferences*. Beverly Hills, CA: Sage Publications, Inc.

World Bank (2005) *Pakistan Country Gender Assessment Bridging the Gender Gap: Opportunities and Challenges*. Washington, DC: The World Bank.

World Bank (2011) *World Development Report 2012: Gender Equality and Development*. Washington, DC: The World Bank.

Yount, K. M. (2001) 'Girls' excess mortality in the Middle East in the 1970s and 1980s: patterns, correlates and gaps in research'. *Population Studies*, 55(3): 291–308.

Zeng, Y., P. Tu, B. Gu, Y. Xu, B. Li and Y. Li (1993) 'Causes and implications of the recent increase in the reported sex ratio at birth in China'. *Population and Development Review*, 19(2): 283–302.

10
Child mortality

Danzhen You, Lucia Hug and Kenneth Hill

Introduction

Child mortality is a key output indicator for child health and well-being, and, more broadly, for social and economic development. It is a closely watched public health indicator because it reflects the access of children and communities to basic health interventions such as vaccination, to medical treatment of infectious diseases, and to adequate nutrition. Among child mortality indicators, the under-five mortality rate (the probability of dying before the fifth birthday) is the most important one given the goal of ending all preventable child deaths under age five. The neonatal mortality rate (the probability of dying within the first 28 days of life) becomes increasingly important because of the growing share of under-five deaths that occur in the neonatal period and the specific health interventions needed to address the neonatal causes of deaths.

Child mortality is a major component of population studies. Knowledge of recent decline of child mortality is crucial for a better understanding of overall mortality change and as a possible predictor of fertility transition. As mortality transition begins, mortality rates usually decline first at young ages. For populations lacking comprehensive civil registration systems, mortality estimates for older ages are often based on models fitted using data about child mortality. Improvements in child mortality have a larger impact on life expectancy than declines at older ages, and have been responsible for much of the rise in life expectancy around the world in recent decades. In addition, reduction in child mortality used to be regarded as a key trigger for the fertility transition, as it reduces the demand for children by improving the chances of survival to adulthood. Although this is no longer seen as a hard-and-fast causal link, some analyses strongly suggest that continuing high child mortality is a significant barrier to fertility decline in sub-Saharan Africa (Bongaarts 2008). Causation also runs in the other direction, as reductions in fertility contribute to falls in child mortality by enabling parents to devote more time and resources to their children. With fertility decline, risk factors of child mortality also decline: fewer births occur at very short birth intervals, births become better spaced and there are fewer women who are either very young or very old when they have children.

Several studies have analysed social and economic background factors and demographic risk factors for child mortality. Researchers have identified a negative relationship between per capita income and level of child mortality and a clear association of higher mortality with lower income but found also great variability among countries, indicating that factors other than income levels such as efficiency of health systems, play an important role in determining levels of under-five mortality (Hill et al. 1999). Studies on demographic risk factors of child mortality have shown that birth intervals, birth order, size at birth, and mother's age impact on the survival chances of children (Cleland and van Ginneken 1988; Gakidou et al. 2010; Hobcraft et al. 1985). Children who are born within short birth intervals, as first births or as high parity births, and those who are born to very young or old mothers are associated with higher mortality risks. The educational attainment of mothers is also an important factor for child survival (Hobcraft et al. 1984; Rutstein 2000; Gakidou et al. 2010). Mother's education can mean that children receive better economic benefits, including better housing, sanitation and health care, and more educated mothers make better use of preventive and medical treatments for child and maternal health. Mosley and Chen (1984) have provided a framework which assumes that socioeconomic, cultural and health system background factors operate through a set of proximate determinants that include maternal factors (age, parity, birth interval), environmental conditions (air, food/water/fingers, skin/soil/inanimate objects, insect vectors), nutrient deficiencies (calories, protein, micronutrients), injury (accidental, intentional) and personal illness control (preventive measures, medical treatment) that directly influence the health status of children. Although it is not possible to translate the framework in a quantifiable model, it has helped to define the factors with the largest impact on child survival (Hill 2003). The impact on child mortality of water and sanitation at the household level has been shown by Fink et al. (2011).

According to the United Nations Inter-agency Group for Child Mortality Estimation (UN IGME), the developing world as a whole has experienced continuous declines in levels of child mortality from 1960 to 2015. Under-five mortality has dropped from an average of more than 200 per 1,000 live births in 1960 to around 100 per 1,000 by 1990, and has declined further to about 50 deaths per 1,000 by 2015 (UN IGME 2015). Asia, the continent with the second highest child mortality rate in the world, has experienced tremendous progress in reducing child mortality in the past few decades. However, progress has not been equal across age groups, sub-regions, countries and different subgroups within countries. This chapter discusses the progress that Asia has made in the past few decades in improving child survival as well as the issues and challenges that Asia faces to further reduce child mortality, using the child mortality estimates generated by the UN IGME (UN IGME 2015; UNICEF 2015). It focuses on the following five topics: levels and trends in child mortality, gender gaps in child mortality, mortality disparities by social-economic status, risk factors of child mortality and leading causes of child deaths.

Data sources

The Millennium Development Goal (MDG) number 4 called for a reduction of the under-five mortality rate by two-thirds between 1990 and 2015 (UN 2000). The newly agreed Sustainable Development Goals (SDGs) have set the target of ending preventable deaths of newborn babies and children younger than five years by 2030, with all countries aiming to reduce neonatal mortality to at least as low as 12 deaths per 1,000 live births and under-five mortality to at least as low as 25 deaths per 1,000 live births under SDG number 3, which seeks to ensure healthy lives and promote well-being at all ages. As global momentum and investment for accelerating child survival to meet the newly agreed SDG targets have increased, monitoring progress at the global and country levels has become even more critical. Evidence-based estimation of child mortality is a cornerstone for tracking progress towards SDG targets and for planning national and global health strategies, policies and interventions on child health. The UN IGME produces annual updates, typically released in September, of neonatal, infant and under-five mortality levels and trends for all United Nations member states. These UN IGME estimates are among the latest available information on child mortality to provide a basis for assessing progress and reaching consensus for action, and are therefore used in this chapter.

The UN IGME was established in 2004 to improve monitoring of progress towards achievement in child survival goals, and to enhance the capacity of countries to produce timely estimates of child mortality. It is led by UNICEF, and also includes the WHO, the United Nations Population Division and the World Bank. The group is advised by an independent Technical Advisory Group of leading experts in areas of demography and biostatistics (UN IGME 2015).

Civil registration systems are the preferred source of data on child mortality because they collect information as events occur and cover the entire population. However, many developing countries, including most of the countries of Asia, lack fully functioning civil registration systems that accurately record all births and deaths. Therefore national household surveys are the primary sources of data on child mortality for most developing countries. Nationally-representative estimates of child mortality can also be derived from census or sample registration systems. The UN IGME compiles all available nationally-representative data on child mortality. Country-specific estimates are then obtained by applying a statistical model to all data that meet the quality standards established by the UN IGME, and extrapolated to a common reference year. More information about the UN IGME and a detailed technical description of the methodology used by the UN IGME are available elsewhere (Alkema and New 2014; Alkema et al. 2014; UN IGME 2015; You et al. 2015).

Levels and trends in child mortality

Under-five mortality and burden of under-five deaths

Much of the news on child survival in Asia is heartening. From 1970 to 2015, the under-five mortality rate fell by 77 per cent, from 151.1 deaths per 1,000 live births to 34.3 (Table 10.1 and Figure 10.1a). Over the same period, the annual number of under-five deaths has fallen from 11.8 million to an estimated 2.6 million.

Encouragingly, the past decades have witnessed an acceleration of progress in lowering the under-five mortality rate in Asia. The annual rate of reduction has increased to 4.5 per cent in

Table 10.1 Estimated under-five mortality rate and under-five deaths (in thousands) by continent, 1970, 1990 and 2015

Region	Under-five mortality rate (deaths per 1,000 live births)			Under-five deaths (in thousands)		
	1970	1990	2015	1970	1990	2015
Africa	240.4	164.1	76.3	3,830	4,150	3,062
Americas	93.4	42.5	14.7	1,293	678	223
Asia	151.1	86.8	34.3	11,758	7,739	2,597
Europe	33.3	17.3	6.1	352	164	48
Oceania	52.1	34.5	23.8	24	17	15

Notes: In 1970, the population coverage for Africa was 88.7%, Asia: 94.7%, Americas: 99.9%, Europe: 84.9% and Oceania: 98.0%. For 1990 and 2015, the population coverage in all regions was 100%.
Source: UN IGME (2015).

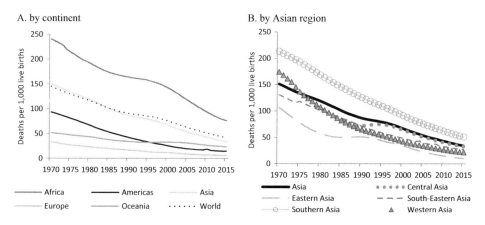

Figure 10.1 Under-five mortality rates, 1970–2015
Source: Authors' analysis based on UN IGME (2015).

the period 2000–2015 from 2.6 per cent in the 1990s – thanks to more effective and affordable treatments, innovative ways of delivering critical interventions to the poor and excluded, and sustained political commitment.

Despite these gains, children under age five in Asia still face much higher risks of dying than those in Europe, the Americas and Oceania. The under-five mortality rate in Asia in 2015 is almost 6 times the average rate of European countries, 2.3 times the average for the Americas and 1.4 times the average of Oceania. As a result of the combination of the second highest under-five mortality rate and the largest share of the world's population of children under age five (55 per cent in 2015), Asia currently bears the second highest burden of under-five deaths in the world. While its share has declined from 68 per cent in 1970, Asia still accounted for 44 per cent of all global under-five deaths in 2015.

Wide variations in under-five mortality are found across the five regions of the continent. Southern Asia has consistently experienced the highest under-five mortality rates over 1970–2015, and Eastern Asia the lowest rates (Figure 10.1b). Central Asia had similar levels of under-five mortality and similar rates of decline to Western Asia and South-Eastern Asia in the 1980s, but has been surpassed by the other two regions in the rate of reduction due to its mortality stagnation in the early 1990s. Since then, under-five mortality rates in Central Asia have remained the second highest in Asia.

Among the five regions, Eastern Asia has made the fastest progress in reducing under-five mortality – mainly driven by China, followed by Western Asia and South-Eastern Asia. Only Eastern Asia has reduced its under-five mortality rate by more than two-thirds since 1990 – with a reduction of 80 per cent – and has therefore met the MDG 4 target. All other regions did not achieve the MDG 4 target in time.

At the country level, substantial variations in the under-five mortality rate are found (Figure 10.2). In 1970, among 29 Asian countries with available data, under-five mortality rates ranged from 17.5 deaths per 1,000 live births in Japan to 329.3 deaths per 1,000 live births in Yemen. Eight countries (Afghanistan, Bangladesh, Bhutan, India, Maldives, Nepal, Oman and Yemen) had an under-five mortality rate of more than 200 deaths per 1,000 live births. In 2015, all 48 Asian countries with available data had reduced the under-five mortality rate to less than 100 deaths per 1,000 live births (Map 10.1). However, levels of under-five mortality still varied greatly across countries, ranging from 2.7 deaths per 1,000 live births in Cyprus, Japan and

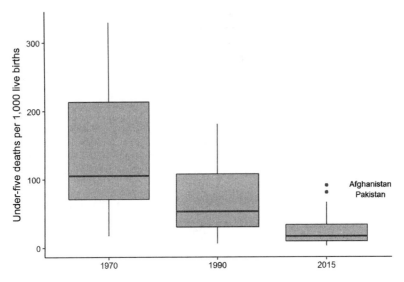

Figure 10.2 Distribution of under-five mortality rate in Asia, 1970, 1990 and 2015
Note: Afghanistan and Pakistan are two outliers in the distribution.
Source: Authors' analysis based on UN IGME (2015).

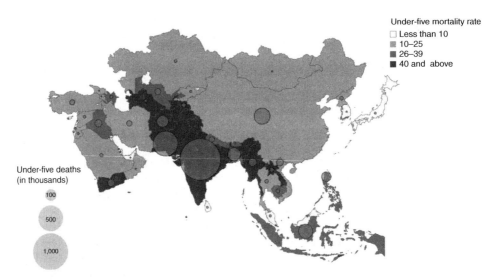

Map 10.1 Under-five mortality and under-five deaths in countries in Asia in 2015
Note: The size of the bubbles represent the number of under-five deaths per thousand live births.
Source: Authors' analysis based on UN IGME (2015).

Singapore to 91.1 in Afghanistan. In the period 1990–2015, 41 countries reduced the under-five mortality rate by at least 50 percent; among these countries, 22 (Armenia, Bahrain, Bangladesh, Bhutan, Cambodia, China, Cyprus, Georgia, Indonesia, Iran, Kazakhstan, Kyrgyzstan, Lebanon, Maldives, Mongolia, Nepal, Oman, Saudi Arabia, Thailand, Timor-Leste, Turkey and Yemen) achieved a reduction of two-thirds or more. The least progress in relative terms was recorded in Afghanistan, Brunei, Democratic People's Republic of Korea, Iraq, Pakistan, Turkmenistan and Uzbekistan, all achieving a reduction of less than 50 per cent. Detailed estimates for under-five mortality rate, neonatal mortality rate and annual rate of reduction for countries and regions in Asia are provided in Appendix Table 10.1.

Asia as a whole has reduced the number of under-five deaths significantly over the last few decades. The annual number of under-five deaths is a function of mortality rates and numbers of children under five. Up to the 1990s, the population of Asia under age five increased, but it began to decline around 2000 (UN 2015; UNICEF 2014); numbers of deaths declined steeply – about 25,000 and 14,000 fewer children died each day in 2015 than in 1970 and 1990, respectively. Within the continent, because of the increasing share of the population of children under age five in Southern Asia where child mortality remains highest, under-five deaths are increasingly concentrated in that region. In the early 1970s, about half of the under-five deaths on the continent occurred in Southern Asia, but this proportion has increased to more than 70 per cent in recent years. In 2015 almost two million children died before reaching their fifth birthday in Southern Asia alone, accounting for almost a third of global under-five deaths. In 2015, more than nine out of ten under-five deaths in Asia occurred in just ten countries – India (46 per cent), Pakistan (17 per cent), China (7 per cent), Indonesia (6 per cent), Bangladesh (5 per cent), Afghanistan (4 per cent), the Philippines (3 per cent), Myanmar (2 per cent), Iraq (1 per cent) and Yemen (1 per cent).

Declines in under-five mortality rates in Asian countries were associated with increases in GDP per capita from 1990 to 2015. However, the data in Figure 10.3 indicate that some low- and lower-middle-income countries such as Nepal and Yemen have achieved great percentage declines in under-five mortality, particularly after 2000, with relatively small increases in GDP levels. Studies on improvements in child survival have highlighted the importance of interventions such as national vitamin A supplementation programmes and vaccination schemes. In addition, improved health sector efficiency may have contributed to decreases in under-five mortality in several countries without large increases in per capita income (Hill et al. 1999).

Although all Asian countries have experienced declines in the under-five mortality rate, an increasing number of under-five deaths have been observed in several countries during some

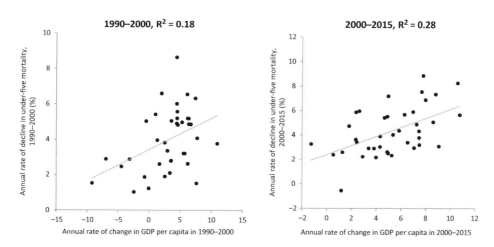

Figure 10.3 Annual rate of decline in under-five mortality rate and annual rate of change in GDP per capita (per cent) in 1990–2000 and 2000–2015 by countries in Asia
Source: Authors' analysis based on UN IGME (2015) and World Bank, International Income Distribution Database (I2D2), GDP per capita estimates published in 2016 (see http://data.worldbank.org/indicator/NY.GDP.PCAP.CD).

years due to the rising population of children under age five. For example, trends for Pakistan show an increasing number of under-five deaths before 1990 and for the period 2007–2010. Similarly, the number of under-five deaths in the Philippines rose between 1970 and the mid-1980s even though the mortality rate was constant or declining, and Timor-Leste experienced a growing number of under-five deaths in the early 1990s.

Neonatal mortality and burden of neonatal deaths

The first 28 days of life – the neonatal period – represent the most vulnerable time for a child's survival. Reducing neonatal mortality is increasingly important not only because the proportion of under-five deaths that occur during the neonatal period is increasing as under-five mortality rates fall, but also because the health interventions needed to address the major causes of neonatal deaths generally differ from, and tend to require greater health sector investment than, those needed to address the primary causes of deaths at older ages.

Asia as a whole has reduced the neonatal mortality rate by 53 per cent, from 40.4 deaths per 1,000 live births in 1990 to 19.1 in 2015; the comparable decline for under-five mortality overall is 60 per cent. Despite the decline, newborns in Asia still face much higher risk of dying than newborns in Europe, where the neonatal mortality rate is 3.4 deaths per 1,000 live births in 2015. Among Asian countries, Pakistan has the highest neonatal mortality rate in 2015 – 45.5 deaths per 1,000 live births – significantly higher than the continent's lowest neonatal mortality rate of 0.9 deaths per 1,000 live births, observed in Japan.

It is encouraging to see that Eastern Asia and Central Asia have accelerated progress in reducing neonatal mortality rates in 2000–2015 compared to 1990–2000, driven by many countries in these regions including China, Democratic People's Republic of Korea, Mongolia, Kazakhstan, Kyrgyzstan, Tajikistan, Turkmenistan and Uzbekistan.

As a result of the declining trends in both neonatal mortality rates and numbers of live births, Asia has reduced the number of neonatal deaths from 3.6 million in 1990 to 1.4 million in 2015, and lowered its share of global neonatal deaths from 71 per cent to 54 per cent. Still, Asia has the highest burden of neonatal deaths in terms of numbers among all continents.

The ratio of the neonatal mortality rate to the under-five mortality rate in Asia has increased from 0.47 in 1990 to 0.56 in 2015, as a result of a slower decline of the mortality rate in the neonatal period than in other periods. The annual rate of reduction for mortality among children aged 1–59 months has been much faster than that for neonatal mortality across all regions in Asia except Eastern Asia (Figure 10.4). The trend has resulted in a narrowing gap between Asia and Europe, where this ratio has remained almost constant over the last two decades (0.53 in 1990 and 0.56 in 2015). This trend has also resulted in a rapid increase in the proportions of under-five deaths occurring in the neonatal period. In 2015, the proportion of under-five deaths that occurred in the neonatal period in Asia (55 per cent) was similar to the proportion in Europe (56 per cent) and the Americas (52 per cent).

At the country level, most Asian countries have experienced an increasing trend in the ratio of the neonatal mortality rate to the under-five mortality rate, with the exception of a few countries that have reached very low levels of mortality including Japan, Israel, Kuwait and Singapore. The ratios across countries indicate wide variations in the composition of child mortality by age with three-quarters of the ratios ranging between 0.46 to 0.56 in 2015.

The change in the distribution of under-five deaths by age is closely linked to the change in causes of death, as the main causes of newborn deaths generally differ from the causes of deaths in other age groups. Later in this chapter, the main causes of child death in Asia will be discussed.

Child mortality

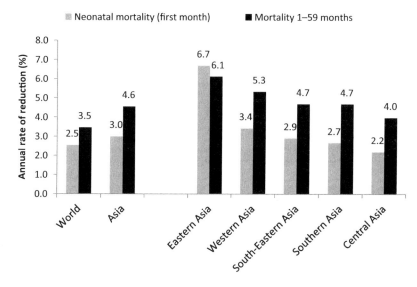

Figure 10.4 Average annual rate of reduction (per cent) in the neonatal mortality rate, and in the mortality rate from 1 to 59 months, by Asian regions, 1990–2015
Source: Authors' analysis based on UN IGME (2015).

Gender gaps in child mortality

Generally, girls tend to have better biological endowments than boys for survival to age five (Waldron 1998). The sex ratio for under-five mortality, defined as the ratio of male to female under-five mortality rates, is usually above one, meaning the mortality risk is higher for male under-fives than for female under-fives.

However, the sex ratio in child mortality may vary naturally depending on mortality levels and the associated cause of death distribution, and may therefore change over time as mortality declines. With declining mortality levels (males and females combined) the survival advantages of girls tend to become more pronounced (Hill and Upchurch, 1995; Tabutin and Willems 1998; Drevenstedt et al. 2008). Gender gaps can also be impacted by other factors and unusually high or low sex ratios may be the result of differential treatment of boys and girls. In several countries, mostly in Asia, under-five mortality rates for boys are lower than those for girls. Identifying these countries and the underlying causes for their atypically low or high mortality sex ratios is important in order to address gender discrimination in treatment of boys or girls.

A recent study by Alkema et al. (2014) has developed a robust model which has been adopted by the UN IGME, to estimate mortality sex ratios and to identify countries with outlying mortality sex ratios. The model provides estimated mortality sex ratios and female mortality for each country over time, for infant mortality (under age 1), child mortality (age 1 to 4) and under-five mortality. It also allows calculation of the expected female mortality, based on the estimated male mortality level and the global pattern of mortality sex ratios. Regions and countries are defined as *outliers* in a specific year if the absolute value of the point estimate for excess female mortality exceeds one per 1,000 live births for the excess infant and under-five mortality rates, and one per 1,000 survivors up to age 1 year for the excess child mortality rate, and if the posterior (revised) probability that the excess female mortality is either negative or positive exceeds 90 per cent (Alkema et al. 2014).

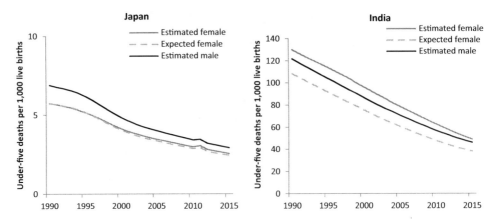

Figure 10.5 Expected female and estimated female and male under-five mortality in Japan and India, 1990–2015
Source: UN IGME (2015).

In 2015 Asia had the lowest sex ratio for under-five mortality (1.04) among all continents. Asia's sex ratio has been identified as an outlier, with an excess under-five female mortality of four deaths per 1,000 live births and an estimated female under-five mortality that is 1.15 times higher than the expected female mortality. The outlying sex ratio for Asia in 2015 is mainly driven by Southern Asia – the only region in Asia with an estimated female under-five mortality rate higher than expected. In 2015, the female excess under-five mortality rate in Southern Asia is nine deaths per 1,000 live births and the estimated female mortality is 1.21 times higher than the expected female mortality rate. Since 1990, the number of regions with an outlying sex ratio in Asia has declined. While Eastern Asia and Western Asia had outlying under-five mortality sex ratios (lower than expected) in 1990, their sex ratios in 2015 fall within the expected range. In Central Asia and South-Eastern Asia, however, the sex ratios in 1990 were higher than expected, indicating lower than expected female under-five mortality rates. For Central Asia this still applied for 2015.

Among Asian countries, India's estimated female under-five mortality is far higher than expected, while in Japan estimated and expected female under-five mortality are almost identical (Figure 10.5). Overall, the number of countries in Asia experiencing outlying sex ratios with higher than expected female under-five mortality has fallen from 13 in 1990 to 6 in 2015. Detailed country estimates for the sex ratio in under-five mortality, estimated male and female under-five mortality and expected female under-five mortality for all countries in Asia are provided in Appendix Table 10.2.

For infants, the highest global excess female infant mortality rate is observed in India with 7.3 deaths per 1,000 live births in 2015, and a female mortality rate about 20 per cent higher than expected (Figure 10.6). The excess female infant mortality rate in India has declined from 9.3 deaths per 1,000 live births in 1990, while the ratio of estimated to expected female infant mortality has increased from 1.12 in 1990 to 1.24 in 2015. Overall, nine Asian countries had an outlying infant mortality sex ratio with higher than expected female infant mortality in 1990, and in all cases their excess female infant mortality has decreased since then. Declines in the excess female mortality since 1990 have been related mainly to decreases in the overall mortality level (Alkema et al. 2014). As of 2015, India, Iran and Jordan remain outliers with higher than expected female infant mortality.

Child mortality

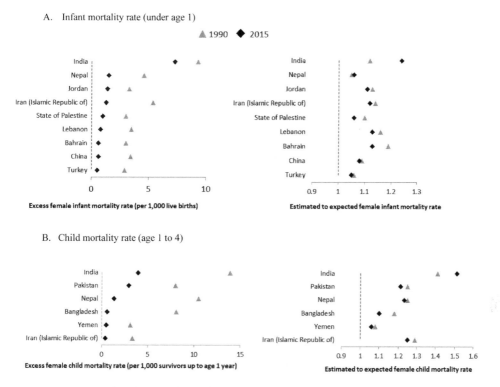

Figure 10.6 Excess female mortality and ratio of estimated to expected female mortality for countries in Asia with outlying sex ratios and higher female mortality than expected, 1990 and 2015
Source: UN IGME (2015).

Fewer Asian countries experience an outlying sex ratio in child mortality (age 1 to 4 years) with a higher than expected female child mortality, compared with the comparable number of infant mortality outliers. In 2015, the highest excess female child mortality rate is observed in India with 3.9 deaths per 1,000 survivors up to age 1 year, followed by Pakistan with 2.9 and Nepal with 1.3. In India the estimated female child mortality in 2015 is about 50 per cent higher than expected (Figure 10.6), compared to around 20 per cent for Pakistan and Nepal. Excess female child mortality in India has declined from 13.9 in 1990 to 3.9 in 2015, while the ratio of estimated to expected female child mortality has increased from 1.41 to 1.51. In Bangladesh, the ratio of estimated to expected female child mortality has declined from 1.18 in 1990 to 1.10 in 2015, and the country's excess child mortality rate has dropped from 8.1 to 0.6. For the other four outlying countries in Asia with higher than expected female child mortality, Nepal, Iran, Pakistan and Yemen, excess child mortality has declined in the last 25 years although the ratios of estimated to expected female child mortality have not changed substantially.

Findings from previous studies have suggested male preference for India and a few other countries (Alam et al. 2007; Arokiasamy 2007; Krishnan et al. 2012; Li et al. 2004; Yount 2001) and pinpointed causes of outlying sex ratios such as male preference in the provision of vaccinations (Rammohan et al. 2014). Information about factors that might have caused outlying sex ratios in other countries is very scarce. Explanation needs to be sought for countries with outlying sex ratios, and action should be undertaken if sex discrimination is present.

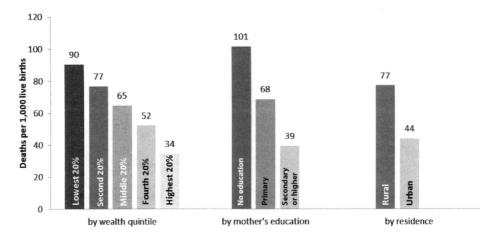

Figure 10.7 Under-five mortality rate by wealth quintile, mother's education and residence for countries in Asia, 2005–2013
Note: Data are based on the most recent 15 MICS or DHS surveys in participating countries since 2005.
Source: Authors' analysis based on MICS and DHS surveys.

Mortality disparities by social-economic status

Wide variations in child mortality are found not only across regions and countries, but also within countries. Disaggregated data from household surveys for 15 Asian countries in recent years (Armenia (2010), Azerbaijan (2006), Bangladesh (2011), Cambodia (2010), Georgia (2005), India (2005), Indonesia (2012), Jordan (2012), Kyrgyzstan (2012), Maldives (2009), Nepal (2011), Pakistan (2012), Philippines (2008), Tajikistan (2012), Timor-Leste (2009)) suggest that in the global push to achieve child survival targets, progress in reducing child mortality has been uneven.

Children from poorer households remain disproportionately vulnerable. Under-five mortality rates are, on average, more than twice as high for the poorest 20 per cent of households as for the richest 20 per cent in the Asian countries studied (Figure 10.7). Mortality is also more likely to strike children in rural areas. Children in rural areas are about 1.8 times more likely to die before their fifth birthday than those in urban areas.

Similarly, mother's education remains a powerful determinant of inequality. Children of mothers with primary school or above education are more likely to survive than children of mothers without such education (Figure 10.7).

The mortality disparities are observed for all age groups of children under age five. However, the disparities by wealth quintile and mother's education are more prominent for children aged 1–4 and less prominent for newborns in the Asian countries studied, probably relating to different causes of deaths. For children aged 1–4, those living in poorer households and whose mothers have no education are four times more likely to die than those in the richest households and whose mothers have secondary or higher education.

Risk factors of child mortality

Survey data for 15 Asian countries give important indications on mortality risks associated with the age of the mother, birth interval, birth order and size at birth (Figures 10.8 and 10.9). Children born to mothers under age 20 have a mortality rate at least 1.5 times higher than

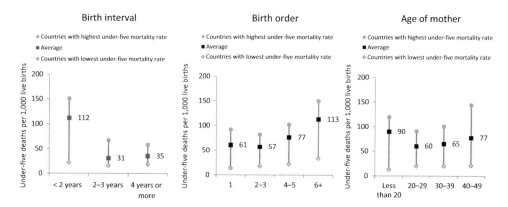

Figure 10.8 Under-five mortality rate by birth interval, birth order and age of mother for countries in Asia, 2005–2013
Notes: Data are based on the most recent MICS or DHS surveys in participating countries since 2005. Data by birth interval are based on 15 surveys, data by birth order on 14 surveys, and data on age of mother are based on 13 surveys.
Source: Authors' analysis based on MICS and DHS surveys.

Figure 10.9 Neonatal mortality rate by birth size for countries in Asia, 2005–2013
Note: Data are based on the most recent 14 MICS or DHS surveys in participating countries since 2005.
Source: Authors' analysis based on MICS and DHS surveys.

children born to mothers in their twenties or thirties; children born to mothers over age 40 have higher mortality rates than those born to women between 20 and 39, but lower than those of children born to young mothers under age 20.

One of the strongest factors associated with child mortality risk is the birth interval preceding the child's birth. The under-five mortality rate for children with preceding birth intervals of less than two years is more than three times higher than that for children with a preceding interval of 2–3 years. Short birth intervals are a particularly significant risk factor in the first year and become less important for children aged 1–4. Data from 15 Asian countries also show that high birth order is associated with higher mortality risk. Children born as fourth or fifth children have a higher mortality risk than children born as first, second or third. The mortality is even more elevated for children born as sixth children. However, the association between high parity and child mortality may not be driven by a physiological link between parity and mortality; it can be largely attributed to differences in the background characteristics of mothers who complete reproduction with high fertility versus low fertility. The background characteristics of mothers with high fertility tend to be related to higher health risks for their children irrespective of the order the children are born in (Kozuki et al. 2013). Small birth size (as reported by mothers) may also be associated with an increased risk: survey data show that newborns reported as being of 'very small' or 'small' birth size have higher neonatal mortality rates than newborns with 'average' or 'large' size at birth (Figure 10.9), particularly in high mortality countries. These findings confirm the earlier results from Hobcraft et al. (1985) that demographic factors and especially birth intervals are related to the survival chances of children under age five.

Leading causes of child deaths

Renewing the promise of survival for children requires tracking and addressing the leading causes of deaths. Infectious diseases (such as pneumonia and diarrhoea), undernutrition and neonatal complications are responsible for the vast majority of under-five deaths globally as well as in Asia (UNICEF 2015).

The cause of death distribution varies significantly with the level of under-five mortality. Whereas preterm birth complications, congenital abnormalities and injuries have become the major causes of death in low mortality countries, infectious diseases still remain a major cause of death for children in high-mortality countries (UNICEF 2015). Worldwide, the leading causes of death among children under five in 2015 include preterm birth complications (18 per cent), pneumonia (15 per cent), diarrhoea (9 per cent), intrapartum related complications (12 per cent), neonatal sepsis (7 per cent) and malaria (5 per cent) (Liu et al. 2016; UNICEF 2015). In Asia, preterm birth complications have been the main killer of children under age five, accounting for 24 per cent of the 2.6 million under-five deaths in 2015, a proportion similar to the one in Europe. Pneumonia and diarrhoea, which are mostly preventable, account for 15 and 8 per cent respectively of all under-five deaths in the continent (Figure 10.10). These proportions remain much higher than in Europe, where pneumonia and diarrhoea account for only 6 and 1 per cent respectively of all under-five deaths. While malaria killed more than 1,000 children under five years of age worldwide every day in 2015, 96 per cent of the deaths were in sub-Saharan Africa; few Asian children have died of malaria in recent decades.

Asia has seen major declines in child deaths due to infectious diseases in the last decade, thanks to expanded efforts against such diseases. The most dramatic proportional fall has been in tetanus deaths, which have plummeted by more than 85 per cent between 2000 and 2015. Child deaths from measles (74 per cent) and diarrhoea (64 per cent) have also dropped by more than 60 per cent over the same period. Pneumonia was the leading cause of death of Asian children under age five in 2000, causing 19 per cent of all under-five deaths, but since 2005 it has been the second major cause, having been replaced as the most important cause by preterm complications. In addition, the number of under-five deaths caused by pneumonia has declined by 60 per cent from 2000 to 2015.

Nonetheless, infectious diseases, which are most often diseases of the poor and which therefore represent a marker of equity, still remain prevalent in the continent of Asia. Leading infectious diseases (including pneumonia, diarrhoea, malaria, AIDS, pertussis, tetanus, measles, meningitis and sepsis) together accounted for 35 per cent of all Asian under-five deaths in 2015.

As the proportion of under-five deaths that occur in the neonatal period increases over time, addressing neonatal complications is increasingly important. Southern Asia had the highest

A. 2000

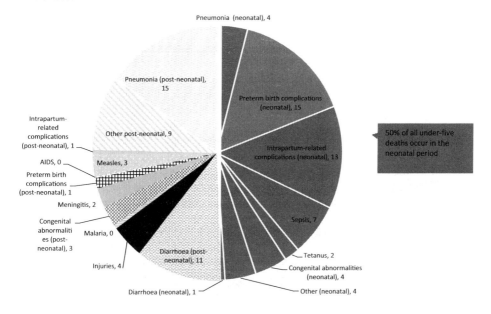

B. 2015

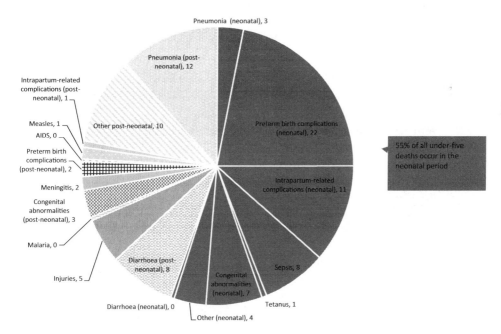

Figure 10.10 Distribution of deaths among children under five in Asia, by cause, 2000 and 2015
Source: Authors' analysis drawing on WHO and Maternal and Child Epidemiology Estimation Group (MCEE) estimates (2015).

proportion of under-five deaths caused by diseases and complications occurring in the neonatal period in 2015, with 6 of 10 under-five deaths occurring in the neonatal period, and Central Asia had the lowest proportion (about 50 per cent). Among the 1.4 million neonatal deaths in Asia, preterm birth complications (40 per cent), intrapartum related birth complications (21 per cent), neonatal sepsis (14 per cent) and congenital abnormalities (12 per cent) are the main causes. Regional variations in the composition of causes of death are substantial. The proportion of under-five deaths due to diarrhoea in Eastern Asia (3 per cent) is less than in Southern Asia (9 per cent), Central Asia (7 per cent), South-Eastern Asia (7 per cent) and Western Asia (5 per cent). However, Eastern Asia has a higher share of under-five deaths due to injury than other regions, particularly Southern Asia; injury accounted for 16 per cent of under-five deaths in Eastern Asia in 2015, but only 5 per cent in Southern Asia.

Cross-country comparisons show a wide variation among countries in the proportions of under-five deaths attributable to specific causes. In Afghanistan, pneumonia and diarrhoea account for a third of all under-five deaths (20 per cent die from pneumonia and 12 per cent from diarrhoea); similarly pneumonia and diarrhoea cause 31 per cent of all under-five deaths in Timor-Leste. For India – a country with a relatively high under-five mortality rate of 48 deaths per 1,000 live births – the leading cause of death is preterm birth complications, which account for 27 per cent of all under-five deaths, above the Asian average of 24 per cent. Preterm birth complications account for a similar share of under-five deaths in countries like Georgia, Lebanon and Qatar. The number two cause of death in India is pneumonia, accounting for 15 per cent of all child deaths or 180,000 deaths; around 1 in 10 children in Bangladesh, Nepal and Pakistan die from sepsis. In Japan, Syrian Arab Republic and China 12 to 17 per cent of all under-five deaths are caused by injuries (Table 10.2). Such variations indicate that optimal programmatic approaches for child survival will differ from country to country.

Successes and challenges

Asia as a whole has made substantial progress in reducing child mortality in the past few decades – the continent has saved the lives of more than 68 million children under age five since 1990 to 2015. This progress is associated with improved health behaviours, improved coverage of effective interventions to prevent or treat the most important causes of child

Table 10.2 Ten countries in Asia with highest proportion (%) of estimated under-five deaths caused by pneumonia, diarrhoea or injury, 2015

Pneumonia		Diarrhoea		Injury	
Timor-Leste	21	Syrian Arab Republic	14	China	17
Afghanistan	20	Afghanistan	12	Syrian Arab Republic	12
Philippines	19	Laos	11	Japan	12
Tajikistan	17	India	10	Republic of Korea	10
Laos	17	Timor-Leste	10	Qatar	10
Indonesia	17	Pakistan	9	Saudi Arabia	10
Turkmenistan	17	Turkmenistan	8	Oman	9
Cambodia	17	Tajikistan	8	Philippines	9
Myanmar	16	Philippines	8	Jordan	9
Yemen	16	Yemen	7	Armenia	9

Source: Authors' analysis using WHO and Maternal and Child Epidemiology Estimation Group (MCEE) estimates (2015).

mortality and improvements in socioeconomic conditions. For example, significant progress has been achieved in terms of sanitation; in 1990 only one-third of the population of Asia was using an improved sanitation facility, compared to 66 per cent in 2015. Open defecation decreased from 32 per cent to 16 per cent over the same period (WHO and UNICEF 2015). The proportion of births attended by skilled health personnel has increased from 69 per cent in 1990 to 84 per cent in 2015 for Asia as a whole, and the number of women with at least four antenatal care visits has risen from 28 per cent to 52 per cent over the same period. In Eastern and Central Asia almost every woman gives birth with skilled attendance (UNICEF global databases 2016).

The enormous progress in child survival in some countries including Bangladesh, China and Nepal suggests that child mortality can decline rapidly in low- and middle-income countries if the political will and resources exist to maintain long-term focus. The 'Success Factors' studies by the Partnership for Maternal, Newborn and Child Health (PMNCH), WHO, World Bank and the Alliance for Health Policy and Systems Research (AHPSR) in 2014 identified factors that have contributed to the rapid child mortality decline in ten fast-track countries, of which six are from Asia. The studies suggest that underpinning the diverse approaches used by the ten fast-track countries is a common commitment to focus on results and to continue investing where the potential health benefits are greatest, such as in maternal and newborn care. It is also clear that strong health sectors, supported by modern data management systems, play an important role in accelerating progress on maternal and child health. In Bangladesh, the coordinated efforts of Community Health Workers and NGOs, working under the umbrella of the national Expanded Programme on Immunization (EPI), have saved many children's lives. Immunization coverage in vaccines against tuberculosis (BCG), diphtheria-tetanus-pertussis (DTP3), polio (Pol3) and measles (MCV) in the country has risen from less than 2 per cent in 1985 to at least 65 per cent in 1990, and to at least 88 per cent coverage in 2015 (WHO Regional Office for South-East Asia 2016). Over the past few decades, China has made intensive policy and planning efforts to improve health, including strengthening and upgrading infrastructure for health as well as for drinking water and sanitation to serve all levels of society. Nepal introduced the National Health Policy in 1991 and has implemented a series of effective programmes at different levels of the health system, focused on improving maternal and newborn outcomes, such as the community-based Integrated Management of Childhood Illness Programme, the National Immunization Programme and the National Newborn Care Package. In 2001, about 12 per cent of women in Nepal gave birth with the help of a skilled birth attendant; this rate has risen to 54 per cent in 2014 (UNICEF global databases 2016). The successful stories in improving maternal and child survival in these countries have provided evidence on strategies that can be used to accelerate progress elsewhere.

This chapter not only summarizes great achievements made in lowering child mortality in Asia to date, but also reveals the glaring disparities in child survival across regions and countries, as well as within countries, that we must address if we are to achieve more sustainable and more equitable progress towards SDG targets and beyond. Children in Afghanistan, which has the highest under-five mortality rate in the continent, are more than 30 times more likely to die before their fifth birthday than children in Japan or Singapore. Reaching the most vulnerable children in poorer countries and households is essential to further reduce child mortality in Asia. Furthermore, reducing gender gaps in child mortality in a few Asian countries, including India, Nepal and Pakistan, is needed to further improve gender equity in Asia.

Despite the substantial progress in reducing child mortality in Asia, the unfinished business of child survival looms large. Currently, nine countries in Asia are still classified as high mortality countries with an under-five mortality rate of 40 or more deaths per 1,000 live births. Among

48 Asian countries with available data, less than half (22) have met the MDG 4 target by 2015. Asia as a whole has failed to meet the MDG target.

Infectious diseases that are readily preventable or treatable with proven, cost-effective interventions are still killing millions of Asian children each year. Actions must be taken immediately to save these children's lives by expanding effective preventive and curative interventions. At the same time, plans must be made for the future. Discussions and consultations have been undertaken globally on setting the post-2015 agenda for child and maternal health. Governments, the United Nations and its agencies, civil society groups, and the private sector are rallying a broad coalition to renew the world's promise to give every child the best possible start in life. The SDG agenda has set a target of an under-five mortality rate of 25 or fewer deaths per 1,000 live births by the year 2030 for all countries (United Nations 2015). It is estimated that six Asian countries (Afghanistan, Laos, Myanmar, Pakistan, Timor-Leste and Turkmenistan) need to accelerate progress in order to meet this target. Accelerating progress in these countries to achieve the SDG by 2030 could save the lives of 2 million children between 2016 and 2030. Finishing the unfinished business is not only about reaching the SDG targets. It is about ending preventable child deaths by targeting the leading causes of death and by reaching children, mothers and families everywhere – no matter how poor or marginal.

Appendix

Appendix Table 10.1 Estimated under-five mortality rate, neonatal mortality rate and annual rate of reduction, 1970, 1990 and 2015

Country name or region	Under-five mortality rate (deaths per 1,000 live births)			Annual rate of reduction (%)		Neonatal mortality rate (deaths per 1,000 live births)		Annual rate of reduction (%)
	1970	1990	2015	1970–1990	1990–2015	1990	2015	1990–2015
World	145	91	43	2.3	3.0	36	19	2.5
Asia	151	87	34	2.8	3.7	40	19	3.0
Central Asia		73	33		3.2	28	16	2.2
Kazakhstan		53	14		5.3	22	7	4.6
Kyrgyzstan		65	21		4.5	25	12	3.1
Tajikistan		108	45		3.5	32	21	1.8
Turkmenistan		91	51		2.3	30	23	1.1
Uzbekistan		72	39		2.4	31	20	1.7
Eastern Asia	106	51	10	3.7	6.4	28	5	6.7
China	113	54	11	3.7	6.5	30	6	6.7
Japan	18	6	3	5.1	3.4	3	1	4.1
Korea DPR		43	25		2.2	22	14	1.9
Korea Republic	53	7	3	10	2.9	3	2	2.1
Mongolia		108	22		6.3	32	11	4.2
South-Eastern Asia	131	72	27	3.0	3.9	28	13	2.9
Brunei		12	10		0.7	6	4	1.6
Cambodia		117	29		5.6	41	15	4

Appendix Table 10.1 (Cont.)

Country name or region	Under-five mortality rate (deaths per 1,000 live births)			Annual rate of reduction (%)		Neonatal mortality rate (deaths per 1,000 live births)		Annual rate of reduction (%)
	1970	1990	2015	1970–1990	1990–2015	1990	2015	1990–2015
Indonesia	166	85	27	3.4	4.5	30	14	3.2
Laos		162	67		3.6	55	30	2.4
Malaysia	56	17	7	6.1	3.5	9	4	3.3
Myanmar	179	110	50	2.4	3.2	47	26	2.3
Philippines	84	58	28	1.8	2.9	20	13	1.8
Singapore	27	8	3	6.3	4.2	4	1	5.5
Thailand	100	37	12	5	4.4	20	7	4.5
Timor-Leste		176	53		4.8	56	22	3.7
Vietnam	86	51	22	2.6	3.4	24	11	3.0
Southern Asia	213	126	51	2.6	3.6	57	29	2.7
Afghanistan	308	181	91	2.7	2.7	53	36	1.6
Bangladesh	224	144	38	2.2	5.4	63	23	4
Bhutan	272	134	33	3.5	5.6	44	18	3.5
India	213	126	48	2.6	3.9	57	28	2.9
Iran		58	16		5.2	27	10	4.1
Maldives	261	94	9	5.1	9.6	43	5	8.7
Nepal	268	141	36	3.2	5.5	59	22	3.9
Pakistan	189	139	81	1.5	2.1	64	46	1.4
Sri Lanka	71	21	10	6.1	3.1	14	5	3.9
Western Asia	175	65	22	4.9	4.4	28	12	3.4
Armenia		50	14		5	23	7	4.5
Azerbaijan		95	32		4.4	36	18	2.7
Bahrain	77	23	6	6	5.2	15	1	10.5
Cyprus		11	3		5.7	6	2	5.3
Georgia		48	12		5.6	25	7	4.9
Iraq	115	54	32	3.8	2.1	27	18	1.5
Israel		12	4		4.3	6	2	4.4
Jordan	90	37	18	4.5	2.9	20	11	2.6
Kuwait	71	18	9	6.9	2.9	10	3	4.7
Lebanon	63	33	8	3.3	5.5	21	5	5.9
Oman	228	39	12	8.8	4.9	17	5	4.8
Qatar	66	21	8	5.8	3.8	11	4	4.4
Saudi Arabia		44	15		4.5	22	8	4.2
State of Palestine		44	21		3	22	12	2.5
Syria	105	37	13	5.2	4.2	17	7	3.5
Turkey	187	75	14	4.6	6.8	33	7	6.1
United Arab Emirates	98	17	7	8.9	3.5	8	4	3.4
Yemen	329	126	42	4.8	4.4	44	22	2.8

Note: Cells are left blank where data are not available.
Source: UN IGME (2015).

Appendix Table 10.2 Sex ratio in under-five mortality, estimated male and female under-five mortality and expected female under-five mortality, 1990 and 2015

Country	Sex ratio of under-five mortality		Estimated male under-five mortality rate (deaths per 1,000 live births)		Estimated female under-five mortality rate (deaths per 1,000 live births)		Expected female under-five mortality rate (deaths per 1,000 live births)	
	1990	2015	1990	2015	1990	2015	1990	2015
Afghanistan*+	1.05	1.08	186	95	176	87	168	83
Armenia	1.22	1.25	55	16	45	13	45	13
Azerbaijan	1.19	1.18	103	34	87	29	90	28
Bahrain*	1.07	1.08	24	6	22	6	19	5
Bangladesh*	1.04	1.16	147	40	141	35	132	33
Bhutan	1.1	1.23	140	36	127	30	126	29
Brunei Darussalam	1.19	1.19	13	11	11	9	11	9
Cambodia	1.15	1.27	125	32	109	25	111	26
China*	1.09	1.13	56	11	52	10	47	9
Cyprus	1.23	1.2	12	3	10	3	10	2
DPR Korea	1.2	1.24	47	28	39	22	39	22
Georgia	1.26	1.27	53	13	42	11	44	11
India*+	0.94	0.94	122	46	130	49	108	38
Indonesia	1.17	1.27	91	30	78	24	80	24
Iran*+	1.01	1.09	58	16	57	15	49	13
Iraq	1.17	1.21	58	35	50	29	49	28
Israel	1.15	1.16	12	4	11	4	10	4
Japan	1.21	1.16	7	3	6	3	6	2
Jordan*+	1.09	1.12	38	19	35	17	31	15
Kazakhstan*	1.29	1.34	59	16	46	12	49	13
Kuwait	1.19	1.16	19	9	16	8	16	8
Kyrgyzstan	1.19	1.25	71	24	59	19	60	19
Laos	1.13	1.2	172	73	152	61	156	62
Lebanon*	1.1	1.09	34	9	31	8	28	7
Malaysia	1.27	1.22	19	8	15	6	15	6
Maldives	1.14	1.22	100	9	88	8	88	8
Mongolia*+	1.35	1.49	123	27	92	18	110	21
Myanmar	1.16	1.22	118	55	102	45	105	46
Nepal*+	1.01	1.13	141	38	140	34	126	31
Oman	1.19	1.21	43	13	36	10	35	10
Pakistan*+	1.04	1.09	141	85	136	77	125	73
Philippines	1.21	1.26	64	31	53	25	55	25
Qatar	1.2	1.19	23	9	19	7	18	7
Republic of Korea	1.06	1.16	7	4	7	3	6	3
Saudi Arabia*	1.11	1.14	47	16	42	14	38	13
Singapore	1.19	1.16	8	3	7	3	7	2
Sri Lanka	1.19	1.22	23	11	19	9	18	9
State of Palestine*	1.13	1.19	47	23	42	19	39	18
Syrian Arab Republic	1.18	1.22	40	14	34	12	33	11
Tajikistan	1.18	1.25	117	50	99	40	103	41
Thailand*	1.31	1.29	42	14	32	11	34	11

Appendix Table 10.2 (Cont.)

Country	Sex ratio of under-five mortality		Estimated male under-five mortality rate (deaths per 1,000 live births)		Estimated female under-five mortality rate (deaths per 1,000 live births)		Expected female under-five mortality rate (deaths per 1,000 live births)	
	1990	2015	1990	2015	1990	2015	1990	2015
Timor-Leste	1.09	1.18	183	57	168	48	165	47
Turkey*	1.09	1.18	78	15	71	12	67	12
Turkmenistan*	1.29	1.33	102	59	79	44	88	49
United Arab Emirates	1.26	1.23	18	8	15	6	15	6
Uzbekistan*	1.26	1.3	80	44	63	34	68	36
Vietnam*	1.26	1.32	57	25	45	19	48	20
Yemen	1.09	1.19	132	46	121	38	118	37

Notes: *Outlying country in 1990, +Outlying country in 2015.
Source: UN IGME (2015).

References

Alam, N., J. van Ginneken and A. Bosch (2007) 'Decreases in male and female mortality and missing women in Bangladesh'. In I. Attané, C. Z. Guilmoto (eds.) *Watering the Neighbour's Garden: The Growing Demographic Female Deficit in Asia*. Paris: CICRED. Pp. 161–182.

Alkema, L., F. Chao, D. You, J. Pedersen and C. C. Sawyer (2014) 'A systematic assessment of national, regional and global sex ratios of infant, child and under-five mortality and identification of countries with outlying levels'. *The Lancet Global Health*, 2(9): e521–e530. Available from: http://dx.doi.org/10.1016/S2214-109X(14)70280-3.

Alkema, L. and J. R. New (2014) 'Global estimation of child mortality using a Bayesian B-spline bias-reduction method'. *Annals of Applied Statistics*, 8(4): 2122–2149. Available from: http://dx.doi.org/10.1214/14-AOAS768.

Alkema, L., J. R. New, J. Pedersen, D. You and the Technical Advisory Group of the United Nations Inter-agency Group for Child Mortality Estimation (2014) 'Child mortality estimation 2013: an overview of updates in estimation methods by the United Nations Inter-agency Group for Child Mortality Estimation'. *PLoS ONE*, 9(7): e101112. Available from: http://dx.doi.org/10.1371/journal.pone.0101112.

Alkema, L. and D. You (2012) 'Child mortality estimation: a comparison of UN IGME and IHME estimates of levels and trends in under-five mortality rates and deaths'. *PLoS Medicine*, 9(8): e1001288. Available from: http://dx.doi.org/10.1371/journal.pmed.1001288.

Arokiasamy, P. (2007) 'Sex ratio at birth and excess female child mortality in India: trends, differentials and regional patterns'. In I. Attané and C. Z. Guilmoto (eds.) *Watering the Neighbour's Garden: The Growing Demographic Female Deficit in Asia*. Paris: CICRED. Pp. 49–72.

Bongaarts, J. (2006) 'The causes of stalling fertility transitions'. *Studies in Family Planning*, 37(1): 1–16.

Bongaarts, J. (2008) 'Fertility transitions in developing countries: progress or stagnation?' *Studies in Family Planning*, 39(2): 105–110.

Cleland, J. G. and J. K. van Ginneken (1988) 'Maternal education and child survival in developing countries: the search for pathways of influence'. *Social Science and Medicine*, 27: 1357–1368.

Drevenstedt, G. L., E. M. Crimmins, S. Vasunilashorn and C. E. Finch (2008) 'The rise and fall of excess male infant mortality'. *Proceedings of the National Academy of Sciences of the United States of America*, 105: 5016–5021.

Fink, G., I. Günther and K. Hill (2011) 'The effect of water and sanitation on child health: evidence from the demographic and health surveys 1986–2007'. *International Journal of Epidemiology*, 40(5): 1196–1204. Available from: http://dx.doi.org/10.1093/ije/dyr102.

Gakidou, E., K. Cowling, R. Lozano and C. L. J. Murray (2010) 'Increased educational attainment and its effect on child mortality in 175 countries between 1970 and 2009: a systematic analysis'. *Lancet*, 376(9745): 959–974.

Guillot, M., P. Gerland, F. Pelletier and A. Saabneh (2012) 'Child mortality estimation: a global overview of infant and child mortality age patterns in light of new empirical data'. *PLoS Medicine*, 9(8): e1001299. Available from: http://dx.doi.org/10.1371/journal.pmed.1001299.

Hill, K. (2003) 'Frameworks for studying the determinants of child survival'. *Bulletin of the World Health Organization*, 81(2): 138–139.

Hill, K., R. Pande, M. Mahy and G. Jones (1999) *Trends in Child Mortality in the Developing World: 1960 to 1996*. New York: UNICEF.

Hill, K. and D. Upchurch (1995) 'Gender differentials in child health: evidence from the DHS'. *Population and Development Review*, 21(1): 127–151.

Hill, K., D. You, M. Inoue, M. Z. Oestergaard and the Technical Advisory Group of the United Nations Inter-agency Group for Child Mortality Estimation (2012) 'Child mortality estimation: accelerated progress in reducing global child mortality, 1990–2010'. *PLoS Medicine*, 9(8): e1001303. Available from: http://dx.doi.org/10.1371/journal.pmed.1001303.

Hobcraft, J. N., J. W. McDonald and S. O. Rutstein (1984). 'Socio-economic factors in infant and child mortality: a cross national comparison'. *Population Studies*, 38(2): 193–223.

Hobcraft, J. N., J. W. McDonald and S. O. Rutstein (1985) 'Demographic determinants of infant and early child mortality: a comparative analysis'. *Population Studies*, 39(3): 363–385.

Kozuki, N., E. Sonneveldt and N. Walker (2013) 'Residual confounding explains the association between high parity and child mortality'. *BioMed Central Public Health*, 13(suppl. 3): S5.

Krishnan, A., N. Ng, S. K. Kapoor, C. S. Pandav and P. Byass (2012) 'Temporal trends and gender differentials in causes of childhood deaths at Ballabgarh, India – need for revisiting child survival strategies'. *BioMed Central Public Health*, 12: 555.

Li, S., C. Zhu and M. W. Feldman (2004) 'Gender differences in child survival in contemporary rural China: a county study'. *Journal of Biosocial Science*, 36: 83–109.

Liu, L., S. Oza, D. Hogan, Y. C. Chi, J. Perin, J. Zhu, J. E. Lawn, S. Cousens, C. Mathers and R. E. Black (2016) 'Global, regional, and national causes of under-5 mortality in 2000–15: an updated systematic analysis with implications for the Sustainable Development Goals'. *Lancet*, 388(10063): 3027–3035.

Mosley, W. H. and L. C. Chen (1984) 'An analytical framework for the study of child survival in developing countries'. *Population and Development Review*, 10(suppl.): 25–45.

Pedersen, J. and J. Liu (2012) 'Child mortality estimation: appropriate time periods for child mortality estimates from full birth histories'. *PLoS Medicine*, 9(8): e1001289. Available from: http://dx.doi.org/10.1371/journal.pmed.1001289.

PMNCH, WHO, World Bank and AHPSR (2014) 'Success factors for women's and children's health: policy and programme highlights from ten fast-track countries'. Geneva: WHO.

Rammohan, A., N. Awofeso and K. Iqbal (2014) 'Gender differentials in the timing of measles vaccination in rural India'. *Demographic Research*, 30: 1825–1848.

Rutstein, S. O. (2000) 'Factors associated with trends in infant and child mortality in developing countries during the 1990s'. *Bulletin of the World Health Organization*, 78(10): 1256–1270.

Sawyer, C. C. (2012) 'Child mortality estimation: estimating sex differences in childhood mortality since the 1970s'. *PLoS Medicine*, 9(8): e1001287. Available from: http://dx.doi.org/10.1371/journal.pmed.1001287.

Silva, R. (2012) 'Child mortality estimation: consistency of under-five mortality rate estimates using full birth histories and summary birth histories'. *PLoS Medicine*, 9(8): e1001296. Available from: http://dx.doi.org/10.1371/journal.pmed.1001296.

Tabutin, D. and M. Willems (1998) 'Differential mortality by sex from birth to adolescence: the historical experience of the West (1750–1930)'. In United Nations, Deptartment of Economic and Social Affairs, Population Division (ed.) *Too Young to Die Genes or Gender?* New York: United Nations.

UNICEF (2014) *Generation 2030 Africa*. New York: UNICEF.

UNICEF (2015) *Committing to Child Survival: A Promise Renewed Progress Report 2015*. New York: UNICEF.

UNICEF global databases (2016) *Based on DHS, MICS and Other Nationally Representative Surveys* (accessed 21 August 2016).

United Nations (2000) *United Nations Millennium Declaration 2000*. New York: United Nations. Available from: www.un.org/millennium/declaration/ares552e.pdf (accessed 21 August 2014).

United Nations (2014) *The Millennium Development Goals Report 2014*. New York: United Nations.

United Nations, Department of Economic and Social Affairs, Population Division (2015) *World Population Prospects: The 2015 Revision.* Available from: http://esa.un.org/unpd/wpp.

United Nations General Assembly (2015) *Transforming our World: The 2030 Agenda for Sustainable Development.* Available from: https://sustainabledevelopment.un.org/content/documents/21252030%20Agenda%20for%20Sustainable%20Development%20web.pdf (accessed 8 December 2016).

United Nations Inter-agency Group for Child Mortality Estimation (UN IGME) (2015) *Levels & Trends in Child Mortality: Report 2015.* New York: UNICEF.

Waldron, I. (1998) 'Sex differences in infant and early childhood mortality: major causes of death and possible biological causes'. In United Nations, Deptartment of Economic and Social Affairs, Population Division (ed.) *Too Young to Die Genes or Gender?* New York: United Nations.

Walker, N., K. Hill and F. Zhao (2012) 'Child mortality estimation: methods used to adjust for bias due to AIDS in estimating trends in under-five mortality'. *PLoS Medicine*, 9(8): e1001298. Available from: http://dx.doi.org/10.1371/journal.pmed.1001298.

WHO and Maternal and Child Health Epidemiology Estimation Group (MCEE) (2015) *Estimates.* Available from: www.who.int/gho/child_health/mortality/causes/en/ (accessed 12 December 2016).

WHO and UNICEF (2015) *Progress on Sanitation and Drinking Water – 2015 Update and MDG Assessment.* Geneva: WHO/UNICEF.

WHO Regional Office for South-East Asia (2016) *EPI Factsheet Bangladesh 2015.* New Delhi: WHO. Available from: www.searo.who.int/entity/immunization/data/bangladesh.pdf?ua=1 (accessed 12 December 2016).

You, D., L. Hug, S. Ejdemyr, P. Idele, D. Hogan, C. Mathers, P. Gerland, J. R. New and L. Alkema (2015) 'Global, regional and national levels and trends in under-5 mortality between 1990 and 2015, with scenario-based projections to 2030: a systematic analysis by the UN Inter-agency Group for Child Mortality Estimation'. *Lancet*, 386(10010): 2275–2286.

Yount, K. M. (2001) 'Excess mortality of girls in the Middle East in the 1970s and 1980s: patterns, correlates and gaps in research'. *Population Studies*, 55: 291–308.

11

Changes in old-age mortality since 1950

Danan Gu, Patrick Gerland, Kirill Andreev, Nan Li, Thomas Spoorenberg, Gerhard Heilig and Francois Pelletier

Introduction

Like many countries in other continents, Asian countries have witnessed a significant decline in old-age mortality since the middle of the last century. For Asia as a whole, life expectancy at age 65 (for both sexes combined) rose from 9.7 years in 1950–1955 to 15.7 years in 2010–2015, a net increase of 6.0 years. This was the second largest increase after Oceania (6.6 years) and exceeded that in Europe (4.9 years), Latin America (5.9 years), North America (5.4 years) and Africa (3.6 years) (United Nations Population Division 2015a).

Recent studies have shown a steady decline in adult mortality in Asia along with a wide variation in levels, trends and gender differences (Zhao 2011), yet little is known about mortality at old ages. Analysing the levels and trends of mortality at old ages in Asia would improve our understanding of mortality and health transitions in Asia and the world. This chapter provides an overview of the levels and trends in mortality at old ages in Asia, focusing on countries with available and relatively reliable data. We first discuss regional trends and country-specific variations in life expectancy at age 65, followed by an examination of gender differences in life expectancy and death rates. We then analyse changes in age-specific death rates among the elderly populations and their contribution to the improvement in life expectancies at age 65 from 1950 to 2015. Next we investigate the association between socioeconomic development and life expectancy at age 65, concluding with projections of future trends in life expectancy at age 65. We rely on data from the 2015 Revision of the World Population Prospects (WPP) (United Nations Population Division 2015a) together with datasets from other sources to achieve this. Six countries/territories (Cambodia, Macao Special Administrative Region (China), Brunei Darussalam, Bhutan, Maldives and Timor-Leste) with small populations and less reliable data than other Asian countries have been excluded from our analysis.

Trends in life experience at age 65

Figure 11.1 shows that life expectancy at age 65 (hereafter e_{65}) for both sexes combined increased 6.0 years, from 9.7 years in 1950–1955 to 15.7 years in 2010–2015. This increase is the second largest after Oceania among all regions. In spite of such progress, e_{65} in Asia today is still below

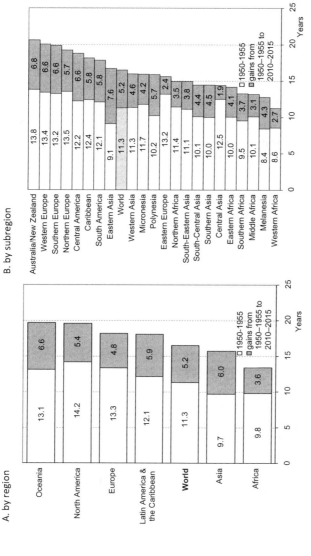

Figure 11.1 e_{65} (both sexes combined) in 1950–1955 and gains from 1950–1955 to 2010–2015 by region and subregion
Source: United Nations Population Division (2015a).

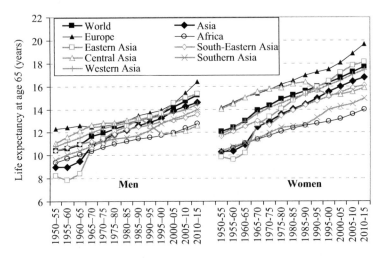

Figure 11.2 e_{65} for subregions in Asia and selected regions, 1950–2015
Source: United Nations Population Division (2015a).

the world average, higher than in Africa but below that in other regions. When the world and Asian populations are further divided, only Eastern Asia's e_{65} surpassed the world average but it was still well below that of many European subregions. In other Asian subregions, e_{65} is only slightly higher than in most African subregions.

Figure 11.2 presents the five-yearly trajectories of e_{65} from 1950 to 2015 for the subregions of Asia, together with Africa and Europe. Before 1965, Asia's e_{65} (for both men and women) was similar to that in Africa and about two years below the world average. However, old-age mortality in Asia declined much faster than in Africa and the gap of e_{65} between Asia and the world has narrowed since 1965. This improvement is mainly attributable to the remarkable progress made in Eastern Asia, whose e_{65} moved from the bottom of the five subregions in Asia before 1965 to the top after 1990. Eastern Asia took just ten years from 1960–1965 to 1970–1975 to close its two-year gap to the world average, mainly because of the progress made by China.

Figure 11.2 further reveals that before 1990 e_{65} in Central Asia usually ranked at the top for both women and men. After the collapse of the former Soviet Union in the early 1990s, however, e_{65} in Central Asian countries fell substantially so that in 2010–2015 this subregion ranked the lowest for men and the second lowest for women among the five subregions. South-Eastern Asia had a slight decline in 1970–1975 for both sexes, attributable to wars and social upheavals in the subregion. Overall, a wide subregional disparity in e_{65} has persisted in Asia over the last six decades, although subregional ranks have reshuffled somewhat in the period.

Despite subregional underperformance compared with the world and some developed regions, several Asian countries have made substantial advancement in e_{65}, surpassing many countries in Europe and North America. For example, Japan, Hong Kong and Singapore had risen to the top layer of e_{65} in the world by 2010–2015. These countries, which had a relatively high e_{65} in 1950–1955, also achieved greater gains from 1950 to 2015 compared to other Asian countries. On the other hand, many Asian countries remained in the lower layer of e_{65} in both 1950–1955 and 2010–2015. In other words, there was a considerable variation among Asian countries in both the level of, and the change in, e_{65} over the period 1950–2015.

Figure 11.3 shows changes in e_{65} from 1950 to 2015 for each Asian country by subregion. Most countries show steady growth in e_{65} over the period, although the trajectories of several

Changes in old-age mortality since 1950

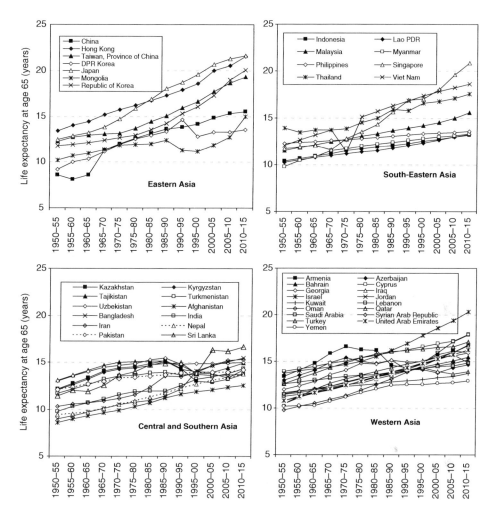

Figure 11.3 e_{65} (both sexes combined) in Asia by country, 1950–2015
Source: United Nations Population Division (2015a).

countries are noteworthy, showing a stagnation or even a reversal pattern in some periods. Before 1965 China ranked at the bottom of Eastern Asian countries, having had a decline in e_{65} in 1960–1965, primarily due to a famine. By 1975, however, it had achieved a full recovery and a large gain in e_{65}, thanks to a large reduction in old-age mortality resulting from national campaigns against infectious diseases and the promotion of healthcare programmes in the countryside (Wang et al. 2005). Between 1975 and 2000, the gain in e_{65} in China was relatively small, although life expectancy at birth increased substantially. Mongolia witnessed a decline in e_{65} in the early 1990s, with worsened economic and social welfare systems due to the collapse of the former Soviet Union (Mungunsarnai and Spoorenberg 2012). However, Mongolia has witnessed a steady recovery since 1995. The Democratic People's Republic of Korea (hereafter DPR Korea) also had a decline in e_{65} in the late 1990s due to a famine but its recovery has been very limited so far (Spoorenberg and Schwekendiek 2012).

In South-Eastern Asia, Vietnam witnessed a big decline in 1970–1975 due to war. While Singapore ranked in the middle of the region in the 1950s, it ranked at the top in 2010–2015.

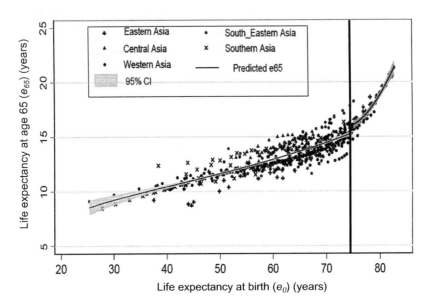

Figure 11.4 Association between e_{65} and e_0 (both sexes combined) in Asia
Notes: Data included all Asian countries under study from period 1950–1955 to 2010–2015. Predicted is the regression line; 95% CI = 95% confidence interval from the regression.
Source: United Nations Population Division (2015a).

Most countries in Central Asia witnessed a deterioration in old-age survival following the collapse of the former Soviet Union and the recovery in these countries has been limited. The trend in Central Asia is consistent with mortality changes at other ages (see Guillot, Gavrilova and Pudrovska 2011; Wang et al. 2012). In Southern Asia, Bangladesh had a decline in e_{65} in 1970–1975 because of a devastating cyclone, yet made a full recovery in the subsequent five years. Afghanistan has had a slow but steady growth in e_{65} despite frequent wars and civil conflicts. It is an outlier in the subregion, as noted by other researchers (e.g. Bulled and Sosis 2010). In Western Asia, e_{65} in some countries of the former Soviet Union (e.g. Armenia, Azerbaijan) began to decline or stagnate after 1970, consistent with findings by other scholars (see Duthé et al. 2010).

Figure 11.4 plots e_{65} against life expectancy at birth (hereafter e_0) for Asian countries from 1950–1955 to 2010–2015. The scatter plot and regression line of predicted e_{65} reveal a clear association between these two indicators. When e_0 is below 75 years, an increase of ten years in e_0 is associated with an increase of 1.25 years in e_{65}. However, once e_0 reaches 75 years, the slope of the regression line changes abruptly, so that a ten-year increase in e_0 is associated with a roughly five-year increase in e_{65} based on experiences in Asian countries over the last 65 years (or more accurately, based on experience from Japan, Singapore, Republic of Korea and Hong Kong over the last one or two decades). This implies that once e_0 reaches a relatively high level (e.g. 75 years), additional improvement in e_0 will increasingly be due to mortality reduction at old ages. This finding is in accordance with previous research (Eggleston and Fuchs 2012; Hummer et al. 2009; Vaupel 1986), and the next chapter of this handbook.

Another major aspect of recent changes in old-age mortality is their gender difference. Women generally live longer than men as shown in the following chapter. Yet the gender difference in life expectancy (women's life expectancy minus men's) is not uniform across Asian countries. Figure 11.5 shows the gender difference in e_{65} over the period 1950–2015 for Asia and its five subregions, together with Africa and Europe. For Asia as a whole, in 1950–1955 women at age

Changes in old-age mortality since 1950

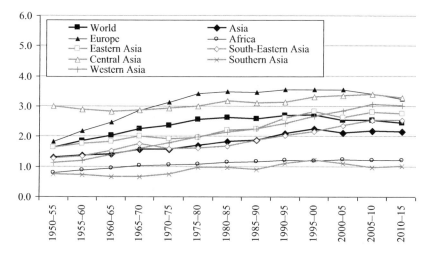

Figure 11.5 Gender difference in e_{65} (years) for subregions in Asia and selected regions
Source: United Nations Population Division (2015a).

65 lived about 1.3 years more on average than men of the same age. In 2010–2015, this difference exceeded two years. Central Asian countries had the largest gender difference, which slightly increased from 3.0 years in the period 1950–1995 to 3.5 years thereafter. Southern Asian countries had the smallest gender difference in e_{65}, less than one year during most of the study period.

Of the three regions shown in Figure 11.5, gender differences have been largest in Europe and smallest in Africa, with Asia somewhere in between. Furthermore, the differences between Asia and Europe in terms of the gender gap have increased, from less than 0.5 years in 1950–1955 to more than one year in 1960–1965 and onwards. The Asia-Africa difference of the gender gap was also less than 0.5 years in 1950–1955, but it exceeded one year in 1990–1995 and remained at 0.9–0.95 years thereafter.

A closer investigation reveals that in most Asian countries the gender difference in e_{65} increased between 1950 and 2015, although the gap was below three years in most countries and below two years in many countries, as shown in Figure 11.6. In Eastern Asia, four countries/territories (Japan, Hong Kong, DPR Korea and Republic of Korea) had a gender difference greater than three years. The increasing gender difference in Japan after 1980 is mainly attributable to the greater reduction in mortality from stroke and heart disease in women compared with men (Gu et al. 2013). The Republic of Korea had a steady increase in the gender difference from 1950 to 1985, but a declining trend after 1985. The declining trend is likely attributable to equal improvement in mortality from the major causes of death in both sexes (Gu et al. 2013). China's gender difference in e_{65} was around two years over the study period. Mongolia had a very small sex differential in e_{65}, around one year from 1950 to 1990, although this has increased more recently.

With exceptions of Singapore and Vietnam, women's e_{65} in all countries in South-Eastern Asia surpassed that of men by less than three years. In Vietnam, the gender difference spiked in the late 1960s due to the Vietnam War. Although its gender difference narrowed after the war, the gap has been growing again since the early 1980s. The increasing gender difference observed in Singapore after 1990 is likely because of a greater reduction in cardiovascular disease mortality in women compared with men (Gu et al. 2013). In Central and Southern Asia and in Western Asia, all countries have a gender difference of less than three years with exceptions of Turkey and the states of the former Soviet Union.

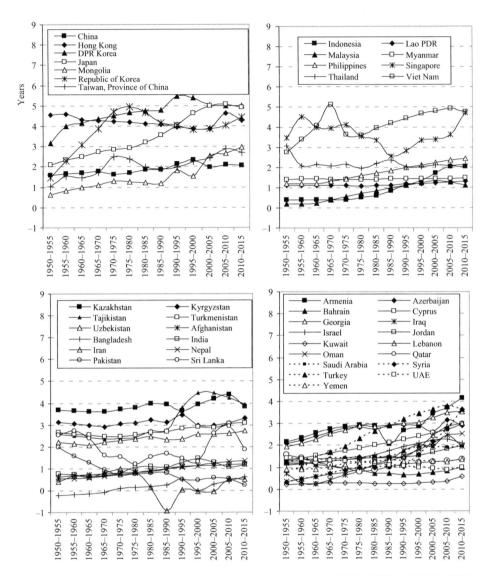

Figure 11.6 Gender difference in e_{65} (years) in Asia by country, 1950–1955 to 2010–2015
Source: United Nations Population Division (2015a).

The underlying mechanism for gender inequity in life expectancy is inadequately studied and difficult to interpret (Hummer et al. 2009). However, there is a consensus that the gender difference reflects a combination of sex differences in biological and genetic make-up and exposures to the risks of morbidity and mortality. These differences include different roles in productive activities and human reproduction, different status in the family and society, and different risky behaviours (Hummer et al. 2009; Rogers et al. 2010; Staetsky 2009; Zhao 2011). For example, marriage is associated with lower mortality and increased longevity for both men and women, even for the oldest-old. However, elderly men probably benefit more from marriage (Zhu and Gu 2010). In comparison with their female counterparts, they are more likely to live with their partners because men tend to be older than their wives or partners.

While men's higher socioeconomic status would benefit their longevity, the variation in their education is usually greater than that of women (Hummer et al. 2009). Furthermore, in comparison with women, men are more likely to engage in risky behaviours such as smoking, excessive drinking, less exercise and poor diet (Rogers et al. 2005). Studies have found estrogen could reduce concentrations of low-density lipoproteins cholesterol (LDL) and increase concentrations of high-density lipoprotein (HDL) cholesterol, whereas testosterone could increase blood concentrations of LDL and decrease concentrations of HDL cholesterol, causing men to be more likely than women to have cardiovascular diseases and stroke. Sex-associated hormones can also modulate immune responses and thus directly influence the outcome of infection, which affects survival and longevity (Candore et al. 2006).

Declines in age-specific death rates and their contribution to rising e_{65}

The two upper panels of Table 11.1 show that from 1950–1955 to 2010–2015, old-age mortality in all five age groups fell more rapidly in Asia than in other regions, with exceptions of Oceania and Latin America (for ages 80 and above). For Asia as a whole, the death rate at ages 65–69 fell by more than 60 per cent in 2010–2015 compared to 1950–1955. However, the relative reduction in the age-specific death rate decreases with advancement of age. At ages 85+, the death rate in Asia has fallen by 37 per cent in the last 65 years.

Table 11.1 also shows that the pace of mortality decline at old ages has varied considerably across subregions. Over the past 65 years, Eastern-Asia had the greatest relative decline in death rates across all five age groups among 22 subregions in the world, with more than 70 per cent decline for ages 65–69 and a 44 per cent decline for ages 85+. Central Asia had the smallest decline in death rates among subregions in Asia, with a 31 per cent decline for ages 65–69 and a 5 per cent decline for ages 85+. The relative decline in Central Asia after age 75 is the smallest of all regions in the world. Additional comparisons of the decline in mortality from 1950 to 2015 between women and men reveal a greater decline among women than men in most countries and most age groups (not shown). Countries with a larger decline in male than female mortality were mainly found in Southern Asia (such as Pakistan and Sri Lanka) with a few in Western Asia (such as the United Arab Emirates).

Findings of a more dramatic decline in mortality among the youngest-old than the oldest-old are in accordance with a recent study in seven European countries (Janssen, Kunst and Mackenbach 2007). However, despite a smaller percentage decline in the death rate at oldest-old ages compared with youngest-old, the absolute reduction in the death rate (in percentage points) is larger due to the higher mortality at oldest-old ages. Indeed, the impact of the reduction at oldest-old ages should not be underestimated considering the number of deaths saved due to the reduction in mortality at these ages.

In most countries and most ages, women had a similar or greater mortality decline than men, despite their lower mortality (not shown). Such a persistent or widening gender gap is consistent with the finding by Ricketts (2014) who showed that the gender gap was persistent or slightly widened in middle or low income countries, although it was reduced in high income countries in the 1995–2010 period. This is possibly because women benefit more from improved gender equality than men in less developed countries, while men gain more from improved gender equality in more developed countries (Medalia and Chang 2011). In sum, considering the substantial decline in mortality in Asian countries, especially in those countries with a relatively high life expectancy at birth for both men and women at the beginning of the period, the large reduction in old-age mortality over the past 65 years

Table 11.1 Age-specific death rates in 2010–2015 and percentage reduction compared with 1950–1955 by region and subregion of Asia (both sexes combined)

	Ages 65–69	Ages 70–74	Ages 75–79	Ages 80–84	Ages 85+
Death rates in 2010–2015					
World	0.023	0.037	0.057	0.087	0.165
Africa	0.035	0.055	0.086	0.132	0.226
Asia	0.026	0.041	0.063	0.096	0.176
Europe	0.017	0.027	0.045	0.075	0.159
Latin America and the Caribbean	0.019	0.030	0.047	0.072	0.147
Northern America	0.014	0.022	0.038	0.063	0.144
Oceania	0.013	0.021	0.037	0.063	0.146
Percentage reduction in death rates from 1950–1955 to 2010–2015					
World	54.7	51.6	48.9	45.6	33.5
Africa	44.2	42.6	40.4	37.7	29.2
Asia	62.4	58.1	54.2	49.7	36.6
Europe	49.3	50.1	48.7	46.7	34.4
Latin America and the Caribbean	55.0	54.6	54.1	53.0	41.6
Northern America	56.4	54.9	50.6	45.6	28.8
Oceania	64.2	62.9	58.3	52.9	34.5
Death rates in 2010–2015					
Eastern Asia	0.021	0.035	0.056	0.088	0.170
South-Eastern Asia	0.029	0.045	0.069	0.105	0.185
South Asia	0.032	0.049	0.073	0.108	0.186
Central Asia	0.031	0.048	0.074	0.113	0.197
Western Asia	0.022	0.037	0.062	0.101	0.195
Eastern Europe	0.026	0.039	0.063	0.100	0.188
Australia/New Zealand	0.010	0.017	0.032	0.058	0.146
Middle Africa	0.036	0.056	0.089	0.138	0.235
Percentage reduction in death rates from 1950–1955 to 2010–2015					
Eastern Asia	71.9	67.3	63.2	58.3	43.7
South-Eastern Asia	42.9	41.9	40.8	39.1	30.5
South Asia	51.2	47.1	43.8	40.0	29.3
Central Asia	30.9	25.9	19.9	13.8	4.5
Western Asia	55.0	50.6	46.3	41.3	28.3
Eastern Europe	27.1	29.9	29.0	27.7	20.3
Australia/New Zealand	69.1	66.5	61.0	54.2	33.1
Middle Africa	40.5	38.1	34.9	31.1	22.4

Note: Percentage reduction = 100* [(value in 1950–1955) − (value in 2010–2015)]/(value in 1950–1955).
Source: United Nations Population Division (2015a).

indicates that further improvements are still possible in the future, even in countries with very low mortality.

By applying Arriaga's (1984) approach for decomposing life expectancy attributable to improvements in mortality for a given age, we have estimated the contribution that mortality decline in each age group makes to the increase in e_{65} from 1950–1955 to 2010–2015.[1] Table 11.2 presents the relative contribution of each age group to the gain in e_{65} by sex and subregion in Asia, as well as other regions.

Table 11.2 Years gained in e_{65} from 1950–1955 to 2010–2015 and the percentage contribution by age-specific mortality by sex and region and subregion

	Women						Men					
	Gains (yrs) e_{65}	65–69 %	70–74 %	75–79 %	80–84 %	85+ %	Gains (yrs) e_{65}	65–69 %	70–74 %	75–79 %	80–84 %	85+ %
World	5.61	33	28	21	12	6	4.79	40	29	18	9	4
Asia	6.47	40	30	18	8	3	5.62	45	30	16	6	2
Africa	3.78	38	31	19	9	3	3.37	41	31	18	7	2
Europe	5.51	24	27	24	16	9	4.09	28	28	23	14	7
Northern America	6.71	28	27	22	14	8	5.00	32	28	21	12	6
LAC	5.35	23	26	23	16	12	5.20	33	29	21	12	6
Oceania	6.62	25	27	23	15	10	6.39	35	30	20	10	5
Eastern Asia	8.24	41	30	18	8	3	7.11	49	30	15	5	1
South-Eastern Asia	4.42	33	29	21	11	5	3.15	36	30	20	10	4
Central Asia	1.82	37	31	20	9	3	1.53	49	31	15	5	1
Southern Asia	4.60	43	29	17	8	3	4.34	41	30	18	8	3
Western Asia	5.59	34	30	21	11	4	3.67	41	30	18	8	3

Note: LAC indicates Latin America and the Caribbean.
Source: The authors' own calculation based on the life tables of each country in the 2015 Revision of the WPP.

In Asia and Africa, the percentage contribution of each age group to the increase in e_{65} was more or less similar for both men and women. The predominant contribution was made by mortality decline at ages prior to 80 years, although Asia experienced a greater absolute decline in mortality than Africa across all five age groups. Specifically, for women in Asia and Africa, mortality decline at ages below 80 years (hereafter youngest-old ages) accounted for more than 85 per cent of the improvement in e_{65}, compared with a less than 15 per cent contribution from ages 80 and older (hereafter oldest-old ages). For men, the comparable figures for Africa and Asia were 91–92 per cent and 8–9 per cent, respectively. Compared with those in Africa and Asia, the percentage contributions made by mortality decline at youngest-old ages were smaller and those by the decline at oldest-old ages were larger in other regions. In Europe and Northern America, for example, the age-group contributions were around 72–74 per cent for youngest-old ages and 26–28 per cent for oldest-old ages among women, and 77–83 per cent and 17–23 per cent, respectively, among men. In comparison with these regional variations, the variation in the sex-age patterns of percentage contribution across Asia's five subregions was relatively small. However, there were marked subregional variations in the number of years gained in e_{65} among Asian subregions. In all the subregions except Southern Asia, the share of the contribution made by mortality decline at age 75 and above was greater for women than men.

According to epidemiological or health transition theory (Omran 1998), cerebrovascular and cardiovascular diseases, cancers and other non-communicable diseases increasingly become leading causes of death, once mortality caused by infectious diseases reaches a low level. There is evidence in some Asian countries of greater cerebrovascular and cardiovascular mortality indicating 'the age of delayed degenerative diseases' (Olshansky and Ault 1986; Robine 2001), similar to observations in some countries in Europe (Glei, Meslé and Vallin 2011; Janssen, Mackenbach and Kunst 2004; Mackenbach and Garssen 2011; Meslé and Vallin 2011; Vallin and Meslé 2001; Zhao and Kinfu 2005; Zhao 2011) and Latin America (Palloni and Pinto-Aguirre 2011) over the period 1950–2000. Some Asian countries, especially Japan, Hong Kong, Republic of Korea and Singapore, are entering or have already entered the fourth stage of epidemiologic transition characterized by declining cardiovascular mortality, ageing population, lifestyle modification and resurgent diseases (Omran 1998).

Socioeconomic development and e_{65}

Studies suggest that economic growth, improvement in educational attainment and urbanization have been major contributors to the increase in e_0 (e.g. Bulled and Sosis 2010; Cervellati and Sunde 2011; Lin et al. 2012; Rogers and Wofford 1989). We thus examined the associations between three basic socioeconomic factors and e_{65} over the period 1950–1955 to 2010–2015.[2] The basic socioeconomic indicators comprise average years of schooling among the population aged 65 or older, urbanization (proportion of urban population) and GDP per capita.[3] The bivariate linear correlation coefficients between e_{65} and these three variables range from 0.41 to 0.68.[4]

High-fertility may diminish per capita resources, which may have a negative effect on life expectancy. Slow decline in, or persisting, high fertility may also be related to health risks such as maternal mortality or may cause some vicious cycles that can have negative effects on life expectancy (Becker, Murphy and Tamura 1990; Caldwell 2000). Some researchers argue that there is a link between life expectancy and fertility (e.g. Bulled and Sosis 2010; Langner 1996), but it depends on the stage of demographic transition that a population is experiencing (e.g. Kabir 2008; Mondal and Shitan 2014). When mortality declines from high to low (as in most Asian countries over the last 65 years), the level of fertility is a good proxy for the stage of demographic transition. We thus included TFR in our modelling of e_{65}. TFRs were obtained from the 2015 Revision of the WPP (United Nations Population Division 2015a). As there may be a quadratic association between e_{65} and TFR, we added a square term of TFR in the regression.[5] To account for regional variation, we further added a regional control variable in all models.

Our results reveal that without controlling any other socioeconomic covariates, an increase of $1,000 in GDP per capita in Asian countries could add roughly 0.17 years to e_{65}; an increase of one year of schooling among the elderly population could add 1.20 years to e_{65}; and increasing the urban proportion by ten percentage points could add 0.89 years to e_{65}. However, these effects tended to be attenuated as the levels of the socioeconomic factors increase (because their quadratic terms were all significant and negative); and these effects also tended to be attenuated when all three variables are simultaneously present in the model.[6]

When TFR and its quadratic terms were included in the model, the main effects of the three socioeconomic factors were further attenuated. This suggests that some associations between e_{65} and the three socioeconomic development indicators could be explained by the level of TFR. In the presence of all three socioeconomic indicators, a decrease of one child in TFR when TFR was between 3 and 4 could add 0.74 years to e_{65}, whereas the added years to e_{65} could be 1.4 when TFR was between 2 and 1. As the level of TFR approximately reflects the demographic transition stage, our results imply that improvement in e_{65} is normally slower for countries at Stage Two of the demographic transition (characterized by high fertility and low mortality), compared with those in Stage Three (characterized by low fertility and low mortality). This supports the argument that the link between life expectancy and fertility likely depends on the stage of the demographic transition that a given population is experiencing (Bulled and Sosis 2010: 271).

Subregional difference in observed associations between socioeconomic development factors, TFR and e_{65} are worth mentioning. Compared to Eastern Asia (and Southern Asia), Central and Western Asia had a lower gain in e_{65} from each unit increase in GDP per capita, in the absence of other covariates. Central Asia also had a smaller gain in e_{65} from each unit increase in urbanization compared with Eastern Asia (and Southern Asia). When all three economic development indicators were simultaneously taken into consideration, Southern Asia and Western Asia tended to have a lower gain in e_{65} than Eastern Asia. However, no subregional difference was found when TFR and its quadratic term were additionally present. Overall, the three socioeconomic factors and TFR could explain two-thirds (R^2 =0.668) of the variation in e_{65} found among Asian countries between 1950 and 2015, implying that these factors had strong associations with the level of mortality in the older population (i.e. e_{65}) in Asia.

These results are in line with the classic linkage between economic growth and life expectancy at birth (also called the Preston curve) (Bulled and Sosis 2010; Cutler, Deaton and Lleras-Muney 2006; Gu et al. 2013; Preston 1975; Pritchett and Viarengo 2010; Tapia Granados 2012). This assumes that economic growth could affect life expectancy either directly through improved living conditions, or indirectly through facilitating advances in medical technology, rising educational levels, improved food security, sanitation and infrastructure, development of social welfare systems and reduced poverty (Janssen, Kunst and Mackenbach 2006). The diminishing effect of economic growth on life expectancy gains when GDP per capita reaches a certain level may be because mortality is more strongly associated with health-related risk behaviour in countries in the third or fourth stage of the health transition (Omran 1998). For example, some scholars have found that the large improvement in life expectancy in the Japanese elderly population is attributable to individual healthy behaviours and lifestyles, such as healthy diets, regular exercise and high community participation, in addition to a good nationwide healthcare system, medical advancements, high incomes, strong family relations and filial piety traditions (Ikeda et al. 2011; Rogers and Crimmins 2011).

Literature has persistently shown that higher education or human capital investment that improves health literacy and other knowledge is at least as important as economic growth in determining the overall health or mortality of a society (Muller 2002). A high level of educational attainment in a society may also mean that the government has implemented public health projects and social welfare programmes that directly contribute to health improvement of its citizens. Without controlling for GDP per capita and education, the association between the growth of urbanization and e_{65} is negative. This result is not uninterpretable. Research has shown that although urbanization contributes significantly to economic growth, it has also been linked with environmental degradation, urban poverty, social inequity, housing shortage, unhealthy lifestyles, crime and other social problems that are unfavourable to human health and well-being, especially when the urban percentage is below 70 per cent (Stephens 1995; Weiss 2001).

Overall, during the period 1950–2015, gains in e_{65} in Eastern and South-Eastern Asia were in accordance with their socioeconomic development and urbanization processes. This is because economic development is a major driving force behind factors that have reduced old-age mortality, in particular, higher living standards, better living and working environments, sufficient nutritional intake, and better availability of and accessibility to health care (Zhao 2011). Of course, various other factors such as certain social practices and traditions, income equity, health awareness and knowledge, and risk-preventing behaviour have also likely contributed to mortality reduction (Zhao 2011). Studies in other developing countries and areas such as Latin America suggest that economic growth plays an important role in explaining the variation in mortality, but years of schooling is always a potent driver of lower mortality (Palloni and Pinto-Aguirre 2011). We

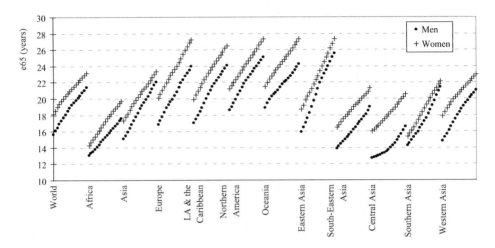

Figure 11.7 Projected e_{65} from 2015–2020 to 2095–2100 for regions and subregions in Asia
Source: United Nations Population Division (2015a).

speculate that gains in e_{65} are mostly rooted in improved standards of living and nutritional status, as well as in the creation of massive infrastructure for water and sewage that reduces communicable disease.

Future prospects

This section presents the projected e_{65} for Asian countries from 2015 to 2100 from the 2015 Revision of the WPP, based on the medium variant of mortality scenario. The scenario is the median value of e_{65} that is estimated using a Bayesian hierarchical model approach with empirical time series data points for each country from 1950 to 2015 (United Nations Population Division 2015b). The projected e_{65} was obtained from country-specific life tables (or model schedules in some cases) corresponding to projected e_0 in each period from 2015 to 2100. The underlying assumption for future trajectories of old-age mortality (or life tables), based on empirical evidence from the Human Mortality Database, is that the share of deaths at older ages in a population will increase with the progress of e_0, and mortality improvement is driven mainly by its decline at old ages. The mathematical formulas and principles on how to estimate future age patterns of mortality improvement can be found elsewhere (Andreev, Gu and Gerland 2013; Li, Lee and Gerland 2013). Overall, the UN projections for e_0 and e_{65} tend to be somewhat optimistic (Oeppen and Vaupel 2002), rather than pessimistic (Carnes and Olshansky 2007).

Figure 11.7 shows that both males' and females' e_{65} in Asia will exceed the world average by the end of the twenty-first century, from its lower levels today. By 2050 e_{65} in Central Asia is projected to continue its slower growth trend of e_{65} for men as compared to other Asian subregions. Eastern Asia will continue to take the lead among Asian subregions and surpass all regions by 2100, ranking the top on the list for both males and females. e_{65} in Southern Asia is projected to grow more quickly and the male e_{65} is projected to exceed the world average by 2100, although female e_{65} is still projected to be lower than that of the world population by 2100. South-Eastern Asia is projected to have similar paces in e_{65} to those of the world for both males and females, although its e_{65} is projected to be still below the world average in the rest of the century. Some countries/territories in Eastern Asia and South-Eastern Asia which enjoy the highest e_{65} in the world today are projected to retain their leading positions to the end of the century.

Concluding remarks

This chapter provides a glimpse into the trends of e_{65} and the age and sex patterns of old-age mortality for Asian countries from 1950 to 2015. While mortality transitions in these populations took place at different times, and under different political systems, levels of socioeconomic development and living conditions, as noted in the literature (see Attané and Barbieri 2009; Tabutin and Schoumaker 2005; Véron 2008), the changes in age patterns and sex differentials in old-age mortality have shown certain common features. Specifically, most countries have made significant progress in the past six decades in lowering mortality among older adults. Compared to men, women have experienced a faster mortality decline and greater gains in e_{65}, despite their lower mortality and higher life expectancy. The youngest-old adults witnessed a relatively greater decline in mortality than the oldest-old, and consequently mortality decline at these ages contributed more to the gain in e_{65} than that at older ages. Finally, countries with relatively high e_{65} in 1950 also experienced a larger gain between 1950 and 2015 compared with other countries.

This chapter showed that as far as sex differentials in mortality were concerned, there was a notable division between some Asian populations. Their experiences not only provide further support to the theories of the demographic and epidemiological transitions, but also offer new insights that enrich our knowledge of these changes. By decomposing changes in e_{65} attributable to mortality decline by age and sex, the chapter provides a fuller picture of the links between changing age patterns of mortality and improving life expectancy in Asian populations.

The changes in e_{65} from 1950 to 2015 in Asian countries suggest there is room for a further reduction in old-age mortality in every country. This finding supports a likely steady increase in human life expectancy in the foreseeable future (Oeppen and Vaupel 2002). The decline in old-age mortality will continue, even in countries that have already achieved the lowest mortality in the world. This could be a driving force in changes of overall life expectancy in Asia in the future, although the challenge in how to accurately forecast mortality after age 65 remains (Favero and Giacoletti 2011). Furthermore, old-age mortality improvement will occur in the presence of great disparities in mortality levels across countries, gender differences and age patterns, as argued by other researchers with respect to adult mortality (e.g. Zhao 2011).

It has been argued that when mortality at old ages is high, improvements in healthcare systems and economic and social progress are necessary for an increase in e_{65}, yet once old-age mortality falls to a moderate or low level, further increases depend also on individual health behaviours such as diet, exercise, cigarette smoking and compliance with medical protocols (Crimmins, Preston and Cohen 2011; Glei, Meslé and Vallin 2011; Preston and Ho 2009; Vallin and Meslé 2001). These factors are powerful enough to create mortality gaps among countries experiencing different political and economic trends (Caselli and Vallin 2006). It is important to determine when the other countries in Asia will reach the levels of life expectancy of Japan today (see Figure 11.3), which countries are in the vanguard of increased life expectancy, and what factors are responsible for such progress. Our findings have implications in these areas. In some high mortality countries, expansion of social security, public health campaigns and other health programmes are required in the future; whereas in low mortality countries, investment in sophisticated medical technology and long-term, or lifetime, treatments are usually needed to further lower mortality from cancer and cardiovascular and other degenerative diseases (Zhao 2011).

There are several limitations with this study which necessitate caution in interpreting the results. First, only few countries/territories in Asia are internationally recognized as having good demographic data (e.g. Japan, Hong Kong, Singapore); most lack a nationwide vital registration system and regular censuses. Despite a long-standing astrological tradition for remembering an individual's birth dates in some Eastern and South-Eastern Asian countries (Gu et al. 2013), under-reporting at young ages and age exaggeration at old ages are not uncommon in these countries. Therefore, even if the WPP estimates were derived from relatively systematic analysis of every country with available data, the estimates for Asian countries would not be free from error. Furthermore, results for nearly a quarter of Asian countries or areas in the WPP were derived from model schedules, which may not reflect the 'actual' values. Such data quality issues continue to hinder a more complete understanding of older adult mortality patterns in Asian populations. Nevertheless, we believe such biases would not alter the general trends of old-age mortality in the countries of Asia and especially at the regional level. More effort in data collection – especially for the less statistically developed countries – and more research on continued efforts to systematically analyse the available data, are clearly needed.

Second, because of the lack of available data, we did not analyse causes of death. This is addressed in Chapter 13 by Colin Mathers. Analysis of causes of death is important for providing a much clearer picture of how changes in the causes of death have been responsible for trends in life expectancy and death rates observed at old ages (Attané and Barbieri 2009; Gu et al. 2013).

Third, the analysis of the association between socioeconomic development and old-age mortality presented in the study has been relatively simple: because life expectancy and economic growth are endogenous (Aísa and Pueyo 2004), their relationship could be bi-directional. Furthermore, the association between socioeconomic development and life expectancy is likely to be region-specific (Bulled and Sosis 2010), so our results may not be applicable to countries outside Asia. Furthermore, a growing body of evidence has suggested that individual social, behavioural and genetic factors, and their interactions, are important associates or determinants of health and mortality (Hernandez and Blazer 2006; Hoffmann 2008), in addition to the neighbourhood environment (Kawachi and Berkman 2003). It is hypothesized that improvement in life expectancy is due to a combination of improved knowledge about health behaviours, advancement in medical technology, improved health care and personal hygiene, public health interventions, housing, nutrition and socioeconomic status (Hummer et al. 2009). This implies that more comprehensive investigations of old-age mortality and an expanded range of socioeconomic development indicators based on more robust analytical methods that include both macro- and micro-levels are necessary to shed light on the topic. As more micro-level longitudinal datasets capturing these factors are becoming available in the region (Kaiser 2013), comprehensive studies integrating these factors under a multilevel framework are clearly warranted. At the country level, we did find data on the prevalence of overweight persons, the prevalence of cigarette smoking, and that of pension coverage. However, we did not include these data in our statistical analyses because they are only available for the most recent period and are not available for all countries in Asia. Global effort in collecting time series data on risk behaviours at the country or subnational level is necessary.

Fourth, the future projections of e_{65} in the WPP were mainly derived from projected e_0 using a Bayesian hierarchical model (Raftery et al. 2012), together with either projected age-sex-specific mortality patterns from the Human Mortality Database, extrapolated into the future, or with age-sex-specific mortality patterns from extended model life tables (Andreev, Gu and Gerland 2013; Li, Lee and Gerland 2013). These projections have considerable uncertainties. Compared to the estimates for the 1950–2015 period, they should be interpreted with caution. The purpose of presenting projected e_{65} was to provide a general picture of possible trajectories should the average trajectories in the past 65 years persist.

In spite of the above limitations, this chapter makes a value-added contribution to the existing literature by providing a general overview of the trends in old-age mortality in Asian countries, about which little is known. Our findings could be informative for the understanding of the health transition as well as for policy-formulation on population ageing.

Notes

1 The total change in e_{65} (i.e. $\Delta = e_{65}^2 = e_{65}^1$) from 1950–1955 to 2010–2015 attributable to mortality change over the corresponding period is defined by

$$\Delta_x = \left[\frac{l_x^1}{l_{65}^1} \left(\frac{{}_5 L_x^2}{l_x^2} - \frac{{}_5 L_x^1}{l_x^1} \right) + \frac{T_{x+5}^2}{l_{65}^1} \left(\frac{l_x^1}{l_x^2} - \frac{l_{x+5}^1}{l_{x+5}^2} \right) \right]$$

for age groups from 65–69 to 80–84 and by

$$\Delta_{85} = \left[\frac{l_{85}^1}{l_{65}^1} \left(\frac{T_{85}^2}{l_{85}^2} - \frac{T_{85}^1}{l_{85}^1} \right) \right]$$

for age group 85+. The percentage share by each age group is defined by $100 \star (\Delta_x / \Delta)$.

2 Because of the structure of our data, linear regressions with panel-corrected standard errors (-xtpcse-) were employed in our analyses to ensure the standard errors were robust to each country having a different variance of the disturbances, and to each country's observations being correlated with those of other countries through time (see StataCorp 2011: 379–383). This approach is one form of multilevel analysis with fixed effects for each country. In all models, we included quadratic terms if they were significant.

3 The data of average years of schooling among the population aged 65 or older were obtained from www.barrolee.com (Barro and Lee 2013). The data for the 2010–2015 period were extrapolated from the periods of 2000–2005 and 2005–2010. Data on GDP per capita were from the World Bank (as measured in the constant 2010 US$ price). GDP per capita data were available only after 1960 and there were some missing values for some countries. Thus, the number of data points of GDP per capita available for each country varies. Urbanization data were from the 2014 *Revision* of the *World Urbanization Prospects* (United Nations Population Division 2014).

4 We checked multicollinearity to ensure that the value of the variance inflation factor (VIF) of each variable in every model was less than ten in linear regressions (e.g. Hair et al. 2009). The quadratic terms for expected years of schooling and urbanization were excluded when all three socioeconomic factors were present in the model because inclusion of these quadratic terms would violate the assumption for no multicollinearity across variables, and because they were not significant in multivariate models.

5 In analytical models, we modified the level of TFR by subtracting 2.3 (the average replacement level for all Asian countries from 1950 to 2015). This modification was to ensure no violation of the assumption of no multicollinearity between variables in the regression. Such a modification does not alter the relative distribution (not shown). The coefficients for modified TFR and the quadratic term of TFR varied slightly from the unmodified ones. The estimates of e_{65} from regressions between modified and unmodified TFR were identical.

6 When all three socioeconomic development variables and their quadratic terms were included in the model, both the main effect and the quadratic term of the urban proportion were not significant. Therefore, we dropped the quadratic term of the urban proportion in the model that included these three variables. Once the qudratic term of the urban proportion was removed from the model, the main effect of the urban proportion was significant ($p<0.05$).

References

Aísa, R. and F. Pueyo (2004) 'Endogenous longevity, health and economic growth: a slow growth for a longer life?' *Economics Bulletin*, 9(3): 1–10.

Andreev, K., D. Gu and P. Gerland (2013) 'Age pattern of mortality improvement by level of life expectancy at birth with applications to mortality projections'. Paper presented at the 2013 Annual meeting of the Population Association of America. 11–13 April 2013, New Orleans. Available from: http://paa2013.princeton.edu/papers/132554 (accessed 15 September 2013).

Arriaga, E. E. (1984) 'Measuring and explaining the change in life expectancies'. *Demography*, 21(1): 83–96.

Attané, I. and M. Barbieri (2009) 'The demography of East and Southeast Asia from the 1950s to the 2000s: a summary of changes and a statistical assessment'. *Population (English Edition)*, 64: 9–146.

Barro, R. J. and J. W. Lee (2013) 'A new data set of educational attainment in the world, 1950–2010'. *Journal of Development Economics*, 104: 184–198. Data are available from: www.barrolee.com (accessed 9 December 2016).

Becker, G., K. Murphy and R. Tamura (1990) 'Human capital, fertility and economic growth'. *Journal of Political Economy*, 98(5): 12–37.

Beltrán-Sánchez, H., S. H. Preston and V. Canudas-Romo (2008) 'An integrated approach to cause-of-death analysis: cause-deleted life tables and decompositions of life expectancy'. *Demographic Research*, 19(35): 1323–1350.

Bulled, N. L. and R. Sosis (2010) 'Examining the relationship between life expectancy, reproduction, and educational attainment: a cross-country analysis'. *Human Nature*, 21: 269–289.

Caldwell, J. (2000) 'Rethinking the African *AIDS* epidemic'. *Population and Development Review*, 26(1): 117–135.

Candore, G., C. R. Balistrerl, F. Listi, M. P. Grimaldi, S. Vasto, G. Colonna-Romano et al. (2006) 'Immunogenetics gender, and longevity'. *Annals of the New York Academy of Sciences*, 1089: 516–537.

Carnes, B. A. and S. J. Olshansky (2007) 'A realist view of aging, mortality and future life expectancy'. *Population and Development Review*, 33(2): 367–381.

Caselli, G. and J. Vallin (2006) 'Geographical variations of mortality'. In G. Caselli, J. Vallin and G. Wunsch (eds.) *Demography: Analysis and Synthesis*, 2: 207–234. London: Academic Press.

Cervellati, M. and W. Sunde (2011) 'Life expectancy and economic growth: the role of demographic transition'. *Journal of Economic Growth*, 16: 99–133.

Crimmins, E. M., S. H. Preston and B. Cohen (eds.) (2011) *International Differences in Mortality at Older Ages: Dimensions and Sources*. Washington, DC: The National Academies Press.

Cutler, D., A. Deaton and A. Lleras-Muney (2006) 'The determinants of mortality'. *Journal of Economic Perspectives*, 20(3): 97–120.

Duthé, G., I. Badurashvili, K. Kuyumjyan, F. Meslé and J. Vallin (2010) 'Mortality in the Caucasus: an attempt to re-estimate recent mortality trends in Armenia and Georgia'. *Demographic Research*, 22: 691–732.

Eggleston, K. N. and V. R. Fuchs (2012) 'The new demographic transition: most gains in life expectancy now realized late in life'. *Journal of Economic Perspective*, 26(3): 137–156.

Favero, C. A. and M. Giacoletti (2011) 'Progress in medicine, limits to life and forecasting mortality'. Institutional Members: CEPR, NBER and Università Bocconi, Working Paper No. 406. Milano, Italy.

Glei, D. A., F. Meslé and J. Vallin (2011) 'Diverging trends in life expectancy at age 50: a look at causes of death'. In E. M. Crimmins, S. H. Preston and B. Cohen (eds.) *International Differences in Mortality at Older Ages: Dimensions and Sources*. Washington, DC: The National Academies Press. Pp. 17–67.

Gu, D., P. Gerland, K. Andreev, N. Li, T. Spoorenberg and G. Heilig (2013) 'Old-age mortality in Eastern and South-Eastern Asia'. *Demographic Research*, 29: 999–1038.

Guillot, M., N. Gavrilova and T. Pudrovska (2011) 'Understanding the "Russian mortality paradox" in Central Asia: evidence from Kyrgyzstan'. *Demography*, 48(3):1081–1104.

Hair, J., W. Black, B. Babin and R. Anderson (2009) *Multivariate Data Analysis*, Seventh Edition. Upper Saddle River, NJ: Prentice Hall.

Hernandez, L. M. and D. G. Blazer (eds.) (2006) *Gene, Behavior, and Social Environment: Moving Beyond the Nature/Nurture Debate*. Washington, DC: The National Academic Press.

Hoffmann, R. (ed.) (2008) *Socioeconomic Differences in Old Age Mortality*. New York: Springer Publisher.

Hummer, R. A., R. G. Rogers, R. K. Masters and J. M. Saint Onge (2009) 'Mortality patterns in late life'. In P. Uhlenberg (ed.) *International Handbook of Population Aging*. New York: Springer Publisher. Pp. 521–542.

Ikeda, N., E. Saito, N. Kondo, M. Inoue, S. Ikeda, T. Satoh et al. (2011) 'What has made the population of Japan healthy?' *Lancet*, 378: 1094–1105.

Janssen, F., A. Kunst and J. Mackenbach (2006) 'Association between gross domestic product throughout the life course and old-age mortality across birth cohorts: parallel analyses of seven European countries, 1950–1999'. *Social Science & Medicine*, 63: 239–254.

Janssen, F., A. Kunst and J. Mackenbach (2007) 'Variations in the pace of old-age mortality decline in seven European countries, 1950–1999: the role of smoking and other factors earlier in life'. *European Journal of Population*, 23: 171–188.

Janssen, F., J. P. Mackenbach and A. E. Kunst (2004) 'Trends in old-age mortality in seven European countries, 1950–1999'. *Journal of Clinical Epidemiology*, 57: 203–216.

Kabir, M. (2008) 'Determinants of life expectancy in developing countries'. *The Journal of Developing Areas*, 41(2): 185–204.
Kaiser, A. (2013) 'A review of longitudinal datasets on ageing'. *Journal of Population Ageing*, 6(1): 5–27.
Kawachi, I. and L. F. Berkman (2003) *Neighborhoods and Health*. New York: Oxford University Press.
Langner, G. (1996) 'Fertility of population as a function of the attained level of life expectancy in the course of human evolution'. *Historical Social Research*, 21(4): 24–55.
Li, N., R. Lee and P. Gerland (2013) 'Extending the Lee-Carter method to model the rotation of age patterns of mortality decline for long-term projections'. *Demography*, 50(6): 2037–2051.
Lin, R. T., Y. M. Chen, L. C. Chien and C. C. Chan (2012) 'Political and social determinants of life expectancy in less developed countries: a longitudinal study'. *BMC Public Health*, 12(85): 1–8.
Mackenbach, J. P. and J. Garssen (2011) 'Renewed progress in life expectancy: the case of the Netherlands'. In E. M. Crimmins, S. Preston and B. Cohen (eds.) *International Differences in Mortality at Older Ages: Dimensions and Sources*. Washington, DC: The National Academies Press. Pp. 369–384.
Medalia, C. and V. W. Chang (2011) 'Gender equality, development and cross-national sex gaps in life expectancy'. *International Journal of Comparative Sociology*, 52(5): 371–389.
Meslé, F. and J. Vallin (2011) 'Historical trends in mortality'. In R. G. Rogers and E. M. Crimmins (eds.) *International Handbook of Adult Mortality*. New York: Springer Publisher. Pp. 9–47.
Mondal, M. N. I. and M. Shitan (2014) 'Relative importance of demographic, socioeconomic and health factors on life expectancy in low- and lower-middle-income countries'. *Journal of Epidemiology*, 24(2): 117–124.
Muller, A. (2002) 'Education, income inequality, and mortality: a multiple regression analysis'. *British Medical Journal*, 324: 23–25.
Mungunsarnai, G. and T. Spoorenberg (2012) 'Did the social and economic transition cause a health crisis in Mongolia? Evidences from age- and sex-specific mortality trends (1965–2009)'. In J. Dierkes (ed.) *Change in Democratic Mongolia: Social Relations, Health, Mobile Pastoralism and Mining*. Leiden: Brill. Pp. 9–47.
Oeppen, J. and J. W. Vaupel (2002) 'Broken limits to life expectancy'. *Science*, 296: 1029–1031.
Olshansky, J. S. and A. B. Ault (1986) 'The fourth stage of the epidemiologic transition: the age of delayed degenerative disease'. *Milbank Memorial Fund Quarterly*, 64: 355–391.
Omran, A. R. (1998) 'The epidemiologic transition theory revisited thirty years later'. *World Health Statistics Quarterly*, 51: 99–119.
Palloni, A. and G. Pinto-Aguirre (2011) 'Adult mortality in Latin America and the Caribbean'. In R. G. Rogers and E. M. Crimmins (eds.) *International Handbook of Adult Mortality*. New York: Springer Publisher. Pp. 114–132.
Preston, S. H. (1975) 'The changing relation between mortality and level of economic development'. *Population Studies*, 29(2): 231–248.
Preston, S. H. and J. Ho (2009) 'The US health care system and lagging life expectancy: a case study'. PSC Working Paper Series. PSC 09-01. Philadelphia: Population Studies Center, University of Pennsylvania. Available from: http://repository.upenn.edu/psc working papers/11 (accessed 12 May 2013).
Pritchett, L. and M. Viarengo (2010) 'Explaining the cross-national time series variation in life expectancy: income, women's education, shifts and what else?' Human Development Research Paper, No. 2010/31. New York: United Nations Development Program.
Raftery, A. E., N. Li, H. Ševčíková, P. Gerlandand and G. K. Heilig (2012) 'Bayesian probabilistic population projections for all countries'. *Proceedings of the National Academy of Sciences*, 109(35): 13915–13921.
Ricketts, C. F. (2014) 'Re-examining the gender gap in life expectancy: a cross country analysis'. *International Journal of Humanities and Social Science*, 4(10): 38–51.
Robine, J. M. (2001) 'Redefining the stages of the epidemiological transition by a study of the dispersion of life spans: the case of France'. *Population: An English Selection*, 13(1): 173–194.
Rogers, R. G. and E. M. Crimmins (eds.) (2011) *International Handbook of Adult Mortality*. New York: Springer Publisher.
Rogers, R. G., B. G. Everett, J. M. Saint Onge and P. M. Krueger (2010) 'Social, behavioral and biological factors and sex differences in mortality'. *Demography*, 47(3): 555–578.
Rogers, R. G., R. A. Hummer and P. M. Krueger (2005) 'Adult mortality'. In D. L. Poston Jr. and M. Micklin (eds.) *Handbook of Population*. New York: Springer Publishers. Pp. 283–309.
Rogers, R. G. and S. Wofford (1989) 'Life expectancy in less developed countries: socioeconomic development or public health?' *Journal of Biosocial Science*, 21(2): 245–252.

Spoorenberg, T. and D. Schwekendiek (2012) 'Demographic changes in North Korea: 1993–2008'. *Population and Development Review*, 38(1): 133–158.

Staetsky, L. (2009) 'Diverging trend in female old age mortality: a reappraisal'. *Demographic Research*, 21: 885–914.

StataCorp (2011) *Stata Longitudinal-Data/Panel-Data Reference Manual: Release 12.0*. College Station, TX: Stata Corporation.

Stephens, C. (1995) 'The urban environment, poverty and health in developing countries'. *Health Policy and Planning*, 10(2): 109–121.

Tabutin, D. and B. Schoumaker (2005) 'The demography of the Arab World and the Middle East from the 1950s to the 2000s: a survey of changes and a statistical assessment'. *Population* (English Edition), 60(5–6): 505–616.

Tapia Granados, J. A. (2012) 'Economic growth and health progress in England and Wales: 160 years of a changing relation'. *Social Science & Medicine*, 74: 688–695.

United Nations Population Division (2014) *The World Urbanization Prospects: The 2014 Revision*. Available from: http://esa.un.org/unpd/wup/index.htm (accessed 12 December 2016).

United Nations Population Division (2015a) *The World Population Prospects: The 2015 Revision*, CD-ROM Edition. Available from: http://esa.un.org/unpd/wpp/index.htm (accessed 12 December 2016).

United Nations Population Division (2015b) *The World Population Prospects: The 2015 Revision, Methodology of the United Nations Population Estimates and Projections. ESA/P/WP.242*. Available from: https://esa.un.org/unpd/wpp/publications/Files/WPP2015_Methodology.pdf (accessed 12 December 2016).

Vallin, J. and F. Meslé (2001) 'Trends in mortality in Europe since 1950: age-, sex- and cause-specific mortality'. In J. Vallin, F. Meslé and T. Valkonen (eds.) *Trends in Mortality and Differential Mortality (Population Studies, 36)*. Strasbourg: Council of Europe Publishing. Pp 283–309.

Vaupel, J. W. (1986) 'How change in age-specific mortality affects life expectancy'. *Population Studies*, 40(1): 147–157.

Véron, J. (2008) 'The demography of South Asia from the 1950s to the 2000s: a survey of changes and a statistical assessment'. *Population* (English Edition), 63(1): 9–90.

Wang, H., L. Dwyer-Lindgren, K. T. Lofgren, J. K. Rajaratnam, J. R. Marcus, A. Levin-Rector et al. (2012) 'Age-specific and sex-specific mortality in 187 countries, 1970–2010: a systematic analysis for the Global Burden of Disease Study 2010'. *Lancet*, 380: 2071–2094.

Wang, H., W. Yip, L. Zhang, L. Wang and W. Hsiao (2005) 'Community-based health insurance in poor rural China: the distribution of net benefits'. *Health Policy and Planning*, 20(6): 366–374.

Weiss, M. (2001) 'Productive cities and metropolitan economic strategy'. A theme paper presented to the United Nations International Forum on Urban Poverty (IFUP), Fourth International Conference. Marrakech, Morocco. 16–19 October 2001. Available from: www.globalurban.org/prod_cities.htm (accessed 18 August 2010).

World Bank (2016) *World Bank List of Economies*. Available from: http://databank.worldbank.org/data/home.aspx (accessed 10 December 2016).

Zhao, Z. (2011) 'Adult mortality in Asia'. In R. G. Rogers and E. M. Crimmins (eds.) *International Handbook of Adult Mortality*. New York: Springer Publisher. Pp. 133–150.

Zhao, Z. and Y. Kinfu (2005) 'Mortality transition in East Asia'. *Asian Population Studies*, 1(1): 3–30.

Zhu, H. and D. Gu (2010) 'The protective effect of marriage on health and survival: does it persist at oldest-old ages?' *Journal of Population Ageing*, 3–4: 161–182.

12
Age patterns and sex differentials in mortality

Yan Yu and Zhongwei Zhao

Introduction

Life expectancy at birth increased from 42 years in 1950 to 70 years in 2010 in Asia (United Nations Population Division 2013). This dramatic mortality improvement is largely attributable to socioeconomic development, improvement in living standards and advancement in medical technology and health care that have been achieved by many countries in Asia. Some other Asian countries, however, have experienced slow socioeconomic development with past or ongoing military conflicts or social unrest, and their mortality improvement has been relatively slow. The preceding two chapters have described the trajectories in child and old-age mortality. This chapter includes all age groups in the analysis and examines age patterns and sex differentials in mortality in Asia.

The search for age variations or patterns of mortality has a long tradition in demographic research and can be approached in different ways. For example, the Gompertz law uses a mathematical (exponential) model to characterize the relationship between age and mortality rate, whereas the Coale-Demeny model life tables classify age-specific mortality schedules into four families (North, South, East and West) to accommodate distinct and persistent variations in the age patterns of mortality at similar overall mortality levels (Preston et al. 2001). Changes in age-specific mortality are closely related to both the overall mortality level and its mortality decline. In the early stages of the epidemiological transition, the level of mortality is high. Mortality reductions are greater in the younger ages where deaths caused by infectious diseases are dominant. When diseases related to infection and malnutrition are brought under control, and man-made and degenerative diseases become more visible, mortality falls to a lower level and its reductions shift to the older age groups (Omran 1971; Olshansky and Ault 1986). In this chapter, we analyse mortality change, investigating whether and how the change varies across age groups, and how the age variations are dependent on initial overall mortality level as well as on historical time and country or territory.

For a combination of biological, social and behavioural reasons, the probability of dying varies between men and women. While it is not uncommon for female mortality to be higher than male mortality in some, especially historical populations, women tend to live longer than men, and the sex gap in longevity tends to widen as mortality levels decline (Preston 1976; Vallin

1993). This chapter first examines age patterns of mortality change among males and females separately, followed by an analysis of sex differences in life expectancy at birth and how the sex differences vary across mortality levels and countries and territories.

Up to the present, most investigations of age and sex patterns of mortality have been conducted using data collected in Western populations (Preston et al. 2001). While there has been early inquiry and, more recently, a growing body of research into mortality trends in developing countries including those in Asia (e.g. Stolnitz 1965; Preston 1976; United Nations (UN) 1982; Gu et al. 2013; Zhao 2011; Zhao and Kinfu 2005), such studies are still limited. The UN *World Population Prospects* (WPP) published life tables for individual populations for the first time in its 2012 *Revision*. Using these data, we examine mortality change in Asian countries and territories over the past 60 years. Documenting this change provides basic facts about population dynamics in Asia. Furthermore, Asia's geographical, historical and sociocultural diversity constitutes a unique laboratory to study and understand mortality determinants in general.

In the remainder of this chapter, we first explain the data used in the study, including their limitations. We then present the changes in life expectancy at birth observed in Asian countries and territories between 1950 and 2015, summarizing the overall trend and describing three clusters of countries and territories that deviate from the general trend. Changes in life expectancy at birth are the product of changes in age-specific mortality. These changes and their sex differentials are analysed in the next three sections. In the final section we discuss key findings.

Data and their limitations

For each individual population, we use mortality data for three time points between 1950 and 2015. For the 50 Asian countries and territories as defined by the UN (United Nations Population Division 2013), life tables for 1950–1955, 1980–1985 and 2010–2015 were obtained from the WPP 2012 *Revision*; for Taiwan, life tables for 1954, 1982 and 2012 were extracted from official statistics published by the Taiwan government (1954 is the earliest year where the age grouping is comparable to the one used in WPP). We analysed mortality change in two 30-year periods: between 1950–1955 and 1980–1985; and between 1980–1985 and 2010–2015. In this chapter, the general mortality level in a population is indicated by life expectancy at birth (e_0).

As mentioned above, the existing mortality literature is based mostly on data from Western populations because there is a lack of suitable data that can be used to construct life tables for non-Western countries. Life table quantities are calculated from age-specific mortality rates or probabilities. The ideal data sources are death counts from vital registrations (as the numerator) and census population counts (as the denominator). If either type of data is lacking, representative survey data and deaths reported in the census are often used as substitutes. If these data sources are not available, age-specific mortality data would have to be derived from model-based estimation. In fact, data quality checking and estimation have been among the main purposes of mortality models (Preston et al. 2001).

The availability of mortality data in Asia has been improving but there are still gaps. Around the year 1950, in the less developed parts of Asia that exclude Cyprus, Israel, Japan and the former Soviet republics, 'complete' vital registration with at least 90 per cent of all deaths recorded existed in only three countries and territories (that is, Hong Kong, Singapore and Peninsular Malaysia); Sri Lanka was added to this list by 1975 (UN 1982). For the WPP 2012 Revision, model-based estimation was required to obtain age-specific mortality data for 12 Asian countries (Afghanistan, Brunei Darussalam, Indonesia, Iraq, Jordan, Laos, Lebanon, Myanmar, Nepal, Palestine, Timor-Leste and Yemen) (United Nations Population Division 2014). As the estimation procedure typically involves using the Coale-Demeny West model, which as mentioned earlier has embedded age patterns, it is possible that the age pattern shown in the UN mortality data is an artefact of, or affected by, the estimation. Even for populations where suitable types of data exist, the available data may not be of sufficient quality. For example, we note that there are large discrepancies between the 2010 and 2012 Revisions of the WPP for the mortality data of Vietnam, where the completeness and reliability of death registration are ongoing issues (Merli 1998; Rao et al. 2010). In this chapter, rather than individual populations, we focus on the overall trends across 51 Asian countries and territories, and clusters of countries and territories. Data limitations should be kept in mind when interpreting the results.

Mortality trends 1950–2015 and variations across Asia

Changes in e_0 (in number of years) are calculated for two consecutive equal periods, between 1950–1955 and 1980–1985 and between 1980–1985 and 2010–2015. Results are plotted against the e_0 values recorded in the populations at the beginning of each period (initial e_0), separately for females (Figure 12.1) and males (Figure 12.2). It is clear that e_0 has increased for all Asian female and male populations in both time periods, and the magnitude of increase is negatively related to initial e_0, so that at higher initial values, the increases in e_0 tend to be smaller.

In addition to the actual values, Figures 12.1 and 12.2 show two straight lines which are based on regressing the increase in e_0 on the initial e_0.[1] The regression line indicates the average or expected change in e_0 (along the y-axis) at each initial e_0 value (along the x-axis). For example, when initial e_0 is 40 years, female e_0 is expected to increase by 21.6 years over a 30-year period in Asia; when initial e_0 is 60 years, the expected female gain is 12.2 years. The linear regression captures the overall trend rather well up to the stage where initial e_0 reaches 70 years, and fits well in both time periods. Additional analysis of the two time periods (not shown) finds that time differences in the relationship between initial e_0 and e_0 increase are rather small.

In Figures 12.1 and 12.2, some clusters of populations are located substantially below or above the regression line, indicating that in these populations, the gains in e_0 are considerably smaller or greater than those expected from initial e_0. Three clusters are of interest: one with faster than expected improvement in mortality, which we call vanguards, and two with slower than expected mortality improvement, which we call laggards. The vanguard cluster includes Japan, Hong Kong, Israel, Singapore, Taiwan, Macao, Republic of Korea[2] and Lebanon, and may also include countries such as Cyprus, Brunei Darussalam and Vietnam. These 11 countries and territories are geographically diverse and can be found in Eastern, South-Eastern and Western Asia,[3] and all have a female e_0 exceeding 80 years in 2010–2015.

In contrast, one lagging cluster comprises the eight former Soviet republics of Armenia, Georgia, Azerbaijan, Kazakhstan, Uzbekistan, Kyrgyzstan, Tajikistan and Turkmenistan. It is noteworthy that in the early 1950s, these countries were at an advanced mortality level similar to that in the vanguard group, with female e_0 exceeding 55 years in both clusters. However, a divergence occurs afterwards. Comparing populations with similar initial e_0 in 1950–1955, the female e_0 gain in the following 30 years is smaller in Armenia and Georgia than in Hong Kong and Japan (7.9 and 8.8 vs. 12.4 and 15.7 years), in Azerbaijan, Kazakhstan, Uzbekistan and Kyrgyzstan than in Macao and Brunei Darussalam (7.1, 10.3, 10.2 and 10.9 vs. 13.1 and 14.0 years), and in Tajikistan and Turkmenistan than in Vietnam (9.7 and 10.2 vs. 16.0 years). The gaps in e_0 gains between the two clusters also occur among males. In additional analysis, we observe that the relatively slow mortality improvement in the former Soviet cluster is already evident in the early 1960s. In the second period between 1980–1985 and 2010–2015, the former Soviet bloc has a lower initial e_0 than the vanguard group, and continues to make smaller gains in e_0 compared with the regression line or the vanguard group. As a consequence of six decades of slower than expected

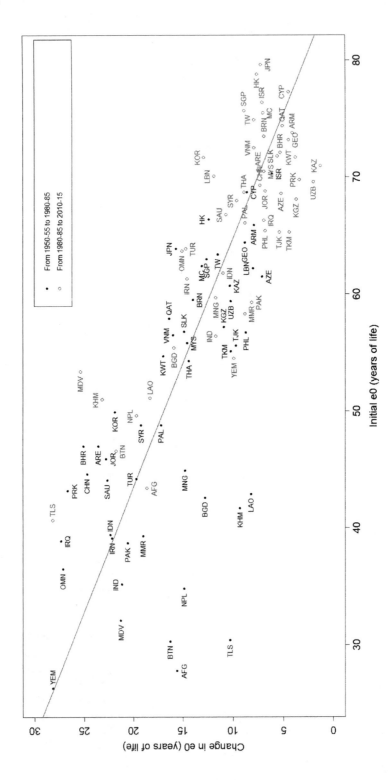

Figure 12.1 Change in e_0 vs. initial e_0, by time period, females, Asia

Notes: HK for Hong Kong, MC for Macao, TW for Taiwan and the other symbols are country ISO codes. The straight line is based on regressing change in e_0 on initial e_0 (change in $e_0 = 40.43 − 0.47*e_0$; $R^2 = 0.75$). All 102 data points are used except AFG, BTN, IRQ, LAO and NPL in the first period, MDV in the second period, and KHM and TLS in both time periods. The excluded observations are considered influential according to the Cook's distance statistic.

Sources: United Nations Population Division (2013) and 1954, 1982 and 2012 Taiwan life tables (http://sowf.moi.gov.tw/stat/Life/quary-1age.htm#taiwan-a-title.gif).

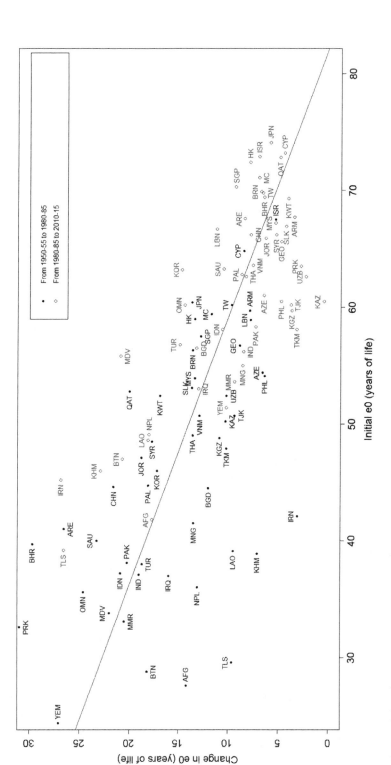

Figure 12.2 Change in e_0 vs. initial e_0, by time period, males, Asia

Notes: HK for Hong Kong, MC for Macao, TW for Taiwan and the other symbols are country ISO codes. The straight line is based on regressing change in e_0 on initial e_0 (*change in e_0 = 35.68 − 0.43*e_0; R^2 = 0.63*). All 102 data points were used except AFG, BHR, KHM, LAO and PRK in the first period, and IRN and TLS in both time periods. The excluded observations are considered as influential according to the Cook's distance statistic.

Sources: United Nations Population Division (2013) and 1954, 1982 and 2012 Taiwan life tables (http://sowf.moi.gov.tw/stat/Life/quary-1age.htm#taiwan-a-title.gif).

improvement in mortality, female e_0 values in the former Soviet republics move from the highest or upper medium levels at the start of the study period to below the median of Asian populations in 2010–2015, with none reaching 80 years and most being around 70 years.

The third cluster consists of several countries in Southern and South-Eastern Asia, including Laos, Cambodia, Nepal, Timor-Leste, Bhutan, Afghanistan, Myanmar, Pakistan, India, Maldives, Bangladesh and probably also Mongolia. Mortality improvement is slow in this cluster, but unlike the slowly-improving former Soviet bloc, these countries generally start with low e_0 values. While their progress in lowering mortality is remarkable, the improvement is not as impressive as that observed in some other populations with similar mortality levels (e.g. Saudi Arabia or Indonesia) or extrapolated from populations with lower mortality (as indicated by the regression lines in Figures 12.1 and 12.2).

The clustering tends to be stable over the study period. The country groups with faster or slower than expected mortality improvement in the first 30-year period tend to have faster or slower than expected improvement in the second 30 years. However, there are exceptions and several countries in the third cluster do not fall behind in mortality improvement in the second period. In Bangladesh, for example, female e_0 exceeds 70 years in 2010–2015. This achievement has been described as 'exceptional' (Chowdhury et al. 2013). Here, we find that the Bangladeshi gains in e_0 between 1980–1985 and 2010–2015 (15.9 years for females and 13.3 years for males) exceed the expected values, but are not unprecedented historically or unique in contemporary populations. Other countries where female and male gains in e_0 over the second period are substantially larger than expected include Laos, Cambodia, Nepal, Timor-Leste, Bhutan and Maldives. However, in Pakistan and among males in India and Mongolia, mortality improvement in the second period continues to be substantially smaller than expected.

Both male and female populations exhibit the two features of a negative and almost linear relationship between initial mortality level and subsequent mortality improvement, and population clusters with faster or slower than expected improvement. However, although the two regression lines have similar slopes, the male intercept is smaller than the female one, indicating that at each mortality level, the expected gain in e_0 is smaller among males than among females. Related to this, there are sex differences in the distributions of initial e_0 values and e_0 gains. The initial e_0 values (shown on the x-axis in Figures 12.1 and 12.2) are less spread out among males than among females: the range in initial e_0 is 24.4 to 74.1 years for males and 26.3 to 79.6 years for females. At each initial mortality level, however, the gain in e_0 (shown on the y-axis in Figures 12.1 and 12.2) is generally more spread out among males, and the R^2 statistic of the regression analysis is smaller for males, indicating that the linear regression explains less variation among male than female populations. As a result of men's greater dispersion along the vertical axis but smaller dispersion along the horizontal axis, the clustering of vanguards and laggards in mortality improvement appears weaker among men.

Age patterns of mortality change

The physiology, socioeconomic conditions and behavioural characteristics of human beings differ by age, leading to a different causal structure of deaths across age groups. An age-specific analysis helps to understand the multifactorial processes underlying the mortality transition. Mortality further varies by sex, as noted earlier. This section, however, focuses on the age variations. We analyse the age patterns of mortality change separately by sex, but focus on their regularities common to both sexes. A later section is devoted to the sex variations in mortality change. We classify each population into six age groups (0, 1–14, 15–44, 45–64, 65–84 and 85+), and as mentioned above, use the e_0 value to indicate mortality level. We use life tables to examine mortality change between 1950–1955 and 1980–1985 and between 1980–1985 and 2010–2015. Two mortality indicators are calculated: (1) percentage change in age-specific death probabilities and (2) the contribution of age-specific mortality reduction to the gain in e_0.

Figure 12.3 shows proportional decline in age-specific death probabilities in the two time periods for females (the graphs on the left) and males (the graphs on the right). In each of the four panels, countries and territories are grouped into four categories according to their initial e_0. The list of countries and territories in each e_0 category is shown in Table 12.1. There are strong variations across age groups in the magnitude of mortality decline. Mortality change is greater for the three youngest age groups than for those aged 45 and above. The median values for females fall into the 49–82 per cent range for the first three age groups (0, 1–14 and 15–44), 29–43 per cent for the 45–64 age group, and 8–15 per cent for the 65–84 group. The corresponding ranges for males are, respectively, 33–79 per cent, 14–47 per cent and 3–28 per cent.

The pattern that the magnitude of decline in the death probability decreases from younger to older ages holds generally across mortality levels and time periods. In the older ages, however, there is some evidence that mortality reduction accelerates at lower mortality levels. For the 65–84 age group, the median percentage decline in the first period increases steadily with initial e_0 from 8 per cent to 15 per cent among females, and more moderately from 8 per cent to 10 per cent among males. In the second period, in populations with an initial e_0 over 50, mortality decline at ages 65–84 increases from 9 per cent to 21 per cent among females, and from under 4 per cent to 28 per cent among males. Mortality improvement in the 45–64 age group also becomes more notable in the second period when e_0 exceeds 50 years. The accelerated mortality decline in the older ages at lower mortality levels can be further examined in terms of gains in life expectancy.

Figure 12.4 shows the contributions of age-specific mortality change to the gain in e_0 in each of the two 30-year periods, which are calculated using Arriaga's decomposition procedure (Preston et al. 2001). Each age component can be interpreted as the contribution made by mortality change over the time period in that particular age group to the total gain in e_0, incorporating both the direct effect and indirect and interaction effects (ibid.).

The age components of e_0 gains decrease consistently from younger to older age groups when initial e_0 is below 70. Thus, for the majority of the populations under observation, the gains in e_0 are dominated by mortality improvement in the younger ages. In fact, for females, when e_0 is below 70 years, mortality decline in the first or second age group makes the largest contribution of all six age groups to years of life gained in all populations except Japan in the first period, Democratic People's Republic of Korea and Cambodia in both periods, and Iraq and Bhutan in the second period. In all these exceptions, the largest component is attributable to mortality reduction at ages 15–44. In most of these countries, this is related to the end of military conflicts and a reduction in mortality from violent deaths.

It is notable, however, that a transition stage seems to begin when initial e_0 reaches 60–69 years. At this stage, while the gains in e_0 continue to be dominated by infancy and childhood, improvement in older age mortality begins to gain momentum: the female and male age-specific components are largest in the first or second age group, but do not decrease in the older ages until the last age group of 85+ years. When initial e_0 exceeds 70 years, the contributions of the four middle age groups increase steadily with age, and in 10 of 20 female populations and four of seven male populations at this mortality level, mortality improvement at ages 65–84 makes the largest contribution to the gain in e_0 in the following 30 years.

In addition to comparing the age components against each other, we can observe the shifting contributions of changes in age-specific mortality to the gains in e_0 by examining each age component against initial e_0. The first three age components of gains in e_0 (representing ages

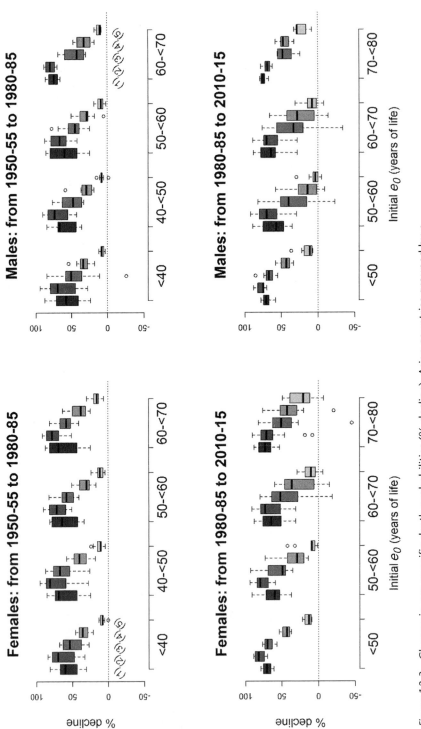

Figure 12.3 Change in age-specific death probabilities (% decline), Asian countries grouped by e_0

Notes: Shades of grey indicate five age groups: (1) age 0, (2) ages 1–14, (3) 15–44, (4) 45–64 and (5) 65–84. The 60–<70 e_0 level in the first time period includes the observation for Israeli females with e_0 of 70.3 years. Due to space limitation, the observation for Iran males at ages 15–44 in the first time period is not shown, with initial e_0 of 42.1 years and % change of −243. Key elements of the box plots: height of the box for the interquartile range (IQR), the bar within the box for the median, the lower whisker for the larger of the minimum mortality change value and 1.5 IQR plus the lower quartile, the upper whisker for the smaller of the maximum mortality change value and 1.5 IQR plus the upper quartile, and circles for outliers.

Sources: United Nations Population Division (2013) and 1954, 1982 and 2012 Taiwan life tables (http://sowf.moi.gov.tw/stat/Life/quary-1age.htm#taiwan-a-title.gif).

Table 12.1 List of Asian countries and territories by life expectancy (e_0)

Life expectancy (e_0)	Female	Male
1950–1955		
Less than 40 years	Afghanistan, Bhutan, India, Indonesia, Iran, Iraq, Maldives, Myanmar, Nepal, Oman, Pakistan, Timor-Leste, Yemen	Afghanistan, Bahrain, Bhutan, Cambodia, India, Indonesia, Iraq, Laos, Maldives, Myanmar, Nepal, North Korea, Oman, Pakistan, Saudi Arabia, Timor-Leste, Turkey, Yemen
40 to less than 50	Bahrain, Bangladesh, Cambodia, China, Jordan, Laos, Mongolia, North Korea, Palestine, Saudi Arabia, South Korea, Syria, Turkey, United Arab Emirates	Bangladesh, China, Iran, Jordan, Kyrgyzstan, Mongolia, Palestine, South Korea, Syria, Thailand, Turkmenistan, United Arab Emirates
50 to less than 60	Brunei Darussalam, Kuwait, Kyrgyzstan, Malaysia, Philippines, Qatar, Sri Lanka, Tajikistan, Thailand, Turkmenistan, Uzbekistan, Vietnam	Armenia, Azerbaijan, Brunei Darussalam, Georgia, Hong Kong, Kazakhstan, Kuwait, Lebanon, Macao, Malaysia, Philippines, Qatar, Singapore, Sri Lanka, Tajikistan, Uzbekistan, Vietnam
60 to less than 70	Armenia, Azerbaijan, Cyprus, Georgia, Hong Kong, Japan, Kazakhstan, Lebanon, Macao, Singapore, Taiwan	Cyprus, Israel, Japan, Taiwan
70 and greater	Israel	–
1980–1985		
Less than 50 years	Afghanistan, Bhutan, Nepal, Timor-Leste	Afghanistan, Bhutan, Cambodia, Iran, Laos, Nepal, Timor-Leste
50 to less than 60	Bangladesh, Cambodia, India, Laos, Maldives, Mongolia, Myanmar, Pakistan, Yemen	Bangladesh, India, Indonesia, Iraq, Kyrgyzstan, Maldives, Mongolia, Myanmar, Pakistan, Turkey, Turkmenistan, Yemen
60 to less than 70	Azerbaijan, China, Indonesia, Iran, Iraq, Jordan, Kyrgyzstan, North Korea, Oman, Palestine, Philippines, Saudi Arabia, Syria, Tajikistan, Thailand, Turkey, Turkmenistan, Uzbekistan	Armenia, Azerbaijan, Bahrain, Brunei Darussalam, China, Georgia, Jordan, Kazakhstan, Kuwait, Lebanon, Malaysia, North Korea, Oman, Palestine, Philippines, Saudi Arabia, South Korea, Sri Lanka, Syria, Taiwan, Tajikistan, Thailand, United Arab Emirates, Uzbekistan, Vietnam
70 to less than 80	Armenia, Bahrain, Brunei Darussalam, Cyprus, Georgia, Hong Kong, Israel, Japan, Kazakhstan, Kuwait, Lebanon, Macao, Malaysia, Qatar, Singapore, South Korea, Sri Lanka, Taiwan, United Arab Emirates, Vietnam	Cyprus, Hong Kong, Israel, Japan, Macao, Qatar, Singapore

Sources: United Nations Population Division (2013) and 1954, 1982 and 2012 Taiwan life tables (http://sowf.moi.gov.tw/stat/Life/quary-1age.htm#taiwan-a-title.gif).

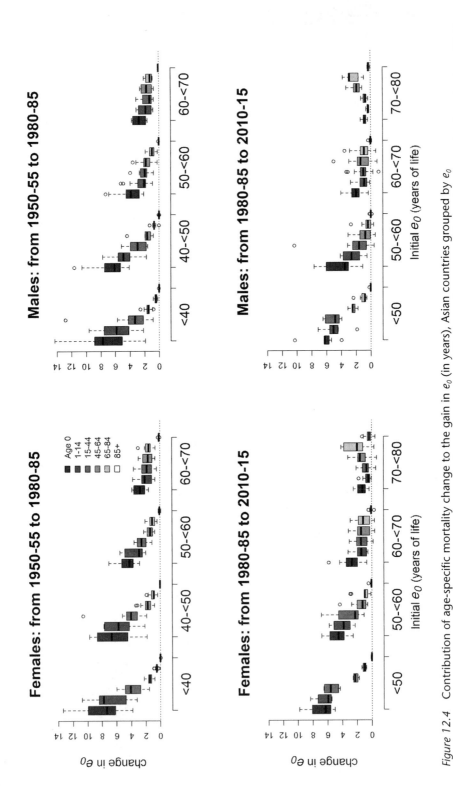

Figure 12.4 Contribution of age-specific mortality change to the gain in e_0 (in years), Asian countries grouped by e_0

Notes: The 60–<70 e_0 level in the first time period includes the observation for Israel females with e_0 of 70.3 years. Due to space limitation, three observations for males at ages 15–44 are not shown: Iran (initial e_0 of 42.1 years; age component of -9.7 years) and Iraq (37.0; -2.6) in the first time period, and Iran (45.2; 17.5) in the second period. For key elements of the box plots see notes for Figure 12.3.

Sources: United Nations Population Division (2013) and 1954, 1982 and 2012 Taiwan life tables (http://sowf.moi.gov.tw/stat/Life/quary-1age.htm#taiwan-a-title.gif).

0–44 years) decrease as initial e_0 increases. In contrast, the three components due to mortality decline at middle and old ages do not decrease; when e_0 reaches the 60s or higher, the years of life gained from mortality decline at ages 65–84 and 85+ increase with initial e_0.

To sum up, there are systematic variations across mortality levels in age-specific mortality change. Generally the decline of age-specific mortality starts at young ages and extends gradually to older age groups. Largely because of that, the contributions of age-specific mortality reduction to the gain in e_0 decrease from the younger to older ages until initial e_0 reaches the 60s. When mortality reaches or is around this level, the age patterns begin to shift. When e_0 is 60–69 years, the age components of e_0 gain flatten out, and when e_0 reaches 70 and above, the largest component is attributable to mortality improvement in the 65–84 age group.

We have so far focused our discussion on the central tendencies of age-specific mortality change, and noted that the central tendencies are in general similar between the first and second time periods. This is consistent with the earlier observation that the roughly linear relationship between initial mortality level and gain in e_0 does not vary substantially with time (Figures 12.1 and 12.2). However, when examining the distributions of age-specific mortality change, we observe some differences between the two time periods. In the period between 1950–1955 and 1980–1985, the scatter of mortality change data points (both proportional decline in mortality and years of life gained) is wider for the first three age groups than for the middle and old ages, and this pattern does not vary across initial e_0 values. In the period between 1980–1985 and 2010–2015, the spread of the distributions narrows for infant and child mortality, but widens for adult and old-age mortality, compared with the first period. A related difference between the first and second time periods is that negative values of mortality decline (that is, mortality increases or deteriorations) are not observed in the first period, but do exist in the second period in some adult and older age populations. These temporal differences in the distributions of age-specific mortality change relate to the three population clusters with faster or slower than expected mortality improvement, as noted previously. These are further discussed in the following section.

Age patterns of fast or slow mortality change

In the period between 1950–1955 and 1980–1985, mortality improvement in the 11 vanguard populations does not deviate much from the straight-line negative relationship between initial e_0 and the gain in e_0. e_0 in all these countries and territories is below 70 years in 1950–1955, except for Israeli females, and the largest component of the gain in e_0 in the following 30 years is due to mortality decline in the first or second age group, except for Japanese females. However, what makes the vanguard group stand out from other Asian populations is adult mortality improvement: in seven female and eight male vanguard populations, mortality decline at ages 15–44 or 45–64 makes the first (in the case of Japanese females) or second largest contribution to the longevity gain, compared with just six female and five male populations in the rest of Asia.

The speed of adult mortality decline among the vanguards can be best seen in the case of Japanese females. The success story of Japan's rising longevity in the post-World War II era has been well documented, but mostly in its own terms or in comparison with Western populations at different mortality levels. The Asian context allows for a comparison at similar mortality levels. In 1950–1955, Japanese female e_0, at 63.9 years, ranks sixth in Asia and infant mortality is higher than in Israel and Taiwan, child mortality is higher than in Singapore, Georgia, Armenia, Cyprus and Israel, and young adult mortality is higher than in 11 Asian populations (Israel, Taiwan, Cyprus, Hong Kong, Armenia, Georgia, Singapore, Azerbaijan, Kazakhstan, Uzbekistan and Tajikistan). By 1980–1985, Japanese females have achieved the lowest adult mortality as well as the lowest infant and child mortality in Asia, and mortality reductions have already shifted to old age. In this 30-year period, Japanese infant and child mortality decline have contributed 5.9 years of life gained, but this is smaller than the combined contribution of 6.6 years ascribable to mortality reductions at ages 15–64 years. The Japanese case stands out among the vanguard group in furthering longevity at the right tail of the e_0 distribution in Asia.

In the second period, the vanguard populations maintain their pace of mortality decline but age patterns shift. Mortality change accelerates in the middle and old ages. For example, in comparison with the first period, the percentage decline in the 45–64 age group increases in the second period in eight female and eight male vanguards. The acceleration in mortality decline is even stronger for those aged 65–84, with a greater percentage decline in the second period in ten female and 11 male vanguards. The contribution of mortality reduction at ages 65–84 to the gain in e_0 is the largest of all age groups in 11 female and ten male populations in the second period, but in none in the first period.

In contrast, the eight former Soviet republics experience slower than expected mortality improvement from the early 1950s. In the first period, the smaller gains in e_0 are mainly due to the slower improvement of mortality under age 45. Mortality decline at ages 45 and above is also relatively small. However, in most populations when initial e_0 is 55–65 years, the magnitude of mortality reduction at ages 45–64 tends to be small, the exception being the vanguard countries with fast improvement discussed above.

In the second period, the infant and child mortality decline in the former Soviet republics is smaller than in other Asian populations with similar mortality levels, which is consistent with the observation that infant mortality deteriorated in Russia after the breakup of the USSR in the early 1990s (Shkolnikov and Meslé 1996). The impact on the sluggish e_0 gain, however, is less than that of the older groups, because the level of infant and child mortality is already fairly low after 1980–1985. In the second period, as in the European portion of the former Soviet countries (Shkolnikov et al. 1998), a slowdown or even reversal in adult and old-age mortality decline is observed in Central Asia and the Caucasus. Adult or old-age mortality increases among females in four countries (Azerbaijan, Kazakhstan, Uzbekistan and Kyrgyzstan) and males in six countries (Armenia, Kazakhstan, Uzbekistan, Kyrgyzstan, Tajikistan and Turkmenistan). The largest proportional mortality increase is observed for the 15–44 age group in Kazakhstan (rising by 46 per cent for females and 34 per cent for males), and would have produced a drop in e_0 if not for the improvement in infant and child mortality. While there is no reversal of age-specific mortality in the remaining populations, mortality decline in the adult and old age groups is slow (the maximum decline being 35 per cent, observed for women aged 15–44 in Georgia), and the improvement in e_0 is small, much smaller than the gains in other Asian countries at similar mortality levels. These results for age-specific mortality change over the two 30-year periods indicate that the slow mortality improvement in the former Soviet republics in Central Asia and the Caucasus is persistent over time and pervasive at various stages of life, suggesting a scenario of systemic societal devaluation of life and health (Shkolnikov and Meslé 1996; Field 1995) exacerbated by the collapse of the political system and ensuing social dysfunction.

For the third cluster, their smaller gains in e_0 in the first period are mainly due to the slower improvement of mortality among infants, children and young adults. The slow improvement in the most populous Southern Asian countries from the early 1950s to the early 1970s has been noted in an early UN study and attributed to widespread poverty, lack of education, poor sanitary and health conditions and malnutrition (UN 1982). Several of these populations have been involved in protracted military conflicts. These conflicts not only take a toll on lives, of adults in particular, but also hamper economic and social development and prevent the implementation of public health programmes.

Between 1980–1985 and 2010–2015, several countries in the third cluster are lifted out of military conflicts and are no longer falling behind in mortality improvement. Poverty, however, is still persistent and pervasive; under the socioeconomic constraints, diseases (e.g. child and maternal malnutrition) and injuries continue to be serious concerns. The burden of disease data show that in the 2000–2012 period, the contributions of road injuries and other unintentional injuries to the loss of healthy years of life in this third cluster, except for the Maldives, are among the highest in Asia (see Chapter 13). Adults in the prime of life and actively engaged in social and economic production are likely to be most vulnerable to accidental death. Thus, the adverse adult mortality conditions in this third cluster contrast sharply with the rapid adult mortality decline experienced by the vanguard group at similar mortality levels.

Sex differentials in mortality change

The systematic variations between mortality level and mortality change are generally similar between males and females. There are, however, notable sex differences. Figure 12.5 shows the differences between female and male life expectancies at two time points (1950–1955 and 2010–2015), plotted against female life expectancy. Except for Iran, India, Bangladesh, Maldives, Nepal, Jordan and China in 1950–1955, women live longer than men in all countries and territories at both time points. Moreover, the sex gap in life expectancy widens at lower mortality levels. When female e_0 is less than 40 years, the median sex gap in e_0 is less than 1 year, but the female advantage increases to over 4 years when their e_0 exceeds 70 years.

A comparison of changes in female and male age-specific mortality in Figure 12.3 shows that mortality decline is greater for females than males in all age groups across mortality levels until e_0 reaches approximately 70 years. For example, at ages 15–44, the median reduction in mortality in the first time period is greater for females than males by 3.5 percentage points when e_0 is below 40 years, by 19 percentage points when e_0 is 40–49 years, and by seven percentage points when e_0 is 60–69 years. From 1980–1985 to 2010–2015, the respective female surpluses are 3, 19 and 3 percentage points. These sex differences are consistent with the earlier observation that at a given mortality level, the expected gain in e_0 is greater for females than males (Figures 12.1 and 12.2). They indicate an increasingly lower mortality for females than for males, i.e., an expansion of female mortality advantage at relatively low mortality levels.

When female e_0 reaches 70–79 years, the female advantage in proportional decline in mortality mostly vanishes or reverses, which may suggest a catch-up in male mortality improvement. It should be emphasized, however, that these sex differences are based on comparing the sexes at the same e_0 level, and female and male populations involved in this comparison may not come from the same country. The 19 female populations with e_0 exceeding 70 years in 1980–1985 are spread across a mix of vanguards, laggards (mostly in the former Soviet republics) and other countries, whereas the seven comparable male populations are in Qatar and six vanguards. Under the more common approach of comparing female and male mortality changes in the same country (e.g. Figure 12.5), there is no clear evidence yet that sex differentials in mortality are narrowing; compared with their male compatriots, females are typically at a more advanced stage of the mortality transition. These two approaches (i.e. comparing female and male mortality changes at the same mortality level vs. in the same country) provide different perspectives on the sex differentials and are complementary.

The positive relationship between e_0 and sex differentials in mortality likely reflects sex-specific causal structures of death and changes in these sex differences at different stages of the mortality transition. Early in this transition, success is achieved in the control against infectious diseases, to which women are generally more vulnerable than men because of a variety

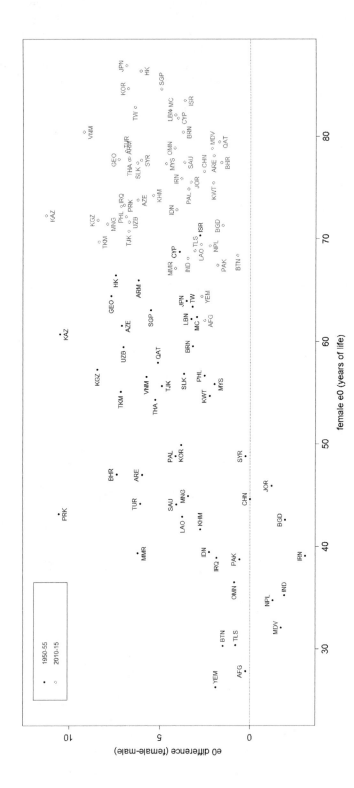

Figure 12.5 Sex differences in e_0 (years of life), by female e_0, Asia

Note: HK for Hong Kong, MC for Macao, TW for Taiwan and the other symbols are country ISO codes.

Sources: United Nations Population Division (2013) and 1954, 1982 and 2012 Taiwan life tables (http://sowf.moi.gov.tw/stat/Life/quary-1age.htm#taiwan-a-title.gif).

of factors that are compounded by poor economic development, limited health care and high fertility. In contrast, behaviour-related and external causes of death, to which men are more susceptible, are contingent on the broad social context and tend to increase at certain stages of socioeconomic development. The greater male susceptibility to external mortality is clearly seen in military conflicts. Because of the Iran-Iraq war, for example, the male probability of dying at ages 15–44 increases by 243 per cent in Iran and 26 per cent in Iraq between 1950–1955 and 1980–1985, and these mortality deteriorations are responsible for 9.7 and 2.6 years of life lost in the respective male populations. In contrast, mortality among young female adults in Iran and Iraq continues to improve, contributing 2.7 and 5.0 years of life gained, respectively.

The greater male susceptibility to behaviour-related mortality risks permeates most aspects of adult life. Traffic accidents and HIV-AIDS mortality are responsible for high male mortality in Thailand, for example (Carmichael 2011). Cause-specific mortality for Kyrgyzstan (Guillot et al. 2013) indicates that excessive alcohol drinking and smoking likely underlie the excess male mortality in the former Soviet countries, especially in the middle and old ages when the ageing process starts and degenerative diseases are prominent. In this sense, the sex differences in mortality in Asia do not deviate from the Western experience, where excess male mortality from cardiovascular and respiratory diseases and cancer is largely responsible for the expansion of sex differentials across time and space (Preston 1976; Lopez 1983).

In addition to the broad trends, mortality sex differentials are persistently low or high in certain groups of Asian countries. Over the 60-year period, the sex gap in e_0 is persistently small (about 2 years or lower) in a group of Southern Asian countries, including Bhutan, Afghanistan, Pakistan, Nepal and Bangladesh and in Yemen. The narrow sex gap in these countries is largely due to female mortality disadvantage in infancy and childhood (see also Chapter 10) and among young adults, and likely results from a combination of sociocultural and environmental factors. Low social status, for example, could inhibit access to adequate nutrition and care among young girls and lead to high fertility among young women, and is compounded by poverty and the hot climate where infectious diseases such as diarrhoea are endemic. In a regression analysis of causes of death in an international sample of populations up to the 1960s, Preston (1976) suggested that poor nutrition, combined with discrimination against females, would increase mortality disadvantage for females, in particular from infectious diseases.

A small sex gap in e_0 (about 2 years) also exists in 2010–2015 in some Gulf countries (e.g. Bahrain, Kuwait, Qatar and United Arab Emirates). The small sex differentials have previously been observed in data from the World Health Organization (Zhao 2011). Our additional analysis also shows that this narrow gap is already evident in 1980–1985 (not shown in Figure 12.5), and exists mainly in the middle and old ages. For example, in the 45–64 age group, the proportional decline in mortality is greater for males than for females in Bahrain, Qatar and United Arab Emirates between 1950–1955 and 1980–1985 and between 1980–1985 and 2010–2015, and in Kuwait between 1980–1985 and 2010–2015. There has been little demographic research on mortality in the Gulf countries. Public health research shows the high prevalence of overweight and obese persons and metabolic complications in these countries, higher than that in the West and higher for females than males in the region (Mabry et al. 2010; Ng et al. 2011). The high prevalence could result from changes in diet and physical activity that are associated with economic and industrial development. That women are more susceptible to these conditions than men could be related to sex differences in physical activity and autonomous behaviour, and in stress arising from the conflict between women's expected roles in private and public life (Baglar 2013). As mortality in the middle and old ages is dominated by degenerative diseases, the sex differences in disease prevalence are consistent with the age patterns of sex differentials in mortality uncovered here. Further cause-of-death analysis would be useful for understanding the mortality patterns in the region.

A large sex gap in e_0 (about 7–10 years) is found in the former Soviet republics in Central Asia and the Caucasus. As discussed above, both male and female mortality declines have been slow, or reversed, in the adult and old ages in these countries. However, the unfavourable trends have been stronger for men than for women. The large sex gap in e_0 and marked excess male mortality in the adult and old age groups persist throughout the 60-year period. A cause-of-death analysis of adult mortality in Kyrgyzstan indicates that the excess male mortality is mainly from cardiovascular diseases and external causes and relates to alcohol consumption; and the cause-specific male excess persists in the period between 1980 and 2010 (Guillot et al. 2013). The persistence and causal structure of male mortality disadvantage are closely related to alcohol abuse and risk taking behaviour in the former Soviet countries that affect men more than women. It is noteworthy that within this group of countries, male disadvantage is larger in the more Russified countries and smaller in countries where Islamic influences are stronger. Thus the sex gap in e_0 is largest in Kazakhstan, followed by Kyrgyzstan and Georgia, and smallest in Tajikistan, which borders Afghanistan. Economic factors such as poverty and unemployment may have also acted as triggers of excessive use of alcohol (Murphy 2011).

Discussion

Over the 60-year period between 1950–1955 and 2010–2015, the Asian population as a whole has largely completed the classic epidemiologic transition and experienced rapid mortality decline, representing an important chapter in its history. During this transition, the pace of mortality decline is closely related to initial mortality level. Before e_0 reaches approximately 70 years, there is a negative and almost linear relationship between initial e_0 and the gain in e_0, and for the majority of the populations, the longevity gain is dominated by contributions attributable to mortality reductions under age 15. At lower mortality levels, however, mortality decline in the older ages accelerates and plays an increasingly important role in the e_0 gain. The gains in longevity and shifts in the age patterns of mortality change have taken place in both sexes, but mortality improvement is generally smaller for males than females, and the sex gap in longevity widens at lower mortality levels.

The shifts in the age patterns of change in female and male mortality are related to the shifting causes of death. At high mortality levels, mortality in the youngest age groups is dominated by infectious diseases. As infectious diseases are gradually brought under control, there is little room for further improvement in mortality in the younger ages, and mortality change shifts to the older ages where degenerative and man-made diseases are prominent. Mortality decline in the older ages leads to further gains in longevity. During this process, the two sexes are often subject to the mortality risk factors unevenly, and long-term mortality decline usually begins earlier and is faster among females than among males, leading to an expansion of sex differentials in mortality favouring females. This process has been closely studied for Western populations and Japan (Omran 1971; Olshansky and Ault 1986), and to a limited extent for populations in Eastern Asia (e.g. Hong Kong, Taiwan and the Republic of Korea). As shown here, the structural shifts and expansion of sex differentials have occurred throughout Asia in a fashion that is rather similar to the Western experience.

Besides the overall trend, we detect clusters of Asian populations where mortality improvement is faster or slower than expected from the initial mortality level. A dozen countries and territories in Eastern, South-Eastern and Western Asia have achieved very low mortality even by world standards, whereas two regional clusters lag behind in mortality improvement, one in

Central Asia and the Caucasus, and the other in Southern and South-Eastern Asia. With some exceptions, countries that are slow (or fast) in controlling infectious diseases and improving mortality among children and young adults in the earlier period tend to be slow (or fast) in fighting man-made and degenerative diseases and improving adult and old-age mortality in the later period.

The persistence over time and geo-cultural clustering of disadvantages point to environmental and systemic socioeconomic factors that hinder mortality improvement. While the sustained success in the vanguard group is clearly attributable to their remarkable socioeconomic development, high standards of living, advanced medical technology and services, and effective health care and disease prevention, many of the laggards in the last 60 years have been subject to social unrest and military conflicts that are intertwined with poor, or lack of, socioeconomic development and public health programmes. Furthermore, sex differentials in mortality are unusually large for the former Soviet cluster and unusually small for the Southern and South-Eastern Asian cluster. The co-occurrence may not be coincidental, but is suggestive of the important part played by sociocultural factors in the sex differentials of mortality.

The analysis divided the 60-year period into two subperiods to capture populations and their experiences in improving survival at different stages of the mortality transition. One interesting finding is that at the same mortality level, the general pace and age patterns of mortality change are largely similar between the first and second 30 years across Asia. This is probably because the medical know-how to fight infectious diseases, which are the major killers, was already widely available by the 1950s (e.g. sulfa-drugs, antibiotics and vaccines), and major advances in the treatment of cardiovascular disease and its risk factors (e.g. antihypertensive drugs) occurred in the 1960s and later (Freis 1995). However, the accelerated mortality decline in the older ages in the vanguard group has most likely benefited from the social and technological advances of recent decades. As for societal crises (e.g. wars and instabilities in political regimes), they clearly have immediate impacts on mortality. However, countries that have been able to end conflicts and enjoy peace and stability (e.g. Bangladesh and Bhutan in the second period) are achieving mortality decline that is well up to expectations based on their mortality level.

As for mortality changes in the next few decades, it is reasonable to expect that mortality will continue to decline and life expectancies will continue to increase in perhaps every Asian country and territory, if there is no major war or other disaster. At the moment, there is no indication that this change will soon stop, even in populations with the highest e_0. However, there are considerable uncertainties about these changes. It is less clear whether mortality decline in populations that have been slow in their epidemiological transition will soon catch up to the pace of the frontrunners or other countries. Although some of the laggards, such as Bangladesh, have recently achieved very impressive mortality decline, mortality improvement is far from encouraging in other countries where there have been protracted political and social uncertainties. Lastly, given the persistence of notable sex differentials in some populations, perhaps it is still early to say whether the divergence and subsequent convergence of sex differentials in mortality observed in European and North American countries (Pampel 2002) will soon take place in Asia. Reducing the marked survival disadvantage among male (and in a few cases female) populations remains a major challenge in the foreseeable future.

Acknowledgements

The authors want to acknowledge the partial financial support provided by the ARC Centre of Excellence in Population Ageing Research (project number CE 1000 1029). The authors are grateful to three reviewers and Adrian Hayes for helpful feedback.

Notes

1 The regression includes all data points except for nine female and eight male populations that are assessed as having a large influence on the regression. The excluded female populations are: Laos, Cambodia, Nepal, Timor-Leste, Bhutan and Afghanistan in the first period, and Maldives, Cambodia and Timor-Leste in the second period. The excluded male populations are: Iran, Bahrain, Cambodia, Democratic People's Republic of Korea, Timor-Leste and Afghanistan in the first period, and Iran and Timor-Leste in the second period. The exclusions are based on the Cook's distance statistic (Cook 1977).
2 Female e_0 in the Republic of Korea is only 49.9 years in 1950–1955.
3 We also observe unusually fast mortality decline in the older age groups and larger than expected gains in e_0 in a few other countries, including Oman and perhaps Turkey and Iran, but we have not categorized them as vanguards because of their somewhat lower e_0 (in the lower 60s in 1980–1985 and still in the upper 70s at the end of the study period).

References

Baglar, R. (2013) '"Oh God, save us from sugar": an ethnographic exploration of diabetes mellitus in the United Arab Emirates'. *Medical Anthropology*, 32(2): 109–125.

Carmichael, G. A. (2011) 'Exploring Thailand's mortality transition with the aid of life tables'. *Asia Pacific Viewpoint*, 52(1): 85–105.

Chowdhury, A. M. R., A. Bhuiya, M. E. Chowdhury, S. Rasheed, Z. Hussain and L. C. Chen (2013) 'The Bangladesh paradox: exceptional health achievement despite economic poverty'. *Lancet*, 382(9906): 1734–1745.

Cook, R. D. (1977) 'Detection of influential observation in linear regression'. *Technometrics*, 19(1): 15–18.

Field, M. G. (1995) 'The health crisis in the former Soviet Union: a report from the "post-war" zone'. *Social Science & Medicine*, 41(11): 1469–1478.

Freis, E. D. (1995) 'Historical development of antihypertensive treatment'. In J. H. Laragh and B. M. Brenner (eds.) *Hypertension: Pathophysiology, Diagnosis and Management, Second Edition*. New York: Raven Press, Ltd. Pp. 2741–2750.

Gu, D., P. Gerland, K. Andreev, N. Li, T. Spoorenberg and G. Heilig (2013) 'Old age mortality in Eastern and South-Eastern Asia'. *Demographic Research*, 29(38): 999–1038.

Guillot, M., N. Gavrilova, L. Torgasheva and M. Denisenko (2013) 'Divergent paths for adult mortality in Russia and Central Asia: evidence from Kyrgyzstan'. *PLoS ONE*, 8(10): e75314. Available from: http://dx.doi.org/10.1371/journal.pone.0075314.

Lopez, A. D. (1983) 'The sex mortality differential in developed countries'. In A. D. Lopez and L. T. Ruzicka (eds.) *Sex Differentials in Mortality: Trends, Determinants and Consequences*. Canberra, Australia: Australian National University, Department of Demography.

Mabry, R. M., M. M. Reeves, E. G. Eakin and N. Owen (2010) 'Gender differences in prevalence of the metabolic syndrome in Gulf Cooperation Council countries: a systematic review'. *Diabetic Medicine*, 27(5): 593–597.

Merli, M. G. (1998) 'Mortality in Vietnam, 1979–1989'. *Demography*, 35(3): 345–360.

Murphy, M. (2011) 'Adult mortality in the former Soviet Union'. In R. G. Rogers and E. M. Crimmins (eds.) *International Handbook of Adult Mortality*. Dordrecht, Heidelberg, London and New York: Springer.

Ng, S. W., S. Zaghloul, H. I. Ali, G. Harrison and B. M. Popkin (2011) 'The prevalence and trends of overweight, obesity and nutrition-related non-communicable diseases in the Arabian Gulf States'. *Obesity Reviews*, 12(1): 1–13.

Olshansky, S. J. and A. B. Ault (1986) 'The fourth stage of the epidemiologic transition: the age of delayed degenerative diseases'. *The Milbank Quarterly*, 64(3): 355–391.

Omran, A. R. (1971) 'The epidemiologic transition: a theory of the epidemiology of population change'. *The Milbank Memorial Fund Quaterly*, 49(4): 509–538.

Pampel, F. C. (2002) 'Cigarette use and the narrowing sex differential in mortality'. *Population and Development Review*, 28(1): 77–104.

Preston, S. H. (1976) *Mortality Patterns in National Populations: with Special Reference to Recorded Causes of Death*. New York and London: Academic Press.

Preston, S. H., P. Heuveline and M. Guillot (2001) *Demography: Measuring and Modeling Population Processes*. Oxford, UK and Malden, MA: Blackwell Publishers.

Rao, C., B. Osterberger, T. D. Anh, M. MacDonald, N. T. K. Chúc and P. S. Hill (2010) 'Compiling mortality statistics from civil registration systems in Viet Nam: the long road ahead'. *Bulletin of the World Health Organization*, 88(1): 58–65.

Shkolnikov, V. M., G. A. Cornia, D. A. Leon and F. Meslé (1998) 'Causes of the Russian mortality crisis: evidence and interpretations'. *World Development*, 26(11): 1995–2011.

Shkolnikov, V. M. and F. Meslé (1996) 'The Russian epidemiological crisis as mirrored by mortality trends'. In J. DaVanzo with the assistance of G. Fansworth (ed.) *Russia's Demographic 'Crisis'*. California: RAND Center for Russian and Eurasian Studies. Pp. 113–162.

Stolnitz, G. J. (1965) 'Recent mortality trends in Latin America, Asia and Africa: review and re-interpretation'. *Population Studies*, 19(2): 117–138.

United Nations (1982) *Model Life Tables for Developing Countries*. New York: United Nations Publication.

United Nations Population Division (2013) *World Population Prospects: The 2012 Revision*. Available from: http://esa.un.org/unpd/wpp/Excel-Data/mortality.htm (accessed 24 June 2013).

United Nations Population Division (2014) *World Population Prospects: The 2012 Revision, Methodology of the United Nations Population Estimates and Projections*. New York: United Nations.

Vallin, J. (1993) 'Social change and mortality decline: women's advantage achieved or regained?' In N. Federici, K. O. Mason and S. Sogner (eds.) *Women's Position and Demographic Change*. New York: Oxford University Press. Pp. 190–212.

Zhao, Z. (2011) 'Adult mortality in Asia'. In R. G. Rogers and E. M. Crimmins (eds.) *International Handbook of Adult Mortality*. Dordrecht, Heidelberg, London and New York: Springer. Pp. 133–150.

Zhao, Z. and Y. Kinfu (2005) 'Mortality transition in East Asia'. *Asian Population Studies*, 1(1): 3–30.

13
Trends in causes of death and burden of diseases

Colin D. Mathers

Introduction

Detailed description of the level and distribution of diseases and injuries, and their causes, are important inputs to public health policies and programmes for national governments and for international health agencies and programmes. Closely related statistics on the age, sex and cause distributions of deaths in the Asian region are also important for understanding and assessing demographic trends in mortality and life expectancy, as well as in identifying key determinants and drivers, and in projecting future demographic trends.

The demand is also growing for timely data to monitor progress in health outcomes such as child mortality, maternal mortality, life expectancy and age- and cause-specific mortality rates. Much of the recent focus has been on monitoring progress towards the 2015 targets of the (health-related) Millennium Development Goals (MDGs), including time series and country-level estimates that are regularly updated. But increasingly, the demand is for comprehensive estimates across the full spectrum, including non-communicable diseases (NCDs) and injuries. In the post-2015 development agenda, there is a considerable focus on ending preventable deaths, and an increasing focus in Asia on the NCDs of adulthood and on injuries.

The world has witnessed major gains in life expectancy in recent decades. At the global level both male and female life expectancies have increased by 6 years since 1990, with gains recorded across all country-income groups. In Asia, increases in life expectancy at birth from 1990 to 2012 exceeded the global average in all subregions for women and for men except in Western Asia where it was just under the global average. For men in Eastern Asia and South-Central Asia, the life expectancy gain was almost 7 years, and for women in South-Central Asia it exceeded 9 years. The Asian region includes several countries with some of the highest life expectancies at birth in the world, as well as several countries whose life expectancies are around 20 years lower.

Drawing on data and analyses from the World Health Organization and collaborating UN agencies, and from the Global Burden of Disease (GBD) 2010 study, this chapter provides an overview of changes in patterns of cause of death and burden of disease in Asia, which underlie the above trends and differentials in life expectancies. The chapter also examines their subregional and country-level trends for the years 2000–2012. Diseases that cause a large number of deaths are clear public health priorities, but mortality statistics alone do not capture the burden caused by chronic diseases, injuries and mental health disorders. A substantial body of work in the last two decades has focused on the quantification of such disease burden using a summary measure that includes both disability (or loss of full health) and premature death, and gives extra weight to diseases that primarily affect younger people, since mortality at younger ages results in a greater loss of years of life.

The initial GBD study was commissioned by the World Bank to provide a comprehensive assessment of disease burden in 1990 from more than 100 diseases and injuries, and from ten selected risk factors (Murray and Lopez 1996a, 1996b; World Bank 1993). As well as generating a comprehensive and consistent set of estimates of mortality and morbidity by age, sex and region for the world, the GBD study introduced a new metric – the Disability Adjusted Life Year (DALY) – to simultaneously quantify the burden of disease from premature mortality and the non-fatal consequences of over 100 diseases and injuries. One lost DALY can be thought of as one lost year of 'healthy' life (either from death or through illness/disability), and total DALYs (quantifying the burden of disease) as a measure of the gap between the current health of a population and an ideal situation where everyone in the population lives into old age in full health. DALYs are calculated by adding years of life lost for deaths (YLL) and equivalent years of healthy life lost due to ill-health and disability (YLD), which are described in more detail later in the chapter.

Drawing on extensive databases and information provided by member states, WHO produced updated GBD estimates for years 2000 to 2004, incorporating substantial improvements in data and methods (WHO 2008, 2009). This was followed by the GBD 2010 study, led by the Institute for Health Metrics and Evaluation at the University of Washington, with key collaborating institutions including WHO, Harvard University, Johns Hopkins University and the University of Queensland. The GBD 2010 study was funded by the Bill & Melinda Gates Foundation, and also drew on wider epidemiological expertise through a network of expert working groups. The results were published in a series of papers in the Lancet in December 2012 (Murray et al. 2012a; Murray et al. 2012b; Lozano et al. 2012; Vos et al. 2012) and welcomed by the WHO as representing an unprecedented effort to improve global and regional estimates of levels and trends in the burden of disease.

To meet WHO's need for comprehensive global health statistics, which bring together WHO and inter-agency estimates for all-cause mortality and priority diseases and injuries, as well as drawing on the work of academic collaborators including the Institute for Health Metrics and Evaluation, updated Global Health Estimates for mortality, causes of death and disease burden have been prepared and released (World Health Organization 2013a, 2014a). Drawing on the WHO Global Health Estimates and results from the GBD 2010 study, this chapter further examines trends and differentials in causes of death and burden of disease in Asia. It identifies groups of countries at different stages of the epidemiological transition and with different patterns of mortality and morbidity. Their cause of death patterns and changes are examined in terms of absolute numbers of deaths, death rates and causal contributors to increases in life expectancy. Finally, projection results of future trends in causes of death for years up to 2050 are presented for the Asian region.

Asian data on mortality and causes of death

Death registration data containing useable information on cause of death distributions are available for around 100 countries, the majority of these in the high income group, Latin America and the Caribbean, Europe and Central Asia. The WHO Mortality Database (WHO 2014b) includes information on cause of death from national death registration systems for 28 of the 49

Asian countries, although the coverage and quality of the cause of death information is highly variable. The proportion of deaths coded to ill-defined causes varies from around 5–10 per cent in countries such as Japan and Singapore, to more than 40 per cent in Sri Lanka and Thailand.

Neither China nor India has complete national registration for deaths, but both countries have partial death registration systems supplemented by sample cause-of-death data collections which are designed to be nationally representative. Taking into account only the actual deaths recorded in the sample systems for China and India, the overall coverage of death registration for the Asian region in the years 2000–2012 is approximately 28 per cent. In other words, slightly less than one-third of deaths in Asia are registered and information on cause of death collected. Death registration coverage varies from 53 per cent in Western Asia down to 22 per cent in Eastern Asia. If systems with coverage of 85 per cent or more are considered to provide representative information on causes of death, along with the sample systems of China, then the proportion of Asian deaths for which useable cause of death information is available ranges from 42 per cent in South-Eastern Asia to 98 per cent in Eastern Asia, with a regional average of close to two-thirds.

The original GBD study and the latest 2010 study developed methods and approaches to make estimates for causes of death and for disease burden for which there was limited data and considerable uncertainty, to ensure that causes with limited information were not implicitly considered to have zero burden and hence ignored by health policymakers. The summary results presented here draw on WHO and UN Inter-agency analyses together with GBD 2010 results to present our best assessment of the situation and trends for Asia.

WHO life tables have been revised and updated for all member states for years 1990–2012, drawing on the UN *World Population Prospects 2012 Revision* (UN Population Division 2013), recent analyses of all-cause and HIV mortality for countries with high HIV prevalence, vital registration data, and UN-IGME estimates of levels and trends for under-five mortality (WHO 2014c). Total deaths by age and sex were estimated for each country by applying the WHO life table death rates to the estimated de facto resident populations prepared by the UN Population Division in its 2012 *Revision* (UN Population Division 2013). They may thus differ slightly from official national estimates for corresponding years.

Diseases and injuries are classified in the GBD using a tree structure based on the International Classification of Diseases. The highest level of aggregation consists of three broad cause groups: Group I (communicable, maternal, perinatal and nutritional conditions), Group II (non-communicable diseases), and Group III (injuries). Group I causes are those conditions that typically decline at a faster pace than all-cause mortality during the epidemiological transition, and occur largely in poor populations. They have been the particular focus of the health-related Millennium Development Goals during 1990–2015 and are also referred to below as 'MDG conditions' for brevity.

The cause-specific mortality and burden of disease estimates for Asian countries summarized in this chapter are drawn from the 2014 Revision of the WHO Global Health Estimates (WHO 2014a) which provide a comprehensive and comparable set of cause of death estimates from year 2000 to 2012. These estimates are consistent with and incorporate UN agency, inter-agency and WHO estimates for population, births, all-cause deaths and specific causes of death, including the most recent death registration data for all countries where it was assessed as of reasonable quality (Liu et al. 2012; WHO 2014d). These estimates also include updated assessments for specific causes of death by WHO programmes and inter-agency groups. These causes include tuberculosis, HIV (UNAIDS 2013), malaria (WHO 2013b), measles and pertussis (Simons et al. 2012; WHO 2011), maternal mortality (WHO, UNICEF et al. 2014), cancers (Ferlay et al. 2013) and road traffic accidents (WHO 2013c). GBD 2010 study estimates (Lozano et al. 2012) were used for other causes in countries without useable vital registration data or other nationally representative sources of information on causes of death.

Cause-specific mortality data for China were available from two sources – the sample vital registration system data for years 1987 to 2010 (China Ministry of Health 2013a) and summary deaths tabulations from the Diseases Surveillance Points system for years 1995–1998 and 2004–2010 (China CDC 2012; China Ministry of Health 2013b). For estimates of causes of death under age five, a separate analysis was undertaken based on an analysis of 206 Chinese community-based longitudinal studies that reported multiple causes of child death (Rudan et al. 2010).

Analysis of causes of death for India was based on data over a period of 3 years (2001–2003) recorded by the Million Death Study (Registrar General of India 2009; Jha et al. 2006), a comprehensive study based on verbal autopsy that assigned causes to all deaths in areas of India covered by the Sample Registration System. Both the Chinese Diseases Surveillance Points system and the Indian Million Death Study use verbal autopsy methods to assign cause of death for deaths outside hospitals. The GBD 2010 also relied heavily on verbal autopsy data for other countries without information on causes of death. Such methods naturally produce more uncertain attribution of cause of death than physician diagnosis. Additionally, categorical assignment of cause of death is inherently difficult for diseases without distinctive symptoms, such as malaria in children, or some forms of cardiovascular disease in older adults.

The results reported below include estimates of cause-specific deaths even for Asian countries or subregions with limited death registration data, based on the best possible assessment of the available evidence. While these estimates will have wider uncertainty ranges than those for regions with more data, their exclusion would result in a potentially biased picture of the patterns of global mortality.

Trends in disease and injury causes of death

Substantial declines in the risk of premature mortality over the last two decades reflect considerable progress in reducing death rates for infectious, perinatal, maternal and nutritional conditions (Figure 13.1). This set of conditions has been the focus of the MDG, whose health goals targeted HIV, tuberculosis, malaria, child mortality and maternal mortality. In all Asian subregions, death rates for this group of broadly 'MDG conditions' (including all infectious diseases) declined by around 30 to 40 per cent, although their share of total mortality remains relatively high in South-Eastern Asia (at 23 per cent) and South-Central Asia (at 28 per cent). Overall crude death rates for cardiovascular diseases, cancer and other non-communicable diseases fell slightly in Western Asia, but rose by around 10 to 20 per cent in other Asian subregions, largely reflecting population ageing rather than increases in age-specific risks of death.

Figure 13.2 shows the broad contributions of major causes of death to overall mortality risk for countries in the Asian region for year 2012. Three small countries with a population of less than 1 million have been excluded from this graph. Death rates are age-standardized to the WHO world standard population (Ahmad et al. 2001) to allow cross-country comparison of mortality risks un-confounded by differences in population age structure. Countries are ranked in order of increasing total death rates, from Japan and Singapore at the top (lowest level) to Yemen, Turkmenistan and Afghanistan at the bottom (highest mortality level).

There are considerable variations across Asian countries in overall mortality risks and the contribution of the MDG conditions to these risks is clear. China, at eighteenth rank with relatively low total mortality risk, has a very low contribution of MDG conditions, whereas India, at 37th rank, is one of the countries with a still relatively large contribution of MDG conditions.

Colin D. Mathers

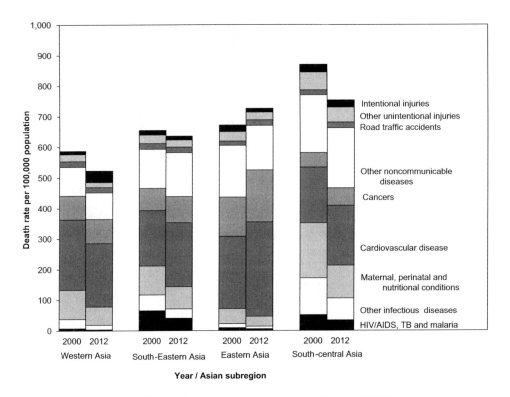

Figure 13.1 Cause-specific death rates, Asian subregions, 2000 and 2012
Source: WHO Global Health Observatory (WHO 2014e).

The countries in the Asia region with highest mortality risk comprise a mix of countries such as Yeman, Afghanistan and Myanmar with high mortality from MDG conditions, and countries in Western Asia such as Kazakhstan and Turkmenistan, with relatively low mortality from MDG conditions but very high mortality from cardiovascular disease.

Figure 13.3 summarizes the leading causes of death overall in the Asian region in 2000 and 2012. The four leading causes of death have remained unchanged from 2000 to 2012: stroke, ischaemic heart disease, chronic obstructive pulmonary disease and lower respiratory infections (principally pneumonia). These account for a rising proportion of deaths (from 37 per cent in 2000 to 41 per cent in 2012) mainly because of population ageing, rather than any increase in age-specific risks. The leading infectious causes in 2000 have all declined as a proportion of total deaths, as have MDG causes such as prematurity, birth asphyxia and birth trauma. Apart from cardiovascular diseases, a number of cancers have also increased in importance as causes of death, as have road injuries. The latter reflect the increasing levels of road vehicle ownership and use in Asian countries such as China and India.

Table 13.1 shows the top 15 causes of death in each of the Asian subregions in 2012. Stroke is the leading cause of death in Eastern Asia and South-Eastern Asia, causing substantially more deaths than ischaemic heart disease. This relationship is reversed in South-Central Asia and Western Asia. Stomach cancer is the sixth leading cause of death in Eastern Asia, although it does not appear in the top 15 causes in any of the other subregions. South-Eastern Asia is the only subregion where HIV/AIDS appears in the top 15 causes.

Causes of death and burden of diseases

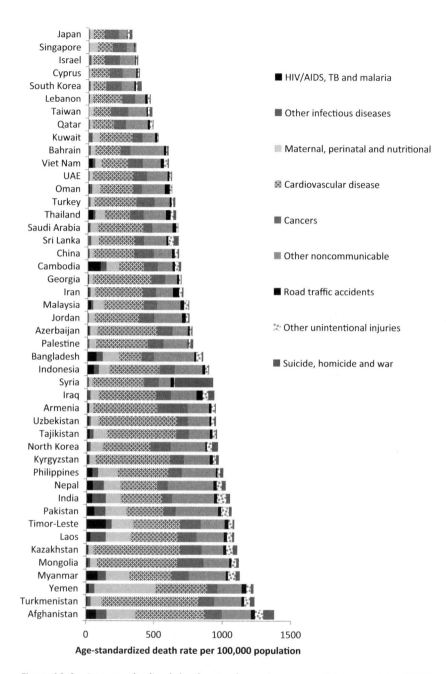

Figure 13.2 Age-standardized death rates for major causes, Asian countries, 2012
Source: WHO Global Health Observatory (WHO 2014e).

The total numbers of deaths or overall death rates from specific causes do not necessarily provide a good metric for informing public health priorities for the Asian region. Such measures, for example, assign the same weight to a death at age 80 as at age 30 or even at 1 year of age. The preponderance of NCDs such as ischaemic heart disease and cerebrovascular disease in

ASIA, 2000					ASIA, 2012			
Cause	Deaths (000s)	% deaths	Rank		Rank	Cause	Deaths (000s)	% deaths
Stroke	3434	12.4	1		1	Stroke	4520	14.9
Ischaemic heart disease	2563	9.2	2		2	Ischaemic heart disease	4033	13.3
Chronic obstructive pulmonary disease	2484	9.0	3		3	Chronic obstructive pulmonary disease	2485	8.2
Lower respiratory infections	1826	6.6	4		4	Lower respiratory infections	1452	4.8
Diarrhoeal diseases	1203	4.3	5		5	Trachea, bronchus, lung cancers	928	3.1
Tuberculosis	998	3.6	6		6	Diabetes mellitus	822	2.7
Preterm birth complications	778	2.8	7		7	Road injury	795	2.6
Birth asphyxia and birth trauma	641	2.3	8		8	Diarrhoeal diseases	785	2.6
Self-harm	609	2.2	9		9	Preterm birth complications	655	2.2
Road injury	598	2.2	10		10	Tuberculosis	638	2.1
Trachea, bronchus, lung cancers	567	2.0	11		11	Hypertensive heart disease	617	2.0
Diabetes mellitus	533	1.9	12		12	Liver cancer	560	1.8
Hypertensive heart disease	507	1.8	13		13	Cirrhosis of the liver	543	1.8
Cirrhosis of the liver	499	1.8	14		14	Self-harm	534	1.8
Kidney diseases	444	1.6	15		15	Stomach cancer	523	1.7
Stomach cancer	441	1.6	16		16	Kidney diseases	520	1.7
Liver cancer	417	1.5	17		17	Falls	459	1.5
Falls	355	1.3	18		18	Birth asphyxia and birth trauma	349	1.1
Neonatal sepsis and infection	354	1.3	19		19	Colon and rectum cancers	330	1.1
Congenital anomalies	347	1.3	20		20	Asthma	299	1.0
Asthma	284	1.0	22		22	Congenital anomalies	290	1.0
Colon and rectum cancers	219	1.0	26		27	Neonatal sepsis and infection	224	0.8

Figure 13.3 Leading causes of death, Asia, 2000–2012
Source: WHO Global Health Observatory (WHO 2014e).

Table 13.1 Fifteen leading causes of deaths in each of the Asian subregions, 2012

Rank	Eastern Asia			Rank	South-Eastern Asia		
	Cause	Deaths (000s)	% deaths		Cause	Deaths (000s)	% deaths
1	Stroke	2,547	21.8	1	Stroke	642	16.5
2	Ischaemic heart disease	1,672	14.3	2	Ischaemic heart disease	409	10.5
3	COPD	1,072	9.2	3	Lower respiratory infections	274	7.0
4	Lung cancer	707	6.0	4	Diabetes	190	4.9
5	Liver cancer	440	3.8	5	Tuberculosis	156	4.0
6	Stomach cancer	392	3.4	6	COPD	143	3.7
7	Lower respiratory infections	369	3.1	7	Road injury	119	3.1
8	Road injury	297	2.5	8	Cirrhosis of the liver	103	2.6
9	Hypertensive heart disease	269	2.3	9	Kidney diseases	96	2.5
10	Diabetes	268	2.3	10	Hypertensive heart disease	92	2.4
11	Oesophageal cancer	214	1.8	11	Lung cancer	92	2.4
12	Colorectal cancer	205	1.8	12	HIV/AIDS	78	2.0
13	Self-harm	183	1.6	13	Liver cancer	73	1.9
14	Falls	130	1.1	14	Asthma	67	1.7
15	Kidney diseases	127	1.1	15	Preterm birth complications	66	1.7

Causes of death and burden of diseases

Table 13.1 (Cont.)

Rank	South-Central Asia			Rank	Western Asia		
	Cause	Deaths (000s)	% deaths		Cause	Deaths (000s)	% deaths
1	Ischaemic heart disease	1,697	12.6	1	Ischaemic heart disease	255	20.2
2	COPD	1,237	9.2	2	Stroke	155	12.3
3	Stroke	1,176	8.7	3	Lower respiratory infections	77	6.1
4	Lower respiratory infections	733	5.4	4	Conflict and legal intervention	74	5.9
5	Diarrhoeal diseases	698	5.2	5	Road injury	42	3.3
6	Preterm birth complications	518	3.8	6	Lung cancer	34	2.7
7	Tuberculosis	424	3.1	7	COPD	34	2.7
8	Road injury	336	2.5	8	Diabetes	33	2.6
9	Diabetes	330	2.4	9	Hypertensive heart disease	28	2.2
10	Self-harm	307	2.3	10	Preterm birth complications	27	2.1
11	Cirrhosis of the liver	302	2.2	11	Congenital anomalies	22	1.7
12	Falls	288	2.1	12	Kidney diseases	21	1.7
13	Kidney diseases	276	2.0	13	Rheumatic heart disease	19	1.5
14	Birth asphyxia and birth trauma	253	1.9	14	Birth asphyxia and birth trauma	16	1.3
15	Hypertensive heart disease	228	1.7	15	Colorectal cancer	15	1.2

Source: WHO Global Health Observatory (2014e).

cause-of-death rankings is therefore potentially misleading and may not appropriately reflect the impact of premature mortality. YLL is a measure of premature mortality that takes into account both the frequency of death and the age at which it occurs.

YLL due to premature mortality are calculated from the number of deaths at each age multiplied by a global standard life expectancy of the age at which death occurs. For the YLL reported by WHO, the standard life table is based on the projected frontier life expectancy for 2050, with a life expectancy at birth of 92 years (WHO 2013a). The standard reference life table is intended to represent the potential maximum life expectancy of an individual at a given age, and is used for both males and females. A death at birth will thus result in 92 YLL, a death at age 30 in 62.1 YLL, and a death at age 70 in 23.2 YLL. In the calculation of these results, the age weighting and time discounting applied in previous versions of GBD studies have not been used. The overall pattern of premature mortality in Asian countries is summarized below in terms of YLL.

During the period 2000–2012, a major shift occurred in the main causes of YLL, away from MDG conditions and towards NCDs and injuries, with the proportion of YLL due to MDG conditions declining in almost every country in the Asian region. Countries in which MDG conditions were responsible for the most YLL in 2000 are generally those in which the greatest reductions have taken place. Countries are, however, in very different stages of this epidemiological transition (Figure 13.4). For example, there are five Asian countries in which MDG

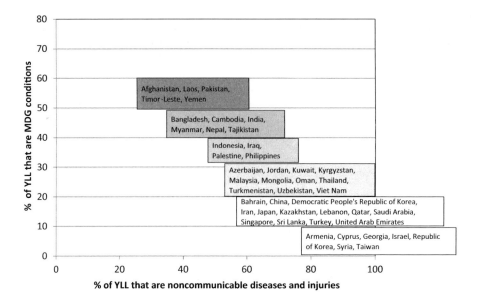

Figure 13.4 Progression through the epidemiological transition in Asia
Notes: Countries are grouped into boxes according to the ten percentage point range in which their % of YLL that are MDG conditions falls. The horizontal placing of the box gives an approximate indication of the complementary % of YLL that are non-communicable diseases and injuries.
Source: WHO Global Health Observatory (WHO 2014e).

conditions are still responsible for more than 50 per cent of all YLL. At the other end of this epidemiological shift, there are seven countries in which MDG conditions cause less than ten per cent of all YLL. Syria is only in this latter group because of the very high injury contribution to YLL from the civil war underway in 2012.

Causes of disability and lost health

The Disability Adjusted Life Year (DALY) extends the concept of years of life lost due to premature death (YLL) to include equivalent years of 'healthy' life lost from living in states of poor health or disability. The latter is quantified through the years of (equivalent healthy) life lost due to disability (YLD), estimated for a particular cause in a particular time period as follows:

YLD = number of prevalent cases × disability weight.

The 'valuation' of time lived in non-fatal health states formalizes and quantifies social preferences for different states of health as *disability weights*. These weights can also be described as health state valuations or health state preferences. In the formulation of the DALY, the disability weight is conceived of as quantifying the relative loss of health for different conditions or states, and does not carry any implication about quality of life, or the overall value of a life lived in particular health or disability states. Disability weights were completely revised for the GBD 2010 study based on data collected from 13,902 individuals in household surveys in five countries, supplemented by an open-access web-based survey of 16,328 people (Salomon et al. 2012).

YLD estimates are restricted to loss of health experienced by individuals, and do not take into account other aspects of quality of life or well-being, or the impacts of a person's health

Causes of death and burden of diseases

Asia, 2000					Asia, 2012			
Cause	YLD (000s)	%YLD	Rank		Rank	Cause	YLD (000s)	%YLD
Major depressive disorder	36106	9.9	1	→	1	Major depressive disorder	43638	10.2
Iron-deficiency anaemia	29230	8.0	2	⤫	2	Back and neck pain	30828	7.2
Back and neck pain	24648	6.8	3		3	Iron-deficiency anaemia	27611	6.4
COPD	15489	4.2	4	→	4	COPD	19817	4.6
Alcohol use disorders	13559	3.7	5	→	5	Alcohol use disorders	15403	3.6
Anxiety disorders	11965	3.3	6	⤫	6	Hearing loss	14949	3.5
Hearing loss	10403	2.9	7		7	Anxiety disorders	14408	3.4
Diabetes	9704	2.7	8	→	8	Diabetes	13472	3.1
Refractive errors	9417	2.6	9	⤫	9	Falls	11445	2.7
Migraine	9295	2.6	10	⤫	10	Migraine	11404	2.7
Falls	8598	2.4	11	⤫	12	Refractive errors	10044	2.3

Figure 13.5 Ten leading causes of years lost due to disability (YLD) in Asia, 2000–2012
Source: WHO Global Health Observatory (WHO 2014e).

condition on other people (except as far as they experience directly assessed losses of health themselves). Estimates of YLD presented here for Asian countries draw on the GBD 2010 analyses (Vos et al. 2012), with selected revisions to disability weights and prevalence estimates as described in a WHO Technical Paper (WHO 2013a).

There is much less variation in overall YLD rates per 1,000 population across the Asian subregions, than in YLL rates or mortality rates. The total YLD rate in 2012 for South-Central Asia was 108 per 1,000 of the population compared to 91 per 1,000 of the population for Eastern Asia. This differential of 19 per cent is lower than the corresponding YLL differential of 81 per cent. Most of the YLD rate differential is due to the subregional variation in the contribution of MDG conditions.

The overall burden of non-fatal disabling conditions is dominated by a relatively short list of causes, particularly a number of mental disorders, musculoskeletal disorders and sense organ disorders. In Asia, mental and neurological disorders are the most important causes of disability, accounting for around one-third of YLDs among adults aged 15 years and over. The ten leading causes of YLD are shown in Figure 13.5 for Asia as a whole in 2000 and 2012. The three leading causes of disability are non-fatal conditions: major depressive disorder, back and neck pain, and iron-deficiency anaemia (although suicide is a major fatal consequence for depressive disorders). Several of the other conditions in the top ten list are also non-fatal conditions: hearing loss, anxiety disorders and migraine. Alcohol use disorders include alcohol dependence and problem use. Refractive errors include uncorrected vision loss due to short sightedness, long sightedness and astigmatism.

The disabling burden of neuropsychiatric conditions is almost the same for males and females, but the major contributing causes are different. While depression is the leading cause for both males and females, the burden of depression is 60 per cent higher for females than males. Females also have a higher burden from anxiety disorders, migraine and senile dementias. In contrast, the male YLD for alcohol and drug use disorders is six times higher than that for females, and accounts for almost one-third of the male neuropsychiatric burden.

Vision and hearing loss account for nearly 10 per cent of YLD in Asia. Curable or treatable disorders of vision (cataracts and refractive errors) cause 4 per cent of YLD, as does adult-onset hearing loss.

Burden of disease

As noted earlier, the Global Burden of Disease analyses use the DALY to quantify total loss of healthy years of life from disease or injury, including potential years of life lost due to mortality

Colin D. Mathers

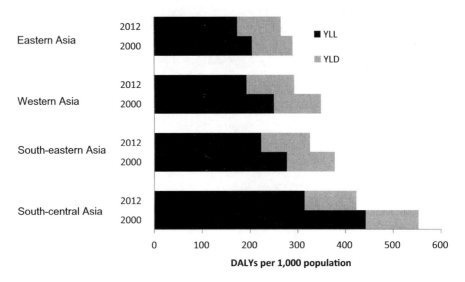

Figure 13.6 YLL and YLD contributions to total DALY rates, Asian subregions, 2000 and 2012
Source: WHO Global Health Observatory (WHO 2014e).

(YLL) and equivalent healthy years of life lost due to living in states of disability or less than full health (YLD). Total DALYs (or the burden of disease) can be thought of as a measurement of the gap between the current health of a population and an ideal situation where everyone in the population lives into old age in full health. DALYs for a specific disease or injury cause are calculated as the sum of the YLL from that cause and the YLD for prevalent cases of the disease or injury (for a given age, sex and year).

DALY rates have declined in all the subregions of Asia from 2000 to 2012 with declines ranging from 8 per cent in Eastern Asia to almost 25 per cent in South-Central Asia (Figure 13.6). These declines have mainly come from reductions in YLL. The YLD rates have changed only slightly across this period, with small increases in overall rates in all subregions except South-Central Asia where rates decreased very slightly. Because of the much smaller variation in YLD rates across the subregions, YLD represent a larger proportion of DALYs in the lowest burden subregions. China (almost all Eastern Asia) now has DALY rates similar to those of many Latin American countries and lower than those in some low- and middle-income European countries.

Figure 13.7 shows a more detailed cause breakdown of DALY rates for the subregions of Asia. It is clear that most of the variation is due to the MDG conditions. The large contribution of the 'Other non-communicable diseases' category includes the YLD for mental disorders, sense disorders and musculoskeletal disorders as well as other DALYs relating to digestive diseases, diabetes and other NCDs. For children, the MDG conditions are the dominant cause of DALY loss. Injury DALYs are concentrated in young adult ages, whereas at older ages the DALYs are dominated by the NCDs, particularly cardiovascular diseases.

Table 13.2 summarizes the 15 leading causes of burden of disease in each of the Asian subregions in 2012. With some exceptions, these are broadly similar: stroke, ischaemic heart disease and lower respiratory infections are in the top five causes in all subregions. Chronic obstructive lung disease is high in the DALY rankings in Eastern Asia and South-Central Asia reflecting the high levels of male smoking and also of exposure to indoor air pollution through use of solid fuel cooking stoves and ambient (outdoor) air pollution. Road injury is also in fourth or fifth

Causes of death and burden of diseases

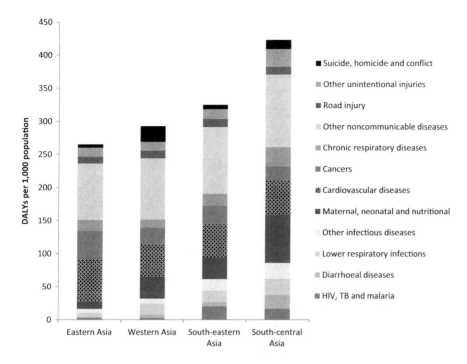

Figure 13.7 Major cause contributions to DALY rates, Asian subregions, 2012
Source: WHO Global Health Observatory (WHO 2014e).

position in Eastern Asia and South-Eastern Asia, reflecting the increasing use of road vehicles and relatively poor enforcement of driving regulations.

Preterm birth complications is the leading cause of DALYs in South-Central Asia, reflecting high levels of preventable neonatal deaths in some of the larger countries of this subregion. Diarrhoeal diseases, birth asphyxia and birth trauma, neonatal sepsis and congenital malformations are also in the top 15 causes for this subregion. Conflict is the second leading cause of DALYs in Western Asia in 2012, largely because of the civil war in Syria.

Major depressive disorders are in the top 15 causes in all subregions, as well as other conditions with few direct deaths but large disability (anxiety disorders, back and neck pain, adult-onset hearing loss and disorders associated with alcohol use). More than half of disease burden in most Asian countries is now from NCDs, ranging from 50 per cent in South-Central Asia to almost 80 per cent in Eastern Asia.

Risk factors and determinants of health

As part of the Global Burden of Disease project, a unified framework for comparative risk assessment (CRA) was developed using a systematic and consistent approach to the assessment of the changes in population health (deaths or DALYs) which would result from modifying the population distribution of exposure to a risk factor or a group of risk factors (Ezzati et al. 2004; Ezzati et al. 2006; WHO 2009). In the CRA framework, the burden of disease due to the observed exposure distribution in a population is compared with the burden from an alternative 'theoretical minimum risk' distribution which is defined consistently for different risk factors.

Table 13.2 Fifteen leading causes of burden of disease, Asian subregions, 2012

Rank	Eastern Asia Cause	DALYs (000s)	% DALYs	Rank	South-Eastern Asia Cause	DALYs (000s)	% DALYs
1	Stroke	51,704	12.1	1	Stroke	14,226	7.2
2	Ischaemic heart disease	34,296	8.0	2	Ischaemic heart disease	10,247	5.2
3	COPD	22,104	5.2	3	Lower respiratory infections	10,099	5.1
4	Road injury	16,601	3.9	4	Major depressive disorder	7,319	3.7
5	Lung cancer	15,967	3.7	5	Road injury	7,304	3.7
6	Major depressive disorder	13,866	3.2	6	Tuberculosis	6,745	3.4
7	Back and neck pain	12,923	3.0	7	Preterm birth complications	6,361	3.2
8	Liver cancer	12,429	2.9	8	Diabetes	6,192	3.1
9	Diabetes	11,981	2.8	9	COPD	5,988	3.0
10	Alcohol use disorders	9,413	2.2	10	HIV/AIDS	4,543	2.3
11	Stomach cancer	9,063	2.1	11	Congenital anomalies	4,494	2.3
12	Falls	8,802	2.1	12	Birth asphyxia and birth trauma	4,072	2.0
13	Lower respiratory infections	8,596	2.0	13	Diarrhoeal diseases	3,966	2.0
14	Self-harm	6,757	1.6	14	Back and neck pain	3,876	2.0
15	Other hearing loss	5,856	1.4	15	Iron-deficiency anaemia	3,657	1.8

Rank	South-Central Asia Cause	DALYs (000s)	% DALYs	Rank	Western Asia Cause	DALYs (000s)	% DALYs
1	Preterm birth complications	48,441	6.4	1	Ischaemic heart disease	5,891	8.3
2	Ischaemic heart disease	45,441	6.0	2	Conflict and legal intervention	4,606	6.5
3	Lower respiratory infections	41,281	5.5	3	Lower respiratory infections	3,785	5.4
4	COPD	40,045	5.3	4	Major depressive disorder	3,409	4.8
5	Diarrhoeal diseases	38,429	5.1	5	Stroke	3,400	4.8
6	Stroke	28,107	3.7	6	Road injury	2,860	4.0
7	Birth asphyxia and birth trauma	25,382	3.4	7	Preterm birth complications	2,546	3.6
8	Road injury	21,089	2.8	8	Congenital anomalies	2,037	2.9
9	Iron-deficiency anaemia	19,535	2.6	9	Diabetes	1,965	2.8
10	Major depressive disorder	19,049	2.5	10	Back and neck pain	1,713	2.4
11	Tuberculosis	18,027	2.4	11	Birth asphyxia and birth trauma	1,643	2.3
12	Self-harm	17,504	2.3	12	Iron-deficiency anaemia	1,592	2.3
13	Neonatal sepsis	17,075	2.3	13	COPD	1,455	2.1
14	Congenital anomalies	15,894	2.1	14	Anxiety disorders	1,295	1.8
15	Diabetes	13,965	1.8	15	Diarrhoeal diseases	1,220	1.7

Source: WHO Global Health Observatory (2014e).

Because most diseases are caused by multiple risk factors acting together, and because some risk factors act through others, attributable fractions for multiple risk factors for the same disease can add to more than 100 per cent. In other words, the joint attributable burden of several risk factors combined may be less than the sum of the individual attributable burdens. For this reason, attributable burden estimates for individual risk factors presented below should not be added across risk factors.

The Global Burden of Disease 2015 study estimated deaths and DALYs attributable to the independent effects of 79 risk factors and clusters of risk factors for 195 countries for years 1990–2010 (GBD 2015 Risk Factors Collaborators 2016). Table 13.3 summarizes the ten leading risk factors in the four Asian subregions, in terms of their attributable deaths in 2012. The joint effect of a range of dietary risks was the leading risk factor cause of attributable deaths in all four regions, followed by high blood pressure, and smoking (in two of the four regions). The

Table 13.3 Ten leading risk factors for attributable deaths, Asian subregions, 2012

Rank	Eastern Asia Cause	Deaths (000s)	% deaths	Rank	South-Eastern Asia Cause	Deaths (000s)	% deaths
1	Dietary risks	3,521	31.0	1	Dietary risks	866	22.1
2	High blood pressure	2,577	22.7	2	High blood pressure	801	20.5
3	Smoking	2,073	18.3	3	Smoking	555	14.2
4	Ambient air pollution	1,202	10.6	4	High fasting plasma glucose	437	11.2
5	High fasting plasma glucose	970	8.5	5	High total cholesterol	262	6.7
6	High total cholesterol	809	7.1	6	High body-mass index	242	6.2
7	Household air pollution	697	6.1	7	Ambient air pollution	233	6.0
8	High body-mass index	663	5.8	8	Household air pollution	205	5.2
9	Alcohol use	657	5.8	9	Impaired kidney function	185	4.7
10	Impaired kidney function	428	3.8	10	Alcohol use	153	3.9

Rank	South-Central Asia Cause	Deaths (000s)	% deaths	Rank	Western Asia Cause	Deaths (000s)	% deaths
1	Dietary risks	2,681	19.2	1	Dietary risks	253	24.4
2	High blood pressure	2,253	16.2	2	High blood pressure	242	23.4
3	High fasting plasma glucose	1,434	10.3	3	High body-mass index	132	12.8
4	Ambient air pollution	1,376	9.9	4	Smoking	122	11.8
5	Household air pollution	1,302	9.3	5	High total cholesterol	116	11.2
6	Smoking	1,084	7.8	6	High fasting plasma glucose	114	11.0
7	High total cholesterol	978	7.0	7	Ambient air pollution	86	8.3
8	High body-mass index	678	4.9	8	Impaired kidney function	54	5.2
9	Impaired kidney function	645	4.6	9	Low physical activity	45	4.4
10	Alcohol use	401	2.9	10	Occupational risks	21	2.0

Source: Global Burden of Disease Study 2015 (2016).

dietary risks include dietary salt (which contributes to high blood pressure), lack of fruit, lack of vegetables and lack of nuts, among other factors. As shown in Table 13.3, although the ranks of these risk factors are similar across regions, there is a considerable variation in the size of their population-attributable fractions for deaths.

Smoking is the third or fourth ranked cause of attributable mortality in all the Asian subregions except South-Central Asia (where it is sixth), with attributable fractions of total mortality ranging from 12 per cent in Western Asia to 18 per cent in Eastern Asia in 2012. Tobacco smoking remains one of the leading entirely preventable causes of mortality in Asian region, and its attributable burden is increasing, unlike in developed regions. Ambient air pollution and household air pollution (mainly due to solid fuel use) are also among the leading risk factors in most of these regions. A recent update by WHO has estimated that more than 70 per cent of the 7 million global deaths attributable to air pollution occur in the WHO regions of Western Pacific (which includes China) and South-Eastern Asia (WHO 2014f).

Several risks that primarily affect childhood communicable diseases, including unimproved water and sanitation and childhood micronutrient deficiencies, fell in rank between 1990 and 2012, and no longer appear in the top ten risk factor causes of mortality in the Asian region.

In Asia, as in other developing regions, the contribution of different risk factors to disease burden has changed substantially, with a shift away from risks for communicable diseases in children towards those for non-communicable diseases in adults. These changes are related to the ageing population, decreased mortality among children younger than five years, changes in cause-of-death composition and changes in risk factor exposures. The extent to which the epidemiological shift has occurred, and what the leading risks currently are, varies greatly across Asian subregions.

Projections of causes of death to 2050

We used updated WHO projections of mortality and causes of death 2011–2030 (WHO 2013d). These projections are an update of previous projections released in 2006 (Mathers and Loncar 2006) and in 2008 (WHO 2008), and use methods similar to those applied in the original GBD study (Murray and Lopez 1996a). A set of relatively simple models was used to project future health trends for baseline, optimistic and pessimistic scenarios, based largely on projections of economic and social development, and using the historically observed relationships of these with cause-specific mortality rates.

These updated projections have been prepared using the Global Health Estimates cause of death results for the year 2011 as a starting-point. The methods used are essentially the same as those previously published, with the following updates and revisions. Gross national income projections were updated using recent projections of real growth per annum in income per capita from the World Bank (2012a, 2012b), International Monetary Fund (2011) and OECD (2012). Human capital (average years of schooling for adults) estimates and projections were updated (Barro and Lee 2010) and projected using the International Futures project base case (Hughes et al. 2013). The projection regression equations were recalibrated and HIV projections updated as described elsewhere (WHO 2008).

Large declines in mortality between 2011 and 2050 are projected for communicable, maternal, perinatal and nutritional causes in Asia (Figure 13.8). Total HIV/AIDS deaths are projected to rise from 326,000 in 2011 to a maximum of 361,000 in 2015, and then to decline to 244,000 in 2030 and 123,000 in 2050, under a baseline scenario that assumes that coverage with antiretroviral drugs continues to rise at current rates to a maximum of 80 per cent. Tuberculosis deaths are projected to decline at an even faster rate, from 672,000 in 2011 to 214,000 in 2050.

Causes of death and burden of diseases

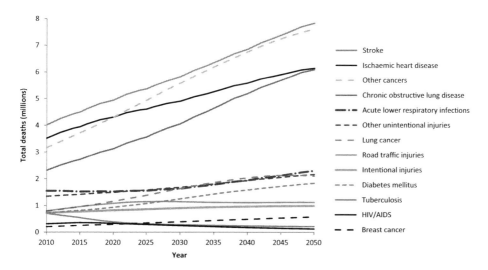

Figure 13.8 Projected deaths in Asia from selected causes, 2010–2050
Source: Author's calculations based on WHO projections of causes of death (WHO 2014e).

Ageing of populations in this region, associated with reductions in infectious, maternal and childhood risks of death, will result in significantly increasing total deaths mostly due to chronic diseases. Cancer deaths are projected to almost double from 4.3 million in 2011 to 7.6 million in 2030, and deaths from ischaemic heart disease and stroke to increase from 7.8 million in 2011 to 10.7 million in 2030. Lung cancer deaths are projected to increase substantially from 823,000 in 2011 to 1.6 million in 2030 and 2.1 million in 2050.

The projected 28 per cent increase in Asian deaths due to injury between 2011 and 2030 is also largely associated with population growth, and increases in population numbers are projected to more than offset small declines in age-specific death rates for most causes of injury. Road traffic accident deaths are projected to increase from 830,000 in 2011 to 1,140,000 in 2030, primarily due to increased motor vehicle ownership and use, and then to decline to 1,120,000 in 2050 as Asian countries increasingly address road safety issues.

Death rates are strongly age dependent for most causes, so changes in the age structure of a population may result in substantial changes in the number of deaths, even when the age-specific rates remain unchanged. The relative impact of demographic and epidemiological change on the projected numbers of deaths by cause is shown in Figure 13.9. The change in the projected numbers of deaths in Asia from 2011 to 2050 can be divided into three components (WHO 2008). The first is *population growth*, which shows the expected increase in deaths due to the increase in the total size of the population, assuming there are no changes in age distribution. The second is *population ageing*, which shows the additional increase in deaths resulting from the projected changes in the age distribution of the population from 2011 to 2050. Both these population-related components are calculated assuming that the age and sex-specific death rates for causes remain at 2011 levels. The final component, *epidemiological change*, shows the increase or decrease in numbers of deaths occurring in the 2050 population due to the projected change from 2011 to 2050 in the age- and sex-specific death rates for each cause.

For most MDG conditions, the projected reduction in number of deaths from 2011 to 2050 is due mostly to epidemiological change, and population ageing has little effect. For NCDs, demographic changes in all regions will tend to increase total deaths substantially, even though

Colin D. Mathers

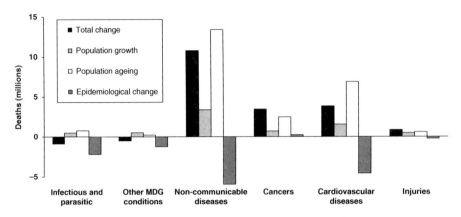

Figure 13.9 Decomposition of projected changes in annual numbers of deaths in Asia from selected cause groups, 2010–2030
Source: Author's calculations based on WHO projections of causes of death (WHO 2013d).

age- and sex-specific death rates are projected to decline for most causes, other than for lung cancer. The impact of population ageing is generally much more important than population growth. The total epidemiological change for injuries is small in Asia, because the projected increase in road injury death rates is offset by projected decreases in death rates for other unintentional injuries. Demographic change is more important than epidemiological change for injuries, though both types of change are small compared to those for diseases.

Conclusions

The analyses presented here reinforce the conclusions of the original GBD study about the importance of including non-fatal outcomes in a comprehensive assessment of Asian population health. They have also confirmed the growing importance of NCDs in the low- and middle-income countries of Asia.

The epidemiological transition in Asian countries has resulted in a 40 per cent reduction in the per capita disease burden due to MDG conditions (communicable, maternal, perinatal and nutritional conditions) since 2000. However, the MDG conditions remain a substantial cause of DALYs in the South-Central Asian region responsible for 38 per cent of total DALYs in 2012.

The burden of NCDs is increasing, accounting for 60 per cent of the Asian burden of disease (all ages), an 11 percentage point increase from estimated levels in 2000. Implementation of effective interventions for Group I diseases (communicable, maternal, perinatal and nutritional conditions), coupled with population ageing and the dynamics of risk for NCD in many Asian countries, are the likely causes of this shift.

The injury contribution to Asian burden of disease has remained largely unchanged at around 11 per cent. Road injuries, suicide and conflict are the leading causes of burden of disease in several Asian subregions. In Western Asia, 30 per cent of the entire disease and injury burden among males aged 15–44 is attributable to injuries, including road traffic accidents, violence and self-inflicted injuries, compared to around 17–23 per cent in other Asian subregions. Additionally, injury deaths are noticeably higher for women in some parts of Asia, in part due to high levels of suicide and violence.

These results clearly illustrate the 'double burden' of disease faced by the poorer developing countries of South Asia and Central Asia. Countries that are still struggling with 'old' and 'new' infectious disease epidemics must now also deal with the emerging epidemics of chronic, non-communicable disease such as heart disease, stroke, diabetes and cancer.

References

Ahmad, O. B., C. Boschi-Pinto, A. D. Lopez, C. J. L. Murray, R. Lozano and M. Inoue (2001) *Age Standardization of Rates: A New WHO Standard* (Technical report). GPE Discussion Paper Series: No.31. Geneva: World Health Organization.

Barro, R. J. and J. Lee (2010) *A New Dataset of Educational Attainment in the World, 1950–2010. NBER Working Paper 15902*. Cambridge, MA: National Bureau of Economic Research.

China Ministry of Health (2013a) *Unpublished Tabulations – Vital Registration System Cause-of-Death Data Submitted Annually to WHO*. Beijing: China Ministry of Health.

China Ministry of Health (2013b) *Cause-of-Death Data from Chinese Disease Surveillance Points 2004–2009*. Beijing: China Ministry of Health.

Chinese CDC (2012) *National Disease Surveillance System Monitoring Causes of Death 2010*. Chinese Center for Disease Control and Prevention. Beijing: Military Medical Science Press.

CRED (2013) *EM-DAT: The CRED International Disaster Database*. Belgium: Université Catholique de Louvain, 2013. Available at: www.emdat.be/disaster-list (accessed 27 September 2013).

Ezzati, M., A. D. Lopez, A. Rodgers and C. J. L. Murray (eds.) (2004) *Comparative Quantification of Health Risks: Global and Regional Burden of Disease Attributable to Selected Major Risk Factors*. Geneva: World Health Organization.

Ezzati, M., S. Vander Hoorn, A. D. Lopez et al. (2006) 'Comparative quantification of mortality and burden of disease attributable to selected major risk factors'. In A. D. Lopez, C. D. Mathers, M. Ezzati, D. T. Jamison and C. J. L. Murray (eds.) *Global Burden of Disease and Risk Factors*. New York: Oxford University Press. Pp. 241–396.

Ferlay, J., I. Soerjomataram, M. Ervik et al. (2013) *GLOBOCAN 2012 v1.0, Cancer Incidence and Mortality Worldwide: IARC CancerBase No. 11 [Internet]*. Lyon: International Agency for Research on Cancer. Available from: http://globocan.iarc.fr (accessed 13 January 2014).

GBD 2015 Risk Factors Collaborators (2016) 'Global, regional and national comparative risk assessment of 79 behavioral, environmental and occupational, and metabolic risks or clusters of risks, 1990–2015: a systematic analysis for the Global Burden of Disease Study 2015'. *Lancet*, 388: 1659–1724.

Global Burden of Disease Study 2015 (2016) *Results*. Seattle, United States: Institute for Health Metrics and Evaluation (IHME). Available from: http://ghdx.healthdata.org/gbd-results-tool.

Hughes, B. B. et al. (2013) *The International Futures (IFs) Modeling System*, Version 6.32. Frederick S. Pardee Center for International Futures, Josef Korbel School of International Studies, University of Denver. Available from: www.ifs.du.edu.

International Monetary Fund (2011) *World Economic Outlook 2011: Slowing Growth, Rising Risks*. Available from: www.imf.org/external/pubs/ft/weo/2011/02/pdf/text.pdf (accessed 12 June 2013).

Jha, P., V. Gajalakshmi and P. C. Gupta et al. (2006) 'Prospective study of one million deaths in India: rationale, design and validation results'. *PLoS Medicine*, 3(2): e18.

Liu, L., H. L. Johnson, S. Cousens et al. for the Child Health Epidemiology Reference Group of WHO and UNICEF (2012) 'Global, regional, and national causes of child mortality: an updated systematic analysis for 2010 with time trends since 2000'. *Lancet*, 379: 2151–2161.

Lozano, R., M. Naghavi, K. Foreman et al. (2012) 'Global and regional mortality from 235 causes of death for 20 age groups in 1990 and 2010: a systematic analysis for the Global Burden of Disease Study 2010'. *Lancet*, 380(9859): 2095–2128.

Mathers, C. D. and D. Loncar (2006) 'Projections of global mortality and burden of disease from 2002 to 2030'. *PLoS Medicine*, 3(11): e442.

Murray, C. J. L. and A. D. Lopez (1996a) *The Global Burden of Disease: a Comprehensive Assessment of Mortality and Disability from Diseases, Injuries and Risk Factors in 1990 and Projected to 2020*. Cambridge: Harvard University Press.

Murray, C. J. L. and A. D. Lopez (1996b) *Global Health Statistics*. Cambridge: Harvard University Press.

Murray, C. J., M. Ezzati, A. D. Flaxman et al. (2012a) 'GBD 2010: a multi-investigator collaboration for global comparative descriptive epidemiology'. *Lancet*, 380(9859): 2055–2058.

Murray, C. J., T. Vos, A. D. Flaxman et al. (2012b) 'Disability-adjusted life years (DALYs) for 291 diseases and injuries in 21 regions, 1990–2010: a systematic analysis for the Global Burden of Disease Study 2010'. *Lancet*, 380: 2197–2223.
Murray, C. J., M. Ezzati, A. D. Flaxman et al. (2012c) 'GBD 2010: design, definitions and metrics'. *Lancet*, 380: 2063–2066.
Organization for Economic Cooperation and Development (OECD) (2012) *OECD Economic Outlook, Volume 2012, Issue 1*. Paris: Organization for Economic Cooperation and Development.
Registrar General of India (2009) *Causes of Death in India in 2001–2003*. New Delhi: Government of India.
Rudan, I., K.Y. Chan, J. S. Zhang et al. (2010) 'Causes of deaths in children younger than 5 years in China in 2008'. *Lancet*, 375(9720): 1083–1089.
Salomon, J. A., T. Vos, D. R. Hogan et al. (2012) 'Common values in assessing health outcomes from disease and injury: disability weights measurement study for the Global Burden of Disease Study 2010'. *Lancet*, 380: 2129–2143.
Simons, E., M. Ferrari, J. Fricks et al. (2012) 'Assessment of the 2010 global measles mortality reduction goal: results from a model of surveillance data'. *Lancet*, 379(9832): 2173–2178.
UN Population Division (2011) *World Population Prospects: The 2010 revision*. New York: United Nations.
UN Population Division (2013) *World Population Prospects: The 2012 Revision*. New York: United Nations.
UNAIDS (2013) *2013 UNAIDS Report on the Global AIDS Epidemic*. Geneva: UNAIDS.
Vos, T., A. D. Flaxman, M. Naghavi et al. (2012) 'Years lived with disability (YLDs) for 1160 sequelae of 289 diseases and injuries, 1990–2010: a systematic analysis for the Global Burden of Disease Study 2010'. *Lancet*, 380: 2163–2196.
WHO, UNICEF, UNFPA, United Nations Population Division and World Bank (2014) *Trends in Maternal Mortality: 1990 to 2013*. Geneva: World Health Organization.
World Bank (1993) *World Development Report 1993. Investing in Health*. New York: Oxford University Press for the World Bank.
World Bank (2012a) *Global Economic Prospects 2012*. Washington, DC: The World Bank.
World Bank (2012b) *World Development Report 2012*. Washington, DC: The World Bank.
World Health Organization (2008) *The Global Burden of Disease: 2004 Update*. Geneva: World Health Organization.
World Health Organization (2009) *Global Health Risks*. Geneva: World Health Organization.
World Health Organization (2011) *Final Report: Global Pertussis Burden Expert Elicitation*. Geneva: World Health Organization.
World Health Organization (2013a) 'WHO methods and data sources for Global Burden of Disease Estimates 2000–2011'. *Global Health Estimates* (Technical Paper), WHO/HIS/HSI/GHE/2013.4. Geneva: World Health Organization.
World Health Organization (2013b) *World Malaria Report 2013*. Geneva: World Health Organization.
World Health Organization (2013c) *Global Status Report on Road Safety 2013: Supporting a Decade of Action*. Geneva: World Health Organization.
World Health Organization (2013d) *Projections of Mortality and Causes of Death, 2015 and 2030*. Available from: www.who.int/healthinfo/global_burden_disease/projections/en/ (accessed 26 March 2014).
World Health Organization (2014a) 'WHO methods and data sources for country-level causes of death 2000–2012'. *Global Health Estimates* (Technical Paper), WHO/HIS/HSI/GHE/2014.7. Geneva: World Health Organization.
World Health Organization (2014b) *WHO Mortality Database*. Available from: www.who.int/healthinfo/mortality_data/en/index.html.
World Health Organization (2014c) 'WHO methods for life expectancy and healthy life expectancy'. *Global Health Estimates* (Technical Paper), WHO/HIS/HSI/GHE/2014.5. Geneva: World Health Organization.
World Health Organization (2014d) 'CHERG-WHO methods and data sources for child causes of death 2000–2012'. *Global Health Estimates* (Technical Paper), WHO/HIS/HSI/GHE/2014.6. Geneva: World Health Organization.
World Health Organization (2014e) *Global Health Observatory [online database]*. Geneva: World Health Organization. Available from: www.who.int/gho.
World Health Organization (2014f) *Burden of Disease from Household Air Pollution for 2012*. Geneva: World Health Organization.

14
HIV/AIDS in Asia

Binod Nepal

This chapter provides an overview of HIV/AIDS in Asia. It begins with a summary of the development of HIV/AIDS in the world and a critique of the available data. It then examines the development of the epidemic in Asia and cross-national patterns and trends in HIV/AIDS. This is followed by an examination of the populations and subpopulations that are most affected by the disease, the forces shaping the epidemics in these populations and the major efforts made in this region to control the epidemic. Finally, the chapter discusses recent developments and emerging challenges in combating HIV/AIDS. In this chapter, HIV *prevalence* refers to the proportion of people with HIV (total cases) in a population at a point of time, and the term *incidence* refers to new cases over a year.

Background

The disease or health condition characterized by an unusual immune deficiency which later came to be known as acquired immune deficiency syndrome (AIDS) was initially detected in the United States in 1981 (CDC 1981). The first cases of AIDS were found primarily among homosexual men in the United States and Europe. Within a few years, two research teams led by Galo in the United States and Montagnier in France independently identified the disease with the virus later named human immunodeficiency virus (HIV) (Gallo 2002; Montagnier 2002). The virus has two types, HIV-1 and HIV-2. HIV-1 is the most widespread strain and responsible for the current global pandemic and HIV-2 is confined mainly in West Africa and to a limited extent in Europe and India (Durban Declaration 2000; Takebe et al. 2004; Kandathil et al. 2005). Here, the term HIV refers to either type of HIV, unless otherwise specified. Almost all HIV infections in Asia are HIV-1.

In the early years of the AIDS epidemic, the origin of the virus was poorly known and remained scientifically as well as politically contentious. The viral agent, HIV, is believed to have existed in Africa since the 1930s or so (Korber et al. 2000). One very contentious hypothesis posited that the virus spread through contaminated oral polio vaccine (made using tissues from chimpanzees with a similar virus) administered to the inhabitants of Equatorial Africa in the late 1950s (Elswood and Stricker 1994). However, most researchers have discounted this theory (Worobey et al. 2004). One well received theory is that the Simian Immunodeficiency Virus present in some species of African chimpanzees may have crossed to humans during hunting and butchering (Gao et al. 1999; Hahn et al. 2000). This appears plausible as transmission of retroviruses from primates to people is still occurring in Africa (Wolfe et al. 2004). Keele et al. (2006) found Simian Immunodeficiency Virus in faeces of chimpanzees in the forests of Cameroon. They suggested that HIV might have spread from Cameroon to Congo, where the HIV epidemic probably first took off, through people travelling along the Congo River. The exact location of the origin of the virus and how exactly it crossed the species barrier to infect humans are yet to be established.

The march of AIDS continued worldwide from the 1980s onwards. Later estimates by the Joint United Nations Programme on HIV/AIDS (UNAIDS 2013) indicated that, in 1990, about eight million people were living with HIV/AIDS, about two million individuals were newly infected with HIV and nearly 300,000 people were estimated to have died of AIDS worldwide. While the number of people living with HIV/AIDS continues to grow, reaching 35 million in 2012, the speed of the pandemic has slowed. The epidemic probably peaked in the late 1990s when the number of new infections began to decline after a record 3.7 million new cases in 1997 (UNAIDS 2013). AIDS-related deaths are estimated to have peaked by the mid-2000s. Despite a declining rate of new infections, the absolute number of people living with HIV/AIDS continues to grow, owing to life-prolonging treatment and population growth (Bongaarts et al. 2008; UNAIDS 2013).

Though the outlook of the AIDS pandemic has improved, it continues to be a matter of concern in Asia for a number of reasons. As the infection is preventable, any loss of life from this disease can be seen as a reflection of a failure of health policy and human behaviour. Even a small rise in the HIV incidence can reflect massive numbers of new infections because of the huge population base. Some sections of the population continue to experience high infection levels, and comprehensive responses covering all aspects of prevention and care are yet to be instituted in many countries. This chapter expands on these themes by assessing the epidemic patterns, the forces influencing the epidemic, evolution of policy responses and likely future trends.

Data collection developments and limitations

Data on HIV/AIDS epidemiology in the Asia region has gradually improved with wider demographic coverage and an expansion in the data collected. The populations targeted for monitoring have expanded from, initially, persons diagnosed with AIDS, to those who present at carefully selected reporting sites (particularly antenatal clinics, ANC), at-risk subpopulations, and finally national populations surveyed through Demographic and Health Surveys (DHSs). While early reporting focused on the collection of biological data, this has been expanded to include behavioural information which can shed light on the context of the epidemic. This section outlines the various data collection approaches adopted by different countries in the region over time.

Data collection was initially limited to persons who had been diagnosed with AIDS. AIDS case reporting was the only method of gathering data in the early years of the epidemic and continues to be the sole method in some countries. As AIDS-defining illnesses generally appear 5–10 years following HIV infection (Durban Declaration 2000), reported cases of AIDS belatedly provide an indirect measure of the underlying and preceding HIV epidemics. Case reporting is ineffective in resource-limited settings where only a few AIDS patients come into contact with the health system, diagnosis may be less than ideal and reporting is not always timely and accurate (World Health Organization (WHO) and UNAIDS 2000). In these circumstances, the reported cases of AIDS alone would not reflect the true state of the epidemic, and would underestimate the actual number of people living with the virus.

HIV sentinel surveillance was introduced in the late 1980s to collect data from ANC attendees, as a proxy for the general population. The method provides an opportunity to collect timely and more generalizable information than AIDS case reporting by collecting epidemiological information early on. People are screened for HIV/AIDS when they come into contact with health systems at ANC, sexually transmitted disease (STD) clinics, tuberculosis clinics and blood banks. HIV biomarkers may also be collected from samples of key subpopulations (often described as at-risk groups) such as people who inject drugs (PWID) at rehabilitation centres and sex workers at brothels.

However, sentinel surveillance surveys do not collect background information of individuals tested for HIV. Therefore, the HIV sentinel surveillance approach, by itself, offers limited opportunity to understand the context of the epidemic. HIV sentinel surveillance also suffers from selection bias. The ANC visit rate in resource-limited countries in Asia, especially in Southern Asia, is low and utilization is skewed in favour of urban, educated and wealthier women (Abou-Zahr and Wardlaw 2003). A Cambodian study indicated that data drawn through HIV sentinel among ANC attendees could have overestimated the HIV prevalence in rural areas (Saphonn et al. 2002). This problem can vary across locations, depending primarily on the coverage of antenatal care practices. Estimated national prevalence data will be further biased if they are derived as crude averages of site-specific rates, without properly accounting for underlying population differences. In China, concerns were raised in 2002 that the surveillance system was inadequate because HIV testing was confined to official surveillance systems, not all most-at-risk groups were targeted, and the sentinel sites varied over time (Hesketh et al. 2002).

HIV data collection improved in the late 1990s with the introduction of a more comprehensive system, dubbed 'second generation surveillance' (WHO and UNAIDS 2000). In this approach both biological and behavioural information are collected from samples of the population, or local at-risk subpopulations, depending on how widespread the epidemic is (WHO and UNAIDS 2000; Family Health International (FHI) 2000). Where HIV prevalence exceeds one per cent of the general population, population-based behavioural and serological surveys are considered appropriate. Alternatively, in concentrated epidemics where HIV prevalence is high in most-at-risk groups but less than one per cent in the general population, only the groups at risk are monitored. In low-level epidemics, surveillance systems focus largely on the presence of and changes in risky behaviours.

The biological and behavioural data obtained from second generation surveillance surveys are not necessarily collected from the same individuals. Where HIV surveillance is implemented in clinical or similar settings, second generation surveillance emphasizes collecting a minimum of socio-demographic information about the subject and linking it with population-based survey information collected in the relevant catchment area (FHI 2000; Rehle et al. 2004). In Asian settings where multiple, overlapping at-risk groups exist, the number of people living with HIV is estimated by combining direct estimates from samples and indirect estimates from populations. The mix of data from ANC and most-at-risk group surveillance is combined with demographic data to derive estimates and projections of HIV cases by age-groups, AIDS cases, AIDS deaths and paediatric AIDS cases (Stover 2004). As case reporting is likely to underestimate actual HIV/AIDS cases, these indirect estimates are used as the main means of assessing levels and trends of national and subnational epidemics.

The biennial Global Report of UNAIDS contains national estimates sourced from the reports of government agencies of individual countries and provides a major source of international comparative data on HIV/AIDS prevalence and incidence. The methods used are simple enough to apply in a country or territory with limited input data. However, input data quality can be affected by the geographic coverage and representativeness of surveys conducted among at-risk subpopulations, as well as the accuracy of the population size estimates. Depending on the coverage of antenatal care practices, ANC-based surveillance estimates may not necessarily represent the general population prevalence. Nevertheless, by the early 2000s most of the low- and middle-income countries of Asia were assessed as having fairly good surveillance systems in place (Garcia-Calleja et al. 2004). Hence the national estimates are considered to be reasonably reliable.

Since the early 2000s, HIV testing has been integrated into population-based surveys, particularly the DHSs. This has provided opportunities to link serological information with socio-demographic information and has led to a revision of prevalence estimates. India is perhaps the best known example where estimates of HIV prevalence were hotly contested until the early 2000s. In 2005, surveillance surveys indicated that 0.9 per cent (range 0.5–1.5 per cent), or 5.6 million adults (range 3.4–9.3 million), were living with HIV/AIDS in India (UNAIDS 2006). However, the 2005–2006 DHS, which was the first population-based survey to collect HIV biomarkers in India, arrived at a much lower adult HIV prevalence of 0.28 per cent (range 0.23–0.33 per cent) (International Institute for Population Sciences and Macro International 2007). This prompted a significant downward revision in India's national HIV/AIDS estimates for 2005, from over 5 million (UNAIDS 2006) to below 3 million (National AIDS Control Organization [India] 2009).

The downward revision is attributed to improvements in methodology and in the quantity and quality of information available from multiple sources and an increasing number of sentinel sites. The consistently lower estimates of HIV prevalence observed in population-based surveys in India and Cambodia (National Institute of Public Health and ORC Macro 2006; International Institute for Population Sciences and Macro International 2007) indicate that surveillance surveys have much room for improvement in consistency, quality and coverage.

Behavioural surveillance surveys (i.e. repeated cross-sectional surveys of defined populations), designed to monitor behavioural indicators in selected population groups over time (FHI 2000), provide important supportive information. However, Demographic and Health Surveys in Asia have not asked women routinely about their sexual behaviour. Male modules, introduced in the DHSs in the early 2000s, have collected data on male sexual behaviour (Nepal 2010). Yet initially, DHS reports either dropped the information on male sexual behaviour (for example, Bangladesh in 2004 (NIPRT 2005)) or published selective information (for example, the Philippines in 2003 (NSO 2004)).

For many years into the epidemic, statistics on HIV/AIDS and vulnerable populations were treated with high sensitivity, making it difficult for independent institutions to access the information. In China, for example, some local authorities were reluctant to know, or let others know, about AIDS in their area as they believed that information-sharing would reflect poorly on the localities and their officials (UN Theme Group on HIV/AIDS in China 2002).

Overall, epidemiological information systems for HIV/AIDS have evolved from case reporting to a more comprehensive approach with wider demographic coverage. In India, for example, sentinel surveillance has been extended beyond ANC attendees to cover key at-risk groups such as female sex workers (FSW), PWID and men who have sex with men (MSM), as well as bridging groups such as migrants and long distance truckers (National AIDS Control Organization [India] 2012). The most important development has been the collection of serological and behavioural data from samples of the general population. These developments in HIV/AIDS statistics have enabled a more informed assessment of epidemics in the region.

Emergence of HIV in Asia

The global epidemic started to grip Asian countries a few years after it took hold in the United States and sub-Saharan Africa. While initial cases of AIDS were found among Western tourists and locals returning from the West and neighbouring countries, major outbreaks were often reported among PWID. Thailand was the first country in Asia to experience an explosive epidemic that emerged among injecting drug users in the late 1980s in Bangkok, though initial cases of AIDS were identified in the mid-1980s among homosexuals who had come into contact with foreigners in gay bars (Smith 1990). The epidemic soon moved to female sex workers and their clients and eventually to women in general. By the early 1990s, Thailand came to be seen as an epicentre of Asia's HIV epidemic (Horn 2010). In the 1990s, notable outbreaks of HIV were identified among PWID in several other countries or territories including Malaysia, Vietnam, Myanmar, Nepal, Manipur (North-East India), Yunnan Province of China and Indonesia, before the infection became noticeable in other groups. Cambodia was a notable exception where heterosexual transmission was the sole driver of the epidemic. Indonesia experienced a major surge in HIV infections only at the end of the 1990s, mostly among PWIDs, except for West Papua Province where the epidemic was driven by heterosexual transmission.

HIV was seeded through the medical use of contaminated blood in Japan in the 1980s and in China in the early 1990s. Haemophiliac patients in Japan were infected when using HIV contaminated blood products imported from the United States and this mode of transmission dominated the reported cases of HIV/AIDS until the early 1980s (Kihara et al. 1997). In China, local farmers in many remote villages in the eastern region acquired HIV during commercial collection of blood, a process in which plasma was extracted and the remainder of the blood was transfused back to the donors so they could keep donating at short intervals. Nearly one in ten donating adults (8.9 per cent) were identified with HIV in the early 2000s in some parts of eastern China where plasma sale was popular during 1992–1995 (Wu et al. 2001).

Cross-national patterns and trends

While the overall HIV prevalence across Asia continues to remain much lower than in sub-Saharan Africa, the sheer size of this region, accounting for over 60 per cent of the global population, has always attracted international attention to the region's HIV epidemic. Even a small rise in HIV prevalence would reflect millions of new HIV cases. In the early years when little was known about the epidemic, it was difficult to rule out the possibility of larger epidemics in a region dominated by resource-limited economies.

In 2012, the highest national prevalence of HIV/AIDS for any Asian country was 1.1 per cent in Thailand, followed by Cambodia (0.8 per cent) and Myanmar (0.6 per cent). All other countries in Asia had less than 0.5 per cent prevalence at the national level (Table 14.1). All of the high prevalence countries – Thailand, Cambodia and Myanmar – form a neighbourhood in South-Eastern Asia, making this region the most affected part of Asia. With 0.1 per cent to 0.4 per cent adult HIV prevalence, Laos, Singapore, Indonesia, Malaysia and Vietnam can be considered as moderate prevalence countries by Asian standard. Other countries in South-Eastern Asia either have low prevalence, less than 0.1 per cent, or no estimates are available.

National prevalence among adults aged 15–49 was estimated to be less than 0.1 per cent in 2011 in all of the countries in Eastern Asia. Of the estimated 830,000 HIV carriers in Eastern Asia, 780,000 (94 per cent) were in China, followed by 15,000 in South Korea and 7,900 in Japan (UNAIDS 2012).

Table 14.1 Total population, number of people living with HIV and HIV prevalence among people who inject drugs and female sex workers, Asia

Major area, region, country or area	Population ('000) 2010[a]	Number of persons with HIV 2012[b]	Adult HIV prevalence (%) 2012[c]	Women's share of population ages 15+ living with HIV (%) 2012[d]	PWID HIV prevalence (%) 2000s[e]	FSW HIV prevalence (%) 2005–2012[f]
Eastern Asia[1]	1,593,571					
China	1,359,821	780,000[g]	<0.1[g]	30[g]	–	0.6
DPR Korea	24,501	–	–	–	–	–
Japan	127,353	7,900[g]	<0.1[g]	30[g]	–	–
Mongolia	2,713	<1,000[g]	<0.1[g]	–	–	0.0
Republic of Korea	48,454	15,000[g]	<0.1[g]	28[g]	–	–
Central Asia	61,694					
Kazakhstan	15,921	19,000[g]	0.2[g]	42[g]	9.2	1.3
Kyrgyzstan	5,334	8,700	0.3	18	8.0	1.6
Tajikistan	7,627	12,000	0.3	37	14.7	2.8
Turkmenistan	5,042	–	–	–	–	–
Uzbekistan	27,769	30,000	0.1	27	15.6	3.2
Southern Asia	1,681,407					
Afghanistan	28,398	4,300	<0.1	35	3.4	0.2
Bangladesh	151,125	8,000	<0.1	36	1.35	1.1
Bhutan	717	1,100	0.2	–	–	–
India	1,205,625	2,100,000	0.3	39	11.15	4.9
Iran	74,462	71,000	0.2	27	15.0	–
Maldives	326	<100	<0.1	–	–	–
Nepal	26,846	49,000	0.3	31	41.39	1.7
Pakistan	173,149	87,000	<0.1	28	10.8	0.6
Sri Lanka	20,759	3,000	<0.1	–	–	0.2
South-Eastern Asia	597,097					
Brunei Darussalam	401	–	–	–	–	–
Cambodia	14,365	76,000	0.8	55	22.8	13.9
Indonesia	240,676	610,000	0.4	39	42.5	–
Lao PDR	6,396	12,000	0.3	45	–	1.0
Malaysia	28,276	82,000	0.4	15	10.3	10.7
Myanmar	51,931	200,000	0.6	33	42.6	9.4
Philippines	93,444	15,000	<0.1	16	1.0	0.3
Singapore	5,079	3,400[g]	0.1[g]	30	–	0.0
Thailand	66,402	440,000	1.1	47	42.5	1.8
Timor-Leste	1,079	–	–	–	–	2.8
Vietnam	89,047	260,000	0.4	28	33.85	3.0
Western Asia	231,671					
Armenia	2,963	3,500	0.2	–	–	0.6
Azerbaijan	9,095	10,000	0.2	11	–	1.1
Bahrain	1,252	–	–	–	0.3	–
Cyprus	1,104	–	–	–	0.0	–

Table 14.1 (Cont.)

Major area, region, country or area	Population ('000) 2010[a]	Number of persons with HIV 2012[b]	Adult HIV prevalence (%) 2012[c]	Women's share of population ages 15+ living with HIV (%) 2012[d]	PWID HIV prevalence (%) 2000s[e]	FSW HIV prevalence (%) 2005–2012[f]
Georgia	4,389	6,600	0.3	21	–	1.3
Iraq	30,962	–	–	–	–	–
Israel	7,420	8,500[g]	0.2[g]	31[g]	2.94	–
Jordan	6,455	–	–	–	–	–
Kuwait	2,992	–	–	–	–	–
Lebanon	4,341	–	–	–	–	0.0
Oman	2,803	–	–	–	11.8	–
Qatar	1,750	–	–	–	–	–
Saudi Arabia	27,258	–	–	–	0.14	–
State of Palestine	4,013	–	–	–	–	–
Syrian Arab Republic	21,533	–	–	–	–	–
Turkey	72,138	5,500[g]	<0.1[g]	30[g]	2.65	–
United Arab Emirates	8,442	–	–	–	–	–
Yemen	22,763	19,000	0.1	43	–	0.0

Note: [1] Hong Kong SAR and Macao SAR of China are not included; '–' indicates data not available.
Sources: [a] United Nations Population Division (2013); [b,c] UNAIDS (2013); [d] Author's estimates from UNAIDS (2013); [e] Mathers et al. (2008); [f] Prüss-Ustün et al. (2013); [g] Estimates for 2011 from the 2012 Global Report (UNAIDS 2012).

Southern Asia has had the largest concentration of HIV carriers in Asia, most of them in India. In 2012, India was home to an estimated 2.1 million people living with HIV/AIDS, the third largest number in the world behind the two African countries of South Africa (6.1 million) and Nigeria (3.4 million) (UNAIDS 2013). However, adult HIV prevalence in India was only 0.3 per cent, much lower than both South Africa (17.9 per cent) and Nigeria (3.1 per cent) (UNAIDS 2013). This was the highest national prevalence in Southern Asia, equal to Nepal (0.3 per cent) and comparable to Bhutan (0.2 per cent), two small neighbours which share an open border with Northern India. Nationally, HIV prevalence was 0.2 per cent in Iran and less than 0.1 per cent in the other countries in Southern Asia.

Central Asia has been identified as an emerging HIV hotspot since the early 2000s. Estimates of adult HIV prevalence were 0.3 per cent in Kyrgyzstan and Tajikistan in 2012 and 0.2 per cent in Kazakhstan in 2011. Limited information is available about the number of people with HIV in Western Asia. The highest adult HIV prevalence was 0.3 per cent in Georgia, followed by 0.2 per cent in Armenia, Azerbaijan and Israel. A few countries had 0.1 per cent or less adult HIV prevalence and no estimates were available for other countries.

Improved data and estimates demonstrate that the HIV epidemic in Asia started to stabilize or decline around the late 1990s, led by countries such as Thailand and Cambodia which had experienced major outbreaks in the 1990s (Figures 14.1 and 14.2). Thailand, Cambodia and Myanmar – which were once feared to be heading towards explosive epidemics – recorded more than 50 per cent decline in the rate of new HIV infections between 2001 and 2011 (UNAIDS

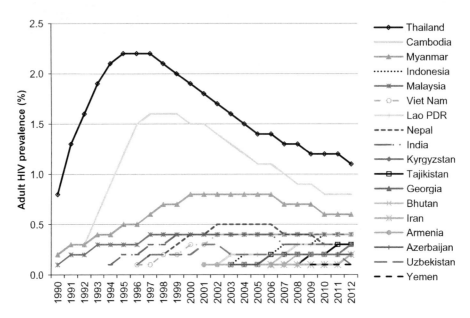

Figure 14.1 HIV prevalence among adults aged 15–49 years, selected countries of Asia
Source: UNAIDS (2013).

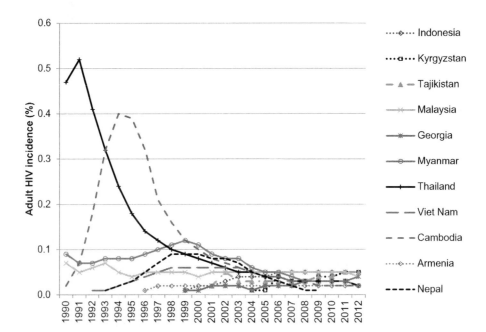

Figure 14.2 Adult HIV incidence, selected countries of Asia
Source: UNAIDS (2013).

2012). Malaysia experienced a more than 25 per cent fall in HIV incidence in the same period, and two Southern Asian countries, India and Nepal, recorded over 50 per cent decline in the rate of new HIV infections (UNAIDS 2012).

However, the HIV incidence has trended upward in some countries. The rate of new HIV infections increased by over 25 per cent between 2001 and 2011 in two countries in Southern Asia, Bangladesh and Sri Lanka; two countries in South-Eastern Asia, Indonesia and the Philippines; and two countries in Central Asia, Kazakhstan and Kyrgyzstan (UNAIDS 2012). The absolute numbers and prevalences of people with HIV are low in these countries. The estimated incidence in these countries is much lower (below 0.1 per cent) than the incidence (0.4–0.5 per cent) in Thailand and Cambodia at the peak of their epidemics (Figure 14.2). The upward trend in HIV infections in these countries, especially in Southern and South-Eastern Asia, is partly due to the expansion of epidemics among MSM and transgender communities.

Affected populations and population groups

While the national prevalence of HIV is low across countries in Asia, there are considerable behavioural, socio-demographic and geographic variations within and among countries. A common feature of the epidemics in Asia is that infection levels are very low among the population in general, but very high among certain key population groups such as PWID, FSWs and men who buy sex, and MSM.

PWID are the most affected groups in Asia. They are present in most Asian countries and often have reported HIV infection levels many times higher than in the adult population in general (Table 14.1). Where unsafe needle sharing has been widespread, the majority of PWID surveyed have been found to be infected, for example, in some locations in Manipur state of India (Panda et al. 2001), Nepal's capital of Kathmandu, Vietnam's northern port city of Hai Phong, Indonesia's capital Jakarta and Myanmar's border town of Lashio (Commission on AIDS in Asia 2008). Fortunately, these high infection levels among PWID have not caused the overall adult HIV prevalence to soar to similarly alarming levels because the population of PWID is small, usually below one per cent of the adult population aged 15–64 years, except in Malaysia where it has been estimated to be slightly higher at 1.3 per cent (Mathers et al. 2008).

Female sex workers constitute another well-known affected group in Asia. Commercial sex work is reportedly widespread in almost all Asian countries. Women selling sex are estimated to account for less than one per cent of the adult female population aged 15 years and over except in a few countries such as Nepal (1.6 per cent) and the Philippines (2 per cent) (Prüss-Ustün et al. 2013). Levels of HIV infection among FSWs are normally not as high as those among PWID but are often much higher than in the adult population in general (Table 14.1). Recent modelling has estimated that about two to nine per cent of HIV infections in adult females in Eastern and South-Eastern Asia are attributable to the occupational risk factor of female sex work (Prüss-Ustün et al. 2013).

HIV infections are often seeded into FSW communities and then channelled outside into the wider population by their male clients. The percentage of men visiting sex workers varies widely across Asia. Some estimates suggest that up to 20 per cent of men in Thailand and Cambodia, and up to 10 per cent in some parts of India and China, visit sex workers at least once a year (Commission on AIDS in Asia 2008). The male clients are largely migrants or people involved in mobile occupations. These are described as bridge groups in the AIDS literature because of their role in bringing infections from core groups such as FSWs to their sex partners or wives. Seasonal migrants and mobile populations are found to have HIV prevalences higher than in the adult population in general in several areas of Asia. For example, in 2010–2011 surveillance in India, single male migrants and truckers in several locations had more than one per cent HIV prevalence (National AIDS Control Organization [India] 2009), compared to the overall prevalence of 0.3 per cent among adults (Table 14.1). In China, long distance truck drivers were found to have 3.3 times higher risk of HIV infection than the population in general (Zhang et al. 2013). A 2005 review showed that the HIV prevalence among fishermen was higher than that in the adult population in general in Cambodia (18.2 per cent), Myanmar (16.1 per cent), Thailand (6.9 per cent), Malaysia (4 per cent) and Indonesia (1.4), countries for which information was available (Kissling et al. 2005).

MSM are an emerging, but little understood, high risk group in Asia. New HIV epidemics among MSM and transgender people are documented in several Asian countries, with over 10 per cent infected in some areas, including cities in China, Taiwan, India, Myanmar and Thailand (van Griensven and de Lind van Wijngaarden 2010). In Asian regions, the highest HIV infection levels among MSM are estimated to be 15 per cent in Southern and South-Eastern Asia, followed by 7 per cent in Central Asia (including Eastern Europe), 5 per cent in Eastern Asia and 3 per cent in Western Asia (including Northern Africa) (Beyrer et al. 2012). Rising infections among MSM are reported in Thailand, cities in China (Beyrer et al. 2012) and at least four states of India (National AIDS Control Organization [India] 2012).

In Asia, HIV epidemics are predominantly urban phenomena. The commercial sex and drug markets operate in cities and sentinel surveys are also often conducted in cities. The population-based surveys in Cambodia, India and Vietnam demonstrate that infection levels are higher among women and men living in urban than rural areas (Table 14.2). In most other countries there is limited information to quantify urban–rural differentials in HIV infection.

An emerging feature of the Asian epidemics is the narrowing of the gender gap in HIV infections. Infections in many Asian populations started among PWIDs, who were predominantly men, or the infections occurred between small groups of female sex workers and their large male clientele. As the epidemics matured, PWIDs and male clients of sex workers have started to infect their female sex partners, resulting in a gradual increase in the share of women among the people living with HIV. In Malaysia, for example, the female to male ratio of reported cases increased from 1:99 in 1990 to 1:10 in 2000 and 1:4 in 2011 (Ministry of Health [Malaysia] 2012). Where heterosexual transmission is the overwhelmingly dominant mode of transmission and the epidemic has been established longer, as in Cambodia, men and women are almost equally infected. In contrast, where injecting drug use is a dominant driver and the epidemic is relatively newer, as in Vietnam and Pakistan, the people with HIV are predominantly men (Table 14.1).

HIV predominantly infects people in their prime adulthood but the age pattern varies by gender. Population-based surveys in Cambodia and Vietnam illustrate that infected women are likely to be younger than men, with HIV prevalence among women peaking in the late 20s to early 30s, and that among men peaking in the early to late 30s. However, this age pattern is less apparent in India (Table 14.2). In terms of marital status, HIV prevalence is skewed towards persons who have experienced marital dissolution. Divorce, separation and widowhood may push individuals to risky behaviours. Sex workers in India, for example, were disproportionately divorced, separated or widowed women (Dandona et al. 2006).

The role of socioeconomic factors in the HIV epidemics remains contentious (Greener and Sarkar 2010; Whiteside 2001). Studies in sub-Saharan Africa suggest that inequality, rather than absolute wealth, could be more strongly associated with the risk of HIV, with the poor being at higher risk of acquiring HIV in more prosperous regions and the better off being at greater risk in poorer regions (Fox 2012). The Commission on AIDS in Asia (2008) observed that where HIV prevalence is less than 0.4 per cent, most of the people living with HIV belong

Table 14.2 Differentials in HIV prevalence among women and men aged 15–49 years

	India		Cambodia		Vietnam	
	Women	Men	Women	Men	Women	Men
All	0.22	0.36	0.6	0.6	0.2	0.9
Age groups						
15–19	0.07	0.01	0.0	0.1	0.0	0.0
20–24	0.17	0.19	0.6	0.2	0.0	1.8
25–29	0.28	0.43	1.3	0.6	1.1	1.1
30–34	0.45	0.64	0.8	1.2	0.9	2.5
35–39	0.23	0.53	0.7	1.3	0.0	1.8
40–44	0.19	0.41	0.3	0.7	0.0	0.0
45–49	0.17	0.48	1.0	1.3	0.0	0.0
Residence						
Urban	0.29	0.41	1.3	1.4	0.3	2.0
Rural	0.18	0.32	0.5	0.4	0.2	0.4
Marital status						
Never married	0.03	0.16	0.1	0.1	0.0	1.1
Married/living together	0.19	0.45	0.7	0.9	0.3	0.6
Divorced/separated	1.14	1.91	1.1	2.0	–	–
Widowed	1.51	0.13	2.9	4.1*	–	–
Wealth quintile						
Poorest	0.18	0.39	0.5	0.3	–	–
Second	0.20	0.31	0.4	0.1	–	–
Middle	0.24	0.31	0.4	0.2	–	–
Fourth	0.34	0.52	0.8	0.7	–	–
Richest	0.12	0.24	0.9	1.5	–	–

Note: – no data published or sample size too small; * based on fewer than 50 unweighted cases.
Sources: India National Family Health Survey (NFHS-3), 2005–06 (International Institute for Population Sciences and Macro International 2007); Cambodia Demographic and Health Survey, 2005 (National Institute of Public Health and ORC Macro 2006); Vietnam Population and AIDS Indicator Survey, 2005 (General Statistical Office (GSO)/National Institute of Hygiene and Epidemiology (NIHE) and ORC Macro 2006).

to lower income groups; where the epidemic is more widespread, the infection levels skew towards wealthier people. The limited data available from population-based surveys in India and Cambodia indicate that the relationship between HIV prevalence and household wealth is not established (Table 14.2). As vulnerability to HIV can be multidimensional (Greener and Sarkar 2010), material wealth alone cannot explain socioeconomic variations in HIV infections. Without comprehensive analyses of data from household and at-risk populations, it may be premature to draw conclusions about the role of specific socioeconomic factors in HIV infections in Asia.

The characterization of affected populations is based on the dominant mode of transmission. Though behaviours underlying most HIV transmissions in Asia are important, they are but one aspect of individuals' many identities. Detailed examination of socioeconomic, demographic and geographic attributes is standard practice in most social research but remains scant in HIV/AIDS literature. However, the collection of biological and behavioural data relevant to HIV in recent DHSs has started to provide opportunities to examine socio-demographic and spatial differentials in HIV/AIDS.

Major forces shaping the epidemics

Injecting drug use and commercial sex work, two major risk behaviours responsible for most HIV epidemics in this region, were present in several Asian countries prior to the arrival of HIV. Sex industries and injecting drug markets in Asia evolved from old practices that began to draw commercial interest during the colonial period in the seventeenth to nineteenth centuries and, together with modernization, grew into their present forms in the late twentieth century. A combination of urbanization, industrialization, migration and military deployment have transformed traditional prostitution into a large, modern sex industry (Boonchalaksi and Guest 1994; Truong 1990; Brown 2001) which has evolved to generate a significant share of national economies (Lim 1998). In Thailand, most of the clients of the modern sex industry are local men, though external factors such as tourism and military deployment have motivated local authorities to tolerate the industry (Boonchalaksi and Guest 1994). In China, prostitution started to flourish in the 1980s when the country turned to the market economy (Smith 2005). The arrival of the United Nations Transitional Authority in Cambodia (UNTAC), which consisted of military and civilian police personnel from a number of Asian, African and other countries, is believed to have acted as a catalyst for the emergence of an organized form of prostitution in the 1990s (Heng and Key 1995; Sales 1996).

The networks of sex industries, drug markets, and internal and external population movements, including the flow of migrant labourers, have induced many local epidemics and kept them active by interconnecting them. HIV epidemics have simply travelled the paths of these established risk networks. For example, background forces such as drug trafficking, population mobility and conflict have contributed to the emergence and formation of HIV epidemics in and around the Greater Mekong subregion, a region made up of China's Yunnan Province, Burma, Laos, Thailand, Cambodia and Vietnam. The Golden Triangle, a major opium producing area at the heart of this region, experienced unsafe injecting practices and explosive HIV epidemics in the late 1980s and 1990s. Beyrer et al. (2000) mapped four heroin trafficking routes emerging from Myanmar and connecting neighbouring countries: from Myanmar's eastern border to China's Yunnan Province; from Eastern Myanmar going north to Yunnan, and west to Xinjiang Province; from Myanmar and Laos, through Northern Vietnam, to China's Guangxi Province; and from Western Myanmar to India's north-eastern state of Manipur. Cross-border movement and sexual and injecting networking among PWID and sex workers are likely to have spread HIV across border cities in Nepal and India (Nepal 2007b). In Central Asia also, the areas with a high number of reported cases of HIV/AIDS are located along the migration and drug trafficking routes (Renton et al. 2006).

Many of the people identified as sex workers and drug injectors are migrants or mobile people. The sex industry operates by maintaining a steady flow of new sex workers and creates a high turnover of women pulled from various places. A biannual follow up of low-price brothels in Bali, Indonesia, found that about half of the sex workers were new in each round (Ford et al. 2002). In Vietnam, the majority of karaoke-based sex workers in Hai Phong (66 per cent) and Da Nang (57 per cent) and one-tenth of street-based sex workers in those provinces had lived there for less than a year (Tung et al. 2001). Women and girls of Myanmar were reported to cross borders to Thailand and Yunnan Province of China to work as hospitality girls (Chantavanich et al. 2000). Cross-border mobility along the Thai-Cambodia border was once dominated by refugee movement. More recently it is dominated by mobility related to work and trade. The emergence of an active sex industry serviced by Cambodian and Vietnamese women and girls in Thailand's border town of Poipet is an example (Chantavanich et al. 2000). Along the Vietnam-Cambodia border in the Mekong Delta, Vietnamese men and women slip through the border to engage in commercial sex since these activities can occur more freely in Cambodia than Vietnam.

Many injecting drug users are mobile people, and they not only share injecting equipment with their local peers, but also with people from other locations (Nepal 2007b; Beyrer et al. 2000). As Beyrer et al. (2000) noted, PWIDs crossed the borders – from North-Eastern India to Mandalay (Myanmar), and from Guangxi (China) to Vietnam – to purchase drugs, test their quality through self-injections, and also share drugs and injecting equipment with local suppliers. A 2001 survey reported that about 10 per cent of Vietnamese PWIDs had taken drugs by injection in other provinces in the preceding year, and some of them shared needles on those occasions (Tung et al. 2001). In the early 1990s, most of the drug injectors surveyed in a detoxification centre in north-eastern Malaysia reported a history of travel to Thailand and many of them had contracted HIV through sharing drug injecting equipment while across the border (Singh and Crofts 1993). UNTAC personnel who used to frequent Thailand for holidays were implicated in seeding HIV in Cambodia (Ledgerwood 1994).

More conducive to the spread of HIV is the fact that commercial sex and illegal drug use are not distinct but overlapping phenomena. For example, a 2002 study of male injecting drug users in three Indonesian cities reported that over two-thirds of drug injectors were sexually active, about a half had multiple partners, two-fifths had had sex with a female sex worker and only 10 per cent used condoms consistently in the past year (Pisani et al. 2003). A study in Hanoi reported that 27–46 per cent of female sex workers used drugs and 79–85 per cent of the users injected, often using contaminated equipment (Tran et al. 2005).

Population movement and mixing have contributed to the spread of HIV to otherwise unlikely populations and places, especially the rural areas. People whose occupation requires them to stay away from their families for an extended period of time have been found to have a higher prevalence of HIV than the population in general (Nepal 2010). When they return home, they bring HIV as well and transmit it to their sexual partners, as for example, in the rural communities in western Nepal (Poudel et al. 2003). In India also, widespread male labour migration of mostly less-educated migrants who are poorly aware of preventive methods, is argued to be a continuous catalyst for HIV epidemics (Sinha 2013). In Thailand, migration to cities and sex tourism have been implicated in circulating HIV from urban to rural areas (Leisch 1997). Internal population mobility in China has attracted considerable interest with regard to HIV epidemics because the floating population of rural-to-urban temporary migrants is seen as a significant force circulating HIV between cities and rural China (Tucker et al. 2005; Yang 2004; Hu et al. 2006; Anderson et al. 2003; Smith 2005). Temporary migrants, who are largely poor, rural, single men, have been over-represented among people with sexually transmitted diseases including HIV (Yang 2004). Several provinces with a high incidence of sexually transmitted infections have also had high immigration rates (Tucker et al. 2005).

Increasing population movements within and across national borders in Asia are associated with growing economic and demographic disparities. People from less prosperous places are legally and illegally migrating to countries and cities with more prosperous economies and labour shortages. Most low-skilled labour migrants work in disadvantaged circumstances deprived of human rights, family reunion and settlement opportunities (Abella 2005) and thus constitute a large pool of vulnerable people. Feminization of migration has occurred owing to the increased demand for domestic workers in some advanced or rising economies such as Hong Kong, Singapore, Taiwan and Malaysia, as well as for female entertainers in Japan (Asis 2005). The heterogeneous and changing demographic and economic institutions have increasingly fostered these population movements which, in some instances, are interwoven with human trafficking and prostitution, and facilitators of HIV epidemics.

Major efforts in controlling the epidemics

A holistic approach involving both behaviour-modifying prevention programmes and treatment is required to tackle HIV epidemics. Such programmes are highly dependent on the perceptions and resolve of policymakers. The development of effective and large scale responses in Asian countries has been taking place at diverse paces and with varying degrees of enthusiasm. Early years were defined by denial, doubt and indifference to HIV epidemics and were influenced by historical impressions that sexually transmitted diseases were Western diseases. There was also a long-held negative image towards groups such as PWIDs and FSWs who were most exposed to the epidemic (Nepal 2007a).

In the 1980s, when AIDS was newly detected, initial cases found in Asian countries were mostly among foreigners or overseas returnees. In the West, AIDS was found mainly among homosexual communities. This unusual disease was erroneously characterized as a 'gay plague' (Fee and Krieger 1993: 1477). Ignorance about AIDS was widespread. This might have prompted Asian governments to dismiss the potential challenge of the disease, as they did not accept the existence of homosexuality in Asian societies (Nepal 2010).

Though the epidemic began to spread significantly in the early 1990s, for many years denial and doubt prevailed over recognition and action. AIDS was seen as a foreigners' disease or a disease of certain marginal groups. For example, Cambodians thought that AIDS was a problem of other countries and could be contracted only from sex workers (Nariddh 1994). In the Philippines, AIDS was mainly identified with lower class prostitutes and homosexual men who had contact with foreigners (Tan et al. 1990). Taiwanese authorities classified labourers from Southern and South-Eastern Asia into the highest risk category likely to pass HIV to innocent locals (Hsu et al. 2004). Amidst the doubts, some prevention programmes were also initiated, though often on a small scale by the non-government sector.

As international collaboration against the AIDS pandemic began to galvanize in the 1990s, Asia's policymakers began to realize the consequences of inaction. The recognition of AIDS as a development challenge, and the implementation of government-initiated national anti-AIDS programmes, which began in the 1990s in Thailand and Cambodia, were being considered favourably in neighbouring countries. For the first time in 2003, on the occasion of the World AIDS Day, the Chinese Premier shook hands with an HIV/AIDS patient in Beijing, and asked the local governments to make concerted efforts for better prevention and control (*China Daily* 2003). Responses to the epidemic started to become more comprehensive.

Success stories, to varying degrees, began to emerge from within the region. Thailand's 100 per cent condom use programme was a policy model that proved to be effective in reducing the spread of HIV through commercial sexual activities, though it was at times criticized as being coercive (Marten 2005; Loff et al. 2003). Later endorsed and encouraged by United Nations agencies as the best practice to control HIV infections (UNAIDS 2000; WHO/WPRO 2004), the 100 per cent condom use programme was first conceptualized and piloted in Ratchaburi province of Thailand. With the nationwide implementation of the programme in 1992, condom use in commercial sex work rose to 90 per cent in some places and STD infections declined from 6.5 infections per 1,000 population in 1989 to 2.1 per 1,000 population in 1992 (Rojanapitayakorn 1993). One significant finding was that HIV infections among 21-year-old Thai army conscripts declined from a peak of four per cent in June 1993 to 2.5 per cent in December 1994 and just over one per cent in 2004 (Rojanapithayakorn 2006).

Cambodia was the second country to pilot this programme in 1998 in Sihanoukville, before expanding it to other provinces in around 2000. From the early 2000s, this model began to be adopted in other Asian countries including Vietnam, China, Myanmar, Philippines, Mongolia,

Laos and Indonesia. One obstacle was that condom use was never a norm in the developing societies of this region. Some countries had successful family planning movements which boosted use of other contraceptive methods to very high levels. Yet acceptance and use of condoms remained insignificantly low. AIDS prevention policies had to change this norm to make condoms acceptable to male clients of sex workers. Nevertheless, the prevention programmes targeted towards the most-at-risk populations were efficacious in promoting behaviour change and reducing the incidence of HIV (Tan et al. 2012).

Despite high infection levels among PWID, the harm reduction approach, which includes a needle-syringe exchange programme as its core element, remained a very controversial model for many years into the HIV epidemic. Harm reductionists continued to advocate needle-syringe exchange to contain the spread of HIV among intravenous drug users (Reid and Costigan 2002). However, governments declined to implement this programme, fearing that support for a harm reduction approach would induce a further rise in illicit drug use. In some countries, small projects were run by non-government organizations despite hostile political and legal environments. These efforts provided a basis for evidence-based advocacy. A move towards creating a more supportive legal and political environment, leading to the implementation and scaling up of harm reduction programmes, started to emerge in the 2000s in countries such as China, Indonesia, Malaysia and Vietnam which had experienced significant transmissions through unsafe needle sharing (Chatterjee and Sharma 2010; Narayanan et al. 2011; Ball 2007).

Since the early 2000s, antiretroviral therapy (ART) programmes have begun in the developing Asian nations, led by high-burden countries such as Thailand in 2000 and Cambodia in 2001 (Srikantiah et al. 2010). Access to life-prolonging antiretroviral therapy has emerged as an important method of HIV prevention, as it has helped reduce the viral load in HIV carriers and also reduce transmission of the virus (WHO et al. 2013; Cohen et al. 2013). Universal access to ART, defined as more than 80 per cent of people with HIV/AIDS receiving the treatment, can have a population-level impact (WHO et al. 2013). While by 2012 some high-burden countries such as Cambodia and Thailand had achieved or were nearing the universal access goal, the treatment coverage in many other countries was well below the 80 per cent threshold (Table 14.3). The coverage of treatment for children with HIV is lagging behind in the region (Srikantiah et al. 2010). Access to treatment for prevention of mother-to-child transmission is slowly evolving, especially in Southern and South-Eastern Asia. In 2012, only one in five pregnant women with HIV in Southern and South-Eastern Asia was estimated to be receiving antiretrovirals for the prevention of mother-to-child transmission (UNAIDS 2013).

Hopes and challenges

The global AIDS pandemic has passed the phase of 'panic and despair' and has entered the stage of 'hope and confidence'. The disease never spread in Asia to the degree seen in sub-Saharan Africa. Cambodia, Myanmar and Thailand, the most affected Asian countries, have reversed their overall epidemics (UNAIDS 2012). All high-income and some low- and middle-income countries and territories of this region have never progressed beyond the low stage of the epidemic. Yet sensitivity towards the epidemic remains high for this populous part of the globe, as any complacency can result in a substantial increase in HIV prevalence (Commission on AIDS in Asia 2008).

Modelling based on improved sets of data and methods has indicated an optimistic outlook for Asia. The Asian Epidemic Model, designed for situations with multiple most-at-risk groups, shows that adult HIV prevalence could have reached 8–10 per cent in countries such as Thailand and Cambodia where about 20 per cent of adult men visited sex workers, and 5 per cent in parts

Table 14.3 Estimated per cent of adults with HIV in need of antiretroviral therapy receiving the treatment (based on WHO 2010 Guidelines), selected countries of Asia, 2012

	Per cent
Cambodia	82
Thailand	76
Philippines	76
Georgia	71
Vietnam	58
Lao PDR	54
India	51
Myanmar	46
Malaysia	42
Sri Lanka	35
Armenia	34
Nepal	33
Uzbekistan	31
Kyrgyzstan	29
Tajikistan	27
Bangladesh	27
Maldives	26
Azerbaijan	24
Indonesia	18
Yemen	15
Pakistan	14
Iran	13
Bhutan	11
Afghanistan	9

Source: UNAIDS (2013).

of India and China where 10 per cent of men visited sex workers (Commission on AIDS in Asia 2008). The epidemic did not reach those levels owing to timely interventions (Ainsworth et al. 2003; Commission on AIDS in Asia 2008). After a comprehensive analysis, the Commission on AIDS in Asia (2008) concluded that, as heterosexual networking is low in the population in general, HIV epidemics in Asia could not be sustained in the absence of transmission among most-at-risk groups, such as people buying and selling sex, PWID and MSM.

While massive epidemics seem to have been averted, the region is far from safe. High HIV prevalences are being recorded among MSM and transgender populations in several countries (van Griensven et al. 2010, van Griensven and de Lind van Wijngaarden 2010; Pisani et al. 2004; UNAIDS 2013). Labour migration and mobility remain important factors channelling HIV within and between countries (Saggurti et al. 2012; Nepal 2007b; Beyrer et al. 2000; Sinha 2013) as many migrants and mobile people are not easily reached through prevention programmes. The epidemic is gradually affecting more females with the transmission of the virus from injecting drug users and male clients of sex workers to their low risk partners, as reflected in the rising share of women among all HIV carriers in Asia from 21 per cent in 1990 to 35 per cent in 2009 (UNAIDS 2010).

The persistence of stigma and discrimination against at-risk groups and people living with HIV continues to undermine the emerging political resolve against the epidemic. The criminalization of people engaged in behaviours such as injecting drug use, sex work and male-to-male sex, which dominate HIV transmission in Asia, is argued to have weakened the prevention efforts in the region (Csete and Dube 2010).

While antiretroviral treatment has been shown to be effective in slowing the spread of HIV, achieving and maintaining universal access to ART remain a big challenge. With their weak health care systems, the developing economies of this region were slow in instituting effective treatment and care. For example, in 2003, the number of HIV-positive persons per doctor was over 11,000 in Vietnam, compared to 24 in Japan (TREAT Asia 2004). In the absence of universal health care, identifying every individual with HIV can be a very ambitious goal for the developing countries of the region. In addition, while ART has shown promising results in preventing heterosexual transmissions of HIV, its effectiveness in preventing transmission through male-to-male sex and injecting drug use is yet to be established (Cohen et al. 2013). Sociopolitical challenges that hinder behaviour-change policies, such as stigma and discrimination against members of key groups and poor health infrastructure, can also slow the progress towards universal access to ART.

To the extent that unsafe practices persist in the sex industry and drug market, the HIV epidemic in the region is likely to persist. In the absence of widespread sexual networking in the population in general, a significant increase in the epidemic is unlikely (Commission on AIDS in Asia 2008; Caldwell 2006). However, an increase or resurgence of the epidemic to some extent cannot be ruled out, at least in the developing economies which have underdeveloped and underfunded health and social care systems. HIV epidemics can find favourable space in societies that are poorly governed, inequitable and socioeconomically disadvantaged (Over 1998; Mahal 2001; Drain et al. 2004; Menon-Johansson 2005) if behavioural risk factors are also present. Any complacency can trigger new outbreaks, though not on the same scale as in sub-Saharan Africa.

In conclusion, Asia enjoys a low HIV prevalence overall and an optimistic prospect. However, given the large population base in this region, even a low prevalence reflects a considerable number of people living with the virus, a large proportion of whom are not receiving the recommended medication. Epidemics in the high-burden countries of Thailand, Cambodia and Myanmar have peaked and are likely to maintain their downward trajectory as long as prevention and treatment programmes are maintained. India and China, where the epidemic was once feared to be growing explosively, have managed to maintain it at a low level. However, the epidemic is expanding in a number of countries, notably Indonesia and the Central Asian countries, where a major surge in infections started relatively late. Injecting drug use and commercial sex were major drivers of the epidemic in the 1990s. More recently, male-to-male sex has surfaced as a new driver of the epidemic. The emergence of multiple at-risk groups has slowed down the pace of decline of mature epidemics and propelled newer epidemics.

Behavioural and geographic heterogeneity is a common feature of HIV epidemics in Asia. There are many localized epidemics concentrated in key groups such as PWID, sex workers and their clients, and MSM, and connected through population mobility and mixing. The image is less of a comprehensive network than of a complex spider-web stretching over vast social distances, trapping unsuspecting victims. The presence of multiple at-risk groups means that elimination of infections in one group or area is not enough to tackle the epidemic. The virus can continue to spread through other groups that are outside the scope of current prevention policies. As the HIV epidemics in this region are immensely heterogeneous in scale, scope and timing of occurrence, the future depends on how well governments are able to eliminate the widespread discrimination against people's behaviours, mobility and sexual identity. Without more tolerant and realistic approaches, any hope of controlling HIV in Asia could evaporate.

References

Abella, M. I. (2005) 'Social issues in the management of labour migration in Asia and the Pacific'. *Asia-Pacific Population Journal*, 20(3): 61–86.
Abou-Zahr, C. and T. Wardlaw (2003) *Antenatal Care in Developing Countries: Promises, Achievements and Missed Opportunities – An Analysis of Trends, Levels and Differentials, 1990–2001*. Geneva: World Health Organization.
Ainsworth, M., C. Beyrer and A. Soucat (2003) 'AIDS and public policy: the lessons and challenges of "success" in Thailand'. *Health Policy*, 64(1): 13–37.
Anderson, A. F., Z. Qingsi, X. Hua et al. (2003) 'China's floating population and the potential for HIV transmission: a social-behavioural perspective'. *AIDS Care*, 15(2): 177–185.
Asis, M. M. B. (2005) 'Recent trends in international migration in Asia and the Pacific'. *Asia-Pacific Population Journal*, 20(3): 15–38.
Ball, A. L. (2007) 'HIV, injecting drug use and harm reduction: a public health response'. *Addiction*, 102(5): 684–690.
Beyrer, C., S. D. Baral, F. van Griensven et al. (2012) 'Global epidemiology of HIV infection in men who have sex with men'. *Lancet*, 380(9839): 367–377.
Beyrer, C., M. H. Razak, K. Lisam et al. (2000) 'Overland heroin trafficking routes and HIV-1 spread in South and South-East Asia'. *AIDS*, 14(1): 75–83.
Bongaarts, J., T. Buettner, G. Heilig et al. (2008) 'Has the HIV epidemic peaked?' *Population and Development Review*, 34(2): 199–224.
Boonchalaksi, W. and P. Guest (1994) *Prostitution in Thailand*. Nakhon Pathom, Thailand: Institute of Population and Social Research.
Brown, T. L. (2001) *Sex Slaves: The Trafficking of Women in Asia*. London: Virago.
Caldwell, J. C. (2006) 'Will HIV/AIDS levels in Asia reach the level of sub-Saharan Africa?' *Asia-Pacific Population Journal*, 21(1): 3–9.
Centers for Disease Control and Prevention (CDC) (1981) 'Pneumocystis Pneumonia – Los Angeles'. *Morbidity and Mortality Weekly Report*, 30(21): 1–3.
Chantavanich, S., A. Beesey and S. Paul (2000) *Mobility and HIV/AIDS in the Greater Mekong Subregion*. Bangkok: Asian Development Bank.
Chatterjee, A. and M. Sharma (2010) 'Moving from a project to programmatic response: scaling up harm reduction in Asia'. *International Journal of Drug Policy*, 21(2): 134–136.
China Daily (2003) 'Premier's handshake highlights fight against AIDS'. *China Daily*, 1 December.
Cohen, M. S., M. K. Smith, K. E. Muessig et al. (2013) 'Antiretroviral treatment of HIV-1 prevents transmission of HIV-1: where do we go from here?' *Lancet*, 382(9903): 1515–1524.
Commission on AIDS in Asia (2008) *Redefining AIDS in Asia: Crafting an Effective Response*. New Delhi: Oxford University Press.
Csete, J. and S. Dube (2010) 'An inappropriate tool: criminal law and HIV in Asia'. *AIDS*, 24: S80–S85.
Dandona, R., L. Dandona, G. A. Kumar et al. (2006) 'Demography and sex work characteristics of female sex workers in India'. *BMC International Health and Human Rights*, 6(1): 5.
Drain, P. K., J. S. Smith, J. P. Hughes et al. (2004) 'Correlates of national HIV seroprevalence: an ecologic analysis of 122 developing countries'. *Journal of Acquired Immune Deficiency Syndromes*, 35(4): 407–420.
Durban Declaration (2000) 'The Durban declaration'. *Nature*, 406(6791): 15–16.
Elswood, B. F. and R. B. Stricker (1994) 'Polio vaccines and the origin of AIDS'. *Medical Hypotheses*, 42(6): 347–354.
Family Health International (FHI) (2000) *Behavioral Surveillance Surveys (BSS): Guidelines for Repeated Behavioral Surveys in Populations at Risk of HIV*. Arlington: FHI.
Fee, E. and N. Krieger (1993) 'Understanding AIDS: historical interpretations and the limits of biomedical individualism'. *American Journal of Public Health*, 83(10): 1477–1486.
Ford, K., D. N. Wirawan, B. D. Reed et al. (2002) 'The Bali STD/AIDS study: evaluation of an intervention for sex workers'. *Sexually Transmitted Diseases*, 29(1): 50–58.
Fox, A. M. (2012) 'The HIV-poverty thesis re-examined: poverty, wealth or inequality as a social determinant of HIV infection in sub-Saharan Africa?' *Journal of Biosocial Science*, 44(4): 459–480.
Gallo, R. C. (2002) 'Historical essay: the early years of HIV/AIDS'. *Science*, 298(5599): 1728–1730.
Gao, F., E. Bailes, D. L. Robertson et al. (1999) 'Origin of HIV-1 in the chimpanzee Pan troglodytes troglodytes'. *Nature*, 397(6718): 436–441.

Garcia-Calleja, J. M., E. Zaniewski, P. D. Ghys et al. (2004) 'A global analysis of trends in the quality of HIV sero-surveillance'. *Sexually Transmitted Infections*, 80(suppl. 1): i25–i30.

General Statistical Office (GSO)/National Institute of Hygiene and Epidemiology (NIHE) and ORC Macro (2006) *Vietnam Population and AIDS Indicator Survey 2005*. Calverton, Maryland, USA: General Statistical Office (GSO), National Institute of Hygiene and Epidemiology (NIHE) [Vietnam] and ORC Macro.

Greener, R. and S. Sarkar (2010) 'Risk and vulnerability: do socioeconomic factors influence the risk of acquiring HIV in Asia?' *AIDS*, 24: S3–S11.

Hahn, B. H., G. M. Shaw, K. M. De et al. (2000) 'AIDS as a zoonosis: scientific and public health implications'. *Science*, 287(5453): 607–614.

Heng, M. B. and P. J. Key (1995) 'Cambodian health in transition'. *British Medical Journal*, 311(7002): 435–437.

Hesketh, T., Z. W. Xing and D. Lin (2002) 'Editorial on epidemiology of HIV in China was misleading'. *British Medical Journal*, 325(7362): 493–494.

Horn, R. (2010) *Getting It Right – Case Studies on Paediatric HIV Treatment, Care and Support in Thailand and Cambodia*. Bangkok: UNICEF East Asia and Pacific Regional Office.

Hsu, M. L., W. C. Lin and T. S. Wu (2004) 'Representation of "Us" and "Others" in the AIDS news discourse: a Taiwanese experience'. In E. Micollier (ed.) *Sexual Cultures in East Asia: The Social Construction of Sexuality and Sexual Risk in a Time of AIDS*. London: Routledge Curzon. Pp. 183–222.

Hu, Z., H. Liu, X. Li et al. (2006) 'HIV-related sexual behaviour among migrants and non-migrants in a rural area of China: role of rural-to-urban migration'. *Public Health*, 120(4): 339–345.

International Institute for Population Sciences and Macro International (IIPS) (2007) *National Family Health Survey (NFHS-3), 2005–06, India, Volume I*. Mumbai: International Institute for Population Sciences.

Kandathil, A. J., S. Ramalingam, R. Kannangai et al. (2005) 'Molecular epidemiology of HIV'. *Indian Journal of Medical Research*, 121(4): 333–344.

Keele, B. F., F. Van Heuverswyn, Y. Li et al. (2006) 'Chimpanzee reservoirs of pandemic and nonpandemic HIV-1'. *Science*, 313(5786): 523–526.

Kihara, M., S. Ichikawa, M. Kihara et al. (1997) 'Descriptive epidemiology of HIV/AIDS in Japan, 1985–1994'. *Journal of Acquired Immune Deficiency Syndromes & Human Retrovirology*, 14: S3–S12.

Kissling, E., E. H. Allison, J. A. Seeley et al. (2005) 'Fisherfolk are among groups most at risk of HIV: cross-country analysis of prevalence and numbers infected'. *AIDS*, 19(17): 1939–1946.

Korber, B., M. Muldoon, J. Theiler et al. (2000) 'Timing the ancestor of the HIV-1 pandemic strains'. *Science*, 288(5472): 1789–1796.

Ledgerwood, J. L. (1994) 'UN peacekeeping missions: the lessons from Cambodia'. *Asia Pacific Issues*, 11: 1–10.

Leisch, H. (1997) 'AIDS research and prevention strategies in Thailand'. *Geographische Rundschau*, 49(4): 226–230.

Lim, L. L. (ed.) (1998) *The Sex Sector: The Economic and Social Bases of Prostitution in Southeast Asia*. Geneva: International Labour Office.

Loff, B., C. Overs and P. Longo (2003) 'Can health programmes lead to mistreatment of sex workers?' *Lancet*, 361(9373): 1982–1983.

Mahal, A. (2001) 'The human development roots of HIV and implications for policy: a cross-country analysis'. *Journal of Health & Population in Developing Countries*, 4(2): 43–60.

Marten, L. (2005) 'Commercial sex workers: victims, vectors or fighters of the HIV epidemic in Cambodia?' *Asia Pacific Viewpoint*, 46(1): 21–34.

Mathers, B. M., L. Degenhardt, B. Phillips et al. (2008) 'Global epidemiology of injecting drug use and HIV among people who inject drugs: a systematic review'. *Lancet*, 372(9651): 1733–1745.

Menon-Johansson, A. (2005) 'Good governance and good health: the role of societal structures in the human immunodeficiency virus pandemic'. *BMC International Health and Human Rights*, 5(1): 4.

Ministry of Health [Malaysia] (2012) *Global AIDS Response Country Progress Report Malaysia 2012*.

Montagnier, L. (2002) 'A history of HIV discovery'. *Science*, 298(5599): 1727–1728.

Narayanan, S., B. Vicknasingam and N. M. H. Robson (2011) 'The transition to harm reduction: understanding the role of non-governmental organisations in Malaysia'. *International Journal of Drug Policy*, 22(4): 311–317.

Nariddh, M. C. (1994) 'Myths about AIDS in Cambodia'. *Aidscaptions*, 1(3): 20–21.

National AIDS Control Organization [India] (2009) *Annual Report 2008–2009*. Delhi: NACO.

National AIDS Control Organization [India] (2012) *HIV Sentinel Surveillance 2010–11: A Technical Brief*. Delhi: NACO.

National Institute of Population Research and Training (NIPRT), Mitra and Associates and ORC Macro (2005) *Bangladesh Demographic and Health Survey 2004*. Dhaka, Bangladesh and Calverton, Maryland, USA: National Institute of Population Research and Training, Mitra and Associates and ORC Macro.

National Institute of Public Health, National Institute of Statistics [Cambodia] and ORC Macro (2006) *Cambodia Demographic and Health Survey 2005*. Phnom Penh, Cambodia and Calverton, Maryland, USA: National Institute of Public Health, National Institute of Statistics and ORC Macro.

National Statistics Office (NSO) [Philippines] and ORC Macro (2004) *National and Demographic and Health Survey 2003*. Calverton, Maryland, USA: NSO and ORC Macro.

Nepal, B. (2007a) 'AIDS denial in Asia: dimensions and roots'. *Health Policy*, 84(2–3): 133–141.

Nepal, B. (2007b) 'Population mobility and spread of HIV across the Indo-Nepal border'. *Journal of Health, Population, and Nutrition*, 25(3): 267–277.

Nepal, B. (2010) *HIV/AIDS in Asia: Facts, Faces and Forces*. Saarbrücken: Lambert Academic Publishing.

Over, M. (1998) 'The effect of societal variables on urban rates of HIV infections in developing countries'. In M. Ainsworth, L. Fransen and M. Over (eds.) *Confronting AIDS: Evidence from the Developing World*. Brussels: European Commission. Pp. 39–51.

Panda, S., L. Bijaya, N. S. Devi et al. (2001) 'Interface between drug use and sex work in Manipur'. *National Medical Journal of India*, 14(4): 209–211.

Pisani, E., Dadun, P. K. Sucahya, O. Kamil and S. Jazan (2003) 'Sexual behavior among injection drug users in 3 Indonesian cities carries a high potential for HIV spread to noninjectors'. *Journal of Acquired Immune Deficiency Syndromes*, 34(4): 403–406.

Pisani, E., P. Girault, M. Gultom et al. (2004) 'HIV, syphilis infection and sexual practices among transgenders, male sex workers, and other men who have sex with men in Jakarta, Indonesia'. *Sexually Transmitted Infections*, 80(6): 536–540.

Poudel, K. C., J. Okumura, J. B. Sherchand et al. (2003) 'Mumbai disease in far western Nepal: HIV infection and syphilis among male migrant-returnees and non-migrants'. *Tropical Medicine and International Health*, 8(10): 933–939.

Prüss-Ustün, A., J. Wolf, T. Driscoll et al. (2013) 'HIV due to female sex work: regional and global estimates'. *PLoS ONE*, 8(5): e63476.

Rehle, T., S. Lazzari, G. Dallabetta et al. (2004) 'Second-generation HIV surveillance: better data for decision-making'. *Bulletin of the World Health Organization*, 82: 121–127.

Reid, G. and G. Costigan (2002) *Revisiting 'The Hidden Epidemic': A Situation Assessment of Drug Use in Asia in the Context of HIV/AIDS*. Melbourne: Centre for Harm Reduction, Burnet Institute.

Renton, A., D. Gzirishvilli, G. Gotsadze et al. (2006) 'Epidemics of HIV and sexually transmitted infections in Central Asia: trends, drivers and priorities for control'. *International Journal of Drug Policy*, 17(6): 494–503.

Rojanapityakorn, W. (1993) '"100 percent" condom use seeks to slow HIV spread'. *Network*, 13(4): 30, 32.

Rojanapithayakorn, W. (2006) 'The 100% condom use programme in Asia'. *Reproductive Health Matters*, 14(28): 41–52.

Saggurti, N., B. Mahapatra, S. Sabarwal et al. (2012) 'Male out-migration: a factor for the spread of HIV infection among married men and women in Rural India'. *PLoS ONE*, 7(9).

Sales, P. M. (1996) 'Cambodia after UNTAC: the ambivalent legacy of a United Nations peace keeping operation'. *Pacific Review*, 8(1): 81–92.

Saphonn, V., L. B. Hor, S. P. Ly et al. (2002) 'How well do antenatal clinic (ANC) attendees represent the general population? A comparison of HIV prevalence from ANC sentinel surveillance sites with a population-based survey of women aged 15–49 in Cambodia'. *International Journal of Epidemiology*, 31(2): 449–455.

Singh, S. and N. Crofts (1993) 'HIV infection among injecting drug users in north-east Malaysia, 1992'. *AIDS Care*, 5(3): 273–281.

Sinha, K. (2013) 'Mass economic migration: the greatest threat to HIV control in India'. *British Medical Journal*, 346: f474.

Smith, C. J. (2005) 'Social geography of sexually transmitted diseases in China: exploring the role of migration and urbanisation'. *Asia Pacific Viewpoint*, 46(1): 65–80.

Smith, D. G. (1990) 'Thailand: AIDS crisis looms'. *Lancet*, 335(8692): 781–782.

Srikantiah, P., M. Ghidinelli, D. Bachani et al. (2010) 'Scale up of national antiretroviral therapy programs: progress and challenges in the Asia pacific region'. *AIDS*, 24(suppl. 3): S62–S71.

Stover, J. (2004) 'Projecting the demographic consequences of adult HIV prevalence trends: the Spectrum Projection Package'. *Sexually Transmitted Infections*, 80(suppl. 1): i14–i18.

Takebe, Y., S. Kusagawa and K. Motomura (2004) 'Molecular epidemiology of HIV: tracking AIDS pandemic'. *Pediatrics International*, 46(2): 236–244.
Tan, J. Y., T. B. Huedo-Medina, M. R. Warren et al. (2012) 'A meta-analysis of the efficacy of HIV/AIDS prevention interventions in Asia, 1995–2009'. *Social Science & Medicine*, 75(4): 676–687.
Tan, M. L., A. de Leon, C. O'Donnell et al. (1990) 'Philippines: focusing on the hospitality women'. *The Third Epidemic: Repercussions of the Fear of AIDS*. Budapest: Panos Institute. Pp. 200–203.
Tran, T. N., R. Detels, H. T. Long et al. (2005) 'Drug use among female sex workers in Hanoi, Vietnam'. *Addiction*, 100(5): 619–625.
TREAT Asia (2004) *Expanded availability of HIV/AIDS drugs in Asia creates urgent need for trained doctors.* Available from: www.amfar.org.
Truong, T. D. (1990) *Sex, Money, and Morality: Prostitution and Tourism in Southeast Asia*. London: Zed Books.
Tucker, J. D., G. E. Henderson, T. F. Wang et al. (2005) 'Surplus men, sex work and the spread of HIV in China'. *AIDS*, 19(6): 539–547.
Tung, N. D., N. Tuan, T. V. Hoang et al. (2001) *HIV/AIDS Behavioral Surveillance Survey, Vietnam, 2000: BSS Round 1 Results*. Hanoi: National AIDS Standing Bureau and Family Health International.
UN Theme Group on HIV/AIDS in China (2002) *HIV/AIDS: China's Titanic Peril*. Beijing.
UNAIDS (2000) *Evaluation of the 100% Condom Programme in Thailand*. Geneva: UNAIDS.
UNAIDS (2006) *2006 Report on the Global AIDS Epidemic*. Geneva: UNAIDS.
UNAIDS (2010) *Global Report: UNAIDS Report on the Global AIDS Epidemic 2010*. Geneva: UNAIDS.
UNAIDS (2012) *Global Report: UNAIDS Report on the Global AIDS Epidemic 2012*. Geneva: UNAIDS.
UNAIDS (2013) *Global Report: UNAIDS Report on the Global AIDS Epidemic 2013*. Geneva: UNAIDS.
United Nations Population Division (2013) *World Population Prospects: The 2012 Revision*. New York: United Nations.
van Griensven, F. and J. W. de Lind van Wijngaarden (2010) 'A review of the epidemiology of HIV infection and prevention responses among MSM in Asia'. *AIDS*, 24: S30–S40.
van Griensven, F., A. Varangrat, W. Wimonsate et al. (2010) 'Trends in HIV prevalence, estimated HIV incidence and risk behavior among men who have sex with men in Bangkok, Thailand, 2003–2007'. *Journal of Acquired Immune Deficiency Syndromes*, 53(2): 234–239.
Whiteside, A. (2001) 'Demography and economics of HIV/AIDS'. *British Medical Bulletin*, 58(1): 73–88.
WHO, UNICEF and UNAIDS (2013) *Global Update on HIV Treatment 2013: Results, Impact and Opportunities*. Geneva: World Health Organization.
Wolfe, N. D., W. M. Switzer, J. K. Carr et al. (2004) 'Naturally acquired simian retrovirus infections in central African hunters'. *Lancet*, 363(9413): 932–937.
World Health Organization (WHO) and UNAIDS (2000) *Second Generation Surveillance for HIV: The Next Decade*. Geneva: WHO.
World Health Organization Regional Office for the Western Pacific (WHO/WPRO) (2004) *Experiences of 100% Condom Use Programme in Selected Countries of Asia*. Geneva: World Health Organization.
Worobey, M., M. L. Santiago, B. F. Keele et al. (2004) 'Origin of AIDS: contaminated polio vaccine theory refuted'. *Nature*, 428(6985): 820.
Wu, Z., K. Rou and R. Detels (2001) 'Prevalence of HIV infection among former commercial plasma donors in rural eastern China'. *Health Policy and Planning*, 16(1): 41–46.
Yang, X. (2004) 'Temporary migration and the spread of STDs/HIV in China: is there a link?'. *International Migration Review*, 38(2): 212–235.
Zhang, X., E. P. F. Chow, D. P. Wilson et al. (2013) 'Prevalence of HIV and syphilis infections among long-distance truck drivers in China: a data synthesis and meta-analysis'. *International Journal of Infectious Diseases*, 17(1): e2–e7.

15
Population distribution

Christophe Z. Guilmoto and Sébastien Oliveau

This chapter aims at providing an overview of population distribution in Asia at various scales. Asia is taken here in the usual United Nations definition, and comprises the 51 countries and territories forming a triangle with the Bosporus to the west, Japan to the north-east and Indonesia to the south-east, as the three corners.[1] It includes China and India, which are the two most populated nations in the world. With the addition of Indonesia, Pakistan, Bangladesh and Japan, six out of the ten largest populations are in Asia. While there are a few Asian countries with less than a million inhabitants, such as the Maldives in the Indian Ocean and Bhutan in the Himalayas, Asia is made up mostly of nations with large populations, and 24 among them have more than 20 million inhabitants. This chapter will examine the main features of the spatial distribution of population in Asia, by stressing the geographical and demographic variations observed across the continent, and by presenting some of the main factors that have influenced the settlement patterns observed today. The spatial distribution of Asia's population is particularly skewed in comparison with that of other continents. We will also review the recent population dynamics and see how they are likely to alter the population distribution within Asia.

The changing share of Asia's population in the world

With a total population estimated at 1.4 billion in 1950, Asia already represented no less than 55.4 per cent of the world's population.[2] Yet its formidable demographic increase over the following decades, of close to 2.0 per cent per year, brought Asia's population total to 3.7 billion at the beginning of the twenty-first century and its share climbed to more than 60.7 per cent of the world's total. Asia is expected to cross the 5 billion threshold by 2036. This preeminence stems primarily from the presence of the two demographic giants that are China and India. With more than 1.2 billion inhabitants, each represents a larger population than any other continent and they jointly correspond to more than 36 per cent of the world's total. The third largest country by population size (United States) is only about a quarter of that for China or India. It may also be pointed out that Asia includes several other countries such as Indonesia, Pakistan, Bangladesh and Japan that are ranked fourth, sixth, eighth and tenth respectively by population size.

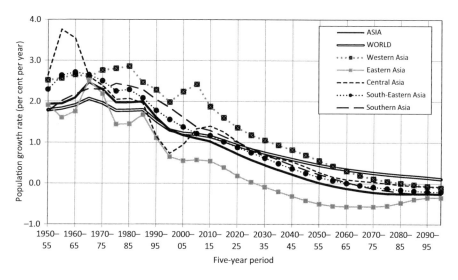

Figure 15.1 Annual population growth per region, 1950–2100
Source: United Nations (2013).

Yet in spite of the continuing demographic growth anticipated until the middle of the twenty-first century, the beginning of the millennium has marked an historical downturn in Asia's population surge; it is exactly at this juncture that its relative share in the world has started to level off. It is now expected to decline at a sustained pace in the near future, falling back to 55 per cent of the world's total by 2050 and perhaps close to 45 per cent at the end of the current century, following recent population forecasts by the United Nations Population Division. As these trends suggest, this turnaround is related directly to Asia's declining population growth rate vis-à-vis the rest of the world's growth rate. Estimates provided in Figure 15.1 demonstrate that Asia's annual population increase will be consistently below the world's average during the twenty-first century, and that the gap may reach 0.5 per cent per year by 2070. This downturn, associated with a net population decrease anticipated in Asia after 2050, is of course closely linked to its rapid fertility decline. However, it also highlights the importance of the first couple of decades of the twenty-first century in shaping Asia's relative demographic share of global population. This chapter should therefore be read as a description of Asian population at its apex, on the eve of an irreversible demographic decline.

The rest of this section will review recent demographic differentials across the continent, with a special emphasis on the variations in growth rates observed within Asia due to their implications for the relative distribution of population within Asia. Because Eastern Asia will experience the lowest growth rates, and in contrast Western Asia the highest, we highlight a comparison between those two regions in this section. Before that, however, we consider a longer-term perspective based on available population estimates for more ancient periods. In view of the lack of reliable population figures in several Asian countries before 1950,[3] these estimates obviously need to be taken with caution, but they offer an illuminating overview of population trends. The most reliable source stems from the HYDE project that has compiled and revised all previous available demographic estimates for the last 300 years, with more speculative figures referring to the entire Holocene period starting about 11,760 years ago (Goldewijk et al. 2010, 2011).[4]

According to these estimates, people were already living in Asia in very early human history, and population in the continent had already reached more than 100 million at the beginning of

Christophe Z. Guilmoto & Sébastien Oliveau

Table 15.1 Various population estimates for Asia during the Holocene

Year	Population (in millions)		Density		Period	Annual growth rates (%) World	
	Asia	% of world's population	Asia	World		Asia (%)	World (%)
–10000 BC	0.7	30.4	0.03	0.02			
0 AD	106.7	56.7	4.9	1.4	10000 BC–0	0.05	0.04
1700	366.4	60.7	7.7	2.2	0–1700	0.07	0.07
1800	656.8	66.4	16.8	4.5	1700–1800	0.59	0.50
1900	902.2	54.5	41.5	12.3	1800–1900	0.32	0.52
1950	1335.7	52.5	61.4	19.0	1900–1950	0.79	0.86
2000	3419.0	55.6	157.2	45.8	1950–2000	1.90	1.78

Note: Figures differ from other estimates quoted in this chapter because Asia's definition in the HYDE database excludes the Middle-East and the former Soviet Union.
Source: HYDE 3.1 database (Goldewijk et al. 2010).

the Christian era (Table 15.1). Even though Europe was already densely populated, Asia's population density was also close to five persons per sq. km and comparable to that of Europe. This level was three times higher than in the rest of the world. The annual demographic growth rate was estimated at 0.7 per 1,000 and the gap between Asia and the rest of the world was almost imperceptible, but its cumulative impact over more than ten centuries was significant. In fact, the share of Asia in the global population gradually increased and reached a peak in 1800 at 66.4 per cent. At that time, Asia had a density close to 17 persons per sq. km, a level that the rest of the world would only reach one and a half centuries later.

The ensuing period was, however, characterized by a relative decline in Asia's population in contrast with the spectacular demographic evolution of Latin and North America as well as the steady population growth observed in Europe and Russia. This growth was linked firstly to agricultural expansion by settlers in the Americas and in Russia, and also to industrialization and urbanization processes in most of Europe. Asia did not benefit from any increase in croplands nor from industrial economic development, during the nineteenth and first half of the twentieth century. In addition to the colonial predicament of the region, China was affected by a succession of major internal and international conflicts and subsistence crises, while India also suffered from epidemics and famines until 1950. In spite of Asia's subsequent record growth during the last 50 years, the continent as a whole has never recovered from the relative demographic stagnation observed through 1800–1950 (Goldewijk 2005).

Starting from 1950, we have more detailed demographic estimates at both national and subnational levels based on census results. We will also use population forecasts till 2050. These figures show how the distribution of population within Asia has been subject to significant changes during the last six decades and the extent of growth differentials in the future. Beyond the mere effect of demographic forces such as steady mortality decline, the twentieth century finally witnessed a formidable agricultural expansion in most Asian countries – such as Indonesia, India, Vietnam and the Philippines – which combined with the Green Revolution after 1960 to reverse the Malthusian pressure on rural areas (Goldewijk and Ramankutty 2004; Hazell 2009).

Asia's relative size in the world population has not increased uniformly since 1950, nor is the forecast until 2050 and beyond parallel for all 51 countries and territories.[5] As Figure 15.1 demonstrates (see also Table 15.2), population growth has been notably faster in Western Asia since the 1950s. The number of inhabitants in this mostly arid subregion rose by a factor of 4.5 in the

Table 15.2 Population, urbanization, growth rates and density: Asian countries

	Population ('000)			Urban (%)	Annual growth rates (%)	Density (inhabitant/ sq. km)
	1950	2010	2050	2010	2010–2050	2010
World	2,525,779	6,916,183	9,550,945	51.6	1.15	50.6
Asia	1,395,749	4,165,440	5,164,061	44.4	1.03	130.5
Central Asia	17,499	61,694	86,154	40.7	1.4	15.4
Southern Asia	492,799	1,681,407	2,312,026	32.2	1.29	247.7
Eastern Asia	666,249	1,593,571	1,605,341	54.4	0.55	135.1
South-Eastern Asia	167,986	597,097	787,535	44.1	1.17	132.8
Western Asia	51,216	231,671	373,006	67.4	1.88	48.0
Afghanistan	7,451	28,398	56,551	23.2	2.39	43.5
Armenia	1,354	2,963	2,782	64.1	0.18	99.4
Azerbaijan	2,896	9,095	10,492	53.4	1.11	105.0
Bahrain	116	1,252	1,835	88.6	1.66	1,803.3
Bangladesh	37,895	151,125	201,948	27.9	1.19	1,049.5
Bhutan	177	717	980	34.8	1.60	15.3
Brunei Darussalam	48	401	546	75.6	1.35	69.5
Cambodia	4,433	14,365	22,569	19.8	1.75	79.3
China	543,776	1,359,821	1,384,977	49.2	0.61	141.7
China, Hong Kong SAR	1,974	7,050	8,004	100.0	0.74	6,414.5
China, Macao SAR	196	535	797	100.0	1.78	20,562.5
Cyprus	494	1,104	1,356	70.3	1.08	119.3
DPR Korea	10,549	24,501	27,076	60.2	0.53	203.3
Georgia	3,527	4,389	3,563	52.7	−0.39	63.0
India	376,325	1,205,625	1,620,051	30.9	1.24	366.8
Indonesia	72,592	240,676	321,377	49.9	1.21	126.4
Iran	17,119	74,462	100,598	68.9	1.30	45.2
Iraq	5,719	30,962	71,336	66.5	2.89	70.6
Israel	1,258	7,420	11,843	91.8	1.30	335.1
Japan	82,199	127,353	108,329	90.5	−0.08	337.0
Jordan	449	6,455	11,510	82.5	3.50	72.2
Kazakhstan	6,703	15,921	20,186	53.7	1.04	5.8
Kuwait	152	2,992	6,342	98.2	3.61	167.9
Kyrgyzstan	1,740	5,334	7,976	35.3	1.35	26.7
Laos	1,683	6,396	10,579	33.1	1.86	27.0
Lebanon	1,335	4,341	5,316	87.1	3.04	417.4
Malaysia	6,110	28,276	42,113	72.0	1.61	85.7
Maldives	74	326	504	40.0	1.89	1,092.9
Mongolia	780	2,713	3,753	67.6	1.49	1.7
Myanmar	17,527	51,931	58,645	32.1	0.84	76.8
Nepal	8,140	26,846	36,479	16.7	1.15	182.4
Occupied Palestinian Territory	932	4,013	8,906	74.1	2.51	666.6
Oman	456	2,803	5,065	73.2	7.89	9.1
Pakistan	37,542	173,149	271,082	35.9	1.66	217.5
Philippines	18,580	93,444	157,118	48.6	1.71	311.5
Qatar	25	1,750	2,985	98.7	5.90	159.1

(continued)

Christophe Z. Guilmoto & Sébastien Oliveau

Table 15.2 (Cont.)

	Population ('000)			Urban (%)	Annual growth rates (%)	Density (inhabitant/ sq. km)
	1950	*2010*	*2050*	*2010*	*2010–2050*	*2010*
Republic of Korea	19,211	48,454	51,034	82.9	0.53	486.8
Saudi Arabia	3,121	27,258	40,388	82.1	1.85	12.7
Singapore	1,022	5,079	7,065	100.0	2.02	7,436.3
Sri Lanka	8,076	20,759	23,834	15.0	0.81	316.4
Syrian Arab Republic	3,413	21,533	36,706	55.7	0.67	116.3
Taiwan	7,562	23,146	21,371	72.8	0.24	639.5
Tajikistan	1,532	7,627	15,093	26.5	2.43	53.3
Thailand	20,607	66,402	61,740	33.7	0.30	129.4
Timor-Leste	433	1,079	2,087	28.0	1.66	72.6
Turkey	21,238	72,138	94,606	70.5	1.22	92.1
Turkmenistan	1,211	5,042	6,570	48.4	1.27	10.3
United Arab Emirates	70	8,442	15,479	84.0	2.52	101.0
Uzbekistan	6,314	27,769	36,330	36.2	1.35	62.1
Vietnam	24,949	89,047	103,697	30.4	0.95	268.5
Yemen	4,661	22,763	42,497	31.7	2.30	43.1

Sources: Population and density: United Nations (2013); Urbanization: United Nations (2012).

60 years until 2010. The progression was even more spectacular in the Arabian Peninsula where the populations of small Gulf countries such as Qatar, Kuwait, Bahrain and the United Arab Emirates have increased more than tenfold from 1950 to 2010. Although by far the least populous of Asia's subregions, Western Asia is likely to witness a similar record population growth over the coming decades. Demographic forecasts predict faster (by more than 0.5 per cent) annual population growth in Western Asia than in the rest of the continent, until 2050. Rapid natural increase in most of these countries, coupled with a considerable inflow of immigrants to the oil-producing countries, account for one of the fastest paces of demographic growth ever observed. To this specific subregion, we should add the case of individual countries such as Afghanistan and Timor-Leste, where delayed fertility decline will cause a near threefold demographic increase during the next four decades. If we restrict the focus here to larger countries, then it is in Pakistan and the Philippines that growth over the 1950–2050 period will be the most remarkable; the population is estimated to increase by a factor of seven during these hundred years, or double the average Asian increase.

On the other hand, growth has been rather modest, and will continue to be so, in more developed areas of Asia. A net demographic decline is forecast from 2010 to 2050 in countries such as Japan and South Korea, and as a result the share of Eastern Asia in Asia's population will shrink. Eastern Asia's lower population growth is the direct product of its dramatic fertility decline. However, the evolution of the growth rate in this region has been complex: the first decades after 1950 witnessed a succession of demographic ups and downs, such as the great Chinese famine of 1958–1961, followed by a spectacular recovery and subsequent demographic 'echoes', but the overall trend became steadier after 1980, highlighting a gradual slowing down in population growth. Eastern Asia's annual demographic growth has decreased steadily since then, reaching 1 per cent in 1990 and 0.5 per cent today. Within 15 years, it is likely to become negative. As in Eastern Asia, the smaller countries of Armenia and Georgia that are part of the Western Asia subregion, are also poised to record a population loss in the future as a consequence of persistent below-replacement fertility levels, with the additional effect of massive emigration from the Caucasus region.

The overall impact of these country-specific differentials in demographic growth is a gradual redistribution of Asia's population. Thus, Western Asia's share in Asia has grown from 4 per cent in 1950 to 6 per cent today, and it is expected to reach 8 per cent by mid-century. Similarly, the share of Southern Asia has risen from 35 per cent in 1950 to 41 per cent today and should reach 47 per cent in 2050, owing to the rapid growth forecast for Pakistan and Afghanistan, and the sustained growth observed in India where the fertility decline has been slower than anticipated. The fastest decline in birth rates has negatively affected the demographic share of Eastern Asian countries, which used to account for almost 50 per cent of Asia's population in 1950, as compared to the forecast of about 29 per cent by 2050 and even lower values in the following decades. Japan, once the third-largest country in Asia after China and India, will be surpassed by Indonesia, Pakistan, Bangladesh and the Philippines by the middle of the century.

Population densities

Table 15.2 provides an overview of some key demographic characteristics of the 51 Asian countries and territories, starting with population estimates in 1950, 2010 and 2050, and the current rates of demographic increase. We have added data on population densities as well as on urbanization levels, as a first indication of the major variations in the distribution of population across the continent. As our further analysis will show, national averages tend to conceal significant variations in density levels within countries.

Interestingly, Asia as a whole – with more than 130 inhabitants per sq. km – appears to be five times more densely inhabited than Africa, America or Europe, which have an average density of 26.4. Contrary to what its high density would intuitively suggest, Asia is less urbanized than other continents, an apparent paradox that can be explained by its especially dense rural settlements patterns. Within Asia, there is in fact no significant positive or negative correlation between the overall density and urbanization; some of the low-density countries such as Kazakhstan and Mongolia also happen to be highly urbanized, while others such as Bangladesh display both extremely high density levels and moderate urbanization. The disaggregated spatial analysis discussed below will also show that some rural areas display elevated density levels.

Population density varies strikingly across countries. If we leave aside the specific case of small islands – from Bahrain to Singapore and Hong-Kong – that are highly or totally urbanized, we observe that population density levels range from two persons per sq. km in Mongolia to 1,050 persons in Bangladesh. A different way to illustrate these regional disparities across Asian nations is by considering Kyrgyzstan, Sri Lanka and Bangladesh, three countries with roughly similar land surfaces, yet with populations as varied as 5, 21 and 149 million inhabitants respectively, in 2010.

Comparing densities at the national level fails, however, to give a fair idea of population distribution within Asia, since populations within most countries tend to both concentrate in specific areas such as river basins and avoid other areas such as arid tracts (Small and Cohen 2004), though India is somewhat an exception with a few cities in arid zones (Balk et al. 2009). Sparsely inhabited lands that are almost entirely unpopulated lie next to subregions of extreme density levels in many countries, from Iran to China and Indonesia. Rescaling our analysis from Asia as a whole to subnational units, we observe that density has an obviously fractal dimension in the

Christophe Z. Guilmoto & Sébastien Oliveau

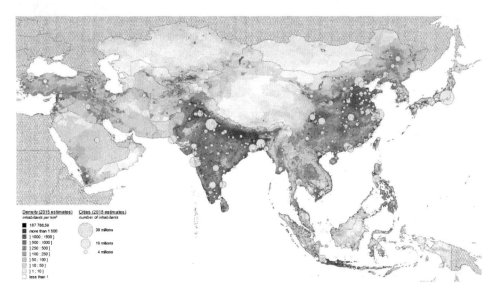

Map 15.1 Population density in Asia, 2015
Sources: CIESIN (2005); United Nations (2012).

sense that the heterogeneity in population density between countries is hardly greater than that observed within individual countries and even within individual subregions.[6]

We will therefore rely on another set of disaggregated data for Asia, derived from the 'Gridded Population of the World: Future Estimates', for our analysis of population dispersion and concentration in Asia.[7] This source provides subnational figures for all Asian countries based on census results. The number of administrative units in this database is close to 100,000 for Asia alone, compared to the 51 countries and territories for which the United Nations Population Division provides demographic estimates. It has been used here to draw a detailed map of estimated density levels across Asia in 2015. We have added on Map 15.1 the 2015 estimated populations for the 323 largest Asian cities, drawn from the United Nations database of cities with population larger than 750,000 inhabitants (United Nations 2012). Note that extremely high density areas typical of metropolitan conurbations are largely indiscernible on a map drawn at the all-Asia scale.[8]

Map 15.1 reveals a multifaceted picture of human settlements across Asia, ranging from desert areas to some of the densest population concentrations in the world. Three large high-density macro-regions emerge across Asia. The first block is located in Western Asia and includes in particular Turkey and Western Iran, as well as the Caucasus, the Mediterranean coast and the former Mesopotamia. It obviously corresponds to a northern extension of the Fertile Crescent associated with the Neolithic Revolution, towards the Anatolian Plateau and the Turkish littorals. The second block encompasses the entire Indian subcontinent, enclosed by the Baluchistan desert to the west, the Himalayas to the north, mountainous forested areas to the east, and the Indian Ocean to the south. The third major block is made of East China (roughly Imperial China at the time of the Han Dynasty), broadened to Korea and Japan. In comparison to these three macro-regions, the remaining territories of South-Eastern Asia, Central Asia and the Arabian Peninsula present a far more fragmented picture, with several isolated population concentrations surrounded by sparsely inhabited tracts. Incidentally, these three macro demographic regions correspond to what are perceived as the world's major cradles of civilization, with distinct linguistic, ethnic and religious features that clearly delineate population groups up to today.

A closer geographical examination leads to the identification of more distinct and homogeneous areas, sharing typical demographic features. We will use high and low density to single out some of the most prominent regions, in terms of land area and population concentration. If we start our review with the most populated areas, two compact regions distinctly emerge with density levels above 500 or even 1,000 persons per sq. km: the Ganges Plains in India and Bangladesh, and the Central Plains (Zhongyuan) along the Yellow River (Huang He) in East China. These two lowland areas enjoy, at different periods of the year, both annual monsoon rains and runoff from mountains located in a different climatic region (the Tibetan Plateau). The former area is the larger and more populated of the two, with more than 500 million inhabitants living in this basin. It includes the world's most important deltaic region, in which the Ganges joins the Brahmaputra before flowing into the Indian Ocean. Geographically, it is part of the Indo-Gangetic Plains that also encompasses the Indus valley in Pakistan and the Punjab, where density is also often above 1,000 inhabitants per sq. km. By comparison, the Yellow River Plain and especially its densest lower reaches centred on Henan are of somewhat smaller size, but the entire basin supports no less than 400 million people. Geographically speaking, however, the Yellow River basin tends to blend with the lower Yangtze region. In fact, the Yellow River used to flow southward until the nineteenth century and the limits of its alluvial basin are blurred. These areas in China and India constitute a unique profile of massive concentrations of rural population not found anywhere else in world. China's case is even more striking, as 91 per cent of the population lives east of the Heihe-Tengchong line (or the Hu line), in a group of provinces that includes the Northern plains and South-East China.[9]

Seven other regions with high population densities appear on our map, starting with Java in Indonesia where local human density is consistently above 500 inhabitants per sq. km, with higher figures observed in the western and central parts of the island. Compared to Java's 133 million inhabitants, the next population concentration in Asia in the Sichuan basin, covering most parts of the current provinces of Sichuan and Chongqing along the Yangtze River (Chang Jiang) and its tributaries, is hardly less populated with almost 110 million inhabitants. The Sichuan region stands out as a somewhat unique example of a remarkable population concentration located far away from a sea coast (Shanghai is 2,500 km downstream from Chongqing), set against the sparsely populated Tibetan Plateau that lies to the west and from where the Yangtze pours down. In fact, another high-density area in China lies further downstream, centred on Wuhan in Hubei province and extending towards Nanjing, Shanghai and the coast. Three additional, narrower regions with exceptional human density are also distinguishable on our map. The first is the Red River (Song Hong) Delta region in north Vietnam that represents the cradle of Vietnamese civilization. While the region includes the cities of Hanoi and Haiphong, it is, however, a mostly rural area with a long agricultural rice-growing tradition. In several of its constituting provinces, population density in the Red River Delta exceeds 1,000 persons per sq. km. The second region is the state of Kerala in southwestern India, whose average population density (860 inhabitants per sq. km) is nearly three times higher than in the rest of the country and exceeds 1,500 in some coastal districts. The Philippines and Japan constitute the last high-density zones, with national averages above 300 inhabitants per sq. km and limited variation across administrative regions.

The demographic concentration along the major river basins represents the first basic principle of the population distribution across Asia.[10] We have stressed the role of the Indus, Ganges, Brahmaputra, Yellow River, Yangtze and their tributaries in Asia's population geography. This logic is also replicated at a smaller scale and we easily identify smaller population concentrations on the map: along the Tigris and Euphrates in the Middle East; along the Narmada, Kaveri, Godavari and Krishna in Peninsular India; along the Irrawaddy in Myanmar; and along the Chao Phraya and Mekong in continental South-Eastern Asia. The close resemblance between the maps of population density and local hydrography is no coincidence. The availability of permanent water provided by these major waterways is the key to irrigation and cereal cultivation, and is especially essential for growing rice. Along with appropriate terrain and climatic conditions, permanent access to water makes multiple cropping possible, with both demand for intensive labour and exceptionally high yield per hectare, compared to rain-fed and other agricultural systems.[11] These rich agricultural regions have long been able to sustain high population densities, including ancient commercial towns and royal cities.

The urban structure is, however, not the mere outgrowth of population concentrations across Asia.[12] While many historical capitals such as Baghdad, Hanoi, Delhi, Nanjing, Beijing and Xi'an are indeed located in Asia's main water basins, the urban system is far more diverse, and many metropolises have emerged over the last two centuries. As a matter of fact, the distribution of cities on our map points to a second guiding principle of population settlement in Asia along the sea coast. Coastal cities include some of Asia's large metropolises, from Istanbul, Karachi and Mumbai to Shanghai, Tianjin and Tokyo. Of the ten largest urban agglomerations in Asia, only two (Delhi and Beijing) are located away from the sea. High density in littoral areas proceeds partly from favourable climatic conditions such as higher rainfall and fertile delta zones, but the distinct role of urbanization in the process of population concentration is also significant. New port cities have appeared over the last two hundred years under the influence of colonial powers, and the development of many coastal metropolises of today, such as Ho Chi Minh City, Karachi, Mumbai, Kolkata and Shanghai, started during the late nineteenth century. Yet the extraordinary expansion of coastal cities over the last 30 years is, of course, linked to Asia's rapid economic development and its export-oriented growth. Many of these Asian conurbations are located in low-elevation areas and are therefore especially prone to the future effects of climate change. In fact, Asia contains eight of the ten largest fragile countries in terms of population, with about half of the population of Vietnam and Bangladesh residing in vulnerable coastal areas. According to one count, in 2000, 466 million people lived in these exposed low-elevation coastal zones.[13] The overall health risks of climate change for Asian cities, however, go beyond rising seas and represent a major challenge for future urban concentration (Kovats and Akhtar 2008).

A third type of high-density area is a typical Asian settlement pattern described as *desakota*, a word derived from Indonesian meaning 'countryside-town' and used by geographer Terry McGee to describe mixed rural–urban regions.[14] *Desakota* areas are rural areas characterized primarily by high human density (above 200 people per sq. km), but also by close access to cities and intense population mobility.[15] Agriculture remains a significant part of the local economy, but its role has gradually faded due to the development of industries and services. *Desakota* resist a simple classification as rural or as urban because of their composite nature. These settlements are not really towns nor part of the urban sprawl in terms of their morphology and historical development, nor can they be confused with the countryside from an economic and demographic viewpoint. The concept of *desakota* therefore captures a typically Asian settlement pattern, lying in-between villages and towns. In most cases, these areas were dominated by rice cultivation, but today they are characterized by mixed land use combining agriculture, industry, commerce and residential areas, and by a parallel blend of diversified activities such as trade, transport and industry, apart from residual agriculture. Intense demographic mobility and trade intimately link *desakota* areas to urban centres.

While this notion was initially developed to describe situations in Indonesian Java, it was found applicable to many other high-density areas in Asia that were neither primarily urban nor agricultural. Examples of *desakota* regions abound in China, India, Pakistan and the Philippines. Almost the entire state of Kerala in India (barring mountainous areas) can fall in this category; its few cities and towns are immersed into a continuous 'rural' space with few large village centres, but a continuous high-density settlement with more than 500 inhabitants per sq. km. Agriculture (rice and coconut) has not disappeared, but represents only a secondary source of employment and income to the local population. Kerala is a rather singular area for such an exceptional population density since it is not associated with any major river basin. This is true also for the island of Java and other *desakota* areas in China, where local handicraft, industry and more recently, services, have long supplanted the economic role of agriculture in sustaining high population densities. Provinces around Shanghai, from Jiangsu to Zhejiang, provide further illustrations of former rich agricultural regions that have witnessed a continuous change in land use and decrease in cultivated areas under the influence of gradual industrialization. While still lacking a formal urban morphology, these rural areas have acquired most social and economic characteristics of urban areas, such as access to modern sanitation and communication, and are characterized by density levels usually higher than 500 people per sq. km.

In contrast, our map of population densities also points to the presence of large areas which appear almost uninhabited. As elsewhere, these areas tend to be landlocked and located far away from the coastline. In Asia, in spite of high-density pockets such as Sichuan in China or the smaller Fergana Valley in Central Asia, population tends to decrease with increasing distance from the sea coast. This rule is even stronger when extended to distance from the coastline and from all waterways. The two largest blocks of barren lands, with densities that are on average below one inhabitant per sq. km, are found in Central and Eastern Asia. The first one covers more than half of Kazakhstan and extends to neighbouring Uzbekistan and Kyrgyzstan. The second block is even larger, and centres on the Taklimakan desert (Tarim basin) in West China and on the Gobi desert along the China-Mongolia border. The Taklimakan is a 1,000 km long depression, with barely any vegetation and very few oases. This inhospitable dry terrain stretches to the south towards the Tibetan Plateau and the Himalayas. While it is a sparsely populated mountainous area, it represents Asia's water tower, providing water to the Brahmaputra, Indus, Ganges, Mekong, Yangtze and Yellow Rivers, thus irrigating Southern, Eastern and South-Eastern Asia. The Gobi desert to the north is even longer (1,600 km), and much larger than the Taklimakan desert. It is also reported to be expanding continuously through a rapid process of desertification, linked to the reduction of grasslands on its edges, at a rate of about 2,000 sq. km per year in China (Yang et al. 2005). Taken together, the Gobi and Taklimakan deserts occupy more than 1.5 million sq. km. Other low-density areas found in the Arabian Peninsula, in Iran and in Indonesia, are rather small in comparison. Even smaller population concentrations are also visible in more arid parts of Central and Eastern Asia, such as along the Syr Darya River in Uzbekistan and along the historical northern Silk Road in China. The lack of access to water and arable land has given rise to a very uneven settlement pattern, in which towns and cities predominate and villages are few and far between. Urban settlements can become the focal points for demographic growth, as the large cities of Urumqi in China and Tashkent in Uzbekistan illustrate.

Deserts are, however, never completely empty and Asian deserts are no exception to the rule. Western China is a good example. Even if densities are very low away from cities and agricultural areas, traces of settlements dating back to the Neolithic period are found across Xinjiang and adjacent provinces in West China. Permanent human settlements and villages have tended to centre on oases, and to rely on elaborate water management systems (*karez*). Turpan in Xinjiang provides a typical example of such a settlement, with hundreds of wells, tunnels and canals, which have long sustained large populations. In addition, population-based maps do not accurately reflect the presence of nomadic groups, and this is especially the case for the Kazakh steppes and Mongolia. In the latter country, pastoralism has long been a dominant force and is based on the constant mobility of a large part of the population, making it as much an economic base as a way of life (Barfield 2011). Nomads occupy extensive territories of seasonal steppes and mountain pastures, through complex migratory movements with their herds that can be vertical (up and down the mountains) as well as horizontal (across the steppes). The Deccan Plateau in India, a vast semi-arid region where agriculture is mostly rain-fed, provides another illustration of the complexity of settlement patterns, since it is characterized by relatively high population densities and the presence of cities with millions of people such as Hyderabad and Nagpur.

In some countries like Turkey, India and the Philippines, populations are on the whole more uniformly distributed than in the rest of Asia where extreme density differentials often prevail. This spatial demographic heterogeneity is illustrated by the contrast between empty West China and the high density levels observed in East China. These imbalances have fuelled specific migration streams from the densest rural areas towards less populated regions. An extreme case is provided by the oil-producing countries of the Middle East, which have attracted millions of temporary migrants to expand their workforces. While the departure to the Gulf region of migrants from Pakistan, India and the Philippines has had a tremendous impact on the local economies of their regions of origin, it has proved too modest to affect the overall demographic growth in these countries, especially as it is based on short-term moves.

In contrast, the permanent resettlement of internal migrants within given countries has had a more visible demographic impact.[16] It has boosted the growth in some peripheral frontier areas in West China, Malaysia, Thailand, Central Vietnam and some Indonesian islands. Contrary to the effects of urbanization, these internal migrations have mostly been rural-rural and have been linked to land development or reclamation. Many governments across Asia have supported voluntary colonization programmes as a solution to rural saturation.[17] The Indonesian transmigration project is probably the best-known example and was directed towards less populated islands such as Sumatra, Kalimantan, Sulawesi and Papua, with Java providing most out-migrants. These programmes were based on selective incentives for relocation, such as support during migration and access to land and employment, but there was also a significant spontaneous component to these internal migrations fuelled by new economic opportunities. An additional illustration stems from westward migrations observed within China since the twentieth century, across the Hu line mentioned earlier. This has resulted in a more rapid demographic progression in West China (Yue et al. 2003). These policies may not have had a visible impact on the areas of origin such as Java or the alluvial plains of China and Vietnam, but they have often displaced the population composition of the target, that were as a rule less populated and occupied by ethnic and religious minorities with limited political power. Indigenous populations of these destination regions often find themselves now in a minority in urban areas and at times in their entire ancestral regions, a situation that carries significant political risks as recent cases of tension and civil unrest in China attest. The demographic absorption capacity of the last rural frontiers in Asia appears nowadays limited, compared to the lure of more urbanized, densely populated regions.

The distribution of population across Asia

The mapping of population densities across Asia suggests extreme variations between uninhabited steppic regions and major world conurbations. Excluding countries with the smallest territories, we find indeed in Asia, the world's lowest density in Mongolia and the highest in Bangladesh. However, to examine more formally the geographical dispersal and concentration of Asia's inhabitants across its extent, we have used a Lorenz curve to compare the spatial and demographic distributions. In the graph shown below, the areas of countries and subcountry units are arranged by cumulative area on the x-axis, while cumulative population itself is represented on the y-axis. The curvature of the function provides a graphical representation of the inequality in population distribution within Asia and reflects the degree of spatial concentration. Thus, if Asian populations were equally spread from Turkey to Japan, the Lorenz curve would be close to a straight equality line. The difference between the observed Lorenz curve and the equity line is in fact proportional to the Gini coefficient.

The computation has been done at country level, based on 2010 population estimates from the United Nations. Yet, in the case of Asia, this procedure based on country totals is distorted by the fact that two single units, China and India, account for more than 61 per cent of Asia's total. As noted earlier, each of these two countries has a total population larger than that of any other continent. In addition, these countries are at the same time characterized by high levels of subregional heterogeneity in density, with regional densities ranging from less than 20 inhabitants per sq. km in Qinghai (China) and in Arunachal Pradesh (India), to more than 750 in Jiangsu (China) and in Bihar (India). We have, therefore, disaggregated Asia's three most populated countries into subregional units. We have used here China's provinces, India's states and Indonesia's provinces in our computations, now based on a total of 48 countries and 99 subregions, instead of the 51 countries and territories for which we have statistics. The subregional partition was not necessary for countries such as Japan and Bangladesh where density variations are less pronounced and populations smaller. We could not disaggregate the figures for Pakistan – whose inhabitants tend to concentrate along the Indus River and are rather scarce in desert and mountainous regions – for lack of recent regional census figures.

The resulting graph (Figure 15.2) summarizes the extremely skewed population distribution in Asia. The first empty quarter of Asia – which includes in particular Mongolia, Kazakhstan, Tibet and Indonesia's Papuan provinces – accounts for no more than 1 per cent of its population.[18] This curve further demonstrates that half of the continent's surface – including, in addition to these, large territories such as Iran and Saudi Arabia in the near-East, China's Xinjiang, Gansu and Inner Mongolia provinces in Eastern Asia, and most northern Indonesian islands in South-Eastern Asia – shelters a mere 6 per cent of the population, amounting to less than 14 million inhabitants (less than Delhi's population). It takes, in fact, 87 per cent of Asia's less populated regions to reach half of Asia's population, and the remaining 13 per cent of its surface carries the second half.

The remarkable demographic concentration in high density areas is also visible on the Lorenz curve, since the last quarter of the population inhabits about 4 per cent of the continent's surface. This quarter includes as expected, all metropolitan areas in our dataset from Singapore to Beijing municipality. It includes for instance, Jakarta province, an Indonesia metropolitan region of 9.6 million inhabitants squeezed on 664 sq. km, which is part of a larger Jabodetabek conurbation of 28 million people extending to Banten and West Java provinces. Population density in Jakarta nears 15,000 inhabitants per sq. km. Yet the most populated quarter of Asia's population also comprises a significant number of still predominantly rural regions such as the entire country of Bangladesh, India's Uttar Pradesh state, Indonesia's Javanese provinces and China's Shandong province.

The Lorenz curves in Figure 15.2 show that population distributions in Asia are far more spatially skewed than in the rest of the world.[19] While Europe (without Russia) emerges as the most evenly populated continent due to the absence of semi-arid, steppic and densely-forested areas, Africa and the Americas also appear to have less skewed population distributions than Asia, in spite of the vast and largely uninhabited parts found in the Sahel, North Canada and inland Brazil. Half of the continental surface accounts for 23 per cent of Europe's population, 20 per cent of America's and 15 per cent of Africa's, as against a mere 6 per cent of Asia's population total. In other words, Asia is characterized by the most extreme forms of population distributions found in the world.

Christophe Z. Guilmoto & Sébastien Oliveau

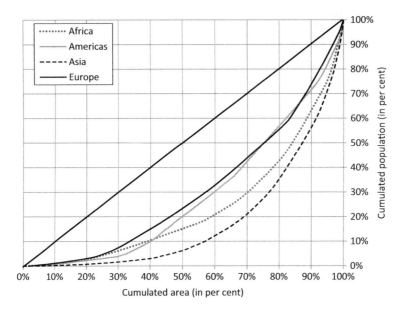

Figure 15.2 Lorenz Curve of population concentration in four different continents, 2010
Sources: United Nations (2013); Provincial figures are from the censuses of China (2010), India (2011) and Indonesia (2010).

These findings raise new questions for future research. One relates to the long-term evolution of this spatial distribution, for which we have limited evidence in view of the almost complete absence of disaggregated demographic estimates before the beginning of the twentieth century. Over the last decades, there has been a complex interplay between higher natural growth in inland regions that are both less developed and less densely inhabited, and migration towards more urbanized growth poles often located closer to coastal areas. It remains difficult to predict how these contradictory trends will evolve once fertility has reached low levels, i.e. when spatial mobility becomes a far more decisive factor of demographic growth than the natural increase.[20] A further question relates to the linkages between economic growth and population concentration (World Bank 2009). Agricultural expansion tends to deconcentrate population by directing migrants towards less densely populated pioneer areas. The process is still at work in some Indonesian islands east and north of Java, and in large swathes of West China. Yet, population density has also been associated with Asia's rapid economic growth during the last three decades, especially along the coast which happens to be ecologically most vulnerable, while sparsely populated inland regions have not developed at the same pace (Bloom et al. 1999).

Conclusion

This chapter has reviewed the spatial distribution of Asia's population at its demographic apex – when the share of Asia in the world peaked at 61 per cent at the turn of the twenty-first century. This dominance is both a product of its dense settlement patterns inherited from the past and of its record population growth during the twentieth century, to which China and India have contributed to a considerable extent. Owing in large part to an average population density five times higher than in other world regions, with high growth rates over the past six decades, Asia is by far the most populated continent with its 4.2 billion inhabitants in 2010, and it will remain so even as it enters an era of irreversible decline over the current century.

Closer examination of the population distribution within Asia and within its countries has, however, demonstrated the substantial uneven distributions in population across regions. These variations follow some of the basic physiographic principles of population geography: densities are often highest along the coastline and rivers, and diminish with altitude. Interestingly, no simple climatic principle emerges linking population distribution with rainfall or average temperature, except for the avoidance of the most arid climate observed in landlocked regions. At the same time, desert areas have progressed and central Asia now represents the greatest concentration of dryland degradation in the world due to erosion, physical deterioration, and decrease in vegetation cover (Lepers et al. 2005). This mechanism is illustrated by the slow colonization of West China by Han settlers and the encroachment on grasslands (McNeill 2006). Elsewhere in Asia, dense forests that used to check the progression of human settlements – as illustrated by the population distribution of South-Eastern Asia – have shrunk rapidly during the last century (Basnyat 2009). The process of deforestation started earlier in China, but has been especially dramatic in South-Eastern Asia over the last 60 years and is linked closely to the advance of modern agriculture. In fact, large-scale deforestation is also associated with a rapid increase in cropped areas through most of South-Eastern Asia.

The concentration of population along the coastline – which current modes of export-oriented development are only reinforcing – is a well-known source of environmental risk in many Asian countries such as Japan, India and Vietnam.[21] Unequal development is now the main driver of population redistribution, and agricultural systems are therefore bound to play a lesser role in determining future demographic trends (Huang and Bocchi 2009). Economic density (output per sq. km), which tends to attract migration, has been shifting increasingly towards urban and peri-urban areas over the recent decades.

At a higher scale, variations in population both across and within Asian countries are a product of the past, and point to the cradle of major Asian civilizations. These formidable population concentrations have been made historically possible by the combination of extremely rich agricultural systems and sophisticated water management technologies that have sustained rural population densities higher than in Europe, with the additional contribution of monsoon rains in most Asian countries. The rapid population increase during the previous century has only accentuated Asia's demographic dominance, and within it, the weight of China and India that represent more than 35 per cent of the world's population. Population redistribution within Asia has been directed mostly towards urban areas, and its present moderate level of urbanization suggests that this process of rural–urban migration, along with more migration between towns and cities, will continue unabated during the current century. This will lead to a faster decline of population growth in the countryside, accompanied by population stabilization in most parts of rural Asia.

Notes

1 Asia encompasses here, Turkey (including the Eastern Thrace), the Middle East (excluding Egypt) and the South Caucasus, but it does not include the Asian part of Russia (Siberia and the Far East). As a result, we have left out from our purview, the Siberian and Far Eastern districts of Russia located east of the Ural mountain range. This huge territory spread over 13 million sq. km had a relatively modest population of about 26 million in 2010.
2 Unless otherwise stated, all demographic parameters and estimates underlying this chapter derive from the 2013 United Nations population estimates for 1950–2010 (United Nations 2013). Population forecasts up to 2100 are based on the medium variant projections from the same source. Subregional figures quoted for individual countries are however taken from the latest national census reports.

3 With the exception of the Ottoman census of 1831, the first modern censuses in Asia date from the second half of the nineteenth century for the British colonies (India, Pakistan, Bangladesh, Myanmar, Sri Lanka and Malaysia). During the first half of the twentieth century, census operations were introduced in Indonesia, Japan and Thailand, but countries such as China, the Philippines, Iran and Vietnam had to wait until after World War II.
4 Population estimates from the HYDE database are described in particular in Goldewijk et al. (2010, 2011). Others sources can be found in Durand (1977) and Maddison (2007). See also Livi-Bacci (2012).
5 On Asia's population growth, see notably James (2011), East-West Center (2002), and Guilmoto and Jones (2016).
6 Examples of provinces with significant density disparities include Sichuan and Shanxi provinces in China, Rajasthan state in India, Sulawesi and Kalimantan provinces of Indonesia, provinces of central Vietnam, as well as Punjab and Sind provinces of Pakistan. In these subnational entities, extremely densely populated rural areas coexist with forested, mountainous or desert terrains devoid of any significant population settlements. It is, however, beyond the scope of this chapter to measure the fractal complexity of population density in Asia.
7 GPW data come from CIESIN/Columbia University/CIAT (2005). See also Balk et al. (2005) for more detail. Other sources of disaggregated population mapping include the LandScan dataset of 'ambient population' (Dobson et al. 2000) and the HYDE estimates (Goldewijk et al. 2010).
8 Night-time satellite imagery provides an alternative source for identifying conurbations, but this procedure may generate additional difficulties of interpretation (Sutton et al. 2001).
9 This is the so-called Hu line – running from Heilongjang to Yunnan provinces – imagined in 1935 by geographer Hu Huanyong. Figures quoted here are from Yue et al. (2003).
10 On the case of South-Eastern Asia, see Hirschman and Bonaparte (2012).
11 Rain-fed agriculture is most vulnerable, as it is dependent on the irregular monsoon precipitations in Asia. See Wang (2006).
12 On urban distribution, see notably McGranahan et al. (2007), Bulkeley (2013) and UN-Habitat (2008).
13 These figures are based on the rather high threshold of 10 metres. See McGranahan et al. (2007).
14 McGee (1991). See also DST (2008) for a more recent perspective. See also World Bank (2009) for a detailed description of settlement patterns and density.
15 A more comprehensive definition of urban agglomerations combines density (above 150 per sq. km), population totals and connectivity (see Nallari et al. 2012).
16 On internal migration in Asia, see for instance Deshingkar (2006) and Fan (2008). See Hugo (2005) on international migrations.
17 Forced displacement constitutes a distinct case of population redistribution. Asia has a record number of refugees and internally displaced persons. Major dams have also led to large numbers of relocations.
18 For a comparison with the spatial distribution of the global human population, see Small and Cohen (2004).
19 Australia also presents an extremely skewed population distribution, but it is not considered here because of its limited population (24 million in 2015).
20 This situation is already illustrated by the case of China's major metropolises. In Beijing and Shanghai, the natural increase is already negative owing to ultra-low fertility levels, but the massive influx of migrants led to population growth greater than 40 per cent during the previous decade.
21 Population growth is, however, only one in a long list of factors associated with environmental degradation in Asia. See AASA (2011).

References

Association of Academies of Sciences in Asia (AASA) (2011) *Towards a Sustainable Asia: Green Transition and Innovation*. Heidelberg, Dordrecht, London, New York and Beijing: Springer and Science Press.
Balk, D. et al. (2005) 'The distribution of people and the dimension of place: methodologies to improve the global estimation of urban extents'. In *International Society for Photogrammetry and Remote Sensing, Proceedings of the Urban Remote Sensing Conference*. Pp. 14–16.
Balk, D. et al. (2009) 'Mapping urban settlements and the risks of climate change in Africa, Asia and South America'. In J. M. Guzmán et al. (eds.) *Population Dynamics and Climate Change*. New York: UNFPA-IIED. Pp. 80–103.
Barfield, T. (2011) 'Nomadic pastoralism in Mongolia and beyond'. In P. Sabloff (eds.) *Mapping Mongolia: Situating Mongolia in the World from Geologic Time to the Present*. Philadelphia: Penn Museum Press. Pp. 104–124.

Basnyat, B. (2009) *Impacts of Demographic Changes on Forests and Forestry in Asia and the Pacific*. Working Paper No. APFSOS II/WP/2009/08. Bangkok: FAO.

Bloom, D. E., D. Canning and P. N. Malaney (1999) *Demographic Change and Economic Growth in Asia*. CID Working Paper No. 15. Cambridge, MA: Harvard University.

Bulkeley, H. (2013) *Cities and Climate Change*. London: Routledge.

Center for International Earth Science Information Network (CIESIN)/Columbia University and Centro Internacional de Agricultura Tropical (CIAT) (2005) *Gridded Population of the World, Version 3 (GPWv3): Population Density Grid, Future Estimates*. Palisades, NY: NASA Socioeconomic Data and Applications Center (SEDAC).

Census of China (2010) Available from: www.stats.gov.cn/tjsj/pcsj/rkpc/6rp/indexce.htm.

Census of India (2011) Available from: www.censusindia.gov.in/2011-Common/CensusData2011.html.

Census of Indonesia (2010) Available from: http://sp2010.bps.go.id/.

Deshingkar, P. (2006) 'Internal migration, poverty and development in Asia: including the excluded'. *IDS Bulletin*, 37: 88–100.

Dobson, J. E. et al. (2000) 'LandScan: a global population database for estimating populations at risk'. *Photogrammetric engineering and remote sensing*, 66(7): 849–857.

DST (2008) *Re-imagining the Rural-Urban Continuum*. Kathmandu, Nepal: Institute for Social and Environmental Transition.

Durand, J. D. (1977) 'Historical estimates of world population: an evaluation'. *Population and Development Review*, 3(3): 253–296.

East-West Center (2002) *The Future of Population in Asia*. Honolulu: East-West Center.

Fan, C. C. (2008) *China on the Move: Migration, the State and the Household*. Oxon: Routledge.

Goldewijk, K. K. (2005) 'Three centuries of global population growth: a spatial referenced population (density) database for 1700–2000'. *Population and Environment*, 26(4): 343–367.

Goldewijk, K. K., A. Beusen and P. Janssen (2010) 'Long-term dynamic modeling of global population and built-up area in a spatially explicit way: HYDE 3.1'. *The Holocene*, 20(4): 565–573.

Goldewijk, K. K. and N. Ramankutty (2004) 'Land cover change over the last three centuries due to human activities: the availability of new global data sets'. *GeoJournal*, 61(4): 335–344.

Goldewijk, K. K. et al. (2011) 'The HYDE 3.1 spatially explicit database of human-induced global land-use change over the past 12,000 years'. *Global Ecology and Biogeography*, 20(1): 73–86.

Guilmoto, C. Z. and G. W. Jones (eds.) (2016) *Contemporary Demographic Transformations in China, India and Indonesia*. Dordrecht: Springer.

Hazell, P. B. R. (2009) *The Asian Green Revolution*. IFPRI Discussion Paper 911.

Hirschman, C. and S. Bonaparte (2012) 'Population and society in Southeast Asia'. In L. Williams and P. Guest (eds.) *Demography of Southeast Asia*. Southeast Asia Program. Ithaca: Cornell University. Pp. 5–41.

Huang, Y. and A. M. Bocchi (eds.) (2009) *Reshaping Economic Geography in East Asia*. Washington, DC: World Bank.

Hugo, G. (2005) *Migration in the Asia-Pacific Region*. A paper prepared for the Policy Analysis and Research Programme of the Global Commission on International Migration.

James, K. S. (2011) 'India's demographic change: opportunities and challenges'. *Science*, 333(6042): 576–580.

Kovats, S. and R. Akhtar (2008) 'Climate, climate change and human health in Asian cities'. *Environment and Urbanization*, 20(1): 165–175.

Lepers, E. et al. (2005) 'A synthesis of information on rapid land-cover change for the period 1981–2000'. *BioScience*, 55(2): 115–124.

Livi-Bacci, M. (2012) *A Concise History of World Population*. Chichester: John Wiley & Sons.

Maddison, A. (2007) *The World Economy, Volume 1: A Millennial Perspective Volume*. Paris: OECD.

McGee, T. G. (1991) 'The emergence of desakota regions in Asia: expanding a hypothesis'. In N. S. Ginsburg, B. Koppel and T. G. McGee (eds.) *The Extended Metropolis: Settlement Transition in Asia*. Honolulu: University of Hawaii. Pp. 3–25.

McGranahan, G., D. Balk and B. Anderson (2007) 'The rising tide: assessing the risks of climate change and human settlements in low elevation coastal zones'. *Environment and Urbanization*, 19(1): 17–37.

McNeill, J. R. (2006) 'Population and the natural environment: trends and challenges'. *Population and Development Review*, 32(S1): 183–201.

Nallari, R., B. Griffith and S. Yusuf (2012) *Geography of Growth: Spatial Economics and Competitiveness*. Washington, DC: World Bank.

Small, C. and J. E. Cohen (2004) 'Continental physiography, climate and the global distribution of human population'. *Current Anthropology*, 45(2): 269–277.
Sutton, P., D. Roberts, C. Elvidge and K. Baugh (2001) 'Census from heaven: an estimate of the global human population using night-time satellite imagery'. *International Journal of Remote Sensing*, 22(16): 3061–3076.
UN-Habitat (2008) *State of the World's Cities 2008/9: Harmonious Cities*. London: Earthscan.
United Nations (2012) *World Urbanization Prospects: The 2011 Revision*. New York: Population Division, Department of Economic and Social Affairs.
United Nations (2013) *World Population Prospects: The 2012 Revision*. New York: Population Division, Department of Economic and Social Affairs.
Wang, B. (2006) *The Asian Monsoon*. Springer: Berlin/Heidelberg.
World Bank (2009) *World Development Report 2009: Reshaping Economic Geography*. Washington, DC: World Bank.
Yang, X. et al. (2005) 'Desertification assessment in China: an overview'. *Journal of Arid Environments*, 63(2): 517–531.
Yue, T. X. et al. (2003) 'Numerical simulation of population distribution in China'. *Population and Environment*, 25(2): 141–163.

16
The urbanization of low- and middle-income Asia

Mark R. Montgomery and Deborah Balk

Across the famously diverse regions of Asia, all low- and middle-income countries have at least one fundamental experience in common: their populations are growing steadily more urban. Some countries are already more than half urban; the remainder are on course to attain urban majorities in the next decade or two. The emergence of a remarkable number of large cities and mega-urban regions throughout Asia has justifiably seized the attention of journalists and scholars alike. Yet nearly half of Asia's urban dwellers reside in small and intermediate-size cities and towns, a demographic fact that too often goes unnoticed. These smaller places vary enormously in their economies, revenue bases and governance capacities. Some lie within the commuting zones of vibrant large cities, thereby participating in and drawing benefits from nearby economic powerhouses. Other small places stand apart, all but disconnected from the economic circuits that energize regional and national growth.

Accompanying the Asian urban transformation is a rising concern over the sustainability of cities, especially in view of the risks posed by extreme-event disasters and climate change. Such risks figure prominently in the newly crafted 2015–2030 Sustainable Development Goals (SDGs).[1] In marked contrast to the earlier Millennium Development Goals, the SDGs give specific and detailed consideration to the ways in which urban places and people are integral to national social and economic development. As the monitoring systems of the SDGs are put into place over the next few years, we can expect the implications of Asian urbanization for social and economic well-being to be documented in unprecedented detail.

To effectively monitor progress towards the SDGs, urban social, demographic and risk data will need to be integrated in detailed, spatially-specific frameworks for policy and planning (Balk and Montgomery 2015). Twenty years ago, the notion of uniting socioeconomic and environmental data in a detailed spatial frame might have been thought far-fetched. But over the past decade, remarkable advances have been achieved in the ability to measure and monitor the spatial features of urbanization at the level of individual cities, towns and even neighbourhoods. With the aid of newly accessible satellite imagery and comparatively easy-to-use derived products, researchers who were once confined to the study of national urban tabulations can now envision the local and regional manifestations of urban change in astonishing geographic detail.

The possibilities for visualizing the land-cover aspects of urbanization are bringing new life to long-standing theoretical conceptions, by which multiple two-way connections among cities, towns and rural villages are envisioned in terms of networks of settlements. Spatial data should also help to refine and clarify the status of smaller cities and towns, perhaps allowing policymakers to identify linkages in transport and communication that could better connect them to promising urban and rural markets. National urban totals and percentage shares will remain relevant to development policy for some time to come, but increasingly, we believe, policymakers will begin to think of interventions directed to specific network nodes, aiming to enhance the connections between settlements. This spatial vision of networks of cities has recently been made explicit in China's *National New-Type Urbanization Plan* of 2014, but it has long informed the transport and infrastructure policies of South Korea and other forward-thinking countries of the region (World Bank 2013).

In research circles, much well-justified enthusiasm has greeted the newly-available land-cover imagery and related spatial data. On occasion the excitement over the arrival of these new materials has tended to obscure one awkward fact: satellites do not (yet) count people, to say nothing of their social and economic characteristics (e.g. age, sex, education, poverty level, occupation and so on). Countries must still deploy the old-fashioned, conventional demographic tools – mainly population censuses and surveys – to get an accounting of these fundamentally important features.

If the analysis of census and survey data presents few new challenges for trained demographers, much still remains to be learned about how best to distribute these data to improve local and national governance. Some Asian countries (most notably, India) have made impressive strides in presenting disaggregated census data in their full spatial detail to local and state governments as well as researchers. Unfortunately, this practice is still far from being the norm across the region. Technical challenges and worries about confidentiality have not prevented countries in Latin America and elsewhere from collecting, analysing and publishing spatially specific socioeconomic information for the benefit of their policymakers, researchers and civil societies. It would be surprising and disappointing – a significant opportunity lost – if the national statistical offices of Asian countries did not join with these data and governance trend-setters.

Spatial perspectives may also help to bring the needs of rural populations into the picture. International bodies have often called for recognition and support of urban–rural linkages and advocated holistic planning in the name of inclusive development, but in the past these pleas tended to have a somewhat dutiful and *pro forma* quality. There is good reason to think that urban–rural connections will be treated more seriously in the SDGs than they have been previously. Many observers would now agree with Hugo (2003), who wrote with reference to the Asia-Pacific region:

> One of the most salient features of urban areas in the region [is] the complex and strong linkages they have with rural areas and the high degree of population mobility which occurs along those linkages. This movement has blurred the distinctions between urban and rural areas with many people working in urban areas while keeping their family in and spending long periods themselves in rural areas.

As the conversation around the SDGs moves from the articulation of broad goals to the refinement of specific targets and indicators, a consensus is emerging that MDG-like national-level scorecards of progress simply will not suffice: given the overarching aim of monitoring inclusive human development, *subnational* data-systems must be put in place that employ spatially disaggregated data to gauge where progress is occurring and where effort needs to be intensified.

This chapter focuses on the low-and middle-income countries of Asia where the bulk of future urban population growth will take place (Japan is therefore excluded). Drawing upon indicators collected by the United Nations Population Division, the first section reviews national levels and trends in urbanization in these countries, as well as changes in the number and expected growth of the larger agglomerations. The graphs and tables of this section are organized according to UN subregion to better communicate the extraordinary heterogeneity of developing Asia as a whole. Against this background the second section explores the experiences of selected countries in more detail, drawing out specific features that would not be evident in the UN's national-level indicators and illustrating the potential value of new settlement-specific and other spatially coded demographic data. Here we review innovations in Asian data-collection, research and urbanization policies. In the third section we combine demographic with spatial–environmental data to illustrate how the newly available empirical materials can provide estimates of the exposure of urban populations to the risks of natural disasters and climate change. The fourth section concludes.

The demography of urbanization and settlement growth

This section begins with an overview of urbanization as it has been estimated from national definitions by the United Nations Population Division, and then proceeds to examine what is known of the development of individual cities and agglomerations. We close the section with an account of recent ongoing research that aims to measure Asian urbanization on a scientifically comparable basis.

A long-standing difficulty in measuring urban population totals and percentages is the diversity of meanings given to the term *urban*, as evidenced in the variety of definitional criteria that are applied by national statistical offices in Asia and elsewhere.[2] The terms *city* and *urban settlement* are also variously defined. In a country such as India, the statistical authorities maintain what is, in effect, two sets of books: a given settlement can be classified as urban for the purposes of the national census, but this classification can differ from the settlement's formal political–legal–administrative status. In India, the formal designation determines which national-level development funds can be accessed by local and state governments; in some cases these governments perceive an advantage to having large, dense villages remain formally rural. Additional political–economic considerations can come into play in establishing the boundaries of cities. In China, for example, the boundaries of large 'cities' delineate what amounts to planning regions, and purposely include rural as well as urban-dwellers. This practice – however well-justified it may be – has the effect of inserting a wedge between counts of city and urban population.

An additional consideration has to do with the distinction between individual cities and towns and the spatially contiguous agglomerations of urban population composed of such individual settlements. Because of the emergence in developing Asia of a historically unprecedented number of megacities with over 10 million residents, as well as other enormous urban agglomerations, some care is needed in clarifying both the conceptual and measurement issues entailed in the notion of 'agglomeration'.

These concerns are, of course, not unique to Asia. Frustrated by the country-specific complexities of definition, demographers have long sought to measure urban and city populations on a scientifically comparable basis with consideration of only a few central criteria: population density thresholds; cut-off points having to do with the total populations of contiguous places each of which exceeds the density threshold; and increasingly, measures of *connection* such as commuting zones or the equivalent where data sources allow. As spatially-coded demographic data become more detailed and more plentiful, this long-sought goal of comparability has now come almost within reach. In the current enthusiasm for scientific standardization, however, formal jurisdictional boundaries are either being down-played or ignored in favour of more easily manipulated raster grid-cells of population. Yet jurisdictional boundaries remain important in delineating the spatial reach of local government authority and service delivery. For the foreseeable future, we would argue, scientifically standardized estimates should complement but not supplant the political–economic definitions of urban and city populations.

Urbanization trends: totals, percentages, growth rates

The evolution of total urban and rural populations from 1950 to 2000 is charted in Table 16.1, with near-term UN projections given for 2025 and more speculative forecasts for 2050. To keep the subregional variations in context, it bears mentioning that the population of Central Asia is and will evidently remain relatively small, paling by comparison with the enormous populations of the Eastern and Southern Asia subregions.

Figure 16.1 recasts the estimates in terms of the urban percentages of national population. As can be seen in this figure, Western Asia achieved its urban majorities long ago – this is no doubt due in part to the difficulties of sustaining any sizeable rural populations in what is a highly arid region. Southern Asia is forecast to be the last of the Asian subregions to cross the majority-urban threshold (an event predicted to occur only in the late 2040s). However, the estimates and trends for this region are much influenced by India, where public finance and related political-economy issues have had considerable influence on urban definitions. (Some researchers believe that Indian urban percentages are artificially low, as will be discussed.) The trends and forecasts for Eastern Asia will surely need monitoring as China proceeds with its *National New-Type Urbanization Plan* of 2014, an exercise being conducted on a scale so massive that it must be without historical precedent. As the outlines of this effort become clearer, urban forecasts for Eastern Asia will doubtless be undergoing substantial revision.

The sheer size of the governance challenge facing Asian national, provincial and municipal governments is suggested by Figure 16.2, which depicts the net additions to urban populations taking place in each five-year period since 1950. The net urban gains in Central Asia appear to have been almost nil over the last half-century with little change anticipated for the future, and there has been comparatively little change in Western Asia. The experiences of these small subregions stand in stark contrast to the additions to urban populations expected in Eastern Asia – estimated to peak at nearly 200 million per five-year period and then forecast to decline as 2050 is approached – and the substantial continuing additions expected to occur in the Southern and South-Eastern regions of developing Asia, which are predicted to pass 100 million per five-year period and continue with no slackening in sight.

A different picture of urban change is conveyed by estimates and forecasts of urban population growth rates. It is noteworthy that across all subregions of developing Asia, including Eastern, South-Eastern and Southern Asia where large absolute increases have been recorded and are expected to continue, urban population growth rates are generally on the decline (Figure 16.3). The UN foresees growth rates falling well below two per cent in all subregions, with zero urban growth rates expected by 2050 in Eastern Asia. Again, however, we would caution that all forecasts for Eastern Asia will need adjusting to align with China's evolving urbanization development strategy.

These urban growth rate declines are due to in part to the demographic fundamentals that either produce or at least systematically accompany urbanization. They owe much to the rapid fertility declines that began decades ago in Eastern and much of South-Eastern Asia, following closely on the heels of mortality decline, with the sequence repeated (if not quite as rapidly nor

Table 16.1 Total urban and rural population, low- and middle-income Asian countries, 1950–2050 by subregion

Subregion	Total Urban Population					Total Rural Population				
	1950	1975	2000	2025	2050	1950	1975	2000	2025	2050
Central Asia	5,715	16,367	22,870	31,345	46,416	11,785	20,603	32,177	42,807	39,736
Eastern Asia	73,580	189,732	518,197	1,018,365	1,126,146	502,906	780,909	840,713	520,206	349,495
South-Eastern Asia	26,065	74,040	199,681	370,922	507,726	141,921	244,617	324,727	325,227	279,810
Southern Asia	78,951	177,891	420,685	788,252	1,213,612	413,849	657,300	1,027,166	1,209,786	1,098,416
Western Asia	14,732	48,324	117,108	214,830	295,448	36,486	50,359	66,396	80,306	77,560

Source: United Nations (2014).

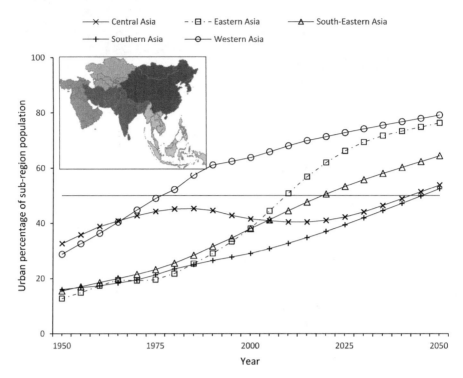

Figure 16.1 Urban percentage of subregional population, low- and middle-income Asian countries, 1950–2050
Source: United Nations (2014).

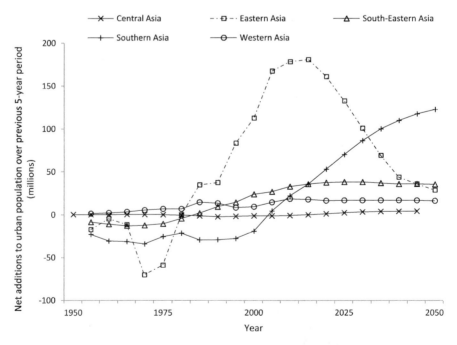

Figure 16.2 Urban population growth less rural growth in previous five years, by subregion of Asia, 1950–2050
Note: Calculated as $\Delta U(t) - \Delta R(t)$, with the 5-year change in the urban population of the subregion defined as $\Delta U(t) = U(t) - U(t-5)$ and similarly for $\Delta R(t)$, the rural population change.
Source: United Nations (2014).

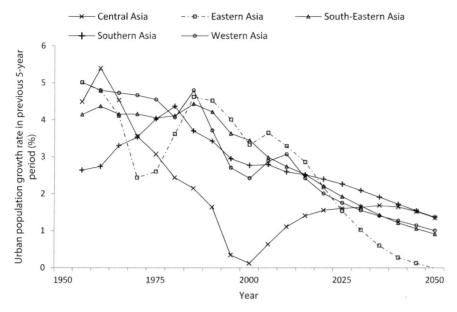

Figure 16.3 Urban population growth rates in previous five years, by subregion of Asia
Note: Percentage growth rate for time t − 5 to t calculated as r (t) = 100 · ln (U (t)/U (t − 5)) /5, with U (t) being the urban population of the subregion at time t.
Source: United Nations (2014).

with a comparable depth of decline) across the wider Asian region. A lengthy treatment of the interrelationships between urbanization and demographic rates can be found in the Panel on Urban Population Dynamics (PUPD 2003) volume, which identifies the quantity-quality trade-off between levels of fertility and children's schooling as a key mechanism in urban settings. Across Asia, fertility levels are generally much lower in cities and towns than in the countryside, and school enrolment percentages are markedly higher.[3] The urban demographic transformation is thus associated, over the long term, with lower rates of labour force growth (stemming, with a lag, from lower fertility) and higher levels of human capital per potential worker, both of these being associated with higher income per worker in economic models of GDP growth.

The PUPD (2003) also emphasizes a point that has generally escaped many commentators: the greater part of global urban population growth – roughly 60 per cent in most accounts – is due to the natural increase of urban populations, that is, to the excess of urban births over urban deaths, rather than to the combination of in-migration and reclassification. This surprising 60–40 split is partly produced by the nature of urban age structures, which have a notable 'bulge' in the prime reproductive ages, a bulge that comes from the combination of low fertility (which pinches in the base of the population pyramid) and urban in-migration between the ages of 15 and 30 in most countries. The UN's national assessments of the roles of natural increase versus migration/reclassification have been reconfirmed at the subnational level for India (Bhagat and Mohanty 2009). Giving a detailed breakdown of these contributions over the 1991–2001 period, they find that natural increase accounted for 57.6 per cent of urban growth overall, whereas net migration accounted for 20.8 per cent. In Gujarat the migration share reached 36 per cent – the highest share recorded among Indian states at the time.

However, in India and elsewhere in Asia, the share of natural increase in urban population growth is expected to decline as urban total fertility rates continue to fall. Indeed, China has long presented the largest exception to the '60–40' UN rule of thumb, owing to a unique combination of circumstances: its unusually low levels of fertility (especially urban fertility) achieved as early as the late 1970s; the institutional suppression of migration via the imposition of strict *hukou* controls until 1980; and the subsequent lifting and refashioning of these controls to allow massive rural-to-urban migration to fuel export-oriented growth.

Populations of cities and urban agglomerations

We confront difficult conceptual and measurement issues in distinguishing individual settlements and municipal jurisdictions, on the one hand, from urban agglomerations, on the other. On the conceptual front, it is important to recognize that urban residents and economic actors live and operate within multiple units or scales. An urban household lives in a neighbourhood, some of whose functions and public services may be delivered by a local government. Other services and functions, however, may be supplied by higher-tier governments whose responsibilities extend across multiple local jurisdictions. An individual urban-dweller's web of social, work, transport and civic networks may thus connect multiple localities and distinct settlements; so, too, might the economic networks by which an urban firm acquires its labour and inputs and supplies its outputs. Hence, when we say that an urban resident 'lives in' a megacity, this should not obscure the importance of the smaller units and jurisdictions in which that individual also simultaneously lives. The notion of 'agglomeration' is perhaps helpful in sketching the outer boundaries or envelope of individual connections, but the very local, small-scale connections can remain exceedingly important.

The settlement–agglomeration distinction also presents daunting empirical challenges. Ever since it began to monitor urbanization on a systematic worldwide basis in the late 1970s, the United Nations Population Division has sought to collect information on the populations of urban agglomerations, preferring this indicator to one based on the population residing within formal municipal or administrative boundaries (which it describes as *cities proper*). There is good theoretical justification for this stance, but its empirical implementation has proven to be quite difficult. The low- and middle-income countries supplying population data to the Population Division do not necessarily collect urban population counts in units of agglomerations; and even when agglomeration-level populations are reported, the encompassing boundaries are not. The UN has thus been in the awkward position of collecting data on the population of agglomerations whose spatial extents are, on the whole, simply unknown.

These long-standing data deficiencies make it especially difficult to interpret the UN estimates of urban population according to size class of settlement – for some countries and settlements, the 'size class' is determined by the population of the city proper; for others, it is the population of the agglomeration; for still others, the population unit goes unspecified; and for quite a number of countries, the meaning of size class has varied not only over time but also by within-country location. These ambiguities and imprecisions are of special concern for Asia, given the unusual prominence of large urban agglomerations in the region.

The Population Division begins to monitor a given city's population (or, where possible, that of an agglomeration) once that city has passed the 100,000 threshold (apart from capital cities, which are tracked whatever their size). No systematic effort is exerted to reconstruct the histories of urban places below 100,000 persons. Hence, the number of such places is not recorded in the UN's database. The total population of urban areas under 300,000 is estimated by the difference between the country's total urban population and the sum of the populations of all urban areas in the country that exceed 300,000 residents. (A separate accounting is possible for areas in the 100,000–300,000 range, but these calculations are not published in *World Urbanization Prospects*.)

The urbanization of Asia

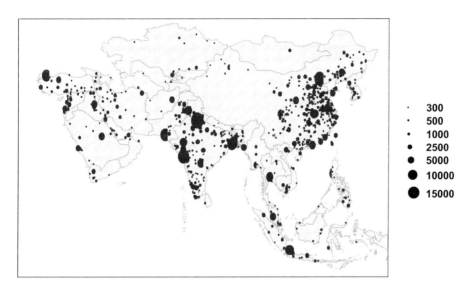

Map 16.1 Urban agglomerations of 300,000 population and above in developing Asia, in 2015. Size of circle indicates estimated population (in thousands)
Source: United Nations (2014).

Likewise, forecasts of total urban population by city size class depend on two distinct forecasting procedures: forecasts of total urban population rely on the UN's methods for projecting total national populations and the urban share of the total. For the larger places exceeding 300,000 in size, city-specific forecasts are prepared and then aggregated into size classes. Map 16.1 presents Asia showing urban agglomerations of at least 300,000 population. Table 16.2 lists the largest urban agglomerations in each Asian subregion.

Despite the common impression that the largest places dominate the urban scene in Asia, we find that in 2015 megacities were estimated to hold a mere 11.9 per cent of all urban residents. Small cities and towns below 300,000, by contrast, account for 41.4 per cent of the total, and the two smallest size classes combined for nearly half of all urban-dwellers in the region (47.6 per cent). Yet the megacities loom far more vividly than smaller cities and towns in the mind's eye and the research literature. Perhaps the mega-agglomerations are more important in development terms than their urban population shares would suggest, but the comparison of shares underscores the need to bring smaller cities and towns into the development conversation.

When set against this overall pattern, in which smaller urban places are numerically significant, a striking feature of the UN's near-term forecasts is the sharp anticipated decline in the percentages of urban dwellers living in such small places. Apart from South-Eastern Asia, where little in the way of trend is evident, substantial and not entirely plausible declines are forecast in the smaller-city shares over the period from 2000 to 2030. The direction and magnitude of this prediction is surprising given the tendency for large agglomerations to have slower rates of population growth, due to the lower fertility rates characteristic of large cities and the costs stemming from size and congestion that tend to discourage in-migration. These counter-balancing forces have been well-documented by the UN and incorporated in its city growth forecasts. Because the UN's (preferred) measurement unit is that of the urban agglomeration, part of this projected shift away from smaller places of residence must somehow come from the absorption

Table 16.2 Largest urban agglomerations in 2015, by subregion of developing Asia

Urban Agglomeration	Population (000s)	Urban Agglomeration	Population (000s)
Central Asia		**Southern Asia**	
Aktyubinsk	416	Tehran	8,432
Karaganda	496	Lahore	8,741
Namangan	521	Hyderabad	8,944
Shymkent	746	Chennai	9,890
Ashgabat	746	Bangalore	10,087
Astana	759	Kolkata	14,865
Dushanbe	822	Karachi	16,618
Bishkek	865	Dhaka	17,598
Almaty	1,523	Mumbai	21,043
Tashkent	2,251	Delhi	25,703
Eastern Asia		**Western Asia**	
Dongguan	7,435	Kuwait City	2,779
Chengdu	7,556	Sana'a	2,962
Wuhan	7,906	Izmir	3,040
Seoul	9,774	Aleppo	3,562
Shenzhen	10,749	Tel Aviv-Jaffa	3,608
Tianjin	11,210	Jiddah	4,076
Guangzhou	12,458	Ankara	4,750
Chongqing	13,332	Riyadh	6,370
Beijing	20,384	Baghdad	6,643
Shanghai	23,741	Istanbul	14,164
South-Eastern Asia			
Bandung	2,544		
Surabaya	2,853		
Hanoi	3,629		
Yangon	4,802		
Singapore	5,619		
Kuala Lumpur	6,837		
Ho Chi Minh City	7,298		
Bangkok	9,270		
Jakarta	10,323		
Manila	12,946		

Source: United Nations (2014).

of what were once relatively free-standing smaller cities and towns into larger agglomerations. Unfortunately, the UN has not offered much by way of analysis to elucidate the sources of these less-than-persuasive near-term forecasts.

More convincing evidence comes from careful, country-specific studies. Park et al. (2011) analyse the percentage of urban population living in cities of different sizes in Korea, showing steady increases in percentages living in cities of size 200,000 to 500,000, 500,000 to 1 million, and 1 million and above; there have been correspondingly steady declines in the percentages living in smaller cities and towns. Greater Jakarta has also been closely scrutinized, with Mamas and Komalasari (2008) providing a detailed analysis of its development (also see World Bank 2012). This massive agglomeration, often now termed 'Jabodetabek', comprises DKI Jakarta, the regencies (*kabupaten*) of Bogor, the municipality of Bogor (*kotamadya*), the

The urbanization of Asia

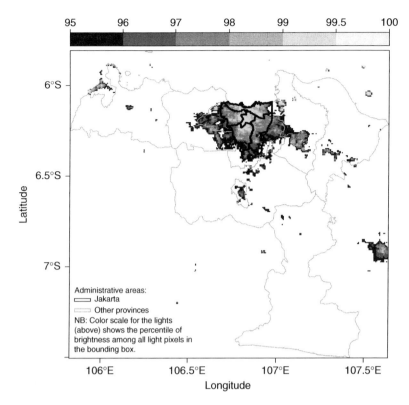

Map 16.2 Urbanized areas in the Greater Jakarta region, as indicated by VIIRS night-time lights
Source: Map produced by authors based on VIIRS night-time lights, see https://ncc.nesdis.noaa.gov/VIIRS/ and Indonesian Administrative Boundaries, www.gadm.org/.

municipality of Depok and the regencies of Tangerang and Bekasi. Map 16.2, which is based on night-time lights imagery for the region, indicates the variations in population concentration within Jabodetabek.[4] The UN population estimate for Jakarta in 2015 is 10.3 million persons. Yet even by 1990, according to Douglass and Jones (2008), the population of the mega-urban region of Jakarta had reached 13 million.[5] The difference with the UN count is mainly attributable to the units in which population is recorded: the UN figure refers only to Jakarta's 'core' administrative units, that is, the *city proper* in the UN classification. This example illustrates how much can be gained in understanding via access to spatially-coded census data – available to both Mamas and Komalasari (2008) and Douglass and Jones (2008) – or public-domain remote-sensing proxies for population, such as the night-lights depicted in Map 16.2.

The ongoing search for scientific comparability

Remarkable progress has been made over the past five years in assembling the data and testing methods to investigate the population of urban agglomerations on a comparable basis, relatively free of the variation in national definitions that we have mentioned. Several major international strands of work, each based on spatially detailed population data collected from national statistical offices, are buttressed by satellite and ancillary spatial data. Deuskar and Stewart (2016) describe the current status of these collaborative and intertwined projects, and discuss some preliminary results that, if confirmed, could substantially alter our understanding of urbanization in Asia.

The Global Human Settlements Layer (GHSL) relies on a remarkable archive of LANDSAT data covering the period from 1975 to the present. The research team has devised machine-learning methods to identify structures and built-up areas at resolutions as detailed as 30–300 square metres (Pesaresi et al. 2013). Working with the Gridded Population of the World (GPW) team at CIESIN, which gathers spatially detailed population counts from national statistical offices, the joint research group allocates the population data only to the grid cells that are estimated to be built-up (Freire et al. 2015). This approach is a modernization of the methods applied in the earlier Global Rural–Urban Mapping Project, which relied upon night-time lights rather than LANDSAT imagery to spatially allocate population. The WORLDPOP project also begins with spatially detailed population data from national statistical offices, but applies a different machine-learning algorithm to estimate population density grids incorporating a variety of additional spatial covariates, including information on roads, the locations of health facilities, land cover and – in new and ongoing work – estimates of structures from the GHSL project (Stevens et al. 2015). This approach distributes population in areas in which there is no satellite evidence of structures, and thus tends to spread population in a more diffuse fashion than the GHSL–CIESIN methods.

Meanwhile, a European Commission research team has devised analogous methods of defining urban agglomerations based on population density, size and commuting zones – data available for Europe and high-income countries more generally – and is examining the implications of less-ambitious approaches applicable in low-income countries that lack commuting-zone data. Each of these international research teams is focusing on definitions of clusters of urban settlement based on population density thresholds and a minimum size criterion for the total populations of contiguous areas that are at least as dense as the chosen thresholds. Work for Europe suggests that a density threshold of 1,500 persons per sq. km, when combined with size criteria of 50,000 residents, gives a meaningful portrait of large urban clusters in that region of the world; and densities of 300+ inhabitants and a total population of 5,000, appear to describe well Europe's smaller urban clusters. Outside Europe, however, the question of what density and size criteria to apply is the subject of ongoing intensive investigation. One preliminary finding appears to be sufficiently robust to deserve mention. Deuskar and Stewart observe:

> …South Asia is more urbanized and Latin America is less urbanized than figures based on national definitions indicate … This finding is consistent in our study using both sources of input data, as well as in Agglomeration Index analysis done by others previously (Uchida and Nelson 2010).
>
> *(Deuskar and Stewart 2016: 6, 8)*

For India in particular, Deuskar and Stewart note that 'India has a large number of small, dense settlements which would be counted [as urban] if we select a high density threshold but a low size threshold'.

Research suggesting understatement of urbanization in southern India has also been conducted by Denis and Marius-Gnanou (2011), who define Indian urban clusters in terms of contiguous built-up areas at a specified density of buildings and a total population size of at least 10,000 residents. Application of these definitions puts India's urban percentage at 37.5 per cent in 2001, a full ten points above the official estimate of 27.1 per cent that was derived from the 2001 census. Bhagat and Mohanty (2009: 8) point to Kerala, a southern Indian state, as an instructive example:

> The relatively low urbanization (26 per cent) in Kerala is an artefact of the rural–urban definition problem. Making the distinction more difficult in Kerala is the high density of population everywhere in the state (Visaria 1997) and the disinclination of the state government to grant municipal status to large villages.

The last point is drawn out by World Bank (2013: 25): '[L]ocal politicians may not want to be classified as urban, because, once designated a statutory town, the local government may lose preferential treatment in intergovernment transfers and public resources'.

In India, these challenges to measurement are well known if not yet satisfactorily resolved. The approach that the Indian statistical authorities have taken involves the designation of 'census towns' as urban settlements, not in the legal sense but for the narrower purposes of the country's decennial census.[6] The comparison of the southern state of Kerala to India as a whole in Figure 16.4 demonstrates the implications. Across India, data from the 2011 census put the urban percentage of the country at 35.1 per cent, with census towns accounting for only 4.2 percentage points of the total. In the state of Kerala, however, roughly 50.8 per cent of the population is urban, a total well above the all-India average, with census towns accounting for almost 29 percentage points of this total. Had the census towns of Kerala been ignored, only 21.9 per cent of the state's residents would have been counted as urban.

New and under-studied developments

This section describes several recent Asian developments in urban data-gathering, dissemination, methodology and policy. First, we describe how following the 2011 population census, Indian statistical authorities began to make freely available highly disaggregated population and

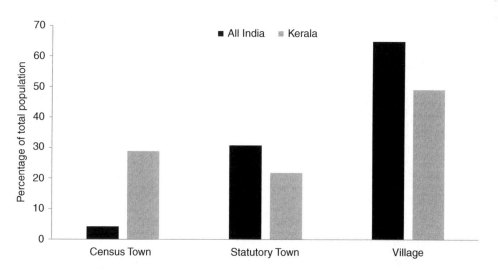

Figure 16.4 Percentages of India's population, and that of Kerala state, living in census towns, statutory towns and rural villages, according to the census of 2011
Source: Authors' calculations using data from www.censusindia.gov.in/2011census.

socioeconomic data at the level of individual settlements. This commitment to open-source information provision is still rare in Asia – nothing of the kind has been seen in China – but follows the lead of a number of countries in Latin America, which in the late 1990s began to put such detailed settlement data on the Internet. Second, we address the need to understand more fully the concept of urban connectedness, not only through internal migration but also through commuting, seasonal migration and new networks of communication. The discussion then turns from methods and data to innovations in policy. China is today engaged in a massive urban-focused social experiment of unparalleled ambition. Quantities of physical and human capital are being invested in the construction and inter-linkage of new urban settlements, the largest of which are to be situated within enormous planning regions that span the country, and China is taking steps to reform its *hukou* system to enable rural-to-urban migrants to participate as full first-class citizens in their urban homes.

Innovations in provision of urban socioeconomic data: the example of India

A continuing source of frustration to scholars of urbanization in the developing countries of Asia is the lack of demographic and social information compiled at the level of cities and towns (PUPD 2003). Although sample surveys may not allow credible statistical generalizations to be made for city units, the same cannot be said of the data collected in national censuses. The problem has been that these census data are rarely disaggregated and made available at the city level for the benefit of local governments and interested researchers. Within China, for example, access to census data is still tightly restricted to a small circle of selected researchers, with no general opening-up in sight.

India may be the single Asian exception to the general rule. Beginning with the results of the 1991 census, its national statistical office has prepared tabulations of a large set of census-collected variables at the individual settlement level, for places ranging in size from the tiniest of rural villages to towns and upward to the largest of India's municipalities. For some years the existence of these tabulations was known only to specialists, perhaps because the data were sequestered in CD-ROMS under the heading of 'primary census abstracts'. But as India's national statistical office has moved more aggressively to establish a presence on the Internet – a development that has proceeded rapidly since the 2011 census, and which has been strongly encouraged by India's transformative right-to-information laws that aim to democratize access to information – it has placed these collections more firmly in the public domain. Today, settlement-specific census abstracts can be freely downloaded for the 1991, 2001 and 2011 censuses – tabulations for the latter cover no fewer than 650,000 individual settlements, each geographically located according to subdistrict or the equivalent. A great range of variables that would be especially useful for socioeconomic and climate risk analysis is thus available.

Commuting and related forms of urban connection

Many researchers have advocated the replacement of simplistic urban–rural classifications by graduated measures of urban-ness, with degrees of urban connection assigned to rural villages and towns. The fact that people keep a foot in both rural and urban environments, and that places may also have the character of both sectors, has prompted calls for scientific measures that better capture the realities. Nearly 30 years ago, Terry McGee and other observers of urbanization in Asia saw signs of the emergence of zones of space that were neither obviously urban nor obviously rural in nature, having some features in common with both sectors. McGee termed these new spaces *desakota zones*, a hybrid term carrying the sense of both city and countryside (McGee

1987). Other researchers noted that binary urban–rural classifications are just as inadequate for people as they are for places: many people participate in both ends of the urban–rural spectrum through migration and receipt of remittances, and through a myriad of indirect connections formed by consumer and producer markets.

In particular, migration serves as one strategy by which individuals and households can extract benefits (whether in the short or long term) from spatially focused development taking place at a distance from their home communities (World Bank 2009, 2011). The existence of short-term internal migration flows has long been acknowledged by demographers, but the major international survey programmes – the Demographic and Health Surveys (DHS), and the Multiple Indicator Cluster Surveys (MICS) – rarely include even rudimentary questions on the topic. The task of measuring internal migration has thus been left to national population censuses, which generally do not have the luxury of probing into its short-term and seasonal aspects.

In Asia, the importance of internal migration has been examined in some depth in several recent and wide-ranging reviews giving particular attention to the experiences of China and India (Chandrasekhar and Sharma 2015; Charles-Edwards et al. 2016; Kundu and Saraswati 2016; Liang and Song 2016). Less attention has been given to short-term moves and commuting, another form of linkage over space that is emerging as a research issue in the region and which clearly warrants more study. The general neglect of mobility in conventional demographic surveys has prompted researchers to look elsewhere for insight, with much recent attention given to the possibilities suggested by mobile phone data (Lu et al. 2016).

Mamas and Komalasari (2008) cite estimates for Indonesia suggesting that over one million people commute on a daily basis to the Jakarta metropolitan region. Sharma and Chandrasekhar (2014) and Kundu (2014) explore commuting in India, giving attention to the population living in the 'urban shadow' just beyond the administrative boundaries of cities. Sharma and Chandrasekhar (2014) find that in 2009–2010, some 12.2 million non-agricultural workers commuted from rural to urban areas (or vice-versa) on a daily basis. About two-thirds of these commuters (8.1 million, just over 8 per cent of the total rural workforce) travelled from rural to urban settings, while 4.4 million persons (or five per cent of the urban workforce) commuted to rural areas. The number of commuters is nearly double that counted in 1993–1994. As noted by Sharma and Chandrasekhar (2014: 5), 'Individuals living closer to the city and with transport connectivity will try to take advantage of the wage gradient and miniscule rents in rural areas by commuting to the nearby urban areas'. Commuting is thus the product of a balancing between workplace location and home residence, entailing simultaneous consideration of wages, transport costs and rents. In the aggregate, commuting acts much like longer-stay forms of migration, contributing to the integration of rural and urban labour and product markets.

Given the lack of attention to migration and mobility in international demographic survey programmes, and the limited abilities of population censuses to inquire into the details, considerable interest has been aroused by the potential of mobile phone records and social media such as Twitter to provide insight. One instructive recent account is that of Lu et al. (2016) for Bangladesh, which employed data on mobile call records for some six million users collected over a period that spanned Cyclone Mahasen, which struck the country in May 2013. The researchers were keen to see whether population displacement caused by the cyclone could be detected in phone records. They concluded that while Cyclone Mahasen brought about some displacement, the amount was dwarfed by the routine but massive number of short-term and seasonal moves to, from and through the affected region in the period before and after the storm. Lu et al. (2016: 4) write that 'The findings illustrate the profound significance of seasonality in migration and the importance of taking these into account in the planning, executing and interpretation of migration surveys'.

China: revolutions in definitions and policies

Kam Wing Chan, a specialist in the study of Chinese urbanization (2009: 1), has observed that 'China has probably the world's most complex and confusing urban and city statistical data, with multiple indicators of city/urban population and a complicated administrative system'. As described by Chan (2010), China's city-system is hierarchical: provincial-level cities form its apex; and ranging below them in the hierarchy are deputy-provincial cities, provincial capitals, prefecture-level cities, county-level cities and towns in the lowest urban tier.

Since the mid-1950s, Chinese citizens have been classified into one of two de jure statuses – either 'non-agricultural' (effectively urban) or 'agricultural' – in what Chan has likened to an internal passport system. Well into the 1970s, citizens holding urban *hukou* had access to an array of state-guaranteed sources of grain, jobs, housing and other services, whereas rural *hukou* holders enjoyed no comparable benefits. Yeh (2011) argues that this two-tier system effectively suppressed urban population growth until the late 1970s.[7]

At that juncture, however, China's adoption of an aggressive export-led growth strategy made it necessary to open the door to substantial flows of rural-to-urban migrant labour. The exclusions and discrimination of the *hukou* system nevertheless continued to serve a purpose: by allowing the receiving cities to exclude migrants from public services and benefits, the budgetary consequences of labour migration were kept in check. By 2005, as Chan and Wang (2008) note, credible estimates of the size of the 'floating population' placed it at 147 million migrants or more, and the contradictions and inequities of the system were beginning to prompt calls for reform. In the early 2000s, some city-specific tinkering and waivers began to be permitted, and in 2014, Chinese authorities proposed to abolish the *hukou* system for small and medium-sized cities, while maintaining a version of it in larger cities. If they are fully implemented, even these partial policy reforms are likely to have immense significance for urban and rural well-being. In order to fully appreciate these developments, it is necessary to understand the myriad of city and urban definitions in China, as well as who is officially counted by its National Bureau of Statistics (NBS).[8]

As Chan has shown – see Figure 16.5 – the implications of the de facto approach to tabulating residence are especially pronounced in China's coastal cities, where the need for migrant labour has been greatest. In these cities, but also more generally, taking a de facto approach affects both city population sizes and growth rates, thus altering many *per capita* measures of urban economic performance. For example, the population of Shanghai's city districts was 14.35 million in 2000 and rose to 22.32 million in 2010 on a de facto basis, whereas de jure residence in these districts (i.e. considering only residents with urban *hukou*) increased over the period from 11.37 to 13.43 million, a far more modest change (Chan 2009).

The National New-Type Urbanization Plan and Hukou reforms

In March 2014, China launched a new urbanization agenda that will introduce significant additional reforms and guide targeted investments through 2020, by which time the urban share of total population is forecast to increase by another ten percentage points, to 60 per cent. The most remarked-upon aspect of the plan concerns the proposed transformation of the *hukou* system. Much of China's urban growth and remarkable national economic performance has come from the internal migrants who lack urban *hukou* – and who have therefore lacked access to the consumption benefits, better-quality schooling and social services that *hukou* residents can enjoy. The new plan proposes not to abolish the system across the whole of the country, but at least to

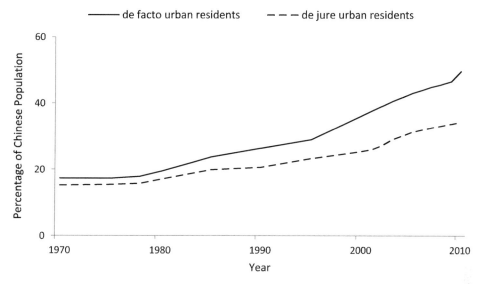

Figure 16.5 Percentage share of de facto and de jure urban residents in China's population, 1970–2010
Source: Chan (2012), updated by author.

do so for towns and small-to-intermediate-size cities, while leaving the system largely intact (for now) in the largest urban places.

Chan (2014) has set out a careful analysis of the implications of these partial reforms. As he notes, the largest new obligations that the Chinese state will assume have to do with expanded responsibility for urban old-age pensions and health care. Because the 'floating population' migrants who would gain eligibility for such social benefits are still relatively young, these costs will likely be felt mainly in the future, as the migrants age. In Chan's view, the pay-offs to reform are more immediate, being both economic in nature (freer mobility of labour, choice of occupation and expanded access to housing and schooling, all of which may stimulate productivity and raise domestic consumption) and more broadly social and political, involving the difficult-to-quantify benefits that flow from giving the formerly excluded migrants new opportunities to participate as first-class citizens in the various arenas of urban public life.

The new plan envisions massive public investment in transport and other infrastructure – which may well exceed one trillion US dollars over the period (EYGM Limited 2014) – with attention to forging connections among clusters of cities across the country. The new plan also ushers in public finance reforms to equip local urban governments with the fiscal tools they will need to better support city growth. Until recently, local governments in China have been heavily dependent on one-off long-term leases of land to private enterprises to secure funding for their recurrent expenses, an unsustainable practice that critics charge has spawned inequities and led to ill-planned, environmentally unsound development (Bai, Chen and Shi 2012).

Climate change and extreme-event risks in urban Asia

Many Asian countries, such as India, Indonesia and the Philippines, face a full menu of extreme-event risks. Such risks manifest themselves differently across the landscape of any one country,

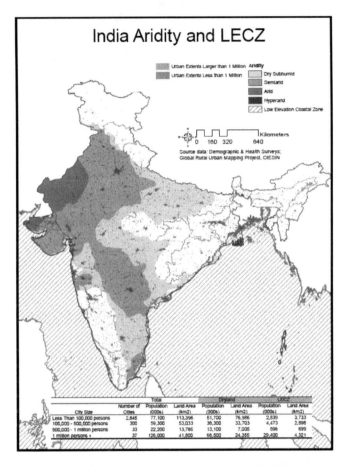

Map 16.3 India's low-elevation coastal zone and arid regions, with locations of cities indicated in night-time lights imagery
Source: Map produced by authors with data and methods described in Balk et al. (2009b).

as do the characteristics of the population exposed to them. Hence, spatially detailed demographic and environmental risk data must be combined to generate adequate risk profiles (Balk et al. 2009b). Here we concentrate on two of the most important risks in the region: flooding and water scarcity. As Map 16.3 indicates for India, there can be a great deal of spatial variation across one country in the incidence of these two risks, which afflict both the rural and urban populations of the country. The recently-released settlement data for India will allow the socio-economic composition of the population at risk to be examined in some detail. Elsewhere in Asia, however, the matching of demographic data to spatial risk zones is still in its very earliest stages.

According to current forecasts, sea levels will gradually but inexorably rise over the coming decades, placing large coastal urban populations under threat around the globe. Alley et al. (2007) foresee increases of 0.2 to 0.6 metres in sea level by 2100, a development that will be accompanied by more intense typhoons and hurricanes, storm surges and periods of exceptionally high precipitation. Many of Asia's largest cities are located in coastal areas that have long been cyclone-prone. Mumbai saw massive floods in 2005, as did Karachi in 2007 (Kovats and Akhtar

2008; World Bank 2008). A coastal flood model used with the climate scenarios developed for the Intergovernmental Panel on Climate Change (IPCC) suggests that the populations of the areas at risk, and the income levels of these populations, are critical factors in determining the health consequences of such extreme-weather events (Kovats and Lloyd 2009).

Whether from coastal or inland sources, urban flooding risks in developing countries stem from a number of factors: impermeable surfaces that prevent water from being absorbed and cause rapid runoff; the general scarcity of parks and other green spaces to absorb such flows; rudimentary drainage systems that are often clogged by waste and which, in any case, are quickly overloaded with water; and the ill-advised development of marshlands and other natural buffers. When flooding occurs, faecal matter and other hazardous materials contaminate flood waters and spill into open wells, elevating the risks of water-borne, respiratory and skin diseases (Ahern et al. 2005; Kovats and Akhtar 2008).

The urban poor are often more exposed than others to these environmental hazards, because the only housing they can afford tends to be located in environmentally riskier areas, the housing itself affords less protection, and their mobility is more constrained. The poor are likely to experience further indirect damage as a result of the loss of their homes, population displacement, and the disruption of livelihoods and networks of social support (Hardoy and Pandiella 2009). Kovats and Akhtar (2008) detail some of the flood-related health risks: increases in cholera, cryptosporidiosis, typhoid fever and diarrhoeal diseases – describing increases in cases of leptospirosis after the Mumbai floods of 2000, 2001 and 2005 – but caution that the excess risks due to flooding are hard to quantify without adequate baseline data. They also note the problem of water contaminated by chemicals, heavy metals and other hazardous substances, especially for city-dwellers who live near industrial areas.

Estimates of risk exposure in urban Asia

Figure 16.6 summarizes the exposure of Asian urban populations to coastal and inland flooding and to the multiple risks stemming from arid environments. Building on earlier research, Balk, Montgomery, and Liu (2012) have estimated that in 2010, some 250 million Asian urban dwellers faced appreciable risks of inland flooding; in 2025, this number will likely reach 350 million persons.[9] About three-quarters of the urban population of Cambodia is at risk of inland flooding, approximately 35 per cent of the urban populations of Bangladesh, Vietnam, Laos and Thailand, and an estimated one-fifth of the urban population of China and 12 per cent of India. Cities in three Asian countries – Bangladesh, China and India – dominate the highest risk category for inland flood frequency (i.e. flooding at least every other year). Coastal flooding would appear to be an even greater threat, confronting over 300 million residents of low-elevation coastal zones (LECZ) in 2010 and a predicted 430 million in 2025. In contrast to inland flood risk, the risk of coastal flooding in Asian cities is heavily concentrated in the South-Eastern Asian subregion, with all countries situated here (except landlocked Laos) having high proportions of their population at risk. An estimated half of the city residents of Bangladesh, 20 per cent of Taiwanese urbanites, and 18 per cent of China's urban dwellers are at risk of coastal flooding.

Across Asia, serious challenges are also presented at the other end of the water spectrum, that is, by seasonal and perennial water scarcity. Much of the land area of Asia is either arid or semi-arid (McDonald et al. 2011). Of the 22,000 towns and cities in Asia enumerated by Balk and colleagues, slightly fewer than 3,000 are found in the LECZ, and close to 9,000 face some sort of inland flood risk – but some 11,000 cities are located in dryland regions. This total includes over 80 cities with more than 1 million inhabitants. Cities in India and China are prominent on the risk list, as would be expected, but so are cities in Pakistan, Iraq, Burma, Uzbekistan and Turkey

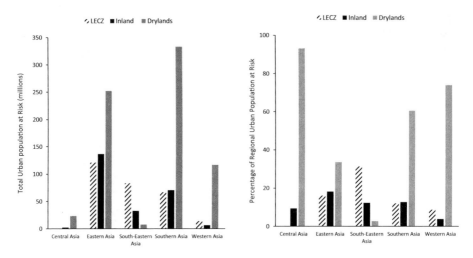

Figure 16.6 Urban populations in low-elevation coastal zone (LECZ), inland flood zones and drylands, expressed in terms of total urban residents and in percentages of subregional urban population
Source: Authors' calculations.

among others. Using a combination of hydrological and demographic approaches to estimate per-capita water availability, McDonald et al. (2011) estimate that currently, 150 million people worldwide live in cities with perennial water shortage, defined as having less than 100 litres per person per day of sustainable surface and groundwater flow within the urban extent. By 2050, demographic growth alone will drive this figure to almost 1 billion people. Climate change over the period is expected to induce water shortage for an additional 100 million persons. (The number of urban-dwellers facing seasonal shortages is even higher.) In the drylands ecosystems that are expected to face increasing water scarcity, the agricultural practices suitable to an earlier era may well be seriously disrupted, and this may magnify the normal flows of migration between rural and urban areas and might also increase urban food prices, thus placing both the urban and the rural poor under stress. Water scarcities in some cases will affect urban power derived from hydroelectricity as well as the access to and cost of drinking water. To date, the research literature has hardly touched these urban-specific implications.

Urban adaptation to flood risks

Bangladesh, which in many respects has been a leader and international model in climate adaptation efforts in general, provides a striking example of how the lack of national-level attention to cities and the urban poor can inhibit and even disable urban climate risk adaptation. According to Banks, Roy and Hulme (2011), none of the three major countrywide assessments – the Poverty Reduction Strategy Paper (PRSP) for Bangladesh (2005), the National Adaptation Plan of Action (2005) and its successor, the Bangladesh Climate Change Strategy and Action Plan (2008) – consider the climate risks to which poor urban-dwellers are exposed. As Banks, Roy and Hulme (2011) explain, the neglect of the urban poor in national-level strategies has left something of an institutional vacuum at the local level, leaving municipal governments without clear national mandates (or funding) for adaptation and discouraging non-governmental organizations from investing effort in links between urban communities and local government.

Building these connections is essential to the longer-term success of urban climate adaptation, because community groups cannot carry the full adaptation burden on their own. Satterthwaite (2011: 339–340) writes, 'Community organizations cannot design and build the city infrastructure that is so important for resilience to storms and heavy rainfall…. [Nor can they] ensure good management of land use for expanding cities so that new developments avoid dangerous sites and are served with infrastructure'.

Urban adaptation and disaster plans throughout Asia have met with limited success, in large part because one or more of the full complement of necessary actors is absent from the planning or implementation stages (Ahammad 2011; Bahadur and Tanner 2014). See www.adpc.net for an informative summary of adaptation efforts underway throughout Asia.

Conclusions

Over the next few decades, the Asian region will experience the effects of two great worldwide trends: urbanization and climate change. Neither is an overnight development, but much remains to be done scientifically, and in the realm of policy and governance, to meet the implications of these powerful forces. While identifying in broad strokes what is known about urbanization in Asia – in particular, that much population growth can be expected to take place in its smaller cities and towns – this chapter has also highlighted important deficits in the knowledge base. The energies devoted by the international community to the crafting of the SDGs have succeeded in producing a thoughtful agenda for the 2015–2030 period with an unprecedented and welcome focus on urbanization, but the hard work of establishing monitoring systems and integrating science, government and civil society in the effort, still lies ahead.

With so much of Asia's urbanization yet to unfold, it is especially important that our understanding of urban change is fully informed demographically and spatially. This chapter has put its emphasis on the necessity of spatially-specific data disaggregation to the subnational level, so that local urban authorities can better understand local needs and make an evidence-based case to higher-level authorities for adequate funds to address these needs. Many of the SDG targets and indicators will be monitored with data-collection systems that, at present, simply do not reach down to the level of cities, towns and local governments. Until this deficiency of statistical systems can be remedied, the demographic and socioeconomic information available to support good governance at the local level must be extracted from national population censuses. With great effort and expense, these censuses collect data in fine spatial detail; but in poor Asian countries the data are rarely disaggregated and mapped to allow local governments to make use of the information. Today, the technical barriers that once stood in the way of information provision have all but vanished, and there can be little justification for continuing the practice of sequestering national census data in national statistical offices. We have described one model of good practice in India, but for the future, routine disaggregation and data provision must figure among the most important criteria by which Asian national statistical systems are held to account.

Over the longer term, attention needs to be directed to the *development of local capacities to gather reliable information* on the high-priority items needed for effective local governance. Relatively few local urban governments now possess the in-house abilities to process census and other data; nor do they have the knowledge and experience to know what can be learned from such data that is of local value. To develop municipal capacities for evidence-based governance, continuing technical assistance and support will likely be needed, especially if city-specific surveys are to be fielded to complement national survey programmes and fill the gaps in census data collection. Since a near-majority of Asia's urban residents live in small- and intermediate-sized cities, where mayors and planners operate with little hard information on their populations, and whose municipal staff lack the empirical data they would need to anticipate risks and guide local development, there is an urgent need to focus resources and attention on these small places. But if technical assistance is provided on an ongoing basis by supportive national and international institutions, appropriately guided by the targets set out in the SDGs, there is good reason to hope that investments in these capacities will bear fruit.

Acknowledgements

Analysis in the chapter was supported by the following research grants to Professors Balk and Montgomery: AXA Research Fund and NSF National Science Foundation award #1416860 to the City University of New York, the Population Council, the National Center for Atmospheric Research and the University of Colorado at Boulder.

Notes

1 Goal 11 of the SDGs is expressed in terms of cities, but its central theme focuses on meeting basic needs and reducing inequities in settlements of all types, in part by fostering beneficial urban–rural connections. The targets to be reached by 2030 include: ensuring access to adequate, safe and affordable housing and sustainable transport systems; inclusive and sustainable urbanization plans; and reduction of deaths and loss of livelihood and economic output caused by disasters, with a focus on protecting the poor and people in vulnerable situations; strengthening linkages between urban, peri-urban and rural areas; and improving inclusiveness in urban and regional planning. Goal 11 also aims to reduce the environmental impact of cities.
2 See United Nations (2014). More detail is presented in an informative ILO summary, www.ilo.org/stat/Areasofwork/Compilation/WCMS_389373/lang–en/index.htm, and in the recent Deuskar and Stewart (2016) review.
3 Compelling evidence on lower urban fertility comes from detailed studies of the metropolitan regions of Pacific Asia, which even in the 1990s displayed at- or below-replacement total fertility rates that were substantially below the rates of their countries; see Douglass and Jones (2008: Table 2.1) and Mamas and Komalasari (2008: Table 5.3) for Jakarta.
4 VIIRs two-month composite lights measured in April and October 2012, downloaded from http://ngdc.noaa.gov/eog/viirs.html in July 2014.
5 See calculations by Jones (2008: Tables 3.1, 3.3) and Mamas and Komalasari (2008: Table 5.1), which for the year 2000 give a core population count of 8.3 million residents as against a mega-urban region count of 21.2 million, among whom some 9.4 million live in an 'inner zone' that is adjacent to but lies outside the city proper or administrative core. Estimates in Jones and Mulyana (2015) confirm the continuation of this pattern in 2010.
6 Denis and Marius-Gnanou (2011) provide an excellent comparison of statutory and census towns in India, noting the difficulties of generalization that stem from the discretionary latitude accorded to census officials in designating census towns, which although urban for census purposes remain under the Rural Development and Panchayat Raj administration. A vexing issue for researchers is that census towns can be included in one census but then 'declassified' to rural villages in the next. Declassification to rural status is not as common as promotion to urban status, but it occurs often enough to be demographically important.
7 Also see McGranahan et al. (2014), World Bank and Development Research Center of the State Council, the People's Republic of China (2014), and Bai, Shi and Liu (2014).
8 Since the 1950s, city units have been administratively defined, and include rural counties within the administrative boundary. By the 1990s, many cities already had an administrative area far larger than the urbanized area per se. The spatial administrative structure is as follows (Chan 2009): Outer boundary: the limit of the city (*shi*) administrative unit, which generally comprises both city districts and counties. Thus, this 'city' includes both an urbanized core (high-density built-up area) and extensive rural areas, primarily agricultural but with occasional towns (*zhen*). Urban core, together with some close-in areas, is administratively divided into 'city districts' (*shiqu*), and the surrounding rural areas (with towns) into counties (*xian*). The city districts comprise the administratively defined urban area,

meaning that local governments, social services, etc. are organized along urban lines, while the counties are administratively rural. Together the city districts and counties form a single administrative unit administered from, and bearing the name of, the main city.

Additionally, there are NBS-defined urban areas, according to criteria principally reflecting physical features and de facto population density – an average population density of at least 1,500 per km^2 or contiguity of the built-up area. These statistical areas are rarely in total congruence with the administratively defined urban areas (city districts). The sum of their populations is the basis for the official urban count. The 2000 census published for the first time demographic figures for China that separated all de facto residents from the subset of residents holding urban *hukou*. This fundamental revision in the basis for census population counts has greatly clarified the nature of urbanization in the country.

9   See Balk et al. (2009a) and Balk et al. (2009b) for preparatory research in poor countries more generally. Population-at-risk estimates require fine-scale spatial data and are sensitive to the definitional issues discussed above.

References

Ahammad, R. (2011) 'Constraints of pro-poor climate change adaptation in Chittagong City'. *Environment and Urbanization*, 23: 503–516.

Ahern, M. R. et al. (2005) 'Global health impacts of floods: epidemiological evidence'. *Epidemiologic Reviews*, 27(1): 36–45.

Alley, R. B. et al. (2007) *Summary for Policymakers: Contribution of Working Group I to the Fourth Assessment Report*. Intergovernmental Panel on Climate Change. Available from: www.ipcc.ch (accessed 7 November 2007).

Bahadur, A. V. and T. Tanner (2014) 'Policy climates and climate policies: analyzing the politics of building urban climate change resilience'. *Urban Climate*, 7: 20–32.

Bai, X., J. Chen and P. Shi (2012) 'Landscape urbanization and economic growth in China: positive feedbacks and sustainability dilemmas'. *Environmental Science & Technology*, 46: 132–139.

Bai, X., P. Shi and Y. Liu (2014) 'Realizing China's urban dream'. *Nature*, 509: 158–160.

Balk, D., M. R. Montgomery and Z. Liu (2012) *Urbanization and Climate Change Hazards in Asia*. Report submitted to the Asian Development Bank.

Balk, D. et al. (2009a) 'Understanding the impacts of climate change: linking satellite and other spatial data with population data'. In J. M. Guzmán, G. Martine et al. (eds.) *Population Dynamics and Climate Change*. New York: United Nations Fund for Population Activities (UNFPA), International Institute for Environment, and Development (IIED). Pp. 206–217.

Balk, D. et al. (2009b) 'Mapping urban settlements and the risks of climate change in Africa, Asia and South America'. In J. M. Guzmán, G. Martine et al. (eds.) *Population Dynamics and Climate Change*. New York: United Nations Fund for Population Activities (UNFPA), International Institute for Environment, and Development (IIED). Pp. 80–103.

Balk, D. L. and M. R. Montgomery (2015) 'Spatializing demography for the urban future'. *Spatial Demography*, 3(2): 59–62.

Banks, N., M. Roy and D. Hulme (2011) 'Neglecting the urban poor in Bangladesh: research, policy and action in the context of climate change'. *Environment and Urbanization*, 23(2): 487–502.

Bhagat, R. B. and S. Mohanty (2009) 'Emerging pattern of urbanization and the contribution of migration in urban growth in India'. *Asian Population Studies*, 5(1): 1744–1749.

Chan, K. W. (2009) *What is the True Urban Population of China? Which is the Largest City in China?* Note posted on: http://faculty.washington.edu/kwchan/Chan-urban.pdf.

Chan, K. W. (2010) 'Fundamentals of Chinas urbanization and policy'. *The China Review*, 10(1): 63–94.

Chan, K. W. (2012) 'Crossing the 50 percent population rubicon: can China urbanize to prosperity?' *Eurasian Geography and Economics*, 53(1): 63–86.

Chan, K. W. (2014) *Achieving Comprehensive Hukou Reform in China*. Paulson Policy Memorandum. Chicago, IL: The Paulson Institute. Available from: www.paulsoninstitute.org/wp-content/uploads/2015/04/PPM_Hukou_Chan_English.pdf.

Chan, K. W. and M. Wang (2008) 'Remapping China's regional inequalities, 1990–2006: a new assessment of *de facto* and *de jure* population data'. *Eurasian Geography and Economics*, 49(1): 21–56.

Chandrasekhar, S. and A. Sharma (2015) 'Urbanization and spatial patterns of internal migration in India'. *Spatial Demography*, 3(2): 63–89.

Charles-Edwards, E. et al. (2016) 'Migration in Asia'. In M. J. White (ed.) *International Handbook of Migration and Population Distribution*. New York and London: Springer. Pp. 269–284.

Denis, E. and K. Marius-Gnanou (2011) 'Toward a better appraisal of urbanization in India'. *Cybergeo: European Journal of Geography*. Available from: http://dx.doi.org/10.4000/cybergeo.24798.

Deuskar, C. and B. Stewart (2016) *Measuring Global Urbanization Using a Standard Definition of Urban Areas: Analysis of Preliminary Results*. Draft Working Paper. Washington, DC: World Bank.

Douglass, M. and G. W. Jones (2008) 'The morphology of mega-urban regions expansion'. In G. W. Jones and M. Douglass (eds.) *Mega-Urban Regions in Pacific Asia. Urban Dynamics in a Global Era*. Singapore: National University of Singapore (NUS) Press. Pp. 19–40.

EYGM Limited (2014) *China: Planning for an Urban Future*. China Business Network, EYGM Limited. Available from: www.ey.com/cn/en/issues/driving-growth/ey-china-planning-for-an-urban-future.

Freire, S. et al. (2015) *Combining GHSL and GPW to Improve Global Population Mapping*. EC JRC Global Security and Crisis Management Unit, Joint Research Commission, Ispra, Italy. Conference paper, Milan.

General Economics Division, Planning Commission Government of People's Republic of Bangladesh (2005) *Unlocking the Potential: National Strategy for Accelerated Poverty Reduction*. Bangladesh.

Hardoy, J. and G. Pandiella (2009) 'Urban poverty and vulnerability to climate change in Latin America'. *Environment and Urbanization*, 21(1): 203–224.

Hugo, G. J. (2003) *Urbanisation in Asia: An Overview*. Paper prepared for Conference on African Migration in Comparative Perspective, Johannesburg, South Africa, 4–7 June 2003.

Jones, G. W. (2008) 'Comparative dynamics of the six mega-urban regions'. In G. W. Jones and M. Douglass (eds.) *Mega-Urban Regions in Pacific Asia: Urban Dynamics in a Global Era*. Singapore: National University of Singapore (NUS) Press. Pp. 41–61.

Jones, G. W. and W. Mulyana (2015) *Urbanization in Indonesia*. UNFPA Indonesia Monograph Series 4. UNFPA.

Kovats, S. and R. Akhtar (2008) 'Climate, climate change and human health in Asian cities'. *Environment and Urbanization*, 20(1): 165–175.

Kovats, S. and S. Lloyd (2009) 'Population, climate and health'. In J. M. Guzmán, G. Martine et al. (eds.) *Population Dynamics and Climate Change*. London: United Nations Fund for Population Activities (UNFPA), International Institute for Environment, and Development (IIED). Pp. 164–175.

Kundu, A. (2014) 'India's sluggish urbanization and its exclusionary development'. In G. McGranahan and G. Martine (eds.) *Urban Growth in Emerging Economies: Lessons from the BRICS*. New York: Routledge. Pp. 191–232.

Kundu, A. and L. R. Saraswati (2016) 'Changing patterns of migration in India: A perspective on urban exclusion'. In M. J. White (ed.) *International Handbook of Migration and Population Distribution*. New York and London: Springer. Pp. 311–332.

Liang, Z. and Q. Song (2016) 'Migration in China'. In M. J. White (ed.) *International Handbook of Migration and Population Distribution*. New York and London: Springer. Pp. 285–309.

Lu, X., D. J. Wrathall et al. (2016) 'Unveiling hidden migration and mobility patterns in climate stressed regions: a longitudinal study of six million anonymous mobile phone users in Bangladesh'. *Global Environmental Change*, 38: 1–7.

Mamas, S. G. M. and R. Komalasari (2008) 'Jakarta – dynamics of change and livability'. In G. W. Jones and M. Douglass (eds.) *Mega-Urban Regions in Pacific Asia: Urban Dynamics in a Global Era*. Singapore: National University of Singapore (NUS) Press. Pp. 109–149.

McDonald, R. I., P. Green et al. (2011) 'Urban growth, climate change and freshwater availability'. *Proceedings of the National Academy of Sciences (PNAS)*. Published 28 March 2011 in Online Early Edition, manuscript 2010-11615R.

McGee, T. G. (1987) *Urbanization or Kotadesasi – The Emergence of New Regions of Economic Interaction in Asia*. Honolulu: East-West Center.

McGranahan, G., J. Guoping et al. (2014) 'China's radical urbanisation and bringing capital and labour together step by step'. In G. McGranahan and G. Martine (eds.) *Urban Growth in Emerging Economies: Lessons from the BRICS*. New York: Routledge.

Ministry of Environment and Forests, Government of the People's Republic of Bangladesh (2005) *National Adaptation Programme of Action (NAPA)*.

Ministry of Environment and Forests, Government of the People's Republic of Bangladesh (2008) *Bangladesh Climate Change Strategy and Action Plan 2008*. Dhaka, Bangladesh.

Panel on Urban Population Dynamics (PUPD) (2003) *Cities Transformed: Demographic Change and Its Implications in the Developing World.* M. R. Montgomery, R. Stren, B. Cohen and H. E. Reed, editors. Washington, DC: National Academies Press.

Park, J. et al. (2011) *Urbanization and Urban Policies in Korea.* Korea Research Institute for Human Settlements. Available from: www.krihs.re.kr.

Pesaresi, M., G. Huadong et al. (2013) 'A global human settlement layer from optical HR/VHR RS data: concept and first results'. *IEEE Journal of Selected Topics in Applied Earth Observations and Remote Sensing,* 6(5): 2102–2131.

Satterthwaite, D. (2011) 'Editorial: Why is community action needed for disaster risk reduction and climate change adaptation?' *Environment and Urbanization,* 23(2): 339–349.

Sharma, A. and S. Chandrasekhar (2014) 'Growth of the urban shadow, spatial distribution of economic activities, and commuting by workers in rural and urban India'. *World Development,* 61: 154–166.

Stevens, F., A. Gaughan et al. (2015) 'Disaggregating census data for population mapping using random forest with remotely-sensed and ancillary data'. *PLoS ONE,* 10(2): e0107042.

Uchida, H. and A. Nelson (2010) *Agglomeration Index: Towards a New Measure of Urban Concentration.* Working paper. Washington, DC: The World Bank.

United Nations (2014) *World Urbanization Prospects: The 2014 Revision, Highlights.* New York: United Nations, Department of Economic and Social Affairs, Population Division.

World Bank (2008) *Climate-Resilient Cities: 2008 Primer.* Washington, DC: World Bank.

World Bank (2009) *World Development Report 2009: Reshaping Economic Geography.* Washington, DC: The World Bank.

World Bank (2011) *Migration and Remittances Factbook 2011,* Second Edition. Washington, DC: World Bank.

World Bank (2012) *Indonesia – The Rise of Metropolitan Regions: Towards Inclusive and Sustainable Regional Development.* Washington, DC: World Bank.

World Bank (2013) *Urbanization beyond Municipal Boundaries: Nurturing Metropolitan Economies and Connecting Peri-Urban Areas in India.* Washington, DC: World Bank.

World Bank and Development Research Center of the State Council, the People's Republic of China (2014) *Urban China: Toward Efficient, Inclusive and Sustainable Urbanization.* Washington, DC: World Bank.

Yeh, A. (2011) 'Urban growth and spatial development: the China case'. In E. L. Birch and S. M. Wachter (eds.) *Global Urbanization.* Philadelphia, PA: University of Pennsylvania Press. Pp. 67–85.

17
Asia's international migration

Graeme Hugo

Introduction

Although international migration has a long history in Asia, it has acquired unprecedented scale, diversity and significance in recent decades. At the United Nations Second Asian Population Conference held in Tokyo, Japan, in 1972, international migration was not mentioned in the review of demographic trends in the region over the previous decade (United Nations ECAFE Secretariat 1972). However, four decades later it is among the most significant demographic processes shaping the economic, social and demographic development of all Asian nations. International migration is a topic of unprecedented interest in the region among both governments and the wider community. With newspapers and other media reporting on it daily, the issue is constantly in the public consciousness.

This chapter seeks first to document recent major trends in the various types of international migration in the Asian region. It argues that there are elements in the existing system and in the region which will lead to the perpetuation and enhancement of international migration, regardless of political and economic change and the interventions of government. Second, the chapter discusses some of the major issues which are emerging in the region in relation to migration between nations, and finally, it addresses some important policy issues.

The vast size and cultural, ethnic, political, religious and economic complexities of the Asian region make it difficult to generalize. The region has some of the world's poorest nations, such as Nepal, and wealthy nations such as Singapore. There are vast nations such as India and China and tiny countries which are virtual city-states such as Singapore. Inevitably, in this chapter, there will be generalization across the region but it must be borne in mind that there is huge variation between countries and also within nations.

It should also be pointed out that the exponential increase in significance of international migration in Asia has not been accompanied by a concomitant increase in the amount and quality of related data collection. This is a major constraint to the development of effective migration policy and needs to be addressed systematically. Measuring migration is especially problematic because of the widespread occurrence of undocumented migration. Stock migration data are usually obtained from censuses but only a minority of countries has a full range of the basic questions of relevance to international migration. Moreover, temporary migrants are rarely detected in censuses. A similar situation prevails with respect to migration flow data. While all nations have border control systems, data on arrivals and departures are often not maintained in a way that makes them amenable to analysis, especially departures. The data sometimes exclude movement of nationals and often do not differentiate between short term, long term and permanent movements. Accordingly, any demographic assessment of international migration in the Asian region is limited by the lack of comprehensive and accurate data. Improvement in the collection of both stock and flow data in the region is a crucial priority. Related to this is the lack of capacity in migration management and research in the region, both of which are constraints to improving the effectiveness of migration policy in Asia.

The transformation in international migration in Asia has been shaped by a complex set of political, economic and social developments associated with globalization. However, internationalization of labour markets and trade and the revolution in transport and communication as well as the demographic transformations analysed elsewhere in this volume have also played a major role. In particular the uneven pace and scale of the remarkable decline in fertility, and the associated shifts in age structure, have been influential. Due to the differences among Asian nations in the timing and rate of fertility decline, there are significant differences among countries in the rates of growth (or decline) in their youth populations. Higher income countries like Japan and South Korea have slow growth or even decline in their youth populations, while the lower income nations, especially those in parts of South Asia and the Philippines, will continue to experience growth. This of course has implications for migration since youth groups have high levels of mobility.

Two elements have been especially influential in the increase in migration. The first is the proliferation of social networks. Most Asian international migrants move to a place where they have social capital in the form of relatives or friends already living there. These networks not only encourage and facilitate mobility but also assist the migrant in adjusting to the situation in the destination. The growing size of the Asian diaspora comprises anchors in a rapidly spreading network of connections facilitating migration. The second facilitator is the vast migration industry comprising migration agents, recruiters, travel providers, immigration officials and others who form chains linking Asian communities with overseas destinations and are crucial elements in the migration system.

Trends in international migration

Permanent migration

The United Nations (2013a) estimates that 70.8 million of the 231.5 million people worldwide who live outside the country in which they were born live in Asia. While this is equivalent to only 1.6 per cent of the total Asian population, it is a significant understatement of the impact of international migration in Asia. Table 17.1 shows significant differences between the subregions of Asia in recent change in the number of migrants. Similarly, within these regions there is variation between countries with respect to migration.

A number of trends are evident. The number of Asia's international migrants accounted for one-third of the world total in 1990, but its average annual growth rate was very low in the next decade (0.1 per cent) and well below the world average of 1.2 per cent. As a result, its share of all migrants in the world fell to 28.5 per cent in 2000. Since then, however, the rate of growth in the number of international migrants in Asia increased and reached 2.6 per cent per annum in 2001–2013, which was higher than the world average of 2.2 per cent. As noted by the United Nations (2013b: 2) that during this period, 'Asia added more international migrants than any

Graeme Hugo

Table 17.1 International migration in Asia, 1990–2013

	Number (thousands)			Average rate of change (per cent per year)	
	1990	2000	2013	1990–2000	2000–2013
Asia	49,911	50,415	70,846	0.1	2.6
Central Asia	6,631	5,151	5,472	−2.5	0.5
Eastern Asia	3,961	5,393	7,720	3.1	2.8
South-Eastern Asia	3,200	5,274	9,509	5.0	4.5
Southern Asia	20,202	15,693	15,002	−2.5	−0.3
Western Asia	15,917	18,903	33,144	1.7	4.3
World	**154,162**	**174,516**	**231,522**	**1.2**	**2.2**

Source: United Nations (2013a).

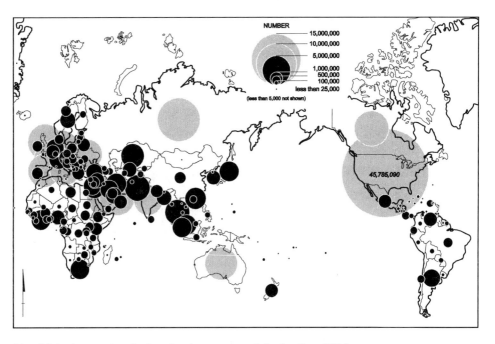

Map 17.1 International migration by country of destination, 2013
Source: United Nations (2013a).

other major area'. Its share of all migrants globally rose to 30.6 per cent in 2013, with the most rapid growth being in Western and South-Eastern Asia.

The increasing significance of Asian countries as destinations of international migrants is part of a global trend towards increasing South–South migration and reflects the higher rates of economic growth in the region than in other parts of the world. Map 17.1 shows the global distribution of international immigrants in 2013 and it indicates the dominance of North America, Europe, Oceania and the Middle East as major destination areas. However, Asia is of increasing importance with 15 of the 30 largest global migration corridors identified by the World Bank (2011) involving an Asian origin or destination or both; these are

Asia's international migration

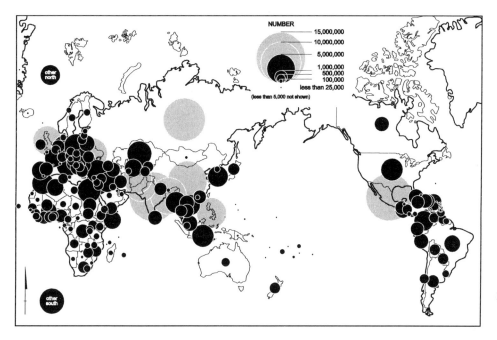

Map 17.2 International migration by country of origin, 2013
Source: United Nations (2013a).

Bangladesh–India, China–Hong Kong SAR, India–United Arab Emirates, China–United States, the Philippines–United States, Afghanistan–Iran, India–United States, India–Saudi Arabia, Indonesia–Malaysia, Vietnam–United States, Pakistan–India, Malaysia–Singapore, India–Bangladesh, South Korea–United States and Pakistan–Saudi Arabia. Map 17.2 shows the distribution of persons living outside their country of birth in 2013 according to their country of *origin*. When comparing this to Map 17.1, it will be noted that Asia is more significant as a region of emigration than it is of immigration. In the World Bank's (2011) list of the 30 largest sources of emigrants, 12 are from Asia compared with 8 of the 30 largest immigration nations.

Asian international movement has also become much more diverse both in terms of the forms that it takes and in terms of the people who move. There has been a significant increase in the movement between Asian nations but also out of, and into, the region. Movement is both forced and unforced, documented and undocumented, permanent and temporary, work related and non-work related.

South-North migration

For more than two centuries the United States, Canada, Australia and New Zealand have been receiving substantial numbers of immigrants but until the late 1960s however, they discriminated in favour of Europeans, so Asian immigration was extremely limited. Since the early 1970s, discrimination on the basis of race, ethnicity or birthplace has been removed and immigrant selection is now based mainly on skills and family reunion and as a result Asian immigration has increased substantially. Table 17.2 shows the rapid growth of Asian communities in the four traditional migration countries. Europe has become an increasingly important destination of

Table 17.2 Australia, USA, Canada and New Zealand: growth (in thousands) of the Asia-Pacific-born population, 1971–2011

	Australia		USA		Canada		New Zealand	
	Asia-born	Pacific-born[a]	Asia-born	Pacific-born	Asia-born	Pacific-born	Asia-born	Pacific-born[b]
1971	167.2	97.2	824.9	41.3	131.8	n.a.	18.0	n.a.
1971–1981 % p.a. increase	8.3	8.2	11.9	6.5	15.2	n.a.	1.7	n.a.
1981	371.6	212.8	39.8	77.6	541.2	n.a.	21.3	n.a.
1981–1991 % p.a. increase	8.3	5.1	7.0	3.0	7.0	n.a.	11.3	n.a.
1991	822.2	349.8	4979.0	104.1	1064.8	41.7	62.1	146.8
1991–2001 % p.a. increase	1.8	2.7	4.8	5.6	5.8	2.3	10.3	1.7
2001	982.5	455.3	7970.0	179.0	1878.0	52.2	165.8	174.3
2001–2006 % p.a. increase	4.2	1.7	3.1	0.3	4.3	2.1	8.7	2.6
2006	1208.7	496.4	9272.6	182.0	2316.6	57.8	251.1	198.6
2006–2011 % p.a. increase	7.5	4.2	4.2	2.8	4.0	4.0	n.a.	n.a.
2011	1738.9	609.2	10629.9	221.2	2822.4	63.6	n.a.	n.a.

Notes: [a] Excludes Australia-born; [b] Excludes New Zealand-born.
Sources: OECD (1995), ABS 1971, 1991, 2001, 2006 and 2011 censuses; US Bureau, 2001 and 2006 censuses, Current Population Survey and 2006 and 2011 American Community Surveys; Statistics Canada, 1971, 1991, 2001, 2006 and 2011 censuses; Gibson and Lennon (1999); Statistics New Zealand, 1971, 1981, 1991 and 2006 censuses.

Asian emigrants. The United Nations found that there were 6.1 million Asia-born persons living in Europe in 2013.

South–North migration out of Asian countries has a number of characteristics. It is predominantly permanent migration where migrant workers seek permanent residence or citizenship at the destination. It is also becoming increasingly selective of highly skilled workers while avenues for low-skilled workers have been reduced. Temporary migration is also increasing in significance under special visas like the H1B in the USA (Martin 2008) and 457 in Australia (Khoo et al. 2003). This is even more selective of highly skilled migrants than permanent migration. Student migration is also important, and associated with this there has been an increase in 'designer' migrants (Simmons 1999), i.e. migrants who first arrive as students, gain their qualifications at the destination and subsequently apply for permanent residence as migrants. There is an increasingly significant nexus between student migration and skilled migration out of Asian countries. Women are also increasingly engaged in this migration. While there is a predominance of movement out of Asia, there are also significant flows in the opposite direction, among which return migration is a major component.

Temporary labour migration

The largest international migration flows influencing contemporary Asian countries are those involving non-permanent contract labour movements. This migration has a long history in Asia (Hugo 2004) but entered a new era in scale and complexity with the 1973 oil price increase and the associated massive demand for workers in the Middle East. South Asian migrant workers had a long history of involvement in the Gulf area but after 1973 their numbers expanded rapidly and large numbers of East and South-East Asians also became involved. In 1975, India and Pakistan contributed 97 per cent of Asian workers to West Asia but this is now less than a third, with the South-East Asian share growing from 2 per cent to more than half. Whereas workers in the early years were mainly involved in infrastructure development, those in more recent times have moved into service occupations. Over time women have become more significant in the migration flows, with many working in domestic service. During the last two decades the destinations of Asian migrant workers have become more diverse, with Asian destinations now accounting for more migrants than the Middle East. Much of the movement is undocumented.

The first, and by far the largest, group of contract workers are unskilled and semi-skilled workers who are employed in low paid, low status, so-called 3D (dirty, dangerous and difficult) jobs that are eschewed by local workers in labour-short economies in Asia and the Middle East. These are drawn predominantly from the South Asian nations, and Indonesia, Thailand, the Philippines, China, Burma and Vietnam. The second group are much smaller in number but still significant, and involve highly skilled professionals drawn mainly from India, Bangladesh, Pakistan, Sri Lanka and the Philippines. They are attracted not only to fast developing, labour-short, Newly Industrializing Countries (NICs) and near NICs, but also to labour-surplus nations like China and Indonesia, where there is a mismatch between the products of the education and training system and the skilled labour demands of a rapidly restructuring and growing economy.

In countries like South Korea, Japan, Taiwan, Singapore, Hong Kong, Brunei, Malaysia and Thailand, the shortage of labour has led to major inflows of workers both documented and undocumented. These countries experienced net emigration in the first three decades of the post-war period but have been through a rapid demographic transition and have become substantial immigration nations. This transition has been much more rapid than it was in Europe (Martin 1993, 1994; Fields 1994; Skeldon 1994; Vasuprasat 1994). Malaysia and Thailand are currently midway through this transition and are recording *both* substantial emigration and significant immigration of workers from nearby labour-surplus nations (Indonesia, Bangladesh and Burma especially). Accurate estimation of the stocks and flows of labour migrants in Asia is not possible because of limited data collection and significant undocumented flows.

One of the most important trends over the last two decades is the growing demand for labour migrants in the so-called Asian Tiger economies where rapid economic growth and an associated growth in employment have been outpacing the rate of growth of the native workforce. The latter is also due to the substantial fertility declines of the 1960s and 1970s, which resulted in cohorts of school leavers in the late 1980s and 1990s being smaller than the generations preceding them.

Student migration

One movement of particular significance is the increasing number of Asians undertaking study outside their homeland, especially in North countries, but increasingly too, in other Asian nations. Table 17.3 presents UNESCO data on the number of students from Asia studying in countries other than their own. This indicates that in 2010, 1.33 million Asian students left home to study abroad with the largest numbers from China, Korea and India. The major destinations are OECD nations. Asia is a major source of foreign students in most of the countries with the largest numbers of such students – USA and Australia (around two-thirds), Germany and the United Kingdom (around one-third).

Student migration is part of the emigration of Human Resources in Science and Technology (HRST) out of Asia, both because of the fact that many students work while studying but especially because for an increasing number of these students their move is a prelude to permanent settlement in the destination. Indeed, OECD nations are increasingly seeing recruitment of overseas students not only as being financially beneficial but also an excellent source of future skilled migrants. Hence, what is potentially a valuable asset to an Asian nation's human resources

Table 17.3 Asian tertiary education international students and their main destinations, 2010

Origin	Number	Top five destinations
Brunei	3,208	UK, Australia, Malaysia, NZ, USA
Cambodia	4,060	Thailand, France, Vietnam, Australia, USA
China	562,889	USA, Australia, Japan, UK, Republic of Korea
Hong Kong	32,842	Australia, UK, USA, Canada, Macao
Macao	1,733	Australia, USA, UK, Hong Kong, Canada
DPR Korea	2,079	Australia, Canada, France, India, Philippines
Indonesia	34,067	Australia, Malaysia, USA, Japan, Germany
Japan	40,867	USA, UK, Australia, Canada, Germany
Laos	3,854	Vietnam, Thailand, Japan, Australia, France
Malaysia	53,884	Australia, UK, USA, Russian Fed, Indonesia
Myanmar	6,288	Russian Fed, Thailand, Japan, USA, Australia
Philippines	11,748	USA, UK, Australia, Saudi Arabia, Japan
Republic of Korea	126,447	USA, Japan, Australia, UK, Canada
Singapore	20,030	Australia, USA, UK, Malaysia, Canada
Thailand	26,233	USA, UK, Australia, Japan, Malaysia
Timor-Leste	3,699	Indonesia, Cuba, Saudi Arabia, Australia, Portugal
Vietnam	47,979	USA, Australia, France, Japan, Russian Fed
Afghanistan	5,757	Iran, Turkey, USA, Germany, Russian Fed
Bangladesh	20,831	UK, Australia, USA, Cyprus, Japan
Bhutan	1,229	India, Australia, Thailand, USA, Canada
India	200,621	USA, UK, Australia, New Zealand, Canada
Iran	38,380	Malaysia, USA, UK, Germany, Canada
Maldives	1,897	Malaysia, Australia, UK, Saudi Arabia, NZ
Nepal	24,238	USA, Australia, Japan, India, UK
Pakistan	34,290	UK, USA, Australia, Sweden, Canada
Sri Lanka	16,135	Australia, UK, USA, Japan, Malaysia
Total	**1,325,285**	**UK, USA, Australia, Canada, Japan**

Source: UNESCO (2012).

and a conduit of knowledge transfer has become a dimension of brain drain. In Australia, for example, in recent years more than a half of immigrants from Asia who settle in the country already have an Australian qualification (Hugo 2005).

North-South and South-South migration

While increased movement from Asia to the OECD nations has been perhaps the major shift in international migration over the last two decades, there have also been significant flows in the other direction and within the region. In Asia the rapid growth and restructuring of national economies have been accompanied by an increasing influx of skilled workers and business people from Europe, North America and Australasia on a mostly temporary, but long term, basis. This has been in addition to significant movement of professionals and other highly skilled workers within the Asian region, largely from countries with education systems producing larger numbers of such workers than their own economies can currently absorb, especially India, the Philippines, Pakistan, Sri Lanka and Bangladesh.

The influx of professionals, business people and technical workers from more developed countries is associated with the massive growth of investment by multinational companies in the Asian region which has seen the transfer of staff from the origin country to Asia. It has been estimated that in 2003 there were 911,062 Japanese citizens living overseas, many in other Asian countries (Iguchi 2005). The mismatches between the education and training systems and labour market skill needs in rapidly growing economies, such as Indonesia, have also led to substantial numbers of expatriate engineers, technicians, accountants, finance and management experts, etc. having to be imported, notwithstanding high levels of local underemployment and unemployment among the educated population (Hugo 1996).

Another element in this flow of migrants is a reverse flow to the South-North migration considered earlier: a 'reverse brain drain'. It refers to the return migration of former migrants who have spent a considerable period living and working in a developed country. This movement has been gathering momentum throughout the late 1980s and 1990s and is associated partly with the burgeoning opportunities in the rapidly growing, restructuring and labour shortage economies of their home countries. Moreover, the dynamism of the economies of their home countries has contrasted with the low growth and economic downturns experienced by some of the developed countries in the early 1990s. In some Asian countries there has been a deliberate policy to attract back former emigrants who have particular technical, professional or business skills (Hugo 1996).

Marriage migration

One of the most significant, albeit neglected, types of growing international mobility in Asia is that related to marriage (Jones 2012a). There are two components. The first occurs because the high level of international movement by young Asians associated with study, tourism and work means that, inevitably, many are going to form relationships with foreigners while abroad. The second element is commodified marriage whereby agents are employed to seek out marriage partners in a foreign country or mail order/online partnering schemes are utilized. The changing role of women in some Asian countries has also resulted in men seeking brides with more 'traditional' values. In several Asian countries with rapidly rising ratios of women with higher levels of education in the cohorts entering marriageable age and continuing attitudes among men favouring hypogamy, less educated and lower status men (especially in rural areas) are finding it increasingly difficult to find brides locally. Moreover in countries such as China, South Korea, India and Singapore, male child preference and sex selective abortion are creating a significant imbalance between the number of young men and young women in the marriage ages.

In the past marriage migration has been directed towards Europe, Australia, New Zealand and North America but the movement is increasingly dominated by mobility within Asia. Marriage migration is becoming increasingly significant in Japan, South Korea, Taiwan and Singapore with the major origin countries being Vietnam, the Philippines, Indonesia and Thailand. It is playing an important role in changing attitudes towards migration in societies which have had a strong anti-migration cultural homogeneity focus. In South Korea, international marriages increased from 11,605 in 2000 to 42,356 in 2005. The numbers have since declined with a tightening of controls on marriage migration agreements but remain substantial. Almost three-quarters of international marriages are of Korean men with foreign women. Another element in the increasing importance of marriage migration is the preference among some groups in the diaspora for spouses from the country of origin. For example, Afghans living outside Afghanistan often choose prospective brides from their home region in Afghanistan and bring them to the destination country (Abbasi-Shavazi et al. 2012).

The increasing level of marriage migration in the region is creating new forms of marriage and family formation and has important implications for family law in both origin and destination countries.

Graeme Hugo

Feminization of Asian migration

One of the most distinctive features of the massive expansion of international migration in Asia over the last two decades has been what has been referred to as the feminization of that movement. Many international migrants, if not the majority, are women. However, it is often difficult to measure the proportion of females because much of their movement occurs outside official migration systems. It is important to study the movements of women separately from those of men, because the patterns, causes, consequences and policy implications of the movement of women can differ from those of men. Also, migrant women are often more vulnerable to exploitation than are men.

Asian countries vary in the extent to which women are represented in labour migration streams, as shown in Table 17.4. Women dominate in two of the major migrant sending nations, the Philippines and Indonesia, whereas in Bangladesh cultural factors have led to women not being permitted to be recruited as labour migrants, although this barrier has been removed in the last decade. The Thai figures are a little misleading in that much female migration is undocumented (Klanarong 2003).

It is apparent, however, that unskilled women predominate among female migrants from Asia. Much of the migration involves women, like men, taking up low wage, low status 3D jobs that are eschewed by local women at the destination. There is greater occupational segmentation among women than is the case among men. There are a relatively small number of occupations among which unskilled female international labour migrants from Asia are concentrated. Paramount here is the occupation of domestic workers. Asia is one of the world's greatest suppliers of female international migrants working in domestic service, not only in other Asian countries but also in other regions, especially the Middle East and Europe. This movement involves more than two million women, mainly from the Philippines, Indonesia, Sri Lanka and Thailand. Since the work is located in the homes of employers, it is open to greater exploitation than working in a factory or other workplace. Some of the other main occupations which unskilled female migrant workers take up in other countries also make them vulnerable to exploitation. One of the most significant of these is working in the so-called entertainment or sex industry.

Table 17.4 Selected Asian out-migration economies: proportion of international labour migrants who are women

Country of origin of international labour migrants	Year	Number of workers sent	Per cent women
Philippines	2010	1,470,826	54.5*
Sri Lanka	2010	267,507	48.8
Thailand	2007	161,917	14.8
Indonesia	2005	474,310	68.5
Vietnam	2006	78,855	34.0
Bangladesh	2007	832,609	4.0

Note: *New hires.
Sources: Philippine Overseas Employment Administration (2011); Sri Lanka Bureau of Foreign Employment (n.d.); Thailand: Kachonpadungkitti (2008); Indonesia: Ananta and Arifin (2008: 22); Vietnam: Angsuthanasombat (2010: 3); Bangladesh: Miah (2008).

Undocumented migration in Asia

As Castles (2003) has pointed out, the overwhelmingly dominant policy model for dealing with migration in Asia is to not allow permanent settlement and to greatly restrict non-permanent migration, especially that of unskilled workers. This is in spite of the existence of a manifest demand for unskilled workers in those Asian nations where native labour forces have ceased to grow because of a long period of low fertility. In Asia the official barriers erected by nation states to the inflow of people have been substantially more resistant to the process of globalization than barriers to information flows and movements of finance and traded goods. Nevertheless, the inequalities, differences and complementarities which have fuelled other flows between nations are impinging equally strongly upon people. With barriers to entering countries, the international migration that occurs outside of official immigration control systems has increased exponentially. Indeed there may be as many undocumented international migrants in Asia as there are officially recognized migrants. However, almost all of the existing research and literature on patterns, causes and consequences of international migration are devoted to considerations of legal, documented migrants. This is hardly surprising given the inherent difficulties in measuring, let alone studying in detail, undocumented migration.

Undocumented labour migration in Asia can be differentiated along a wide spectrum ranging from totally voluntary movement in which the mover controls the migration process, through to kidnapping and trafficking at the other extreme. Labour migrants who control their own movement arrange all their own travel and move along familiar, well established routes. However, in many undocumented moves, middlemen of various types are involved and their control over the migrant workers varies considerably. In some situations the chain of middlemen involved reaches back to the home village and they have strong accountability to the home community. In others, they are all powerful in controlling the information that potential workers receive about the migration process and destination, in determining when they move, how much it costs, where they go and what job they obtain.

These movements grade into trafficking where workers are forced to move and are in indentured situations in the destination country. In some cases, potential migrant workers are purposely misled about the type of work at the destination, the conditions, remuneration, etc. and are 'trapped' at the destination. In others, workers (often women and children) are sold into bonded situations, often by relatives, while at the extreme, people are kidnapped and trafficked across borders against their will. In all cases, their unauthorized status exposes them to the possibility of exploitation and prevents them seeking the protection of authorities at the destination. This can add to the marginalization experienced by many migrant groups.

Migration and development

In addressing the impacts of migration in origin and destination countries, it is important to recognize that migration can and does have both negative and positive impacts. Simplistic pronouncements of migration having an unfailingly positive (or negative) influence on poverty reduction or economic and social development are not helpful. Migration can both support and undermine national and regional attempts to alleviate poverty and encourage development. The crucial issue is that migration can play a positive role and this provides scope for policy intervention which can, on the one hand, facilitate and enhance those elements of migration which have positive effects and also reduce or ameliorate those which have negative impacts. The development of such interventions requires a deep understanding of the complex interrelationship between migration on the one hand and economic development and poverty alleviation on the other.

The discourse on the effects of migration on development is polarized around two schools of thought. On the one hand, the 'brain drain' perspective sees migration impact on origin areas as negative because emigration is selective of the 'best and the brightest', diminishing human capital and constraining development. Others point to the inflow of finance, information and ways of doing things which result from the outflow as being positive for development. Both perspectives have relevance for contemporary international migration in Asia.

A 'brain drain' involving a net loss of skilled persons from less developed nations in Asia and a net gain in the more developed countries elsewhere was recognized as long ago as the 1960s (Adams 1968). More recent analyses (e.g. Carrington and Detragiache 1998; Dumont and Lemaître 2005; Dumont, Spielvogel and Widmaier 2010) have confirmed that emigration rates in Asian countries are higher for skilled groups and that some countries experience a significant brain drain. Moreover, in recent times, destination nations have placed greater emphasis on skill in their selection of immigrants and this, with the increasing global competition for talent and skilled workers (Abella 2005), has exacerbated these tendencies.

A comprehensive analysis by the OECD (Dumont, Spielvogel and Widmaier 2010) has collected data from more than 200 sending nations and 89 receiving nations and calculated emigration rates of highly qualified persons (with a university education) for non-OECD nations. Overall, some 4.3 per cent of all Asia-born persons with a university qualification live outside of their country of birth – a rate which is lower than for Africa (10.6 per cent), Europe (7.8 per cent), Latin America (8.8 per cent) and Oceania (7.2 per cent). Table 17.5 presents the highly skilled emigration rates for a number of Asian countries and a range is evident. As elsewhere, the rates are quite low for large nations like China, India, Indonesia, Japan, Pakistan and Bangladesh, despite the fact that immigrants from these nations are among the largest groups residing in OECD countries. The highest rates are in smaller nations like Brunei, Hong Kong, Macao and the Maldives. However, there are also substantial rates in some medium-sized Asian nations which have become known as important origin countries for skilled migrants. These include the Philippines, Vietnam, Sri Lanka, Cambodia and Laos.

Table 17.5 Emigration rates[a] of tertiary-educated by country of origin, c.2000

Country of origin	Emigration rate (%)	Country of origin	Emigration rate (%)
Afghanistan	4.2	Maldives	11.9
Bangladesh	4.5	Myanmar	1.9
Brunei	19.7	Mongolia	5.4
China	2.0	Malaysia	9.3
Hong Kong, China	16.9	Nepal	2.7
Indonesia	2.4	Pakistan	4.3
India	2.9	Philippines	15.0
Japan	1.0	Singapore	9.1
Cambodia	43.7	Thailand	3.5
South Korea	3.7	Taiwan	6.1
Laos	10.9	Vietnam	18.4
Sri Lanka	28.8		
Macao, China	16.7		

Note: [a] Per cent of tertiary-educated persons born in country of origin now living in another country.
Source: Based on data reported in Dumont, Spielvogel and Widmaier (2010).

Asia's international migration

Despite the low rates of emigration of highly skilled persons from large Asian countries, it would be incorrect to assume that brain drain does not have negative impacts in the region and that there are no net losses of the human resources necessary to foster long-term development in Asia. The loss of even small numbers of the most skilled, most educated and most entrepreneurial can be a significant constraint on development. This is especially the case, for example, in the net loss of doctors, nurses and other health professionals from several Asian countries.

Much of the discussion about potential positive impacts of migration on origin areas relates to remittances. The World Bank (Ratha et al. 2013) has estimated global remittances in 2013 at US$594 billion, some $414 billon being directed towards developing countries. Remittances have continued to increase despite the Global Financial Crisis, and remittances to less developed countries are now almost three times larger than official development assistance and approximately the size of foreign direct investment. Moreover in considering these figures, it must be borne in mind that: 'This amount, however, reflects only transfers through official channels. Econometric analysis and available household surveys suggest that unrecorded flows through informal channels may add 50 per cent or more to recorded flows' (World Bank 2007: 1).

Ratha et al. (2013) project that remittance flows are expected to register an average annual growth rate of over 8 per cent between 2013 and 2016. The three largest recipient countries of remittances in 2013 were Asian – India (US$71 billion), China (US$60 billion) and the Philippines (US$26 billion) – while Bangladesh, Vietnam and Pakistan were also in the top ten.

According to the World Bank (2013), remittances have increased substantially in recent years particularly in countries such as Indonesia, the Philippines and the countries of South Asia, and are the largest source of external funding in several Asian countries, having an impact on the balance of payments. Official estimates of remittances relative to the value of total merchandise exports and imports over the last three decades in several major migrant origin countries in Asia show that the effects vary considerably (Table 17.6). Remittances are generally small in relation to export earnings in the larger countries, especially China and Indonesia. An exception is India where remittances have represented an important share of foreign exchange earnings, especially in recent years. Remittances are significant in all the countries of South Asia, especially in Sri Lanka, Bangladesh and Pakistan. In the Philippines, remittances have made up a major share of foreign exchange earnings for many years.

Diaspora and development

Several Asian countries have growing and substantial diaspora working in high-income countries and there is increasing interest in the role that they can and do play in development, growth and poverty reduction in their origin countries (Newland and Tanaka 2010). First, as discussed above, remittances from the diaspora are larger and a more reliable source of development funds to less developed countries than development assistance. There are two major areas of policy concern with respect to remittances from the diaspora. The first involves initiatives to reduce the transaction costs involved in sending remittances. The World Bank (Ratha et al. 2013) has shown that the global average cost of sending $200 is around 9 per cent. The second area of policy concern relates to creating opportunities for families receiving remittances and returning migrants to invest remittances in productive enterprises.

Second, it is increasingly being realized that diaspora can contribute to development in their home countries in other ways. One of the roles that the diaspora can play is as both a direct source of foreign investment and as an effective agent to channel such investment towards the home country. Biers and Dhume (2000: 38) report that '…several overseas Indians who had reached upper management positions in western multinational companies helped convince their

Table 17.6 Main Asian labour exporting countries: workers' remittances relative to exports and imports in US$ million, 1980–2012

Country	Year	Workers' remittances	Total merchandise Exports (X)	Total merchandise Imports (M)	R X	R M
Indonesia	1980	33	21,908	10,834	0.2	0.3
	1992	264	33,815	27,280	0.8	1.0
	2012	7,212	186,146	190,225	3.9	3.8
Philippines	1980	421	5,744	8,295	7.3	5.1
	1992	2,538	9,790	15,465	25.9	16.4
	2012	24,641	51,995	65,360	47.4	37.7
Thailand	1979	189	5,240	7,158	3.6	2.6
	1992	1,500	32,473	40,466	4.6	3.7
	2012	4,713	229,519	247,590	2.1	1.9
Bangladesh	1980	339	885	2,545	38.3	13.3
	1992	912	1,903	2,527	47.9	36.1
	2012	14,085	25,113	34,132	56.1	41.3
Pakistan	1980	2,048	2,958	5,709	69.2	35.9
	1992	1,574	7,264	9,360	21.7	16.8
	2012	14,007	24,596	44,157	56.9	31.7
India	1980	2,757	11,265	17,378	24.4	15.9
	1992	2,897	19,795	22,530	14.6	12.8
	2012	67,258	293,214	489,394	22.9	13.7
Sri Lanka	1980	152	1,293	2,197	11.8	6.9
	1992	548	2,487	3,470	22.0	15.8
	2012	6,001	9,480	19,087	63.3	31.4
China	1982	564	21,875	19,009	2.6	3.0
	1992	739	84,940	80,585	0.9	0.9
	2012	57,799	2,048,814	1,818,069	2.8	3.2

Sources: Hugo (1995); World Bank Development Report (1979–2012); World Bank Remittances Data (October 2013).

companies to set up operations in India. Hewlett Packard, being a prime example'. It has been suggested that the spectacular economic growth of China and Taiwan in recent years has been influenced heavily by investment from a diaspora of perhaps 30 million Chinese (Lucas 2003). There has been considerable discussion of how Chinese business and social networks have overcome barriers to international trade. Rauch and Trindade (2002) found that the Chinese diaspora have a quantitatively important impact on bilateral trade. Rubin (1996) has shown how Chinese entrepreneurs in the United States are taking their businesses into China. The Indian diaspora, second in size only to that of China, comprises around 20 million people with a total income of US$160 billion – more than a third of India's GDP (Sharma 2003).

Third, the diaspora can be a bridgehead into expansion of the economic linkages of the home nation. Korean Americans were the bridgeheads for the successful penetration of the United States market by Korean car, electronics and white good manufacturers. Canadian based studies have shown that a doubling of skilled migration from Asia saw a 74 per cent increase in Asian imports to Canada (Head and Reis 1998; Lucas 2001).

Fourth, diaspora networks have become important in transmitting information both formally and informally. Levitt (1998: 927) refers to this as *social remittances* – 'the ideas, behaviours, identities and social capital that flow from receiving to sending communities'. It can be the transmission of different ways of doing things and can take the form of networks of professionals sending information. Lucas (2001) has shown how professionals in origin and destination countries have maintained strong linkages so that ideas flow freely in both directions. In Taiwan, meetings of local and diasporic scientists are held. In the scientific world, flows of information are of utmost significance and it may also be that diaspora can play a role in technology transfers. The potential for such interaction to accelerate diffusion of new ideas, products, processes, etc. is considerable. Undoubtedly, the ethnic linkages of Taiwan and India with Silicon Valley have had a major impact on the development of the information technology sector in the home countries and regions (Saxenian 1999).

Return migration

The main way in which net emigration countries have attempted to recoup the human capital of skilled emigrants is through return migration programmes. Some of the major attempts to encourage expatriates to return have been made by Asian countries. Korea and Taiwan (Englesberg 1995), for example, initiated programmes to encourage a 'reverse brain drain' (Chang 1992; Hugo 1996), with some success (Yoon 1992), although it is not clear the extent to which this was due to the programmes and how much was a result of rapid economic development (Lucas 2001). Saxenian (1999) points out that some of the advantages flowing from these activities have been an increase in interaction between Taiwanese and Korean scientists and engineers with expatriate colleagues in the United States, facilitating knowledge transfer, investment and business cooperation (Lucas 2001).

The largest outflow of talent has been from China. A Chinese Academy of Sciences Report (*Asian Migration News*, 1–15 February 2007) estimated that one million Chinese students had left to study abroad in the two decades to 2006 and two-thirds had chosen to remain abroad after graduation. Chinese governments at national and regional levels have put in place a large number of programmes to attract these migrants back on a permanent or temporary basis (Zweig 2006). In addition to national policies to attract back skilled expatriates, individual Chinese provinces, companies and development parks also offer a range of incentives to return, including equivalent salary packages taking into account purchasing power, expenses-paid trips to China, etc. (*Asian Migration News*, 16–30 November 2002). The Chinese government programme offers high salaries, multiple entry-exit visas and access to strictly controlled foreign exchange (*Asian Migration News*, 16 August 2001).

Zweig (2006) points out there has been a 'reverse tide' of returning Chinese since the mid-1990s, with the numbers coming back increasing rapidly although there has not been an increase in the *percentage returning*. He demonstrates that large numbers and levels of government organizations actively promote the return of scholars and students but also that the return wave has been associated with 'political stability, improved housing, better business opportunities and a more vibrant private sector, more modern equipment and management procedures, higher salaries and special incentives' (Zweig 2006: 212–213). The term *Hai Gui* has been applied to this group, and refers to the returning sea turtles that were born onshore, grew up at sea but eventually returned to shore again (Wattanavitukul 2002). Zweig, Changgui and Rosen (2004) have shown that foreign PhDs are worth more than domestic PhDs, not only in terms of perceptions in China but also in their ability to affect technology transfer and capital and bring benefits to China.

More recently, however, the Chinese have concentrated more on engaging with their diaspora, ensuring that they return frequently and maintain intensive contact with colleagues in China (Wescott 2005). There has been a recognition that frequent temporary return and virtual return (through email, etc.) can deliver as big a dividend for China as permanent return.

Graeme Hugo

There is limited experience of government policies and programmes to encourage return migration in other Asian countries (Hugo 1996). Not all have been successful. Malaysia, for example, is a rapidly growing economy with a diaspora of 250,000 skilled workers overseas (Jayasankaran 2003). In 2001, the government initiated a substantial scheme offering tax exemptions on income remitted to Malaysia and on all personal items brought into the country, and granting of permanent resident status to spouses and children. The scheme targeted six key fields – information and communications technology, manufacturing industries, science and technology, arts, finance and medicine – especially in the UK, USA, Singapore, Brunei, Hong Kong and Australia (*Asian Migration News*, 16–30 November 2002). In the first two years of the programme only 104 expatriates returned home (*Asian Migration News*, 1–15 January 2003).

Policy implications

One of the defining characteristics of international migration in Asia has been the increasing involvement of government in seeking to influence the pattern of immigration or emigration in their countries. The United Nations (2013d) conducts a survey of national governments every few years to assess their population policies and has noted a growing 'openness' to immigration, with fewer countries seeking to lower immigration levels. Table 17.7 shows that this has been the case in Asia: in 1996, 46 per cent of reporting countries had policies to lower immigration, but this had been reduced to 28 per cent in 2011. Moreover, the proportion of nations wishing to increase immigration increased from 4 to 15 per cent over the same period.

The United Nations survey also records Asian government attitudes towards emigration and these are presented in Table 17.8. This indicates that there has been a reduction in the proportion of countries seeking to lower emigration, from 30 per cent in 2005 to 19 per cent in 2011. Moreover, the proportion with policies to raise emigration has risen from 7 per cent in 1996 to 26 per cent in 2011. These trends are also evident globally (United Nations 2013d) and reflect the growing recognition that expatriates can have positive impacts on development at home. In this respect, it is interesting to note that there has been a significant increase in the number of Asian countries which have specific policies to facilitate the return of their expatriates. Indeed, there has been a doubling since 1996. It is interesting, too, that some 24 Asian governments have reported having established a special government unit to deal with matters of interest to emigrants and their families living in other countries. However, while globally more than a half of governments have policies to allow their citizens to retain their citizenship of origin without

Table 17.7 Views and policies of Asian governments regarding immigration, 1976–2011

Year	Views on level of immigration				Goal of policies on immigration			
	Too low	Satisfactory	Too high	Total number of countries	Raise	Maintain or no intervention	Lower	Total number of countries
1976	4	32	1	37	4	32	1	37
1986	1	30	7	38	1	30	7	38
1996	1	35	10	46	2	23	21	46
2005	4	30	13	47	4	26	17	47
2011	2	33	12	47	7	27	13	47

Source: United Nations (2013c).

Table 17.8 Views and policies of Asian governments regarding emigration, 1976–2011

Year	Views on level of emigration				Goal of policies on emigration			
	Too low	Satisfactory	Too high	Total number of countries	Raise	Maintain or no intervention	Lower	Total number of countries
1976	4	31	2	37	4	31	2	37
1986	3	28	7	38	5	25	8	38
1996	2	31	13	46	3	32	11	46
2005	7	25	15	47	9	24	14	47
2011	7	28	12	47	12	26	9	47

Source: United Nations (2013c).

restrictions when acquiring another country's citizenship, in Asia only 34.8 per cent allow dual citizenship without restriction and another 15 per cent with some restriction.

It could be argued that one of the most pressing needs in the region is for migration in general, and international labour migration in particular, to be considered by national governments in a more objective way. It is clearly an emotional issue but in many countries, especially in destination nations, there is widespread misunderstanding and misinterpretation of the nature, scale and effects of contemporary international migration of workers. Indeed, one of the concerns is that the international labour migration issue is not even on the 'radar screen' of both formal and informal discussion. There are myths and half-truths abounding about migrant workers and their effects. Stereotypes about involvement in crime, spreading disease, etc. need to be exposed as incorrect and there is a need for both governments and the public more generally to see migrant workers as contributing to, and in some cases constituting an integral part of, the local economy. Indeed, in many cases such workers are necessary for the long term health of the economy. The failure to recognize these realities has led to unrealistic policies and programmes to replace migrant workers with local workers; these programmes and overly restrictive entry policies only encourage the proliferation of underground migration that marginalizes and restricts the rights of migrant workers.

Hence, there would seem to be a need in the region for the wider dissemination of quality research-based information about the reality of labour migration and its effects to policymakers, planners and the general population in destination countries. There is a widespread view in these countries that the whole migrant worker issue revolves around the maintenance of national homogeneity, compliance with immigration regulations and border control. However, there are more positive aspects such as the contribution of workers to the national economy; the fact that most migrant workers wish to maintain strong contact with their home areas and to return to their home country; and the social and cultural benefits of multicultural societies.

What is involved here is a significant shift in culture, and this is one of the most intractable barriers to improving the situation for migrant workers and to enabling labour migration systems to work more efficiently and effectively, as well as equitably and justly.

There is a particular concern in Asia of the need to achieve better practice with respect to international labour migrants, both in origin and destination nations. There is considerable variation between nations in the level of government commitment and in the extent of protection given to labour migrants. For example, the Philippines has developed an array of strategies to protect its migrant workers, while Indonesia until recently has done little.

Civil society is playing an increasing role with respect to migration, internal and international, in Asia although there is considerable variation from country to country in the nature and level of that activity. Most NGO activity in this area is nationally based but there are some emerging regional NGOs which cover several nations. It is particularly important to have NGOs which are active in pairs of origin and destination countries. There are a number of examples of effective NGO activity improving the protection of migrants, providing support for migrants, and also in advocating for the rights of migrants and in lobbying to change policy in both origin and destination countries. In terms of origin countries, the Philippines has the best developed and most comprehensive NGO presence and their role undoubtedly has improved the lot of overseas contract workers from that country.

One of the major constraints on governments in the Asian region is a lack of capacity in the development of efficient and equitable migration systems, which work for the benefit of countries of origin and destination as well as migrants. Countries need to move from a migration governance system which is focused on control, to one which seeks to manage people movement. Migration will continue to occur if there is a good reason for it to occur (demand for workers, persecution, environmental pressures, etc.). To seek to stop it in such circumstances is doomed to failure and simply forces the movement underground and into the hands of illegal and criminal agencies. However, effective migration management requires considerable capacity and infrastructure, and this is lacking in most countries.

There is general agreement that, in the new 'age of migration', countries cannot aspire to stop migration flows but are best advised to develop effective management of that population mobility which maximizes national interest, while preserving the integrity of national borders and human rights. Effective management of migration is very much dependent on international bilateral, regional and multilateral cooperation.

Conclusion

Among all of the massive transformations which have swept across Asia in the last half century, the increase in population mobility has been one of the most striking. There has been an increase in both the scale and complexity of population movement both as a cause and a consequence of the region's dramatic social, economic, political and demographic changes. International migration has been an important part of this change. While there is a great deal of variation between nations, it is clear that demographic, economic and social changes within the region will continue to favour an increase in international movement, as will differences between Asia on the one hand and Europe, North America and Australia-New Zealand on the other.

A major barrier to the development of better understanding and an evidence-based policy relating to international migration in Asia is a lack of comprehensive, relevant and timely data on migration stocks and flows. There is a dire need for a regional initiative to improve the amount and quality of data on international migration. The evidence base on the adaptation of immigrants to destinations, their relationships with the labour market, responses of host communities and the increasing significance of diaspora is extremely limited, and there is a need to improve considerably the capacity to undertake high quality demographic research on international migration in Asia.

International migration is 'here to stay' as a permanent structural feature of Asian economies and societies and must no longer be considered as a temporary, ephemeral phenomenon. As Castles (2003: 22) argues, there is a need in the region to make a 'conceptual leap' with respect to international migration policy, involving, in part, the recognition of the long term significance of migration and settlement in the region. As he correctly states, the conceptual leap '…is not likely to happen quickly, but the human costs of delay may be high'. Migration has the potential to improve the situation of people in poorer countries and to facilitate development in these nations. However, making this happen will be dependent in part on the formulation of a judicious range of migration policies within countries of origin and destination and in achieving a greater degree of cooperation between sending and receiving countries.

References

Abbasi-Shavazi, M. J., R. Sadeghi, H. Mahmoudian and G. Jamshidiha (2012) 'Marriage and family formation of the second generation Afghans in Iran: insight from a qualitative survey'. *International Migration Review*, 46(4): 828–860.

Abella, M. I. (2005) 'Social issues in the management of labour migration in Asia and the Pacific'. *Asia-Pacific Population Journal*, 20(3): 61–86.

Adams, W. (1968) *The Brain Drain*. New York: Macmillan.

Ananta, A. and E. N. Arifin (2008) 'Demographic and population mobility transitions in Indonesia'. Paper prepared for PECC-ABAC Conference on Demographic Change and International Labor Mobility in the Asia-Pacific Region, Seoul, South Korea, 25–26 March. Available from: www.pecc.org.

Angsuthanasombat, K. (2010) 'Situation and trends of Vietnamese labor export'. Available from: www.asian-scholarship.org/asf/ejourn/articles/kannika_a.pdf (accessed 23 September 2010).

Arif, G. M. (2009) *Recruitment of Pakistani Workers for Overseas Employment: Mechanisms, Exploitation and Vulnerabilities*, July. Geneva: International Labour Office.

Asian Migration News, www.smc.org.ph/smc_amn.

Baruah, N. (2013) 'Trends and outlook for labour migration in Asia'. Presentation for the 3rd ADBI-OECD-ILO Roundtable on Labour Migration in Asia: Assessing Labour Market Requirements for Foreign Workers and Developing Policies for Regional Skills Mobility, Thailand, 23–25 January.

Biers, D. and S. Dhume (2000) 'In India, a bit of California'. *Far Eastern Economic Review*, 2 November.

Carrington, W. and E. Detragiache (1998) 'How big is the brain drain?'. IMF Working Paper WP/98/102, Washington.

Castles, S. (2003) 'Migrant settlement, transnational communities and state region'. In R. Iredale, C. Hawksley and S. Castles (eds.) *Migration in the Asia Pacific: Population, Settlement and Citizenship Issues*. Cheltenham, UK: Edward Elgar. Pp. 3–26.

Chang, S. L. (1992) 'Causes of brain drain and solutions: the Taiwan experience'. *Studies in Comparative International Development*, 27(1): 27–43.

Dumont, J.-C. and G. Lemaître (2005) 'Counting immigrants and expatriates in OECD countries: a new perspective'. Conference on Competing for Global Talent, Singapore Management University, Singapore, 13–14 January.

Dumont, J.-C., G. Spielvogel and S. Widmaier (2010) 'International migrants in developed, emerging and developing countries: an extended profile'. OECD Social, Employment and Migration Working Papers No. 114. Available from: www.oecd.org/els/workingpapers.

Englesberg, P. (1995) 'Reversing China's brain drain: the study-abroad policy, 1978–1993'. In J. D. Montgomery and D. A. Rodinelli (eds.) *Great Policies: Strategic Innovations in Asia and the Pacific Basin*. Westport, CT: Praeger.

Fields, G. S. (1994) 'The migration transition in Asia'. *Asian and Pacific Migration Journal*, 3(1): 7–30.

Fitzpatrick, M. (2013) 'Hong Kong's foreign "helpers" fight for equality'. Available from: www.cbc.ca/news/world/hong-kong-s-foreign-helpers-fight-for-equality-1.1304964 (accessed 22 November 2013).

Gibson, J. and E. Lennon (1999) 'Historical census statistics on the foreign-born population of the United States: 1850–1990'. Population Division Working Paper No. 2, US Census Bureau.

Head, K. and J. Reis (1998) 'Immigration and trade creation: econometric evidence from Canada'. *Canadian Journal of Economics*, 31(1): 47–62.

Hu, X. (2012) 'China's young rural-to-urban migrants: in search of fortune, happiness and independence'. Migration Information Source, Population Policy Institute.

Hugo, G. J. (1995) 'Labour export from Indonesia: an overview'. *ASEAN Economic Bulletin*, 12(2): 275–298.

Hugo, G. J. (1996) 'Brain drain and student movements'. In P. J. Lloyd and L. S. Williams (eds.) *International Trade and Migration in the APEC Region*. Melbourne: Oxford University Press. Pp. 210–228.

Hugo, G. J. (2004) 'International migration in the Asia–Pacific region: emerging trends and issues'. In D. S. Massey and J. E. Taylor (eds.) *International Migration: Prospects and Policies in a Global Market*. Oxford: Oxford University Press. Pp. 77–103.

Hugo, G. J. (2005) 'Competing for global talent: the Australian experience'. Paper prepared for Conference on Competing for Global Talent, organized by Wee Kim Centre, Singapore Management University, Singapore, 13–14 January.

Iguchi, Y. (2003) 'Labour market and international migration in Japan – towards the era of new economic partnership in East Asia'. Paper prepared for Workshop on International Migration and Labour Market in Asia, organized by the Japan Institute of Labour, Tokyo, Japan, 6–7 February.

Iguchi, Y. (2005) 'Growing challenges for migration policy in Japan – to cope with regional integration and declining fertility'. Paper given at Workshop on International Migration and Labour Markets in Asia, Tokyo, Japan, 21–22 January.

IHLO (2013) Macau. Available from: www.ihlo.org/HKM/00405.html (accessed 22 November 2013).

Japan Institute for Labour Policy and Training (2012) *Databook of International Labour Statistics 2012*. Japan Institute for Labour Policy and Training.

Jayasankaran, S. (2003) 'The Ireland of Asia'. *Far Eastern Economic Review*, 20(March): 58.

Jones, G. W. (2012a) 'International marriage in Asia: what do we know, and what do we need to know'. In Doo-Sub Kim (ed.) *Cross Border Marriage: Global Trends and Diversity*. Seoul: Korea Institute for Health and Social Affairs.

Jones, G. W. (2012b) 'Population policy in a prosperous city-state: dilemmas for Singapore'. *Population and Development Review*, 38(2): 311–336.

Kachonpadungkitti, C. (2008) 'Managing the labour migration in labour-sending countries – policy development, current management mechanisms, challenges and lessons learnt'. Presentation at Regional Conference on Labour Migration Management in the Process of Regional Integration, Bangkok, Thailand, 27–30 May.

Khoo, S. E., C. Voigt-Graf, G. Hugo and P. McDonald (2003) 'Temporary skilled migration to Australia: the 457 visa sub-class'. *People and Place*, 11(4): 27–40.

Klanarong, N. (2003) 'Female international labour migration from Southern Thailand'. Unpublished PhD thesis, Population and Human Resources, Department of Geographical and Environmental Studies, The University of Adelaide.

Levitt, P. (1998) 'Social remittances: migration driven local-level forms of cultural diffusion'. *International Migration Review*, 32(4): 926–948.

Lucas, R. E. B. (2001) 'Diaspora and development: highly skilled migrants from East Asia'. Report prepared for the World Bank, Boston University, November.

Lucas, R. E. B. (2003) 'The economic well-being of movers and stayers: assimilation, impacts, links and proximity'. Paper prepared for Conference on African Migration in Comparative Perspective, Johannesburg, South Africa, 4–7 June.

Martin, P. (1993) *Trade and Migration: NAFTA and Agriculture*. Washington, DC: Institute for International Economics.

Martin, P. (1994) 'Migration and trade: challenges for the 1990s'. Paper prepared for the World Bank's Development Committee, World Bank, Washington, DC.

Martin, P. (2008) 'Temporary worker programs: US and global experiences'. Available from: www.metropolis.net/policypriority/migration_seminar/PhilipMartinsPaper_e.pdf.

Miah, S. (2008) 'Labour migration scenario of Bangladesh'. Presentation at Regional Conference on Labour Migration Management in the Process of Regional Integration, Bangkok, Thailand, 27–30 May.

Newland, K. and H. Tanaka (2010) *Mobilizing Diaspora Entrepreneurship for Development*. Migration Policy Institute.

Nguyen, N. X. (2003) 'International migration of highly skilled workers in Vietnam'. Paper presented at the Workshop on International Migration and Labour Markets in Asia, Japan Institute of Labour, Tokyo, Japan, 4–5 February.

Norbu, N. (2008) 'Labour migration trends, policies and challenges'. Available from: www.adbi.org/files/2008/05.29.cpp.norbu.country.presentations.bhutan.pdf (accessed 22 November 2013).

Organization for Economic Co-operation and Development (OECD) (1995) *Trends in International Migration: Continuous Reporting System on Migration: Annual Report 1994*. Paris: OECD.

Philippine Overseas Employment Administration (POEA) (2010) 'Commission on Filipinos overseas: stock estimate of overseas Filipinos as of December 2009'. Available from: www.poea.gov.ph/stats/Stock%20Estmate%202009.pdf.

Philippine Overseas Employment Administration (POEA) (2011) *Annual Report 2010*. Republic of the Philippines: POEA.

Ratha, D., C. Eigen-Zucchi, S. Plaza, H. Wyss and S. Yi (2013) 'Migration and remittance flows: recent trends and outlook, 2013–2016'. *Migration and Development Brief 21*. World Bank.

Rauch, J. E. and V. Trindade (2002) 'Ethnic Chinese networks in international trade'. *The Review of Economics and Statistics*, 84(1): 116–130.

Rubin, K. (1996) 'Go West, Look East'. *Far Eastern Economic Review*, 10 October.

Saadi, S. (2011) 'IMU recruits migrant workers, Central Asia Online', 4 August. Available from: http://centralasiaonline.com/en_GB/articles/caii/features/main/2011/08/04/feature-01 (accessed 9 May 2012).

Saxenian, A. L. (1999) *Silicon Valley's New Immigrant Entrepreneurs*. San Francisco: Public Policy Institute of California.

Scalabrini Migration Centre (2012) *Asian Migration Outlook 2011*. Philippines: Scalabrini Migration Centre, Quezon City.

Sharma, A. (2003) 'Come home, we need you'. *Far Eastern Economic Review*, 23(January): 28–29.

Simmons, A. (1999) 'International migration and designer immigrants: Canadian policy in the 1990s'. In M. Castro (ed.) *Free Markets, Open Societies, Closed Borders? Trends in International Migration and Immigration Policy in the Americas*. Miami: North-South Center Press.

Skeldon, R. (1994) 'Turning points in labor migration: the case of Hong Kong'. *Asian and Pacific Migration Journal*, 3(1): 93–118.

Skeldon, R. (2006) 'Recent trends in migration in East and Southeast Asia'. *Asian and Pacific Migration Journal*, 15(2): 277–293.

Soeprobo, T. B. (2005) 'Recent trends in international migration in Indonesia'. Paper prepared for Workshop on International Migration and Labour Market in Asia organized by the Japan Institute for Labour Policy and Training, Japan Institute of Labour, Tokyo, 20–21 January.

Stahl, C. W. and PECC-HRD Task Force (1996) 'International labour migration and the East Asian APEC/PECC economies: trends, issues and policies'. Paper presented at PECC Human Resource Development Task Force Meeting, Brunei, 7–8 June.

United Nations (2013a) *Trends in International Migrant Stock: The 2013 Revision*. New York: United Nations.

United Nations (2013b) *The Number of International Migrants Worldwide Reaches 232 Million, Population Facts, No. 2013/2*, September 2013. Department of Economic and Social Affairs, Population Division.

United Nations (2013c) *World Population Policies 2011*. New York: United Nations.

United Nations (2013d) *Changing Landscape of International Migration Policies, Population Facts, No. 2013/5*, September 2013. Department of Economic and Social Affairs, Population Division.

United Nations Economic Commission for Asia and the Far East (ECAFE) Secretariat (1972) 'The demographic situation in the ECAFE region'. *Asian Population Studies Series*, 28: 69–130.

United Nations Educational, Scientific and Cultural Organization (UNESCO) (2012) 'Opportunities lost: the impact of grade repetition and early school leaving'. *Global Education Digest 2012*. UNESCO Institute for Statistics.

Vasuprasat, P. (1994) 'Turning points in international labour migration: a case study of Thailand'. *Asian and Pacific Migration Journal*, 3(1): 93–118.

Wattanavitukul, P. (2002) 'Hai Gui: the sea turtles come marching home'. Available from: www.apmforum.com/columns/china19.htm.

Wescott, C. (2005) *Promoting Exchanges Through Diaspora*. G-20 Workshop on Demographic Challenges and Migration, Sydney, 27–28 August.

World Bank (1979–2012) *World Development Reports*. New York: Oxford University Press.

World Bank (2007) 'Remittance trends 2006'. *Migration and Development Brief 2, Development Prospects Group*. Washington, DC: World Bank.

World Bank (2011) *Migration and Remittances Factbook 2011*. Washington, DC: World Bank.

World Bank (2013) *Migration and Remittances Data*. Washington, DC: World Bank. Available from: www.worldbank.org/migration (accessed October 2013).

Yin, S. C. (2011) 'Plight of the migrant worker'. *Straits Times*, www.straitstimes.com/Asia/China/Story/STIStory_637189.html.

Yoon, B. L. (1992) 'Reverse brain drain in South Korea: state-led model'. *Studies in Comparative International Development*, 27(1): 4–26.

Yu, T. (2010) 'Number of outbound tourists soaring'. *China Daily*, www.chinadaily.com.cn/bizchina/2010-03/29/content_9654759.htm.

Zhou, M. and G. Cai (2005) 'Migrant workers' adaptation to urban life'. Paper prepared for Urban China Research Network Conference 'Urban China in Transition', New Orleans, Louisiana, 15–16 January.

Zhu, Y. (2004) 'Changing urbanization processes and *in situ* rural-urban transformation: reflections on China's settlement definitions'. In A. Champion and G. Hugo (eds.) *New Forms of Urbanization*. Aldershot: Ashgate. Pp. 207–208.

Zweig, D. (2006) 'Learning to compete: China's efforts to encourage a "reverse brain drain"'. In E. Pang and C. Kuptsch (eds.) *Competing for Global Talent*. Geneva: International Labour Office.

Zweig, D., C. Changgui and S. Rosen (2004) 'Globalization and transnational human capital: overseas and returnee scholars to China'. *The China Quarterly*, 179: 735–757.

18
Forced and refugee migration in Asia

Mohammad Jalal Abbasi-Shavazi and Ellen Percy Kraly

Introduction

Regions throughout Asia have experienced high levels of voluntary and forced population movements. In recent years, forced migrations originating from some Asian countries have contributed to the global scale and complexity of international population movements. According to a recent report by the United Nations High Commission of Refugees (UNHCR), there were 63.9 million persons 'of concern' in the world at the end of 2015, and 46.0 per cent of them (29.4 million) were from Asia. Among those originating from Asian countries, about 9.6 million or about one-third were officially designated as refugees or people in refugee-like situations (UNHCR 2016a).

Despite the increasing volume and complexity of refugee migration and forced population movements, most demographic studies on migration have focused on voluntary or unforced population movements. Although Asia's voluntary migration has been well documented and analysed (Huget 1992; Battistella 2002; Hugo 2005, 2006 and Chapter 17), little attention has been paid to forced migration. This chapter is a step to fill the gap in the demography of refugee migration and forced population movements in Asia. The chapter begins with a brief review of the concept and definitions of forced migration. Available data sources and research on forced population movements in Asia are then examined. Following that, the chapter analyses the levels and patterns of forced migration in Asia, and identifies the major social demographic characteristics of the refugee population. Finally, it discusses the major driving forces of refugee migration and forced population movement in Asia and the implications of this study.

Who are forced migrants and refugees?

In both theory and practice, distinction between voluntary and forced migration is difficult. Most straightforwardly, voluntary migration is the movement of people into another place by their own choice. Voluntary migrants sometimes move as a result of their own desires and motivations to seek a better life and all that entails, including better jobs and economic opportunities, education, marriage and retirement. They choose where they migrate to and can usually return whenever they like. Voluntary migrants have time to prepare for their trip and plan their life in their new location. By contrast, forced migrants are persons compelled to leave their country, region or home to seek safe haven, protection and security. Although both push and pull factors may be involved in the decision and choice of migration, people who migrate voluntarily are generally responding to pull factors in the destination place and are motivated to improve their future prospects for themselves and their families. People who are forced to migrate, on the other hand, are mainly influenced by push factors in the place of origin.

The term 'refugee' has particular meaning in international affairs. Under the 1951 Convention of the United Nations and the 1967 Protocol relating to the Status of Refugees, a refugee is a forced migrant who has crossed an international border and '…owing to a well-founded fear of being persecuted for reasons of race, religion, nationality, membership of a particular social group or political opinion, is outside the country of his nationality and is unable or, owing to such fear, is unwilling to avail himself of the protection of that country; or who, not having a nationality and being outside the country of his former habitual residence as a result of such events, is unable or, owing to such fear, is unwilling to return to it' (UNHCR 1951). The term 'refugee' holds significant legal implications under the international convention and the offices of the United Nations, and thus has great impact on persons seeking safety, security and survival.

Kunz (1973, 1981) was one of the first demographers to develop a conceptual model of forced migration. Grounded in observed patterns of refugee migration, he sought to produce a general model which included the fundamental elements of the refugee process from initial flight to eventual settlement. The model recognizes three stages in the forced migration process – flight, asylum and eventual settlement. Within the first stage of displacement, an important distinction emerges between movers in response to a sudden crisis and those who have responded to a more gradual build-up of the pressure which eventually forces a person or family to move. Kunz (1973) recognizes a number of situations intermediate between acute and anticipating movers. Each component of his conceptual framework offers a basis for prediction and empirical comparison of observed forced population movements.

Crucially, the Kunz model recognizes that after fleeing their home, forced migrants will often first seek a place of temporary protection. This may be a camp set up to provide an initial safe haven for those fleeing or it can involve staying with a friend, family or acquaintance in an area which is secure. Kunz (1973) describes this as a 'midway to nowhere' situation which captures the anomie and uncertainty of transit contexts. The time spent in this situation varies. For some forced migrants there can be a return to the home area once the conflict situation has passed. In fact, return is not always possible and another long-term solution needs to be found. This can be settlement in the transit situation or movement to a third destination. While transit situations can occur in voluntary migration, they are an important differentiating characteristic of forced migration and have not been investigated sufficiently. The spatial processes may proceed in the form of waves initiated by particular events impinging on particular groups of people, which generate subsequent forced migration flows with different characteristics, for example, demographic characteristics (age and sex), social and economic resources (money and education) and vulnerabilities (disabilities and trauma). Kunz's model has been applied by scholars of refugee studies (Meda 2016; George and Jettner 2016; Nair and Bloom 2015; McAuliffe and Jayasuriya 2016).

One important feature of forced migration is that it may result in other forms of migration. A forced migration may create a migration corridor or channel along which other, non-forced migrants move. It can become the basis for the development of a social network linking the origin with the new destination of the forced migrants who send back information and perhaps assist others to move, especially family members (Hugo, Abbasi-Shavazi and Kraly 2017b). Over several decades of responding to emerging humanitarian crises, the UNHCR has expanded its focus from the strict category of 'refugee' defined above, to identify several categories of forced

Table 18.1 Persons of concern to UNHCR

Refugees		Other groups of people of concern	
Refugees	Persons recognized as refugees under the 1951 UN Convention/1967 Protocol, the 1969 OAU Convention, in accordance with the UNHCR Statute, persons granted a complementary form of protection and those granted temporary protection. In the absence of government figures, UNHCR has estimated the refugee population in 25 industrialized countries based on 10 years of individual refugee recognition.	Returned refugees	Refugees who have returned to their place of origin during the last six months.
		Internally displaced persons (IDPs)	Persons who have been forced to leave their homes or places of habitual residence within their country and to whom UNHCR extends protection/assistance. It also includes people in IDP like situations.
		Returned IDPs	IDPs who were beneficiaries of UNHCR's protection and assistance activities and have returned to their place of origin between January and December each year.
People in refugee-like situations	Includes groups of persons who are outside their country or territory of origin and who face protection risks similar to those of refugees but for whom refugee status has, for practical or other reasons, not been ascertained.	Stateless people	Persons not considered nationals by any state.
		Various	Others given protection/assistance.
Asylum seekers	Persons whose application for asylum (international protection) or refugee status is pending at any stage in the asylum procedure.		

Sources: UNHCR (2013b: 15); UNHCR (2013a: 37).

population movement, collectively referred to as 'persons of concern'. The definition of each of these categories is given in Table 18.1.

Although these definitions are useful in identifying persons of concern to the UNHCR, they are not mutually exclusive because forced migrants may belong to more than one group, either concurrently or over time (Van Hear and McDowell 2006). Thus, the line between refugees and other types of migrants is blurred. As Monsuti (2008) argued, both forced and unforced migrants may share a number of social features, individuals may belong to several migration categories at a time or successively, and social networks may also comprise people with different statuses. Richmond (1993) replaced the dichotomy between voluntary and involuntary, or forced, migration with a continuum between 'proactive' and 'reactive' migration. Examples of typical proactive migrants include professionals, entrepreneurs, retired people and temporary workers under contract. Reactive migrants include those who meet the UN convention definition of having a genuine fear of persecution and being unwilling or unable to return, but they may also comprise others reacting to crisis situations caused by war, famine, economic collapse and other disasters. Richmond (1993) argued that there is a continuum between the rational choice behaviour of proactive migrants seeking to maximize net advantage and the reactive behaviour of those whose degrees of freedom are severely constrained. He concluded that a large majority of international migrants (including those generally regarded as 'refugees') fall somewhere between these extremes.

Hugo (2011) differentiated various migration patterns in Asia along a wide spectrum ranging from totally voluntary movement in which the mover controls the migration process, to kidnapping and trafficking at the other extreme. Given the flexibility and continuity of migration, the dichotomy of forced versus unforced migration is no longer held, and thus forced migration should be considered as dynamic and continuous movement involving multiple steps and directions which all need to be analysed as both causes and consequences of this type of migration. In the following discussion, however, we will gravitate to the UN categories of persons of concern given the organization of international statistics on forced population movements and our goal for comparative analysis of forced migration and refugees within countries in Asia.

Studies of forced and refugee migration

The magnitude and occurrence of forced population movements in recent decades suggest that the issues of migration and asylum have risen to the top of the international agenda (Boswell and Crisp 2004) and that forced and refugee migration will be one of the continuing issues in the world in the twenty-first century. Since 2005, the growth of the population of concern has risen from 21.1 million in 2005 to 33.9 million in 2010 and 63.1 million in 2015, an increase of more than 200 per cent in ten years. The refugee population increased from 8.7 million in 2005 to 16.1 million at the end of 2015, and the number of internally displaced persons increased from 6.6 million to 37.5 million over the same period (UNHCR 2016b).

However, despite the persistence of forced migrations and large-scale refugee movements over recent decades and, critically, of protracted refugee situations in countries of asylum (Hugo, Abbasi-Shavazi and Kraly 2017b), most studies on migration have been focused on unforced migration, and little progress has been made towards understanding forced migrations and refugee movements. This is particularly evident among population scientists (Foley 2000: 5; Hugo 2005; Hugo, Abbasi-Shavazi and Kraly 2017a). Scholars (Baker 1983; Harrell-Bond 1988; Hugo 1987; Jacobsen and Landau 2003) have, for a long time, raised concerns as to why this area has remained under-researched. Stein (1981) and Harrell-Bond (1988) noted that refugee research lacks standard texts, theoretical structure, a systematic body of data, and even a firm definition of the subject or the field. The dearth of research by social scientists and demographers on forced and refugee migrations is due to the fact that these types of movements are deemed to be 'outside the domain' of these disciplines (Chan 1990; Jacobsen and Landau 2003), and are stochastic and unpredictable (see Zolberg, Suhrke and Aguayo 1989 for an earlier notable exception). Research on forced and refugee migration also requires a multidisciplinary approach which demands new paradigms, multiple methodologies and collaborative research teams.

The lack of systematic refugee research has partly been due to a narrow focus in which refugee movements are considered 'isolated, localized, sporadic, transitory and non-recurring and temporary events' (Foley 2000: 5; see also Stein 1981; Chan 1987, 1990). As a result, many studies on refugee movements have not been comprehensive, dealing primarily with particular aspects of the refugee experience such as the provision of asylum and protection, assimilation and integration or government policies. Based on these observations, scholars have called for holistic perspectives on refugee movements to investigate all stages of the refugee experience, including the root causes for the mass exodus of people, and the traumatic and often tragic experiences suffered *en route* (Stein 1981; Zetter 1988). Hugo (1987) and Hugo, Abbasi-Shavazi and Kraly (2017b) have called for more innovative, flexible and appropriate research strategies to be adopted. In addition, the dynamics of refugee communities, especially the adaptation patterns of refugees in the origin and host countries and communities, are important areas of research and policy concern (Zetter 1988; Foley 2000; Abbasi-Shavazi and Sadeghi 2014, 2016).

Moreover, there are particular challenges to the study of forced migration and refugees in Asia. First, note should be taken of the size as well as the socioeconomic, cultural and ethnic diversity within the vast region of Asia, and critically within many countries, that challenge generalization of findings on forced population movement. Second, forced migration is arguably a response to unanticipated events or disasters, both unprecedented and recurrent (e.g. floods and famines), and thus the systematic collection of data by governments is often focused on specific aspects of movements and movers, or is altogether impractical. Therefore, the lack of reliable and comprehensive data on the level of forced migration, and particularly on the characteristics of movers, results in an underestimation of the scale of forced movements and an incomplete and inconsistent demographic picture. The UNHCR is the prime organization producing systematic data on refugees and other types of forced population movements for all regions of the world. The following section describes the strengths and weaknesses of international data on forced migration and refugees.

Data sources on forced and refugee migration

The complex nature of forced population movements has produced challenges to empirical analysis, specifically measurement and data collection. Analytic challenges include the classification of 'people on the move' into different categories of migration and mobility based on criteria – ultimately operational definitions – regarding geography, distance and political boundaries, length of absence and stay, and reason, or more appropriately, reasons, for migration. Variations in statistical measures and in availability and quality of data for countries and regions pose significant challenges for efforts aiming at comprehensive and comparative analysis. Appropriate statistical infrastructure for reliable data collection and analysis is also a challenge in the field, particularly given the social, spatial and temporal characteristics of complex humanitarian emergencies.

Under these circumstances there are often multiple data sources for forced population movements including registration and special censuses (see Hovy 2017). Persons for whom assistance is provided by the UNHCR or non-governmental agencies are likely to be documented in administrative systems of aid. In many cases, only refugees or populations of concern to the UNHCR who receive international assistance are counted; forced migrants who self-settle and 'blend in' with the local population might never be counted or estimated, unless their number is large enough that a rise in the local population becomes visible. For these reasons, as Schmeidl (1998) argued, many migration statistics are nothing more than estimates or best guesses about the reality in the field, but nevertheless such estimates are not necessarily without value if certain consistent rules of analysis and interpretation are applied.

The UNHCR has been, for many years, the main comprehensive source of demographic information on refugees and the other categories of persons of concern at the global level. Data collection by the UNHCR started around 1960, with systematic compilation, analysis and dissemination being institutionalized in the 1990s. The scope and role of statistics have evolved steadily to serve as the foundation for protecting displaced populations, monitoring their global trends and assessing UNHCR activities. The UNHCR's database (http://popstats.unhcr.org), launched in 2006, is now one of the main data sources on refugees and forced movements (UNHCR Statistical Yearbook 2014b). The United Nations Relief and Works Agency for Palestine Refugees (UNRWA) also publishes reports about Palestinian refugees (www.unrwa.org).

Methods for collecting data related to forced population movements and refugees include national and special censuses, registrations, and surveys or estimations. Some countries rely on a single method while others use several methods to obtain refugee statistics. The UNHCR attaches a great deal of importance to registration and to the number and social demographic characteristics of refugees, as these are fundamental to its mission for the protection of refugees. Registration of migrants is also a key task of host governments, intergovernmental agencies and non-governmental organizations working in this field. In order to compare forced migration outcomes, data and information should be comparable and reliable. The UNHCR has undertaken triangulation exercises to ensure that data across the various countries are comparable, reliable and credible. For example, in 2012 technical support was provided to Afghanistan, Pakistan, Jordan and Myanmar aimed at improving their data quality (UNHCR Statistical Yearbook 2013b).

Since 2001 the UNHCR has been publishing its *Statistical Yearbook*, which illustrates the richness of data, principally those stemming from the administrative processes maintained by host governments and by the UNHCR (see Hovy 2017). In 2014, 173 countries reported data to the UNHCR; 77 per cent (or 133) countries used registration as the source of measurement; 13 per cent of countries reporting relied on estimation as a source of information on forced migrants (UNHCR 2015). Not surprisingly, reporting countries vary in processes of registering and collecting information on refugees. For example, Iran as one of the main countries of asylum for Afghan refugees conducts *Amayesh* registration, which is administered periodically by the Iranian government in order to identify foreign nationals. Afghan refugees participating in this registration are given *Amayesh* cards enabling them to access various services. In 2015, around 950,000 Afghan refugees held *Amayesh* cards. However, there are around one to two million Afghans who do not have legal status and are undocumented. This group is also diverse and includes Afghans who crossed the border illegally and those whose *Amayesh* card has expired.

As noted earlier, while these censuses, registrations and surveys are valuable sources of information on refugees and forced migrants, complementary sources including interviews and other forms of qualitative data gathering should be implemented in order to provide more meaningful data on the motivations for migration and the experiences of individual migrants. Sample surveys are also valuable sources for the understanding of the dynamics of forced migration, characteristics of movers and adaptation of migrants and refugees in camps or destination places. For instance, the 2010 survey on 'The Socio-economic and Demographic Adaptation of Afghan Youth in Iran' (Abbasi-Shavazi and Sadeghi 2014) and 'The Survey of Afghan Settlement in Australia' (Abbasi-Shavazi, Sadeghi and Hugo 2014) collected information on various aspects of migration from Afghanistan including the characteristics of Afghan refugees, their decision-making process to move, sources of information about destination places, and experiences in the two host societies. Attempts to estimate the numbers and demographic characteristics of people who are internally displaced within their own countries are always a major challenge for researchers and policymakers. To overcome the difficulty, Davies and Jacobsen (2010) used a new methodology for profiling urban internally displaced persons (IDPs) to assess and contextualize the particular needs of this group and to address the implications for humanitarian action.

Demographic research on forced migrants and displaced populations must rely on synthesis of information from multiple sources and methods of data collection, including both quantitative and qualitative approaches. As in all social demographic research, and social research generally, there is tension among demands for generalizability and precision of data, and goals for understanding the causes and consequences of forced migration and displacement at different scales (populations, communities, households and individuals). For comparative and trend analysis, as undertaken here, the statistical resources of the United Nations are invaluable; social surveys and community based and ethnographic research efforts are also critical to understanding the experience of migration and the implications for vulnerable persons at risk of displacement and the search for safe haven.

We rely on UNHCR statistics as the basis for comparative analysis of demographic patterns and trends over time which characterizes forced migration in Asia. Other sources will also be used to draw conclusions on more detailed characteristics of refugees, adaptation patterns and the social demographic behaviour of refugees/migrants in countries of destination/residence. Even drawing on these rich comparative sources, the data used in this paper could not provide a general and comprehensive picture of refugees and forced migration: levels are likely underestimated, and characteristics of registered refugees may be different from those who are not covered in the available data. Furthermore, this analysis of patterns and trends relies on the analysis of stock data of forced migrant and refugee populations, which refer to population counts at one point in time. Measurement of the flows of categories of forced migrants (that is, population movements occurring continuously and measured, for example, through border control) is far from comprehensive, consistent or reliable at the global or Asian regional level.

Levels and trends of forced migration: Asia within a global context

The scale and complexity of forced migration has increased in the world since the beginning of the current century. The number of 'persons of concern' to the UNHCR who have received protection and assistance has increased from 17.0 million in 2003 to 38.7 million in 2013, and to nearly 64 million at the end of 2015. However, the proportion of refugees in this total has fallen from 56.4 per cent (9.6 million persons) in 2003 to 25.2 per cent (16.1 million) at the end of 2015 (UNHCR 2016b).

The rapid increase in the number of persons of concern to the UNHCR has been due to the increase in the number of IDPs – from 4.2 million in 2003 to 37.5 million at the end of 2015. The estimate of the number of migrants who are actually displaced is higher than those who are under the UNHCR protection. A key issue for our purposes is the fact that forced migrants identified by the UNHCR are quite spatially concentrated. For example, people classified as being refugees or in refugee situations, as well as IDPs, are heavily concentrated in Asian and African countries, especially low income and less developed countries.

Table 18.2 shows that at the end of 2015, 63.9 million people were forcibly displaced globally, of whom 16.1 million were identified by the UNHCR and member states as refugees and people in refugee-like situations, approximately 37.5 million were IDPs, and the remaining were returnees, stateless people and asylum seekers whose applications are pending for decision.

Asia was home to around 29.7 million (46.5 per cent) people of concern to the UNHCR, compared with 20.3 million (31.7 per cent) in Africa, and 7.7 million (12 per cent) in Latin America and the Caribbean. More than half (53.9 per cent or around 8.7 million) of the refugees identified by the UNHCR were residing in Asia, while close to 30 per cent lived in Africa. Europe hosted approximately 11.3 per cent of the total number of refugees recorded by the UNHCR.

By the end of 2015, Asia ranked highest among all regions as the region of origin for forced migration with 46.0 per cent of the total population of concern to the UNHCR originating from Asian countries (Table 18.3). Also, close to three-fifths (59.6 per cent) of the world's refugees originated in Asia. Given the large-scale population movements out of Syria in 2016, we

Table 18.2 Persons of concern to UNHCR by region of asylum, end of 2015

Region of asylum	Refugees	Asylum seekers	IDPs	Returnees	Stateless people	Total persons of concern
Africa	4,811,365	1,367,409	11,197,751	1,879,197	1,021,440	20,277,162
Asia	8,694,562	396,662	17,265,028	1,404,938	1,942,856	29,704,046
Europe	1,820,424	1,083,567	1,918,326	78,427	586,848	5,487,592
Latin America & Caribbean	337,698	44,887	7,113,067	26,907	136,585	7,659,144
Northern America	409,090	305,810	-	-	-	714,900
Oceania	48,288	21,606	-	-	-	69,894
Total	**16,121,427**	**3,219,941**	**37,494,172**	**3,389,469**	**3,687,729**	**63,912,738**

Note: See Table 18.1 and UNHCR Global Trends 2015 (2016a) for more detailed definitions of Refugees, Asylum seekers, IDPs, Returnees and Stateless people.
Source: UNHCR (2016a).

Table 18.3 Persons of concern to UNHCR by major region of origin, end of 2015

Region of asylum	Refugees	Asylum seekers	IDPs	Returnees	Stateless people	Total persons of concern
Africa	5,393,331	660,424	11,197,751	1,876,157	0	19,127,663
Asia	9,608,535	1,146,965	17,265,028	1,404,613	0	29,425,141
Europe	507,379	179,656	1,918,326	67,542	0	2,672,903
Latin America & Caribbean	448,302	177,716	7,113,067	26,895	0	7,765,980
Northern America	4,912	603	-	17	0	5,532
Oceania	1,387	799	-	1	0	2,187
Various/ Stateless	157,581	1,053,778	-	14,244	3,687,729	4,913,332
Total	**16,121,427**	**3,219,941**	**37,494,172**	**3,389,469**	**3,687,729**	**63,912,738**

Note: See Table 18.1 and UNHCR Global Trends 2015 (2016a) for more detailed definitions of Refugees, Asylum seekers, IDPs, Returnees and Stateless people.
Source: UNHCR (2016a).

can anticipate a further increase in the share of Asian countries as sources of forced migrations in coming years.

It is also worth noting that while three-quarters of the world's population lived in the Asian and African regions in 2015, more than 93 per cent of refugees originated from these two regions. Only 2.8 per cent of the world's refugees originated from Latin America and 3.2 per cent from Europe.

In 2014, countries in the Asian region were also hosts to the largest number of refugees worldwide. According to the UNHCR, most refugees having fled to neighbouring countries remain in the same region. The major refugee-generating regions hosted around 91 per cent of

Table 18.4 Persons of concern to UNHCR for top ten countries of asylum in Asia, end of 2015

Asian country of asylum	Refugees	Asylum seekers	IDPs	Returnees	Stateless people	Total persons of concern
Syrian Arab Republic	21,113	5,251	6,563,462	3,743	160,000	6,753,569
Iraq	277,701	7,420	4,403,287	7,697	50,000	4,746,105
Pakistan	1,561,162	6,442	1,146,108	676,641	-	3,390,353
Yemen	267,173	9,866	2,532,032	17	-	2,809,088
Turkey	2,541,352	212,408	-	-	780	2,754,540
Afghanistan	257,554	82	1,174,306	335,349	-	1,767,291
Myanmar	-	1	451,089	25,267	938,000	1,414,357
Lebanon	1,070,854	12,139	-	5,238	-	1,088,231
Iran	979,437	42	-	12	-	979,491
Jordan	664,118	24,935	-	-	-	689,053
Total Asia	**8,694,562**	**396,662**	**17,265,028**	**1,404,938**	**1,942,856**	**29,704,046**

Note: See Table 18.1 and UNHCR Global Trends 2015 (2016a) for more detailed definitions of Refugees, Asylum seekers, IDPs, Returnees and Stateless people.
Source: UNHCR (2016a).

refugees from within the same region. A smaller number and proportion of Asian refugees were located outside of Asia (UNHCR 2015).

Nearly three-fifths (59.5 per cent) of the 'total population of concern' were residing in ten countries around the world (Colombia, Democratic Republic of Congo, Iraq, Nigeria, Pakistan, South Sudan, Sudan, Syrian Arab Republic, Turkey and Yemen), and five of them were in Asia. There have been large scale forced migrations initiated by political conflicts, environmental disasters and large-scale construction projects in Asia. Significant proportions of these population displacements have occurred within countries in Asia (Hugo 2005), though international movements have also been large. Both Pakistan and Iran have been the primary host countries for Afghan refugees for the past three decades. In 2013, around 2.8 million registered Afghan refugees were hosted in these two countries. However, in recent years, the number of refugees in these two countries has decreased due to the repatriation of Afghan refugees. The number of refugees (most of them from Syria) in Jordan, Turkey and Lebanon reached 1.7 million in 2013. This number is likely to grow because of the large population flows out of Syria.

Table 18.4 lists the top ten Asian countries of asylum in 2015. These countries in total hosted 41.3 per cent of the total population of concern to the UNHCR. Due to violent conflicts in recent years, the Syrian Arab Republic has witnessed significant population displacement: over one million Syrian refugees were registered during 2015, bringing its total close to 5 million, compared to 3.9 million Syrian refugees at the end of 2014 and 2.5 million at the end of 2013 (UNHCR 2016b).

Table 18.5 shows Asia's top ten countries from which the largest numbers of forced migrants originated. These countries were the origin of 44.4 per cent of total forced displacement, and, notably, 96.5 per cent of forced migrants from Asia. These ten countries were the origin of 55.2 per cent of all refugees, and 92.6 per cent of Asian refugees; 45.9 per cent of all IDPs, and 99.7 per cent of IDPs from the Asian region.

Table 18.5 Persons of concern to UNHCR for top ten countries of origin in Asia, end of 2015

Asian country of asylum	Refugees	Asylum seekers	IDPs	Returnees	Stateless people	Total persons of concern
Syrian Arab Republic	4,872,585	245,844	6,563,462	8,436	-	11,690,327
Iraq	264,107	237,166	4,403,287	11,267	-	4,915,827
Afghanistan	2,666,254	258,892	1,174,306	335,401	-	4,434,853
Yemen	15,896	10,075	2,532,032	13	-	2,558,016
Pakistan	297,835	64,085	1,146,108	676,642	-	2,184,670
Myanmar	451,807	60,659	451,089	25,710	-	989,265
Azerbaijan	9,712	5,230	618,220	-	-	633,162
Philippines	593	1,902	63,174	334,905	-	400,574
Vietnam	313,156	4,372	-	265	-	317,793
Georgia	6,498	9,282	268,416	-	-	284,196
Total Asia	9,608,535	1,146,965	17,265,028	1,404,613	-	29,425,141
Total World	16,121,427	3,219,941	37,494,172	3,389,469	3,687,729	63,912,738

Note: See Table 18.1 and UNHCR Global Trends 2015 (2016a) for more detailed definitions of Refugees, Asylum seekers, IDPs, Returnees and Stateless people.
Source: UNHCR (2016a).

During the last three decades, Afghanistan has generated the largest number of refugees worldwide, with annual numbers varying from 500,000 refugees at the onset of the crisis in 1979 to more than 6.3 million at its peak in 1990. In 2012, one out of every four refugees in the world was from Afghanistan, with 95 per cent of them located in Pakistan and the Islamic Republic of Iran (UNHCR Statistical Yearbook 2013b: 30). At the end of 2015, 2.7 million of the world's refugees originated in Afghanistan; the humanitarian crisis in Syria has taken the scale of international refugee migration to a new level, reaching 4.9 million by the end of 2015. Consequently, Syria has shifted to the top of the list of countries of origin of forcibly displaced people (18.3 per cent of the total at the end of 2015) due to the massive internal displacement of its people (17.5 per cent of all IDPs) resulting from war and conflict. Other significant flows in Asia in 2015 include the outflows from Iraq, Afghanistan, Pakistan and Myanmar.

Demographic characteristics of forced and refugee migrants in Asia

The previous section presented global and regional levels of forced and refugee migration. The first order of demographic analysis in response to humanitarian crises is the estimation of the overall scale of the crisis (population size) and the relative proportions of vulnerable groups within the displaced population, most often measured by age and gender characteristics. Analysis of the demographic characteristics of migrants is also critical for the allocation of resources and services to vulnerable migrants at various stages of displacement and flight (Reed, Haaga and Keely 1998).

Gender is one of the main demographic characteristics of forced migrants, refugees and populations of concern that needs to be analysed in order to identify the degree to which risks, experiences and circumstances vary by gender (Jacobsen and Landau 2003). As noted by Kraly

Forced and refugee migration in Asia

(2017), the 'gender lens' should be applied to demographic analyses of migrants at all stages of the move, including pre-migration in countries of origin, during flight and move, in transit places and camps, and finally, in countries of asylum and resettlement as well as in migrant communities in the host societies. Hugo (2005 and Chapter 17) argued that it is important to study the movements of women separately from those of men as the patterns, causes and consequences, and policy implications of movement for women can differ from those of men. Failure to consider gender in the demography of forced migration weakens the relevance of demographic analysis for prevention of, and response to, complex humanitarian crises (Kraly 2017).

There are other demographic characteristics that need to be taken into account. Disaggregation by age is essential for the understanding of the dynamics of migration, as well as the services necessary for migrant communities. The age of migrants, their marital status, number of children and household composition can all influence the process of migration, vulnerabilities and risks, and services needed for the migrant groups.

Relying on data submitted by countries and international organizations, the UNHCR statistics about populations of concern do not fully cover all characteristics of movers in the countries of asylum and origin. For instance, it has been reported that around 60 per cent of the global population of concern to the UNHCR can be disaggregated by sex, and only 41 per cent can be classified by broad age group. The figures differ for different population of concern categories. Around 90 per cent of returned refugees can be grouped by sex, compared to only 19 per cent of returned IDPs (UNHCR 2011). Hugo (2005) identified the feminization of movement as one of the main features of the massive expansion of international migration in Asia. For several Asian countries of origin, women have formed the majority of emigrants (Hugo 2005). He has also noted some problems in measuring the gender of international migrants when national population data sources were used for many countries in Asia (Hugo 2005). Yet as noted above, data on the age and gender composition of forced migrants and refugees are essential for understanding the risks and vulnerabilities of groups of migrants as well as their need for support and resources within the host societies.

Figure 18.1 illustrates the age and sex composition of populations of concern located in Syria, Iraq and Pakistan, the top three countries of asylum in Asia. It should be noted that the data provided for both males and females are only for the subsets of forced migrant population who are living in refugee camps and settlements. For example, the data on age composition by gender for Syria have been obtained from 29,917 persons and those for Iraq from 285,141 persons, which are far smaller than the total number of forced migrants in these countries. As indicated by the figure, over half of the population of concern in Syria and Pakistan is aged under 18 years (52 per cent and 50.4 per cent, respectively), metrics that are likely to be comparable to the overall populations of these countries. The forced migrant population in Iraq, in contrast, is less youthful and those under 18 years account for 39.7 per cent.

Table 18.6 shows the sex ratio of the population of concern by broad age group in Asia's top ten countries of asylum. Very interesting patterns by age are evident. Overall, the sex ratio of 0–4 and 5–11 age groups is close to normal in more than half of the listed populations of concern to UNHCR, showing a surplus of boys to girls. In these youngest age groups, people seeking asylum in Pakistan have the highest sex ratio, but those in Yemen, Afghanistan, Myanmar and Iran have fewer boys than girls. Sex ratios of those aged 12–17, 18–59 and 60+ are high for those in Pakistan and Turkey, indicating that more males have made their way to these countries of asylum. Sex ratios for the oldest age group, 60+ years, are very high for Syria and Pakistan, and very low for Myanmar, Lebanon and Jordan. The sex selection in migration to Yemen, generally selecting for women, presents an interesting case.

M. J. Abbasi-Shavazi & E. P. Kraly

Table 18.6 Sex ratio, by age group, of populations of concern to UNHCR for top ten countries of asylum in Asia, end of 2015

Country of asylum	Age group					
	0–4	5–11	12–17	18–59	60+	Total
Syrian Arab Republic	103	101	81	90	132	94
Iraq	104	105	121	142	92	126
Pakistan	120	123	121	106	134	115
Yemen	86	89	101	86	113	90
Turkey	107	114	138	189	100	158
Afghanistan	98	108	108	99	117	103
Myanmar	97	103	113	82	84	93
Lebanon	104	105	103	83	79	94
Iran	98	108	108	99	118	103
Jordon	105	109	115	88	57	98

Source: UNHCR (2016a).

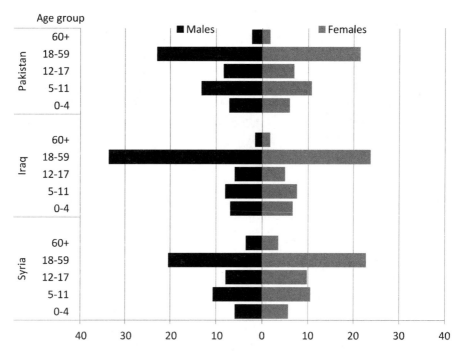

Figure 18.1 Age and sex composition of populations of concern to UNHCR in Syria, Iraq and Pakistan, end of 2015
Source: UNHCR (2016b).

In addition to the age and sex composition of forced migrants, it is important to study from which local area and what region of the country migrants originate, in relation to what region in the destination they tend to settle. In countries where there is ethnic violence, people may move out from an area where particular ethnic groups are located. For example, in Afghanistan, Hazara ethnic groups moved from Herat and Mazar-e Sharif provinces to Iran. They are also located in Tehran and Mashhad, among other provinces. The majority of Hazara Afghans have settled in Iran, while Sunni Pashtuns have migrated to Pakistan as a Sunni dominant country. Those living in Iran have mainly scattered among the native population, particularly in urban areas, while those in Pakistan are mainly located in camps (Abbasi-Shavazi and Sadeghi 2014).

The proportion of refugees living in urban areas at the end of 2015 is estimated at 54.1 per cent (UNHCR 2016b). Earlier figures show 63 per cent of refugees in the Asia and Pacific regions resided in urban or semi-urban areas. Growing numbers of displaced people, both refugees and IDPs, now reside in urban areas rather than camps, but relatively little is known about their precise numbers and demographic characteristics, their basic needs or protection problems. Guterres (2010) and Tibaijuka (2010) emphasized the complexity of the challenges faced by those displaced into urban areas and by those seeking to protect and assist them, and argued for the need for a radical rethinking of approaches by the international community.

The settlement and experience of refugees also depend on policies and programmes at the place of destination. In 2013, 21 countries in Asia and Oceania were signatory to the 1951 Convention relating to the Status of Refugees and the 1967 Protocol by which they agreed to host refugees from other countries. For this reason, refugees may flee to other neighbouring countries, or directly move to the final country of destination by applying for asylum either from another country in the region or elsewhere. Table 18.7 shows the number of refugees from Asia's ten top countries of origin by major countries of asylum (in descending level of settlement). For example, Syrian refugees are living largely in Turkey, Lebanon and Jordan. Afghans have mainly been hosted by Pakistan, Iran and Germany. Refugees from Myanmar are regionally concentrated in Bangladesh, Thailand and Malaysia. The overwhelming majority of Vietnamese refugees are in China, and most Pakistani refugees are in Afghanistan.

While there is diversity in the country of settlement of refugees from Asian countries, we do observe a regional response to refugees from neighbouring states (see also Icduygu 2015).

Table 18.7 Refugees and people in refugee-like situations by top ten Asian countries of origin[a] by major countries of asylum, end of 2015

Country/territory of origin	Country/territory of asylum	Total	Of whom: UNHCR assisted
Syrian Arab Republic	Turkey	2,503,549	2,461,790
	Lebanon	1,062,690	1,062,690
	Jordan	628,223	628,223
	Iraq	244,642	244,642
	Egypt	117,635	117,635
Afghanistan	Pakistan	1,560,592	1,560,592
	Iran	951,142	951,142
	Germany	30,026	-
	Austria	17,458	-
	Sweden	13,064	-
Myanmar	Bangladesh	231,948	31,948
	Thailand	106,349	106,349
	Malaysia	88,637	88,637
	India	15,735	15,735

(*continued*)

Table 18.7 (Cont.)

Country/territory of origin	Country/territory of asylum	Total	Of whom: UNHCR assisted
	USA	1,999	-
Vietnam	China	300,896	*
	France	8,132	-
	Germany	1,357	-
	Switzerland	1,130	-
Pakistan	Afghanistan	257,523	257,523
	Italy	9,202	-
	Canada	7,207	-
	UK	6,319	-
	Germany	4,702	-
Iraq	Germany	51,396	-
	Jordan	33,256	33,256
	Iran	28,268	28,268
	Turkey	24,135	24,135
	Sweden	23,886	-
China	India	110,098	*
	USA	74,020	-
	Canada	11,415	-
	France	3,260	-
	Switzerland	3,022	-
Sri Lanka	India	64,208	-
	France	24,220	-
	Canada	8,807	-
	UK	5,279	-
	Switzerland	4,989	-
Palestine	Egypt	70,021	21
	Iraq	9,250	9,250
	Libya	5,380	5,380
	Algeria	4,016	11
	Cyprus	1,786	99
Iran	Germany	19,763	-
	UK	12,667	-
	Iraq	8,231	8,231
	Turkey	5,262	5,262
	USA	5,216	-
Turkey	Germany	20,281	-
	Iraq	15,557	15,557
	France	10,652	-
	Switzerland	3,544	-
	Italy	2,482	-

Notes: [a] Also includes Palestinians under UNHCR mandate. In the table, '-' indicates the number is 0 or unavailable; * indicates a number between 1 and 4.
Source: UNHCR (2016a).

Among non-Asian countries, Germany is at the top, having received the largest number of Asian refugees especially from Syria, Afghanistan, Turkey, Iraq and Iran.

The results presented in this section suggest the need for further analysis of migrant characteristics in order to understand the demography of migrants and their communities. This will help in providing more reliable information of those in need of services as well as the nature of services needed. Demographic information can thus be integrated into planning for the resettlement, repatriation, and/or adaptation of these migrants in their countries of origin and destination.

Drivers of forced and refugee migration

In recent years, millions of people have crossed borders involuntarily. As Boswell and Crisp (2004: 1–2) noted, the pressures and opportunities arising from globalization – including improved transportation, communications and information technology, the expansion of transnational social networks, and the emergence of a migration industry – have led to an increase in international migration. Insecurity and armed conflict in many of the world's poorest and economically marginalized states have also triggered new waves of displaced people. Forced migration, however, reflects mainly the insecurity and fear due to war, conflict and persecution in the country or place of origin. As an example, Afghanistan has been experiencing war and conflict for the past three decades and it is not surprising that it has been the top source country of refugees for 32 years prior to 2012. Afghanistan is not only included in the list of countries of origin of refugees but it is also one of the countries hosting large number of IDPs, both people who have returned from their country of asylum and those who have been internally displaced from other parts of the country.

History has shown that once a country faces war and conflicts, the surrounding regions and neighbouring countries are likely to be affected by the exodus of people seeking refuge from the associated violence, threats to life and insecurity. Pakistan and Iran have been the two main receiving countries for persons seeking refuge from conflicts in Afghanistan. In addition, millions of Iraqis fled to the neighbouring countries of Jordan, Saudi Arabia, Syria, Egypt, Iran, Lebanon and Turkey during the war in the 1980s and 1990s (UNHCR 2014a).

Civil war can also lead to the forced displacement of people within a country. Most of the persons forcibly displaced in the Middle East are the result of the civil wars in Iraq, Libya, Syria and Yemen as well as from the long-running Israeli-Palestinian conflict. Palestinian refugees have been displaced in Syria, Lebanon, the Gaza Strip, the West Bank and Jordan for decades (www.unrwa.org). As illustrated above, the displacement within and from Syria is dramatic. In South-East Asia, many people, particularly ethnic minorities, have been displaced within Myanmar and have also sought asylum in border regions of Bangladesh and Thailand (see Tables 18.5 and 18.7).

Forced migration in the name of development – 'development-induced displacement' – is a significant form of population displacement associated with the global south and Asia specifically, generating both internal and international movements. 'Mega projects', especially dam construction, have become common, especially in less developed countries where there are escalating demands for electricity and water associated with rapid urbanization (Cernea 1990; Cernea and McDowell 2000). According to Terminski (2012) approximately 15 million people worldwide each year are forced to leave their homes following big development projects (dams, irrigation projects, highways, urbanization, mining, conservation of nature, etc.). Oliver-Smith (2009) and Cernea (2006) have also estimated that the current scale of development-induced displacement amounts to 15 million people worldwide per year.

While development-induced displacement occurs throughout the world, two countries in particular – China and India – are responsible for a large portion of such forced movements. According to Fuggle et al. (2000), the National Research Center for Resettlement in China has calculated that over 45 million people were displaced by development projects in that country between 1950 and 2000. One of the largest cases is the Three Gorges Dam Project located in the lower reaches of the Yangtze River in China. The construction was completed in 17 years and involved a displacement of more than 1.2 million people (Hugo 2008). Taneja and Thakkar (2000) and Mahapatra (1999) pointed out that estimates of displacement in India from dam projects alone ranged from 21 million to 40 million persons during the second part (from 1947 to 1997) of the twentieth century (see also Terminski 2012).

Damage and disruption due to natural disasters such as earthquakes, tsunami and hurricanes can force surviving people and their families to move from their own places of residence. The South-East Asian earthquake and tsunami, which struck on 26 December 2004, affected 12 Asian countries, killing 298,055 people, leaving an estimated five million people in immediate need of assistance and displacing an estimated one to two million (Hugo 2008). The crisis required governments, civil society, humanitarian actors (including non-governmental organizations and donors) and the UN to respond on a scale that had never been seen before (Inderfurth, Fabrycky and Cohen 2005). The 2003 Bam earthquake in Iran not only killed around 30,000 people but also led to displacement of families in other cities, while at the same time many others moved voluntarily to the city of Bam (Hosseini-Chavoshi and Abbasi-Shavazi 2016).

While push factors are the main drivers of forced migration, the question of how the places of destination are selected or emerge is also important in the process of movement. Geographic proximity and relatively low-cost travel, visa-free regimes, common language and historical legacies within regions all work to encourage mobility. Skeldon (2009) argued that 'geography' plays a role where labour shortage and labour surplus nations are 'cheek by jowl'. Another facilitator of the movement of forced migrants to a new destination is cultural and ethno-linguistic similarity between origin and destination countries. These factors have been significant in movements from Syria and Afghanistan to neighbouring countries.

Growing disparity in economic and social development in a region, as well as comparable disparities within countries, is a key driver of many population movements. These sets of factors, and the underlining forces of regional and global economic change, illustrate the analytic challenges of defining whether migrations are forced or voluntary. Hugo (2005 and Chapter 17) argued that there are two main forces behind the increasing level of population movement in Asia. One is the proliferation of social networks. Most Asian international migrants move to a place where they have social capital in the form of relatives or friends already living there. Simich et al. (2003) showed how the need for social support among newly arrived refugees motivated migration decisions and affected their health and well-being. Family members and peers who have migrated previously can provide useful support for newly arrived refugees because they provide personal affirmation of common experiences of both origin and transition. The second important factor is the growth in scale and reach of the international migration industry comprised of migration agents, recruiters, travel providers and immigration officials who form chains linking Asian communities with overseas markets (Hugo 2005).

Summary and conclusions

According to the UNHCR, in 2015 around 29.7 million people have experienced forced displacement throughout Asia. Around two-thirds of all refugees have originated from Asia, while 54 per cent of them were residing in the Asian region. Around 44 per cent of the total population of concern to the UNHCR originated from ten Asian countries. For 32 years Afghanistan ranked as the first refugee-sending country, while Pakistan and Iran were the top two refugee-receiving countries. Since 2013, however, Syria has become the first country of forced migration for its refugee and IDPs.

Generally, but particularly for regions within Asia, forced population movements and migrations have been under-researched. This chapter has examined forced and refugee migration in the Asian region. The lack of comprehensive and standardized data on the scale and patterns of forced migration frustrates consistent analysis and comparison. The processes, dynamics and drivers underlying current and emerging patterns of forced movements require more systematic census and survey data. There is also a critical place for qualitative research on the experiences of forced migrants during stages of flight and settlement, and the implications of forced migration for persons, families and households left behind, and for communities of both origin and settlement. Improvements in data collection are warranted worldwide and particularly in Asia which experiences significant proportions of forced migrants. Furthermore, Jacobson and Landau (2003) have argued that much of the current research on forced migration needs to be strengthened in terms of research design, measurement and analysis.

Despite the large scale of forced migration worldwide and in Asia, there are several questions that have not been addressed due to serious methodological challenges in the study of forced migration. Monsuti (2008) has argued that forced migration research should focus on the strategies of movers and forced migrants: How do people travel? How do they cross zones of warfare and violence as well as international borders? How do migrants send money to their families left in the home country? How do people communicate even if scattered and in spite of the absence of modern facilities in the country of origin? Moreover, research needs to address the consequences of forced migration and movements for receiving communities, particularly given changes in international assistance and local responses to both voluntary and forced migrants. It is also important to underscore that many of these implications are positive (Boswell and Crisp 2004).

Given the population dynamics and patterns presented, programmes of demography and population studies throughout Asia should more actively engage in studies of forced migration and promote research and training in the field of migration generally. Training of, and investment in, a new generation of scholars in the study of forced migration will not only lead to the generation of new knowledge, but also to better data collection, increasingly rigorous research methodologies and more evidence-based interpretations concerning forced migrations in Asia. To be gained is a more clear and effective understanding of the drivers of forced migration and the experiences and contributions of forced migrants and refugees within both the host and home societies. Planning for refugees and forced migration should also include programmes for the integration of refugees in the host societies while facilitating repatriation (United Nations 2013). This process is possible with close and creative collaborations among population scientists in government agencies and civil society within all countries in Asia and beyond.

Acknowledgements

This chapter is dedicated to the late Graeme Hugo for his pioneering work on refugee and forced migration. Graeme was our co-editor for our fourthcoming volume, *Demography of Refugee and Forced Migration*, but he sadly passed away in January 2015. Useful comments from Meimanat Hosseini-Chavoshi, editors, anonymous reviewers, and assistance from Safiyeh Navab-Safavi and Abdullah Mohammadi on this chapter are gratefully acknowledged.

References

Abbasi-Shavazi, M. J. and R. Sadeghi (2014) 'Socio-cultural adaptation of second-generation Afghans in Iran'. *International Migration*, 53(6): 89–110. Available from: http://dx.doi.org/10.1111/imig.12148.
Abbasi-Shavazi, M. J. and R. Sadeghi (2016) 'Integration of Afghans in Iran: patterns, levels and policy implications'. *Migration Policy and Practice*, VI(3): 22–29.
Abbasi-Shavazi, M. J., R. Sadeghi and G. Hugo (2014) 'The 2012 survey of Afghan settlement in Australia: preliminary results'. Unpublished report, Australian Demographic and Social Research Institute, Australian National University, Canberra.
Baker, R. (1983) *The Psychological Problems of Refugees*. Luton: L & T Press.
Battistella G. (2002) 'International migration in Asia vis-à-vis Europe: an introduction'. *Asian and Pacific Migration Journal*, 11(4): 405–414.
Boswell, C. and J. Crisp (2004) 'Poverty, international migration and asylum, policy brief no. 8'. World Institute for Development Economics Research, United Nations University (UNU-WIDER), Helsinki.
Chan, K. B. (1987) 'Looking ahead: toward a framework for research on Indochinese Canadians'. In B. C. Kwok and I. Doreen (eds.) *Uprooting, Loss and Adaptation: The Resettlement of Indochinese Refugees in Canada*. Ottawa: Canadian Public Health Association.
Chan, K. B. (1990) 'Getting through suffering: Indochinese refugees in limbo 15 years later'. *Southeast Asian Journal of Social Science*, 18: 1–18.
Cernea, M. and C. McDowell (2000) *Risks and Reconstruction: Experiences of Resettlers and Refugees*. Oxford: Berghahn Books.
Cernea, M. M. (1990) *Internal Refugees and Development-Caused Population Displacement*. Cambridge: Harvard Institute for International Development, Harvard University.
Cernea, M. M. (2006) 'Development-induced and conflict-induced IDPs: bridging the research divide'. *Forced Migration Review*, Special Issue (December): 25–27.
Davies, A. and K. Jacobsen (2010) 'Profiling urban IDPs'. *Forced Migration Review*, 34: 13–15.
Foley, P. (2000) 'From hell to paradise: the stages of Vietnamese refugee migration under the Comprehensive Plan of Action'. Unpublished Thesis in Demography, Australian National University, Canberra.
Fuggle, R., W. T. Smith, Hydrosult Canada Inc and Androdev Canada Inc (2000) 'Experience with dams in water and energy resource development in the People's Republic of China'. Country review paper prepared for the World Commission on Dams, Cape Town, South Africa.
George, M. and J. Jettner (2016) 'Migration stressors, psychological distress and family – a Sri Lankan Tamil refugee analysis'. *Journal of International Migration and Integration*, 17(2): 341–353.
Guterres, A. (2010) 'Adapting to urban displacement'. *Forced Migration Review*, 34: 4.
Harrell-Bond, B. (1988) 'The sociology of involuntary migration: an introduction'. *Current Sociology*, 36: 1–6.
Hosseini-Chavoshi, M. and M. J. Abbasi-Shavazi (2016) 'Demographic consequences of the 2003 Bam earthquake in Iran'. In H. James and D. Paton (eds.) *The Consequences of Disasters*. Springfield, IL: Charles C. Thomas Publisher Ltd. Pp. 110–126.
Hovy, B. (2017) 'Registration – a sine qua non for refugee protection'. In Hugo, Abbasi-Shavazi and Kraly (eds.) *Demography of Refugee and Forced Migration*. Dordrecht: Springer.
Huget, J. W. (1992) 'The future of international migration in Asia'. *Asian and Pacific Migration Journal*, 1(2): 250–277.
Hugo, G. (1987) 'Postwar refugee migration in Southeast Asia: patterns, problems and policies'. In J. R. Rogge (ed.) *Refugees: A Third World Dilemma*. Totawa, NJ: Rowman and Littlefield Publishers Inc. Pp. 237–253.
Hugo, G. (2005) 'Migration in the Asia-Pacific region'. Paper prepared for the Policy Analysis and Research Programme, the Global Commission on International Migration, Geneva.
Hugo, G. (2006) 'The new international migration in Asia'. *Asian Population Studies*, 1(1): 93–120.
Hugo, G. (2008) 'Migration, development and environment'. IOM Migration Research Series No. 35, International Organization for Migration (IOM), Geneva.
Hugo, G. (2011) 'Irregular international migration in Asia'. Report to OECD International Migration Division.
Hugo, G., M. J. Abbasi-Shavazi and E. P. Kraly (eds.) (2017a) *Demography of Refugee and Forced Migration*. Dordrecht: Springer.
Hugo, G., M. J. Abbasi-Shavazi and E. P. Kraly (2017b) 'Introduction: advancing the demography of forced migration and refugees'. In Hugo, Abbasi-Shavazi and Kraly (eds.) *Demography of Refugee and Forced Migration*. Dordrecht: Springer.

Icduygu, A. (2015) *Syrian Refugees in Turkey: The Long Road Ahead*. Washington, DC: Migration Policy Institute.

Inderfurth, K. F., D. Fabrycky and S. Cohen (2005) 'The 2004 Indian Ocean tsunami: one year report'. The Sigur Center for Asian Studies, Washington.

Jacobsen, K. and L. B. Landau (2003) 'The dual imperative in refugee research: some methodological and ethical considerations in social science research on forced migration'. *Disasters*, 27 (3): 185–206.

Kraly, E. P. (2017) 'Behind and beyond disaggregation by sex: forced migration, gender and the place of demography'. In Hugo, Abbasi-Shavazi and Kraly (eds.) *Demography of Refugee and Forced Migration*. Dordrecht: Springer.

Kunz, E. F. (1973) 'The refugee in flight: kinetic models and forms of displacement'. *International Migration Review*, 7(2): 125–146.

Kunz, E. F. (1981) 'Exile and resettlement: refugee theory'. *International Migration Review*, 15(1–2): 42–51.

Mahapatra, L. K. (1999) 'Testing the risks and reconstruction model on India's resettlement experiences'. In M. M. Cernea (ed.) *The Economics of Involuntary Resettlement: Questions and Challenges*. Washington, DC: World Bank.

Meda, L. (2016) 'A journey without planned destination: traumatic transmigration experiences of refugee children'. *International Migration and Integration*, 18(1): 131–142. Available from: http://dx.doi.org//10.1007/s12134-016-0477-x.

McAuliffe, M. and D. Jayasuriya (2016) 'Do asylum seekers and refugees choose destination countries? Evidence from large-scale surveys in Australia, Afghanistan, Bangladesh, Pakistan and Sri Lanka'. *International Migration*, 54(4): 44–59

Monsuti, A. (2008) 'Afghan migratory strategies and the three solutions to the refugee problem'. *Refugee Survey Quarterly*, 27(1): 58–73.

Nair, P. and T. Bloom (eds.) (2015) *Migration Across Boundaries: Linking Research to Practice and Experience*. London: Routledge.

Oliver-Smith, A. (ed.) (2009) *Development & Dispossession: The Crisis of Forced Displacement and Resettlement*. School for Advanced Research Advanced Seminar Series. SAR Press.

Reed, H., J. Haaga and C. Keely (eds.) (1998) *The Demography of Forced Migration: Summary of a Workshop*. Washington, DC: National Academy Press.

Richmond, A. H. (1993) 'Reactive migration: sociological perspectives on refugee movements'. *Journal of Refugee Studies*, 6(1): 7–24.

Schmeidl, S. (1998) 'Data sources: how much do they differ and why?' In H. Reed, J. Haaga and C. Keely (eds.) *The Demography of Forced Migration: Summary of a Workshop*. Washington, DC: The National Academies Press.

Simich, L., M. Beiser and F. N. Mawani (2003) 'Social support and the significance of shared experience in refugee migration and resettlement'. *Western Journal of Nursing Research*, 25(7): 872–891.

Skeldon, R. (2009) 'Managing irregular migration as a negative factor in the Development of Eastern Asia'. Working Paper No.18, International Labour Organization Asian Regional Programme on Governance of Labour Migration.

Stein, B. (1981) 'The refugee experience: defining the parameters of a field of study'. *International Migration Review*, 15: 320–330.

Taneja, B. and H. Thakkar (2000) 'Large dams and displacement in India'. Cape Town, South Africa: Submission no. SOC166 to the World Commission on Dams.

Terminski, B. (2012) *Environmentally-Induced Displacement. Theoretical Frameworks and Current Challenges*. Université de Liège.

Tibaijuka, A. (2010) 'Meeting humanitarian challenges in urban areas'. *Forced Migration Review*, 34: 8–9.

United Nations (2013) *UN General Assembly on International Migration and Development*, 15 July 2013. New York: UN.

United Nations High Commissioner for Refugees (UNHCR) (1951) *The 1951 Refugee Convention*. Available from: www.unhcr.org/1951-refugee-convention.html.

United Nations High Commissioner for Refugees (UNHCR) (2011) *Statistical Yearbook 2010*. Geneva: UNHCR.

United Nations High Commissioner for Refugees (UNHCR) (2013a) *Displacement the New 21st Century Challenges: UNHCR Global Trends 2012*. Geneva: UNHCR.

United Nations High Commissioner for Refugees (UNHCR) (2013b) *The 2012 Statistical Yearbook*. Geneva: UNHCR.

United Nations High Commissioner for Refugees (UNHCR) (2014a) *Statistics on Displaced Iraqis Around the World*. Available from: www.unhcr.org/461f7cb92.pdf.

United Nations High Commissioner for Refugees (UNHCR) (2014b) *The 2013 Statistical Yearbook*. Geneva: UNHCR.
United Nations High Commissioner for Refugees (UNHCR) (2015) *The 2014 Statistical Yearbook*. Geneva: UNHCR.
United Nations High Commissioner for Refugees (UNHCR) (2016a) *Global Trends: Forced Displacement in 2015*. Geneva: UNHCR.
United Nations High Commissioner for Refugees (UNHCR) (2016b) *Population Statistics Database*. Available from: http://popstats.unhcr.org/en/demographics.
Van Hear, N. and C. McDowell (eds.) (2006) *Containing Forced Migration in a Volatile World*. Oxford: Rowman and Littlefield Publishers Inc.
Zetter, R. (1988) 'Refugee, repatriation and root causes'. *Journal of Refugee Studies*, 1: 99–106.
Zolberg, A., A. Suhrke and S. Aguayo (1989) *Escape from Violence: Conflict and the Refugee Crisis in the Developing World*. London: Oxford University Press.

19
Changing marriage patterns in Asia

Gavin W. Jones

There have been major changes in aspects of marriage in Asian countries over recent decades. In one short chapter, it is not possible to cover effectively a continent as large and diverse as Asia, but in this paper I will concentrate on three of the major regions of Asia – East and South-East Asia, on the one hand, and South Asia, on the other. Together they contain over 90 per cent of Asia's population.[1] The key issues differ between South Asia and the more easterly parts of Asia, largely because their traditional marriage and kinship systems differed, but also because the forces acting to modify these systems have had different intensity in different places. Half a century ago, universal and early marriage were characteristic of almost all of Asia,[2] but child marriage (a high proportion of girls marrying before their sixteenth birthday), while very common in South Asia, was not common in South-East or East Asia, with the exception of some of the Malay populations of Malaysia and Indonesia. The system that produced child marriage was a strongly patriarchal one in which parent-arranged marriage was the unquestioned mechanism for finding a marriage partner.

In East and South-East Asia, traditional arranged marriage systems have almost disappeared, though on the whole, young people still attach great importance to parental approval of their chosen partner. Delayed and non-marriage have contributed to very low fertility in the region. In South Asia, the key issues relate to whether there are any fractures in the arranged marriage system, issues related to continued patterns of early marriage, and the role of consanguineous marriage. The geographic division of issues, of course, is not completely neat. For example, early marriage remains fairly common in some parts of South-East Asia, and consanguineous marriage is prevalent in parts of South-East Asia. Also, in just one South Asian country – Sri Lanka – delayed marriage is as prominent as it is in countries further eastwards.

Kinship systems and marriage arrangement

Before discussing changes in marriage ages, the differences in kinship systems and their effects on both arrangement of marriage and age at marriage need to be considered. Both the Confucianist systems of East Asia and the Hindu system in India emphasized the absorption of the bride into the husband's family, whereas the bilateral kinship systems of most of South-East Asia allow much closer association of the bride with her cognates, and a pattern whereby the newly married couple more commonly lived first with the bride's parents rather than the husband's parents, before establishing an independent household.[3]

The system that is heavily dependant on arranged marriage is strongest in North India. North Indian kinship involves three key principles: marriage is exogamous with only non-relatives marrying; males generally cooperate with agnates, particularly brothers; and females do not inherit. The sexuality of women needs to be carefully controlled to uphold the honour of the family. Husbands and wives should not be too emotionally attached, as this could threaten the unity of the patriarchal family. Girls are married off very young, and are thenceforth cut off from their natal families. There is a saying that 'a woman is concerned not with who her husband will be but with who her mother-in-law will be' (Caldwell 1992: 44). Early marriage (with a considerably older man) helps protect young women's chastity, marks a clear break from their natal families, makes them more likely to accept the structure of authority in their new family, and weakens the husband-wife bond. Writing of fieldwork in rural Karnataka, in South India, Caldwell, Reddy and Caldwell (1982: 706) noted that although great changes had been transforming marriage over the past third of a century, there was no claim of any decline in the significance of arranged marriage, which remained universal.

Many of these principles also operated in Malay-Muslim societies of South-East Asia,[4] in particular the desire to protect family honour by marrying off girls at a young age. However, women could inherit, albeit following the Islamic allocation of half shares. And while patriarchy as a principle was supported by their Muslim religion, in practice spousal relations were much more egalitarian. As a result of the bilateral kinship system, the North Indian pattern of cutting off young wives from their natal family was absent. In the non-Muslim South-East Asian societies – Buddhist Burma, Thailand, Cambodia and Laos, and the Catholic Philippines – choice of spouse was more relaxed than in the Islamic societies of South-East Asia.

In East and South-East Asia, a broad generalization is that at mid-twentieth century, arranged marriage with varying degrees of consultation with the individuals marrying remained the norm, but by the end of the century, it had largely disappeared.[5] The sharp decline in arranged marriage has been clearly documented for Japan, Taiwan, China, Korea and Malaysia (Retherford and Ogawa 2006: Figure 1.9; Thornton and Lin 1994; Martin 1990: 108–109; Tsuya and Choe 1991; Jones 1994: 131–144*)*, and observed elsewhere.

The history of arranged marriage reflects trends in gender and intergenerational relations. Traditional arranged marriage placed considerable power in the hands of parents, and in particular the father. The weakening of the system of arranged marriage throughout East and South-East Asia reflects at a deep level the abdication of this power by the older generation and in particular by males of the older generation. It can be seen as a largely voluntary abdication, clearly related to the remarkable developments in education, increasing urbanization and involvement of women in economic activities outside the household, among other things – which in the public perception are often referred to in the vernacular as 'changing times' (e.g. in Indonesian, *perobahan zaman*), a term which some social scientists may consider excessively vague, but which on the contrary captures the breadth and pervasiveness of the changes referred to.

The weakening of the arranged marriage system in South-East Asian countries is not hard to explain. As these are characterized by bilateral kinship systems and not (except for northern Vietnam[6]) subject to Confucianist influences, there was little underlying structural need for an arranged marriage system. The system therefore crumbled when faced by changing reality in the form of extended education for girls, the effect of this on raising ages at marriage, and the lack of a compelling reason why parents should continue to be the ones choosing the spouse for later-marrying daughters. But this does not explain why the same crumbling took place in

East Asian Confucianist-influenced societies, but not in South Asia, where the arranged marriage system proved to be much more resilient. Part of the explanation may be simply a 'developmental' one: Japan, South Korea, Taiwan and Singapore were the East Asian 'tiger economies' which experienced rapid and sustained economic growth, underpinned by remarkable educational advances, over the four decades from the 1960s onwards. In South Asia, development – whether measured by economic or human development criteria – was much slower, at least until India's recent upsurge in growth. Female education has lagged male, though before concluding from this that lack of female autonomy is a key factor in persistence of arranged marriage, it needs to be noted that arranged marriage is nearly universal in Kerala, where female autonomy is acknowledged to be particularly high. This serves to underline the strong cultural underpinnings of arranged marriage in South Asia.

Most young people in South Asia continue to accept that their parents are the best ones to choose their marriage partners, and have shown little inclination to challenge the arranged marriage system, though there is some movement towards greater consultation with children in the choice of spouse (Jejeebhoy et al. 2013; Desai and Andrist 2010; World Bank 2008: 114–115). By contrast, it is argued that in East Asia, the collapse of the arranged marriage system has not been matched by the emergence of an alternative system, and the dearth of social contacts with the opposite sex is partly responsible for the sharp rise in singlehood (Retherford and Ogawa 2006: 17–18). Reports in the popular press suggest that parents in China and Japan may be getting more involved again in finding partners for their children. There is certainly evidence that in East and South-East Asia, many young people are finding it hard to deal with the lack of an arranged marriage system, though adaptations of various kinds are developing – for example, the involvement of Islamic marriage bureaus serving as matchmaking agencies in Malaysia (Jones 1994: 153) and more broadly, the growth of Internet dating and matchmaking, ranging from many hundreds of small agencies to very large ones such as Sunoo and Duo in Korea and zhenai.com in China. In Singapore, such matchmaking is sponsored by the government (Jones and Gubhaju 2009: 259–260).

The one exception to the persistence of arranged marriage systems in South Asia is Sri Lanka, which in relation to marriage should perhaps be considered to lie in South-East Asia, as it is culturally closer to the Theravada Buddhist countries such as Thailand and Burma than it is to the countries of the Indian subcontinent. Here, arranged marriage dropped sharply over the 20 years from the early 1960s to the early 1980s (from 70 per cent to 32 per cent), according to the Sri Lankan Demographic Change Project (Caldwell 1992: Table 5.1).

Trends towards later and less marriage

In 1960, Asia was characterized by universal marriage (a crude definition of which is fewer than five per cent of women remaining single in their late 40s), with the Philippines and Myanmar the only exceptions, both by a small margin. The contrast with the present time is dramatic. Asia is now home to some of the latest-marrying populations in the world; in Singapore, Hong Kong, Japan and Myanmar the proportion of women reaching their late 40s never-married is around 12 per cent, and is only slightly below 10 per cent in Thailand.

The trend towards later marriage has been universal throughout Asia over the past half century; in East and South-East Asia it has been accompanied by a trend towards less marriage (Jones 2005; Jones and Gubhaju 2009). A summary of trends in the singulate mean age at marriage (SMAM)[7] is given in Table 19.1. This measure is subject to biases when age at marriage is rising, but it does have the advantage of summarizing marriage trends into just one number and it can be readily calculated using census data. Over the 40 years from 1970 to 2010, SMAM for women

Table 19.1 Trends in singulate mean age at marriage, various Asian countries, 1970–2010

Country	1970	1980	1990	2000	2010
Women					
East and SE Asia					
Japan	24.7	25.1	26.9	28.6	29.7
South Korea	23.3	24.1	25.5	27.1	30.1
Taiwan	22.6	23.9	26.0	27.6	30.4
China	20.6	22.4	22.1	23.3	24.7
Hong Kong	23.8	25.3	28.0	29.6	30.3
Thailand	22.0	22.8	23.5	24.1	24.7
Singapore	24.2	26.2	27.0	26.5	27.9
Malaysia	22.1	23.5	24.6	24.9	25.7
Indonesia	19.3	20.0	21.6	22.7	22.2
Philippines	22.8	22.4	23.8	23.9	24.4
Myanmar	21.3	22.4	24.5	25.8	26.1
South Asia					
India	17.7	18.7	19.3	20.2	22.0
Pakistan	19.7	20.2	21.7	22.2	22.7
Bangladesh	16.8	16.9	18.1	18.7	19.4
Sri Lanka	23.5	24.4	25.5	23.7	23.6
Iran	18.5	19.7	19.8	22.4	23.4
Men					
East and SE Asia					
Japan	27.5	28.7	30.4	30.8	31.2
South Korea	27.2	27.3	28.5	30.3	32.9
Taiwan	24.6	25.3	28.8	30.5	32.7
China	n.a.	25.1	23.8	25.1	26.5
Hong Kong	30.2	28.7	29.8	31.9	33.1
Thailand	24.7	24.9	26.0	27.4	28.2
Singapore	27.8	28.4	29.9	30.0	30.3
Malaysia	25.6	26.6	27.9	28.5	27.8
Indonesia	23.8	24.1	25.2	25.9	25.6
Philippines	24.4	24.9	26.3	26.3	27.0
Myanmar	23.9	24.6	26.3	27.6	27.6
South Asia					
India	22.7	23.4	23.9	24.8	25.9
Pakistan	25.7	25.1	26.5	26.1	26.4
Bangladesh	24.0	23.9	25.0	25.3	25.0
Sri Lanka	28.0	27.9	28.3	27.6	n.a.
Iran	25.0	n.a.	23.8	25.3	26.8

Notes: The data used derive from population censuses and nationally representative surveys (mainly Demographic and Health Surveys). The column data do not always refer exactly to the column heading year ending in a zero (1970, 1980, etc.). The main deviations are China 1982 (instead of 1980); Philippines 2007; Myanmar 2007; India 1992–1993; Pakistan 1981, 2007; Bangladesh 1974, 1981, 1991; Sri Lanka 1971, 1981, 1993, 2006–2007; and Iran 1966, 1986, 1996, 2011.
'n.a.' indicates information not available.
Sources: Jones and Gubhaju (2009); Banister (1984); Dommaraju (2008); Sathar and Kiani (1998); United Nations Population Division, World Marriage Data; Demographic and Health Surveys of various countries and years; Japan, Statistical Bureau; Korea, Statistical Information Service; Taiwan, Ministry of the Interior; China, National Bureau of Statistics; Hong Kong, Census and Statistics Department; Thailand, National Statistics Office; Singapore, Department of Statistics; Malaysia, Population and Housing Census; Indonesia, Statistics Indonesia; Philippines, National Statistics Office; India, Office of the Registrar General; Bangladesh, Statistical Yearbooks.

has increased by 5 years in Japan, 6.8 years in Korea, 7.8 years in Taiwan and 6.5 years in Hong Kong. In these countries, SMAM was already relatively high in 1970, and by 2010 was among the highest anywhere in the world, particularly if cohabiting couples in Western countries are included in the married population for purposes of comparison. In South-East Asian countries the rise has not been as spectacular, though the SMAMs for women in the Philippines, Malaysia and Thailand – already around 22 in 1970 – have now reached levels of 24 or 25, and Myanmar has seen a rise of almost 5 years.

Average age at marriage has been rising in South Asian countries as well, though from lower starting points than in East and South-East Asia. For women, the SMAM has risen by over four years between 1970 and 2010 in India, by two and a half years in Bangladesh, by three years in Pakistan and by five years in Iran. In Iran, the rise was particularly striking, given the strong promotion of early marriage in the early post-revolutionary years. It is noteworthy that in Iran's pronatalist phase (1979–1986), during which early marriage was encouraged, the SMAM barely changed. There was then a three and a half year rise in SMAM in the 20-year period between 1990 and 2010, in which pronatalist policies had been abandoned.

In India, there are large regional differences in age at marriage. Women marry relatively late in the South, particularly in Kerala, and relatively early in the North, particularly in Bihar, Madhya Pradesh, Rajasthan and Uttar Pradesh (Visaria 2004: 62; Bhagat 2002). These differences have been discussed as part of a broader difference in female autonomy and demographic behaviour between North and South India (or more strictly north-west and south-east India) by Dyson and Moore (1983).

Another measure of singlehood, the proportion still single at age 30–34, is given in Table 19.2. In East Asia, the revolution in singlehood since 1970 is indicated by rates of singlehood for women in Japan, Taiwan, Korea and Hong Kong climbing from low single digit figures to around 30–35 per cent in 2010. For men, rates have climbed even more – to around 50 per cent. China is a striking exception, with only the beginnings of an upturn apparent. In South-East Asia, Myanmar, Singapore and Thailand are only slightly below the East Asian frontrunners in levels of female singlehood, but Vietnam and Indonesia are far lower. For males in their early 30s in South-East Asia, levels of singlehood are increasing everywhere. Very few women in South Asia remain unmarried at ages 30–34, with the important exception of Iran, where the proportion remaining single more than doubled in the 10 years to 2010.

Singlehood is particularly high in the cities, and for well educated women. In Thailand, among women aged over 30 in 2010, the propoprtion of never-married was twice as high in urban areas as in rural areas (for example, 20 per cent compared with 10 per cent at ages 35–39). As for education, figures for Thailand in 2000 show that the proportion of women still single at ages 35–39 was 7 per cent for those with primary education or less, 14 per cent for those with lower secondary education, 17 per cent for those with upper secondary education, and 23 per cent for those with tertiary education. Similar data for three countries in 2010 are shown in Table 19.3. In Singapore and Korea, in the younger adult ages there are few women with primary school education or less, so the key comparison is between the high school and tertiary educated; in both countries, delayed and non-marriage is considerably higher for the tertiary educated women. In China, the tertiary educated are the only group of women delaying their marriage beyond age 30 in considerable numbers.

For men, the relationship between educational level and marriage is different. In the countries included in Table 19.3, and also in Japan and for Chinese Malaysians, it is the less educated who are less likely to marry, seemingly because of the difficulties they face in the marriage market. Partly as a result of this, there have been rapid increases in the proportion of men from wealthier Asian countries (e.g. Japan, South Korea, Taiwan and Singapore) marrying women

Gavin W. Jones

Table 19.2 Per cent never married at ages 30–34, various Asian countries, 1970–2010

Country	1970	1980	1990	2000	2010
Women					
East Asia					
Japan	7.0	9.0	14.0	27.0	32.5
South Korea	1.0	3.0	5.0	11.0	29.1
China	1.0	0.7	0.6	1.0	5.4
Taiwan	2.0	6.0	12.3	20.8	37.2
Hong Kong	6.0	11.1	21.0	30.0	35.0
South-East Asia					
Singapore	10.0	17.0	21.0	20.0	25.1
Malaysia	5.7	9.9	12.1	12.1	17.9
Thailand	8.1	11.8	14.2	16.2	23.5
Philippines	8.9	11.9	13.4	14.8	15.9
Indonesia	2.2	3.4	4.5	6.9	6.0
Myanmar	9.3	12.8	19.6	25.9	20.8
Vietnam	n.a.	n.a.	11.2	9.7	8.2
South Asia					
India	0.8	1.2	1.8	2.2	2.7
Bangladesh	0.6	1.0	1.1	3.9	1.8
Pakistan	3.0	3.9	3.7	7.2	7.2
Nepal	1.4	3.1	1.9	2.5	2.9
Iran	1.4	n.a.	3.5	6.4	15.5
Men					
East Asia					
Japan	11.7	21.5	32.6	42.9	44.5
South Korea	6.4	7.3	13.9	28.1	50.2
China	9.0	7.0	8.0	10.0	12.6
Taiwan	11.0	12.5	22.7	35.4	54.1
Hong Kong	35.0	27.0	34.0	46.0	55.4
South-East Asia					
Singapore	22.0	22.0	34.0	31.0	37.1
Malaysia	12.2	14.5	20.2	24.4	28.4
Thailand	9.8	10.9	16.4	23.2	36.5
Philippines	13.1	14.4	16.9	20.8	22.4
Indonesia	6.1	6.1	9.4	11.8	12.8
Myanmar	10.3	12.7	19.6	22.4	22.9
Vietnam	n.a.	n.a.	7.5	9.8	13.3
South Asia					
India	7.3	7.1	8.2	8.7	9.7
Bangladesh	5.7	6.3	7.2	12.0	9.0
Pakistan	n.a.	13.8	15.3	16.1	15.3
Nepal	15.7	12.4	12.7	15.7	16.7
Iran	7.0	n.a.	6.0	7.7	16.0

Notes and Sources: As for Table 19.1.

from poorer Asian countries (e.g. China, Vietnam) through marriage brokers (Jones and Shen 2008; Jones 2012; Kim 2008).

Given that singlehood is much more prevalent for well-educated women, an important question is whether the recent rise in singlehood is purely a 'compositional' effect of

Table 19.3 South Korea, China and Singapore: per cent still single women and men, by age and education, 2010

Education Level	Age Groups					
	20–24	25–29	30–34	35–39	40–44	45–49
South Korea						
Women						
None, primary or middle school*	60.2	49.7	35.5	17.4	6.2	2.4
High school	86.1	53.6	23.7	9.8	4.5	2.5
Tertiary	98.0	73.8	31.4	14.8	8.4	5.7
Men						
None, primary or middle school^	92.6	82.3	70.4	54.9	36.4	18.2
High school	96.5	78.9	52.9	31.8	17.6	8.0
Tertiary	99.3	87.2	48.8	22.3	9.7	4.2
China						
Women						
None, primary or middle school	40.2	12.2	4.0	1.4	0.6	0.4
High school	60.0	17.5	4.8	1.6	0.7	0.4
Tertiary	93.1	39.6	9.5	3.6	1.8	1.1
Men						
None, primary or middle school	72.0	37.6	21.8	14.5	10.3	9.0
High school	77.8	31.1	11.0	5.1	2.7	1.8
Tertiary	96.4	53.4	13.5	4.2	1.8	0.9
Singapore						
Women						
None, primary or middle school#	55.1	23.0	12.7	9.4	9.0	9.1
High school	88.0	48.0	24.0	16.5	13.9	13.6
Tertiary	93.1	61.7	28.0	20.7	19.1	18.3
Men						
None, primary or middle school+	88.9	63.9	39.4	29.1	22.7	19.1
High school	97.1	72.0	38.6	21.8	15.3	11.6
Tertiary	97.2	75.7	35.0	16.9	10.9	8.1

Notes: * Only 0.8% of female aged 20–24, 1.1% of those aged 25–29, 1.2% of those aged 30–34, 2.3% of those aged 35–39, 6.7% of those aged 40–44 and 20.1% of those aged 45–49.
^ Only 0.7% of male aged 20–24, 1.2% of those aged 25–29, 1.6% of those aged 30–34, 2.6% of those aged 35–39, 4.8% of those aged 40–44 and 11.8% of those aged 45–49.
# Only 5.4% of female aged 20–24, 5.5% of those aged 25–29, 8.3% of those aged 30–34, 14.2% of those aged 35–39, 22.7% of those aged 40–44 and 33.9% of those aged 45–49.
+ Only 4.2% of male aged 20–24, 4.0% of those aged 25–29, 6.0% of those aged 30–34, 9.8% of those aged 35–39, 19.2% of those aged 40–44 and 32.1% of those aged 45–49.
Sources: Korea (www.kosis.kr); China, National Bureau of Statistics; Singapore, Department of Statistics.

increasing proportions of women in these educational categories, or whether the increase in singlehood is something sweeping through the whole society. It has been shown that, up to 2005 at least, the dramatic trend away from marriage in Japan, Korea and Taiwan has been pervasive across all educational groups, whereas in Thailand, for the Chinese in Peninsular

Malaysia, in Singapore and in China, compositional changes played the dominant role (Jones and Gubhaju 2009).

A decade ago, the rise in singlehood throughout Asia seemed to be inexorable, and indeed it continues to appear this way through most of Asia. However, over the past decade, some important exceptions have emerged. In Indonesia, the earlier steady rise in age at marriage was reversed after 2005, though in 2010 the SMAM was still 3 years higher than it had been in 1970. Singlehood has also declined somewhat in Vietnam and Sri Lanka (see De Silva 2014). Reasons differ. In Indonesia, there appears to be increasing religiosity, and support for early family formation by popular religious figures, including those hosting popular TV programmes (Fealy and White 2008; Weintraub 2011). In Sri Lanka, De Silva (2014) gives a number of reasons: the ending of the marriage squeeze, restriction on abortion services for unmarried females, clearing of education backlogs resulting in earlier completion of education and entry into the labour market, and lower unemployment rates.

Turning to age differences between husbands and wives, these are much wider in South Asia than in East and South-East Asia; in East Asian countries in recent decades, the SMAM for males typically exceeds that for females by between 2 to 3.5 years, and for South-East Asian countries by 1.8 to 3.6 years, whereas in South Asian countries, the differences tend to be more like five or six years. (For earlier evidence from World Fertility Survey data, see Casterline, Williams and McDonald 1986.) Bangladesh is probably the most extreme case; men marry on average more than nine years later than women, indicating large age differences between husbands and wives (National Institute of Population Research and Training, Mitra and Associates and Macro International 2009: 77). The wider age gap in South Asian countries reflects parent-arranged marriage and patriarchal family structures, which typically lead to young ages at marriage for females, whereas males are expected to be in a position both to support a family economically, and to show maturity in taking on the responsibilities of a new family, before entering into marriage, which usually means some delay in marriage.

Over time, the age differences have contracted somewhat in most Asian countries for which there is evidence. For example, in Pakistan, the difference between SMAM for males and females was around 6 years in the 1950–1970 period, but has been around 5 years since the 1980s (National Institute of Population Studies and IRD/Macro International Inc. 1992: Table 7.2); census data show the difference contracting to 3.9 years in 1998 (Nayab 2009). In Iran, the difference in mean age at first marriage in rural areas fell from 5.3 years in 1980 to 4.3 years in 2000, and in urban areas from 5.4 years to 5.0 years (Abbasi-Shavazi, McDonald and Hosseini-Chavoshi 2009: Table 5.2). However, in Peninsular Malaysia, there has been little change. What is clear in Malaysia is that tertiary-educated women tend to have a smaller age gap with their husband, and are more likely than other women to be the same age as, or older than, their husband (Tey 2007: Tables 1 and 8).

Issues arising from rising singlehood

In the traditional, universal marriage systems of Asia, only women with serious physical or mental disabilities were likely to remain single. The situation has now drastically changed in many East and South-East Asian countries. In Japan, around 40 per cent of women are entering their 30s still single, and around 15 per cent of that cohort is likely to remain single when they reach 49.[8] In Indonesia, around 10 per cent of women are entering their 30s still single, though the proportion reaching their 40s still single remains very low. Most East and South-East Asian countries fall between these two extremes. What is the role of singles in these societies? In Japan, many adjustments have been made, but the use of terms such as 'parasite singles' to describe those who remain living at home, and enjoy their good salaries to buy designer clothes and take vacations with friends, shows a degree of tension about the role of singles. In Indonesia, the situation of singles may be more difficult, because a place has not been provided for single adults in community and family activities and ceremonies (Situmorang 2007). Similarly, in Vietnam, while non-marriage has become more acceptable, 'single women are far from being fully accepted by, and integrated in, their families and communities' (Bélanger and Hong 2002: 90). It is perhaps easier for single women in Buddhist countries such as Thailand and Burma, where remaining single to look after aged parents is an accepted role for women.

Given the increasing numbers of singles in their 20s and 30s in many Asian countries, are many of them becoming involved in cohabiting relationships? Data on this is scarce, but in Japan and the Philippines, cohabitation is increasing (Raymo, Iwasawa and Bumpass 2009; Abalos 2014). In Thailand, where both registered and unregistered marriages are recognized in the community, cohabitation is a separate category. Its incidence is low (2.4 per cent among those aged 18–59 in 2006), but higher in Bangkok (10 per cent) (Jampaklay and Haseen 2011: Table 1). In Shanghai, a recent study of young married couples found that 43 per cent had cohabited before marriage, though the great majority were engaged or had clear plans to marry before they cohabited. The study suggests that cohabitation is becoming more acceptable in Chinese cities.[9] Cohabitation may well be increasing in other East and South-East Asian countries, but it remains very uncommon in South Asia.

In many countries of Asia, it is very difficult for singles to access contraceptive advice and services. In many countries of the region, access to contraception by unmarried teenagers is made very difficult. For example, in Mataram, Lombok, women are denied access to family planning in government clinics if they are unable to confirm that they are married; the alternative for single women is to access contraception privately, but 'this requires the cooperation and discretion of a willing doctor, midwife, or chemist and the financial resources to pay the inflated cost of contraception sold in the private sector' (Bennett 2005: 35). In Malaysia, even the private Federation of Family Planning Associations of Malaysia 'has limited its services for young, adolescent and unmarried women to counselling, information, and education, and not any direct services that are not endorsed by government policy' (Chee 2006: 5). There is a clear need to re-think these policies in view of the much longer period young people are exposed to the possibility of pre-marital sexual relations.

Delayed marriage of the magnitude being experienced in many East and South-East Asian countries is sufficient to make a considerable difference in lowering fertility rates, from an accounting point of view, but perhaps more emphasis needs to be placed on the motivation for delaying marriage. Given the stress on quickly having a child after marriage in these societies, a delay in marriage could in many cases be motivated by reluctance to start family formation by those who are worried about the many problems they face in bearing and raising children. These problems include the increasing costs of childrearing, both the direct financial costs and the opportunity costs of women's interrupted career development; societal expectations about intensive parenting and driving children to succeed in a highly competitive world, and the pressures this places on women in particular; and the difficulty for women in finding partners who share their values and expectations, particularly regarding sharing housework and childrearing in a two-income household.

Consanguineous marriage

Consanguineous marriage tends to be prevalent in societies where the interaction between young women and men from outside close kin is highly restricted. It is therefore prevalent in many Islamic societies, as well as non-Islamic communities in South Asia, especially in South India. The most common form of consanguineous unions is between first cousins (Bittles 1994: 562). As noted by Korson (1979: 196), writing of Pakistan, 'with the limitation of sexual segregation among adolescents and adults enforced by the practice of *purdah*, it is only natural that the young men and women are likely to develop close attachments to those relatives they are permitted to see over a period of time, namely, cousins'.

Pakistan does, indeed, have one of the highest rates of consanguineous marriage in the world. Among currently married women aged 15–49 surveyed in the 2006–2007 Pakistan Demographic and Health Survey, only one-third were married to non-relatives, and the proportion was even lower among those aged below 30, suggesting, if anything, a tendency for the practice to increase over time. This increase over time is confirmed by comparing the 2006–2007 Pakistan Demographic and Health Survey with the DHS of 1990–1991 (Nayab 2009). More than half of women in 2006–2007 were married to first cousins. Consanguineous marriage was more common among the rural and less educated population, but even among those with secondary education, 44 per cent were married to first cousins, and among the tertiary educated, 37 per cent (National Institute of Population Studies and Macro International Inc. 2008: Table 6.3).

In India, consanguineous marriage has long been more prevalent in the south, especially in Tamil Nadu. The favoured version is matrilineal cross-cousin (with mother's brother's daughter), or uncle-niece marriage, that is, with sister's daughter (Caldwell 1992: 49; Dyson and Moore 1983). Tamil populations abroad (e.g. in Malaysia) have carried on this tradition; in a survey of Indian (mainly Tamil) women in Malaysian estates in the 1980s, close to 30 per cent had been offered to their maternal uncle, where one was available (though only half of them actually proceeded to the marriage), while one-third were offered in marriage to a cousin, of whom two-thirds married the cousin. In all, some 40 per cent were offered in marriage to a cousin, an uncle, or both (Tan et al. 1988: 44–48).

In Malaysia, not only the Tamils but also the Malays have traditions of marrying close relatives. Malaysia's long-serving Prime Minister, Mahathir Mohamad, famously argued in his book *The Malay Dilemma* (banned until he became prime minister) that the genetic weaknesses resulting from the practice of cross-cousin marriage were part of the reason why Malays were unable to compete successfully with the Chinese in Malaysia.[10] Interestingly, the evidence from the Malay world shows that among Malays in Malaysia, marriage to relatives is not particularly common, and certainly less than in parts of Indonesia, where in places it reaches levels of 30–50 per cent, though the Javanese seem to have lower rates of consanguineous marriage than elsewhere in Indonesia (Jones 1994: 11–13).

It has been frequently argued (e.g. by Goode 1963) that consanguineous marriage will decline with development, urbanization and the decline of arranged marriage. And there is indeed evidence of decline in many parts of the developing world (Tfaily 2005). However, the decline has tended to be slow, and not universal. As noted above, there is no sign of a decline in consanguinity in Pakistan. A recent study for Iran (Abbasi-Shavazi, McDonald and Hosseini-Chavoshi 2008) shows considerable regional variation in levels of consanguinity, and greater incidence in rural areas and among the lesser-educated, lending some support to the argument that it may soon decline, particularly bearing in mind the decline in arranged marriages in Iran. Nevertheless, consanguineous marriage has strong cultural support in Iran, and there is no evidence of a lowered incidence so far.

Many observers stress the undesirable clinical outcomes of close kin marriages, though these adversely affect only a small minority of the families and individuals concerned, and need to be balanced by an understanding of the social and economic benefits of a consanguineous union in the cultural settings of the countries in which they are prevalent. Such benefits include maintenance of family structure and property, financial advantages of keeping dowry or bridewealth payments within the family, a closer relationship between the wife and her in-laws, and greater marital stability.

Problems of continued early marriage

In South Asia, universal marriage remains the norm, and although there has been a decline over time in the proportion of females in the 15–19 age group who are married, the proportion still marrying as teenagers remains very high in Bangladesh, parts of India, Afghanistan and Nepal (Bhagat 1993, 2002). Marriage, though, tends to be at a later age in Pakistan, and at a much later age in Sri Lanka, which in this respect does not fit the South Asian pattern at all.

Before World War II, teenage marriage was the norm throughout South-East and East Asia.[11] The post-war years saw major changes, but in the early 1960s teenage marriage remained the norm in Islamic South-East Asia (Indonesia, Malays in Malaysia, Singapore and Southern Thailand), as well as among the Indian populations of Malaysia and Singapore and, to a lesser extent, in rural Thailand and Myanmar. The median age at marriage for females in the late 1950s was around 17 in Indonesia, for Malays in Malaysia and Singapore, and for Southern Thai Muslims (Jones 1994: Table 3.1). Then it rose dramatically and by 1990 had reached 21 in Indonesia and 24 for Malays in both Malaysia and Singapore.

Table 19.4 shows the percentages of females ever married in the 15–19 age group in various countries and populations. This statistic needs to be interpreted carefully. It is a cross-sectional figure, showing the current marital status of those in the age range 15–19 *at the time of the census*.

Table 19.4 Teenage marriage: per cent of females ever married at ages 15–19, various countries, 1960–2010

Country	1960	1970	1980	1990	2000	2010
East Asia						
South Korea	7.0	2.9	1.8	0.5	0.7	0.4
China	n.a.	n.a.	4.4	4.7	1.2	2.1
Taiwan	10.4	7.2	5.3	2.7	1.6	0.4
Hong Kong	7.0	3.3	3.7	1.6	0.7	0.1
South-East Asia						
Philippines	12.7	10.8	14.1	10.5	10.2*	5.3
Indonesia	40.5	37.4	30.0	18.2	13.3	14.4
Thailand	18.5	19.9	16.7	14.9	12.0	13.5
Malaysia Malays	54.2	22.8	10.5	5.1	3.0	4.8
Malaysia Chinese	10.3	6.0	4.6	2.5	1.8	4.8
Malaysia Indians	53.2	17.0	8.0	6.0	4.0	5.0
Myanmar	n.a.	22.0	16.8	10.7	8.4	7.2
South Asia						
India	70.8	57.1	44.2	35.7	24.9	14.4
Bangladesh	n.a.	70.2	65.8	53.3	48.1	31.5
Nepal	73.9	60.7	50.8	44.0	40.3	28.9
Pakistan	53.4	34.4	29.4	24.9	20.6	10.8
Iran	n.a.	46.1	34.3	33.5	18.6	21.4

Notes: *6.8 if 'common law/live in' are considered to be never married.
Exact reference years for country data same as in Table 19.1. In addition: Nepal, 1961, 1971, 1981, 1996, 2010; Malaysia 1957, and Malaysia data 1957 and 1970 are for Peninsular Malaysia.
Sources: As for Table 19.1.

If 50 per cent of this age group are ever married, it does not mean that half of women marry only at ages 20 and above. Many women aged 15–19 at any particular time are aged 15, 16 or 17, and the fact that they are not yet married does not necessarily mean that they will not marry before reaching age 20. Thus, if 50 per cent of women aged 15–19 are ever married, this implies that a *large majority* of the women in this cohort marry in their teens.

In South Asia, although proportions ever-married at ages 15–19 have fallen very substantially, they remain much higher than in most countries of South-East Asia; in East Asia, teenage marriage has virtually disappeared. However, it is noteworthy that in the first decade of the twenty-first century, sharp declines in percentage of teenagers who are married in India and Pakistan, and slight increases in Indonesia and Thailand, have resulted in a convergence in the incidence of teenage marriage in these four countries.

In India, the proportion of females aged 10–14 who were currently married declined from 6.5 per cent in 1981 to 2.4 per cent in 2001 (Office of the Registrar General and Census Commissioner, India n.d.: 18). The legal age at marriage for women in India is 18. In 2001, one state – Rajasthan – had by far the highest proportion of women who were married before reaching age 18 – 5.4 per cent. It was followed by Madhya Pradesh and Bihar, each 3.2 per cent, Andhra Pradesh, 2.9 per cent, and Uttar Pradesh, 2.8 per cent. The census report commented that these are the known demographically backward states with high birth rates, high infant and maternal mortality rates and low literacy rates. While 18 has been set as the minimum age at marriage for women since 1929 (Haub and Sharma 2006), most Indian women married before age 17 until fairly recently.

In Bangladesh, too, the legal age at marriage for women is 18, but a remarkably large proportion of marriages take place before that age. The 2007 Demographic and Health Survey found that 66 per cent of women aged 20–24 were married before age 18 (see Table 19.5). Although there had been a steady decline in the proportion married before age 18, from 90 per cent among women currently aged 45–49, the fact that two-thirds of young women are still married before the legal age suggests that this particular legislation has little or no meaning. As for the proportion of marriages occurring before age 15, this has fallen rather more sharply, from 65 per cent among women aged 45–49 to 21 per cent among women ages 15–19.

In 1960, South-East Asia could not match the South Asian figure of 70 per cent of females ever married in the 15–19 age group, but among South-East Asian Muslim populations, figures of 50 per cent and more were common – in Malaysia and Singapore, many provinces of Indonesia and in Southern Thailand. Then a decline set in, dramatic in the case of Malaysia and Singapore, much more gradual in the case of Indonesia, such that the percentage ever married in this age group is now above 8 per cent only in Thailand, Indonesia, the Philippines and Myanmar – interestingly, three of them countries with only small Muslim populations.

The trends in early marriage in Indonesia and Bangladesh are compared in Table 19.5, based on DHS data collected in 2007. It is possible that in both countries, the extent of teenage marriage is somewhat overstated, as DHS samples tend to be biased away from single women or women with few children (Hull and Hartanto 2009; Avery et al. 2013). In Bangladesh, there is also evidence of systematic under-reporting of women's age at marriage (Streatfield et al. 2015). Keeping this possible bias in mind, the data show that in both countries, although there has been a gradual decline over time in teenage marriage, it remains quite prevalent in Indonesia and highly prevalent in Bangladesh. In Indonesia, between the cohort of women aged 45–49 and those aged 20–24 (i.e. over a 25-year period), the proportion married before age 15 fell from 17 per cent to 4 per cent; and the proportion married before age 18 fell from 47 per cent to 22 per cent. More than one-third of all women were still marrying in their teens, and of all women currently in their childbearing ages, approximately half married as teenagers. In Bangladesh, the

Table 19.5 Indonesia and Bangladesh: per cent of women married by exact ages 15, 18 and 20, from 2007 Demographic and Health Surveys

Current age	Married before age 15 (%)	Married before age 18 (%)	Married before age 20 (%)
Indonesia			
15–19	1.7		
20–24	4.3	22.0	40.7
25–29	5.1	24.0	43.4
30–34	8.6	28.0	46.4
35–39	9.1	31.7	49.6
40–44	15.1	43.4	59.4
45–49	16.8	46.6	65.0
20–49	**9.3**	**31.6**	**49.8**
Bangladesh			
15–19	21.1		
20–24	32.3	66.2	79.2
25–29	41.3	75.4	86.4
30–34	48.5	81.1	90.2
35–39	47.2	81.8	91.0
40–44	54.4	87.1	94.0
45–49	64.7	90.1	95.3
20–49	**45.2**	**78.0**	**87.8**

Sources: Statistics Indonesia and Macro International (2008).

proportions marrying as teenagers were much higher; two-thirds of young women aged 20–24 were still marrying before age 18, although 18 is the minimum legal age at marriage.

In both Indonesia and Bangladesh, there are legal issues in early marriage. Although the legal age at marriage for girls in Indonesia has been 16 since 1974, in the decade after that, more than 10 per cent of girls were still being married before reaching that age, a figure which had fallen to about 3 per cent by the early years of the twenty-first century. There are a number of reasons why such marriages are still taking place. One is that in some cases, the girl is pregnant and marriage is seen as the only way to preserve family honour. Another is that some parents, and officials responsible for registering such marriages, do not accept that there should be any lower age limit on the age at which girls can be married. Another is that sometimes there is no valid birth certificate for the girl, and therefore no way for the official to verify her age.

There are at least four key problems with early, parent-arranged marriage. First, there is a human rights dimension. Article 16 of the Universal Declaration of Human Rights states that 'marriage shall be entered into only with the free and full consent of the intending spouses'. Second, early marriage is likely to result in early age at first childbirth, which can have adverse health consequences for both mother and child. Third, early marriage is typically a barrier to education. Fourth, women who marry very young, typically to a much older husband, 'are likely to have less power, status, agency and autonomy within the household. In fact, men may choose younger brides for this very reason' (Jensen and Thornton 2003: 10).

Divorce trends[12]

Divorce rates in Western countries rose very substantially – with more than a doubling of the general divorce rate – in the two decades between 1960 and 1980 (Jones, Asari and Djuartika

Table 19.6 General divorce rates (number of divorces per 1,000 population aged 15+), various countries and regions, 1980–2010

	1980	1985	1990	1995	2000	2005	2010
OECD countries							
Australia	3.6	3.3	3.2	3.5	3.3	3.2	2.7
France	2.0	2.5	2.3	2.5	2.4	3.1	2.5
Germany	1.9	2.5	2.0	2.5	2.8	2.8	2.6
United Kingdom	3.8	4.0	3.6	3.6	3.2	3.4	2.7
United States	6.7	6.3	5.9	5.6	n.a.	n.a.	n.a.
Russian Federation	4.7	4.5	4.9	5.7	5.2	5.2	5.8
Asian countries							
Hong Kong	n.a.	1.0	1.2	1.9	2.4	2.5	2.8
Japan	1.6	1.8	1.6	1.9	2.4	2.4	2.3
South Korea	0.9	1.3	1.3	1.6	3.2	3.3	3.1
China	0.0	n.a.	1.0	1.3	1.3	1.7	2.4
Thailand	0.8	0.9	1.2	1.3	n.a.	n.a.	n.a.
Singapore	1.0	1.0	1.6	1.5	1.6	1.9	2.4
Iran	1.1	1.5	1.2	1.0	1.3	1.7	1.8

Notes: The column data do not always refer exactly to the column heading year ending in a zero or 5 (1980, 1985, etc.). The main deviations are Australia 2009 (for 2010); France 1979, 2008; Germany 1991, 2009; United Kingdom 2003, 2008; Russian Federation 2006, 2009; Hong Kong 2009; Japan 2009; South Korea 2009; China 1992, 1997 (for 1995); Thailand 1979, 1992; Iran 2006 (for 2010).
Sources: United Nations Demographic Yearbooks; Singapore, Department of Statistics.

1994: Table 1). Since then these rates have shown little change, although with the rise in cohabitation, divorce trends in these countries are becoming less meaningful as an indicator of dissolution of long-term relationships. In East Asian countries, though, divorce rates have been rising steadily since 1980, particularly in the period since 1990 in the case of Japan, South Korea and Hong Kong (see Table 19.6). The rise in South Korea was particularly sharp between 1995 and 2000 – the period in which the Asian Financial Crisis occurred. The usual risk factors explain only a small part of the rise in Korean divorce over this period, implying 'transformations in normative regimes regarding divorce, which may have accelerated after the economic recession in the late 1990s' (Lee 2006: 127).[13] In China, freeing up of divorce regulations in 2001 and 2003 may have contributed to the sharp rise in divorce rates (almost a doubling) since 2000.[14]

Trends in divorce in East Asia appear, then, to be going the way of the West, and partly for the same reasons. Substantial increases in divorce rates in East Asian countries signify a significant change in circumstances and attitudes to divorce, because in the past divorce carried a considerable stigma, and the pressure to remain in a disharmonious marriage for 'the sake of the children' and also for the sake of appearances and family honour, was very strong. It would appear that factors such as the increasing economic independence of women and the pressures of the big-city environments in which an increasing proportion of East Asians live, are influencing divorce trends. More controversial is the issue of whether East Asian societies are becoming more individualistic and less governed by Confucianist norms.

But in the less wealthy countries of Asia, divorce rates have varied tremendously in the past, from very low rates in South Asian countries to very high rates in the Malay-Muslim populations of South-East Asia. One generalization about trends in divorce that has at least some theoretical basis is that in stable high-divorce systems, 'industrialization' can be expected to lead to declines in divorce rates (Goode 1963: Chapter 8). I have argued that, with regard to the Malay-Muslim populations, it is only when the traditional marriage and kinship systems in these countries are understood, along with the pressures under which they are placed by social and economic developments, that trends in divorce can be understood (Jones 1997; see also Hirschman and Teerawichitchainan 2003). 'Industrialization' led to massive declines in divorce rates in these populations, because divorce had been an escape route from unsatisfactory parent-arranged marriages at very young ages, and when this system of marriage arrangement broke down and love marriages took over, this escape route was no longer needed.

Actually, in very recent years, the falling trend in divorce rates in Malay-Muslim populations of South-East Asia appears to have been reversed, very likely because the factors just mentioned have more than played themselves out, and divorce among these populations is now being driven by similar factors to those operating elsewhere in East Asia, and in the West, for that matter. The rise came first for the Muslim population of Singapore, followed by Malaysia, but it is now clearly evident in Indonesia as well (Cammack and Heaton 2011).

In South Asian societies, too, the underlying marriage system must be understood if lack of increase in divorce rates with 'industrialization' is to be understood. In the marriage systems of the Indian subcontinent, divorce is not a feasible way out of a disharmonious marriage. Unless arranged marriage and patrilocal residence cease to be the norms governing marriage, it seems unrealistic to expect much increase in divorce rates in the region. However, Iran is a South Asian country with a different system: relatively high divorce rates, which declined from 1985 to 1995, then rose significantly over the following 15 years.

Conclusions

Arranged marriage systems in South Asia have proved extremely durable, whereas they have broken down in East and South-East Asia. Age at marriage has risen very substantially in the countries where arranged marriage systems have collapsed, but it has also risen (though to a lesser extent) in the South Asian countries. What can be expected in future? Competing theories abound: Goode's convergence towards the conjugal family form; changes based on ideological factors (Lesthaeghe's second demographic transition, or Thornton's 'development idealism'). Focusing on the two trends that appear to be close to universal in Asian countries in recent times – later and less marriage, and increasing divorce rates – both can plausibly be attributed to either socioeconomic trends (rising incomes, education and urbanization) or ideational change (legitimization of individual self-interest) or, more likely, both. Regressing female education and economic development indicators against indicators of delayed marriage shows that these are powerful predictors of singlehood in Asia (Jones and Yeung 2014). Yet there is good reason to doubt that there will be convergence to one universal pattern. Intercountry differences remain enormous, as do differences within countries, and these differences are by no means fully explained by levels of socioeconomic development, but involve cultural and institutional factors as well.

As argued by Lesthaeghe (2010) there is certainly evidence of individualism and the quest for self-fulfilment in some East Asian countries. But to conclude that rising singlehood is being driven by individualism would be to downplay (among other drivers of rising singlehood) the many existential dilemmas facing increasingly educated women in East Asia. Changes in women's attitude appear to be related more to dissatisfaction with the dilemmas and conflicts that traditional gender roles pose for educated women in a rapidly changing economy than with 'individualism' per se (Jones and Yeung 2014: 1581). The 'marriage package' elaborated by Bumpass et al. (2009) captures this very well. Thornton (1989) has argued in the American context that marriage has become much more discretionary as an adult role, and this point can equally be made for many of the countries of East and South-East Asia. In time, it may become true for countries such as India and Bangladesh as well, but this is unlikely to be in a linear way determined purely by economic development.

Marriage patterns in Asia raise some important issues for policy, though the issues differ between the wealthier and poorer countries of Asia. In some of the poorer countries, the problem of very young marriage is paramount. Legislating minimum ages for marriage appears to have little impact on marriage ages, as minimum ages are flouted openly in countries such as Bangladesh and until fairly recently in India, and a little more circumspectly in countries such as Indonesia. Some form of community consensus about ages below which marriage should not be allowed needs to be developed rather than relying solely on regulations imposed from above. Emphasis needs to be placed on the human rights violations when marriages are arranged at very young ages.

Policymakers and planners also find it hard to come to terms with issues relating to the sexuality of the unmarried. In traditional systems, this was dealt with by ensuring that young women did not remain single for long after reaching puberty. But now the interval between puberty and marriage has lengthened greatly, meaning that the chance of premarital conceptions is heightened. Family planning programmes in the region must face up to the need to provide contraceptive information and services to the unmarried, to avert unnecessarily large numbers of induced abortions and of marriages entered into unwisely to preserve family honour.

In the wealthier countries, the issues are more to do with adaptation of family and social structures to the fact of extended singlehood in a context where young people typically live with parents until they marry, and the family is expected to look after its elderly. Before long, the movement of a generation with high singlehood rates into the older age groups will pose many challenges to social policy.

Notes

1 Central Asia and West Asia are omitted from the analysis for reasons both of space and the author's lack of regional knowledge. The rising trend of international marriage is also omitted for lack of space.
2 Universal marriage is sometimes defined as fewer than five per cent of women remaining single at age 45–49. By early marriage, we mean the vast majority of women marrying before their 25th birthday.
3 For Thai patterns, see Podhisita (1994) and Limanonda (1994). In Thailand, matrilocal residence after marriage is most common in the north-east and the north, whereas in the central region and the urban south, where there are larger proportions of people with Chinese ancestry, neolocal residence or virilocal residence is preferred (Limanonda 1994: 390).
4 In Indonesia, and in the Malay populations of Malaysia, Singapore, southern Thailand and southern Philippines.
5 This generalization of course needs to be more nuanced. For example, in Thailand, arranged marriage was not the norm in the mid-twentieth century, whereas in Cambodia, also a Buddhist country, arranged marriage remains very common, even today. In Indonesia, though arranged marriage is now fairly rare, it probably remains common in some rural areas.
6 See Guilmoto (2012: 37–44).
7 The singulate mean age at marriage is a measure which takes the proportions single in five-year age groups from age 15 to 54 to calculate the average age at which a synthetic cohort of people cease being single, or in other words the mean age at which they cross into a state of marriage.
8 An even higher proportion of Japanese men are likely to remain single on reaching 49 – perhaps 20 per cent.
9 This study was conducted by the State Innovative Institute for Public Management and Public Policy Studies at Fudan University.
10 Because the highest rates of consanguineous marriage tend to be associated with low socioeconomic status, interactions between consanguinity and social variables can complicate assessment of the genetic

effects of human inbreeding. In a survey of the available studies, Bittles (2001) summarizes that the greater likelihood of rare recessive genes inherited from a common ancestor results in morbidity levels some one to four per cent higher in the progeny of first cousins than in the offspring of unrelated couples, and mean excess mortality four per cent higher.

11 The youngest marriages in East Asia appear to have been in Korea, where in 1935, 63 per cent of females aged 15–19 were ever married (Kwon 2007; Xenos and Kabamalan 2005: Fig. 8); and in China, where a study carried out in 11 provinces between 1929 and 1931 found that 72 per cent of women had married before reaching the age of 20 (Croll, 1981: 66–67).

12 For a more detailed discussion of Asian divorce trends, see Dommaraju and Jones (2011).

13 South Korean divorce rates appear to have leveled off since 2003 and to have fallen since the introduction in 2008 of a mandatory deliberation period before a couple could end their marriage (Kim 2009). Interestingly, divorce rates in Taiwan also peaked in 2003.

14 Before 2003, in many areas of China, people who wanted to divorce had to obtain a written certificate from their workplace or neighbourhood committee before the divorce could be finalized. The new Marriage Law in October 2003 only required the couples to present their own residence booklets, identification cards, marriage certificates and their written divorce agreements to obtain their divorce certificates on the spot.

References

Abalos, J. (2014) 'Trends and determinants of age at union of men and women in the Philippines'. *Journal of Family Issues*, 35(12): 1624–1641.

Abbasi-Shavazi, M. J., P. McDonald and M. Hosseini-Chavoshi (2008) 'Modernization or cultural maintenance: the practice of consanguineous marriage in Iran'. *Journal of Biosocial Science*, 40(6): 911–933.

Abbasi-Shavazi, M. J., P. McDonald and M. Hosseini-Chavoshi (2009) *The Fertility Transition in Iran*. Dordrecht: Springer.

Avery, C., T. St Clair, M. Levin and K. Hill (2013) 'The "Own Children" fertility estimation procedure: a reappraisal'. *Population Studies*, 67(2): 171–183.

Banister, J. (1984) 'An analysis of recent data on the population of China'. *Population and Development Review*, 10(2): 241–271.

Bélanger, D. and K. T. Hong (2002) 'Too late to marry: failure, fate or fortune? Female singlehood in rural North Vietnam'. In J. Werner and D. Werner (eds.) *Gender, Household State: Doi Moi in Vietnam*. Ithaca, New York: Southeast Asia Program, Cornell University.

Bennett, L. R. (2005) *Women, Islam and Modernity: Single Women, Sexuality and Reproductive Health in Contemporary Indonesia*. London: Routledge Curzon.

Bhagat, R. B. (1993) 'Female age at marriage in India: temporal trends and regional variations'. In A. Ahmad (ed.) *Social Structure and Regional Development: A Social Geography Perspective*. Jaipur: Rawat Publications.

Bhagat, R. B. (2002) *Early Marriages in India: A Socio-Geographical Study*. Delhi: Rajat Publication.

Bittles, A. H. (1994) 'The role and significance of consanguinity as a demographic variable'. *Population and Development Review*, 20(3): 561–583.

Bittles, A. H. (2001) 'A background summary of consanguineous marriage'. Unpublished manuscript, Centre for Human Genetics, Edith Cowan University.

Bumpass, L. L., R. R. Rindfuss, M. K. Choe and N. O. Tsuya (2009) 'The institutional context of low fertility: the case of Japan'. *Asian Population Studies*, 5(3): 215–235.

Caldwell, B. (1992) 'Marriage in Sri Lanka: a century of change'. Unpublished PhD thesis, Australian National University.

Caldwell, J. C., P. H. Reddy and P. Caldwell (1982) 'The causes of demographic change in rural South India: a micro-approach'. *Population and Development Review*, 8(4): 689–728.

Cammack, M. and T. Heaton (2011) 'Explaining the recent upturn in divorce in Indonesia: development idealism and the effect of political change'. *Asian Journal of Social Science*, 39(6): 776–796.

Casterline, J. B., L. Williams and P. McDonald (1986) 'The age difference between spouses: variations among developing countries'. *Population Studies*, 40(3): 353–374.

Chee, H. L. (2006) 'Health care corporatization in Malaysia and implications for the reproductive health and rights agenda'. Paper presented at International Conference on Population and Development in Asia, in Thailand, Phuket, March 2006.

Croll, E. (1981) *The Politics of Marriage in Contemporary China*. Cambridge: Cambridge University Press.

De Silva, W. I. (2014) 'Still the "Ireland of Asia"? Declining female age at marriage in Sri Lanka'. *Journal of Family Issues*, 35(12): 1605–1623.

Desai, S. and L. Andrist (2010) 'Gender scripts and age at marriage in India'. *Demography*, 47(3): 667–687.

Dommaraju, P. V. (2008) 'Demography, education and marriage age in India'. Unpublished PhD thesis, Arizona State University.

Dommaraju, P. V. and G. Jones (2011) 'Divorce trends in Asia'. *Asian Journal of Social Science*, 39(6): 725–750.

Dyson, T. and M. Moore (1983) 'On kinship structure, female autonomy and demographic behaviour in India'. *Population and Development Review*, 9(1): 35–60.

Fealy, G. and S. White (eds.) (2008) *Expressing Islam: Religious Life and Politics in Indonesia*. Singapore: Institute of Southeast Asian Studies.

Goode, W. J. (1963) *World Revolution and Family Patterns*. New York: The Free Press.

Guilmoto, C. Z. (2012) 'Son preference, sex selection and kinship in Vietnam'. *Population and Development Review*, 38(1): 31–54.

Haub, C. and O. P. Sharma (2006) 'India's population reality: reconciling changes and tradition'. *Population Bulletin*, 61(3): 2–20.

Hirschman, C. and B. Teerawichitchainan (2003) 'Cultural and socioeconomic influences on divorce during modernization: Southeast Asia, 1940s to 1960s'. *Population and Development Review*, 29(2): 215–254.

Hull, T. H. and W. Hartanto (2009) 'Resolving contradictions in Indonesian fertility estimates'. *Bulletin of Indonesian Economic Studies*, 45(1): 61–71.

Jampaklay, A. and F. Haseen (2011) 'Marital unions and unmarried cohabitation in Bangkok, Thailand: are cohabiters different from singles and married people?' *Asian Population Studies*, 7(2): 137–156.

Jejeebhoy, S. J., K. G. Santhya, R. Acharya and R. Prakash (2013) 'Marriage-related decision-making and young women's marital relations and agency: evidence from India'. *Asian Population Studies*, 9(1): 28–49.

Jensen, R. and R. Thornton (2003) 'Early female marriage in the developing world'. *Gender and Development*, 11(2): 9–19.

Jones, G. W. (1994) *Marriage and Divorce in Islamic Southeast Asia*. Singapore: Oxford University Press.

Jones, G. W. (1997) 'Modernization and divorce: contrasting trends in Islamic Southeast Asia and the West'. *Population and Development Review*, 23(1): 95–114.

Jones, G. W. (2005) 'The "flight from marriage" in South-East and East Asia'. *Journal of Comparative Family Studies*, 36(1): 93–119.

Jones, G. W. (2012) 'International marriage in Asia: what do we know, and what do we need to know?' In D. S. Kim (ed.) *Cross-Border Marriage: Global Trends and Diversity*. Seoul: Korea Institute for Health and Social Affairs.

Jones, G. W., Y. Asari and T. Djuartika (1994) 'Divorce in West Java'. *Journal of Comparative Family Studies*, 25(3): 395–416.

Jones, G. W. and B. Gubhaju (2009) 'Factors influencing changes in mean age at first marriage and proportions never marrying in the low-fertility countries of East and Southeast Asia'. *Asian Population Studies*, 5(3): 237–265.

Jones, G. W. and H. H. Shen (2008) 'International marriage in East and Southeast Asia: trends and research emphases'. *Citizenship Studies*, 12(1): 9–25.

Jones, G. W. and W. J. Yeung (2014) 'Marriage in Asia'. *Journal of Family Issues*, 35(12): 1567–1583.

Kim, D. S. (ed.) (2008) *Cross-Border Marriage: Process and Dynamics*. Seoul: Institute of Population and Aging Research, Hanyang University.

Kim, J. (2009) 'South Korea cools off on hot-headed, speedy divorce'. *Reuters*, January 13.

Korson, J. H. (1979) 'Modernization and social change – the family in Pakistan'. In M. S. Das and P. D. Bardis (eds.) *The Family in Asia*. London: George Allen and Unwin.

Kwon, T. H. (2007) 'Trends and implications of delayed and non-Marriage in Korea'. *Asian Population Studies*, 3(3): 223–241.

Lee, Y. J. (2006) 'Risk factors in the rapidly rising incidence of divorce in Korea'. *Asian Population Studies*, 2(2): 113–131.

Lesthaeghe, R. (2010) 'The unfolding story of the Second Demographic Transition'. *Population and Development Review*, 36(2): 211–251.

Limanonda, B. (1994) 'Family formation in rural Thailand: evidence from the 1989–1990 Family and Household Survey'. In L. J. Cho and M. Yada (eds.) *Tradition and Change in the Asian Family*. Honolulu: East-West Center.

Martin, L. G. (1990) 'Changing intergenerational relations in East Asia'. *Annals of the American Academy of Political and Social Science*, 510: 102–114.

National Institute of Population Research and Training, Mitra and Associates and Macro International (2009) *Bangladesh Demographic and Health Survey 2007*. Dhaka, Bangladesh and Calverton, Maryland, US: Mitra and Associates and Macro International.

National Institute of Population Studies and IRD/Macro International Inc. (1992) *Pakistan Demographic and Health Survey 1990/1991*. Islamabad, Pakistan and Columbia, Maryland, US: National Institute of Population Studies and IRD/Macro International Inc.

National Institute of Population Studies and Macro International Inc. (2008) *Pakistan Demographic and Health Survey 2006–2007*. Islamabad, Pakistan: National Institute of Population Studies and Macro International Inc.

Nayab, D. (2009) 'Who marries whom in Pakistan? Role of education in marriage timing and spouse selection'. Paper presented at Session 113: Gender, educational achievement and the marriage market of 26th IUSSP International Population Conference in Marrakech, Morocco, September 2009.

Office of the Registrar General and Census Commissioner, India (n.d.) *Marital Status and Age at Marriage – An Analysis of 2001 Census Data*. Delhi: Office of the Registrar General and Census Commissioner, India, Ministry of Home Affairs.

Podhisita, C. (1994) 'Coresidence and the transition to adulthood in the rural Thai family'. In L.-J. Cho and M. Yada (eds.) *Tradition and Change in the Asian Family*. Honolulu: East-West Center.

Raymo, J. M., M. Iwasawa and L. Bumpass (2009) 'Cohabitation and family formation in Japan'. *Demography*, 46(4): 785–803.

Retherford, R. D. and N. Ogawa (2006) 'Japan's baby bust: causes, implications and policy responses'. In F. R. Harris (ed.) *The Baby Bust: Who Will Do the Work? Who Will Pay the Taxes?* Lanham, Maryland: Rowman & Littlefield.

Sathar, Z. A. and M. F. Kiani (1998) 'Some consequences of rising age at marriage in Pakistan'. *The Pakistan Development Review*, 37(4) part 2: 541–556.

Situmorang, A. (2007) 'Staying single in a married world: never-married women in Yogyakarta and Medan'. *Asian Population Studies*, 3(3): 287–304.

Statistics Indonesia and Macro International (2008) *Indonesia Demographic and Health Survey 2007*. Calverton, Maryland: BPS and Macro International.

Streatfield, P. K., N. Kamal, K. Z. Ahsan and Q. Nahar (2015) 'Early marriage in Bangladesh: not as early as it appears'. *Asian Population Studies*, 11(1): 94–110.

Tan, P. C., P. T. Chan, B. A. Tan, N. P. Tey and R. Rajoo (1988) *A Study of Indian Women in the Estates in Peninsular Malaysia: Social Mixing, Marriage and the Family*. Kuala Lumpur: Faculty of Economics and Administration, University of Malaya.

Tey, N. P. (2007) 'Trends in delayed and non-marriage in Peninsular Malaysia'. *Asian Population Studies*, 3(3): 243–261.

Tfaily, R. (2005) 'First cousin marriages and marital relationships in Egypt, Jordan, Turkey and Yemen'. Paper presented at the 25th International Population Conference of the International Union for the Scientific Study of Population in France, Tours, July 2005.

Thornton, A. (1989) 'Changing attitudes towards family issues in the United States'. *Journal of Marriage and the Family*, 51: 873–893.

Thornton, A. and H. S. Lin (1994) *Social Change and the Family in Taiwan*. Chicago: University of Chicago Press.

Tsuya, N. O. and M. K. Choe (1991) *Changes in Intrafamilial Relationships and the Role of Women in Japan and Korea*. Tokyo: Nihon University Population Research Institute (NUPRI) Research Papers Series 58.

Visaria, L. (2004) 'The continuing fertility transition'. In T. Dyson, R. Cassen and L. Visaria (eds.) *Twenty-First Century India: Population, Economy, Human Development and the Environment*. India: Oxford University Press.

Weintraub, A. N. (ed.) (2011) *Islam and Popular Culture in Indonesia and Malaysia*. London and New York: Routledge.

World Bank (2008) 'Whispers to voices: gender and social transformation in Bangladesh'. *Bangladesh Development Series Paper No. 22*. Dhaka: The World Bank.

Xenos, P. and M. Kabamalan (2005) 'A comparative history of age-structure and social transitions among Asian youth'. In S. Tuljapurkar, I. Pool and V. Prachuabmoh (eds.) *Riding the Age Waves. Population, Resources, and Development: International Studies in Population, Volume 1*. Dordrecht: Springer Verlag.

20
Family and household composition in Asia

Albert Esteve and Chia Liu

Introduction

In this chapter, we examine patterns and trends in household size and living arrangements in Asia with the goal of highlighting the prevalent characteristics of Asian families while showing diversity across countries and changes over time. We combine data from censuses and surveys in 13 countries from 1980 to 2010, focusing on two different perspectives. First, we take the household perspective, in which the household is the main unit of analysis. In doing so, we utilize indicators such as household size, distribution of households by number of members and composition of households by age group. Second, we use the individual as the unit of analysis or take the individual's perspective to identify living arrangements by age for each person within our datasets. For the sake of comparability, we focus on the most common relationships such as parental, spousal and filial affiliations. Such information is often available when household members are recorded by censuses and surveys (De Vos and Holden 1988). The individual's perspective facilitates the disentanglement of the internal structure of domestic groups by showing vertical and lateral forms of coresidence. It is essential to remember that such demographic information alone often cannot explain the forces of change underlying cultural norms. Further qualitative studies targeting specific populations are required to fully understand the reasons for shifts in traditional practices.

Asia is divided into the subregions of East Asia, South Asia, South-East Asia, West Asia and Central Asia. This division is commonly used in demographic and sociological studies on families in Asia (e.g. Quah 2008; Therborn 2004). The countries within each subregion show some degree of similarity with respect to household, kinship and marriage systems. Because of the scope and introductory nature of this chapter, we do not investigate regional and social differences within countries. For example, India is geographically larger and more populated than Europe, with a striking level of internal diversity regarding the force of patrilocality, arranged marriages and gender roles (Chaudhuri and Roy 2009; Therborn 2004). Ethnic diversity is evident in countries like Malaysia, which harbours three main ethnic groups – Malays, Chinese and Indians – each displaying unique preferences for intergenerational coresidence (Chan and DaVanzo 1994). Vietnam is another country that fosters multiple kinship systems: the ethnic Kinh group observes patrilineal customs similar to Confucian China, whereas the Khmer and

Chamic groups are characterized by bilaterality similar to other countries in South-East Asia (Guilmoto 2012).

This chapter provides a panoramic view of residential patterns in Asia, sacrificing the details of the historical, cultural and social influences that drive their internal heterogeneity. Due to the availability of large, harmonized, recently released microdata exemplified by the Integrated Public Use Microdata Series (IPUMS) International, it is possible to conduct a comparative analysis of cross-national living arrangements in countries ranging from the extensively explored China to the lesser-known Mongolia. For countries that are not represented in the IPUMS dataset, evidence is gathered from national statistical offices and other sources.

Background

Families are widely seen as the basic building blocks of a society. They are kinship units consisting of people who are related through birth, marriage or adoption. In contrast, the household consists of one or more persons sharing a dwelling or housing unit (Pressat 1985; McFalls 2007; UN 2016). Due to the constraints of census definitions, this chapter focuses mainly on household composition and family relationships within households, with an emphasis on coresidential patterns with a spouse, parents, married or unmarried children. The terms of 'family' and 'household' are used conjointly in our discussion.

Living arrangement is determined by the interaction of three factors: demographic, economic and cultural. First, demography shapes the context of opportunities for coresidence. Societies with high fertility have larger households than societies with low fertility. Increased life expectancy expands opportunities for intergenerational coresidence as the time of overlapping among generations lengthens. Second, economic and cultural factors are the driving forces behind the materialization of such demographic opportunities for coresidence. In pre-industrial agrarian societies, children relied on parental financial resources, whereas parents counted on filial support as they aged, leading to multigenerational coresidence. Industrialization and wage labour were posited to simplify household structure and increase nuclear households because they reduce intergenerational dependence (Goode 1963). In modern Asian societies, economic factors such as housing availability and affordability force resource sharing through intergenerational coresidence despite the fact that employment has now been extended beyond family businesses, whereas in the past, individuals lived and worked with family members (Chan and DaVanzo 1994; Martin 1989; Chaudhuri and Roy 2009). Third, cultural norms assert substantial influence on intergenerational coresidence through the expectation to fulfil filial duties. Confucianism, which stresses the importance of caring for and respecting elderly family members, serves as a foundation of social norms in countries such as China, Japan, and Taiwan (Sereny 2011; Zimmer and Korinek 2010; Lin et al. 2003; Goody 1961; Thornton and Fricke 1987). Demographic, economic and cultural factors can interact in many complex ways that often produce outcomes inconsistent with evolutionary presumptions such as those proposed by modernization theory.

If we were to pinpoint one remarkable attribute of Asian family life that sets Asia apart from the rest of the world, it would be the importance of intergenerational coresidence. The majority of people in Asia, including the elderly, do not live alone. According to *Living Arrangements of Older Persons Around the World*, published by the United Nations Population Division in 2005, 74 per cent of individuals in Asia who are aged 60 and over live with children or grandchildren, compared to 26 per cent in Europe. Multigenerational households, either in the form of stem or joint families, are widespread in Asia compared to other parts of the world (Ruggles and Heggeness 2008; Bongaarts and Zimmer 2002). The basis of multigenerational households is the exchange in which the elderly benefit from the emotional and financial support of their children, while the children benefit from the family or economic support of their parents. As a region deeply influenced by Confucianism, many countries, especially those in East Asia, hold filial piety as a crucial element of moral integrity (Goode 1963; Zimmer and Kwong 2003; Chu, Xie and Yu 2011). The ideal of filial piety, which demands lifelong devotion to the well-being of one's elders, extends into South Asia with even greater intensity despite the subregion's different religious and moral codes, such as those of Hindus in India and Muslims in Pakistan. South and East Asia remain strongholds of patriarchy, which is manifested in the parental control over children's marriages and the determination of post-marriage patrilocal coresidence. Patrilocality remains a strong institution in countries such as China, India, Pakistan, Japan, Taiwan and South Korea, but its intensity and pace of change vary over time (Chung and Shibusawa 2013; Tsuya et al. 2010; Thornton and Fricke 1987; Martin and Tsuya 1991; Lin et al. 2003; Logan, Bian and Bian 1998; Frankenberg, Chan and Ofstedal 2002).

From the adult children's perspective, patrilocality does not mean that all married sons must live with their parents; however, at least one, usually the eldest, should assume that responsibility. When only one married child, usually a son, lives with his spouse and his parents, the family is often named as a stem family. In contrast, in countries like India many families consist of all married sons and unmarried daughters living together with their parents, and they are regarded as joint-families (Allendorf 2010; Goode 1963). The distinction between a joint and a stem family is thus marked by the existence of a single couple per generation in a stem family versus multiple couples of the same generation in a joint-family. In the traditional, patrilocal stem household system, both men and women marry relatively young and live with the husband's parents (Goody 1961), although there are noticeable variations (Fauve-Chamoux and Ochiai 2009). In the joint-household systems, the percentage of married sons who live with their parents tends to be higher than in stem-household systems because multiple married sons are obliged to live with their elderly parents, with the elderly male as the figurehead (Cain 1986). From the older generation's point of view, a high percentage of parents coreside with their children in both stem and joint-family systems, compared to the nuclear-family system.

Old age support is not confined to the patriarchal system. In a bilateral system, exemplified by Cambodia and Thailand, both sons and daughters are likely to provide personal care to parents through coresidence (Bongaarts and Zimmer 2002). In Thailand, for example, parents often prefer or are expected to coreside with a married daughter (Piotrowski 2008; Knodel, Chayovan and Siriboon 1992; Knodel, Saengtienchal and Sittitrai 1995). Under that system, we expect similar proportions of married men and women to live with parents, whereas in a patriarchal system, we expect to observe a much higher proportion of coresidence between parents and their sons because married sons shoulder the major responsibilities of caring for their parents.

A sizeable literature examines the evolution of family systems in Asia. Modernization theory predicts that as countries advance economically, the pervasiveness of multigenerational living arrangements declines as a result of urbanization, economic development and increased value given to privacy (Goode 1963; Quah 2008). Supporting this theory, we observe that overall, economically advanced countries such as Japan, Taiwan and Korea are experiencing a decline in intergenerational households (Frankenberg, Chan and Ofstedal 2002; Martin and Tsuya 1991), but very little decline has been detected in China, India and Vietnam, despite their substantial economic development in recent decades. In contrast to the prediction of modernization theory, the constraint imposed by housing prices and the shift from parental needs to mutual needs have encouraged continual intergenerational coresidence. High levels of intergenerational coresidence have been found in urban settings due to housing constraints and the high cost of living (Chaudhuri and Roy 2009; Teo 2006; Logan, Bian and Bian 1998; Chan and DaVanzo 1994; Martin 1989). The traditional paradigm built on filial piety, or attendance to parental needs, has also shifted to include attention to children's needs in their life courses, thus creating a more symbiotic living arrangement for both generations (Logan, Bian and Bian 1998). The older generation often assumes a caretaking role for grandchildren and, in some cases, provides housework and financial relief (Frankenberg, Chan and Ofstedal 2002).

The decline of fertility in Asia has raised concerns over old age support in rapidly greying societies. A smaller number of children implies that fewer sons will be available to take on parental care, challenging the traditional patriarchal system of fully relying on sons as old-age insurance. China's One Child Policy, implemented in 1979 following the 'later-longer-fewer' campaign, was the most extreme antecedent of fertility decline (McNicoll 1996). Despite China's fertility decline, there is no evidence of major shifts in intergenerational coresidence (Zimmer and Kwong 2003). It can be speculated that because only one child needs to coreside with his or her parents, provided the rate of childlessness remains low, the decline in fertility should not limit the possibility to continue the traditional system of old age care (Knodel, Chayovan and Siriboon 1992; Knodel, Saengtienchal and Sittitrai 1995). However, almost all countries in Asia show a decline in intergenerational coresidence, to varying degrees. It should be noted that the decline of coresidence does not always imply a weakening of filial-parental ties because adult children may live within a short distance and offer financial or emotional support (Freedman, Chang and Sun 1982; Hermalin 2002; Knodel and Chayovan 2008a, 2008b; Zhao 2001).

Within this context, this chapter examines household size and living arrangements in Asia. We scrutinize whether changes in household size have had an impact on internal household structures with respect to the level of intergenerational coresidence. We explore the prevalence of post-marriage intergenerational coresidence, especially the differences between societies with patriarchal and bilateral household systems. We also examine intergenerational coresidence from both the older and younger generations' perspectives.

Data

The inclusion of countries in this study was conditioned by the availability of data and varies between the first and second parts of the analysis (household and individual perspectives). For the household perspective, we present basic indicators such as average household size, which do not require microdata. The individual perspective, however, is more data demanding and requires individual records to be organized into households. Therefore, the total number of countries included in the analysis from the perspective of the household is larger than that from the perspective of the individual because microdata were not readily available for all of the countries within the scope of the study.

To analyse residential patterns from the household perspective, we examine the average size of households, distribution of households by size, and household composition by age of its members. Data for these analyses are obtained from the United Nations Development Program (for Myanmar), the United Nations Population Fund (for Iran), the Demographic Health Survey (for Bangladesh), the Luxembourg Income Survey (for China, Japan, South Korea and Taiwan), the Integrated Public Use Microdata Series – IPUMS (for Cambodia, China, India, Indonesia, Iran, Malaysia, Mongolia, Nepal, Pakistan, Philippines, Thailand and Vietnam), and each country's statistical offices. Aggregating the above datasets, we created household-level analyses for 25 countries.

To analyse residential patterns from the perspective of the individual, on the other hand, requires more detailed data. Thus, we have relied heavily on the Integrated Public Use Microdata Series International microdata. The IPUMS is an international collaboration between national statistical offices, which has been led by the Minnesota Population Center. IPUMS provides access to harmonized census microdata for research purposes. For our analysis, we have used data from different years for the following 12 Asian countries with a total of 32 samples: Cambodia (1998, 2008), China (1982, 1990), India (1983, 1987, 1993, 1999, 2004), Indonesia (1980, 1985, 1990, 1995, 2000, 2005, 2010), Iran (2006), Malaysia (1980, 1991, 2000), Mongolia (1989, 2000), Nepal (2001), Pakistan (1998), the Philippines (1990, 1995, 2000), Thailand (1980, 1990, 2000) and Vietnam (1989, 2009). Unfortunately, microdata for Japan, Taiwan, South Korea and (for recent years) China are not available via IPUMS or other sources. However, the IPUMS samples provide a wide range of harmonized pointer variables that identify the presence of mother, father, spouse and child for all members within a household. Using these pointer variables, we were able to create three new variables: living with at least one parent, living with spouse and living with at least one child.

Enumeration techniques often vary from census to census regarding how an individual is recorded. Most censuses have followed the de jure approach, such as in India; some were conducted according to the de facto procedure, exemplified by Malaysia; whereas others, namely those in Cambodia (in 2008), Mongolia and Pakistan, used a combination of the two. Considering that the de jure method counts individuals at their official or usual residences, whereas the de facto method records them at their physical locations, the concept of household for countries included in the study is not exactly the same, although the impact on our conclusions is relatively small.

Household perspective

Figure 20.1 shows the average size of households for 25 countries in Asia from 1980 to 2011, and it ranges from 2.4 (Japan, 2010) to 7.3 (Afghanistan, 2008) persons per household. Between those two levels, we observe a cluster of countries where the average size of households was between 3 to 5 persons over the study period. The mean household size was larger than five persons in Laos, Pakistan, the Maldives and Afghanistan. In contrast, the East Asian countries of Japan, South Korea, Hong Kong, Taiwan and China all have smaller households in comparison with other countries included. Overall, changes over time show a decline in household size. Japan has declined from 3.2 persons in 1980 to 2.4 in 2010, China from 4.4 in 1982 to 3.1 in 2010, and India from 5.1 in 1983 to 4.7 in 2004. Despite the overall decline, we do not observe a convergence in household size, but rather that its cross-country differences remain stable over time. The size of the household largely depends on the number of children as indicated by the fact that larger households are often found in countries with higher fertility, but it is also influenced by the presence of other relatives in addition to the spouse and children of the household head. In countries like India, these live-in relatives are likely to be parents-in-law or children-in-law, though they mainly consist of parents-in-law in Indonesia and the Philippines (Bongaarts 2001).

The strong relationship between average household size and the level of fertility is clearly revealed by Figure 20.2, which shows the mean size of households and the share of household members aged 0–17, 18–64 and 65 and above for selected Asian countries with more than one data point. Fertility decline has been taking place throughout Asian countries in recent decades. For Asia as a whole, total fertility fell from 5.8 children per woman in 1950–1955 to 2.2 in 2005–2010 (UN 2013). Over the study period, household size has also declined in all countries. The decline in the share of those aged 0–17, used as proxy for children in this chapter, is the main driver of the reduction in household size. For example, in China, the average number of adults and seniors was constant between 1982 and 1990, but the average number of children decreased, leading to a decrease in household size. Government-led family planning programmes (e.g. in China), along with the rise of women's reluctance to get married due to the inability to

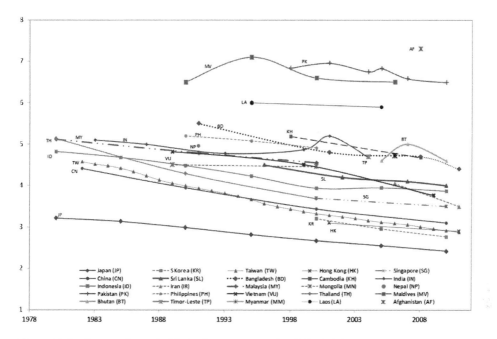

Figure 20.1 Average household size by country, Asia 1980–2010
Sources: National statistical offices, IPUMS – International (2017), Demographic Health Surveys and United Nations data.

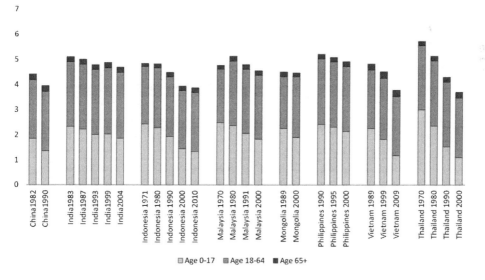

Figure 20.2 Household composition by age groups, selected Asian countries
Source: IPUMS – International (2017).

Albert Esteve & Chia Liu

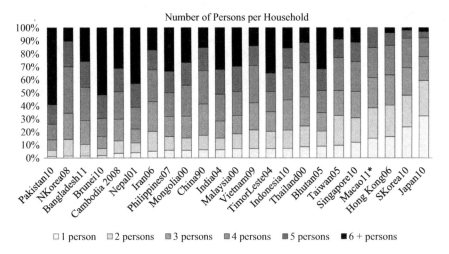

Figure 20.3 Distribution of households by number of members, selected Asian countries
Note: *Macao did not tabulate 6+ person households.
Source: United Nations Statistics and various statistical agencies.

find suitable partners or concerns of having to care for two sets of elderly parents, fear of divorce, etc. have served to effectively decrease the number of children per couple in many countries in Pacific Asia in recent years (Jones 2007).

Figure 20.3 shows the percentage distribution of households by the number of household members. The 23 countries are ordered according to the proportion of one-person households, from the smallest to the largest.

More economically developed Asian countries – such as Japan, South Korea, Hong Kong, Macao, Singapore and Taiwan – cluster around the right side of the chart, whereas developing countries – such as Pakistan, North Korea and Bangladesh – are on the left side of the chart, indicating that more affluent countries have a higher proportion of one-person households. This is consistent with the idea that economic development is highly associated with independent living and communal living is often the result of practical financial necessities (Chaudhuri and Roy 2009; De Vos and Holden 1988). Countries with low proportions of one-person households tend to have high proportions of large households, such as Pakistan and Brunei where more than 50 per cent of households have six or more members. Large households are uncommon, at 2.8, 1.8 and 3.9 per cent for Japan, South Korea and Hong Kong, respectively. However, the correlation between the share of one-person households and the share of very large (with 6+ persons) households is not straightforward. Except for countries with a high proportion of one-person households, the shares of large households vary across the board due to differences in fertility and to the prevalence of intergenerational coresidence.

The individual perspective

Looking into individuals' lives

Past studies of living arrangements have been dominated by household-level analyses. Households are multidimensional entities often comprised of more than one member, each with unique demographic characteristics. Moreover, members are related in diverse ways that are not always

Family and household composition in Asia

easy to analyse (Bongaarts 2001). IPUMS International census microdata offer considerable details about relationships among household members. One of the strengths of using personal records is that the microdata allow a higher level of flexibility for building a standardized framework of analysis for multiple countries in different years. Because it is difficult to obtain longitudinal data on such a scale, we examine living arrangements by age using cross-sectional data. We focus on parental, spousal and filial relationships within households. As an example, Figure 20.4 shows parental, spousal, filial coresidence and individual living for India in 2004 by age and sex.

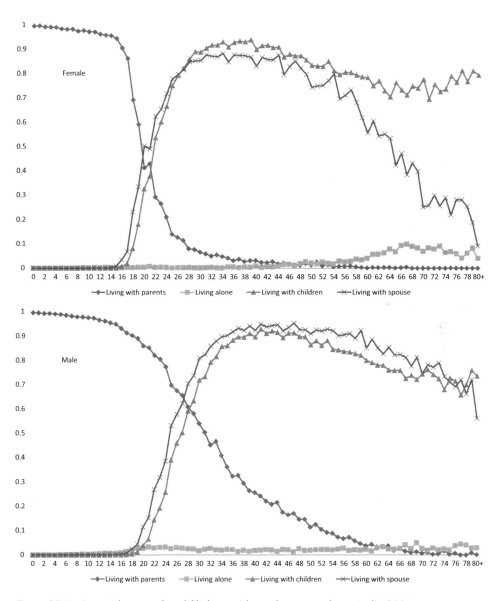

Figure 20.4 Parental, spousal and filial coresidence by age and sex, India 2004
Source: IPUMS – International (2017).

Albert Esteve & Chia Liu

In India in 2004, more than 50 per cent of males coresided with their parents as late as the age of 30, whereas a mere 6.7 per cent of 30-year-old females remained in their parental homes. For the females, living with parents drops drastically between the ages of 15 and 20, which coincides with a sharp rise in the proportion of those who have entered into union. Indian men remain in their parental home even after marriage, and the new bride moves into her husband's home.

With respect to spousal coresidence, Figure 20.4 confirms the universality of marriage in the population. By the age of 35, approximately 85 per cent of women and 90 per cent of men live with a spouse. We observe a drop in spousal coresidence for women starting around age 40, most likely due to widowhood. Men experience a more gradual decline in spousal coresidence at a later age, because they tend to marry younger wives who are more likely to survive them. Living alone is uncommon for both men and women in India, but there is a higher proportion of older women living alone than men, primarily because women tend to outlive their husbands. Women in rural areas are more likely to live alone in comparison with their urban counterparts as their children migrate to urban areas (Chaudhuri and Roy 2009). Living with children lags behind the timing of union formation. Coresidence with children is very common for both men and women in India. By the age of 25 for women and 31 for men, roughly three out of four individuals live with at least one child.

To make cross-national comparisons, we created box plots to visualize the phenomena of living alone, living with parents, living with a spouse, and living with children in 12 selected Asian populations. The graphs below (Figures 20.5–20.8) allow us to visualize differences across countries and between genders by age, as represented by five-year age groups. Detailed data for the box plots are given in the Appendix. For most of the populations the data were collected between 2000 and 2010.

Living alone

Living alone is uncommon in Asia, as shown in Figure 20.5. Young children certainly do not live alone and it is also rare for adolescents or adults to form a solitary household. Compared to the

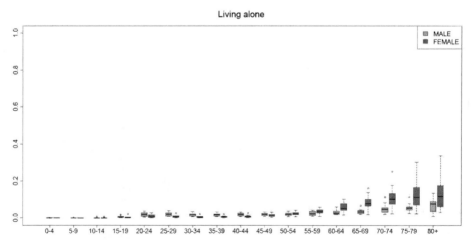

Figure 20.5 Age-specific, between-country variability in living alone by sex, selected Asian countries
Source: IPUMS – International (2017); see Appendix for country-specific details.

Family and household composition in Asia

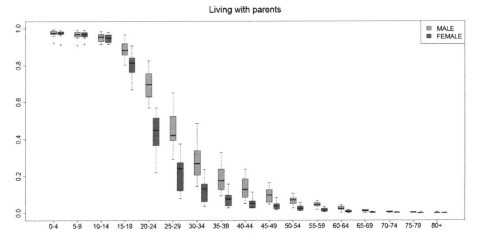

Figure 20.6 Age-specific, between-country variability in living with at least one parent by sex, selected Asian countries
Source: IPUMS – International (2017); see Appendix for country-specific details.

Western world, independent living before marriage is uncommon in Asian countries. Leaving the parental home is conditioned by and closely tied to the timing of partnership formation. Proportions living alone tend to increase with age after people reach 50, and the highest share is observed among those aged 80 and over, particularly among widowed women. Children's migration from rural to urban areas may increase the chance of seniors being left behind in their hometowns to live alone. There are great variations in the proportion of old people living alone. Among individuals aged 80 and over, almost 34 per cent of Iranian women live alone, whereas the share is 11 per cent among the male population. In contrast, only 3 per cent of men or women live alone in Pakistan.

Living with parents

Coresidence with parents decreases with age, either because parents die or children leave their parents' home (Figure 20.6). Prior to age 15, nearly all children live with their parents (Lloyd and Desai 1992). Cross-country differences begin to emerge between the ages of 15 and 49. Women leave the parental home earlier than men because they tend to marry at younger ages (Jones 2005, 2007). This pattern remains despite recent increases in marriage age. Moreover, in patrilineal societies, women are less likely to continue to live with their own parents after marriage.

The proportion of women living with parents experiences a sharp decline between the ages of 15 and 25. Women in India, Pakistan and Nepal leave the parental home at a younger age compared to women in Thailand and China. The proportion of men living with parents dwindles at a more moderate rate between the ages of 20 to 30. Mongolian and Cambodian men are less likely to coreside with parents compared to their Pakistani, Indian and Chinese counterparts. More detailed country-specific results can be found in the Appendix.

To explore the differences among countries and the pervasiveness of post-marriage intergenerational coresidence, we turn to Table 20.1, which shows the percentage of those aged 25–29

Albert Esteve & Chia Liu

Table 20.1 Percentage of children aged 25–29 living with at least one parent, by sex and marital status, selected countries

	All Individuals (%)				Married (%)			
	1980	1990	2000	2010	1980	1990	2000	2010
Male								
Cambodia			20.4	31.6			8.8	12.1
China	48.6	39.7			36.9	30.6		
India	53.6	57.4	61.1	65.3	51.8	53.8	56.4	59.5
Indonesia	26.7	29.8	32.9	41.3	15.9	14.3		17.2
Iran				42.9				12.4
Malaysia	36.8	37.7	38.9		24.0	19.8	17.8	
Mongolia		18.8	29.1			4.7	7.8	
Nepal			53.2				19.9	
Pakistan			53.0				42.6	
Philippines		36.7	41.1			9.4	10.3	
Vietnam		41.1	48.2	52.0		26.3	31.6	35.0
Thailand	30.0	36.4	45.5		14.7	15.9	17.6	
South Korea	69.8	65.1	65.5	64.9	76.2	69.3	61.3	50.3
Female								
Cambodia			23.3	30.3			9.4	11.1
China	11.5	8.9			1.3	1.4		
India	7.7	7.9	9.9	11.2	1.3	0.9	1.2	1.0
Indonesia	14.6	16.1	17.5	24.0	4.9	4.8		10.5
Iran				26.3				0.7
Malaysia	21.3	23.4	24.1		4.6	6.2	6.0	
Mongolia		15.8	24.7			2.8	5.9	
Nepal			7.8				0.9	
Pakistan			13.1				0.7	
Philippines		25.9	28.6			5.1	5.9	
Vietnam		23.7	21.1	19.7		3.6	3.4	3.3
Thailand	28.0	32.8	37.4		12.7	14.9	16.6	
South Korea	10.6	13.9	27.9	47.3	0.2	0.1	0.3	2.0

Note: Cells are left blank where data are not available.
Sources: IPUMS – International (2017); Statistics Korea (KOSTAT).

who live with at least one parent in 13 selected Asian countries and the percentage of parental coresidence for those who are married.

With the exception of Cambodia, Mongolia and Thailand, men are more likely than women to live with their parents. The lower percentage of coresiding with parents for women is due to early entrance into marriage and also to the deeply seated tradition of patrilocality. We subsequently examine only the percentage of 25–29 year old married individuals living with parents. Fewer married children than all children live with parents, but the proportion coresiding with parents remains significant among those married. India shows the highest proportion of men and Thailand shows the highest proportion of women residing with parents after marriage. Sex differentials in post-marriage residential patterns are also striking in some countries. Nearly 60 per cent of all married Indian men live with their parents but only 1 per cent of married Indian women live with their parents. Similarly, approximately 43 per cent of Pakistani married men and less than 1 per cent of Pakistani married women live with their parents.

Gender differences of this kind are less pronounced in Cambodia, Mongolia and Thailand. The data clearly show the influence of different family systems in Asia. In the South Asian countries (e.g. India and Pakistan), where the joint-family system and the patrilocal residential norm prevail, the percentage of married sons living with their parents is high, compared to the extremely low percentage of married daughters. In parts of South-East Asia (e.g. Thailand and Cambodia), the level of intergenerational coresidence is more balanced between men and women because those countries have a bilateral family system (Goody 1961; Knodel, Chayovan and Siriboon 1992; Knodel, Saengtienchal and Sittitrai 1995).

In terms of change over time, intergenerational coresidence shows very little signs of decline in the countries listed below, consistent with the results of previous studies on intergenerational coresidence in developing countries (Ruggles and Heggeness 2008). The coresidence of married sons living with their parents shows no sign of decline in India and displays an upward trend from 51.8 per cent in 1980 to 59.5 per cent in 2010. South Korea shows a dramatic increase in young women living with parents, whereas the same trend is stable for men. At the same time, post-marital coresidence with parents has been decreasing for young men and increasing for young women. These results show that the increase in coresidence with parents among South Korean young women is largely due to the delay of marriage.

Living with a spouse

Spousal coresidence is shaped by the formation and dissolution of the union. In Asian countries, age at marriage differs considerably. Females tend to enter unions at younger ages than men, as indicated by a higher proportion of women than men living with spouses in the age groups of 15–19, 20–24 and 25–29. The share of spousal coresidence peaks for females aged 35–39, and for males at ages 45–49 (see Figure 20.7). The subsequent decline in the level of spousal coresidence, which also takes place at a younger age for women than men, is primarily due to widowhood, separation or divorce.

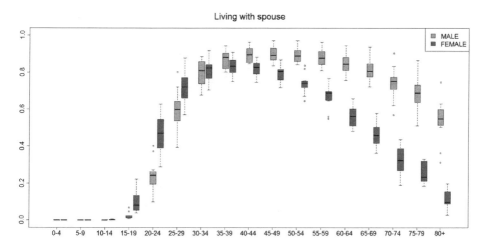

Figure 20.7 Age-specific, between-country variability in living with spouse by sex, selected Asian countries
Source: IPUMS – International (2017); see Appendix for country-specific details.

Delay of marriage for both men and women has occurred throughout Asia (Jones 2005, 2007). Nevertheless, union formation remains prevalent. Cross-national differences are largest at younger ages because the timing of marriage is greatly affected by cultural tradition and its changes. In China, India and Nepal, more women are married by the age of 29 than in Thailand, Cambodia and Mongolia. Marriage among teenage girls is rare in China, Cambodia, Malaysia and Mongolia, whereas it is fairly common in Nepal, Pakistan and India. Nepalese, Chinese and Cambodian men tend to marry younger than their Malaysian and Thai counterparts. Marriage is nearly universal for both genders in all countries, with the exception of Mongolian, Thai and Cambodian women, for whom the proportion of spousal coresidence does not exceed 78 per cent at any age. See Appendix Table 20.2 for country-specific figures.

Living with children

As one might expect from a region where individuals are unlikely to live alone, the practice of intergenerational coresidence is widespread in Asia. From the parent's perspective, as illustrated in Figure 20.8, the highest level of parent-child coresidence in most countries peaks by the time the parent reaches age 40. It then experiences a moderate decline as the children grow up and leave the parental home. One of the notable features of Asian households is that coresidence with children remains high even as children become adults. Women start having children at a younger age than men, and they also spend a longer period of their lives residing with their children.

Coresidence with young children is practically universal, providing few surprises (see Figure 20.8). When parents and children grow older, cross-country variations in such residential patterns become more pronounced. In recent decades, Japan and South Korea have witnessed a sharp decline in intergenerational coresidence among their old populations (see Table 20.2). But such intergenerational coresidence has remained stable in India and shown a modest decrease in China in recent decades. India has the highest level of intergenerational coresidence: more than three-quarters of seniors coreside with children. Overall, despite the differences in the way that

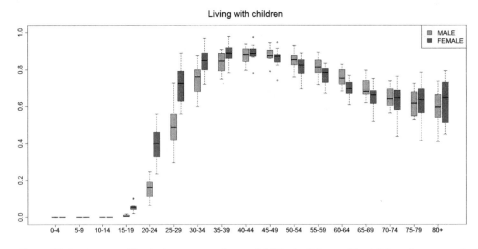

Figure 20.8 Age-specific, between-country variability in living with children by sex, selected Asian countries
Source: IPUMS – International (2017); see Appendix for country specific details.

Table 20.2 Percentage of persons aged 65+ by sex, living with children, selected Asian countries

	Male				Female			
	1980	1990	2000	2010	1980	1990	2000	2010
Cambodia			68.8	67.7			55.1	62.3
China*	67.9	67.6	59.9	51.7	73.6	74.0	68.7	58.6
India	74.5	75.7	76.2	74.1	76.1	77.8	78.6	76.6
Indonesia	62.1	60.9	53.7	57.7	59.2	58.2	47.8	58.6
Iran				59.8				46.1
Malaysia	65.2	66.4	65.6		63.9	66.6	68.1	
Mongolia		52.8	60.7			51.8	58.0	
Nepal			71.6				70.0	
Pakistan			73.2				64.4	
Philippines		62.2	60.9			52.7	55.0	
Vietnam		77.0	74.9	62.0		72.8	72.4	64.9
Thailand	76.3	75.3	66.7		72.5	74.2	70.4	
Japan**	60.6	51.3	41.0	36.9	60.6	51.3	41.0	36.9
Singapore			69.2	63.0			77.4	69.7
South Korea	71.9	59.2	40.4	28.3	74.3	65.9	48.6	34.5
Taiwan		56.4	55.2	49.7		68.3	61.2	54.2

Notes: *2010 data for China is for seniors 60+, as presented by the Centre for Population and Development Studies and Institute of Gerontology; 1980, 1990 and 2000 data are for seniors 65+ (Sun 2013).
**Data by sex not available.
Cells are left blank where data are not available.
Sources: IPUMS – International (2017); Statistics Korea; Statistics Singapore; National Statistics ROC Taiwan; Centre for Population and Development Studies and Institute of Gerontology, Renmin University of China.

households are formed, a high prevalence of intergenerational coresidence remains a dominant feature in Asia.

A comparison of Tables 20.1 and 20.2 shows that the proportion of coresidence with parents among people aged 25–29 has increased slightly in recent years for many countries (as shown in Table 20.1), whereas the proportion of the elderly living with children has not increased but has remained more or less stable (as shown in Table 20.2). This is due to 'ongoing demographic changes that increase the opportunities to reside with parents' such as the rise in age at marriage, 'mortality decline [which] increases the chances that an adult will have a surviving parent', and fertility decline, which entails that 'a smaller group of adult children for each elderly parent increases the chances that any particular child will coreside with a parent' (Ruggles and Heggeness 2008). Although the decline in fertility is often lauded as a positive attribute in a developing country, it provokes the concern that an increasing share of eldercare responsibilities will fall upon a shrinking younger generation (Knodel, Chayovan and Siriboon 1992).

A further examination of the marital status of old people who live with their children finds that women without spouses tend to live with their children, while a higher proportion of men live with both children and a spouse. The latter is related to the fact that many men have a younger wife, and they live with children. In Singapore, for example, 50.9 per cent of men aged 65 or older live with both their spouse and their children, compared to 23.7 per cent of women. Of women aged 65 and over, 46 per cent live with children but without a spouse, in

Table 20.3 Percentage of persons aged 65+, living with married sons or married daughters, selected Asian countries

	Living with married son				Living with married daughter			
	1980	1990	2000	2010	1980	1990	2000	2010
Cambodia			14.9	20.1			8.7	9.2
China	41.8	45.4			1.6	2.0		
India	56.9	59.7	58.7	60.1	1.2	1.0	1.0	1.0
Indonesia	29.5	27.6	17.4	26.8	4.1	4.1	2.2	5.3
Iran				16.2				1.8
Malaysia	33.3	31.4	29.5		3.3	4.8	5.3	
Mongolia		10.4	12.3			6.1	9.0	
Pakistan			47.5				0.6	
Philippines		15	13.5			4.8	5.1	
Vietnam		35.9	38.1			5.5	3.1	
Thailand	30.6	25.4	19.2		13.8	15.4	13.0	

Note: Cells are left blank where data are not available.
Source: IPUMS – International (2017).

comparison with 12.1 per cent in the male population of the same age group (Wong and Teo 2011: Table 7).

In all selected populations, old people have been more likely to live with their married sons than married daughters (see Table 20.3). This pattern has been rather consistent over time. However, in India, Pakistan, China, Vietnam, Iran, Malaysia and Indonesia, the proportion of old people living with married sons is far higher than that living with married daughters. This difference is markedly greater than that found in Mongolia, Cambodia, the Philippines and Thailand, where the proportion of old people living with married sons is fairly close to that living with married daughters.

Conclusion

Family as a crucial part of the social system serves multiple functions that are inclusive of, but not exclusive to, providing a nurturing environment for the young and care and support for the ill and the elderly. Family binds individual life courses through 'unifying the production, distribution, consumption, reproduction, socialization, and transmission of property within and across kinship groups' (Thornton and Fricke 1987: 748). The norms underlying family systems are often supported (influenced or shaped?) by cultures, demographic realities and economic opportunities. Bearing in mind that these three dimensions of underlying forces drive family changes, we must consider the fact that ideals do not dictate practice, and opportunities do not entirely command change. William Goode has noted that 'even though all systems are more or less under the impact of industrializing and urbanizing forces', we cannot assume 'that the theoretical relations between a developing industrial system and the conjugal family system is entirely clear' because the impact of traditional values and cultural norms should be acknowledged (Goode 1963: 369).

In this chapter, we have illustrated that households in Asia have been changing while some of their old elements remain. Large quantitative household surveys and census microdata have allowed us to portray general aggregate measures at the household level while enabling us to contextualize individuals' living arrangements in their family contexts. Although we did not have data for all Asian countries, we have accessed a harmonized set of microdata through IPUMS International, which has facilitated a broad study of 12 countries in Asia. The Luxembourg Income Study Database, United Nations statistics, and national statistical offices also provided aggregate data or supplementary information for some countries and filled in the gap for those for which we have no microdata.

Our analysis shows that household size has declined over recent decades, but family structures have remained stable and they continue to reflect the characteristics of different family systems, which have different impacts on men and women. For women, earlier union formation results in departing from the parental home at a younger age than men. Intergenerational coresidence of young adults usually consists of a married couple and the husband's parents under a patrilocal family system as in China, Japan, South Korea, India, Nepal and Pakistan. However, in countries such as Thailand, the Philippines and some parts of Indonesia, the newlyweds may live with either the husband's or the wife's parents under a bilateral family system (Chung and Shibusawa 2013). Women are more likely to live alone at older ages because of their earlier widowhood compared to men. However, most widows and widowers live with their children, presumably sons, rather than alone, which is an uncommon arrangement in most Asian countries for both genders in nearly all age groups as indicated by Figure 20.5.

Asia's family and household systems have a number of distinctive features that set them apart from those in Europe and the Americas, for example, the importance of intergenerational coresidence of the elderly living with their married children. Previous studies have shown a decline in intergenerational coresidence in some of the economically advanced Asian countries such as Japan and South Korea (Frankenberg, Chan and Ofstedal 2002; Martin and Tsuya 1991; Martin 1989). The decline in household size is primarily due to families having fewer children in general rather than a simplification of household structures. But it is interesting to note that the proportion of elderly living with children has remained stable in countries like India while the proportion of married sons living with parents has been increasing because, presumably, having fewer siblings entails that each child has a higher probability of residing with at least one parent. Differences in household systems are clear from the examination of the propensity of married women and men to live with their parents. Countries having bilateral household systems show a similar proportion of married sons and daughters living with their parents, but those with patrilocal household systems show a higher proportion of married sons than married daughters coresiding with parents.

Fertility decline may put constraints on living arrangements against one's ideal due to a lack of choices in the absence of a son or daughter, but adaptability to such constraints has been observed because Asian parents would rather choose a less-preferred coresidential pattern than live alone (Knodel, Chayovan and Siriboon 1992; Lin et al. 2003). Migration from rural to urban areas may also change household dynamics. However, urban life may not promise household simplification. Instead, housing unaffordability and unavailability encourage coresidence of parents and their married children. The new dynamic that has emerged as social changes have swept Asia is that living arrangements can be shaped by the desires and needs of both the older and the younger generations, as opposed to being the result of solely filial obligations deeply rooted in many Asian societies. For those parents who have not migrated with children into urban areas, living alone is more likely because housing is more affordable in the rural areas (Chaudhuri and Roy 2009; Martin 1989).

This chapter has mainly focused on the coresidence of kin, although family life often extends beyond the roof of a household. For example, some older individuals may elect to live near their children but not in the same household, allowing privacy and daily communication at the same time. This kind of living arrangement is encouraged and supported in Singapore through its housing policies (Teo 2006). In rural Bangladesh, when sons move out of their parental unit upon marriage, they often remain in the same family-owned compound, maintaining close contact with other members of the clan throughout their lives (Amin 1998). Similar arrangements are also found in both Taiwan and China (Freedman, Chang and Sun 1982; Zhao 2001).

In the future, researchers are expected to further examine the unravelling of a revolution of family patterns and living arrangements in the process of demographic transition in other Asian countries which follows the footsteps of their more affluent neighbours: Japan, South Korea, Hong Kong, Macao, Singapore and Taiwan. Because many pre-transition countries were often characterized by different cultural environments, the pace and magnitude of their social and demographic changes tend to vary considerably. The research challenges that we face today will diminish as more coherent, comparable and reliable data become more accessible. Moreover, it may also need time to observe whether the resilience of intergenerational coresidence will endure in the future with further economic advancements and the spread of a media-induced popular culture taking place throughout Asia (Lesthaeghe 2010). New analysis by social class and status will elucidate whether intergenerational coresidence is a practice of necessity or primarily a cultural expression, through examining whether more affluent individuals opt out of intergenerational coresidence (Takagi, Silverstein and Crimmins 2007), or adopt a form of parental care outside of coresidence by choosing 'intimacy at a distance' (Martin and Tsuya 1991). Exploration of internal differences in living arrangements across regions, religious practices, urban and rural settings will also be essential in the quest to decompose current patterns. This chapter has not paid sufficient attention to such details due to data unavailability. With the expansion of data availability, the subject of family life in Asia should be further explored under a wider range of parameters.

Acknowledgements

The authors wish to acknowledge the statistical offices that provided the underlying data that made this research possible: National Institute of Statistics, Cambodia; Statistics Singapore; National Bureau of Statistics, China; Statistics Bureau of Japan; National Statistics, Taiwan; Statistics Korea (KOSTAT); Ministry of Statistics and Programme Implementation, India; BPS Statistics Indonesia, Indonesia; Statistical Centre, Iran; Department of Statistics, Malaysia; National Statistical Office, Mongolia; Central Bureau of Statistics, Nepal; Statistics Division, Pakistan; National Statistics Office, Philippines; National Statistical Office, Thailand; General Statistics Office, Vietnam; Laos Statistics Bureau, Laos; and Bangladesh Bureau of Statistics, Bangladesh.

The authors would like to express their gratitude to the staff of Centre d'Estudis Demogràfics (CED), which provided technical support, substantive comments and useful inputs; and to Hyun Ok Lee for access to Statistics Korea.

The funding of this project is provided by the European Research Council (EQUALIZE, ERC-2014-STG-grant agreement No. 637768) and the Spanish *Ministerio de Economía y Competitividad* (CRISFAM, CSO2015-64713-R).

Appendix

Appendix Table 20.1 Average household size by country, Asia 1980–2010

Country	1980–1984	1985–1989	1990–1994	1995–1999	2000–2004	2005–2009	2010–2013
Japan	3.2	3.1	3.0	2.8	2.7	2.6	2.4
South Korea					3.2	3.0	2.8
Taiwan	4.6	4.4	4.0	3.7	3.3	3.1	2.9
Hong Kong					3.1		2.9
Singapore					3.7		3.5
China	4.4		4.0		3.4		3.1
Sri Lanka				4.5	4.2	4.1	4.0
Bangladesh			5.5		4.8	4.7	4.4
Cambodia					5.2		4.7
India	5.1	5.0	4.8	4.9	4.7		
Indonesia	4.8	4.7	4.5	4.2	3.9	4.0	3.9
Iran						4.1	3.5
Malaysia	5.1		4.8		4.6		
Mongolia		4.5			4.5		
Nepal			5.0				
Pakistan				6.8	6.8	6.6	6.5
Philippines			5.2	5.1	4.9		
Vietnam		4.8		4.5		3.8	
Thailand	5.1		4.3		3.7		
Maldives			6.5	7.1	6.6	6.5	
Bhutan						5.0	4.6
Timor-Leste					4.7		
Burma						4.7	
Laos				6.0		5.9	
Afghanistan						7.3	

Note: Cells are left blank where data are not available.
Sources: Various Statistical Offices, IPUMS – International (2017), Demographic Health Surveys, US Agency for International Development (2015) and United Nations data (2015).

Appendix Table 20.2 Percentage of population residing alone, with at least one parent, with spouse and with at least one child by sex and five-year age group

IPUMS Sample	Age Group	Male Alone	Male Parent	Male Spouse	Male Child	Female Alone	Female Parent	Female Spouse	Female Child
Cambodia 2008	0–4	0.0	95.9	0.0	0.0	0.0	96.1	0.0	0.0
	5–9	0.0	94.7	0.0	0.0	0.0	94.9	0.0	0.0
	10–14	0.1	92.4	0.1	0.0	0.1	92.5	0.0	0.0
	15–19	0.4	88.3	1.1	0.5	0.4	84.2	6.6	4.0
	20–24	0.6	61.3	27.2	18.8	0.4	54.0	43.2	37.3
	25–29	0.9	31.6	66.6	56.9	0.6	30.3	67.2	68.1
	30–34	0.9	17.9	85.3	80.2	0.5	17.8	75.2	81.4
	35–39	0.7	11.7	90.9	88.7	0.8	12.3	77.4	86.7

(continued)

Appendix Table 20.2 (Cont.)

IPUMS Sample	Age Group	Male Alone	Parent	Spouse	Child	Female Alone	Parent	Spouse	Child
	40–44	0.9	8.5	93.7	92.3	1.0	8.4	76.1	88.5
	45–49	0.8	5.5	94.5	92.4	1.9	5.9	72.9	87.4
	50–54	0.8	5.4	91.3	90.9	2.4	4.2	67.0	82.6
	55–59	0.8	4.7	91.5	88.7	3.4	3.1	56.1	79.1
	60–64	1.9	1.9	87.9	80.0	4.2	1.8	48.1	70.4
	65–69	2.0	1.8	84.3	72.9	6.2	0.4	36.3	64.1
	70–74	2.0	0.9	76.7	68.8	5.7	0.3	27.4	61.5
	75–79	3.9	0.2	72.5	63.2	5.9	0.1	22.2	60.5
	80+	0.9	0.6	53.7	57.6	5.2	0.0	9.5	61.9
China 1990	0–4	0.0	99.1	0.0	0.0	0.1	98.5	0.0	0.0
	5–9	0.1	98.6	0.0	0.0	0.1	98.2	0.0	0.0
	10–14	0.1	97.8	0.0	0.0	0.1	97.8	0.0	0.0
	15–19	0.5	95.0	1.7	0.6	0.2	90.7	4.3	2.0
	20–24	1.8	75.7	37.3	24.6	0.6	40.5	55.4	42.3
	25–29	1.9	39.7	80.2	72.7	0.4	8.9	87.8	88.8
	30–34	2.2	26.9	88.5	87.6	0.3	3.8	91.8	96.9
	35–39	2.3	22.1	89.9	90.8	0.3	2.8	90.9	97.9
	40–44	2.7	19.2	89.2	91.5	0.4	2.6	88.1	97.4
	45–49	3.3	15.5	88.0	90.7	0.8	2.2	86.7	94.7
	50–54	3.8	10.8	86.3	87.2	1.3	1.4	83.7	88.8
	55–59	4.3	6.2	84.0	80.9	2.5	0.9	76.7	82.2
	60–64	4.9	2.9	79.4	74.3	4.3	0.3	65.7	74.9
	65–69	6.7	1.1	72.2	66.4	8.1	0.1	50.1	68.4
	70–74	8.3	0.2	62.1	62.6	11.6	0.0	32.7	68.0
	75–79	11.3	0.0	51.2	60.2	13.0	0.0	20.2	69.6
	80+	13.4	0.0	36.3	61.5	15.5	0.0	8.2	69.1
India 2004	0–4	0.0	99.4	0.0	0.0	0.0	99.3	0.0	0.0
	5–9	0.1	98.3	0.0	0.0	0.1	98.1	0.0	0.0
	10–14	0.5	96.7	0.0	0.0	0.2	96.4	0.1	0.0
	15–19	1.5	91.9	1.5	0.3	0.3	80.7	12.8	5.2
	20–24	3.0	82.6	23.6	13.0	0.5	32.7	59.3	48.8
	25–29	2.7	65.3	61.9	49.6	0.2	11.2	81.4	81.2
	30–34	2.2	48.6	84.5	77.1	0.2	5.7	86.8	90.7
	35–39	2.1	32.8	91.7	88.1	0.5	3.5	86.6	92.4
	40–44	2.0	23.8	93.4	90.7	0.8	2.7	84.9	90.7
	45–49	2.2	16.5	92.9	90.0	1.7	1.7	81.3	87.1
	50–54	2.1	10.8	91.8	86.5	2.2	1.3	75.4	83.2
	55–59	2.4	6.7	90.3	83.7	3.1	0.7	69.4	79.8
	60–64	2.6	3.7	85.4	78.9	5.0	0.2	55.5	76.9
	65–69	2.8	1.8	81.4	75.1	7.8	0.1	42.7	75.2
	70–74	2.7	0.8	75.5	73.9	7.3	0.0	26.2	76.5
	75–79	2.8	0.4	70.2	72.0	6.5	0.1	23.5	78.5
	80+	3.0	0.1	56.2	73.6	4.1	0.0	9.1	79.4
Indonesia 2010	0–4	0.0	97.5	0.0	0.0	0.0	97.6	0.0	0.0
	5–9	0.1	96.0	0.0	0.0	0.0	96.0	0.0	0.0
	10–14	0.7	92.9	0.0	0.0	0.7	92.4	0.1	0.0
	15–19	1.9	84.9	1.2	0.5	2.2	75.9	10.4	5.8
	20–24	3.8	64.8	18.8	11.8	2.7	44.0	49.8	40.5
	25–29	2.8	41.2	54.1	43.6	1.2	24.0	75.8	71.9

Appendix Table 20.2 (Cont.)

IPUMS Sample	Age Group	Male Alone	Parent	Spouse	Child	Female Alone	Parent	Spouse	Child
	30–34	2.2	23.8	77.9	71.6	0.8	12.8	85.0	84.8
	35–39	1.8	16.6	86.4	83.2	0.8	7.8	86.6	88.7
	40–44	1.7	12.4	89.8	87.5	1.2	4.9	85.0	86.7
	45–49	1.7	9.4	91.5	87.3	1.9	3.1	81.9	82.4
	50–54	1.8	7.2	91.8	82.8	3.6	2.3	74.3	74.4
	55–59	1.9	5.2	91.1	76.8	6.0	1.1	65.3	67.2
	60–64	2.8	3.3	88.4	68.4	10.2	0.6	51.8	60.7
	65–69	3.6	1.9	85.1	61.9	13.8	0.3	40.6	58.0
	70–74	5.5	0.8	78.1	56.3	17.7	0.1	26.3	57.3
	75–79	5.3	0.4	73.8	54.1	18.0	0.0	18.9	59.5
	80+	7.6	0.1	63.0	52.1	18.1	0.0	9.8	61.1
Iran 2006	0–4	0.0	99.4	0.0	0.0	0.0	99.3	0.0	0.0
	5–9	0.0	99.0	0.0	0.0	0.0	99.0	0.0	0.0
	10–14	0.0	98.4	0.1	0.0	0.0	97.9	0.6	0.1
	15–19	0.3	96.6	1.2	0.4	0.1	84.2	13.9	5.3
	20–24	0.9	80.6	20.1	8.4	0.3	50.4	47.4	31.4
	25–29	1.0	42.9	61.8	41.0	0.3	26.3	71.1	61.9
	30–34	0.9	18.5	86.5	75.2	0.3	14.0	82.7	80.9
	35–39	0.7	10.1	94.4	90.1	0.5	7.5	87.2	89.1
	40–44	0.7	7.4	96.4	93.9	0.6	4.5	88.2	91.5
	45–49	0.9	5.6	97.1	94.6	0.9	2.6	86.6	91.4
	50–54	0.9	4.5	97.2	92.9	2.0	1.7	81.9	87.7
	55–59	1.3	3.1	96.3	89.4	4.1	1.2	75.6	81.3
	60–64	1.8	1.8	94.6	82.9	9.8	0.5	65.0	67.0
	65–69	2.3	0.7	93.8	74.5	16.0	0.3	57.8	51.8
	70–74	4.0	0.2	90.4	61.5	25.1	0.1	43.7	43.8
	75–79	5.5	0.0	86.5	52.8	30.1	0.1	32.6	41.4
	80+	11.1	0.1	74.7	41.0	33.7	0.0	17.1	44.9
Malaysia 2000	0–4	0.0	98.3	0.0	0.0	0.0	98.0	0.0	0.0
	5–9	0.0	97.9	0.0	0.0	0.0	97.8	0.0	0.0
	10–14	0.0	96.9	0.1	0.1	0.0	96.9	0.2	0.1
	15–19	0.8	87.3	0.7	0.4	0.3	86.3	3.9	2.9
	20–24	3.1	60.5	10.0	6.4	1.4	50.7	28.8	23.4
	25–29	4.0	38.9	39.4	29.5	1.2	24.1	63.6	56.0
	30–34	3.1	26.7	67.7	59.9	0.9	13.4	79.1	77.9
	35–39	2.8	17.1	81.3	76.9	1.0	9.0	83.1	84.3
	40–44	2.5	13.4	85.4	83.1	0.9	6.2	83.3	87.4
	45–49	2.5	10.1	88.8	86.2	1.5	5.0	80.9	85.0
	50–54	2.6	7.9	89.0	85.5	2.4	3.7	74.1	79.1
	55–59	3.4	5.2	88.4	79.6	3.7	1.7	69.9	73.9
	60–64	3.1	3.5	85.6	72.4	5.5	0.9	57.6	69.1
	65–69	4.0	1.2	82.4	68.1	9.5	0.3	45.2	66.9
	70–74	5.0	0.8	75.8	65.5	10.8	0.3	29.8	68.5
	75–79	5.0	0.3	72.6	65.4	12.0	0.0	23.0	67.4
	80+	9.3	0.4	60.7	58.6	13.9	0.0	8.9	70.3
Mongolia 2000	0–4	0.0	97.6	0.0	0.0	0.0	97.6	0.0	0.0
	5–9	0.0	95.0	0.0	0.0	0.0	95.2	0.0	0.0
	10–14	0.0	92.8	0.0	0.0	0.0	91.6	0.0	0.0
	15–19	0.9	80.3	1.0	0.4	0.3	76.7	4.3	6.2

(continued)

Appendix Table 20.2 (Cont.)

IPUMS Sample	Age Group	Male Alone	Male Parent	Male Spouse	Male Child	Female Alone	Female Parent	Female Spouse	Female Child
	20–24	2.6	57.0	25.3	19.4	0.4	45.6	40.4	46.7
	25–29	2.4	29.1	58.4	55.0	0.6	24.7	66.7	77.1
	30–34	2.3	14.4	78.2	77.8	0.8	15.3	74.2	87.8
	35–39	1.9	9.5	82.8	83.1	0.6	9.6	76.9	92.8
	40–44	2.9	5.3	84.8	86.4	0.7	6.0	74.7	93.3
	45–49	2.3	4.7	83.6	86.2	1.4	5.0	71.7	87.8
	50–54	2.8	2.6	84.2	82.4	2.4	2.6	64.5	86.8
	55–59	4.2	1.9	80.9	81.5	3.2	2.2	54.9	83.3
	60–64	6.1	0.3	75.6	73.9	4.9	0.3	49.4	72.9
	65–69	4.3	0.0	74.0	66.2	7.8	0.6	36.3	62.3
	70–74	11.4	0.0	57.0	56.4	13.9	0.5	19.0	59.0
	75–79	7.8	0.0	53.4	55.3	18.5	0.0	18.5	53.4
	80+	7.8	0.0	31.2	55.8	21.0	0.0	2.8	50.3
Nepal 2001	0–4	0.0	97.1	0.0	0.0	0.0	97.3	0.0	0.0
	5–9	0.0	96.8	0.0	0.0	0.0	97.0	0.0	0.0
	10–14	0.0	95.0	0.1	0.0	0.0	93.7	0.3	0.0
	15–19	0.8	88.1	6.9	1.8	0.3	66.8	22.3	10.2
	20–24	1.9	72.7	40.1	23.7	0.5	22.1	62.9	55.8
	25–29	1.9	53.2	72.1	58.5	0.4	7.8	78.2	83.5
	30–34	1.7	37.2	86.3	79.6	0.3	4.8	83.4	89.7
	35–39	2.1	25.7	89.6	86.3	0.5	3.4	83.0	91.2
	40–44	2.0	17.9	90.8	88.7	0.9	2.6	82.5	90.2
	45–49	2.4	13.0	89.5	88.7	1.7	2.2	78.8	88.0
	50–54	1.7	8.3	88.8	88.1	2.5	1.4	73.5	83.7
	55–59	1.9	4.6	86.6	85.0	3.7	0.7	67.2	77.7
	60–64	2.5	2.6	82.9	79.8	7.0	0.2	50.6	73.0
	65–69	3.1	0.7	78.1	73.6	7.7	0.2	43.1	68.9
	70–74	4.3	0.7	72.0	70.3	9.6	0.0	32.0	69.1
	75–79	4.9	0.0	63.0	70.4	10.6	0.0	23.1	69.6
	80+	4.3	0.0	50.4	69.6	8.4	0.0	9.8	75.6
Pakistan 1998	0–4	0.0	97.2	0.0	0.0	0.0	97.1	0.0	0.0
	5–9	0.0	97.2	0.0	0.0	0.0	97.1	0.0	0.0
	10–14	0.0	95.8	0.2	0.1	0.0	96.0	0.5	0.1
	15–19	0.6	81.9	4.7	1.6	0.1	68.7	18.4	10.0
	20–24	1.0	67.8	25.0	15.4	0.1	32.6	53.9	45.3
	25–29	1.0	53.0	53.4	42.7	0.1	13.1	75.0	74.6
	30–34	0.8	39.5	73.6	66.7	0.1	6.8	82.2	85.2
	35–39	0.8	28.8	82.1	78.2	0.1	4.4	84.0	88.7
	40–44	1.0	19.7	85.1	83.4	0.2	2.9	83.0	88.8
	45–49	1.1	12.5	86.6	86.3	0.4	1.7	81.2	87.6
	50–54	1.3	7.1	84.5	85.3	0.7	1.2	73.5	81.2
	55–59	1.3	4.4	84.0	85.2	0.8	0.6	69.5	79.2
	60–64	1.9	2.0	79.6	80.8	1.7	0.5	53.5	70.4
	65–69	2.0	1.1	77.1	79.6	1.8	0.2	48.9	70.8
	70–74	2.4	0.7	70.1	73.3	2.4	0.3	33.3	65.8
	75–79	2.6	0.3	65.5	72.5	2.3	0.3	33.0	64.9
	80+	3.0	0.1	53.3	63.2	2.9	0.1	16.0	52.0
Philippines 2000	0–4	0.0	97.5	0.0	0.0	0.0	97.6	0.0	0.0
	5–9	0.0	96.3	0.0	0.0	0.0	96.2	0.0	0.0
	10–14	0.0	94.3	0.2	0.1	0.0	93.1	0.4	0.2

Appendix Table 20.2 (Cont.)

IPUMS Sample	Age Group	Male Alone	Male Parent	Male Spouse	Male Child	Female Alone	Female Parent	Female Spouse	Female Child
	15–19	0.2	88.8	2.3	1.3	0.1	80.1	7.8	5.6
	20–24	0.7	69.3	22.0	16.7	0.3	52.3	37.6	34.2
	25–29	1.1	41.1	54.2	47.8	0.4	28.6	65.5	63.8
	30–34	1.2	22.7	74.1	69.6	0.5	16.1	78.2	79.0
	35–39	1.5	13.7	82.0	80.5	0.6	9.9	82.7	85.7
	40–44	1.6	8.9	85.9	85.2	0.6	6.9	82.4	87.2
	45–49	1.8	6.3	86.4	86.4	0.8	4.9	79.9	85.8
	50–54	2.1	4.9	85.7	84.6	1.6	3.5	75.2	82.3
	55–59	2.8	3.3	84.6	81.2	2.6	2.5	69.0	76.4
	60–64	3.4	1.9	82.5	76.2	4.1	1.2	61.6	68.9
	65–69	3.8	1.2	79.5	68.1	5.6	0.7	52.8	60.7
	70–74	5.6	0.5	74.9	60.2	8.7	0.3	42.4	54.0
	75–79	5.8	0.3	67.4	53.2	8.9	0.3	31.9	51.4
	80+	7.6	0.3	56.1	51.8	9.6	0.1	19.8	48.1
Vietnam 2009	0–4	0.1	96.7	0.0	0.0	0.1	96.8	0.0	0.0
	5–9	0.0	96.9	0.0	0.0	0.0	96.7	0.0	0.0
	10–14	0.1	96.7	0.0	0.0	0.1	96.5	0.0	0.0
	15–19	0.5	91.8	2.4	1.2	0.6	83.1	8.4	4.6
	20–24	1.6	75.6	25.2	17.8	1.8	41.1	46.9	39.5
	25–29	1.7	52.0	61.4	52.9	1.2	19.7	72.9	73.2
	30–34	1.3	30.7	83.6	80.2	0.8	10.4	82.6	88.0
	35–39	1.2	20.9	89.9	88.7	0.9	7.2	83.7	90.9
	40–44	1.4	14.7	92.3	90.7	1.5	5.5	82.5	88.7
	45–49	1.5	10.9	93.4	87.6	3.0	4.4	79.0	83.0
	50–54	1.9	8.1	92.9	81.3	4.2	3.6	75.0	76.5
	55–59	2.1	5.8	92.4	76.8	5.5	2.6	68.6	72.2
	60–64	2.3	4.2	90.5	71.7	8.5	1.4	58.9	67.0
	65–69	3.0	1.9	87.8	67.1	10.8	0.6	50.7	65.5
	70–74	3.5	0.8	83.4	60.6	12.8	0.2	41.8	63.5
	75–79	5.6	0.3	76.4	58.1	15.1	0.1	32.3	62.3
	80+	8.5	0.0	59.2	60.6	16.9	0.0	15.2	67.5
Thailand 2000	0–4	0.0	92.1	0.0	0.0	0.0	91.2	0.0	0.0
	5–9	0.0	90.8	0.0	0.0	0.0	91.4	0.0	0.0
	10–14	0.1	91.5	0.2	0.1	0.1	91.4	0.2	0.0
	15–19	0.7	86.6	2.3	0.9	0.6	82.2	7.5	5.6
	20–24	2.3	69.9	17.5	10.8	2.2	57.0	32.4	29.5
	25–29	3.9	45.5	45.6	36.9	2.6	37.4	57.0	55.8
	30–34	3.5	27.1	69.6	61.3	2.2	23.6	70.4	72.0
	35–39	3.2	17.8	80.2	74.8	2.2	15.8	75.0	78.2
	40–44	3.3	11.9	84.7	79.7	2.6	11.4	75.5	78.0
	45–49	3.0	8.2	87.1	79.0	3.2	8.4	73.1	74.2
	50–54	3.4	5.7	87.6	75.9	3.8	5.7	70.4	69.7
	55–59	3.9	4.3	87.1	71.7	4.6	3.4	64.6	68.1
	60–64	4.2	2.2	83.6	68.4	6.2	1.6	57.0	67.2
	65–69	4.4	1.4	79.9	66.7	7.0	0.6	46.7	67.1
	70–74	5.4	0.4	71.8	65.7	7.6	0.3	35.5	69.7
	75–79	6.1	0.3	64.7	65.4	7.8	0.1	25.8	73.4
	80+	6.8	0.1	52.6	70.3	7.1	0.0	13.4	77.0

Source: IPUMS – International (2017).

References

Allendorf, K. (2010) 'The quality of family relationships and use of maternal health-care services in India'. *Studies in Family Planning*, 41(4): 263–276.

Amin, S. (1998) 'Family structure and change in rural Bangladesh'. *Population Studies*, 52(2): 201–213.

Bongaarts, J. (2001) 'Household size and composition in the developing world in the 1990s'. *Population Studies*, 55(3): 263–279.

Bongaarts, J. and Z. Zimmer (2002) 'Living arrangements of older adults in the developing world: an analysis of demographic and health survey household surveys'. *The Journals of Gerontology Series B: Psychological Sciences and Social Sciences*, 57(3): 145–157.

Cain, M. (1986) 'The consequences of reproductive failure: dependence, mobility and mortality among the elderly of rural South Asia'. *Population Studies*, 40(3): 375–388.

Chan, A. and J. DaVanzo (1994) 'Ethnic differences in parents' coresidence with adult children in Peninsular Malaysia'. *Journal of Cross-cultural Gerontology*, 11(1): 29–59.

Chaudhuri, A. and K. Roy (2009) 'Gender differences in living arrangements among older persons in India'. *Journal of Asian and African Studies*, 44(3): 259–277.

Chu, C. Y. C., Y. Xie and R. R. Yu (2011) 'Coresidence with elderly parents: a comparative study of Southeast China and Taiwan'. *Journal of Marriage and Family*, 73(1): 120–135.

Chung, I. W. and T. Shibusawa (2013) *Contemporary Clinical Practice with Asian Immigrants: A Relational Framework with Culturally Responsive Approaches*. New York: Routledge.

De Vos, S. and K. Holden (1988) 'Measures comparing living arrangements of the elderly: an assessment'. *Population and Development Review*, 14(4): 688–704.

Fauve-Chamoux, A. and E. Ochiai (eds.) (2009) *The Stem Family in Eurasian Perspective: Revisiting House Societies, 17th-20th Centuries, Volume 11*. Bern: Peter Lang.

Frankenberg, E., A. Chan and M. B. Ofstedal (2002) 'Stability and change in living arrangements in Indonesia, Singapore and Taiwan, 1993–99'. *Population Studies*, 56(2): 201–213.

Freedman, R., M. C. Chang and T. H. Sun (1982) 'Household composition, extended kinship and reproduction in Taiwan: 1973–1980'. *Population Studies* 36: 395–411.

Goode, W. J. (1963) *World Revolution and Family Patterns*. New York: Free Press of Glencoe.

Goody, J. (1961) 'The classification of double descent systems'. *Current Anthropology*, 2(1): 3–25.

Guilmoto, C. Z. (2012) 'Son preference, sex selection and kinship in Vietnam'. *Population and Development Review*, 38(1): 31–54.

Hermalin, A. I. (ed.) (2002) *The Well-Being of the Elderly in Asia: A Four-Country Comparative Study*. Ann Arbor: University of Michigan Press.

IPUMS – International (2017) Integrated Public Use Microdata Series, International: Version 6.5 [dataset]. Minneapolis: Minnesota Population Center. http://doi.org/10.18128/D020.V6.5.

Jones, G. W. (2005) 'The "flight from marriage" in South-east and East Asia'. *Journal of Comparative Family Studies*, 36(1): 93–119.

Jones, G. W. (2007) 'Delayed marriage and very low fertility in Pacific Asia'. *Population and Development Review*, 33(3): 453–478.

Knodel, J. and N. Chayovan (2008a) 'Older persons in Thailand: a demographic, social and economic profile'. *Ageing International*, 33(1): 3–14.

Knodel, J. and N. Chayovan (2008b) 'Intergenerational relationships and family care and support for Thai elderly'. *Ageing International*, 33(1): 15–27.

Knodel, J., N. Chayovan and S. Siriboon (1992) 'The impact of fertility decline on familial support for the elderly: an illustration from Thailand'. *Population and Development Review*, 18(1): 79–103.

Knodel, J., C. Saengtienchal and W. Sittitrai (1995) 'Living arrangements of the elderly in Thailand: views of the populace'. *Journal of Cross-Cultural Gerontology*, 10(1–2): 79–111.

Lesthaeghe, R. (2010) 'The unfolding story of the second demographic transition'. *Population and Development Review*, 36(2): 211–251.

Lin, I. F., N. Goldman, M. Weinstein, Y. H. Lin, T. Gorrindo and T. Seeman (2003) 'Gender differences in adult children's support of their parents in Taiwan'. *Journal of Marriage and Family*, 65(1): 184–200.

Lloyd, C. B. and S. Desai (1992) 'Children's living arrangements in developing countries'. *Population Research and Policy Review*, 11(3):193–216.

Logan, J. R., F. Bian and Y. Bian (1998) 'Tradition and change in the urban Chinese family: the case of living arrangements'. *Social Forces*, 76(3): 851–882.

Martin, L. G. (1989) 'Living arrangements of the elderly in Fiji, Korea, Malaysia and the Philippines'. *Demography*, 26(4): 627–643.
Martin, L. G. and N. O. Tsuya (1991) 'Interactions of middle-aged Japanese with their parents'. *Population Studies*, 45: 299–311.
McFalls Jr, J. A. (2007) 'Population: a lively introduction'. *Population Bulletin*, 58(4): 1–40.
McNicoll, G. (1996) *Governance of Fertility Transition: Regularity and Duress*. New York: Population Council, Research Division.
Piotrowski, M. (2008) 'Migrant remittances and household division: the case of Nang Rong, Thailand'. *Journal of Marriage and Family*, 70(4): 1074–1087.
Pressat, R. (1985) *The Dictionary of Demography* (edited by C. Wilson). Oxford: Blackwell Reference.
Quah, S. R. (2008) *Families in Asia: Home and Kin*, Second Edition. Oxon and New York: Routledge.
Ruggles, S. and M. Heggeness (2008) 'Intergenerational coresidence in developing countries'. *Population and Development Review*, 34(2): 253–281.
Sereny, M. (2011) 'Living arrangements of older adults in China: the interplay among preferences, realities and health'. *Research on Aging*, 33(2): 172–204.
Sun, J. (2013) 'Current situation and changing patterns of living arrangement of Chinese elderly: an analysis based on data from the fifth and sixth censuses of China'. *Population Research*, 37(6): 35–42.
Takagi, E., M. Silverstein and E. Crimmins (2007) 'Intergenerational coresidence of older adults in Japan: conditions for cultural plasticity'. *The Journals of Gerontology Series B: Psychological Sciences and Social Sciences*, 62(5): 330–339.
Teo, P. (2006) *Ageing in Singapore: Service Needs and the State*. London and New York: Routledge.
Therborn, G. (2004) *Between Sex and Power: Family in the World, 1900–2000*. London: Routledge.
Thornton, A. and T. E. Fricke (1987) 'Social change and the family: comparative perspectives from the West, China and South Asia'. *Sociological Forum*, 2(4): 746–779.
Tsuya, N. O., F. Wang, G. Alter and J. Z. Lee (2010) *Prudence and Pressure: Reproduction and Human Agency in Europe and Asia, 1700–1900*. Cambridge, MA: The MIT Press.
US Agency for International Development (2015) *Demographic Health Surveys Stat Compiler [dataset]*. Rockville, Maryland: The DHS program.
United Nations, Department of Economic and Social Affairs, Population Division (2005) *Living Arrangements of Older Persons Around the World*. New York: United Nations.
United Nations, Department of Economic and Social Affairs, Population Division (2013) *World Population Prospects: The 2012 Revision, Highlights and Advance Tables*. Working Paper No. ESA/P/WP.228. Available from: https://esa.un.org/unpd/wpp/publications/Files/WPP2012_HIGHLIGHTS.pdf.
United Nations Statistics Division (2015) *Demographic Yearbook 2015. Series R, No. 45*. New York: United Nations.
United Nations Statistics Division – Demographic and Social Statistics (2016) *Household and Families*. New York: United Nations. Available from: http://unstats.un.org/unsd/demographic/sconcerns/fam/fammethods.htm (accessed 12 December 2016).
Wong, Y. M. and Z. Teo (2011) 'The elderly in Singapore'. *Statistics Singapore Newsletter*, 1–9 September.
Zhao, Z. (2001) 'Registered households and micro-social structure in China: residential patterns in three settlements in Beijing area'. *Journal of Family History*, 26: 39–65.
Zimmer, Z. and K. Korinek (2010) 'Shifting coresidence near the end of life: comparing decedents and survivors of a follow-up study in China'. *Demography*, 47(3): 537–554.
Zimmer, Z. and J. Kwong (2003) 'Family size and support of older adults in urban and rural China: current effects and future implications'. *Demography*, 40(1): 23–44.

21
Asia's demographic transition
Variations and major determinants

Minja Kim Choe

Demographic transition describes the general pattern of decline in mortality and fertility observed since 1800 in most populations. Prior to the transition, levels of both mortality and fertility are high, mortality fluctuates due to natural calamities and epidemics, fertility is rather stable and there is little change in population size over the long run. At the early (first) stage of demographic transition, mortality begins to fall gradually due to better nutrition and hygiene which results in lower mortality from infectious diseases, although fertility remains high. This stage is followed by a period of rapid decline in mortality due to better control of infectious diseases through vaccinations and public health programmes, with a concurrent slow decline in fertility. During this (second) stage the population grows rapidly. The third stage of demographic transition is characterized by a slow decline in mortality due to lower mortality from chronic diseases, and a rapid decline in fertility through fertility control and delayed childbearing. At the end of the third stage, mortality and fertility levels reach equilibrium at low levels and population size does not change much. The fourth stage of demographic transition is characterized by low mortality with a slight upward trend due to population ageing, and a decline in fertility to below replacement level. The first three stages of demographic transition are sometimes called the 'first demographic transition', and the fourth stage the 'second demographic transition' (Caldwell 1976; Lesthaeghe 1995; van de Kaa 1987).

Globally, the demographic transition process progressed slowly during the 1800s but has accelerated greatly since 1950. Mortality decline has increased life expectancy from 27 years in 1800 to 47 years in 1950, and an expected 81 years in 2100. Total fertility has declined from 6.0 children per woman in 1800 to 5.0 in 1950 and an expected 2.0 in 2100. The net effect of these declines in mortality and fertility has been global population growth from just below 1 billion in 1800 to 1.65 billion in 1900, 2.52 billion in 1950 and 6.07 billion in 2000 (Lee 2003: 168).

During the second half of the twentieth century Asian countries represented all stages of demographic transition, from the very early stage of high levels of both mortality and fertility, to the post-transition stage of very low mortality and below replacement fertility. Cultural, political and socioeconomic conditions also vary widely among Asian countries. This chapter examines the variations and major determinants of the demographic transition in Asian countries. It first examines trends and variations in life expectancy from 1950–1955 to 2005–2010, together with indicators of mortality, total fertility rate (TFR), and fertility among young women. This is followed by an overview of how mortality and fertility are related to indicators of cultural and political background, economic and social conditions and public health programmes in various countries. An effort is made to interpret these results in the framework of demographic transition theory. Next, illustrative examples are presented and discussed to give further insights into the interplay of key determinants of mortality and fertility. For the analyses, we rely heavily on national and regional level data compiled by the United Nations Population Division, the World Health Organization (WHO) and the World Bank. Country statistics as well as statistics for the five regions of Eastern Asia, Central Asia, South-Eastern Asia, Southern Asia and Western Asia are examined.

Mortality transition in Asia and its variations

The decline of mortality in Asia over the 60 years since 1950 has been spectacular. Life expectancy at birth is a summary measure of the mortality condition at a given time, and is estimated synthetically from age-specific mortality rates at that time. Figure 21.1 shows the trends in life expectancy for the five regions of Asia, as well as the whole of Asia and the world. During the 60-year period since 1950, average life expectancy in Asia has increased by more than 28 years from 42 to 70, six years more than the world average. Within Asia, life expectancy increased in every region, but by different amounts following varying trends.

For example, in Central Asia life expectancy declined temporarily during the politically and economically unstable period around 1990, and then recovered at a much slower pace than before 1985. Eastern Asia and Western Asia show the largest increases in life expectancy with quite different historical patterns. In Eastern Asia life expectancy increased spectacularly during the period from 1950 to 1975 and moderately after that. The region's rapid increase in life expectancy from 1950 to 1975 was dominated by the large reduction of mortality in China. Rapid expansion of the Chinese public health system in the 1960s and 1970s, together with a concurrent reduction in poverty and improvements in sanitation, have contributed greatly in reducing Chinese mortality, especially for infants and children, after a period of very high mortality caused by great famine and economic hardship (Banister and Hill 2004). On the other hand, in Western Asia, which includes many oil-producing countries, living standards and other conditions affecting mortality have improved rapidly and continuously, resulting in a steady rise in life expectancy.

It is notable that in the 1950–1955 period, life expectancy in Asia as a whole and in all regions except Central Asia was lower than the world average, but in 2005–2010 life expectancy in Asia as a whole, as well as in three of its regions, exceeded the world average. Even in Southern Asia, where life expectancy was below the world average in 2005–2010, the increase over the last 60 years has been greater than the world average, and comparable to the increase in Eastern Asia.

Comparing mortality trends across the five regions of Asia reveals an interesting pattern, but is nonetheless limited by summarizing the histories of 51 countries into five regional groups. Figure 21.2, showing the distribution of countries according to life expectancy at selected time periods from 1950–1955 to 2005–2010, provides another view of the mortality transition in Asia. It shows that the intercountry variation in life expectancy has been narrowing over time, mostly by the disappearance of countries with very low levels of life expectancy (below 50 years). The difference between the highest and lowest life expectancy was 41 years in 1950–1955 but only 24 years in 2005–2010. In China and India, two countries each with a population exceeding one

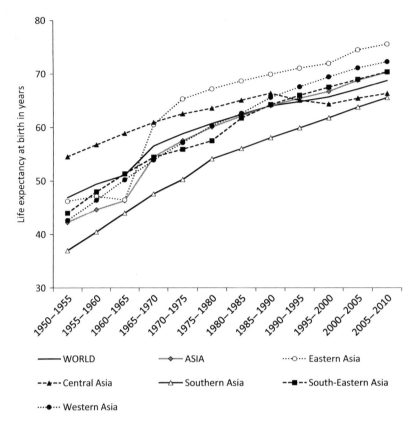

Figure 21.1 Trends in life expectancy at birth: world and regions in Asia
Source: United Nations Population Division (2013).

billion, state/provincial variations are large. For example, in India, estimated life expectancy for the 2002–2006 period was 74 years in Kerala and 58 years in Jharkhand (Government of India 2008). In China, estimated life expectancy was over 75 in Shanghai and Beijing and below 67 in Qinghai, Tibet, Yunnan and Guizhou (China National Bureau of Statistics 2003: 118). In this chapter, we limit our analysis to the country level.

Life expectancy, although very useful as a summary measure of mortality, does not capture the cause of death patterns which underlie trends and differentials in mortality. The Global Burden of Disease study introduced a new metric, the Disability Adjusted Life Year (DALY) as a measure indicating the loss of healthy life, either through death or illness/disability. Total DALYs is a measurement of the gap between the current health of a population and an ideal situation where everyone in the population lives into old age in full health (see Chapter 13). DALYs can be computed for a single cause of death, groups of causes of death, and all causes of death. We use DALYs for each of three broad causes of mortality/disability to indicate the position of the country in the health transition.

Figure 21.3 shows the average DALYs among countries in Asia for three major categories of mortality/disability: DALYs due to communicable diseases (Type 1), DALYs due to non-communicable diseases (Type 2), and DALYs due to injuries (Type 3). Countries have been classified into three groups according to the level of overall mortality as measured by life expectancy

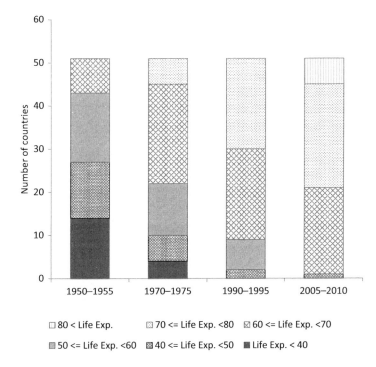

Figure 21.2 Distribution of countries in Asia according to the life expectancy at birth for both sexes, selected years between 1950 and 2010
Source: United Nations Population Division (2013).

in the period 2005–2010. Thirteen countries with life expectancy below 67 years in 2005–2010 are classified as 'high mortality' countries. Twenty-five countries with life expectancy of at least 67 years but below 75 years in 2005–2010 are classified as 'medium mortality' countries. Thirteen countries with life expectancy of 75 years or greater in 2005–2010 are classified as 'low mortality' countries (see Table 21.1).

Although the average DALYs in each mortality/disability category declines as we move from high mortality countries to low mortality countries, the relative declines are quite different among the three types of DALYs. Figure 21.3 shows that the burden of non-communicable diseases exceeds that from communicable diseases and injury in all groups of countries, regardless of mortality level. In addition, the *absolute* difference of DALYs between the high and low mortality countries is greatest for non-communicable diseases, but the *relative* difference is largest for communicable diseases. As a result, the burden of non-communicable diseases as a proportion of all causes of mortality/disability is greater in low mortality countries than in high mortality countries. The burden from injuries is small at all levels of mortality, and declines with the level of mortality in a country.

Furthermore, variations of DALYs within each category of countries are quite large, with especially large variations in the DALYs due to communicable diseases in high mortality countries (see Figure 21.4). We also observe that, for each of the three types of DALY, there are large overlaps in the DALYs ranges across the three categories of countries. For example, many countries in the medium mortality category have higher Type 1 and Type 2 DALYs than countries in the high mortality category. The variations in Type 2 DALYs are quite similar for each country

Minja Kim Choe

Table 21.1 Asian countries classified by the mortality level in 2005–2010

Classification	Life expectancy in 2005–2010	List of countries
High mortality	Below 67	Afghanistan, Bhutan, Cambodia, India, Kazakhstan, Laos, Mongolia, Myanmar, Pakistan, Tajikistan, Turkmenistan, Timor-Leste, Yemen
Medium mortality	67 or higher but below 75	Armenia, Azerbaijan, Bangladesh, Bahrain, China, Georgia, Indonesia, Iran, Iraq, Jordan, Kyrgyzstan, Kuwait, Lebanon, Malaysia, Nepal, North Korea, Occupied Palestinian Territory, Oman, Sri Lanka, Philippines, Saudi Arabia, Thailand, Turkey, Uzbekistan, Vietnam
Low mortality	75 or higher	Brunei Darussalam, Cyprus, Hong Kong, Israel, Japan, Macao, Maldives, UAE, South Korea, Qatar, Singapore, Syria, Taiwan

Note: In this classification, Hong Kong, Macao, Taiwan and Occupied Palestinian Territory are treated as countries.
Source: United Nations Population Division (2013).

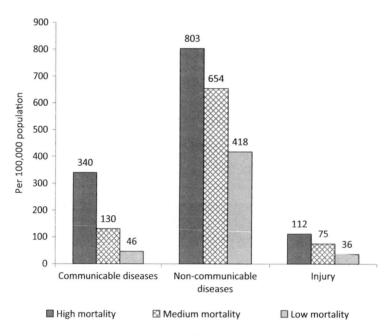

Figure 21.3 Age-standardized DALYs by three major causes of death and disability in three groups of countries classified by their level of mortality
Note: High mortality countries (13) have life expectancy below 67 years (estimated for the period 2005–2010); medium mortality countries (25) have life expectancy 67 years and above but below 75; low mortality countries (13) have life expectancy 75 years and over.
Source: World Health Organization (2012).

category. On the other hand, variations in Type 1 DALYs and Type 3 DALYs are very large in high mortality countries but very small in low mortality countries. Clearly, the mortality transition is dominated by an initial rapid reduction in mortality from communicable diseases, followed by a slower decline in mortality from non-communicable diseases.

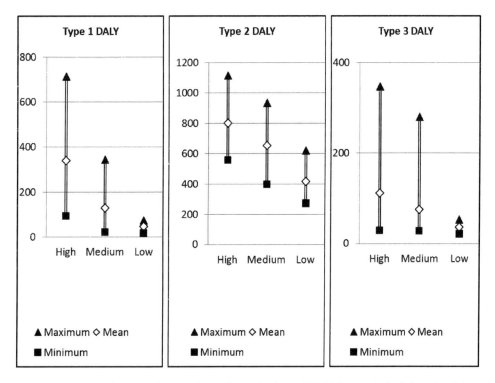

Figure 21.4 Distribution of age-adjusted DALYs (per 100,000 population) by three broad categories of causes among Asian countries grouped by level of mortality (High, Medium, Low), 2007
Notes: Type 1 DALYs are due to communicable diseases; Type 2 to non-communicable diseases; and Type 3 are due to injury. A country's level of mortality is defined as in Figure 21.3.
Source: World Health Organization (2012).

Fertility transition in Asia and its variations

The fertility decline in Asia over the 60 years since 1950 has been even more spectacular than the decline in mortality over the same period (see Chapter 5). The period total fertility rate (TFR) summarizes the fertility level at a given time in terms of the average number of children a woman would have in her lifetime, estimated synthetically from age-specific fertility rates at that time. Figure 21.5 shows the trends in average TFR for the five regions of Asia, as well as for the whole of Asia and the world. In Asia, average TFR declined by 3.6 children per woman or 61 per cent from 1950–1955 to 2005–2010. This is much larger than the decline in the world average: 2.4 children per woman or a 49 per cent decline. Within Asia, Eastern Asia experienced the most spectacular decline in average TFR: a decline of nearly four children per woman or 72 per cent from the 1950–1955 level of nearly 5.6 children per woman to 1.6 children per woman. The smallest decline in TFR was in Central Asia where the decline was less than 50 per cent, or just over 2.5 children per woman. The relatively small decline in Central Asia is partly due to its relatively low TFR at the beginning of the period. In other regions, the decline in TFR was slightly less than 3.5 children, amounting to a decline of between 50 and 60 per cent.

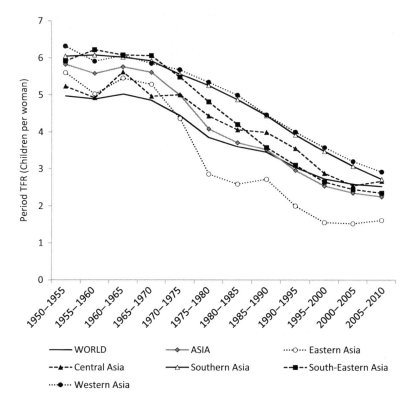

Figure 21.5 Trends in period total fertility rates: world and regions in Asia
Source: United Nations Population Division (2013).

Country level variations in TFR for selected years are shown in Figure 21.6. Unlike the decline in mortality which shows a narrowing of variation, the fertility decline in Asia shows increasing intercountry variation over time. This is a result of persisting high fertility in some countries, combined with fertility declines to very low levels at varying speeds in some other countries. The variation in TFR was especially large in 1990–1995, when TFR was well below replacement level in a number of countries but remained at five children per woman or higher in some other countries. A TFR of 2.1 children per woman is considered to be the replacement level of fertility because if fertility persists at this level for a long time with a constant level of mortality, the total population size remains unchanged.

The number of countries with below-replacement fertility has increased substantially since 2000. In 2005–2010, twenty out of 51 Asian countries had period TFR below replacement level. Among those, TFR was below 1.5 children per woman in seven countries. A TFR below 1.5, commonly referred to as the lowest-low level (Kohler, Billari and Ortega 2002), is associated with late childbearing and very low fertility among women under 25 years of age. For countries with lowest-low TFR, the fertility rate among women of ages 20–24 is very low and the range of fertility is very small. Analysis shows that the fertility rate among women aged 20–24 has a uniquely narrow range among countries with lowest-low TFR.

In the following sections, we review the cultural, political, economic, and social conditions of the countries in Asia and examine how these conditions are related to levels and trends of mortality and fertility.

Asia's demographic transition

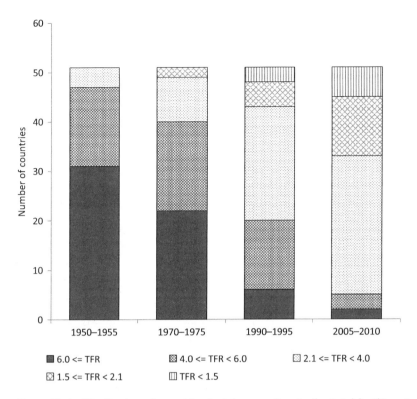

Figure 21.6 Distribution of countries in Asia according to the total fertility rate, selected years between 1950 and 2010
Source: United Nations Population Division (2013).

Cultural, political, economic and social conditions of Asian countries

International agencies such as the WHO (2012), the Population Division of United Nations Department of Economic and Social Affairs (2013), UNESCO (2009) and the World Bank (2013) routinely collect internationally comparable data on potential determinants of mortality and fertility, such as indicators of economic status, environment, education and public health programmes and policies. For many Asian countries, however, this information is available only for recent times. Therefore, examination of the causes or determinants of mortality and fertility is limited to the most recent period, 2005–2010. We examine how the levels of mortality and fertility of a country in 2005–2010 are related to the country's cultural, political, economic and social conditions at the time shortly before 2005–2010. First, we give an overview of potential determinants. Table 21.2 shows the broad cultural, political, economic and social conditions of Asian countries at the beginning of the twenty-first century. The table shows data for the five regions of Asia for convenience, but we also discuss country level variations.

Of 45 countries with data, seven countries (Armenia, Bangladesh, North Korea, Iraq, Japan, the Maldives and South Korea) are characterized by one dominant ethnic group comprising more than 95 per cent of the population. At the other end of the spectrum, eight countries (Afghanistan, Bahrain, Indonesia, Kuwait, Nepal, UAE, the Philippines and Qatar) do not have a major ethnic group, the largest ethnic group amounting to less than 50 per cent of the

401

Table 21.2 Cultural, political, economic and social characteristics of the countries in five regions of Asia

	Eastern Asia	Central Asia	Southern Asia	South-Eastern Asia	Western Asia
Per cent of population belonging in the major ethnic group, 2005	97	75	65	64	75
Per cent of population belonging in the major religion, 2005	49	77	83	70	85
Per cent of countries that had war or major civil unrest since 1990	0	100	33	18	47
GDP per capita in 2002 ($PPP)	13,035	2,548	2,464	10,324	15,549
Per cent of workers in farming occupation	24	33	43	34	17
Secondary school enrolment ratio (%), women, 2007	96	86	34	60	79
Per cent of population living in urban areas, 2005–2010	68	40	31	46	73
Gini index, 2000	37	34	40	42	59
Per cent of women in non-agricultural occupations, 2007	45	47	21	40	27
Female/male ratio of secondary school enrolment, 2007	101	95	81	99	90
Per cent of children 12–23 months old immunized against measles, 2007	96	96	87	82	85

Sources: United States Central Intelligence Agency (2013) for ethnicity, religion and war; UNESCO (2009) for education; and World Bank Group (2013) for other indicators.

population. In terms of religion, eight countries (Cambodia, Iran, the Maldives, Saudi Arabia, Thailand, Timor-Leste, Turkey and UAE) are dominated by one religion, with 95 per cent or more of the population reported as following a single religion. Interestingly, ethnic identity and religious affiliation do not always coincide. Some multi-ethnic countries, such as Afghanistan, Turkey and Thailand are dominated by one religion while the populations of mono-ethnic countries such as South Korea and Lebanon are characterized by diverse religious affiliations. It is likely that in countries characterized by multi-ethnicity or multi-religion, the demographic transition may begin with a specific group but slowly progress nationally. In countries characterized by homogeneous ethnicity and religion, the demographic transition may start late but once it begins, it is likely to progress rapidly (Coale and Watkins 1986).

Politically, some countries in Asia, such as Thailand and Nepal, have maintained independence without major civil unrests or wars for the past 60 years. All countries in Central Asia, as well as Cambodia and Timor-Leste in South-Eastern Asia, obtained independence less than 25 years ago. Many countries in Western Asia have experienced major civil unrests or wars during the past 15 years. Political instability is likely to be associated with high levels of period mortality, at least temporarily. The relationship between political instability and fertility may vary. On the one hand, political instability may disrupt family life such as marriage and the living arrangements of married couples, resulting in low fertility. On the other hand, political instability may have only

Asia's demographic transition

a small impact on family life but a large detrimental effect on family planning programmes and access to contraceptives, resulting in higher levels of fertility.

Economic conditions vary widely among the 51 countries in Asia. Below we consider two economic indicators: GDP per capita (a measure of income level) and the percentage of workers in farming occupations (level of industrialization). As of 2007, the GDP per capita (in international dollars, adjusted for purchasing power parity) was under $2,000 in six countries (Afghanistan, Azerbaijan, Cambodia, Kyrgyzstan, Laos and Nepal), and over $30,000 in six countries (Brunei, Japan, Kuwait, Qatar, Singapore and UAE) (World Bank 2013). Of 27 countries with data on industrialization, in seven countries less than five per cent of workers have farming occupations (Cyprus, Israel, Japan, Jordan, Saudi Arabia, Singapore and UAE), while in four countries more than half of the workers are in farming occupations (Bhutan, Cambodia, Georgia and India). Most of the countries with no data have a large proportion of workers in farming occupations. Demographic transition theory contends that economic development and industrialization are associated with lower mortality and lower fertility in general.

Three measures of social conditions are considered: the secondary school enrolment ratio (in 2007), percentage of the population living in urban areas (2005–2010) and the Gini index of income in 2000. Of 28 Asian countries with information on the secondary school enrolment ratio for 2007, the country average was 71 per cent. However, it was below 30 per cent in six countries: three in Southern Asia (Afghanistan, Bangladesh and Pakistan), two in South-Eastern Asia (Myanmar and Laos), and one (Iraq) in Western Asia. The proportion of the population living in urban areas varies greatly among Asian countries as well. Among 47 countries with data for 2007, the urban population comprised less than 30 per cent in eight countries, mostly in Southern and South-Eastern Asia, and more than 85 per cent in five countries in Western Asia as well as Singapore and Japan. The Gini index for 2000 is available for 32 countries, ranging between 27 and 54. Kazakhstan and Cyprus show the lowest income inequality, and Thailand and Sri Lanka the highest. Social development, characterized by higher levels of urbanization, income equality and education, especially among women, is likely to be associated with lower mortality and fertility during the second through fourth stages of demographic transition in particular.

In addition to the measures of general social conditions above, we consider two indicators of the status of women: the female/male ratio of secondary school enrolment in 2007, and the percentage of women in non-agricultural occupations. Among Asian countries the average female/male ratio of secondary school enrolment in 2007 was quite high, at 93 per cent. It was, however, very low in Yemen, Azerbaijan and Afghanistan (World Bank Group 2013). A higher status of women is associated with lower fertility, especially fertility among young women during the fourth stage of demographic transition.

We now examine the effects of countries' cultural, political, economic and social conditions on levels of mortality and fertility. The relationships between a determining factor and indicators of mortality and fertility are measured by bivariate correlation coefficients. Due to the small number of observations (51 countries) and frequent missing data, multivariate statistics are not used.

Effects of cultural, political, economic and social conditions on mortality and fertility

Measures of mortality and fertility

Three indicators of mortality are examined for each country: life expectancy as the overall measure of mortality, under-five mortality as a measure of mortality due to preventable causes, and the percentage of deaths due to communicable diseases as a measure of the country's stage in the health transition. The strength of the association of a determinant of mortality may vary somewhat depending on which indicator of mortality is used. For example, if a determining factor mainly affects mortality from non-communicable diseases, its association with communicable diseases would be weaker than its association with overall mortality indicated by life expectancy (Caselli 1991; Caldwell 1993, 2001; Olshansky and Ault 1986; Omran 1971, 1998; Preston 1975).

For the analysis of fertility, we use two indicators: period TFR in 2005–2010 as the overall indicator of fertility, and the age-specific fertility rate among women of ages 20–24 in 2005–2010 as an indicator of delayed childbearing during the fourth stage of demographic transition. Asian fertility transition during the 60-year period occurred in two broad phases. The first was the transition from high fertility, more than five or six children per woman, to replacement level fertility, corresponding to the first through third stages of demographic transition (or the 'first demographic transition'). The second phase was the transition from replacement level fertility to very low fertility, corresponding to the fourth stage of demographic transition (or the 'second demographic transition'). Theorists find that the first phase is achieved mainly by reduction in the desired number of children and in unwanted childbearing at older ages of women (Becker 1960; Bongaarts and Potter 1983; Caldwell 1982; Davis and Blake 1956; Easterlin 1975). The second phase of fertility transition is associated mainly with delayed childbearing, and to a lesser degree, an increase in childlessness. Delayed childbearing is measured by the fertility rate among women of ages 20–24 (Brewster and Rindfuss 2000; Lesthaeghe 1995; McDonald 2000, 2006; Kohler, Billari and Ortega 2002).

Effects of ethnicity and religion

For mortality, the ethnic population composition has a small but statistically significant correlation with mortality due to communicable diseases, but no statistically significant correlation with overall mortality or under-five mortality (top panel of Table 21.3). In other words, ethnically homogeneous countries have a smaller proportion of deaths due to communicable diseases than do ethnically heterogeneous countries. It is likely that public health programmes for prevention of communicable diseases can be implemented more effectively in countries with homogeneous ethnic composition. The population composition by religion does not have a statistically significant relationship with any of the mortality indicators we examined.

For fertility, ethnic composition is not significantly related to either TFR or fertility among young women (top of Table 21.4). In contrast, religious composition has some effect on fertility. In countries where one religion dominates, the fertility rate among women aged 20–24 is significantly higher than in other countries. In four of seven countries with the highest fertility rates among women aged 20–24, most people are Muslims. Among the other three countries, the dominant religion is Roman Catholic in one country (Timor-Leste) and Hinduism in two others (India and Nepal). In many countries where nearly all people are Muslim, Roman Catholic or Hindu, delayed childbearing which represents one of the characteristics of the fourth stage of demographic transition had not happened by 2010. It is interesting to note that while period TFR is very high in five of these seven countries, it is low (less than three children per woman) in India and Nepal. Thus, a low level of overall fertility does not necessarily imply low fertility among young women.

Effects of war and civil unrest

Many countries in Asia, especially those in Central Asia and Western Asia, have experienced major civil unrest or war during the last 15 years. Not surprisingly, these countries have higher

Table 21.3 Correlation between indicators of mortality and socioeconomic conditions, c.2007

	Life expectancy at birth, 2005–2010	Under-five mortality, 2005–2010	Per cent of deaths due to communicable diseases, 2008
Per cent of population belonging in the major ethnic group, 2005	0.19	−0.11	−0.31*
Per cent of population belonging in the major religion, 2005	−0.21	0.17	0.11
Per cent of countries that had war or major civil unrest since 1990	−0.33*	0.34*	0.00
Log GDP per capita in 2002	0.77*	−0.73*	−0.60*
Per cent of workers in farming occupation	−0.75*	0.75*	0.55*
Secondary school enrolment ratio, women, 2007	0.77*	−0.73*	−0.85*
Per cent of population living in urban areas, 2005–2010	0.68*	−0.64*	−0.61*
Gini index, 2000	0.17	−0.28	0.06
Per cent of women in non-agricultural occupations, 2007	0.24	−0.29	−0.27
Female/male ratio of secondary school enrolment, 2007	0.57*	−0.67*	−0.29
Children 12–23 months old immunized against measles (%)	0.46*	−0.50*	−0.38*
Fertility rate among women age 15–19, 2005–2010	−0.68*	0.67*	0.56*

Note: * indicates the correlation is statistically significant.
Sources: As for Table 21.2.

Table 21.4 Correlation between indicators of fertility and socioeconomic conditions, c.2007

	Total fertility rate	Fertility rate among women age 20–24
Per cent of population belonging in the major ethnic group, 2005	−0.22	−0.23
Per cent of population belonging in the major religion, 2005	0.25	0.31*
Per cent of countries that had war or major civil unrest since 1990	0.38*	0.52*
GDP per capita in 2002	−0.50*	−0.74*
Per cent of workers in farming occupation	0.07	0.54*
Secondary school enrolment ratio, women, 2007	−0.62*	−0.54*
Per cent of population living in urban areas, 2005–2010	−0.36*	−0.59*
Gini index, 2000	−0.19	−0.21
Per cent of women in non-agricultural occupations, 2007	−0.57*	−0.28
Female/male ratio of secondary school enrolment, 2007	−0.56*	−0.59*
Under-five mortality, 2005–2010	0.66*	0.76*

Note: * indicates the correlation is statistically significant.
Sources: As for Table 21.2.

mortality than others in the 2005–2010 period, including both overall mortality and under-five mortality. The effect of war on fertility is positive: countries that experienced major civil unrest or war during the last 15 years had higher fertility rates in 2005–2010 than other Asian countries. It is likely that an earlier period of civil unrest or war has resulted in higher fertility in 2005–2010 due to couples making up for their temporary postponement of childbearing.

Effects of economic conditions

In general, high income and industrialization are associated with low mortality and morbidity because high income countries are likely to have more hygienic environments, improved nutrition and better medical services (WHO 2012). Not surprisingly, income as measured by GDP per capita, and the extent of industrialization measured by the proportion of workers in farming occupations, are both correlated with the three indicators of mortality in Asian countries. The strength of the association is stronger for overall mortality than for under-five mortality and mortality due to communicable diseases. This is because mortality due to infectious diseases, especially for infants and children, can be reduced substantially by effective public health programmes even when a country's economic conditions are not favourable to low mortality (Choe and Chen 2005).

The relationship between economic conditions and fertility is quite complex. In general, the fertility rate declines as a result of two main trends: a decline in women's desired number of children and a decline in unwanted childbearing. The desired number of children declines during a period of economic development due to lower infant and child mortality, increasing costs of raising children, and a decrease in the perceived value of children. Unwanted childbearing declines mainly due to the greater availability, acceptance and accessibility of contraceptive methods. Decline of period TFR is also caused by delayed childbearing which occurs during a period of economic development. We also find that high income levels are correlated with lower levels of overall fertility and fertility among young women (Table 21.4).

According to our data, the proportion of workers in farming occupations is not significantly correlated with overall fertility but is correlated with fertility among young women. Thus the level of industrialization is not associated with overall fertility in the recent period. This may be attributed to the availability of family planning programmes in less industrialized countries. However, late childbearing is associated with industrialization (Table 21.4). In more industrialized countries, young women are drawn to paid employment outside the home and are likely to postpone marriage and childbearing. In addition, at later stages of industrialization, families perceive the cost of having children to outweigh the perceived value of children, and choose to have small families (Kohler, Billari and Ortega 2002).

Effects of education, urbanization, income distribution and the status of women

Countries with higher rates of secondary school enrolment have significantly lower mortality (on all three indicators) and lower fertility (both TFR and fertility among young women). A higher level of education, especially among women, is associated with lower levels of morbidity and mortality because better educated women and their families are likely to have greater knowledge about preventing diseases and seeking appropriate care when sick. A higher level of women's education is associated with lower fertility because better educated women are more likely to prefer smaller families, have better access to family planning and be effective users of contraceptive methods. They are also more likely to be employed after completing their education and to postpone marriage and childbearing.

Urbanization is associated with lower mortality. In general, residents in urban areas have a higher standard of living, better sanitation and better access to medical facilities, resulting in lower mortality (on all three indicators). The association between urbanization and fertility is more complex. The relationship between urbanization and fertility is likely to be similar to the relationship between women's education and fertility discussed above. In addition, urban living is likely to be associated with increased labour force participation among women, and higher costs of childcare and education. These conditions are likely to result in lower fertility among young women.

At similar levels of income, countries with a more equitable distribution of income are likely to have lower levels of mortality than countries where most income is concentrated among a small proportion of the population. In countries with high income inequality, it is highly likely that there are subsets of the population exposed to high risks of morbidity and mortality, especially of infectious diseases, and this can result in high national levels of morbidity and mortality. Nevertheless, we do not have evidence that the Gini index is significantly related to mortality or fertility in Asian countries when tested by bivariate correlation coefficients.

The relationship between the proportion of women in non-agricultural occupations and mortality is not statistically significant on any of the three measures we are using. This indicator of the status of women, however, does have a statistically significant correlation with overall fertility: a higher proportion of women in non-agricultural occupations is related to lower fertility in Asian countries. Women who are employed in non-agricultural occupations prefer to have smaller families because working outside the home is difficult if raising a large number of children. Women employed in non-agricultural occupations therefore tend to have lower fertility. The proportion of women in non-agricultural occupations, however, is not significantly associated with delayed childbearing. The lack of a significant association in terms of the correlation coefficient may be due to the relationship being non-linear.

The second measure of the status of women, the female/male ratio of secondary school enrolment, is significantly related to both mortality and fertility. Countries with a higher female/male enrolment ratio have lower mortality and lower fertility. Women's ability to provide a healthy family life style and health care for the family improves when their level of education relative to men improves (Hobcraft 1993; Desai and Alva 1998). The combination of women's increased status within the family and better education therefore tends to lower the mortality of their family members.

In terms of fertility, a higher status of women will result in their greater autonomy, lower unwanted fertility and lower fertility overall. A higher status of women is also related to non-traditional attitudes among women towards marriage and childbearing, to late childbearing and to increased childlessness, resulting in low fertility among young women.

Effects of public health programmes

Increased coverage of child immunization reduces child mortality, and, as a consequence, improves life expectancy (WHO 2007). Studies document that even when income and education levels are low, effective child immunization programmes reduce under-five mortality substantially (Choe and Chen 2005). Data from Asian countries confirm this relationship. In countries where the immunization coverage is high, the share of mortality due to infectious diseases is lower (Table 21.3).

To a lesser degree, family planning programmes can reduce fertility from high to moderate levels even under unfavourable economic and social conditions (Tsui 2001). The last panel of Table 21.4 shows that higher under-five mortality is associated with higher overall fertility as well as higher fertility among young women, consistent with the well-known interdependency of child mortality and fertility.

Illustrative examples of mortality and fertility transition

In the process of demographic transition, the many factors which influence the processes of mortality and fertility decline do so interactively, so that the impacts of some factors become stronger or weaker depending on the values of other factors. The illustrative examples that follow provide further insights into these interactions among determinants.

Mortality transition in four South-Eastern countries

Among countries in South-Eastern Asia, Vietnam has experienced the largest increase in life expectancy during the last 60 years. Economic growth in Vietnam has been quite recent, following the 'doi moi' policy (socialist-oriented market economy) adopted in 1986. This is likely to be one of the main factors explaining Vietnam's rapid increase in life expectancy since 1985. An additional factor, however, is that the Gini index in Vietnam is the lowest among South-Eastern Asian countries indicating relatively even distribution of income within the country. This is likely to accelerate the decline of mortality at the national level by minimizing the proportion of the population in high risk groups, especially for mortality due to communicable diseases and other traditional causes.

In the Philippines, where the gain in life expectancy during the last 50 years was the smallest among countries in South-Eastern Asia, the economy has grown at a very slow rate although educational attainment is higher than in other South-Eastern Asian countries. This pattern suggests that, in general, income has a larger effect on mortality reduction than does the level of education.

Malaysia and Indonesia are two neighbouring countries where both life expectancy and the economy have improved steadily during the last 50 years. Both countries have had similar rates of increase in GDP per capita, but life expectancy has increased much more in Indonesia than in Malaysia during the last 60 years. This pattern is likely due to the fact that 60 years ago mortality was much higher in Indonesia than in Malaysia, and the deaths due to communicable diseases and other traditional causes which were more prevalent in Indonesia than Malaysia could be reduced rapidly with economic growth. Both Indonesia and Malaysia are multi-ethnic countries, with no single ethnic group comprising more than 50 per cent of the population. However, religious affiliation is more homogeneous in Indonesia, where nearly 90 per cent of the population are Muslim compared to 60 per cent in Malaysia. Indonesia also has a lower Gini index reflecting greater income equality than Malaysia. These factors have enabled public health programmes in Indonesia to run more effectively, accelerating the mortality transition (Frankenberg 1995).

Mortality transition in China and Kazakhstan

China has achieved a remarkable improvement in life expectancy during the last 60 years, largely due to a decline in mortality among children under age five. The pace of decline of under-five mortality, however, has been uneven and does not parallel the pace of economic development. The decline in under-five mortality since 1990 has been much slower than the decline during the period prior to 1990, in spite of accelerated economic development since 1990 (Choe and Chen 2005; Chen, Xie and Liu 2007). This unusual pattern can be explained by the history of

China's public health system. It was expanded to cover nearly all of the country's population in the 1960s and 1970s, with a concurrent reduction in poverty and improvements in sanitation. As a result, there was a large reduction in under-five mortality in the period prior to 1990 (Banister and Hill 2004). On the other hand, the economic reforms of the 1980s resulted in changes to the healthcare system that widened mortality gaps among some population groups. Development of the health insurance system lagged behind the pace at which the healthcare system was privatized. Furthermore, economic growth during the 1990s was uneven across the country, resulting in increased income inequality. Many poor rural residents did not have medical insurance by the late 1990s. There was a related decline in the coverage of child immunization, so that in 2001 only 79 per cent of children were immunized against measles, a drop of nearly 20 per cent since 1990 (Riley 2004).

Kazakhstan and other countries in Central Asia experienced increases in mortality in the 1990s, followed by a slow recovery in the 2000s. Before independence from the Soviet Union in 1991, Kazakhstan's healthcare system was part of the Soviet Union's planned healthcare system which was successful in providing adequate services to most of the population at that time. Soon after independence, however, Kazakhstan experienced a sharp economic contraction and drastically reduced funding for public-health programmes, resulting in increases in mortality and morbidity over the next ten years. Although the National Health Insurance System was launched in 1995 to address this problem, it collapsed in 1999 due to inefficiency caused by mismanagement and corruption. A slow recovery is now in progress with the assistance of international aid (Academy of Preventive Medicine 1999).

Fertility transition in three Eastern Asian countries

During the second half of the twentieth century, Japan, South Korea and China have experienced rapid economic growth and fertility decline. Economic growth began early in Japan in the mid-1950s and continued into the 1990s, and fertility decline began early in the late 1940s from a high TFR of 4.5 children per woman. South Korea's economic growth began about a decade later in the late 1960s, and fertility decline began at about the same time from a very high TFR of 6.0 children per woman. China's economy grew at a slow pace until 1990 and then accelerated very rapidly. China's fertility decline preceded this period of rapid economic growth, starting from a high level of 6.0 children per woman in the early 1960s.

The pattern of fertility decline in Japan during the second half of the twentieth century has been quite different from that in South Korea and China. In Japan, TFR stayed at about replacement level from the mid-1950s to the mid-1970s and then resumed its slow decline, reaching the lowest-low level of 1.5 children per woman in 1992. In contrast, South Korea and China experienced continuing fertility decline to the lowest-low level of TFR in 1997, with only a brief pause around the replacement level of fertility. Since then, the TFR in all three countries has been below 1.5 children per woman. Apparently, the TFR trends in these three countries are not fully explained by such factors as economic conditions, education and urbanization. Studies on fertility change in these countries conclude that much of the differences are due to their different population policies and family planning programmes (Choe and Park 2006; Chen et al. 2009).

Summary and discussion

Asian countries have experienced rapid demographic transition characterized by declines in mortality and fertility over the 60-year period since 1950. There is, however, wide variation among countries in their starting and ending levels and the pace of transition. The large cross-country variation in mortality has reduced with declining mortality. The rapid mortality transition during the last 60 years in large part reflects rapid economic development, industrialization and urbanization, and increases in education. Other factors including efficient public health programmes, increases in the status of women and income equality can accelerate the mortality transition. To a lesser degree, a homogeneous culture can also enhance the mortality transition. Meanwhile war, major civil unrest and a sudden change in political and economic systems can disrupt the transition.

Fertility in Asian countries has shown very rapid overall decline, with wide intercountry variations in the speed and extent of the decline. As of 2005–2010, period TFR was below replacement level in 20 of 51 Asian countries but remained at more than four children per woman in five countries. A high level of income is associated with a low level of overall fertility. Greater industrialization and a higher status of women are associated with both lower overall fertility and delayed childbearing, and the association is stronger for delayed childbearing.

References

Academy of Preventive Medicine (Kazakhstan), and Macro International, Inc. (1999) *Kazakhstan Demographic and Health Survey 1999*. Calverton, MD: Macro International, Inc.
Banister, J. and K. Hill (2004) 'Mortality in China 1964–2000'. *Population Studies*, 58(1): 55–75.
Becker, G. S. (1960) 'An economic analysis of fertility'. In Universities-National Bureau (ed.) *Demographic and Economic Change in Developed Countries*. Princeton, NJ: Princeton University Press. Pp. 225–256.
Bongaarts, J. and R. G. Potter (1983) *Fertility, Biology, and Behavior: An Analysis of the Proximate Determinants*. New York: Academic Press.
Brewster, K. L. and R. R. Rindfuss (2000) 'Fertility and women's employment in industrialized nations'. *Annual Review of Sociology*, 26: 271–296.
Caldwell, J. C. (1976) 'Toward a restatement of demographic transition theory'. *Population and Development Review*, 29(3): 419–443.
Caldwell, J. C. (1982) *Theory of Fertility Decline*. New York: Academic Press.
Caldwell, J. C. (1993) 'Health transition: the cultural, social and behavioural determinants of health in the Third World'. *Social Science and Medicine*, 36: 125–135.
Caldwell, J. C. (2001) 'Population health in transition'. *Bulletin of World Health Organization*, 79: 159–160.
Caselli, G. (1991) 'Health transition and cause specific mortality'. In R. Schofield, D. Reher and A. Bideau (eds.) *The Decline of Mortality in Europe*. Oxford: Clarendon Press. Pp. 68–96.
Chen, J., R. D. Retherford, M. K. Choe, X. Li and Y. Hu (2009) 'Province-level variation in the achievement of below-replacement fertility in China'. *Asian Population Review*, 5(3): 309–328.
Chen, J., Z. Xie and H. Liu (2007) 'Son preference, use of maternal health care and infant mortality in China'. *Population Studies*, 61(2): 161–183.
China National Bureau of Statistics (2003) *Statistical Yearbook, 2003*. Beijing: China National Bureau of Statistics.
Choe, M. K. and J. Chen (2005) 'Health transition in Asia: implications for research and health policy'. In UNESCAP, *Health and Mortality in Asia and the Pacific Region, Asian Population Studies Series No. 163*. Pp. 37–57.
Choe, M. K. and K. Park (2006) 'Fertility decline in South Korea: forty years of policy-behavior dialogue'. *Korea Journal of Population Studies*, 29(2): 1–26.
Coale, A. J. and S. C. Watkins (1986) *Decline of Fertility in Europe*. Princeton, NJ: Princeton University Press.
Davis, K. and J. Blake (1956) 'Social structure and fertility: an analytic framework'. *Economic Development and Cultural Change*, 4(3): 211–235.
Desai, S. and S. Alva (1998) 'Maternal education and child health: is there a strong causal relationship?' *Demography*, 35(1): 71–81.
Easterlin, R. A. (1975) 'An economic framework for fertility analysis'. *Studies in Family Planning*, 6(3): 54–63.
Frankenberg, E. (1995) 'The effects of access to health care on infant mortality in Indonesia'. *Health Transition Review*, 5(2): 143–163.
Government of India (2008) *SRS Based Abridged Life Table 2002–2006*. New Delhi: Office of the Registrar General, Ministry of Home Affairs, Government of India.

Hobcraft, J. (1993) 'Women's education, child welfare, and child survival: a review of the evidence'. *Health Transition Review*, 3(1): 159–175.

Kohler, H. P., F. Billari and J. A. Ortega (2002) 'The emergence of lowest-low fertility in Europe during the 1990s'. *Population and Development Review*, 28(4): 641–680.

Lee, R. (2003) 'The demographic transition: three centuries of fundamental change'. *Journal of Economic Perspectives*, 17(4): 167–190.

Lesthaeghe, R. J. (1995) 'The second demographic transition in Western countries: an interpretation'. In K. O. Mason and A.-M. Jensen (eds.) *Gender and Family Change in Industrialized Countries*. Oxford: Clarendon Press. Pp. 17–62.

McDonald, P. (2000) 'Gender equity, social institutions and the future of fertility'. *Journal of Population Research*, 17: 1–16.

McDonald, P. (2006) 'Low fertility and the state: the efficacy of policy'. *Population and Development Review*, 32: 485–510.

Olshansky, J. and A. B. Ault (1986) 'The fourth stage of the epidemiologic transition: the age of delayed degenerative diseases'. *The Milbank Quarterly*, 64(3): 355–391.

Omran, A. R. (1971) 'The epidemiologic transition: a theory of the epidemiology of population change'. *Milbank Memorial Fund Quarterly*, 49(4): 509–538.

Omran, A. R. (1998) 'The epidemiologic transition theory revisited thirty years later'. *World Health Statistics Quarterly*, 51(2-3-4): 99–119.

Preston S. (1975) 'The changing relation between mortality and socioeconomic development'. *Population Studies*, 29: 231–248.

Riley, N. E. (2004) *China's Population: New Trends and Challenge*. Washington, DC: Population Reference Bureau.

Tsui, A. (2001) 'Population policies and family planning in Asia's rapidly developing economies'. In A. Mason (ed.) *Population Change and Economic Development in Asia: Challenges Met, Opportunities Seized*. Stanford, CA: Stanford University Press. Pp. 413–444.

United Nations, Department of Economic and Social Affairs, Population Division (2013) *World Population Prospects: The 2012 Revision*.

United Nations Education, Scientific, and Cultural Organization (UNESCO) Institute of Statistics (2009) *UIS Data Centre, Fact Sheets*.

United States Central Intelligence Agency (2013) *The World Fact Book*. Available from: www.cia.gov/library/publications/the-world-factbook/geos/ja.html.

van de Kaa, D. J. (1987) 'Europe's second demographic transition', *Population Bulletin*, 42(1): 1–57.

World Bank Group (2013) *World Development Indicators 2013*. Washington, DC: World Bank.

World Health Organization (2007) *The World Health Report 2007: A Safer Future*. Geneva: WHO.

Word Health Organization (2012) *Global Burden of Disease*. Geneva: WHO.

22
Human capital formation in Asia 1970–2010

Samir KC and Wolfgang Lutz

Introduction

In this chapter we focus on trends in human capital in Asia since 1970. Human capital is a concept often used by economists to capture the productive potential of a society. It is distinct from physical and financial capital and as such enters a production function as the variable capturing the input in terms of labour. Hence human capital is often quantified as the number of working-age individuals in a society according to their skill levels. Since skills are difficult to measure directly (because this requires individual testing) the highest level of educational attainment is often taken as a proxy for skills. The most frequently used indicator of human capital is the mean years of schooling of the adult population above age 15 or 20. The weakness of this approach is that the same value can result from very different educational attainment distributions, and the latter have been shown to be highly relevant for economic growth in addition to the mean level (Lutz, Crespo Cuaresma and Sanderson 2008). For this reason we focus primarily on changes in the educational attainment distribution of the population by age and sex.[1] Education in Asia has a centuries-long tradition and has typically been held in high esteem, yet until recently formal education was mostly restricted to small segments of the population. Historically, countries had their own forms of schooling, ranging from Brahman education in Hinduism to Confucian education to Madrasah education. Later education was influenced by colonizing forces or influences from the West. Japan spearheaded this movement with the introduction of American style education during the Meiji period which then spread to Korea and China. In South Asia, the British introduced Western education. In Central Asia there was considerable Russian influence. However there is only fragmentary statistical information before the 1960s about the extent to which these types of education reached the general population.

For more recent history the statistical information is much richer. Educational attainment level by age and sex is a standard component of all modern censuses and there is also a growing number of representative surveys. Unfortunately the available data tends to be very uneven using different definitions of education categories across countries and over time as well as showing large gaps for many countries. For this reason the UNESCO Institute of Statistics, which collects and harmonizes data provided by member governments, stopped publishing detailed time series data on human capital. In this situation several academic groups have been making

Human capital formation in Asia 1970–2010

their own attempts to estimate consistent human capital data through combining the fragmentary attainment data with somewhat more complete (but in other respects more problematic) information on past school enrolment levels. Among the best known efforts to construct time series for large numbers of countries are Barro and Lee (2013) and de la Fuente and Doménech (2006), both of which rely heavily on interpolation. Meanwhile the International Institute for Applied Systems Analysis (IIASA) and the Vienna Institute of Demography have estimated the most comprehensive and consistent data set using methods of multidimensional demographic back projections (Lutz et al. 2007). The basic idea is as follows: if we have reliable information about the number of men and women in different age and educational attainment groups in a base year – say 2000 – then we can go back along cohort lines to reconstruct the attainment distributions of younger age groups in earlier years. For example, if we know for a certain country how many women there are in 2010 aged 60–64 who do not have any formal education, then we can reconstruct how many women without education were in the age group 20–24 in 1970. The only two possible sources of error for which we have to make adjustments are migration and differential mortality by level of education. Using this principle consistent time series of educational attainment distributions have been reconstructed by age and sex for 171 countries back to 1970 (Goujon et al. 2016) using a consistent set of baseline data (Bauer et al. 2012). The results were validated against all available empirical evidence from older censuses and surveys and adjusted where the reason for a discrepancy – such as changes in the educational composition of migration over time – could be identified (Speringer et al. 2015). Special adjustments were made for the open-ended highest age groups and for the higher education levels where people can still get a degree at older ages. These demographic back projections have the advantage that the definitions of educational attainment categories, which in many countries have changed over time, become consistent. The resulting data sets are used in this chapter to describe the pattern of changing human capital of the adult population in all of Asia as well as in many individual countries from 1970 to 2010.

Changes in educational attainment 1970–2010

The population of Asia roughly doubled over the past four decades, from 2.12 billion in 1970 to 4.14 billion in 2010 (United Nations 2013). The increases in human capital during this period are even more dramatic. To demonstrate this we distinguish six educational attainment categories based on UNESCO's International Standard Classification of Education (ISCED) (see Table 22.1).

Asia experienced a significant decline in the proportion of adult men and women (aged 15 years or above) without any formal education from almost half of the total adult population (49 per cent) in 1970 to less than 18 per cent in 2010. The proportion with some primary or completed primary education marginally declined from 32 per cent in 1970 to 25 per cent in 2010. This category of education is a transient state from a state of no education to a state of completed basic education – which is often 8 years of schooling, also known as lower secondary education or ISCED 2. The most spectacular improvement in education in Asia was for men and women in the lower secondary category: it increased from less than 20 per cent in 1970 to almost 57 per cent in 2010. Figure 22.1 (looking at total population, including children) gives a graphical representation of these trends.

Figure 22.1 also illustrates the sequencing of education expansion in Asia. Growth in lower categories paves the way for subsequent growth in higher categories. The transition rate from lower secondary (ISCED 2) to upper secondary (ISCED 3), for example, has slightly increased from 50 per cent in 1970 to 54 per cent in 2010. The overall increase in the proportion with

Table 22.1 Definition of educational attainment categories used in this study

Category	ISCED 1997 level
No education	No level or ISCED 0
Incomplete primary	Incomplete ISCED 1
Primary	Completed ISCED 1; Incomplete ISCED 2
Lower secondary	Completed ISCED 2; Incomplete ISCED 3
Upper secondary	Completed ISCED 3; Incomplete ISCED 4 or 5B
Post-secondary	ISCED 4 & 5B (first diploma, shorter post-secondary courses)
	ISCED 5A & 6 (longer post-secondary courses, post-graduate level)

Note: For further details see Bauer et al. (2012).

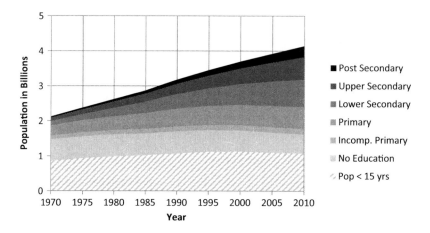

Figure 22.1 Changes in the stock of human capital in Asia, as described by the number of persons age 15 and over in six different education categories
Note: Children under 15 are included without distinguishing their education level.
Source: Based on data reported in Goujon et al. (2016).

upper secondary has increased more than threefold during the same period from 10 per cent in 1970 to 31 per cent in 2010. Similarly the proportion of adult population with post-secondary education has increased as well, from 2 up to 10 per cent during the same period.

The age group 15 years and over represents the stock of human capital for all adult cohorts pooled together and thus hides significant inter-cohort differences that result from the rapid increase in educational enrolment and attainment in recent cohorts. In order to understand the dynamics of improving human capital in Asia, it is helpful to disaggregate the broad age categories into finer age groups (Figure 22.2). In all societies most formal education is concentrated in young ages. Hence the transitions to higher educational levels for individual cohorts can be assumed to be essentially completed by certain ages. The age group 15–19 is proper to study the completed transition from no formal education to some primary or completed primary education as most of the transition would have taken place by the age of 15. Likewise for lower secondary completion the appropriate age group is 20–24, for upper secondary it is 25–29, and for tertiary age 30–34. In countries with a higher level of human development, most of the completions might have already occurred in ages younger than those stated above; however, in many developing countries these age groups are appropriate mainly due to some late entry into education, repetition of grades and postponements in the attainment of higher level education.

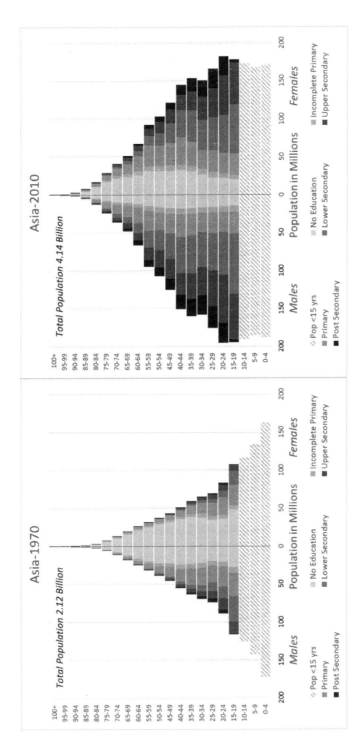

Figure 22.2 Population distribution by age, sex and educational attainment level in Asia, 1970 and 2010
Source: Based on data reported in Goujon et al. (2016).

In an earlier version of the back projection (Lutz et al. 2007), all education transitions had strictly happened by the age-groups stated above for respective education levels. While this rule largely holds true for the current period, exploring the new data (Goujon et al. 2016) for the period 1970–2010, we found that in many countries transitions to higher education level were happening at later ages than those mentioned above. For this reason, for the same ages we will use the proportions that the cohort will eventually attain by age 30–34, for example, the proportion without education for the cohort aged 15–19 years in 1970 will be the proportion without education for the same cohort 30–34 years old in 1985. For ease of reference, the education proportion for each age-group is a reference to the eventual cohort proportion.

There are also some specific age groups that are of particular interest for addressing specific issues. For example, the age group 20–39 is especially important for the economic productivity of a population (Lutz, Crespo Cuaresma and Sanderson 2008). The age group 15–44 (or more specifically 20–39) is of interest in studies examining the fertility and education link. The age group 65 and over is often used to indicate old age in conventional measures. In the following analysis we use proportions, absolute numbers and gaps (ratio or difference) as indicators to describe the changing human capital distributions. For single indicators to summarize the entire distribution in one number we use the mean years of schooling and the proportion of women aged 20–39 with at least junior secondary education.

Primary education

As already noted, Asia has seen a significant decline in the proportion of the population with no education. All countries in the region saw declines; however, in some countries the rate of decline was faster than in others (Figure 22.3). In 1970, 39 out of 42 countries with available data had more than 10 per cent of the adult population (aged 15 and over) with no education. Japan, Georgia and Kazakhstan had less than 5 per cent.

In 1970, there were five countries with over 75 per cent of adults who had never been to school, concentrated in South Asia (except in the case of Timor-Leste with 95 per cent) – namely

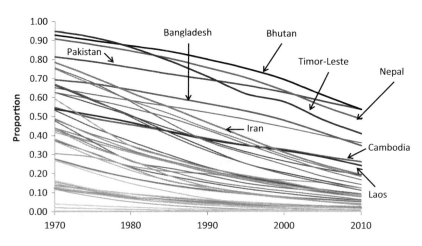

Figure 22.3 Trends in the proportion of the population aged 15 years and above with no formal education, 43 Asian countries, 1970–2010
Source: Based on data reported in Goujon et al. (2016).

Bhutan (91 per cent), Nepal (88 per cent), Pakistan (79 per cent) and Iran (75 per cent). By 2010, except Iran (17 per cent), the first four countries continued to remain the countries with the highest proportion without education although the ranking was reversed, with Pakistan (51 per cent) having the higher proportion without education followed by Bhutan (49 per cent), Nepal (43 per cent) and Timor-Leste (35 per cent). In 1970, India (62 per cent) had a smaller proportion without education than Bangladesh (70 per cent). However, by 2010 with faster educational expansion in Bangladesh (31 per cent), India (34 per cent) took the place of Iran (in 1970) as the country with the fifth highest proportion without education in Asia.

In 1970, in the countries of Western Asia the majority of the adult population was without formal education. Saudi Arabia (73 per cent) had the highest proportion followed by Iraq (72 per cent), Palestine (65 per cent), Jordan (62 per cent) and Syria (58 per cent).

Countries with the next smallest proportions without education were in South-East Asia and East Asia, Laos (55 per cent) and Cambodia (52 per cent) having the highest proportions with no education, followed by China (49 per cent), Malaysia (48 per cent), Myanmar (42 per cent) and Indonesia (41 per cent).

In South Korea, 32 per cent of the adult population over 15 years was without education. Thailand (31 per cent) had a similar proportion as South Korea followed Singapore (29 per cent) and Vietnam (26 per cent). The Philippines (13 per cent) had the second lowest proportion of people without education in the region (after Japan). Finally, all former Soviet Union countries in Central Asia had more than 80 per cent of the adult population with at least some schooling. In summary, in 1970 South Asia was the least educated region followed by West Asia, South-East and East Asia, and Central Asia.

This ranking of regions has not changed much over the last 40 years. A few countries have shown extraordinary growth in their population's level of education while several have shown very slow improvements. In South Asia, Nepal experienced the highest level of decline in the proportion without education (45 percentage points in 40 years), whereas Pakistan and India experienced the lowest level of decline (less than 29 percentage points). In South-East Asia, Cambodia and Laos made modest improvements but still have around a quarter of their populations without education. In the rest of Asia, countries have made significant improvement such that the proportion of uneducated is less than 20 per cent, with 27 countries having less than 10 per cent.

So far, we have shown how countries in Asia transformed from largely uneducated societies into societies with more than 80 per cent having some education. The fundamental transformation of the societies went along cohort lines, a process that has been labelled 'demographic metabolism' (Lutz 2013), with the younger better-educated cohorts moving up the age pyramid (flows of human capital) and gradually improving the average stock of human capital. In the following section, we focus on the changing educational attainment of the younger cohorts to examine the most recent changes in education.

When we focus on the youngest age group of 15–19, we observe a heterogeneous pattern. While Pakistan's improvement in enrolment has resulted in a decline in the proportion with no education by half, from 69 per cent in 1970 to 35 per cent in 2010, the improvement since 1970 in other countries starting with lower levels of education has been considerably faster – for example, Timor-Leste (79 to 6 per cent), Bhutan (79 to 22 per cent) and Nepal (75 to 18 per cent). In 1970 India was a relatively advanced South Asian country in terms of educating people, with less than half (49 per cent) of 15–19 year olds having no schooling experience; however, India's speed of improvement has been the slowest in the region. Bangladesh has made significant progress, already better than many countries in the South Asia region in the year 1970 with

57 per cent without education, declining to 12 per cent by 2010. Iran (55 to 3 per cent) has succeeded in sending almost all of its young population to school.

In 1970, as mentioned earlier, most countries in West Asia were farther along than countries in South Asia. Among 15–19 year olds, in 1970 the proportion with no education was highest in Iraq (40 per cent), followed by Saudi Arabia (39), Syria (38), Palestine (31) and Jordan (33 per cent), with the rest of the countries in the region at below 25 per cent. By 2010, all countries had achieved almost universal (incomplete) primary education among 15–19 year olds. The reason Iraq has not made progress is most likely due to the many wars and turmoil that the country has gone through during the last three decades.

In East and South-East Asia, among 15–19 year olds, Laos had 39 per cent with no education in 1970, followed by Cambodia (30 per cent), Myanmar (19), Indonesia (16), China (14) and Malaysia (12 per cent). The rest of the countries in the region had a proportion with no education of less than 10 per cent and were considered to have achieved almost universal (incomplete) primary by 1970. By 2010, all countries had achieved universal completed primary education.

Lower and upper secondary education

In Asia as a whole, the proportion with at least lower secondary education completed among the total adult population (aged 20 years and over) has increased rapidly from 16 per cent in 1970 to 55 per cent in 2010. This has had a significant positive impact on health and socioeconomic well-being (KC and Lentzner 2010; Lutz, Crespo Cuaresma and Sanderson 2008). In 1970, Bangladesh (9 per cent with at least lower secondary education), Pakistan (9 per cent) and India (13 per cent) performed relatively better than countries in South-East Asia, namely Cambodia (4 per cent) and Thailand (7 per cent). Laos (9 per cent) and Indonesia (9 per cent) had levels similar to Bangladesh and Pakistan; China, Vietnam, Malaysia and Myanmar were in the range of 13–16 per cent; and Philippines (22 per cent) and Singapore (26 per cent) were the forerunners among the South-East Asian countries. It is interesting to note that, in 1970, in Pakistan the progression ratio from primary completed (14 per cent) to lower secondary completed (9 per cent) was 0.61 which is remarkably high. This is an indication of accessibility in certain regions (e.g. urban areas) of the country, whereas in Cambodia the progression ratio was very low (0.27).

In East Asia in 1970, Japan (54 per cent) had a very high level of lower secondary graduates while South Korea (29 per cent) had only slightly more than half of Japan. Many Central Asian countries had higher proportions than in Japan; the highest observed were in Georgia (64 per cent) and Armenia (64 per cent). The majority of countries with the lowest level of lower secondary education in 1970 were in Southern and Western Asia.

By 2010 the picture had changed dramatically – Cambodia (22 per cent) was the country with the lowest level of at least lower secondary graduates, followed by Bhutan (28), Bangladesh (29) and Pakistan (31 per cent). It is also interesting to note that India and China had exactly the same proportion of people (13 per cent) with completed lower secondary schooling in 1970; by 2010, China (66 per cent) had progressed much faster than India (42 per cent). Remarkable changes have also occurred in Malaysia, Saudi Arabia, Mongolia, South Korea, Bahrain, Jordan and Singapore, where the proportion of adults with at least lower secondary education has increased by more than 50 percentage points. While no countries had a proportion greater than 65 per cent in 1970, by 2010 eleven countries had more than 80 per cent, and all countries in Central Asia had more than 90 per cent (which can be considered close to universal lower secondary education).

So far we have described the change in the stock of adult human capital between two points, 1970 and 2010, where the trends were smooth because the stock has great inertia. To see how

Human capital formation in Asia 1970–2010

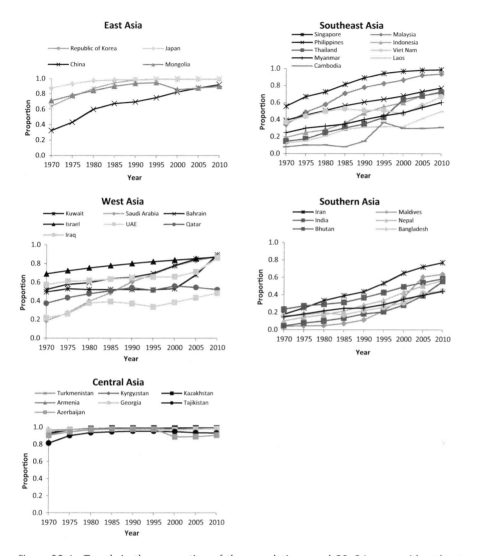

Figure 22.4 Trends in the proportion of the population aged 20–24 years with at least completed lower secondary education
Source: Based on data reported in Goujon et al. (2016).

trends in education transitions (flows of human capital, the new entrants to the stock of human capital) have changed over time, we can look at the evolution of the proportions with at least lower secondary education among 20–24 year olds in individual countries.

Figure 22.4 reveals a number of country-specific peculiarities in the evolution of education of the age group 20–24, which reflects trends in enrolment rates (flows) some 10–15 years before. In South-East Asia, for instance in Cambodia, we see a discontinuation of the increasing trend after 1995. This refers to the birth cohorts after 1970 that were of primary and junior secondary school age in the 1980s, which is likely associated with the serious political problems around that time. Vietnam also saw a discontinuation of the improving trends that could be associated with the later periods of the Vietnam War and its aftermath.

Other countries such as Thailand saw a clear acceleration in the educational attainment of young adults after 1995. In East Asia, China saw very rapid improvements in schooling levels of this age group up to 1985, followed by a decade of less improvement and a subsequent acceleration since 1995. Today China has virtually universal lower secondary education of its young adult population. It thus follows in the footsteps of Singapore, Japan and South Korea that have all achieved universal lower secondary education.

When we examine completion rates of upper secondary education (ISCED 3), in 2010, we find two East/South-East Asian countries – South Korea (98 per cent, world's highest) and Singapore (93 per cent) – have very high proportions among 25–29 year olds which is a result of the highest level of expansion in absolute terms, from a level close to 30 per cent in 1970 to a more than threefold increase. Malaysia and Saudi Arabia also saw an impressive expansion, by almost 60 and 56 per cent respectively. In relative terms, the expansion was impressive in many countries in South-East Asia and West Asia. Also, in Iran the proportion increased from under 5 per cent in 1970 to 46 per cent in 2010; even at the level of the entire adult population age 25 and above, the increase was from 3 per cent in 1970 to 33 per cent in 2010. As illustrated in Figure 22.5, however, Asia still has a number of countries with less than a quarter of the young population (aged 25–29) in this education category.

Tertiary/post-secondary education

We finally turn to the trends in the highest educational category, which includes all completed post-secondary academic education programmes that can range from two-year programmes to a bachelor, master or doctoral degree.

Among the Asian countries, Georgia (in many respects more European than Asian) stands out as having particularly high levels of post-secondary education. In 1970, it already had the highest level of post-secondary education among the adult population above age 30 (22 per cent) and still retains the highest level in 2010 (52 per cent). When examining the flows in Georgia (i.e. the proportion of post-secondary graduates in the age group 30–34, which was 38 per cent in 1970 and 54 per cent in 1980), the subsequent cohorts stagnated between 1980 and 2000, after which the proportion increased to 60 per cent in 2010 (Figure 22.6). Despite the stagnation, the overall stock has consistently increased as the population ages and a larger population with a higher education replaces the older, smaller and less educated cohorts.

The Central Asian countries, like other former Soviet Union countries, have a generally higher level of education stock which increased rapidly. Except for Kazakhstan and Armenia, after the collapse of the Soviet Union the proportion in the adult population nearly stagnated. Focusing on the young adults aged 30–34, Figure 22.6 shows that in those countries the transitions to post-secondary education actually had a declining trend. The same is true for Mongolia and some countries in West Asia.

In East, South-East and Southern Asia, however, there is a near universal trend of a rapid increase of post-secondary education. The proportion of the age group 30–34 with post-secondary education is surprisingly high in the Philippines, increasing from 12 to around 34 per cent over the last 40 years, which may have to do with the large enrolment in nursing schools. Other countries in South-East Asia such as Thailand and Malaysia also made good progress with Cambodia, Laos and Vietnam lagging behind, although Vietnam later saw a rapid increase.

Among the three star performers (Japan, Singapore and South Korea), an interesting pattern appeared with respect to tertiary/post-secondary education. In 1970, Japan had around 7.4 per cent of its entire adult population above age 30 with post-secondary education, which was clearly higher than South Korea (4 per cent) and Singapore (4.8 per cent). Over the past 40 years

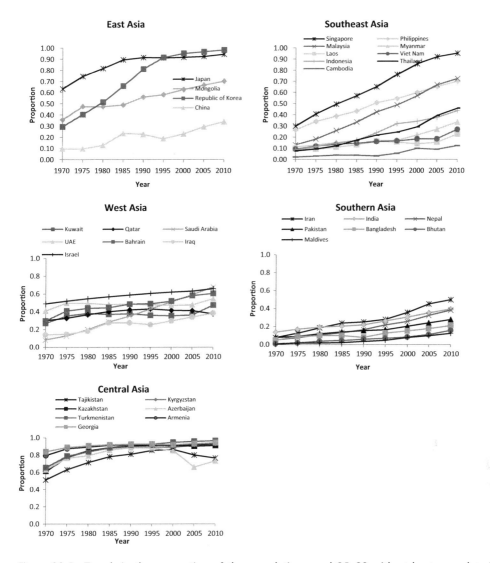

Figure 22.5 Trends in the proportion of the population aged 25–29 with at least completed upper secondary education
Source: Based on data reported in Goujon et al. (2016).

all three countries saw a very fast increase in this indicator: Singapore now lies at the top with 43 per cent, followed by Japan (33 per cent) and South Korea (32 per cent). Singapore surpassed Japan by 1995.

When looking at the age group 30–34 in 1970 (indicative of recent flows at that time), in East and South-East Asia, the proportion with post-secondary education was highest in Japan (13 per cent), followed by the Philippines (12), Singapore (11) and South Korea (8 per cent). Japan accelerated for some time until 1990 (43 per cent) and slowed afterwards, so that by 2010 the proportion was 57 per cent. While Japan slowed down, Singapore and South Korea continued to rapidly increase. The Philippines on the other hand increased relatively slowly.

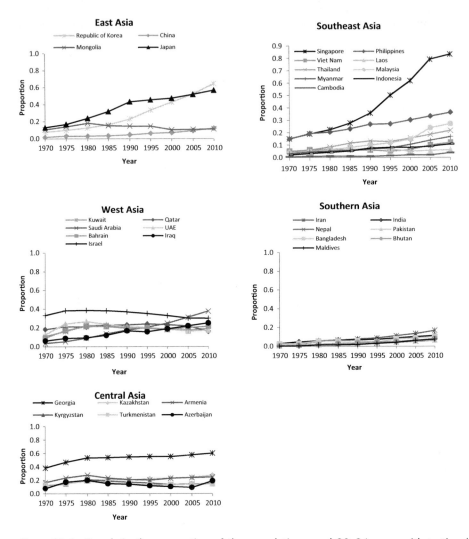

Figure 22.6 Trends in the proportion of the population aged 30–34 years with tertiary/post-secondary education
Source: Based on data reported in Goujon et al. (2016).

How high should post-secondary education go? There is an ongoing and still largely inconclusive policy discussion in the most advanced Asian countries as well as in Europe on whether there is, or should be, a limit to the number of people with tertiary education. In particular, the Government of Singapore is seriously considering whether it is still advantageous for the country to have among their young cohorts 90 per cent or more with completed post-secondary education. While the discussions of the social and economic desirability of very high levels of tertiary education are one issue, another is the analysis of global trends in transitions to post-secondary education. Here, statistical data (such as that given in Figure 22.6) not only show some temporary stagnations in some countries but also no systematic saturation or convergence to any level other than 100 per cent (Barakat and Durham 2014). While this may seem far from the reality of current labour markets in many countries, on the other hand a society where all

Human capital formation in Asia 1970–2010

young people stay in some sort of education until age 21–22 does not look like an impossible scenario. There has been surprisingly little scientific discussion about this issue, possibly due to the lack of consistent time series data to assess the consequences of different educational attainment distributions.

Gender differences

The issue of gender inequality is a serious concern not only for Asia but also around the world. Differences in education between girls and boys lie at the heart of, and are the reason for, many other forms of gender inequality in the labour market as well as in private life. Therefore, statistical data about differences between the education of men and women over time are a very important indicator for progress in gender equity. If we know how gender differentials recently developed for young adults, we have at the same time a powerful predictor for likely future societal level trends in this important issue.

We focus here on the gender gaps in the age group 20–39 since this is the main reproductive age span and matters the most for the education differential in fertility and other family related issues. Among the various possible education indicators, we use the proportion who have completed at least lower secondary education. As discussed before, this summary indicator has high discriminatory power with respect to many of the consequences of education, and also to some extent captures the distributional aspect in addition to the average level of education.

The first line in Table 22.2 clearly shows that for Asia as a whole the gender gap in education has significantly narrowed over the past four decades. While the proportions for young men and women have both significantly increased, this has occurred more rapidly for women. On average for all of Asia in 1970, only 16 per cent of young women had completed lower secondary education, while the proportion for men was double that (32 per cent). In 2010, 70 per cent of Asian men and 63 per cent of Asian women in the age group 20–39 had completed lower secondary education. The gap has narrowed from 16 to 8 percentage points. This closing of the gender gap occurred in every single Asian country although to greatly differing degrees.

In 1970, the differentials were strongest in South Asia and West Asia. The proportions with lower secondary education in India and Pakistan differed by more than a factor of three – in India 9 per cent for women versus 26 per cent for men. In Nepal it was 2 per cent of women versus 10 per cent of men. In Saudi Arabia only 3 per cent of women and 20 per cent of men had secondary education. In the countries of the former Soviet Union, in 1970 education levels were the highest and the gender gap was the lowest. Again, Georgia stands out with 87 per cent of men and 85 per cent of women. In Japan the gap for this level of education was also fairly small: 77 per cent for men and 70 per cent for women.

By 1990 the gap had narrowed in virtually every country. In India, the proportions 'only' differed by a factor of two as compared to more than three in 1970. Over those 20 years in Nepal the proportion of women in this education category increased from 2 to 9 per cent. In Iran it increased from 5 to 27 per cent, and in Saudi Arabia it increased from 3 to 31 per cent. By 1990, Japan and the former Soviet republics reached near universal lower secondary education for both men and women. And in South Korea and Singapore, the proportion of women in this category jumped to 87 and 75 per cent, respectively.

By 2010 the number of countries where near universal lower secondary education was reached for both young men and women was 12 out of the 43 listed in Table 22.2. In some countries women have surpassed men in terms of this education indicator. In Thailand, 71 per cent of women in the age cohort had completed lower secondary education compared to only 59 per cent of men. In the Philippines, it is 76 per cent of women as compared to 71 per cent

Table 22.2 Percentage of population with at least lower secondary education for men and women in the age group 20–39, for Asian countries in 1970, 1990 and 2010

Country	1970 Male	1970 Female	1990 Male	1990 Female	2010 Male	2010 Female
Asia	**0.32**	**0.16**	**0.56**	**0.39**	**0.70**	**0.63**
Southern Asia						
Bangladesh	0.18	0.03	0.29	0.13	0.40	0.35
Bhutan	0.04	0.00	0.19	0.07	0.42	0.35
India	0.26	0.09	0.42	0.21	0.59	0.45
Iran	0.15	0.06	0.44	0.27	0.73	0.67
Maldives	0.01	0.03	0.09	0.05	0.52	0.54
Nepal	0.10	0.02	0.32	0.09	0.58	0.39
Pakistan	0.18	0.05	0.33	0.12	0.47	0.30
East Asia						
China	0.31	0.14	0.70	0.51	0.88	0.83
Hong Kong	0.42	0.28	0.72	0.68	0.95	0.93
Japan	0.77	0.70	0.97	0.96	0.99	0.99
Macao	0.41	0.27	0.64	0.58	0.87	0.90
Mongolia	0.59	0.41	0.85	0.84	0.88	0.95
South Korea	0.56	0.32	0.92	0.87	1.00	0.99
South-East Asia						
Cambodia	0.08	0.03	0.15	0.06	0.39	0.24
Indonesia	0.17	0.09	0.41	0.30	0.66	0.63
Laos	0.21	0.03	0.34	0.14	0.49	0.36
Malaysia	0.28	0.15	0.68	0.59	0.90	0.91
Myanmar	0.28	0.15	0.41	0.29	0.54	0.50
Philippines	0.31	0.27	0.52	0.53	0.71	0.77
Singapore	0.46	0.30	0.78	0.73	0.97	0.97
Thailand	0.13	0.07	0.31	0.25	0.60	0.72
Timor-Leste	0.00	0.00	0.17	0.08	0.51	0.44
Vietnam	0.36	0.13	0.55	0.45	0.57	0.55
West Asia						
Armenia	0.85	0.82	0.98	0.98	0.98	1.00
Azerbaijan	0.75	0.46	0.93	0.88	0.95	0.93
Bahrain	0.42	0.17	0.61	0.59	0.78	0.86
Georgia	0.87	0.85	0.96	0.97	0.98	0.98
Iraq	0.19	0.07	0.39	0.23	0.56	0.47
Jordan	0.34	0.12	0.61	0.51	0.79	0.81
Kuwait	0.49	0.27	0.52	0.53	0.61	0.70
Lebanon	0.31	0.23	0.60	0.59	0.77	0.83
Palestine	0.19	0.04	0.53	0.35	0.74	0.70
Qatar	0.37	0.17	0.46	0.50	0.46	0.70
Saudi Arabia	0.20	0.03	0.55	0.29	0.84	0.79
Syria	0.18	0.06	0.35	0.20	0.37	0.37
Turkey	0.19	0.09	0.42	0.22	0.61	0.46
UAE	0.46	0.24	0.61	0.62	0.68	0.82
Central Asia						
Kazakhstan	0.79	0.75	0.99	0.98	0.99	0.99
Kyrgyzstan	0.75	0.65	0.98	0.98	0.99	0.99
Tajikistan	0.80	0.52	0.95	0.89	0.96	0.91
Turkmenistan	0.87	0.77	0.98	0.98	1.00	1.00

Source: Based on data reported in Goujon et al. (2016).

of men. Even in the countries that had the most extreme gaps in 1970 there has been a very substantial narrowing.

While it still will take time for this massive closing of the gender gap in lower secondary education to filter through to higher levels of education and to older segments of the population, it could still represent the basis for a forthcoming gender revolution in Asia. Since the skills acquired in lower secondary education are an important prerequisite for social empowerment and participation, the significant progress in closing the gender gap described in this section should not be underestimated in terms of its implications for the future.

Labour force participation

Labour force participation is another relevant dimension of human capital, measuring the proportion of an age group that is in the labour force (i.e. either employed, self-employed or actively looking for a job). There is even less consistent information on age- and sex- specific labour force participation rates available for the countries of Asia than for education. Here we focus primarily on three big countries as examples – India, Indonesia and South Korea – using data from the International Labour Organization (ILO). Singapore is also included as a very specific and interesting case. Figure 22.7 shows the labour force participation rates for India in 1971 and 2001. In both years the participation rates are much higher for men than for women. For men the participation is close to universal for the age groups 35–44. However, for younger men the rates have declined over the last three decades, presumably due to longer durations in education. What is interesting is that despite the significantly increased life expectancy and better education, labour force participation has marginally declined for men above age 60. This is probably due to incentive structures in the pension system.

For women in India, the participation rate has significantly increased at all ages. For the peak age group for female employment (age group 40–44), participation rates have increased almost by a factor of three from 21 per cent in 1971 to 62 per cent in 2001. This is associated with structural changes in India's economy (from agriculture to industry and services) as well as better female education. It is still an open question whether this increase in female labour force

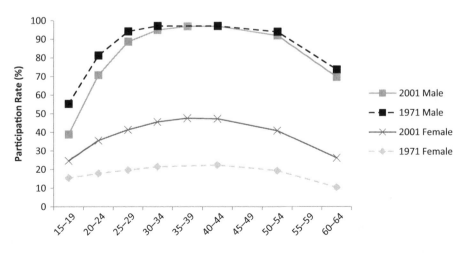

Figure 22.7 Labour force participation rates by age and sex in India in 1971 and 2001
Sources: ILOSTAT, 1971 and 2001 Population Census.

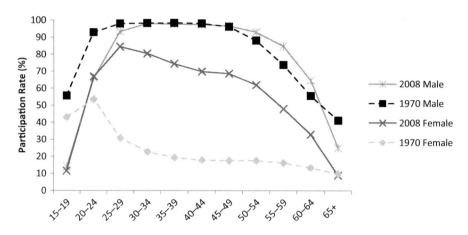

Figure 22.8 Labour force participation rates by age and sex in Singapore in 1970 and 2008
Source: Singapore Government, Ministry of Manpower, Manpower Research & Statistics Department, Comprehensive Labour Force Survey (2008).

participation will continue in the future, but if the experience of more advanced Asian countries is any guide, further increases are very likely.

When we look at the labour force participation pattern in Singapore, the pattern for men looks very similar (Figure 22.8). Both in 1970 and 2008, men in prime working ages have near 100 per cent participation. Also, for younger men the participation rates have dropped over time, presumably due to longer education. Unlike in India, the participation for men above age 50 has increased over the past decades. For women, too, the age profile of labour force participation looks dramatically different from India, both for 1970 and for 2008. In 1970, young women below age 25 had the highest participation rates (around 50 per cent), which may be a consequence of the very different economic structure of Singapore. After that age the rates fall to levels even slightly below that of Indian women in 1970. Since 1970 female labour force participation in Singapore has more than doubled although the curve has maintained the same shape, but shifting a bit to the right; the shift is likely the consequence of longer education. In the age group 25–29 around 85 per cent of women now work. After this peak some women start to drop out of the labour force – presumably for family reasons – and the rate declines slowly to around 70 per cent. The further steep decline after age 50 is likely to be in part a cohort effect: women who once dropped out of the labour force at younger ages (following the old pattern) maintained this pattern for the rest of their lives.

In South Korea (Figure 22.9) the general pattern is not so different from Singapore except that the change in female participation between 1970 and 2012 is not as dramatic. While male participation is above 90 per cent at both points in time, female participation in 1970 showed a small peak in the early 20s followed by a dip which is likely due to childbearing. However, unlike in Singapore, at that time many women returned to the labour market and participation actually reached a peak around age 50. In 2012 the curve for women has still the same shape but is moved up and a bit to the right implying later entry and higher labour force participation at all ages. For China, there is only fragmentary data available for 1982 and 1990. They indicate that the participation rate for women was exceptionally high, around 90 per cent for the broad age group 20–44.

Human capital formation in Asia 1970–2010

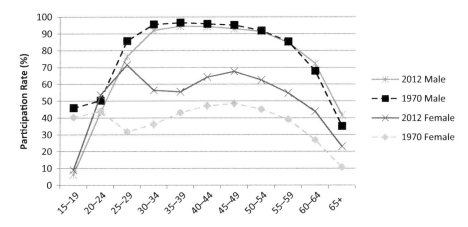

Figure 22.9 Labour force participation rates by age and sex in South Korea in 1971 and 2010
Sources: ILOSTAT, 1971 Population Census and 2012 Labour Force Survey.

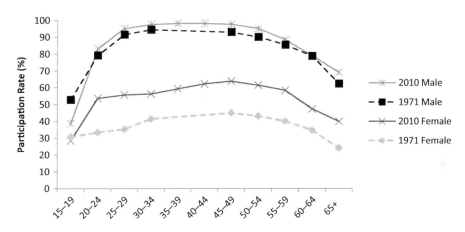

Figure 22.10 Labour force participation rates by age and sex in Indonesia in 1971 and 2010
Sources: ILOSTAT, 1971 Population Census and 2010 Labour Force Survey.

In Indonesia (Figure 22.10) the pattern again resembles an inverted U-shape similar to that of India. A marked difference is that in 2010 the female labour force participation jumps up to over 50 per cent for the age group 20–24 and thereafter increases slowly peaking at 65 per cent at ages 45–49. This implies that most working women are staying in the labour force even after they have children.

Over the past years female labour force participation increased in virtually all countries in Asia but it shows very different age profiles according to cultural and economic conditions. The gender gap in labour force participation rates continues to exist in all countries but it varies greatly across Asia. While countries with large Islamic populations often have very large gender gaps, countries in South-East Asia and Central Asia tend to have minimal gender gaps. Figure 22.11 shows data for male and female labour force participation rates for the age group 30–34 for the latest available year (which in some cases goes back to the 1990s). Countries are ranked by female labour force participation starting with Laos and China at the top and Iran and Iraq at the bottom.

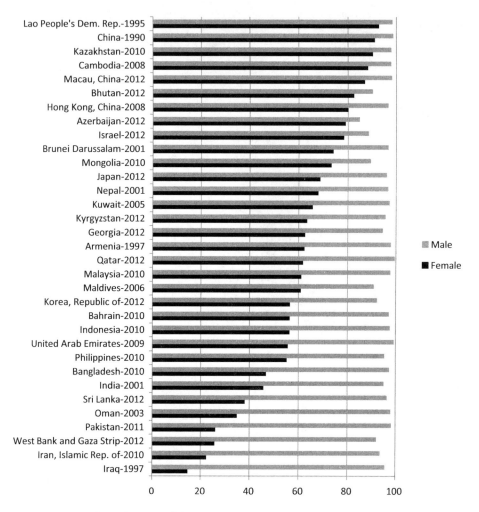

Figure 22.11 Labour force participation rates among men and women aged 30–34 years for countries in Asia (latest available year)
Source: ILOSTAT.

Conclusion

Over recent decades Asia has experienced a stunning expansion of its human capital both for men and women. While in the middle of the twentieth century a high proportion of the continent's population had no or little formal education (with the exception of Japan), it is now home to some of the world's most educated populations – at least for the younger cohorts. Singapore and South Korea (possibly together with Taiwan for which we have no data, and Hong Kong) are the world champions in educational expansion. In 1960, Singapore and Korea were still poor developing countries with very low levels of formal education. However, their development paths then diverged from the bulk of other developing countries through massive investments in human capital, even at times when they were still poor. It can be shown that educational expansion came before economic growth and was a key driver of that growth rather than the other way round (see Lutz, Crespo Cuaresma and Sanderson 2008). The direction of causality can be assessed through the fact that increases in primary and junior secondary school enrolment need to come at least 15–20 years before the better educated cohorts can enter the labour force and make a difference to economic growth and improvements in institutions. Only when it comes to higher education is it plausible to assume that there is a feedback from economic growth to more investments in higher education. In all the successful Asian countries, the rapid expansion of public basic education for both girls and boys clearly preceded the impressive economic growth. The expansion of female education was also a major driver in advancing the fertility transition in Asia (Lutz and KC 2011).

We have also seen in this chapter that in addition to some of the world's most educated countries, Asia is also home to some countries that significantly lag behind. For the two population billionaires, India clearly lags behind China in terms of broad-based basic (lower secondary) education and female education; while in terms of the smaller segments of highly educated men, India had a traditional advantage. The two Islamic countries Iran and Pakistan offer another interesting comparison because in 1970 they were in almost identical demographic conditions, both growing at 2.6 per cent a year with TFRs around 6.5. In both countries only 5 per cent of women aged 20–39 had completed lower secondary education in 1970. However, Iran then started to invest massively in universal basic education, including female education, while Pakistan made only very slow progress. By 2010, 67 per cent of young Iranian women had junior secondary education compared to only 30 per cent in Pakistan. As a consequence, Iran experienced the world's most rapid national level fertility decline with current TFR levels around 1.8 while Pakistan still has a TFR of 3.5. Life expectancy in Iran today is ten years higher than in Pakistan.

In every Asian country the young cohorts are better educated than the older ones and in some countries these inter-cohort differences are very dramatic. Since the relentless process of demographic metabolism (Ryder 1965; Lutz 2013) will continue over the coming decades and the less educated older cohorts will be replaced by the much better educated younger ones, there is no doubt that the future human capital of Asia will be much stronger than today's. There is no reason for complacency, however, particularly in countries where fertility rates are still high, and hence the further expansion of education remains an uphill battle. If rapid population growth coincides with a possible weakening of education efforts, then school enrolment rates may actually decline and the positive momentum of human capital formation may be lost.

Acknowledgements

The authors are very grateful to Elke Loichinger for providing the data for the section on labour force participation. Partial support for this work was provided by the European Research Council (ERC) Advanced Investigator Grant focusing on 'Forecasting Societies' Adaptive Capacities to Climate Change' (ERC-2008-AdG 230195-FutureSoc).

Note

1 More detailed studies of human capital also consider the fact that in order to effectively contribute to the formal economy, people not only need to have a certain level of skills (as approximated by level of education) but also need to be in good health and active in the labour market. Therefore, labour force participation and health are further dimensions of human capital. Because health differentials within the labour force are not a major issue in Asia and data on them are scarce, we do not cover this topic here, but we do include a section on trends in labour force participation.

References

Barakat, B. F. and R. E. Durham (2014) 'Future education trends'. In W. Lutz, W. P. Butz and S. KC (eds.) *World Population and Human Capital in the 21st Century*. Oxford: Oxford University Press. Pp. 397–433.

Barro, R. J. and J. W. Lee (2013) 'A new data set of educational attainment in the world, 1950–2010'. *Journal of Development Economics*, 104(September): 184–198.

Bauer, R., M. Potančoková, A. Goujon, and S. KC (2012) 'Populations for 171 countries by age, sex, and level of education around 2010: harmonized estimates of the baseline data for the Wittgenstein Centre projections'. Interim Report IR-12-016. Laxenburg, Austria: International Institute for Applied Systems Analysis. Available from: www.iiasa.ac.at/publication/more_IR-12-016.php.

de la Fuente, A. and R. Doménech (2006). 'Human capital in growth regressions: how much difference does data quality make?' *Journal of the European Economic Association*, 4(1): 1–36.

Goujon, A., S. KC, M. Speringer, B. Barakat, M. Potančoková, J. Eder, E. Striessnig, R. Bauer and W. Lutz (2016) 'A harmonized dataset on global educational attainment between 1970 and 2060 – An analytical window into recent trends and future prospects in human capital development'. *Journal of Demographic Economics*, 82(3): 315–363.

International Labour Organization (ILO). *ILOSTAT database*. Available from: www.ilo.org/ilostat.

KC, S. and H. Lentzner (2010) 'The effect of education on adult mortality and disability: a global perspective'. *Vienna Yearbook of Population Research*, 8: 201–235. Available from: http://dx.doi.org/10.1553/populationyearbook2010s201.

Lutz, W. (2013) 'Demographic metabolism: a predictive theory of socioeconomic change'. *Population and Development Review*, 38: 283–301.

Lutz, W., J. Crespo Cuaresma and W. C. Sanderson (2008) 'The demography of educational attainment and economic growth'. *Science*, 319(5866): 1047–1048.

Lutz, W., A. Goujon, S. KC and W. C. Sanderson (2007) 'Reconstruction of populations by age, sex and level of educational attainment for 120 countries for 1970–2000'. *Vienna Yearbook of Population Research*, 2007: 193–235. Available from: www.oeaw.ac.at/vid/publications/VYPR2007/abstract_Lutz-et-al_Education.html.

Lutz, W. and S. KC (2011) 'Global human capital: integrating education and population'. *Science*, 333(6042): 587–592.

Ryder, N. B. (1965) 'The cohort as a concept in the study of social change'. *American Sociological Review*, 30(6): 843–861.

Singapore Government, Ministry of Manpower, Manpower Research & Statistics Department, Comprehensive Labour Force Survey (2008). Available from: www.mom.gov.sg/newsroom/press-releases/2008/singapore-workforce-2008.

Speringer, M., A. Goujon, J. Eder, S. KC, R. Bauer and M. Potančoková (2015) 'Validation of the Wittgenstein Centre back-projections for populations by age, sex and level of education from 1970 to 2010'. Interim Report IR-15-008. Laxenburg, Austria: International Institute for Applied Systems Analysis (IIASA).

United Nations (2013) *World Population Prospects: The 2012 Revision. Key Findings and Advance Tables*. New York, NY: Department of Economic and Social Affairs, Population Division.

23
The process of population ageing and its challenges

Heather Booth

Introduction

A recurring theme in this handbook is the wide range of different demographic regimes, experiences and expectations found in Asia. Population ageing is no exception. The degree of ageing, measured most simply by the proportion of the population who are aged 65 or older, varied in 2010 from less than 1 per cent in Saudi Arabia to 23 per cent in Japan. This variation is explored in this chapter by considering trends and patterns among the populations of Asia in the context of demographic transition. The chapter then considers the challenges posed by population ageing for the family and the state. First, however, the chapter describes the theoretical process of population ageing and how it is measured.

The process of population ageing

Population ageing is the process of structural transformation from a youthful population with a large proportion in childhood or young adulthood to a mature population with increased proportions at middle and older ages. The process of ageing occurs over several generations due principally to the underlying processes of fertility and mortality, though migration may also have some influence. In the equilibrium of the stable population model,[1] where fertility and mortality rates are constant and there is no migration, the age-sex structure of the population remains constant over time. It is change in demographic rates that produces structural transformation. In reality, demographic rates are subject to continuous change, resulting in an ever-transforming population structure. This process, known as population dynamics, may involve transformation to an older population structure, in other words population ageing, or to a younger population structure, which in this chapter is referred to as 'reverse ageing'. In Asia, most populations are undergoing population ageing.

Population ageing is inextricably linked to demographic transition, which is associated with economic and social development. During the transition, both mortality and fertility decline. Initially, the process of population ageing is driven by declining fertility, which constrains the annual number of births, thereby constraining the relative size of the younger population.[2] In the later stages of the transition, population ageing is driven by declining mortality through increased survival to older ages and an augmented older population.[3] Thus, the process of population ageing is inherent to demographic transition. Two features stem from this: first, population ageing is a finite process that will end, and second, population ageing is unlikely to be reversed to any significant degree. An older, post-transitional age structure is both inevitable and essentially permanent.

It is important to note that population ageing is concerned with population structure and not with population growth or size. However, there is a connection between population structure and growth because they are determined by the same demographic processes. In particular, smaller numbers of births due to fertility decline will produce both population ageing and slower population growth.[4] Thus, population ageing is associated with decelerating growth, and advanced population ageing is associated with low (or possibly negative) population growth. The pace of fertility decline largely determines the degree of population ageing and the deceleration of population growth, while the pace of mortality decline augments population ageing once child and early adult mortality have reached relatively low levels. In other words, the speed of demographic transition is a direct cause of the rapidity and degree of population ageing.

If post-transition fertility and mortality were to remain constant (again assuming no migration), population ageing would cease after a life span of 100 years or so had elapsed, but population growth (which could be negative) would continue. Only if fertility were also at replacement level would growth be zero; such a population is called 'stationary'. If post-transition fertility were below replacement level (whether constant or not), population growth would eventually become negative – in other words, population size would decline – and the ageing of the population would be more advanced. Japan is already experiencing population decline and advanced population ageing stemming from sustained below-replacement fertility. The role of declining mortality in Japan is to constrain population decline while contributing to population ageing.

The process of population ageing may also be affected by large-scale international migration. Relatively recent emigration of young adults (usually for employment) accelerates ageing in the 'sending' population and decelerates ageing in the 'receiving' population; however, these effects are reversed once the migrants reach old age.[5] International migration may be seen as a solution to population ageing (United Nations 2000). International migration and fluctuations in fertility and mortality rates during the course of transition contribute to irregularity in the age-sex structure. The changing relativity between cohorts influences the measures of population ageing.

Measures of population ageing

Population ageing may be measured by several indices, each with different emphases. The four measures used in this chapter provide different information about the common process of population ageing. For three of the measures, the first step is to define the age at which 'old age' begins. In this chapter, 65 years is used as the old-age threshold. Two measures also involve definition of 'child' and 'working age'; the ages 0–14 and 15–64 years are used respectively.

The first, and perhaps the simplest, measure of population ageing is the proportion of the population that is classed as 'old'. A slightly more complex and commonly-used second measure is the old age dependency ratio (OADR), defined as the ratio of the old-age population to the working-age population. The OADR conveys a broadly economic meaning, describing population ageing in terms of the number of old-age persons that each working-age person supports.[6] In this chapter, the OADR is scaled by a factor of 100 to represent the number of old-age persons per 100 working-age persons. Both the proportion classed as old and the OADR are measures of relative population size, influenced not only by the old-age population but also by the younger population.

The OADR is often considered in conjunction with the total dependency ratio (TDR) or the ratio of the combined old-age and child population to the working-age population. The ratio OADR/TDR, or the old-age share of dependency (OASD), is the third measure of ageing (scaled by a factor of 100) used in this chapter. This measure does not directly involve the working-age population.[7]

The measures discussed thus far are all based on population proportions defined by age.[8] An alternative approach is to use a specific proportion or percentile as the definitional criterion for the older population and to identify the associated threshold age.[9] As the population ages, the threshold age increases. The commonly used median age is the threshold for the 50th percentile, delineating the oldest half of the population from the youngest half, and is the fourth measure of ageing used in this chapter.

Whether the definitional focus is an age or a percentile is a matter of perspective about ageing. The use of a specific age as the definitional criterion of 'old', with charting of the population proportion meeting that criterion, presents ageing in terms of a growing older population. Though relative, the growing proportion is widely understood in terms of increasing numbers of older people in the population when in fact decreasing numbers of children due to lower fertility may be the cause. This perspective tends to be negative towards ageing, viewing the old-age proportion of the population as a 'burden' on the productive population (however defined).

In contrast, the use of a specific percentile as the definitional criterion of 'old' presents ageing in terms of an advancing threshold age. This perspective tends to be more positive towards ageing and in effect incorporates the redefinition of 'old age' as longevity increases (or as large cohorts attain older ages). No longer is the older population portrayed as an increasing burden, as their proportion is fixed. This perspective is also more amenable to the notion of healthy life expectancy (Jagger and Robine 2011).

In studying population 'ageing', there is an implicit assumption that the degree of ageing will increase over time. This is the case under demographic transition theory, and commonly occurs in practice. However, instances are also found where the degree of ageing declines over time; in other words, reverse ageing occurs.

Population ageing in Asia: a historical perspective

Trends and patterns

John Knodel (1999: 39) observed that 'For Asia, population ageing lies almost entirely ahead'. Compared with Europe, North America and Oceania, Asia as a whole has so far experienced only moderate population ageing. Figure 23.1 shows that in 2010, 7 per cent of the population of Asia was aged 65 or older, compared with 17 per cent in Europe, 13 per cent in North America and 11 per cent in Oceania. However, the pace of ageing in Asia is accelerating. In recent decades the Asian population has aged significantly. Its age-sex structure has been transformed, most notably the falling proportion of those aged 0–19 during the recent two decades.

In 1950, very few populations had begun the demographic transition, so that the 1950 age-sex structure of the Asian population is typical of most individual populations in Asia at that time. However, the 2010 Asian population structure masks considerable heterogeneity among populations arising from variability in the onset and pace of demographic transition. This heterogeneity is illustrated in Figure 23.2.

In order to summarize population ageing in Asia and yet retain important heterogeneity, groups of populations are considered. These include the four UN-defined regions within Asia: Eastern Asia, South-Central Asia, South-Eastern Asia and Western Asia. The countries of

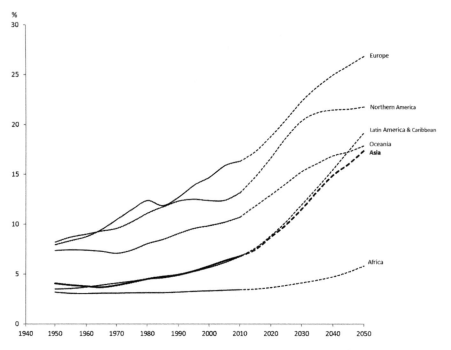

Figure 23.1 Population aged 65+ as a percentage of total population, world regions, 1950–2050
Note: Solid lines are estimates (1950–2010); dashed lines are projections (2011–2050).
Source: United Nations (2012).

each region are shown in Table 23.1. For South-Central Asia, Central Asia is distinguished from Southern Asia in some of the discussion, as the two subregions differ considerably with regard to population ageing. Similarly, the Arab and non-Arab populations of Western Asia are distinguished. As will be seen, the resulting six groups of populations are reasonably homogenous with respect to patterns of population ageing.

Trends in ageing in Asia and the four regions of Asia are seen in Figure 23.3, using the four measures previously introduced. For Asia as a whole, the percentage aged 65 or older was only 4.1 per cent in 1950; after a slight decline, this percentage reached 6.8 in 2010. The OADR declined marginally to 6.6 old-age persons per 100 working-age persons in 1965 and then increased steadily to 10.1 in 2010. The OASD declined from 10.0 per cent in 1950 to 8.2 per cent in 1965, and then increased to reach 21.1 per cent in 2010. The median age of the Asian population was 22.0 years in 1950, declined to 19.5 years by 1970 and increased to 28.8 years by 2010. The slight decreases in all measures in the first 10–20 years were a result of increasing child proportions due in part to the improved health and survival of women and children in the early stages of demographic transition and in part to a temporary increase in fertility in the first five years. This overall trend was reversed by the onset of fertility decline in the 1960s.

Declining fertility has been the main influence on population ageing in Asia, through the reduction in the relative size of the population aged 0–14. Different fertility experiences, in terms of the onset and speed of decline, have resulted in widely differing degrees of ageing. From the mid-1960s, Eastern Asia diverged from the rest of Asia. By 2010, the population aged 65 or older in Eastern Asia comprised 9.7 per cent of the total, while in the remaining three regions

Population ageing and its challenges

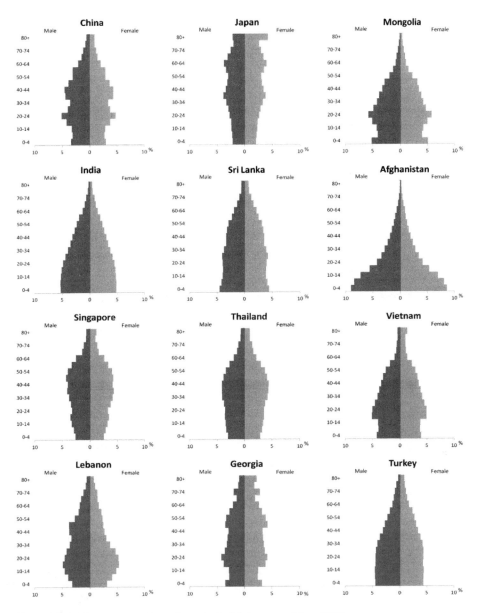

Figure 23.2 Age-sex structures for selected Asian countries, 2010
Source: United Nations (2012).

it comprised only 4.9–5.5 per cent. This divergence is greatest in the OASD (because of the direct effect of the child population as a part of the denominator of this measure). For Eastern Asia, the OASD increased from 9 per cent in 1965 to 35 per cent in 2010, compared with much smaller increases from 7–9 per cent to 14–16 per cent in the remaining three regions over the same period.

The OADR is less sensitive to changing fertility because diminished child proportions reduce the size of the working-age population (the denominator) only gradually and after a delay.

Table 23.1 Regions and subregions of Asia and constituent populations

Eastern Asia	South-Eastern Asia	South-Central Asia	Western Asia
China	Brunei	*South Asia*	*Arab*
Hong Kong	Cambodia	Afghanistan	Bahrain
Japan	Indonesia	Bangladesh	Iraq
Macao	Laos	Bhutan	Jordan
North Korea	Malaysia	India	Kuwait
Mongolia	Myanmar	Iran	Lebanon
South Korea	Philippines	Maldives	Oman
Taiwan	Singapore	Nepal	Qatar
	Thailand	Pakistan	Saudi Arabia
	Timor-Leste	Sri Lanka	Palestine
	Vietnam		Syria
		Central Asia	United Arab Emirates
		Kazakhstan	Yemen
		Kyrgyzstan	
		Tajikistan	*Non-Arab*
		Turkmenistan	Armenia
		Uzbekistan	Azerbaijan
			Cyprus
			Georgia
			Israel
			Turkey

Source: United Nations (2012).

Figure 23.3 shows that the OADR was 6–7 old-age persons per 100 working-age persons in all regions in 1950, with little change during the following two decades. By 2010, the OADR in Eastern Asia had doubled (13 per cent), but it had increased only marginally (to 8 per cent) in the remaining three regions. The median age of the regional populations declined to 18–20 years in 1970 before increasing to 35 years in 2010 in Eastern Asia, and 25–27 years in the remaining regions.

Variation within regions

Figure 23.4 shows trends and differentials in the percentage aged 65 or older in populations within the four regions, highlighting those that differ from, or are influential in determining, the broad regional trend. The patterns in this measure are for the most part also exhibited in the OADR, the OASD and the median age (graphs of these measures are not shown). Figure 23.4 clearly demonstrates the relative homogeneity within the regions (Eastern Asia[10] and South-Eastern Asia) and subregions (Southern Asia, Central Asia, Arab Western Asia and non-Arab Western Asia). Though Asia as a whole is demographically heterogeneous, much of the difference is between rather than within the six population groups.

The demographically-dominant population in Eastern Asia is China. The divergence of Eastern Asia from the remaining regions is attributable to the onset of fertility decline in China in the early 1970s. China's child population peaked as a percentage of the total population in 1965 and then rapidly declined, laying the foundations for population ageing. In 1965, 3.6 per cent of China's population was aged 65 or older, increasing to 8.4 per cent in 2010. Over the

Population ageing and its challenges

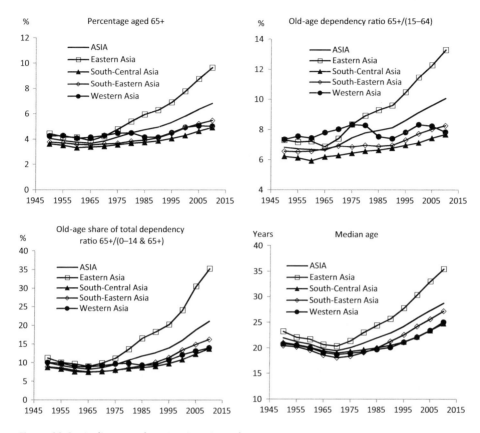

Figure 23.3 Indicators of ageing in Asia and Asian regions, 1950–2010
Source: United Nations (2012).

same period, the OADR increased steadily from 6.6 to 11.4 per cent, the OASD increased from 8.1 to 31.5 per cent, and the median age from 24 to 35 years.

Advanced population ageing makes Japan a clear outlier in Eastern Asia, despite this being the oldest region of the four. Indeed, Japan leads the world in population ageing, with 23 per cent of the population being aged 65 or older in 2010. In the same year, the OADR was 36.0 old-age persons per 100 working-age persons, the OASD reached 63 per cent, and the median age of the population was 45 years. The demographic transition began in Japan in the early twentieth century; by 1950, total fertility was as low as 3.0 births per woman and below-replacement fertility was reached within the next decade (see Chapter 5 of the handbook) with total fertility levels below 1.5 from 1993. However, Japan's continuing population ageing in recent decades is also due to increasing longevity. As discussed in Chapter 11 of the handbook, Japan has the highest life expectancy at age 65 in the world.

Mongolia also stands out from the rest of the region, but it does so because of a very low degree of population ageing. The percentage aged 65 or older was only 3.8 per cent in 2010, which is lower than in 1950. This is attributable to earlier pronatalist policies which contributed to high fertility and delayed fertility decline (Neupert 1994).

The populations of South-Central Asia are grouped into two subregions: Southern Asia and Central Asia. As seen in Figure 23.4, these subregions exhibit different patterns of ageing. The

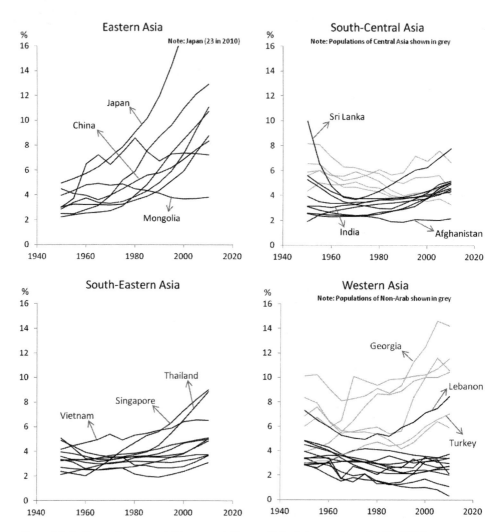

Figure 23.4 Percentage aged 65+, populations within Asian regions, 1950–2010
Source: United Nations (2012).

populations of South Asia were generally younger than the populations of Central Asia in the early part of the period. However, since about 1970 the percentage aged 65 or older has slowly increased in most countries of Southern Asia while it has slowly decreased in most countries of Central Asia.

The most populous and therefore demographically-dominant population in Southern Asia is India. The old-age population comprised 3.2 per cent of the total Indian population in 1965, increasing to only 5.1 per cent in 2010. Over the same period, the OADR increased from 5.8 to 7.8 per cent, the OASD from 7.7 to 14.4 per cent, and the median age from 19.6 to 25.5 years. This slow pace of population ageing in India can largely be attributed to relatively slow fertility decline prior to 1970 (see Chapter 5 of the handbook); the initial decline in mortality would also have served to retard or reverse population ageing.

Population ageing and its challenges

Two exceptions to the general trend in Southern Asia are Sri Lanka and Afghanistan. In Sri Lanka, emigration following independence in 1948 contributed to a relatively large older population in the 1950s, which quickly normalized but increased again after 1970 as a result of relatively early fertility decline. Afghanistan experienced slight reverse ageing, and on all measures ended the period noticeably lower than other populations in the region. In 2010, only 2.2 per cent of the population were aged 65 or older, the OADR was 4.4 per cent, the OASD was 4.3 per cent, and the median age of 15.6 years shows that almost half the population were children – clearly, this lack of population ageing is due to continuing high fertility (Chapter 5 of the handbook) and to some extent by reduced mortality given the low life expectancy in this population.

The Central Asian populations had a relatively high degree of population ageing in 1950 and most experienced an overall decrease, albeit with fluctuation, a pattern resulting mainly from large pre-1950 population losses due to starvation, war and the emigration of the young adult population combined with slow fertility decline (Chapter 5 of the handbook). The single exception to this regional pattern of reverse ageing is Kazakhstan, where the old-age proportion of the population increased from 5.2 per cent in 1965 to 6.7 per cent in 2010. Factors contributing to Kazakhstan's population ageing include a decline in fertility to below-replacement levels during 1996–2003 and return migration after independence in 1991.

Most of the populations of South-Eastern Asia experienced little change in terms of population ageing, and the degree of ageing remains low. Three populations merit further consideration. Singapore experienced rapid population ageing: the old-age proportion increased from 2.6 per cent in 1965 to 9.0 per cent in 2010, attributable to early and rapid fertility decline to below-replacement levels from as early as 1977, reaching less than 1.5 births per woman from 1998. Though life expectancy in Singapore is among the highest in the world, this has relatively little effect on population ageing because the old-age proportion is small. The population structure of Singapore is dominated by large-scale temporary labour migration, inflating total population size and moderating measures of ageing. Over the period 1965 to 2010, the OADR increased from 4.9 to 12.2 per cent, the OASD from 5.7 to 34.2 per cent, and the median age from 18.1 to 37.3 years.

Thailand experienced rapid population ageing after 1990, a legacy of rapid fertility decline between 1970 and 1990 with further declines at below-replacement levels from 1991. The percentage aged 65 or older reached 8.9 per cent in 2010, while the OADR reached 12.4 per cent, the OASD reached 31.4 per cent, and the median age reached 35.4 years.

Population ageing began relatively early in Vietnam, but the pace of change has been moderate. The old-age population is relatively small because of deaths during the Vietnam War (1955–1975) and post-war emigration, and though fertility declined rapidly between 1970 and 2000, the large cohorts born during the war years produced increasing numbers of births until about 1990. Over the period 1965 to 2010, the old-age proportion increased from 5.0 to 6.5 per cent, the OASD increased from 10.2 to 21.8 per cent and the median age from 19.1 to 28.5 years. However, the OADR declined from 9.7 to 9.3 per cent, reflecting the increase in the working age population due to the large cohorts born during and after the war.

The two subregions of Western Asia differ considerably. The Arab populations had lower old-age proportions in 1950 and yet for the most part experienced declining proportions. In contrast, the non-Arab populations experienced higher and, in the latter period, increasing old-age proportions.

Among the Arab populations, high fertility or late fertility decline contributed to reverse ageing, while temporary labour in-migration (see Chapter 17 of the handbook) had the same effect. This group is remarkably homogeneous with respect to both level and trend. Lebanon is the sole exception, with substantially higher old-age proportions over the entire period and rapid population ageing from the mid-1980s. This pattern of ageing can be attributed partly to Lebanon's steady fertility decline, from the relatively moderate 5.7 in the 1950s to 2.1 by 2001 and 1.5 by 2010 (see Chapter 5), and partly to rapid mortality decline (especially more recently at older ages) and relatively recent high rates of emigration (Hourani and Shehadi 1992). Between 1965 and 2010, the old-age proportion of the population increased from 5.3 to 8.4 per cent, the OADR from 9.5 to 12.5 per cent, the OASD from 10.8 to 26.3 per cent and the median age from 18.7 to 28.5 years.

The non-Arab populations are relatively heterogeneous. Georgia is the oldest population in the region, due to very early fertility decline. Total fertility was 3.0 in 1960 and has been below replacement level since 1992. However, stagnating old-age mortality in recent decades has moderated the pace of ageing (Chapter 11 of the handbook). Over the period 1965 to 2010, the old-age proportion increased from 8.1 to 14.2 per cent, the OADR from 13.4 to 20.8 per cent, the OASD from 20.5 to 45.1 per cent and the median age from 28.0 to 37.0 years.

In contrast, Turkey – the most populous country in Western Asia – is characterized by a low degree of population ageing linked to moderate fertility decline, only reaching replacement level in 2010. Between 1965 and 2010, the old-age proportion increased from 3.7 to only 7.1 per cent, the OADR from 6.9 to 10.6 per cent, the OASD from 7.8 to 20.9 per cent, and the median age from 18.6 to 28.3 years.

Divergence and heterogeneity

It is clear that variation in the onset and pace of the demographic transition has resulted in a widening range of experience of population ageing across Asia. The median age provides an easily interpretable indicator of the heterogeneity of ageing. Though at the regional level the median age varies by only 3 years in 1950 and 11 years in 2010 (see Figure 23.3), individual populations vary by as much as 10 years in 1950 and 29 years in 2010. Divergence in the median age of Asian populations is occurring as a result of both ageing and reverse ageing. The maximum median age increased substantially over the 60-year period, from 27.3 years in Georgia in 1950 to 44.9 years in Japan in 2010. Meanwhile, the minimum median age declined by 1.6 years – despite recent increases – from 17.2 years in Jordan to 15.6 years in Afghanistan.

Map 23.1 shows change in the median age between 1950 and 2010 for all populations. The most rapid increases in ageing, as measured by the median age, have occurred in Japan (22.5 years), South Korea (18.8), Taiwan (17.9), Singapore (17.4), Hong Kong (17.3) and Thailand (16.8 years). All of these populations have experienced rapid demographic transition. In contrast, reverse ageing occurred in Timor-Leste (-3.6 years), Iraq (-2.9), Afghanistan (-2.9), Kyrgyzstan (-1.5), Tajikistan (-1.1) and Yemen (-0.7 years). These six populations experienced warfare or significant unrest in previous decades, conditions which contribute to the death or emigration of young adults (many who would now have reached old age), and which tend to favour the maintenance of higher fertility (than might otherwise be the case) to maximize population size or strength. For most populations, however, the median age increased by modest amounts: for 33 of the 51 populations the median age increased by less than 10 years over the 60-year period.

The OASD differentiates more clearly the degree of population ageing. Figure 23.5 shows this measure in 1950 and 2010 by population grouped by region or subregion. It is seen that ageing increases in both degree and heterogeneity, and that there is little similarity in the patterns over time. Figure 23.6 (left-hand graph) further examines the relationship between the OASD in 1950 and 2010. In this figure, the change in the degree of ageing is represented by the vertical

Population ageing and its challenges

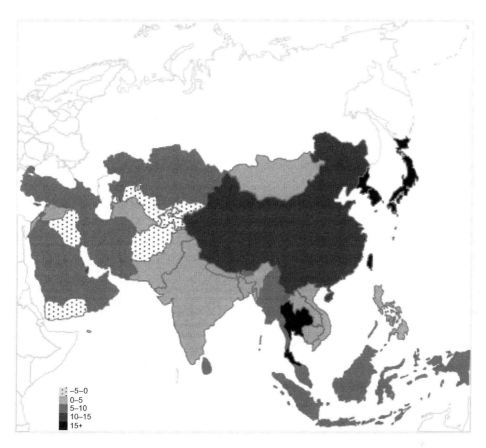

Map 23.1 Countries of Asia showing change in the median age, 1950–2010
Source: United Nations (2012).

distance from the diagonal line: the populations situated below the diagonal experienced reverse ageing, while those above the diagonal experienced ageing. It is seen that more than half of the 51 populations are clustered at low levels of ageing in both 1950 and 2010, indicating that the process of population ageing is still in its early stages in most of Asia. Most of these populations are the Arab countries of Western Asia, and the less-developed countries of South-Central Asia and South-Eastern Asia. Heterogeneity in the OASD in 2010 and its distribution across Asia are seen in Map 23.2.

The process of population ageing is less apparent when change in the OADR, which is also shown in Figure 23.6 (right-hand graph), is considered. Indeed, reverse ageing between 1950 and 2010 is indicated in 24 of the 51 populations, almost double the number identified by the OASD. These temporal decreases in the OADR are the result of an increased working-age proportion of the population due to a reduced child population (see Chapter 24 of the handbook). Map 23.3 shows that in 2010 the OADR was generally low and much less heterogeneous than the OASD. As a measure of population ageing, the OADR is conservative, short-sighted and potentially misleading. Its widespread use to monitor the economic challenges of population ageing is problematic.

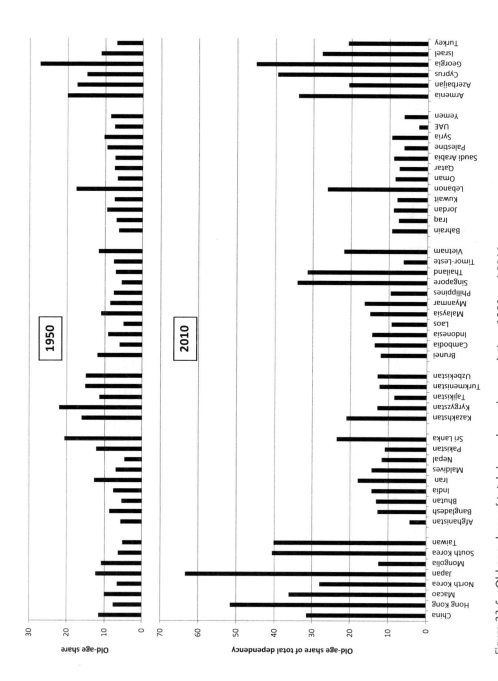

Figure 23.5 Old-age share of total dependency, by population, 1950 and 2010
Source: United Nations (2012).

Population ageing and its challenges

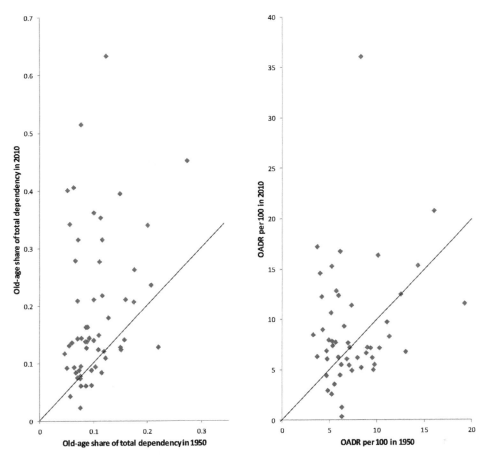

Figure 23.6 Relationship between degree of ageing in 1950 and 2010, old-age share of total dependency and OADR
Source: United Nations (2012).

The challenges of population ageing

Population ageing presents considerable challenges, the most significant of which are the provision of income support and personal care to the old-age population.[11] The magnitude of these challenges varies according to the pace and degree of population ageing, stemming from their different experiences of demographic transition and international migration, in the context of socioeconomic change. While population ageing is conceptualized at the population level, it is reflected in the generational structure of the family, and hence its challenges also occur within the family. In Asia, the provision of support and care for the older population is addressed primarily within the family, though state responses to population ageing are becoming increasingly involved, especially in countries where norms of family support are weakening (Liu, Han, Xiao, Li and Feldman 2015).

Population ageing and the family

Traditionally in most societies, the family (or kin) is the sole source of support in old age. This traditional system of social security is institutionalized in the 'intergenerational contract'[12]

443

Heather Booth

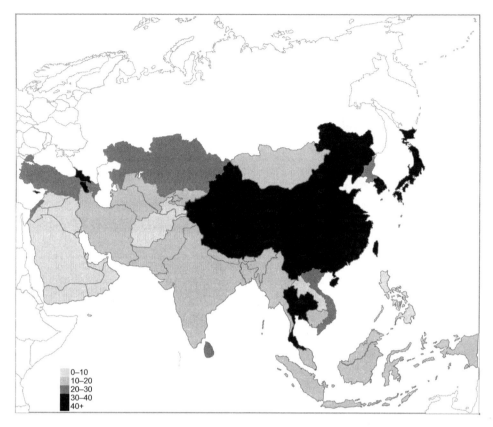

Map 23.2 Countries of Asia showing old-age share of total dependency (per cent), Asia, 2010
Sources: Data from United Nations (2012). Map from http://d-maps.com/pays.php?num_pay=65&lang=en (accessed 25 December 2014).

whereby successive generations care for their parents (or older kin), and in turn are cared for by their children (or younger kin). The intergenerational contract is deeply rooted in the demographic evolution of the population through birth, marriage and death and the associated cultural system (Lee 2007), and has roots in the doctrine of filial piety. Traditionally, the intergenerational contract is operationalized through the multi-generation household.

With the advent of demographic transition and population ageing, the viability of the intergenerational contract is brought into question. Within the family, there are fewer members to provide support and care for each elder. In China, the '4-2-1 problem' arises because the only child is responsible for two parents and four grandparents. This leads to potential hardship not only for the sole supporter (who may also have a dependent child or children) but also for the elders obliged to share the finite support. Though the situation in China is more acute, this problem exists to some degree in many Asian countries.

The challenges of the new demographic balance are compounded by ongoing economic and social change. Successive generations are better educated, more likely to work in the formal sector, more likely to migrate for education or work, more likely to live in an urban environment and, as a result, less likely to live in a multi-generation household. While the current working generation may have higher income, and might thus be considered more able to provide support to ageing parents, the demands on their income are greater, especially in an urban environment.

Population ageing and its challenges

Map 23.3 Countries of Asia showing old-age dependency ratio per 100, 2010
Source: United Nations (2012).

The education of children, often a reason for entering the formal labour market, is also a major expenditure. The working generation is 'squeezed' in terms of their financial responsibilities towards others.

The physical care of the elderly also presents challenges for families in the context of the modern economy, because of the need for proximity and time. In some countries, enhanced longevity has significantly increased the prevalence of frailty, bringing the need for types of care that consume more time and resources. Traditionally, in many parts of Asia, responsibility for the care of aged parents falls on the eldest son, and in particular on his wife, through coresidence. However, the traditional role of the daughter-in-law is incompatible with the increased educational attainment and labour force participation of women. Not only are higher status women asserting their independence, but the daily schedule imposed by formal-sector employment is incompatible with the role of domestic worker and informal carer. The changing status of women presents challenges for informal aged care, and in many populations the norms of family support practices for the elderly are weakening.

Despite the pressures of the modern economy on the working generation, the intergenerational contract or filial piety is largely maintained throughout Asia. Filial obligations towards the older generation are often met through adaptation rather than through traditional practices.

An important adaptation is financial support through private transfers and migrant remittances (including gifts) by children who do not reside with elderly parents. These constitute a significant source of support in countries such as China, Philippines and Vietnam. Living arrangements and the delivery of informal care are also adapted and diversified. In China, daughters are assuming increasing responsibility for elderly parents (Liu, Han, Xiao, Li and Feldman 2015). In Vietnam, rural elders often live near but not with their children, a living arrangement that affords greater independence to both generations while still maintaining daily contact and care. In urban areas, some Vietnamese elders live with a married daughter rather than married eldest son. In other cases, a domestic helper is employed to take care of elderly parent(s) (Hoang 2016). Elders with migrant children may live with a grandchild, and receive financial support from the migrant; this commonly occurs in China (Cong and Silverstein 2008) and Vietnam (Hoang 2016).

These adaptations also involve a shift in intergenerational expectations. Older family members often recognize the pressures on their adult children, leading to changed attitudes and transformed expectations. In Vietnam, children's fulfilment of filial piety is now manifest less in coresidence and domestic work, and more in educational success and a good career, ensuring good returns on the earlier investment by parents. Attitudinal change enables Vietnamese elders to benefit from daughters, who often contribute physically and financially to the well-being of their parents (Hoang 2016).

A significant adaptation is evident in the emergence of private residential aged care, for example in China and Vietnam, though the cost is often prohibitive. At the other extreme, Vietnamese state-run residential accommodation, which was formerly reserved for the destitute, is now accessible on a fee-paying basis to elders whose children have no other way to support them. The considerable social stigma associated with residential aged care is being slowly eroded at both ends of the economic spectrum.

Population ageing and the state

The challenge of population ageing is increasingly being addressed through state responses. These population-level measures address population ageing either directly through policies and programmes or indirectly through legislation enabling public and private employers to provide security in old age. For the state, the major challenge is to institute and regulate sustainable social security systems that provide adequate and affordable income support in old age, while also ensuring a social safety net.[13] In some more advanced economies, the social security systems extend to aged care.

The development of old-age social security programmes in Asia has been relatively slow when compared with other countries at similar levels of development. Indeed, many Asian countries have now reached a point of GDP per capita at which comprehensive welfare systems have historically tended to be implemented (Chomik and Piggott 2014). This is attributable to the strength of the doctrine of filial piety in the dominant religions of the region, most notably the influence of Confucian philosophy in Eastern and South-Eastern Asia, and to concerns that the development of social security systems would undermine the role of the family (Turner 2002). In several countries (for example, China, South Korea, Singapore and Vietnam), family responsibility for older family members is enshrined in law, though this does not preclude state systems.

Contributory social security systems provide income in retirement according to the level of payments made while working. There are two main approaches: unfunded programmes, commonly in the form of a social insurance scheme[14] provided by the state, and pre-funded programmes in the form of an individual or pooled savings scheme[15] in either the public or private sector. The design of social security systems varies across Asia and can comprise complimentary programmes (Chomik 2013).

Social insurance schemes provide an income-based defined-benefit pension for the remaining duration of life. Mandatory social insurance schemes have existed for some years in many countries, including most Arab countries, Japan, South Korea, Pakistan, the Philippines, Thailand and Vietnam (Turner 2002). In addition, the countries of Central and Western Asia that formed part of the former Soviet Union inherited the relatively generous Soviet defined-benefit pension scheme (Falkingham and Vlachantoni 2012).

Population ageing presents a major challenge to the fiscal sustainability of social insurance schemes. In advanced population ageing, a high ratio of pension recipients to contributors threatens the sustainability of schemes, especially those that have relatively low eligibility ages or where working lives have decreased due to later entry to the workforce. In Asia, many countries allow access to pensions at ages as low as 55 for men and 50 for women (OECD 2012). In China, Indonesia and Thailand, indications are that working lives have recently decreased, while India, Japan and Korea also have relatively short working lives (Chen, Eggleston and Li 2012). Raising the retirement age is an appealing solution because it both increases contributions (assuming low levels of older-worker unemployment) and reduces pension eligibility. Other reforms include bringing contributions and benefits into line with each other in the context of increased longevity, through higher contributions or reduced benefits or both, and transitioning from defined-benefit towards defined-contribution systems. Such reforms were hastened in the countries of the former Soviet Union by economic dislocation in the early 1990s (Falkingham and Vlachantoni 2012).

Mandatory workers' savings (defined-contribution) schemes have historically been implemented through provident funds in Brunei, India, Indonesia, Malaysia, Nepal, Singapore and Sri Lanka (Turner 2002). Hong Kong introduced a workers' mandatory provident fund in 2000. Provident funds typically provide lump-sum benefits and thus do not necessarily provide lifelong protection. In recognition of the longevity risk – or outliving one's resources – Singapore and other countries have more recently introduced legislation to compel retirees to take part of their benefit in the form of an annuity providing regular income for remaining life. Private-sector savings schemes have become more widespread with the transition to a market economy in socialist countries such as Cambodia, Laos, Mongolia and Vietnam. However, many such schemes are immature, with members still in the accumulation phase, and substantial retirement benefits have yet to flow. In Vietnam, for example, after satisfying an eligibility constraint of 20 years of contributions, the first pensions were drawn in 2015 (Hoang 2016).

For most of Asia, contributory social security systems are inadequate. The main problems are partial coverage, inequity and a low level of benefit (Park 2012b; Chomik 2013). Typically programmes initially cover (or favour) state employees and the military, and are only later extended to the private sector where they often remain limited to large formal-sector establishments. In Lebanon, for example, only the military and security forces receive pensions and health benefits in retirement, and dependant wives lose these benefits in widowhood, while in the private sector defined benefits take the form of a lump-sum rather than a pension (Abdulrahim, Ajrouch and Antonucci 2015).

China introduced an urban defined-benefit pension system as early as 1951. Initially covering only state and urban collective sectors, Basic Pension Insurance has more recently been extended to urban private enterprises (Qin, Zhuang and Liu 2015). In 2009, the voluntary New Rural Social Pension scheme was introduced, financed primarily through personal accounts and incentivized by government subsidies. Members qualify for a full pension by contributing for at least

15 years. Those aged 65 or older in 2009 receive the basic pension if a family member aged 16 or older participates in the scheme (Qin, Zhuang and Liu 2015). This innovative system combines family support and state social security regulation, providing income security in old age while enabling filial piety obligations to be met through formalized channels. With the passage of time most members will have 'earned' their own defined-benefit pension, but the family-determined safety net will remain.

Similarly, in Vietnam, voluntary social insurance is available to workers in the informal sector and to the unemployed, with a pension eligibility constraint of 20 years of contributions (Hoang 2016). However, for many workers in the informal sector, which accounts for some 50 per cent of the labour force in the ESCAP region[16] (ESCAP 2015), the concept of retirement is inapplicable; labour force participation rates remain high in old age, and the family is the only source of security. In a retrograde development, the reform of social security systems of the countries of the former Soviet Union has often led to the exclusion of the informal sector because of costs to employers (Falkingham and Vlachantoni 2012).

Migrant workers are also disadvantaged in social security systems. In many Arab countries, social insurance schemes historically exclude foreign workers (Turner and Lichtenstein 2002; ILO 2015). In China, 70 per cent of rural–urban migrants have no social insurance; this has been attributed to eligibility being based on household registration and the difficulty of inter-provincial transfers (Qin, Zhuang and Liu 2015).

While various reforms have helped to address some of the inadequacies of social security systems, further steps are needed to promote and achieve fairness and sustainability. Park (2012a) has identified three priorities for states: recognition of the urgency posed by the rapidity of population ageing, the fostering of consumer trust by ensuring the sustainability of social security systems, and the management of the longevity risk through an increased but flexible retirement age. Regarding the latter, it is worthy of note that, due to low retirement ages and increased life expectancy, some Asian populations now live longer on average in retirement than do some populations in the West. The challenge of meeting social security needs is substantial, but Chomik (2013: 1) notes that in many countries the combination of the stage in the demographic transition (or the demographic dividend – Chapters 21 and 24) and the relative immaturity of social insurance programmes actually presents 'the perfect opportunity' to ensure the right balance between fiscal sustainability and adequacy.

Until adequate contributory social security systems are in place, many older Asians will continue to rely on the state safety net (social pension) if such provision exists (Hagemejer and Schmitt 2012). Universal (age-based) safety nets exist in China, Hong Kong, Japan, South Korea, Nepal, Philippines, Thailand and several of the countries of the former Soviet Union. The Five Guarantee System in China was introduced as early as 1956. Targeted (means-tested) safety nets, guaranteeing income security for underprivileged older people, exist in Bangladesh, Mongolia, Sri Lanka and Vietnam, among others. Thailand introduced a targeted social pension scheme in 1993, and in 2009 this allowance was essentially made universal with an eligibility age of 60 years (Suwanrada and Wesumperuma 2012).

However, the value of non-contributory social pensions is very low. The most generous is Japan's National Pension at 16 per cent of the average wage, but others provide at best 5 per cent (Chomik 2013). In the countries of the former Soviet Union, the social pension does not meet the subsistence minimum (Falkingham and Vlachantoni 2012). This situation is echoed across Asia. Nevertheless social pensions provide an important source of income for the poorest sections of the older population, particularly for older women because of their multiple disadvantages in the labour market and over-representation among the poor (Vlachantoni and Falkingham 2012).

In addition to income protection, long-term care is a major area of vulnerability in old age. Social insurance for long-term care exists in only a few countries. Israel's long-term care social insurance scheme, which began in 1988, provides benefits for home-care services (Borowski 2015). Long-term care social insurance was introduced in Japan in 2000 and South Korea in 2008; both schemes are comprehensive in providing benefits for home and institutional care to elders aged 65 or older (and to the younger-old if disabled) (Ozawa and Nakayama 2005; Kang, Park and Lee 2012). However, coverage rates can be low; in South Korea, only 6 per cent of the older population had long-term care insurance in 2012 (Choi 2013). Taiwan plans to introduce long-term care social insurance in 2018 (Nadash and Shih 2013; Taiwan Today 2015).

Social safety nets also encompass long-term care and may take the form of residential aged care. State establishments for the destitute exist in several countries including Malaysia, Vietnam and Singapore. In other settings, the destitute are given shelter by religious establishments, as in the case of Tibetans in Nepal (Childs 2001).

The family, the state and elder well-being

In Asia, the family assumes the major responsibility for old-age support, and does so in a variety of settings shaped by the design and adequacy of state social security systems. The interface between family and state in the provision of old-age support influences the level of support and how it is delivered. The ultimate goal of all systems of old-age support is the well-being of older members of the population (Hermalin 1997). Perspectives differ as to how this is best achieved.

In Singapore, public assistance for older citizens is deliberately kept to a minimum (Park 2012a: 89), while various policies encourage and assist the family to provide support. Coresidence of elderly parents and children was encouraged through tax incentives, preferential housing allocation, and housing design for co-location (Lee 1999). In 2005, 70 per cent of non-institutionalized elders aged 65 or older lived with their children (Singapore Ministry of Social and Family Development 2014).

This focus on living arrangement in the provision of old-age support is shared by Japan and South Korea (Doling and Ronald 2011). In all three countries, the state encourages home ownership and generational co-location as a means of meeting the income needs of older family members and increasing their well-being. Home ownership provides families with the physical, emotional and financial foundation from which to support older members. Further, older home-owners are able to meet their income needs from housing equity, although this has implications for issues of inheritance and intergenerational relations. This perspective is essentially a revival of the traditional multi-generation household model of old-age care.

In Vietnam, recent research shows that the multi-generation household is associated with better subjective well-being. However, the well-being disadvantage of some non-traditional living arrangements (elderly-couple households and elders living with a grandchild) is counterbalanced by material and instrumental intergenerational support (Hoang 2016). Similarly, in rural China, living with a grandchild has been found beneficial in terms of both the financial support and well-being of elders (Cong and Silverstein 2008). These findings suggest that, contrary to common opinion (Knodel 1999), labour migration is not detrimental to the well-being of elderly parents who are left behind.

Different perspectives and designs also affect the efficacy of social safety nets in supporting elder well-being, as demonstrated by comparison of South Korea and Taiwan (Choi and Kim 2010). In South Korea, non-contributory, low-level allowances are household-means-tested, and family support capability is taken into account. In Taiwan, non-contributory, low-level, flat-rate allowances are individual-means-tested, and family support is supplementary. Comparing ten-year outcomes, in South Korea neither public assistance nor family support changed relative to total old-age income, whereas in Taiwan both increased leading to significant reductions in poverty. The Taiwanese system is also more favourable to the fulfilment of filial obligations, supporting social and psychological well-being.

There is mounting evidence that social safety nets are instrumental in reducing elder poverty and increasing well-being, particularly in poorer countries. In Bangladesh, the old-age allowance has improved impoverished older people's ability to meet basic needs, enhanced their status in the household, and improved their psychological well-being (Begum and Wesumperuma 2012). Similar benefits have been identified elsewhere, including Nepal (Samson 2012), Thailand (Suwanrada and Wesumperuma 2012) and Vietnam (Babajanian 2012). Social allowances also enable recipients to invest in livestock or microbusinesses, to meet health costs, and to contribute to social and religious activities (Suwanrada and Wesumperuma 2012). In Vietnam, independent income, no matter how small, supports elder well-being through enabling elders to engage in intergenerational exchanges; and rural elders often live alone, albeit close to family members, so as to qualify by being a 'poor household' for the safety net allowance (Hoang 2016). In China, the New Rural Social Pension has improved the quality of life of elders by increasing their self-confidence and ability to support themselves (Liu, Han, Xiao, Li and Feldman 2015).

Long-term care insurance has also been found to bestow significant well-being benefits, not only for elders but also for their carers. In Israel, insurance reduced the demand for residential aged care, as was intended, and also reduced informal carers' sense of burden, though the benefit tended to supplement rather than substitute the hours of care they provided (Borowski 2015). In Japan, almost all care recipients were satisfied with the care they received, and their family members reported positive impacts on their own lives (Ozawa and Nakayama 2005).

Population ageing and society

Population ageing and old-age security must be viewed as an integral part of wider social development. The ways in which society experiences population ageing derives from the socio-economic context. At the state level, the social security costs of population ageing provide an important imperative for many countries to 'get rich before getting old' (Lee, Mason and Park 2011). However, achieving social security depends as much on the global economy as on the systems in place. The Asian Financial Crisis in 1997 and the Global Financial Crisis of 2007–2008 were significant setbacks for many Asian economies, sometimes resulting in reduced old-age and other benefits. However, Asia recovered with remarkable speed and vigour (Lee and Ofreneo 2014).

While socioeconomic development has enhanced the capacity of states to develop formal social security systems, these are largely financed through the contributions and taxation of the working generation. The operationalization of the financial aspect of the intergenerational contract is thus being transformed. The current working generation are on the cusp of this societal transformation and, in bridging old and new, provides for two generations in old age: the current old-age generation through private transfers and taxation to support safety net schemes, and their own generation through mandatory savings or social insurance schemes. Successive generations expect less and less to depend on their children for old-age security (Ogawa 2008; Hoang 2016), underlining the need to provide for oneself in old age. Thus, the solutions to population ageing can impose a heavy burden on the working generation in the transitional situation, particularly as this generation can expect to live longer in retirement. The older generation are vulnerable to the changes taking place, because they are to a large extent dependent on the degree to which members of the working generation are able to successfully negotiate change.

In Japan, the older generation act as a safety net for children who encounter financial difficulties (Ogawa 2008); that they are able to do so is an outcome of accumulated wealth through Japan's well-established old-age security system.

An important aspect of socioeconomic development is changing gender relations. Gender plays an important role in both population ageing and meeting the challenges of ageing. Population ageing is inextricably linked to the status of women through the latter's role in fertility decline (Mason 2001; McDonald 2000). Old-age security has been traditionally met through gendered cultural practices such as son preference and the subservience of women especially in the role of daughter-in-law. Changing socioeconomic and demographic circumstances exert an influence on such norms. Evidence from rural China shows that when social security is available, son preference is weaker (Ebenstein and Leung 2010). Increasing education and formal sector employment weaken the norms of coresidence with eldest son and the provision of informal aged care by his wife as daughter-in-law. The demographic reality in low fertility populations, especially China, is that many elders (or future elders) do not have a son. Thus, daughters are assuming greater responsibility for elderly parents in such populations. In urban Vietnam, high status women often provide and fund personal and medical care for their own parents and not for their parents-in-law, a change often welcomed by elders (Hoang 2016). Rather than being detrimental to the well-being of elderly parents (Knodel 1999), weakening norms and changing gender relations may be beneficial for some elders.

The incompatibility of the increasing status of women and informal aged care can have far-reaching implications. In parts of South-Eastern Asia, educated women are choosing not to marry, particularly an eldest son, because of filial duties as carer of parents-in-law (Raymo, Park, Xie and Yeung 2015). The 'preferred' son is of reduced benefit if he does not marry as the intergenerational contract is devalued; neither are grandchildren produced. In such situations, social security systems gain importance. Further, low female marriage rates contribute to low fertility, promoting further population ageing.

In contrast, in parts of South Asia, son preference remains strong and the status of women remains low. For these populations, social security systems remain relatively undeveloped: in India, for example, only a small proportion of older men have access to pensions. Widowed Indian women often do not receive entitlements due to being unaware of their rights, and in patrilineal/patrilocal societies may not receive familial support (Dasvarma 2008). In such societies, the intergenerational contract is heavily gender-biased: women are obliged as daughters-in-law to provide aged care for their parents-in-law, but may be denied the same care in widowhood when they need it most. The low status of women is also manifest in high levels of early and arranged marriage and associated early childbearing, which contribute to higher fertility and population growth than would otherwise occur, curtailing population ageing.

The process of population ageing will continue in Asian populations for many decades. By 2050, the population aged 65 or older is expected to comprise 17.4 per cent of the population of Asia (Figure 23.1) and 36.5 per cent of the population of Japan (United Nations 2012). In the longer term, demographic transition theory indicates that population ageing will end and age structures will be much older than they are today. With such prospects, it is highly likely that states will take steps aimed at increasing fertility. Such steps have been implemented in Japan, while China recently abandoned its one-child policy.[17] However, policies aimed at increasing fertility have proved unsuccessful in Japan (Tsuya 2015) and around the world (McDonald 2013). Further, such policies naively assume that the issues of population ageing can be addressed through long-term mitigation. In contrast, and by necessity, families are meeting the challenges of ageing through the adaptation of traditional norms to present-day realities. Rather than focus on the uncertain long term, state policies that support such adaptation, through state social security systems and other enabling measures, would seem more appropriate and may offer synergies. In the short to medium term, how societies meet the social security challenges of population ageing will determine the well-being of the older and working generations alike. The earlier these challenges are addressed, the easier it will be to do so, and the more effective the outcome.

Acknowledgements

The author is grateful to Xiaoguang Jia for research assistance including the creation of figures and tables and to Cuc Hoang for contributing knowledge from her doctoral research on Vietnam. This chapter has benefited from helpful comments from Rafal Chomik and the editors, Zhongwei Zhao and Adrian Hayes.

Notes

1. The stable population model describes a theoretical population in which fertility and mortality rates remain constant and the population is closed to migration. In the long term, the age structure of the population and the population growth rate will become constant. The model can be used to demonstrate the long-term implications of current fertility and mortality rates if they were to persist. For further details, see Preston, Heuveline and Guillot (2001).
2. Fertility decline may not at first result in smaller numbers of births if women of childbearing age are increasing sufficiently to counterbalance the decline. The post-transitional degree of ageing depends on the rapidity of the transition, particularly the pace of fertility decline.
3. In the demographic transition, the initial decline in mortality rates at first benefits younger ages more than older ages, contributing to reverse population ageing. This inhibits the ageing effect of the initial fertility decline both directly and indirectly through an increased proportion of women in the reproductive ages. As the mortality decline continues, it increasingly benefits older ages to a greater degree than younger ages, contributing to population ageing. The threshold for mortality decline to produce population ageing is a life expectancy of about 65 years (Preston, Heuveline and Guillot 2001: 160).
4. Mortality decline will lead to fewer deaths, and hence serve to increase population growth, but as already noted, reduced mortality may lead to either population ageing or reverse population ageing, depending on the level of mortality.
5. Return migration often negates the reversed effect.
6. The OADR is a worker-centric measure. In contrast, the potential support ratio (PSR), which is simply the inverse of the OADR, is elder-centric in that it considers the number of working-age persons providing support for each old-age person.
7. An alternative measure is the 'ageing index' defined as the ratio OADR/YADR where YADR is the young-age dependency ratio or the ratio of the child population to the working-age population. The ageing index is equivalent to the ratio of the old-age and young-age populations; it does not involve the working-age population but contrasts the extremes of the age distribution, both of which contribute to population ageing.
8. More sophisticated measures of ageing, also based on population proportions, take labour force participation into account, so as to replace the crude 'working-age population' by the more meaningful 'working population' and the crude 'old-age' population by the 'retired'. Further refinement is gained by considering the 'scholar/trainee population' rather than the 'young-age population'. The data needed to implement these refinements are not readily available for all Asian countries, necessitating that the less-refined measures be adopted in this chapter.
9. This is the principle used by Sanderson and Scherbov (2013) in the so-called 'characteristics approach' which makes use of life tables; this is beyond the scope of this chapter.
10. Macao and Mongolia do not increase monotonically after 1970.
11. Other challenges include providing opportunities for younger and more educated workers in the context of an older work force seeking to maximize pension benefits, the political challenges of increasing the retirement age, and the political and social impacts of an older and generally more conservative population. The rise of the 'Third Age' (Laslett 1991) also 'requires' a change of attitudes towards ageing; fostering more positive attitudes towards old age often requires leadership and action at the state level.

12 The intergenerational contract is an unwritten agreement between successive generations, which is represented in the cultural practices of the society. It assumes that successive generations will honour the contract by providing care to the parental generation. Thus each generation provides parental care and later receives care. Similarly, each generation provides care to their offspring in childhood. In recent times, the intergenerational contract has undergone renegotiation and reinterpretation in favour of reciprocation between parent and child. See, for example, Croll (2006). In some cultures, a particular family member, such as eldest son or youngest daughter, traditionally bears the responsibility.
13 A strong economy is fundamental to meeting this challenge. For an economic discussion of population ageing in Asia, see Park, Lee and Mason (2012).
14 Social insurance schemes are described as unfunded because the benefit is drawn from current contributions rather than from the beneficiaries' own prior contributions. This form of social security most resembles the principle of the intergenerational contract in that the contributions of the working generation are used to provide benefits to the old-age generation.
15 Pre-funded or funded schemes provide benefits based on the beneficiaries' own invested contributions over their working life.
16 The ESCAP region omits Western Asia.
17 The change to a two-child policy, announced on 29 October 2015 and due to come into effect in 2016, is 'in order to balance population growth and offset the burden of an ageing population' (Xinhua News Agency, 10 November 2015, http://news.xinhuanet.com/english/2015-11/10/c_134802958.htm).

References

Abdulrahim, S., K. J. Ajrouch and T. C. Antonucci (2015) 'Ageing in Lebanon: challenges and opportunities'. *The Gerontologist*, 55(4): 511–518.
Babajanian, B. (2012) 'Social transfers for older persons: implications for policy, practice and research'. In S. W. Handayani and B. Babajanian (eds.) *Social Protection for Older Persons: Social Pensions in Asia*. Manila: Asian Development Bank.
Begum, S. and D. Wesumperuma (2012) 'Overview of the old age allowance programme in Bangladesh'. In S. W. Handayani and B. Babajanian (eds.) *Social Protection for Older Persons: Social Pensions in Asia*. Manila: Asian Development Bank.
Borowski, A. (2015) 'Israel's long-term care social insurance scheme after a quarter of a century'. *Journal of Aging and Social Policy*, 27(3): 195–214.
Chen, Q., K. Eggleston and L. Li (2012) 'Demographic change, intergenerational transfers and the challenges for social protection systems in the People's Republic of China'. In D. Park, S. H. Lee and A. Mason (eds.) *Aging, Economic Growth and Old-Age Security in Asia*. Manila and Cheltenham: Asian Development Bank and Edward Elgar.
Childs, G. (2001) 'Old-age security, religious celibacy and aggregate fertility in a Tibetan population'. *Journal of Population Research*, 18(1): 52–67.
Choi, S. J. (2013) 'Societal response to ageing society in Korea'. In S. J. Choi, J. N Bae, K. J. Min, Y. K. Roh and Y. H. Won (eds.) *Ageing in Korea: Today and Tomorrow*, Third Edition. Korea: Federation of Korean Gerontological Societies.
Choi, Y. J. and J. W. Kim (2010) 'Contrasting approaches to old-age income protection in Korea and Taiwan'. *Ageing and Society*, 30(7): 1135–1152.
Chomik, R. (2013) *Asia in the Ageing Century: Part II – Retirement Income*. Research Brief 2013/02, ARC Centre of Excellence in Population Ageing Research.
Chomik, R. and J. Piggott (2014) *Population Ageing and Social Security in Asia*. Working paper 2014/07, ARC Centre of Excellence in Population Ageing Research.
Cong, Z. and M. Silverstein (2008) 'Intergenerational time-for-money exchanges in rural China: does reciprocity reduce depressive symptoms of older grandparents?' *Research in Human Development*, 5(1): 6–25.
Croll, E. J. (2006) 'The intergenerational contract in the changing Asian family'. *Oxford Development Studies*, 34(4): 473–491.
Dasvarma, G. L. (2008) 'Challenges of Population Ageing: Australia and India'. Paper presented at the Conference on the Economic Implications of Indian Diaspora, Charles Darwin University and Indian Cultural Society, Darwin, June 2008.
Doling, J. and R. Ronald (2011) 'Meeting the income needs of older people in East Asia: using housing equity'. *Ageing and Society*, 32(3): 471–490.

Ebenstein, A. and S. Leung (2010) 'Son preference and access to social insurance: evidence from China's rural pension program'. *Population and Development Review*, 36(1): 47–70.

ESCAP (2015) Table 27.5 Employment by status, 1991–2013. Available from: www.unescap.org/resources/27-employment (accessed 18 May 2015).

Falkingham, J. and A. Vlachantoni (2012) 'Social protection for older people in Central Asia and the South Caucasus'. In S. W. Handayani and B. Babajanian (eds.) *Social Protection for Older Persons: Social Pensions in Asia*. Manila: Asian Development Bank.

Hagemejer, K. and V. Schmitt (2012) 'Providing social security in old age: the international labour organization view'. In S. W. Handayani and B. Babajanian (eds.) *Social Protection for Older Persons: Social Pensions in Asia*. Manila: Asian Development Bank.

Handayani, S. W. and B. Babajanian (eds.) (2012) *Social Protection for Older Persons: Social Pensions in Asia*. Manila: Asian Development Bank.

Hermalin, A. I. (1997) 'Drawing policy lessons for Asia from research on ageing'. *Asia-Pacific Population Journal*, 12(4): 89–102.

Hoang, C. (2016) *Modes of Care for the Elderly in Vietnam: Adaptation to Change*. Unpublished PhD thesis, The Australian National University, Canberra.

Hourani, A. and N. Shehadi (eds.) (1992) *The Lebanese in the World: A Century of Emigration*. London: Centre for Lebanese Studies.

International Labour Organization (ILO) (2015) *Arab States, Areas of Work, Social Security*. Available from: www.ilo.org/beirut/areasofwork/social-security/lang–en/index.htm (accessed 24 November 2015).

Jagger, C. and J. M. Robine (2011) 'Healthy life expectancy'. In R. G. Rogers and E. M. Crimmins (eds.) *International Handbook of Adult Mortality*. New York: Springer. Pp. 551–568.

Jones, G. W., T. H. Hull and D. Ahlburg (2000) 'The social and demographic impact of the Southeast Asian crisis of 1997–99'. *Journal of Population Research*, 17(1): 39–62.

Kang, I. O., C. Y. Park and Y. Lee (2012) 'Role of healthcare in Korean long-term care insurance'. *Journal of Korean Medical Science*, 27(suppl.): S41–S46.

Knodel, J. (1999) 'The demography of Asian ageing: past accomplishments and future challenges'. *Asia-Pacific Population Journal*, 14(4): 39–56.

Laslett, P. (1991) *A Fresh Map of Life: The Emergence of the Third Age*. Cambridge, MA: Harvard University Press.

Lee, H. A. and R. E. Ofreneo (2014) 'From Asian to Global Financial Crisis: recovery amidst expanding labour precarity'. *Journal of Contemporary Asia*, 44(4): 688–710.

Lee, R. D. (2007) 'Demographic change, welfare, and intergenerational transfers: a global overview'. In J. Véron, S. Pennec and J. Legare (eds.) *Ages, Generations and the Social Contract: The Demographic Challenges Facing the Welfare State*. The Netherlands: Springer.

Lee, S. H., A. Mason and D. Park (2011) 'Why does population aging matter so much for Asia? Population aging, economic security and economic growth in Asia'. Chapter 1 in D. Park, S. H. Lee and A. Mason (eds.) *Aging, Economic Growth and Old-Age Security in Asia*. Manila and Cheltenham: Asian Development Bank and Edward Elgar.

Lee, W. K. M. (1999) 'Economic and social implications of aging in Singapore'. *Journal of Aging and Social Policy*, 10(4): 73–92.

Liu, H., X. Han, Q. Xiao, S. Li and M. W. Feldman (2015) 'Family structure and quality of life of elders in rural China: the role of the New Rural Social Pension'. *Journal of Aging and Social Policy*, 27(2): 123–138.

Mason, K. O. (2001) 'Gender and family systems in the fertility transition'. *Population and Development Review*, 27(suppl.): 160–176.

McDonald, P. (2000) 'Gender equity, social institutions and the future of fertility'. *Journal of Population Research*, 17(1): 1–16.

McDonald, P. (2013) 'Low fertility: an East Asia dilemma'. *East Asia Forum Quarterly*, 5(1): 23–24.

Nadash, P. and Y. C. Shih (2013) 'Introducing social insurance for long-term care in Taiwan: key issues'. *International Journal of Social Welfare*, 22(1): 69–79.

Neupert, R. F. (1994) 'Fertility decline in Mongolia: trends, policies and explanations'. *International Family Planning Perspectives*, 20(1): 18–22.

Ogawa, N. (2008) 'The Japanese elderly as a social safety net'. *Asia-Pacific Population Journal*, 23(1): 105–113.

Organisation for Economic Co-operation and Development (OECD) (2012) *Pensions at a Glance Asia/Pacific 2011*. Available from: http://dx.doi.org/10.1787/9789264107007-en (accessed 24 November 2015).

Ozawa, M. N. and S. Nakayama (2005) 'Long-term care insurance in Japan'. *Journal of Aging and Social Policy*, 17(3): 61–84.

Park, D. (ed.) (2012a) *Pension Systems in East and Southeast Asia: Promoting Fairness and Sustainability*. Mandaluyong City: Asian Development Bank.

Park, D. (ed.) (2012b) *Pension Systems and Old-Age Income Support in East and Southeast Asia: Overview and Reform Directions*. Manila and New York: Asian Development Bank and Routledge.

Park, D., S. H. Lee and A. Mason (eds.) (2012) *Aging, Economic Growth and Old-Age Security in Asia*. Manila and Cheltenham: Asian Development Bank and Edward Elgar.

Preston, S. H., P. Heuveline and M. Guillot (2001) *Demography: Measuring and Modeling Population Processes*. Oxford: Blackwell.

Qin, M., Y. Zhuang and H. Liu (2015) 'Old age insurance participation among rural-urban migrants in China'. *Demographic Research*, 33(37): 1047–1066.

Raymo, J. M., H. Park, Y. Xie and W. J. Yeung (2015) 'Marriage and family in East Asia: continuity and change'. *Annual Review of Sociology*, 41: 471–492.

Samson, M. (2012) 'The design and implementation of social pensions for older persons in Asia'. In S. W. Handayani and B. Babajanian (eds.) *Social Protection for Older Persons: Social Pensions in Asia*. Manila: Asian Development Bank.

Sanderson, W. C. and S. Scherbov (2013) 'The characteristics approach to the measurement of population aging'. *Population and Development Review*, 39(4): 673–685.

Singapore Ministry of Social and Family Development (2014) *State of the Elderly in Singapore 2008/2009: Chapter 4 Social Well-being*. Available from: http://app.msf.gov.sg/Research-Room/Research-Statistics/Report-on-the-State-of-the-Elderly (accessed 25 December 2014).

Suwanrada, W. and D. Wesumperuma (2012) 'Development of the old-age allowance system in Thailand: challenges and policy implications'. In S. W. Handayani and B. Babajanian (eds.) *Social Protection for Older Persons: Social Pensions in Asia*. Manila: Asian Development Bank.

Taiwan Today (2015) *ROC Cabinet OKs long-term care insurance bill*. Available from: http://taiwantoday.tw/ct.asp?xItem=231204&ctNode=422 (accessed 25 December 2014).

Tsuya, N. O. (2015) 'Below-replacement fertility in Japan: patterns, factors and policy implications'. In R. R. Rindfuss and M. K. Choe (eds.) *Low and Lower Fertility: Variations Across Developed Countries*. Switzerland: Springer.

Turner, J. (2002) 'Social security in Asia and the Pacific: a brief overview'. *Journal of Aging and Social Policy*, 14(1): 95–104.

Turner, J. and J. H. Lichtenstein (2002) 'Social security in the Middle East: a brief review'. *Journal of Aging and Social Policy*, 14(1): 115–124.

United Nations (2000) *Replacement Migration: Is It a Solution to Declining and Ageing Populations?* New York: United Nations Publication.

United Nations (2012) *World Population Prospects: 2012 Revision*. New York: United Nations. Available from: http://esa.un.org/unpd/wpp/Excel-Data/population.htm (accessed 25 December 2014).

Vlachantoni, A. and J. Falkingham (2012) 'Gender and old-age pension protection in Asia'. In S. W. Handayani and B. Babajanian (eds.) *Social Protection for Older Persons: Social Pensions in Asia*. Manila: Asian Development Bank.

Xinhua News Agency (2015) *Beijing Expected to Implement Two-Child Policy in 2016*. Available from: http://news.xinhuanet.com/english/2015-11/10/c_134802958.htm (accessed 10 November 2015).

24
Demographic dividends

Tomoko Kinugasa

Introduction

In this chapter we discuss the first and second demographic dividends as they have appeared in Asia. The concept of demographic transition provides an important background (see Chapter 21). A country's demographic change as it develops can be stylized in five stages. During the first stage mortality is high, especially among infants, and fertility is also high to balance the high mortality. The second stage is characterized by declining mortality while fertility remains high. Mortality, particularly infant mortality, declines rapidly as the country begins to develop; however fertility does not decline as quickly as mortality, mainly because of enduring cultural norms that still support high fertility. The population size therefore increases dramatically. In the third stage fertility begins to decline. In the fourth stage, both fertility and mortality are low, and population growth stagnates.

The second and third stages are the heart of the 'first demographic transition'. This is a transitory period during which population and age structure change significantly. Compared to European countries, the first demographic transition in Asia began later and did not last as long.[1] In Japan, the first demographic transition started with the country's economic development, including the growth of industry and rising living standards. Southern Asian countries adopted the medical technologies of Western countries, leading to dramatic improvements in health and child survival (Gray 1974; Myint 1980).

A population is often divided into three main age groups: children (under age 15), the working-age population (age 15 to 64) and the elderly (age 65 and above). During the first demographic transition, the share of the working-age population increases and the country tends to benefit from what is called the 'first demographic dividend' (Bloom and Williamson 1998). The decline in fertility during the first demographic transition is also associated with a 'second demographic dividend', however, through its effect on capital accumulation (Mason and Kinugasa 2008). Moreover, as adult mortality starts to decrease following the decline in child mortality, this can lead to an increase in savings among prime-age adults and become a source of the 'second demographic dividend' (Kinugasa and Mason 2007).

In the fifth stage, fertility tends to decline further, becoming much lower than the replacement level. This is called the 'second demographic transition' (van de Kaa 2002; Lesthaeghe

2010). In this stage, the population decreases if low fertility continues for a long time. Some European countries, Japan and South Korea (hereafter, 'Korea') are currently facing the second demographic transition. In Japan, the population has already started to decline, and the population of other Asian countries is expected to decline within the next 50 years.[2] During the second demographic transition, a country cannot benefit from the first demographic dividend, but it can benefit from the second demographic dividend, as will be explained later.

In other words, a demographic transition can lead to a demographic dividend. It is now generally accepted that there are two kinds of demographic dividends. The first demographic dividend refers to an advantageous situation that occurs during the first demographic transition. Here, the size of the working-age population increases relative to the total population, and the proportion of young and old dependants declines. The second demographic dividend refers to factors that influence labour productivity growth. These could include a deepening of capital, as well as an increase in human capital. Measures for the first and second demographic dividends have been suggested by Mason (2005, 2007) and Lee and Mason (2010a).

Mason and Lee (2006) contend that the second dividend is different from the first in the following important respects. First, population ageing causes the first dividend to dissipate, but it is the source of the second dividend. Anticipation of the future decline in the ratio of the younger generation to the older generation can lead to an increase in wealth and, possibly, assets. Second, the first dividend is transitory and its benefits eventually disappear. The second dividend is not necessarily transitory since deepening capital and higher per capita income could become permanent.

Here, the concept of a demographic dividend is explained using a basic equation, with GDP per capita used as the measure of economic growth. First, GDP per capita is decomposed in the following equation:

$$Y/N = (L/N)*(Y/L). \qquad (1)$$

In equation (1), Y denotes the GDP, N the population and L is labour. Then, GDP per capita is expressed as the product of the support ratio (L/N) and labour productivity. Equation (1) can be rewritten in growth terms as follows:

$$gr(Y/N) = gr(L/N) + gr(Y/L), \qquad (2)$$

where gr refers to the growth rate. The growth rate of GDP per capita is the sum of the growth in the support ratio and labour productivity. The growth in the support ratio is referred to as the first dividend; the factors that influence the growth in labour productivity provide the second dividend.

This chapter explains the effects of demographic dividends on an economy, and characterizes the two demographic dividends within the context of Asia. The first section below reviews existing research on the first demographic dividend, and explains how this dividend has contributed to Asia's economic growth. The next section discusses the effect of the second demographic dividend on an economy. The following section presents data for the second dividend as estimated by Mason and Lee (2012), and discusses the socioeconomic conditions that can inhibit its benefits. The final section considers the policy implications of the two dividends, identifying the policies required to maximize their benefits within Asian countries.

Tomoko Kinugasa

The first demographic dividend in Asia

Concept of the first demographic dividend

The first demographic dividend has attracted the attention of many researchers. Numerous countries have experienced the first demographic transition, and in Eastern and South-Eastern Asia, this transition occurred relatively rapidly.

We discuss the first dividend with regard to the population age distribution. The size of the labour force can be influenced significantly by the population age distribution, in particular by the proportion of the population within the working-age group. As mentioned earlier, a population grows rapidly in the middle stage of the first demographic transition. The share of the working-age population declines at the beginning of the first demographic transition, because the number of young dependants increases. Later, the share of the working-age population increases dramatically as the number of children decreases and the children who were previously in the large share of young dependants reach working age. As time passes, the share of the working-age population again begins to decrease, owing to a smaller working-age population and a larger share of elderly dependants. When the first demographic transition ends, the ratio of the labour force to the total population (also known as the support ratio (Mason 2005)) becomes small, and the share of elderly dependants within the total population increases.

Numerous studies have used world panel data to estimate the effects on economic growth brought about by the changes in the working-age population and the dependency ratio. For example, Bloom and Williamson (1998) and Bloom et al. (2000) each found that the population growth rate had a negative effect on the growth rate of GDP per capita, while the growth rate of the working-age population had a positive effect. These studies estimate that demographic transitions could account for around one-third of Eastern Asia's so-called economic miracle. Furthermore, Kelley and Schmidt (2001) found that the fertility rate had a negative effect on economic growth in the same year, but a positive effect on economic growth 15 years later. Later, Kelley and Schmidt (2005) found that the proportion of young and old dependants had a negative effect on economic growth.

On the other hand, it is important to note that the effect of the demographic dividend on an economy depends greatly on the prevailing socioeconomic conditions. The potential for the first dividend to bolster economic growth cannot be realized under adverse conditions. For example, an increase in the working-age population will not stimulate economic growth if many individuals are unemployed. The degree of female participation in the labour force can also influence the contribution of the first dividend. Moreover, the quality of labour will influence the degree to which the working-age population is able to contribute to economic growth.

Estimated first dividend in Asia

Mason (2005, 2007) and Mason and Lee (2006, 2012) calculated the magnitude of the first demographic dividend, based on the growth rate of the support ratio. Their method for calculating the first dividend is described in the Appendix. Figure 24.1 presents the first demographic dividends of various regions in Asia, as estimated by Mason and Lee (2012).[3] If the first dividend in Figure 24.1 is positive (negative), the support ratio in the country is increasing (decreasing); that is, growth of the labour force is faster (slower) than population growth.

Japan experienced a large first dividend after World War II, much earlier than other Asian countries. The first dividend then became negative in 1980, also much earlier than in other Asian countries, and it continues to be negative (and far below zero) after 2010. In Korea, Taiwan and

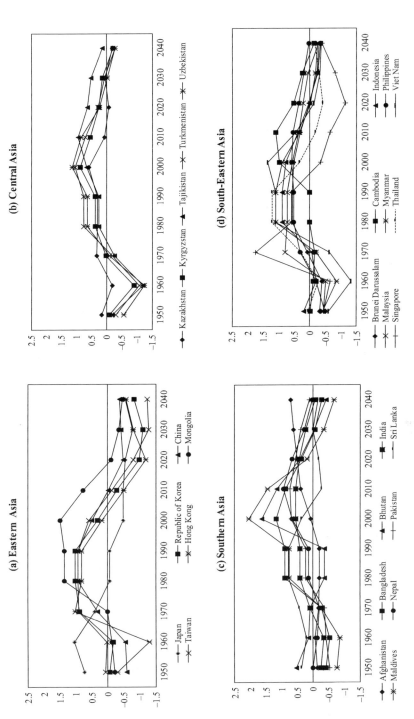

Figure 24.1 The first demographic dividend in Asia

Note: Horizontal axes represent year; vertical axes represent the first dividend in each year (percentage growth).

Source: Based on Mason and Lee (2012).

Hong Kong, the first dividend became positive in 1970. It remained high from 1970 to 1990, before dropping back into the negative in 2010. From 2020 to 2040, it is estimated that the first dividends in Korea and Taiwan will be lower than in Japan. In China, the first dividend became positive in 1970, but not very large, eventually reaching a level similar to Korea and Taiwan in 1980. China experienced a quite rapid demographic transition, with the first dividend dropping to almost zero in 2010. The forecast is that it will remain negative after 2020. The first dividend in Mongolia was large from 1980 to 2000, and was still positive in 2010. However, it is expected that the first dividend will be negative in Mongolia after 2020.

It seems that countries in Central Asia are benefiting from the first dividend later than in Eastern Asia. The first dividend in Central Asia was positive and large from 2000 to 2010, and is expected to remain positive until 2030 or 2040. In Southern Asia, the first dividend was small or negative until 1970. Southern Asia also experienced a larger first dividend overall than Eastern Asia. In Bangladesh and the Maldives, the first dividend was high between 1980 and 2010. In India, benefits from the first dividend have been low, owing to a high youth dependency ratio. It is estimated that India's positive first dividend will continue until 2030, but it is expected to be negative by 2040. Lastly, Sri Lanka's first dividend became negative in 2010, which was earlier than other Southern Asian countries.

In South-Eastern Asia, Malaysia and Singapore experienced a large positive first dividend in 1970. In Singapore, the first dividend was quite large in 1970, but decreased in 1980, before becoming negative in 2000. After 2000, the support ratio in Singapore is expected to continue to decrease. In contrast, Malaysia's positive dividend is expected to continue for far longer, staying positive into 2020–2030, although not at the same high level. Thailand's support ratio became positive in 1970. The country's first dividend peaked between 1980 and 1990, but became negative in 2010 and this is expected to continue. Patterns of change in the first dividends of Indonesia, Myanmar and Vietnam appear to be similar. These countries experienced large first dividends from 1980 to 2000, but all are expected to be negative by 2030. Cambodia, meanwhile, seems to have benefited from its first dividend later than other Asian countries, with a large, positive value from 2000 to 2010. Finally, although the first dividend in the Philippines will not be very large, it is expected to remain positive for a long time.

Figure 24.1 suggests that the first dividend is associated with economic prosperity, at least to some extent. Japan was the first of the Asian countries to benefit; in the 1950s and 1960s it also enjoyed a period of high economic growth. The next to benefit were the newly industrialized economies (NIEs), including Korea, Taiwan, Hong Kong and Singapore, which experienced large first dividends from the 1970s to the 1990s. These were followed by China and some Southern and South-Eastern Asian countries, which had favourable first dividends from the 1980s to the 2000s. It was around this time that the rise of China and the ASEAN countries attracted the attention of researchers. However, not all countries experienced strong economic growth while their first dividends were large. Moreover, it is worth noting that by 2040 the first dividend is estimated to be negative, reflecting declining support ratios, in almost all countries shown in Figure 24.1.

Capital accumulation, human capital and the second demographic dividend

Change in age distribution and capital accumulation

The second dividend is defined as the effect of demographic change on the growth in labour productivity. Mathematically, this dividend is expressed as factors contributing to $gr(Y/L)$ in equation (2). Labour productivity growth is influenced mainly by capital accumulation and growth in human capital. We first examine capital accumulation, which is the result of saving behaviour. In Solow's model (1956), the savings rate is assumed to be constant, and so does not influence the growth rate of GDP per capita. The relationship between population growth and saving was discussed by Coale and Hoover (1958); they argue that high population growth decreases saving because it increases the proportion of the young dependents in the population, and so increases consumption at the expense of saving.

Many studies have found that the age distribution influences the national savings rate, and that the first demographic dividend can greatly increase the national savings rate. According to the basic life-cycle model[4] of Modigliani and Brumberg (1954) and Tobin (1967), individuals are assumed to save for their old age taking into account expected lifetime income. In cases where individuals expect to retire at a certain age, they save while they are young. Then, after they retire, they consume the accumulated funds. According to these two studies, an increase in the population increases the national savings rate because the proportion of the younger generation who can save increases. In the 'variable rate of growth effects' model, Fry and Mason (1982) and Mason (1987, 1988) suggest that a decline in the youth dependency ratio could change the timing of life-cycle consumption. Such a decline could shift the age consumption profile to a later stage of life. According to this model, the savings rate depends on the product of the youth dependency ratio and the rate at which national income grows, as well as on the dependency ratio itself, while the age consumption profile is considered to be in a steady state. The authors supported their theoretical hypothesis with empirical evidence.

The work of Higgins and Williamson (1997) considered the dynamic effects of changes in the youth dependency ratio. They established an overlapping generations model of three generations: children, prime-age adults and the elderly. In analysing the dynamic effect of changes in the age distribution they found, both theoretically and empirically, that the age distribution had an important effect on savings. Lee et al. (2001, 2003) incorporated the age distribution and survival rate into their life-cycle model and simulated the out-of-steady-state effects of demographic change on saving and on the capital-output ratio in Taiwan and the United States.

Changes in life expectancy and capital accumulation

Another major demographic issue that affects capital accumulation is mortality. We focus here on adult mortality.[5] If individuals save only for the purpose of consuming in old age, an increase in adult longevity will increase the amount that prime-age adults save. Yaari (1965) proposed a classic model on lifetime uncertainty and consumption. He analysed how the consumption growth rate differs if bequest motives exist, and how the results are affected by the availability of insurance. Blanchard (1985) later expanded Yaari's model by considering macroeconomic issues. Many authors including Zilcha and Friedman (1985), Strawczynski (1993) and Yakita (2001) have agreed that longer life expectancy results in higher savings by individuals if there is no bequest motive.

Kageyama (2003) has stated that the speed at which life expectancy increases influences the savings rate, with a more rapid increase in life expectancy causing an increase in the rate. The overlapping generations model of Kinugasa and Mason (2007) suggests that the effect of an increase in adult longevity interacts with GDP growth rates. Specifically, an increase in adult longevity increases the national savings rate if the GDP is growing. However, the speed at which adult longevity increases produces a corresponding increase in the national savings rate regardless of the GDP growth rate. Lee et al. (2001) simulated the effects of the survival rate and age

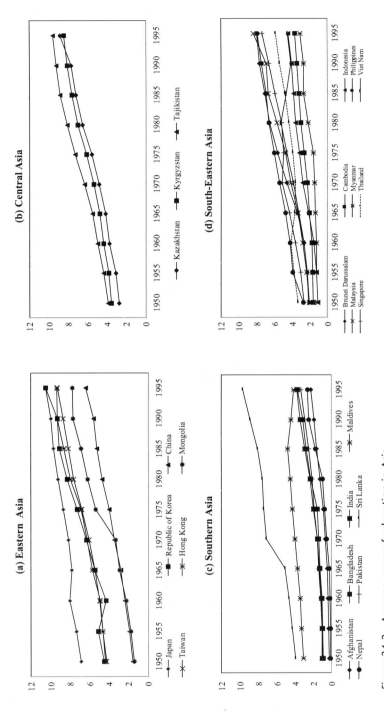

Figure 24.2 Average years of education in Asia

Note: Horizontal axes represent year; vertical axes represent average number of years of education.

Source: Based on Barro and Lee (2013).

distribution on the capital-output ratio, and estimated that the capital-output ratio in Taiwan will rise from its 1950 level of 0.3 to about 5 by 2050.

Some studies have examined the determinants of the savings rate by including life expectancy at birth. Doshi (1994) conducted regression analyses that included life expectancy at birth in the model developed by Leff (1969), and found that it had a significant positive effect on the savings rate. Bloom et al. (2003) included life expectancy at birth in the models of Higgins (1998) and Mason (1987, 1988), and also found a positive effect on the savings rate. Kageyama (2003) estimated the effects of the level and growth rate of life expectancy at birth, and found that an increase in the growth of life expectancy had a significant positive effect on the savings rate. Finally, Kinugasa and Mason (2007) and Mason and Kinugasa (2008) analysed the effects of an increase in adult survival rate on the national savings rate.

Human capital and the second dividend in Asia

Human capital can have a significant influence on economic growth and productivity. Human capital is defined as the quality of labour that influences productivity. The term encompasses education level, experience and health condition of workers, among other factors, with education considered to be especially important. Figure 24.2 presents the average years of total schooling in Asian countries from 1950 to 1995, as calculated by Barro and Lee (2013). According to these data, the average total education level has increased consistently in most Asian countries over this period (see also Chapter 22). This may be largely the result of policies to increase education, but demographic factors can also influence the education level. Becker's theory of the trade-off between quality and quantity states that fewer children means higher education spending per child (Becker 1960; Becker and Lewis 1973; Willis 1973). According to this theory, a decrease in the number of children increases the price of children, which decreases the price of the quality of children. In this case, the demand for quality increases and the demand for quantity of children decreases. The simulation analysis of Lee and Mason (2010a, 2010b) found that lower fertility and mortality lead to higher human capital investment, which can outweigh the problems of a decreasing labour force and an increasing proportion of elderly dependants.

With regard to the demographic effect on human capital, Mason and Lee (2012) clarified two important issues. First, the return on investment in human capital matters to the demographic effects on productivity. The return on education has been estimated in many studies based on the work of Mincer (1974). Psacharopoulos and Patrinos (2004) reviewed studies on the return on education, and found that its level in Asia is average in global terms. The second important issue is the strength of the trade-off between quantity and quality. Lee and Mason (2010a) and Ogawa et al. (2009) used the NTA (National Transfer Accounts) method to calculate the relationship between fertility and human capital, and found that a decline in fertility can induce human capital investment. They estimated the elasticities of the trade-off[5] as -0.68 for all NTA economies, -0.95 in Asian NTA economies and below -1 in Japan, Taiwan and China. Thus, the trade-off is stronger in Asia than in other areas of the world, and is especially strong in Japan and Taiwan.

The second demographic dividend in Asia

Estimated second dividend in Asia

In this section we discuss the second dividend in Asia in terms of capital accumulation. Mason (2005, 2007) and Mason and Lee (2012) calculated the expected value of lifetime total wealth held by those aged 50 and older to estimate the magnitude of the second demographic dividend. The Appendix describes how to calculate the second dividend. Many young working-age adults are responsible for childrearing, making it unlikely that they can save for retirement. However, after age 50 – when most children have reached working age and are therefore independent – these adults tend to concentrate on wealth accumulation.

Figure 24.3 presents the second dividend in Asian countries with calculations based on Mason and Lee (2012). Variation of the second dividend is mainly determined by the survival rate and age distribution of those aged 50 and older. As may be seen in Figure 24.3, the second dividend in Japan has been high, but has been declining slightly. After 2010, it is estimated that the second dividend will continue to decrease gradually, but will remain largely positive until 2040. In Korea, the second dividend was low in 1950, but increased rapidly between 1960 and 2010. Meanwhile, the second dividend in China and Taiwan increased rapidly between 1980 and 2010. It will decline in both after 2010, but is expected to remain positive until 2040. In Central Asia, the second dividend was not especially high until 1990, but it is estimated to increase after 2000. In Southern Asia, most countries will have large second dividends after 2020. Lastly, in most South-Eastern Asian countries, it is estimated that the second dividend will increase rapidly after 2010. Overall, the second dividend will be positive in Asian countries until at least 2040. Therefore, this dividend will benefit Asian economies even after the cessation of the first dividend benefits.

Socioeconomic conditions and the second dividend

Both the first and second dividends have the potential to stimulate economic growth.[7] Here, we discuss the socioeconomic conditions related to capital accumulation in Asia. In order for the second dividend to contribute to capital accumulation, the life-cycle hypothesis should hold. In other words, individuals should save for their consumption after they retire from work. If the socioeconomic conditions of the economy are such that the life-cycle hypothesis does not hold, the second dividend might not benefit the economy sufficiently.

The recent saving patterns in developed Asian countries, such as Japan, Korea, Singapore and Hong Kong, appear to align with the life-cycle model. In the past the Confucian ideology prevailed and it was considered obligatory that children care for their aged parents. However this situation changed dramatically after World War II. In recent years, the number of nuclear households has increased relative to that of traditional stem or extended households[8] (see also Chapter 20). Many elderly individuals in these countries do not depend on support from their children, and younger adults save for their old age. It is possible that Japan and Korea are in a position to enjoy the benefits that come with the second dividend. According to Ogawa et al. (2010), banks and life insurance companies in Japan have been paying more attention to the 'baby boomers' born after World War II. Japan also has a high national savings rate, which has contributed to economic growth.

However, several factors can diminish the benefits of the second dividend, even in high-performing Asian countries. For example, the growth of social security systems can discourage people from saving. If most pensions were governed by a pay-as-you-go scheme, then national saving would likely decrease. Another important factor that can hinder the contribution of the second dividend in Asian society is familial transfer. As noted earlier, the theory supporting second dividend benefits includes that of the life-cycle hypothesis: saving may not increase, even when life expectancy increases, if people do not save for their old age. In many traditional Asian countries, eldercare is based on the assistance of family members. Elderly parents tend to require

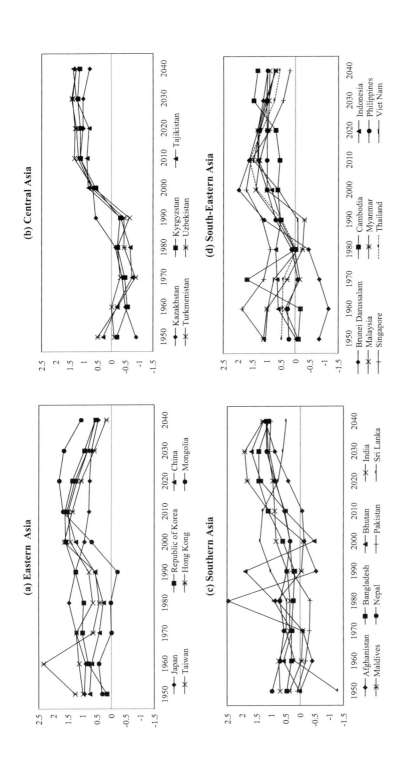

Figure 24.3 The second demographic dividend in Asia

Note: Horizontal axes represent year; vertical axes represent the second dividend in each year (percentage growth).

Source: Based on Mason and Lee (2012).

the assistance of their children in caring for themselves. Moreover, in many Asian countries extended families are very common, and the elderly receive support from the younger generation by living with them under one roof. However, family styles are changing, given the decline in fertility, making it more difficult for the elderly to receive support from a dwindling number of children.[9]

It is also possible that governments and institutions in Asian countries may not recognize the benefits of an increase in adult longevity, and individuals may not really feel that their life expectancy has increased. In addition, an increase in adult longevity may not benefit the economy if there are serious problems such as war, political instability, economic crises or other disasters. Such situations may make people pessimistic about the future, and prevent them from saving.

Policy implications

Thus far we have discussed the characteristics of the two demographic dividends, and how they can influence an economy. We have noted that both the first and second dividends have the potential to bolster economic development, but that this potential may be hampered by unfavourable socioeconomic conditions. Some South-Eastern and many Southern and Central Asian countries will have the opportunity to benefit from the first dividend for a number of decades. These regions can benefit from enacting policies that promote a large labour force. Employment policies that create labour-market flexibility and job opportunities for the working-age population are important. Another essential policy is to increase female labour force participation. In some Asian countries, the status of women remains low, which makes it difficult for these countries to take advantage of a female labour force.

Note that some Asian countries, such as Japan and Korea, no longer benefit from the first demographic dividend. After the first dividend ends, countries tend to experience problems associated with an ageing population, such as a decrease in the labour force and an increase in government expenditure with regard to social security and healthcare. The first dividend bestows a transitory benefit during the demographic transition. Countries currently benefiting from the first dividend should prepare for an ageing society.

The second dividend has recently attracted the attention of demographers and economists, but more policymakers need to heed the opportunity it provides. As discussed above, the second dividend includes demographic factors that can improve labour productivity. Therefore, countries with high support ratios should take advantage of the potential inherent in a high saving rate. Generally, the working-age population tends to save more than the dependent population. If money is saved and subsequently invested effectively, this could help drive economic growth. However, the positive effect induced by the high support ratio will not continue indefinitely.

Capital accumulation induced by higher adult longevity will also be an important source of economic growth. According to Mason (2005, 2007) and Mason and Lee (2012), the second dividend will continue to be positive until 2040 in all Asian countries, based on available data. It is possible that the positive effect of the dividend is largely due to the increase in adult longevity, as well as the relatively large population born in the 1950s and 1960s. In almost all Asian countries, the second dividend is expected to have the potential to foster economic growth.

However, an increase in adult longevity does not always increase economic growth. One possible reason is that familial income transfers predominate in many Asian countries, so that the life-cycle hypothesis does not always hold. Eldercare can be influenced by the culture and norms of each country. Therefore, it is difficult to convince some people to save for their old age rather than assume their children will support them. Policies to increase life-cycle saving might be important. Financial institutions such as banks could benefit from leveraging the potential of individuals aged 50–60 years – who tend to be more dedicated to saving for old age – and should try to promote saving among this age group. Educating people in their 50s and 60s about how to save, in terms of a life plan, may help increase national saving.

The second dividend will be promoted if life expectancy increases. The UN Population Division anticipates that life expectancy will increase in future, but this is not guaranteed. Medical technology has advanced rapidly, and higher-quality healthcare is becoming more available in Asian countries. An increase in income can also increase health conditions related to nutrition. However it remains to be seen whether there are binding biological constraints to improvements in life expectancy. Many factors can decrease life expectancy in modern societies. Therefore, policies that improve health and life expectancy are necessary.

The second dividend is also related to human capital formation. Having fewer children can result in an increase in human capital investment. However, more effort is necessary before the positive effects of the dividend can be realized. In many Asian countries secondary and higher education need to be made available to more people. In addition, the quality of education needs to improve, as this will influence the return on education. As shown by Hanushek and Wößmann (2007), the quality of education is influenced significantly by the quality of teachers, as well as incentives to improve their quality. The government can play a large role in educational improvement by making it accessible to people regardless of income, and should therefore take steps to enact education policies.

In conclusion, the benefit of the first dividend in Asia has either disappeared already or will disappear by 2050. However, the second dividend will continue to benefit most Asian countries beyond this date. Many policymakers are afraid of the negative effects of an ageing population, and these problems do need to be managed carefully (see Chapter 23). However, there are positive aspects to an ageing population, namely those of the second dividend. Therefore, countries facing population ageing should look to take advantage of the second demographic dividend. If they are able to do so, the Asian economy in 2050 could be even stronger than expected.

Acknowledgements

The author would like to thank Andrew Mason and Zhongwei Zhao, as well as the anonymous reviewers for their valuable comments. This research is supported by JSPS KAKENHI Grant Number 26292118 and a grant from the Abe Fellowship Program, assisted by the Social Science Research Council and the American Council of Learned Societies in cooperation with and with funds provided by the Japan Foundation Center for Global Partnership.

Appendix: Measurement of demographic dividends

First demographic dividend

In this Appendix, we briefly explain how to calculate demographic dividends, using the method of Mason (2005, 2007). First, the effective number of consumers (N) and the effective number of producers (L) are defined as follows:

$$N(t) = \sum_{a} \alpha(a) P(a,t) \tag{A.1}$$

$$L(t) = \sum_{a} \gamma(a) P(a,t) \tag{A.2}$$

where '*a*' is age and '*t*' is time period. $P(a,t)$ is the population of age a at time t. $\alpha(a)$ is an age-specific weight for variation in consumption by age, and it is influenced by factors such as physiological needs, culture and preferences. $\gamma(a)$ is age-specific productivity. Output per effective consumer (Y/N) is expressed in equation (2) in the text. Thus, the first demographic dividend is calculated as $gr(L/N)$, and N and L are calculated using equations (A.1) and (A.2).

Second demographic dividend

Mason (2005, 2007) calculated wealth held by those aged 50 and older in order to estimate the magnitude of the second demographic dividend. He did so because many young, working-age adults are responsible for childrearing, and it is likely that they cannot save for retirement; however, after age 50 – when most children have reached working age and are therefore independent – they tend to concentrate on wealth accumulation. The relative per capita age profile of consumption is assumed to be fixed and to shift upward at rate g_c each year; total consumption in year $t + x$ of the cohort born before year b is given by, $\bar{c}(t)e^{g_c x}N(\leq b, t+x)$ where $\bar{c}(t)$ is consumption per effective consumer in year t.[10] The present value (PV) of the future lifetime consumption of the cohort born in year $b = t - a$ or earlier is expressed in the following equation:

$$\bar{c}(t)PVN(\leq b,t) = \bar{c}(t)\sum_{x=0}^{\omega-a} e^{(g_c-r)x}N(\leq b, t+x), \tag{A.3}$$

where ω is the maximum age achieved.

It is assumed that the shape of the per capita cross-sectional age profile of production is fixed and shifting upward at rate g_y. In this case, the total production in year t of the cohort born in year b or earlier is given by $\bar{y}^l(t)e^{g_y x}L(\leq b, t+x)$. In this equation, $\bar{y}^l(t)$ is production or labour income per effective producer, and $L \leq b, t + x$ is the effective number of producers born in year b or earlier. Therefore, the present value of future lifetime production of the cohort born in year $b = t - a$ or earlier is given by

$$\bar{y}^l(t)PVL(\leq b,t) = \bar{y}^l \sum_{x=0}^{\omega-a} e^{(g_y-r)x}L(\leq b, t+x). \tag{A.4}$$

Assuming there is no bequest, the lifetime budget constraint is expressed as

$$W(\leq b,t) = \bar{c}(t)PVC(\leq b,t) - \bar{y}^l(t)PVL(\leq b,t). \tag{A.5}$$

From equation (A.5), we can derive the ratio of wealth to total labour income as

$$w(\leq b,t) = \left[\bar{c}(t)/\bar{y}^l(t)\right]PVC(\leq b,t)/N(t) - PVL(\leq b,t)/L(t) \tag{A.6}$$

where $w(\leq b,t) = W(\leq b,t)/Y^l(t)$. Equation (A.6) can be rewritten as follows:

$$w(\leq b,t) = \left[C(t)/Y^l(t)\right]PVC(\leq b,t)/L(t) - PVL(\leq b,t)/L(t). \tag{A.7}$$

In equation (A.7), $PVC(\leq b,t)/L(t)$ is the present value of the future lifetime production of all persons born in year b or earlier, per effective producer, in year t. The second dividend is calculated in equation (A.7) as the growth rate of wealth among those aged 50 and older. In the calculation, g_y and g_c are assumed to be constant at 0.015, and the ratio of consumption to labour income is equal to 1.0. Mason (2005, 2007) uses the age earning and consumption profiles of the United States in 2000. For simplicity, it is assumed in this model that there is no bequest motive, familial transfer, social security system or changes in retirement.

Notes

1 The first demographic transition started in the early nineteenth century in European countries, but only after World War II in Asian countries.
2 According to the projected population based on medium fertility by the UN Population Division (2013), the populations of Korea, China, Hong Kong, Sri Lanka, Myanmar, Thailand and Vietnam are expected to start decreasing by 2050.
3 This study uses the classifications of Eastern, Central, Southern and South-Eastern Asia as per the typology of the UN Population Division. Western Asia is not included in our Figures because Mason and Lee (2012) only included three countries (Azerbaijan, Armenia and Georgia) from the region.
4 This model assumes that individuals determine their consumption and savings considering lifetime utility and income.
5 Child mortality can also influence capital accumulation as it influences the share of the working-age population.
6 The elasticity of trade-off means the percentage by which human capital investment increases when total fertility rate decreases by one per cent.
7 The empirical analysis conducted by Yamaguchi and Kinugasa (2014) showed that first and second dividends do not necessarily have positive effects on economic growth.
8 The changes observed in the structure of Japanese and Korean families are described by Martin (1990).
9 The current chapter is written from an economic viewpoint. Interdisciplinary discussion is essential for further investigation of this matter. For further details about the family in Asian countries, see Thornton and Fricke (1987), Martin (1990) and Knodel et al. (1995), as well as Chapters 19 and 20 of this volume.
10 $N(\leq b, t + x)$ is the effective number of consumers born in year b or earlier at year t who are alive in year $t + x$. Let $b = t - a$, so that $N(\leq b, t + x)$ is the effective number of consumers 'a' years or older in year t who are still alive in year $t + x$.

References

Barro, R. J. and J. Lee (2013) 'A new data set of educational attainment in the world, 1950–2010'. *Journal of Development Economics*, 104: 184–198.
Becker, G. S. (1960) 'An economic analysis of fertility'. In *Proceedings of Demographic and Economic Change in Developed Countries*. Princeton, NJ: National Bureau of Economic Research.
Becker, G. S. and H. G. Lewis (1973) 'On the interaction between the quantity and quality of children'. *Journal of Political Economy*, 84: S279–S288.
Blanchard, O. (1985) 'Debt, deficits and finite horizons'. *Journal of Political Economy*, 93: 223–247.
Bloom, D., D. Canning and B. Graham (2003) 'Longevity and life-cycle savings'. *Scandinavian Journal of Economics*, 105: 319–338.
Bloom, D. E., D. Canning and P. N. Malaney (2000) 'Demographic change and economic growth in Asia'. In C. Chu and R. Lee (eds.) *Population and Economic Change in East Asia, Population and Development Review*, 26(suppl.): 257–290.
Bloom, D. E. and J. G. Williamson (1998) 'Demographic transitions and economic miracles in emerging Asia'. *World Bank Economic Review*, 12: 419–455.
Coale, A. J. and E. M. Hoover (1958) *Population Growth and Economic Development in Low-Income Countries: A Case Study of India's Prospects*. Princeton, NJ: Princeton University Press.
Doshi, K. (1994) 'Determinants of the saving rate: an international comparison'. *Contemporary Economic Policy*, 12: 37–45.
Fry, M. and A. Mason (1982) 'The variable rate of growth effect in the life cycle model'. *Economic Inquiry*, 20: 426–442.
Gray, R. H. (1974) 'The decline of mortality in Ceylon and the demographic effects of malaria control'. *Population Studies*, 28: 205–229.

Hanushek, E. and L. Wößmann (2007) 'The role of education quality in economic growth'. *World Bank Policy Research Working Paper* 4122.
Higgins, M. (1998) 'Demography, national savings and international capital flows'. *International Economic Review*, 30: 343–369.
Higgins, M. and J. G. Williamson (1997) 'Age structure dynamics in Asia and dependence on foreign capital'. *Population and Development Review*, 23: 261–293.
Kageyama, J. (2003) 'The effects of a continuous increase in lifetime on saving'. *Review of Income and Wealth*, 49: 163–183.
Kelley, A. C. and R. M. Schmidt (2001) 'Economic and demographic change: a synthesis of models, findings and perspectives'. In B. Nancy, A. C. Kelley and S. Sinding (eds.) *Population Matters: Demographic Change, Economic Growth and Poverty in the Developing World*. New York: Oxford University Press.
Kelley, A. C. and R. M. Schmidt (2005) 'Evolution of recent economic-demographic modeling: a synthesis'. *Journal of Population Economics*, 18: 275–300.
Kinugasa, T. and A. Mason (2007) 'Why countries become wealthy: the effects of adult longevity on saving'. *World Development*, 35: 1–23.
Knodel, J., C. Saengtienchai and W. Sittitrai (1995) 'Living arrangements of the elderly in Thailand: views of the populace'. *Journal of Cross-Cultural Gerontology*, 10: 79–111.
Lee, R. and A. Mason (2010a) 'Fertility, human capital and economic growth over the demographic transition'. *European Journal of Population*, 26: 159–182.
Lee, R. and A. Mason (2010b) 'Some macroeconomic aspects of global population aging'. *Demography*, 47(suppl.): S151–S172.
Lee, R. and A. Mason (2011) *Population Aging and the Generational Economy: A Global Perspective*. Cheltenham: Edward Elgar Publishing.
Lee, R., A. Mason and T. Miller (2001) 'Saving, wealth and the demographic transition in East Asia'. In A. Mason (ed.) *Population Change and Economic Development in East Asia: Challenges Met, Opportunities Seized*. Stanford, CA: Stanford University Press.
Lee, R., A. Mason and T. Miller (2003) 'From transfers to individual responsibility: implications for savings and capital accumulation in Taiwan and the United States'. *Scandinavian Journal of Economics*, 105: 339–357.
Leff, N. (1969) 'Dependency rates and savings rates'. *American Economic Review*, 59: 886–896.
Lesthaeghe, R. (2010) 'The unfolding story of the second demographic transition'. *Population and Development Review*, 36: 211–251.
Martin, L. G. (1990) 'Changing intergenerational family relations in East Asia'. *Annals of the American Academy of Political and Social Science*, 510: 102–114.
Mason, A. (1987) 'National saving rates and population growth: a new model and new evidence'. In D. G. Johnson and R. D. Lee (eds.) *Population Growth and Economic Development: Issues and Evidence*. Madison: University of Wisconsin Press.
Mason, A. (1988) 'Saving, economic growth and demographic change'. *Population and Development Review*, 14: 113–144.
Mason, A. (2005) 'Demographic transition and demographic dividends in developed and developing countries'. Paper presented at the United Nations Expert Group Meeting on Social and Economic Implications of Changing Population Age Structure, New York.
Mason, A. (2007) 'Demographic dividends: the past, the present and the future'. In A. Mason and M. Yamaguchi (eds.) *Population Change, Labor Markets and Sustainable Growth: Towards a New Economic Paradigm*. Amsterdam: Elsevier Press.
Mason, A. and T. Kinugasa (2008) 'East Asian development: two demographic dividends'. *Journal of Asian Economics*, 19: 389–400.
Mason, A. and R. Lee (2006) 'Reform and support systems for the elderly in developing countries: capturing the second demographic dividend'. *Genus*, 62: 11–35.
Mason, A. and R. Lee (2012) 'Population, wealth and economic growth in Asia and the Pacific'. In D. Park, R. Lee and A. Mason (eds.) *Aging, Economic Growth and Old-Age Security in Asia*. Cheltenham, UK and Northampton, MA: Edward Elgar Publishing.
Mincer, J. (1974) *Schooling, Experience and Earnings*. New York: National Bureau of Economic Research.
Modigliani, F. and R. Brumberg (1954) 'Utility analysis and the consumption function: an interpretation of cross-section data'. In K. K. Kurihara (ed.) *Post-Keynesian Economics*. New Brunswick: Rutgers University Press.
Myint, H. (1980) *The Economics of Developing Countries*. London: Hutchinson & Co. Ltd.

Ogawa, N., A. Mason, A. Chawla and R. Matsukura (2010) 'Japan's unprecedented aging and changing intergenerational transfers'. In T. Ito and A. K. Rose (eds.) *The Economic Consequences of Demographic Change in East Asia*. Chicago and London: University of Chicago Press.

Ogawa, N., A. Mason, A. Chawla, R. Matsukura and A. C. Tung (2009) 'Declining fertility and the rising cost of children: what can national transfer accounts say about low fertility in Japan and other Asian countries?' *Asian Population Studies*, 5: 289–307.

Psacharopoulos, G. and H. Patrinos (2004) 'Returns to investment in education: a further update'. *Education Economics*, 12: 111–134.

Solow, R. M. (1956) 'A contribution to the theory of economic growth'. *Quarterly Journal of Economics*, 70: 65–94.

Strawczynski, M. (1993) 'Income uncertainty, bequests and annuities'. *Economic Letters*, 42: 155–158.

Tobin, J. (1967) 'Life cycle savings and balanced growth'. In W. Fellner (ed.) *Ten Economic Studies in the Tradition of Irving Fisher*. New York: Wiley.

United Nations, Department of Economic and Social Affairs, Population Division. (2013) *World Population Prospects: The 2012 Revision*, CD-ROM Edition.

Thornton, A. and T. E. Fricke (1987) 'Social change and the family: comparative perspectives from the West, China and South Asia'. *Sociological Forum*, 2: 746–779.

van de Kaa, D. J. (2002) 'The idea of a second demographic transition in industrialized countries'. Paper 6th Welfare Policy Seminar, National Institute of Population and Social Security, Tokyo, 29 January.

Yaari, M. E. (1965) 'Uncertain lifetime, life insurance and the theory of the consumer'. *The Review of Economics Studies*, 32: 137–150.

Yakita, A. (2001) 'Uncertain lifetime, fertility and social security'. *Journal of Population Economics*, 14: 635–640.

Yamaguchi, M. and T. Kinugasa (2014) *Economic Analyses Using the Overlapping Generations Model and General Equilibrium Growth Accounting for the Japanese Economy: Population, Agriculture and Economic Development*. Singapore: World Scientific.

Willis, R. (1973) 'A new approach to the economic theory of fertility behavior'. *Journal of Political Economy*, 81: S14–S64.

Zilcha, I. and J. Friedman (1985) 'Saving behavior in retirement when life horizon is uncertain'. *Economic Letters*, 17: 63–66.

25
Population and environment in Asia

Adrian C. Hayes

Reviews of the state of the natural environment in Asia disclose serious and growing problems – much of the land is degraded, freshwater lakes, rivers and aquifers are increasingly polluted, and even the air is toxic and unfit to breathe in many of the region's cities (UNESCAP 1990, 2005; UNESCAP and ADB 1995; UNESCAP, ADB and UNEP 2012). Such environmental problems are the result of human populations making more and more demands on natural resources and ecological services, and this in turn is due to population growth and economic development (Royal Society 2012). Although not all of the causal mechanisms involved are precisely understood or thoroughly documented there is a growing consensus that current trends in the human use of natural resources are not sustainable in the long term.

'Population and environment' is the label given to the field of inquiry – interdisciplinary but with a strong demographic core – which examines the way human populations interact with the ecosphere, and it is this perspective we adopt in this chapter. The subject matter is complex, broad in scope, and the details of population-environment interactions vary depending on all kinds of geographical and cultural factors (Hunter 2000). We cannot hope to cover the topic comprehensively for Asia in a single chapter. Instead we concentrate on a limited number of key aspects of population-environment interactions, and illustrate using data mostly from the five largest countries in each of the four Asian subregions (as defined by the United Nations Population Division).

The chapter is organized as follows. The first section gives a brief overview of alternative approaches used by population-and-environment researchers and outlines the approach used in this chapter. The second introduces a commonly-used approach to assess the different contributions of population growth and economic growth to environmental change in Asia. The third section discusses major changes in population composition, specifically urbanization and the rise of the middle class, as drivers of resource use and environmental change. The fourth reviews trends in natural resources use in the region, focusing on water and energy, together with their environmental and social consequences. The chapter closes with a brief note on how population-environment interactions in Asia relate to the goals of sustainable development. From a global perspective the case of Asia is especially interesting since although the region contains roughly 60 per cent of the world's population it occupies only 20 per cent of its land area and contains 30 per cent of global freshwater resources. Many of the dilemmas inherent in population-environment interactions can be seen in their extreme form in Asia. How the countries of Asia manage their natural environments over the next couple of decades is of interest to people everywhere.

Theoretical perspectives on population and environment

A wide range of theoretical and methodological approaches have been used to analyse population-environment interactions. The main research emphases have been on the way the environment has been used, managed or exploited to provide natural resources, both renewable (land, water, air) and non-renewable resources (minerals, metals and fossil fuels); the way populations dispose of their waste in the environment and generate pollution; the way population-environment interactions change with time, particularly in response to population growth, economic development, rising affluence or consumption, and technological change; and on the way other social and cultural factors such as taboos, gender roles, inheritance practices, wars, conquest, disease and political economy can influence or modulate any of these interactions. There has also been considerable research looking at causal impacts in the reverse direction, that is, on the impacts of environmental constraints and change on the dynamics of human populations, and on their cultures and opportunities for development.[1]

The choice of variables used in quantitative analysis often reflects the disciplinary backgrounds of the researchers and is highly constrained by the availability of reliable data. Nevertheless theoretical understanding in the field has been cumulative and the last two decades have seen the incorporation of 'complexity science' (Liu et al. 2007) and more precise and rigorous empirical analysis. On the population side, there is more attention given to the process and structure of populations as well as their size and growth rates (e.g. Lutz et al. 2002); on the environment side, there is more attention given to understanding the organization of entire ecosystems, not just the specific resources needed by different economies (e.g. Hummel et al. 2009; Liu et al. 2015).

One well-known approach to analysing population-environment interactions is known as 'IPAT': environmental *I*mpact equals the product of *P*opulation size, the average level of *A*ffluence among members of the population, and the environmental impact caused by the *T*echnology per unit of affluence consumed (Ehrlich and Holdren 1971). Although the IPAT identity is limited in its empirical applications due to its simplicity (Hayes 1995), it is still widely used along with other conceptual tools to organize basic arguments in the field (see, for example, Royal Society 2012 and IEA 2014); so long as its limitations are borne in mind IPAT is still helpful. The main limitation, however, is that since it is defined as a mathematical identity it cannot take into account explicitly the way the P, A and T variables contributing to impact are themselves interdependent. The way it is commonly applied also masks the effects due to changes in the composition of populations. Research suggests many of these interdependencies are not linear but depend on the organization of populations, environments and their interactions.

Acknowledging these complexities, the approach used in this chapter is broadly social-ecological (Figure 25.1). Human activity everywhere involves four kinds of resources: human resources are embodied in the members of human populations; social resources – in the sense of households, interpersonal networks and social institutions, or simply the 'rules of the game' – are embedded in social organization (Dasgupta 2005); physical resources are embodied in infrastructure and the built environment (based on available technologies); and natural resources are provided by, and extracted from, the natural environment. All human activity – including the production and consumption of 'goods and services' – can be regarded as constituted by these four kinds of resources, organized and processed in different ways and quantities. A person's access

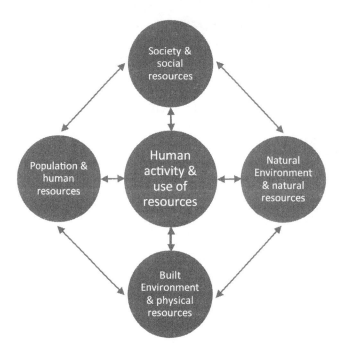

Figure 25.1 Social-ecological systems
Source: Based on Hayes (1995).

to these resources largely determines their well-being and quality of life. From an economic perspective these four kinds of resources are regarded as kinds of capital. Money is a medium of exchange that people use to trade in the rights to use these different kinds of resources.

How these four kinds of resources or capital are produced, exchanged and consumed in social-ecological systems (SESs), viewed across all scales from individual households to global society, are among the most basic stories we can narrate about population-environment interactions. In particular, the production, exchange and consumption of resources always have consequences for the 'parent' SESs from which the relevant resources are drawn (i.e. specific populations, societies, and built and natural environments), and also for other more 'distant' SESs which may be affected via more indirect causal pathways (e.g. waste products produced in one location can pollute the natural resources used by a population in another). Some properties of SESs can be explained in terms of natural laws while others can only be explained in terms of cultural meanings and social processes; a comprehensive analysis of any empirical SES depends on insights from both the natural sciences and the social sciences. It is also worth noting, given contemporary interests in sustainable development (Sachs 2015), that the outcomes of specific population-environment interactions may be assessed relative to some or all of the explicit values associated with sustained economic growth, environmental sustainability and social equity.

Population change, consumption and the environment

The impact a population has on its environment depends on its size and the characteristics of its activities. For non-human animal species the vast bulk of their physical consumption is used to maintain physiological metabolism and sustain reproduction. Human beings are unique in the way they use natural resources to produce cultural artefacts and develop social institutions, the significance of which can extend far beyond their contribution to physical survival. Modern industrial societies in particular are distinguished by the extent to which they consume goods and services that have been produced using inanimate sources of energy, especially fossil fuels.

Human activities are so varied in their characteristics we cannot expect to analyse their environmental impact in detail using a single metric, but a fruitful starting point when considering modern societies is to consider gross domestic product (GDP), an aggregate measure of the market value of all goods and services produced in a country in a given year.[2] Other things being equal, as GDP grows so does the demand for land, water and atmospheric resources, for environmental 'sinks' for the disposal of waste products and pollutants, and for a range of other 'ecological services' (MEA 2005). A set of national GDPs, constructed consistently over time, gives a preliminary sense of the relative magnitudes of total consumption in different countries, and consequently of the physical demands they place on the natural environment, and how these quantities are changing over time.

The economies of many of Asia's developing states and territories have grown impressively during the last several decades. Figure 25.2 shows the size of GDP (estimated in purchasing power parity relative to the US dollar in 2005[3]) for the five largest countries in each of Asia's four subregions during 1975–2010.[4] Regarding the single largest country in each subregion: Turkey's economy grew by a factor of 3.9 during the 35-year period (even after allowing for inflation), China's by an astounding 22.9, Indonesia's by 6.8 and India's by 7.1.[5] In 1975 Japan had the largest economy ($1.7 trillion); by 2010 China's GDP reached $11.3 trillion and India's reached $5.0 trillion, compared to Japan's $4.0 trillion. These statistics represent an enormous increase in the consumption of goods and services.[6]

The causes and consequences of increasing aggregate consumption (including the demands this places on the natural environment) can be assessed more clearly if we decompose a country's annual GDP growth rate into two components, the annual population growth rate and the annual GDP per capita growth rate, respectively (Royal Society 2012).[7] Table 25.1 shows the decomposition of GDP growth rates for the same 20 countries in Figure 25.2; and Figure 25.3 gives a visual representation of the same decomposition for the largest country in each subregion. We see that China's rapid growth in GDP can be attributed increasingly over the four decades to real growth in average GDP per capita and by the end of the period population growth contributed very little: annual GDP growth averaged 6.0 per cent during the 1970s, and of this 4.2 percentage points could be attributed to per capita GDP growth and 1.7 percentage points to population growth;[8] by the first decade of the present century GDP growth averaged 10.0 per cent, of which 9.4 percentage points could be attributed to per capita growth and only 0.6 points to population growth. The decline in the contribution of population growth is similar in the other three countries although fluctuations in the magnitude of GDP growth per capita are more apparent.

The broad pattern in these data is clear. Throughout Asia the prevailing trend is a decline in population growth rates from the 1970s to the 2000s (see Chapters 5 and 21), despite some small peaks in several countries in between.[9] Trends in GDP per capita growth, on the other hand, are not so consistent: Bangladesh, China, India and Vietnam all trend up; Japan, Korea and Thailand go up, then down; Indonesia and Iran go down, then up; and Malaysia, Pakistan and Turkey fluctuate. Nevertheless the overall trend for most Asian countries has been up, and for some countries the exceptionally rapid increase in GDP per capita during the last quarter century is unprecedented.[10]

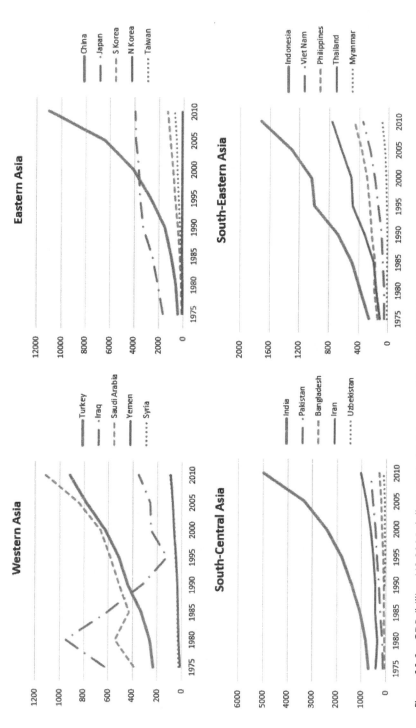

Figure 25.2 GDP (billion US 2005 dollars, PPP), 20 Asian countries, 1975–2010
Source: Based on IEA data from IEA (2014).

Table 25.1 Attribution of average annual rate of growth of GDP to average annual rate of growth of population and of GDP per capita, 20 Asian countries, 1970s–2000s

		Average annual growth rates					Average annual growth rates		
		GDP	Pop	GDP/Pop			GDP	Pop	GDP/Pop
Western Asia					**Eastern Asia**				
Turkey	70s	3.8	2.3	1.6	China	70s	6.0	1.7	4.2
	80s	5.1	2.2	2.9		80s	8.9	1.5	7.4
	90s	3.6	1.5	2.1		90s	9.9	1.1	8.9
	00s	3.8	1.3	2.5		00s	10.0	0.6	9.4
Iraq	70s	7.2	3.2	4.0	Japan	70s	4.3	1.2	3.1
	80s	−10.8	2.45	−13.2		80s	4.5	0.5	4.0
	90s	−2.4	3.1	−5.5		90s	1.1	0.3	0.9
	00s	3.2	2.6	0.6		00s	0.8	0.1	0.7
Saudi Arabia	70s	11.9	5.3	6.6	South Korea	70s	8.4	1.6	6.8
	80s	−0.6	5.0	−5.7		80s	9.3	1.2	8.1
	90s	2.7	2.2	0.5		90s	6.3	0.9	5.4
	00s	5.2	3.1	2.2		00s	4.1	0.5	3.6
Yemen	70s	10.1	2.7	7.4	North Korea	70s	11.1	1.8	9.3
	80s	5.3	4.0	1.2		80s	6.5	1.5	5.0
	90s	5.5	3.9	1.6		90s	−3.6	1.2	−4.8
	00s	4.2	2.7	1.5		00s	−0.3	0.7	−1.1
Syria	70s	9.5	3.5	6.0	Taiwan	70s	10.7	2.0	8.7
	80s	2.2	3.3	−1.1		80s	7.4	1.3	6.0
	90s	4.9	2.7	2.2		90s	6.1	0.9	5.2
	00s	4.8	2.7	2.1		00s	3.8	0.4	3.4
South-Central Asia					**South-Eastern Asia**				
India	70s	3.1	2.3	0.8	Indonesia	70s	7.7	2.4	5.2
	80s	5.4	2.2	3.2		80s	6.2	2.1	4.1
	90s	5.4	1.8	3.6		90s	4.1	1.6	2.6
	00s	7.2	1.5	5.8		00s	5.1	1.4	3.7
Pakistan	70s	5.0	3.1	2.0	Vietnam	70s	0.7	2.3	−1.6
	80s	6.1	3.3	2.8		80s	5.6	2.1	3.5
	90s	3.9	2.6	1.3		90s	7.3	1.6	5.7
	00s	4.1	1.9	2.3		00s	6.4	1.1	5.3
Bangladesh	70s	1.5	2.2	−0.7	Philippines	70s	5.8	2.8	3.0
	80s	3.7	2.6	1.0		80s	1.7	2.7	−1.0
	90s	4.7	2.1	2.6		90s	2.8	2.3	0.6
	00s	5.7	1.3	4.3		00s	4.7	1.8	2.8
Iran	70s	2.3	3.1	−0.8	Thailand	70s	6.8	2.5	4.4
	80s	2.0	3.7	−1.7		80s	7.6	1.8	5.8
	90s	3.7	1.6	2.1		90s	4.4	1.0	3.4
	00s	5.1	1.2	3.8		00s	4.2	0.6	3.6
Uzbekistan	70s	n.a.	n.a.	n.a.	Myanmar	70s	4.7	2.4	2.3
	80s	n.a.	n.a.	n.a.		80s	1.3	2.0	−0.7
	90s	−0.2	1.9	−2.1		90s	6.9	1.4	5.5
	00s	6.7	1.5	5.2		00s	11.4	0.7	10.7

Note: The rate of growth of Pop added to the rate of growth of GDP/Pop does not always exactly equal the rate of growth of GDP because of rounding errors.
Source: Based on IEA data from IEA (2014).

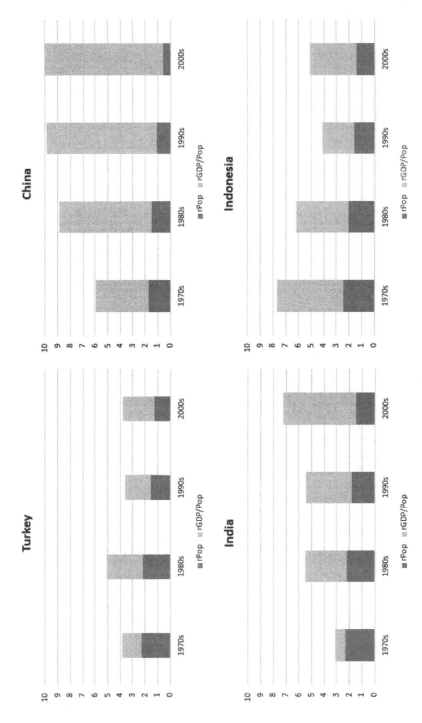

Figure 25.3 Attribution of average annual rate of growth of GDP to average annual rate of growth of population (rPop) and of GDP per capita (rGDP/Pop), Turkey, China, Indonesia and India, 1970s–2000s
Source: Based on IEA data from IEA (2014).

Rapid urbanization and the rise of the middle class in Asia

We have seen that if we decompose GDP growth in Asian countries into population growth and growth in average GDP per capita then the relative contribution of population growth tends to decline over time. This does not mean that population change is no longer important, however. As average GDP per capita grows in a country it does not do so uniformly throughout the population: inevitably the income and wealth of some population groups grows faster than others. It is important therefore to consider the changes in population composition when examining how economic growth impacts on the environment. In Asia two sources of population heterogeneity are especially important, rapid urbanization and the rise of the so-called middle class.

Urbanization and the use of natural resources

In the developing countries of Asia, GDP growth is concentrated in the growing urban areas (Dobbs et al. 2011), and urban people have on average higher incomes and consume more goods and services than rural people. Urbanization is a major driver of household income and aggregate consumption. In this subsection we examine the level of urbanization, the speed and scale of change and the 'form' of urbanization (see also Chapter 16).

Figure 25.4 shows estimates of the level of urbanization from 1950–2010 and projections through to 2050 for the same 20 countries as before. Japan urbanizes first, with over 50 per cent already urban in 1950. South Korea urbanizes rapidly in the post-War period and has caught up with Japan by the end of the mid-1990s at close to 80 per cent, although Japan has experienced a new spurt in urbanization since then. China's population was around 12 per cent urban in 1950 and reached an estimated 56 per cent in 2015; it is projected to reach 69 per cent by 2030 and around 76 per cent by 2050. In Western Asia, Turkey's level of urbanization is 73 per cent in 2015 and Saudi Arabia's 83 per cent. In South-Eastern Asia, both Indonesia and Thailand exceeded 50 per cent at the beginning of the current decade, while Vietnam reached 30 per cent and is expected to reach 50 per cent around 2040. India's urbanization is slow by comparison but it is steadily growing and expected to reach 50 per cent by mid-century. Bangladesh starts from a low base but has now overtaken India. Although Japan has already reached 90 per cent urban and cannot be expected to urbanize much more, the UN projections anticipate continuing increases in all the other countries shown and suggest that Asia will be about 54 per cent urban by 2025 and 64 per cent by 2050. Dobbs et al. (2011: 28) anticipate that by 2025 'nine of the world's top 25 cities ranked by GDP will be located in Asia, up from two in 2007'.

The speed and scale of these shifts to urban living across much of Asia are unprecedented (ADB 2012: 3–46). UN estimates and projections suggest that the urban population in China alone will grow by more than 415 million during the first two decades of this century, which is more than the 2015 total population of the US, the UK and Australia combined. Urbanization has been taking place in the world for centuries but the speed and scale of the process in Asia today contribute to some distinctive patterns in both the form of urbanization and the associated population-environment interactions.

Marcotullio (2003), building on the work of McGranahan and others (Jacobi et al. 2001), distinguishes three 'agendas' of urban environmental challenges. The brown agenda comprises environmental challenges due to population density, especially water supply, sanitation and infectious diseases; in the grey agenda they are due to the negative aspects of industrial production, especially water and air pollution; and in the green agenda they are due to the high rate of human consumption and include issues such as ecosystem health, ozone depletion and greenhouse

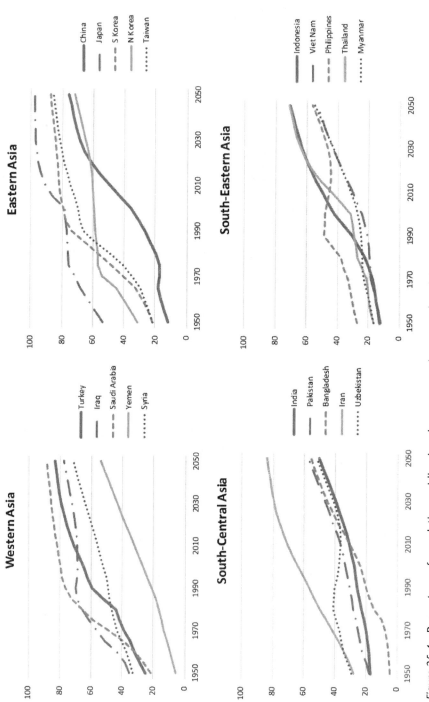

Figure 25.4 Percentage of population residing in urban areas, estimates and projections, 20 Asian countries, 1950–2050
Source: UNPD (2014).

gas emissions. This suggests a simple typology of urban population-environment interactions in terms of urban land use and environmental challenges. At one extreme are low-income cities, still relatively unchanged by globalization, that are struggling with brown issues. Writing around the turn of the century, Marcotullio lists Phnom Penh, Hanoi, Ho Chi Minh City, Vientiane, Yangon and Ulaanbaatar as examples. At the other extreme are the high-income capital-exporting cities of Asia – Tokyo, Seoul and Taipei – 'the sites of concentrations of transnational corporation headquarters, multinational banks, producer- and business-services'. These cities have 'multi-nodal structures' and 'are expanding outwards, leaving workers with longer commutes, as many of the jobs remain in the inner-city area. Manufacturing industries have decentralized from the centre while advanced services are concentrated in the core regions of the city' (Marcotullio 2003: 237).[11] Populations living in these conglomerations have to contend with green agenda issues, especially outdoor air pollution and quality-of-life issues such as lack of open space and sprawl-induced ennui. In between are the rapidly industrializing cities, characterized by high inflows of foreign direct investment and extreme inequalities in income and wealth. Marcotullio mentions Bangkok, Beijing, Delhi, Jakarta, Kuala Lumpur, Manila and Shanghai. Rapid urbanization in these cities in particular has resulted in the brown, grey and green environmental challenges becoming concertinaed together in a chaotic fashion in the same urban environment. At the same time that outdoor air pollution from industry and motor vehicles emerges as a major problem, for example, many residents in poor neighbourhoods are still suffering from indoor air pollution from using biomass or coal for cooking and heating.

One way out of this dilemma may be for urban planners to pay more attention to 'urban form' (embracing built environment, land use and social processes).[12] The way the built environment organizes much of the urban population's daily activities is of special interest. Consider, for example, the spatial distribution of an urban agglomeration like the Greater Jakarta region. It consists of a central core of five districts, the Capital City Region, surrounded by an expanding ring of mixed or 'peri-urban' development, and beyond that a growing number of satellite towns of various sizes and characters. Some of the latter are long-established settlements that have gradually been absorbed amoeba-like into the growing urban agglomeration, while others are new towns developed by large consortia of private businesses; additional land may be purchased for future development (Dick and Rimmer 1998). The environmental impact of such large-scale development is massive, but the full extent depends significantly on how the urban form is designed and constructed. If, for instance, many production and consumption functions are integrated within the satellite towns which are themselves designed as 'walking towns' then this spatial pattern of 'bundling' social activities can be relatively environment-friendly, at least in terms of fuel consumption needed for transportation. Alternatively, if many of those who live in satellite towns need to commute into central Jakarta for work and routine amenities, and if public transportation is inconvenient, unsafe or non-existent, then the same overall spatial pattern is associated with chronic car-dependency and a very high rate of fossil fuel consumption by residents – especially if the roads are congested so that even short distances regularly take an hour or two crawling through traffic jams. Currently the second alternative appears closer to reality in Jakarta and many other Asian cities.[13] Future patterns of aggregate consumption and pollution in Asia will depend not just on the level and pace of urbanization but also on the form that it takes (Rosenzweig et al. 2011; Saieg 2013).

The middle class and the use of natural resources

Running in parallel with urbanization is the rapid growth in the number of people with discretionary income to spend – the rise of the so-called 'consuming classes', or simply the 'middle class' (ADB 2010: 3–52; Dobbs et al. 2012). How this new middle class in Asia spends its money is emerging as a major driver of environmental change (Hayes 2014). To assess this we need to consider the size and growth of the class, the money they have to spend, and the values they exercise in deciding how to spend it.

Different researchers define the middle class differently (Kharas 2010; Ravallion 2009). The Asian Development Bank (ADB 2010) defines it in terms of per capita consumption of $2–$20 per day (at 2005 PPP). They estimate that in developing Asia 1.9 billion people were already in the middle class in 2008, while 1.5 billion were still living on less than $2 per day. But the majority of this middle class were still living in the $2–$4 range, leaving them at high risk of falling into poverty in the event of common shocks such as illness, unemployment or too many unwanted pregnancies. The ADB calls these near-poor people lower-middle class. Those living on between $4–$10, that is, those living above subsistence and able to buy at least some nonessential goods, they call middle-middle class; and those consuming $10–$20 a day are upper-middle class. Table 25.2 (top panel) shows the composition of population by expenditure class for 14 Asian countries c.2005.[14] The data show, for example, that by 2005 the middle class in China already accounted for 63 per cent of the population, although more than half of this was in the lower-middle category; in India the middle class accounted for 25 per cent of the population, with more than 80 per cent of this in the lower-middle category.

The bottom panel of Table 25.2 shows the per cent of total annual expenditure spent by each expenditure class. While the middle-middle class of China accounts for 25 per cent of the population it accounts for 39 per cent of aggregate expenditure. It is hard to assemble reliable and consistent time series data for several countries but Figure 25.5 illustrates the general pattern. Of the countries shown India has the lowest average GDP per capita and Malaysia (moving counter-clockwise around the Figure) the highest. In India, 75 per cent of the population are living on less than $2 a day and this class represents just 11 per cent of total expenditures. In Indonesia, this category has declined to 53 per cent of the population but accounts for 29 per cent of expenditures. In China, the middle class already accounts for 63 per cent of the population and 79 per cent of expenditures, but 37 per cent of the population are still living on under $2 a day. In Malaysia, however, the distribution is overall clearly 'middle class' with each of the three middle-class subcategories comprising more population than either the below-$2 or above-$20 classes. We cannot predict how India will continue to develop but we can expect the distribution of expenditure classes by population and total expenditure to shift in a counter-clockwise direction through the patterns displayed in Figure 25.5 towards a distribution that looks more like that of Malaysia c.2005.

The middle class in Asia is growing much faster than the population as a whole, and the per capita income of the middle class is growing faster still. The ADB estimates that while the total population of developing Asia grew by 26 per cent during 1990–2008, the middle class grew by 236 per cent[15] and aggregate income (or expenditure) grew by more than 350 per cent. Asia's growing middle class is, in fact, an engine of economic growth globally as well as regionally, and the expectation is that its growth will continue and will eventually spread through all parts of the region. How middle-class consumer preferences evolve over time and how they might shift towards more 'green consumption' (Peattie 2010) can make a lot of difference to natural-resource consumption in Asia.

It is also apparent that the rise of the middle class involves considerable geographical and social mobility and therefore inevitably involves significant adjustments to established social and cultural institutions. The rise of the middle class brings about a shift in social values. This is an emerging area of research relevant to understanding the environmental impacts of the growing middle class (Ansori 2009; Beng-Huat 2000; Ganguly-Scrase and Scrase 2008; Lange and

Table 25.2 Expenditure classes by per cent of total population and by per cent of total aggregate annual expenditure, selected developing countries of Asia, c.2005

Country and survey year	Expenditure class (daily expenditure per capita)				
	Under $2	$2-$4	$4-$10	$10-$20	Over $20
	Per cent of population				
Eastern Asia					
China (2005)	36.6	34.0	25.2	3.5	0.7
Mongolia (2005)	48.1	39.2	12.4	0.3	0.0
South-Eastern Asia					
Indonesia (2005)	53.1	35.0	10.4	1.2	0.3
Vietnam (2006)	47.6	35.5	14.8	1.9	0.2
Philippines (2006)	44.4	31.5	19.6	3.8	0.7
Thailand (2004)	10.7	33.5	41.7	10.6	3.5
Malaysia (2004)	7.3	27.1	48.1	14.1	3.4
Cambodia (2004)	66.6	24.7	7.4	0.9	0.3
South-Central Asia					
India (2005)	74.8	20.5	4.1	0.5	0.1
Pakistan (2005)	59.7	32.9	6.6	0.6	0.2
Bangladesh (2005)	79.7	16.4	3.5	0.4	<0.1
Uzbekistan (2003)	76.0	19.3	4.1	0.5	0.1
Nepal (2004)	76.7	16.7	5.3	0.9	0.4
Kazakhstan (2003)					
	Per cent of total aggregate annual expenditure				
Eastern Asia					
China	16.2	28.9	38.5	11.8	4.6
Mongolia	25.6	44.8	28.3	1.3	0.0
South-Eastern Asia					
Indonesia	29.2	37.9	23.1	5.9	3.9
Vietnam	23.1	35.9	30.6	9.2	1.2
Philippines	17.2	27.0	35.3	15.5	5.0
Thailand	2.9	15.6	40.6	22.4	18.5
Malaysia	1.8	12.0	44.9	27.7	13.6
Cambodia	36.1	30.6	19.4	5.6	8.3
South-Central Asia					
India	10.9	57.1	21.7	5.4	4.9
Pakistan	37.9	39.9	16.5	3.7	2.0
Bangladesh	57.1	26.8	12.1	3.3	0.7
Uzbekistan	50.5	29.8	13.3	3.5	3.0
Nepal	41.5	23.5	15.9	6.0	13.1
Kazakhstan	5.8	26.2	50.6	16.0	1.3

Note: All expenditure classes and expenditure amounts are based on 2005 PPP $.
Source: Adapted from Chun (2010: Table 4).

Meier 2009; Li 2010; Peattie 2010; Pinches 1999; Robison and Goodman 1996). Compared with powerful elites on the one hand or the poor on the other, the middle class includes the population segments most committed to values aligned with sustained economic growth (Kharas 2010). Furthermore, although middle-class people often display a seemingly insatiable demand

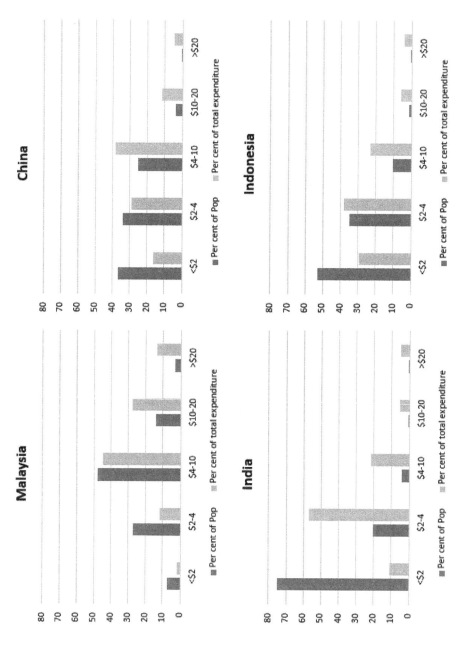

Figure 25.5 Expenditure classes by per cent of total population and by per cent of total aggregate annual expenditure, Malaysia, China, Indonesia and India, c.2005
Source: Based on data from Chun (2010: Table 4).

for goods and services to satisfy their tastes for status, security, comfort and convenience, they also demand, as their prosperity rises, that pollution be removed from their own local environments (and they are willing to pay taxes to see this done) (Myers and Kent 2003; Peattie 2010). Pollution levels, consequently, tend to follow a Kuznets curve, and we see this happening in Asia (ADB 2012: 19–29).[16] Although pollution in Asian countries associated with development and rapid urbanization receives a lot of media attention, some studies suggest that the rate of pollution may be lower than it was in Western countries when they were at similar levels of urbanization (ADB 2012: 26–28).

Trends in resource use and environmental indicators

The continuing growth in aggregate consumption of goods and services in Asia associated with urbanization and the rise of the middle class places enormous demands on the natural environment (Smil 2013).[17] In this section we discuss changes in the use of natural resources, and some environmental and demographic consequences of these changes. Overuse of natural resources and pollution of ecosystems has deleterious consequences for population health, for example, and can exacerbate national security concerns. We consider two vital resources, water and energy.[18]

Water use and pollution

FAO (2003) estimates the total renewable water resources (TRWR) of the world to be around 45,000 cubic kilometres (km^3) a year: about 29 per cent of this is in Asia.[19] Water resources are distributed far from evenly across Asia. They are also exploited differently in different countries, and the health of waterways varies considerably. Table 25.3 (first data column) shows the enormous variation in TRWR per capita among the countries of Asia. According to FAO Aquastat estimates, Indonesia has potentially more than 13,000 cubic metres (m^3) of fresh water per capita per year and Myanmar almost 22,000, while Yemen has barely 220 and Saudi Arabia has to make do with less than 120 m^3 per person per year (FAO 2003). In general TRWR per capita has been declining as a result of population growth. Countries in the arid parts of Western Asia have to use non-conventional water sources like desalinization.

Typically however not all of a country's conventional TRWR are readily available for human use because they are too hard to access or simply located too far from where they are needed. Another constraint is if a significant portion of a country's TRWR comes from rivers originating outside its national borders, resulting in high so-called water dependency ratios (WDR): 91 per cent for Bangladesh, 80 for Syria, and 77 for both Uzbekistan and Pakistan (third data column). The Mekong River is a case in point: its source is high in the Tibetan Plateau, and it courses through Yunnan Province, along the Myanmar-Laos border (where the two countries have WDR estimates 16 and 43 per cent, respectively) and along much of the Laos border with Thailand (49 per cent), through Cambodia (75 per cent) and on to Vietnam (59 per cent). Large hydroelectric schemes built in Yunnan and water use in Laos and Thailand can have dramatic effects on flow and water quality in Cambodia or the annual floods in the river's delta in Vietnam.

A country's level of water security also depends on how the water is actually accessed, distributed and used. Since a population's demand for water is not homogeneous it needs to be 'deconstructed' if it is to be assessed sensibly.[20] Water is needed not just for domestic use in the household, but also crucially for agriculture and industry. Globally, agriculture accounts for 80 per cent or more of freshwater use. The second data column in Table 25.3 gives estimates of average total freshwater withdrawal (TFW) per capita per year. Iraq and Uzbekistan are the largest withdrawers on a per capita basis because they withdraw exceptionally high amounts

Table 25.3 Water resources and water security estimates, 20 Asian countries, c.2005

Country or territory	Water resources		Dep. Ratio %	Water security				
	TRWR per cap. m3/yr	TFW per cap. m3/yr		KD1	KD2	KD3	KD4	KD5
Western Asia								
Turkey	3,439	530	1.0	n.a.	n.a.	n.a.	n.a.	n.a.
Iraq	3,287	2,097	53.3	n.a.	n.a.	n.a.	n.a.	n.a.
Saudi Arabia	118	902	0	n.a.	n.a.	n.a.	n.a.	n.a.
Yemen	223	147	0	n.a.	n.a.	n.a.	n.a.	n.a.
Syria	1,622	746	80.3	n.a.	n.a.	n.a.	n.a.	n.a.
Eastern Asia								
China	2,258	425	0.6	3	4	2	2	2
Japan	3,383	709	0	5	4	2	2	3
South Korea	1,491	525	7.0	5	3	2	2	2
North Korea	3,464	363	13.1	n.a.	n.a.	n.a.	n.a.	n.a.
Taiwan	3,021	n.a.	0	3	3	3	3	3
South-Eastern Asia								
Indonesia	13,381	487	0	2	4	2	3	2
Vietnam	11,406	921	58.9	3	1	1	2	2
Philippines	6,332	872	0	2	4	1	2	2
Thailand	6,527	841	48.8	3	3	2	1	2
Myanmar	21,898	658	15.8	2	3	2	3	1
South-Central Asia								
India	1,880	627	33.9	1	3	1	1	2
Pakistan	1,576	993	76.5	1	4	1	1	1
Bangladesh	8,809	253	91.3	1	3	1	1	1
Iran	1,955	1,243	6.6	n.a.	n.a.	n.a.	n.a.	n.a.
Uzbekistan	2,026	2,015	77.4	3	3	2	2	2

Notes: TRWR = Total renewable water resources; TFW = Total freshwater withdrawal;
KD (key dimension) 1 = Household water security; KD2 = Economic water security; KD3 = Urban water security; KD4 = Environmental water security; KD5 = Resilience to water-related disasters.
A score of 1 is low security ('hazardous') and 5 is high security ('model').
Sources: Water resources data from FAO (2003: 78–82) for TRWR per capita per year, and from Gleick et al. (2014) for TFW per capita per year; water security data from ADB (2013).

for agriculture. For the 19 countries shown with TFW data, Gleick et al. (2014) estimates that the annual withdrawals for agriculture on a per capita basis vary from 134 m^3 (Yemen), 222 m^3 (Bangladesh) and 272 m^3 (China), up to 933 m^3 (Pakistan), 1,143 m^3 (Iran), 1,657 m^3 (Iraq) and 1,813 m^3 (Uzbekistan). Domestic use varies less: from 9 m^3 (Vietnam), 10 m^3 (Yemen) and 25 m^3 (Bangladesh), up to 136 m^3 (South Korea), 141 m^3 (Uzbekistan) and 147 m^3 (Iraq). Variation in withdrawals for industrial use is relatively modest, with the more industrial or rapidly industrializing economies like Japan (127 m^3 per person per year), China (99 m^3) and South Korea (63 m^3) withdrawing more than Saudi Arabia (27 m^3) or Vietnam (37 m^3).

The first major attempt to assess water security systematically for many countries of Asia using a common metric is surprisingly recent. The study (ADB 2013) covers five main uses of freshwater: household water security (KD1), economic water security (agriculture and industry) (KD2), urban water security (KD3), environmental water security (for healthy ecosystems)

(KD4) and resilience to water-related disasters (KD5). Table 25.3 shows estimates for selected countries on a crude scale of 1 (hazardous) to 5 (model).[21]

Regarding household water security (KD1), the ADB finds that although access to safe drinking water has improved impressively in Asia during the last 25 years, access to piped water and sanitation is still well below 50 per cent in many countries, especially in South Asia. As a result water-borne diseases are still endemic through much of Asia. Regarding economic water security (KD2), the report concludes, 'Water is or is likely to become a constraint on economic growth in a number of countries unless a renewed effort is directed towards ensuring water availability in adequate quantities and qualities' (ADB 2013: 31). Agricultural water productivity is particularly low in South Asia, and increased use of groundwater is of concern in both South and East Asia. The situation is especially dire in areas around the Aral Sea, where large-scale irrigation systems for cotton and wheat production dating back to the 1930s have been poorly maintained and are grossly inefficient. Another concern throughout the region is the rising demand for water use in thermal energy production. A World Bank study estimates that 2.3 per cent of China's GDP during the early years of this century was lost because of the combined effects of water scarcity and water pollution. Urban water security (KD3) is generally not high across the region, and the fact that diarrhoeal diseases are endemic in many Asian cities is symptomatic of this (Andrews and Yñiguez 2004; Jacobi et al. 2001; UN-HABITAT 2003).[22]

Improving water security in the first three key dimensions is not a straightforward matter of building more infrastructure to increase supply. The demand in each case needs to be assessed critically, and alternative ways to satisfy the demand need to be evaluated.[23] The failure to distinguish between the 'need' for freshwater where it is an essential resource for consumption (e.g. for drinking) from the 'want' of water to provide a service (e.g. removing waste) where substitutes are available (or where the same water can be recycled and used over and over again) has resulted in many developing countries building larger water infrastructure projects than necessary, often at great cost and with negative social and environmental impacts (Gleick 2003).

Restoring and maintaining the health of rivers and ecosystems (KD4) is another major water-related issue in Asia. The issue here is not whether water is available and accessible for a particular human use, but whether enough of sufficient quality remains in the natural environment after human withdrawals to maintain the health of ecosystems. The pollution of rivers in Asia is strongly associated with population and agricultural density (Economy 2004). In the ADB study, the rivers of Armenia and India were found to be the least healthy.

The human and economic cost of water-related disasters (KD5) is another major security concern. The 2004 Indian Ocean Tsunami caused an estimated 170,000 deaths in Indonesia, 35,000 in Sri Lanka, 18,000 in India and over 8,000 in Thailand. The 2011 floods in Thailand caused damage and economic losses amounting to an estimated $45 billion. Even Japan's sophisticated tsunami warning system could not prevent close to 19,000 deaths from the Tohuku earthquake and tsunami (most from drowning), and the associated flooding of the Daiichi Nuclear Power Plant at Fukushima produced a nuclear waste pollution disaster which will take decades to resolve; total damages and losses are estimated at around $300 billion. Meanwhile climate change is expected to increase the challenge of providing resilience to water-related disasters, especially for densely populated low-lying coastal areas (McGranahan et al. 2007): many of Asia's largest cities are located in such low-lying zones.

Energy use and pollution

Our second example of changes in the use of natural resources is due to the massive growth in the demand for energy. Figure 25.6 shows trends in total primary energy supply (TPES) for 20

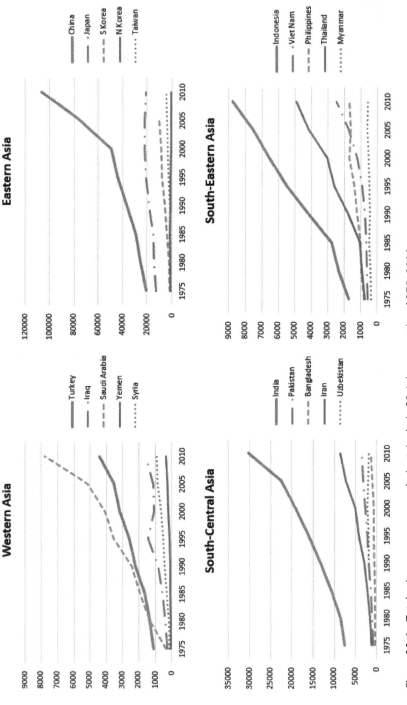

Figure 25.6 Total primary energy supply (petajoules), 20 Asian countries, 1975–2010
Source: Based on IEA data from IEA (2014).

countries.[24] During 1975–2010, the TPES of China (excluding Hong Kong) grew by 422 per cent (from 20,257 to 105,777 petajoules); during the same period the TPES of Turkey grew by 294 per cent, of Indonesia by 409 per cent and of India by 307 per cent. Among the Asian Tigers, South Korea's TPES grew by 922 per cent, Taiwan's by 666 per cent, Singapore's by 586 per cent and Hong Kong's 289 per cent, during 1975–2010. Among developed countries, the TPES of Israel grew by 230 per cent and Japan by 64 per cent during the same years.

Most of this energy is produced by burning fossil fuels (coal, oil and natural gas). Consequently carbon dioxide emissions have increased significantly as well (Figure 25.7). During 1975–2010, the CO_2 emissions of China grew by 576 per cent (from 1,079.3 to 7,294.9 million tonnes); during the same period the growth was 349 per cent for Turkey, 933 per cent for Indonesia and 624 per cent for India. Among the Asian Tigers, South Korea's CO_2 emissions grew by 635 per cent, Taiwan's by 536 per cent, Singapore's by 475 per cent and Hong Kong's 290 per cent. Among developed countries, the TPES of Israel grew by 298 per cent and Japan by 32 per cent during 1975–2010. The trend lines in Figure 25.7 closely mirror those in Figure 25.6 because very little of the energy supply in the countries shown is produced from non-fossil fuel sources. The energy mix by type of fossil fuel is quite variable, however, and although coal provides most of the new energy produced, in most developing countries in the region there is a significant trend to substitute more natural gas (IEA 2015).

While the growth in TPES is essential for improving living standards and reducing poverty, the heavy reliance on fossil fuels has multiple negative consequences for the environment and for population health. Air pollution is now a major population health issue in many parts of Asia (Gong et al. 2012; HEI 2004; Kjellstrom et al. 2007; Shao et al. 2006): the Global Burden of Diseases 2010 study estimates that in China 'around 1.2 million premature deaths and 25 million disability-adjusted life-years annually' can be attributed to air pollution (Lancet 2014: 845). Air pollution is a health risk around the world, but the sheer scale and density of accelerated economic development in China makes the level of risk particularly serious. The problem is not simply with the high concentration of primary airborne pollutants such as SO_2, NO_x and VOCs from burning coal and other fossil fuels,[25] but the way these pollutants oxidize and interact when in high concentrations with other pollutants (especially ozone) to form secondary pollutants, i.e. more airborne particulates, especially the dangerous fine particulates labelled $PM_{2.5}$ (Shao et al. 2006). Another negative consequence of the growing use of fossil fuels is, of course, the contribution of the resulting greenhouse gas emissions to global climate change.

To understand the population-environment dynamics better it helps to introduce the so-called Kaya identity (IEA 2014: 20–21). This is a mathematical identity that decomposes a country's CO_2 emissions into four variables, namely, population size, GDP per capita, the amount of energy used to produce a unit of GDP ('energy intensity') and the amount of carbon dioxide emitted in producing a unit of energy ('carbon intensity'):[26]

$$CO_2 = Pop \times GDP/Pop \times TPES/GDP \times CO_2/TPES.$$

Since the equation is a mathematical identity, it follows that the instantaneous rate of change of the variable on the left-hand side must equal the sum of the rates of change of each of the four variables on the right-hand side. We know the rate of population growth has already declined or begun to decline in most parts of Asia (Chapter 21) and no one is seriously advocating reducing GDP per capita in order to reduce emissions. That leaves energy intensity and carbon intensity open for discussion.

In the case of energy intensity, although total primary energy supply (TPES) has increased considerably in much of the region, the amount of energy it takes to produce one unit of GDP

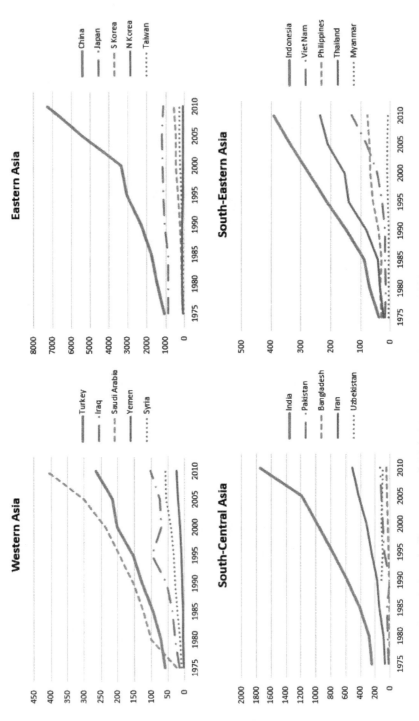

Figure 25.7 CO$_2$ emissions (million tonnes of CO$_2$), 20 Asian countries, 1975–2010
Source: Based on IEA data from IEA (2014).

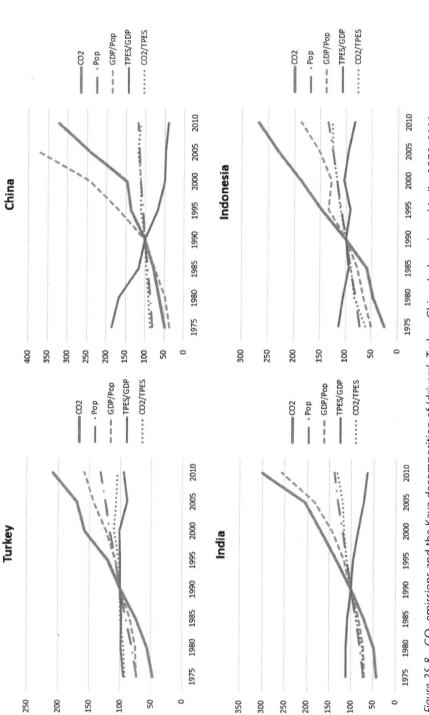

Figure 25.8 CO$_2$ emissions and the Kaya decomposition of 'drivers', Turkey, China, Indonesia and India, 1975–2010
Note: Values for each variable are standardized so that its value for 1990 equals 100.
Source: Based on IEA data from IEA (2014).

has generally declined. Indeed, this is a near-universal trend globally, since there are strong economic incentives to use energy more efficiently. In China in 1975, it took about 40 million joules of primary energy to produce 1 dollar of GDP (in 2005 PPP dollars), while in 2010 it took less than 10 million.[27] It is not only better industrial technology that makes the difference; as we saw in the previous section, designing cities so that people use less energy commuting every day can play a role (Saieg 2013). Although improving energy efficiency is important in combating air pollution and mitigating climate change, it is by itself not enough (UNESCAP, ADB and UNEP 2012).

Reducing carbon intensity can be achieved by extracting energy more efficiently from fossil fuels, or conceivably by developing new technologies like carbon capture and storage, but in terms of commercially viable technologies available today, it requires using less fossil fuels and substituting renewables (and/or nuclear). The countries of Asia have started moving in this direction, although the overall picture is still mixed and fluid. China is heavily dependent on coal, but its carbon intensity appears to have peaked at 73 tonnes of CO_2 per terajoule around 2005 and is now declining (IEA 2014). The carbon intensities of India, Indonesia and Turkey are less but still rising. As suggested in the previous section, the values espoused by the new middle class in Asia could be a major force for accelerating the transformation to low-carbon economies.

Figure 25.8 gives a graphical representation of how CO_2 emissions and their four Kaya 'drivers' have changed relative to their respective values in 1990. In relative terms, GDP per capita during 1990–2010 has grown more rapidly than CO_2 emissions in China, but the reverse is true for Turkey, Indonesia and India.[28] Energy intensity has more than halved during the same period in China and is down about 40 per cent in India, but has only slightly declined in Turkey and Indonesia. Carbon intensity has risen slightly in Turkey and China, more significantly in India and Indonesia. Used as a diagnostic tool the Kaya identity can help identify where a population's activities must change if its CO_2 emissions are to be reduced.

Population change and sustainable development

To find developmental pathways that are more environmentally friendly is now viewed by many as a moral imperative. At the UN Sustainable Development Summit in 2015, the international community renewed a commitment to sustainable development and officially adopted 17 Sustainable Development Goals (SDGs) to guide development efforts during the 15-year period, 2016–2030 (UN 2015). Sustainable development involves managing sustained economic growth in ways that are both environmentally sustainable and socially equitable. Understanding how population change is involved in the causes and consequences of environmental change can help accomplish this.

A population's production and consumption of resources are complex social processes. A single natural resource, say freshwater, can be accessed in a variety of ways (from rain, from rivers and lakes, from aquifers, from treated wastewater and from seawater by desalinization), and used in innumerable ways for countless different purposes. Each production-to-consumption pathway has different costs and benefits over varying timescales for producers, consumers, the population-at-large and the environment. Deconstructing supply and demand shows that a specific resource may be essential for some uses and optional or discretionary for others, and substitutes exist for some purposes and not for others.

Population changes are complex social processes too. For maintaining sustained economic growth in an environmentally friendly way in Asia and increasing social equity at the same time, it is important, for example, that the growth of the middle class is increasingly inclusive and does not take place at the expense of the poor.[29] Acemoglu and Robinson (2012) suggest

Population and environment in Asia

this requires expanding 'inclusive institutions' that support widely distributed prosperity and reducing 'extractive institutions' that protect the rule of elites and extreme wealth inequalities. Monitoring progress towards sustainability requires monitoring changes in well-being and quality of life throughout the whole population.

Many experts agree that making the shift to sustainable development will require more than the usual sticks and carrots of public policy and market instruments, although they remain indispensable (Stern 2007). Deeper levels of system change and societal transformation are needed (O'Rourke and Lollo 2015).[30] What this entails in detail is not yet clear to social scientists and policymakers, but in order to build on the kinds of population-and-environment research discussed in this chapter and make them as relevant as possible to the sustainable development agenda it might be useful to reframe the field as 'population change and sustainable development' (Hayes 2013). Whatever the challenges, we can be confident that as the world's economic centre of gravity moves back towards Asia, it will be the peoples of the region that produce many of the most innovative and successful solutions.

Acknowledgements

The author wishes to thank Susana Adamo, Heather Booth, Alice Sin Yin Chow and Zhongwei Zhao for their very helpful comments on an earlier draft of this chapter.

Notes

1. For important analytical reviews of the population and environment literature see Keyfitz (1991); Hunter (2000); de Sherbinin et al. (2007); Hummel et al. (2013). See also Curran and Derman (2012) and Curran and de Sherbinin (2004).
2. There are serious limitations to the GDP concept when used as a measure of prosperity, especially since it is a far from perfect measure of well-being and it does not measure most of the environmental costs of economic activity, but for practical reasons it still plays an indispensable role in discussions of sustainable development and population-environment interactions. See Costanza et al. (2013) and Sachs (2015).
3. All GDP estimates in this chapter are based on US 2005 dollars in terms of purchasing power parity (PPP) as reported in IEA (2014), unless explicitly stated otherwise. In 2014 the International Comparison Program (ICP) published new estimates for GDP PPP (for all countries normally covered in World Bank reports), and this has led to significant changes for many countries, including most of the developing countries of Asia. IEA (2014) uses these revised estimates.
4. The five largest countries in each region are listed in descending order of size (in the year 2000).
5. Growth was also especially impressive during the period for South Korea (by a factor of 10.6 – Korea graduated to high-income status in the mid-1990s), and Singapore (by a factor of 11.0).
6. Of course measuring the value of economic activities in monetary terms ignores many differences that are relevant for the analysis of their environmental impacts: growth in heavy industry and manufacturing, for example, is likely to have more environmental impact (dollar for dollar) than growth in service activities. The attribution of environmental impact to economic activity is also complicated by international trade, since the impact associated with final consumption of specific goods and services will often be in different countries from where they (or some of their components) are produced. Even so, if we want to understand how the environmental impacts of Asian countries are changing then an appreciation of how their economies are changing in size provides a fruitful starting point.
7. From the point of view of environmental sustainability it matters little if the growth in demand for natural resources is driven primarily by population growth or a rise in per capita consumption (or both). However when designing sound policy it makes a lot of difference, since per capita demand on environmental resources (one person's 'ecological footprint') depends essentially on level of affluence while population size is essentially a scaling factor.
8. The two component rates do not add up exactly to 6.0 per cent because of rounding errors.
9. The city-state of Singapore is an exception: it still has high population growth due to high in-migration for employment.

493

10 The simple decomposition of GDP growth rates displayed in Table 25.1 cannot disclose the causal relations between population growth and growth in GDP per capita, but one can see an association between significant declines in population growth and a surge in GDP per capita in several cases, as postulated by the demographic dividend hypothesis (see Chapter 24): for example, in China since the 1980s, in South Korea and Taiwan already in the 1970s, and in Vietnam during the 1990s and 2000s. It is also worth noting that Bangladesh, Iran, the Philippines and Vietnam all experienced decades where population growth outstripped growth in GDP, entailing negative growth in GDP per capita. Meanwhile low growth in GDP can mean different things for well-being depending on the relative magnitude of population growth: when Vietnam experienced only 0.7 per cent GDP growth per annum in the 1970s (during the American War) this translated into negative growth in GDP per capita since population growth still averaged 2.3 per cent per annum, but when Japan's economy grew at only 0.8 per cent per annum during the 2000s, however, this still represented positive growth in GDP per capita because population growth was down to 0.1 per cent a year.

11 Well-managed entrepôts like Singapore and Hong Kong are excluded from this typology and treated as special cases (Marcotullio 2003: 239).

12 Unfortunately there is currently no generally-accepted theory of urban form which allows us to distinguish clearly the relative environmental impacts of different patterns of agglomeration or to assess which designs are more conducive to reaching the ideals of sustainable development, although many elements of such a theory are becoming increasingly clear (Bettencourt and West 2010; Bertaud 2002; Cuthbert 2006; Glaeser 2011; Levy 1999; Saieg 2013; Satterthwaite 1999; World Bank 2015). We use the term 'urban form' to refer to the distribution and organization of an urban population's activities in space, embracing production, consumption, residential patterns, transportation and communication in both their material and symbolic aspects. Glaeser (2011: 12) writes, 'Transportation technologies have always determined urban form', but it is the political economy and governance of cities that determine the adoption and implementation of technologies (Bai et al. 2010). See also Chow (2014).

13 For another population perspective on Jakarta and a number of other major Asian cities of over 10 million population, see Jones and Douglass (2008).

14 The data derive from household surveys collected by the World Bank. The reference years for the surveys are given in parentheses in Table 25.2.

15 The middle class made up 21 per cent of the population of developing Asia in 1990 and 56 per cent in 2008, or in absolute terms an increase from 565 million to 1.9 billion people.

16 For a critical examination of the hypothesis see Stern et al. (1996).

17 Industrial societies, employing fossil fuels and other modern sources of energy, have quite different 'metabolic regimes' than agrarian societies. Krausmann et al. (2008) estimate that the transition from agrarian to industrial society is associated typically with material and energy use per capita increasing by a factor of around 3 to 5, while material and energy use per unit of land area increases by a factor of anywhere between 10 to 30.

18 The most important population–environment we do not have space to cover is land-use and land-cover change. See Zhao et al. (2006).

19 The focus here is on renewable water resources. Although two-thirds of the planet is covered by water less than 1 per cent is in rivers, lakes and groundwater where it is available to terrestrial ecosystems, and potentially to human populations. Total natural renewable resources (TRWR) for a country is defined as the sum of internal renewable water resources and natural incoming flow originating outside the country. It is estimated as an average over several years, and so in the absence of climate change is considered not to vary with time (FAO 2003: xii).

20 As Gleick (2003: 278) points out, 'The term *water use*, while common, can mean many different things, referring at times to consumptive use and at times to withdrawals of water. Withdrawal usually refers to water removed from a source and used for human needs. Some of this water may be returned to the original source with changes in the quantity and quality of the water, but some may be used consumptively. The term *consumptive use* or *consumption* typically refers to water withdrawn from a source and made unavailable for reuse in the same basin, such as through conversion to steam, losses to evaporation, seepage to a saline sink, or contamination … Thus a power plant may withdraw substantial amounts of water for cooling from a river but use that water in a way that permits it to be returned directly to the river, perhaps a bit warmer, for use by the next downstream user. A farmer may withdraw the same amount of water for irrigation, but the vast majority of it may be used consumptively by plants and become unavailable for any other activity'. Gleick emphasizes there are serious problems with water use data, as well as with definitions.

21 We do not have reliable time series data on water security for many countries but numerous case studies document how the situation is getting more serious in many specific basins, watersheds and localities (e.g. Economy 2004; UNESCAP and ADB 1995: 89–98). In the ADB report (2013) the assessment of a country's level or stage of water security depends on an assessment of various governance factors. Thus stage 1 (hazardous) corresponds to 'Some legislation and policy on water and environment, and inadequate levels of public investment, regulations and enforcement'; by stage 3 (capable) we have 'Continuous capacity building, improved rates of public investment, stronger regulation and enforcement', etc.; and by stage 5 (model) we have 'Sustainable local agencies and services, sustained sources of public financing for water and environment protection and management, sustainable levels of public water consumption', etc. (ADB 2013: 8).

22 Readers may be surprised that even Japan and South Korea only score two on this index. The reason is the index includes several specific measures including flood damage. It is very hard to protect urban areas against all threats to water security.

23 Gleick (2003: 278) illustrates the principle: 'The level of demand for water may have no relationship to the minimum amount of water required to satisfy a particular requirement. Water demand to flush a toilet can range from six gallons in an old, inefficient US toilet, to 1.6 gallons in a model that meets current US standards, to zero gallons in an efficient composting toilet. What is actually being demanded is not a specific amount of water but the service of reliably and safely removing wastes'. Deconstructing the demand for water has important implications for policy.

24 The total primary energy supply (TPES) of a country can be thought of as the total amount of energy used by the domestic economy in a year. It is called 'primary' because it is the total amount taken from nature (from fossil fuels, wind, solar, etc.), before it is converted into another form (like electricity) before final consumption. The unit of measurement is petajoules (or sometimes millions of tonnes of oil equivalent).

25 SO_2, NO_x and VOCs refer to sulphur dioxide, nitrous oxides and volatile organic compounds, respectively, all of which affect human health adversely. Later in the paragraph, $PM_{2.5}$ refers to airborne particulate matter of less than 2.5 microns diameter.

26 The Kaya identity is a useful accounting device but as the IEA (2014: 21) cautions, 'it should be noted that there are important caveats in the use of the Kaya identity. Most important, the four terms on the right-hand side of [the] equation should be considered neither as fundamental driving forces in themselves, nor as generally independent from each other'. Nevertheless the four terms are often described as 'drivers'.

27 One joule can be thought of as the energy it takes to lift a 100 g weight (like a small apple) one metre.

28 The IEA (2014) estimates that for China during 1990–2012 the average annual rate of growth of CO_2 emissions is 6.0%, attributable to average annual growth rates of: Pop 0.8%, GDP/Pop 9.1%, TPES/GDP -4.0%, and CO_2/TPES 0.4%. The last four annual rates do not add up exactly to 6.1% because of rounding errors. Similar rates for Turkey are 4.0%, decomposed into 1.4%, 2.5%, -0.2% and 0.3%, respectively; for Indonesia they are 5.1%, decomposed into 1.5%, 3.3%, -1.2% and 1.5%; and for India 5.7%, attributed to the drivers as 1.8%, 4.8%, -2.1% and 1.4%, respectively.

29 See Kharas's (2010) sobering comparison of the rise of the middle class in South Korea (inclusive) and Brazil (not so inclusive). For analysis of poverty-environment interactions see Hayes and Nadkarni (2001).

30 The Royal Society (2012) puts it thus: 'At present, consumption is closely linked to economic models based on growth. Improving the well-being of individuals so that humanity flourishes rather than survives requires moving from current economic measures to fully valuing natural capital. Decoupling economic activity from material and environmental throughputs is needed urgently for example by reusing equipment and recycling materials, reducing waste, obtaining energy from renewable sources, and by consumers paying for the wider costs of their consumption. Changes to the current socioeconomic model and institutions are needed to allow both people and the planet to flourish … This requires farsighted political leadership concentrating on long-term goals'.

References

Acemoglu, D. and J. A. Robinson (2012) *Why Nations Fail: The Origins of Power, Prosperity and Poverty*. London: Profile Books.

Andrews, C. T. and C. F. Yñiguez (2004) *Water in Asian Cities: Utilities Performance and Civil Society Views*. Mandaluyong City, Philippines: ADB.

Ansori, M. H. (2009) 'Consumerism and the emergence of a new middle class in globalizing Indonesia'. *Explorations*, 9: 87–97.
Asian Development Bank (ADB) (2010) *Key Indicators for Asia and the Pacific 2010*. Mandaluyong City, Philippines: ADB.
Asian Development Bank (ADB) (2012) *Key Indicators for Asia and the Pacific 2012*. Mandaluyong City, Philippines: ADB.
Asian Development Bank (ADB) (2013) *Asian Water Development Outlook 2013*. Mandaluyong City, Philippines: ADB.
Asian Development Bank and Asian Development Bank Institute (ADB and ADBI) (2013) *Low-Carbon Green Growth in Asia: Policies and Practices*. Tokyo: ADBI.
Bai, X., B. Roberts and J. Chen (2010) 'Urban sustainability experiments in Asia: patterns and pathways'. *Environmental Science and Policy*, 13: 312–325.
Beng-Huat, C. (ed.) (2000) *Consumption in Asia: Lifestyles and Identities*. London and New York: Routledge.
Bertaud, A. (2002) 'The spatial organization of cities'. World Development Report Background Paper. Washington, DC: World Bank.
Bettencourt, L. and G. West (2010) 'A unified theory of urban living'. *Nature*, 467: 912–913.
Boyden, S., S. Millar, K. Newcombe and B. O'Neill (1981) *The Ecology of a City and Its People: The Case of Hong Kong*. Canberra: ANU Press.
Chow, A. S. Y. (2014) 'Urban design, transport sustainability and residents' perceived sustainability: a case study of transit-oriented development in Hong Kong'. *Journal of Comparative Asian Development*, 13(1): 73–104.
Chun, N. (2010) 'Middle class size in the past, present, and future: a description of trends in Asia'. ADB Working Paper Series No 217. Mandalulong City, Philippines: ADB.
Costanza, R., G. Alperovitz, H. Daly, J. Farley, C. Franco, T. Jackson, I. Kubiszewski, J. Schor and P. Victor (2013) 'Building a sustainable and desirable economy-in-society-in-nature'. In Worldwatch Institute, *State of the World 2013: Is Sustainability Still Possible?* Washington, DC: Worldwatch Institute. Pp. 126–142.
Curran, S. R. and A. de Sherbinin (2004) 'Completing the picture: the challenge of bringing "consumption" into the population-environment equation'. *Population and Environment*, 26(2): 107–131.
Curran, S. R. and N. Derman (2012) 'Population and environment in Southeast Asia: complex dynamics and trends'. In L. Williams and M. P. Guest (eds.) *Demographic Change in Southeast Asia: Recent Histories and Future Directions*. Ithaca, NY: Cornell University Southeast Asia Program. Pp. 185–208.
Cuthbert, A. R. (2006) *The Form of Cities: Political Economy and Urban Design*. Oxford: Blackwell.
Dasgupta, P. (2005) 'Economics of social capital'. *The Economic Record*, 81(255): S2–S21.
de Sherbinin, A., D. Carr, S. Cassels and L. Jiang (2007) 'Population and environment'. *Annual Review of Environment and Resources*, 32: 345–373.
Dick, H. W. and P. J. Rimmer (1998) 'Beyond the Third World City: the new urban geography of South-east Asia'. *Urban Studies*, 35(12): 2303–2321.
Dobbs, R., J. Remes, J. Manyika, C. Roxburgh, S. Smit and F. Schaer (2012) *Urban World: Cities and the Rise of the Consuming Class*. McKinsey Global Institute.
Dobbs, R., S. Smit, J. Remes, J. Manyika, C. Roxburgh and A. Restrepo (2011) *Urban World: Mapping the Economic Power of Cities*. McKinsey Global Institute.
Economy, E. C. (2004) *The River Runs Black: The Environmental Challenge to China's Future*. Ithaca and London: Cornell University Press.
Ehrlich, P. A. and J. P. Holdren (1971) 'Impact of population growth'. *Science*, 171: 1212–1217.
Food and Agriculture Organization of the United Nations (FAO) (2003) *Review of Water Resources by Country*. Rome: FAO.
Ganguly-Scrase, R. and T. J. Scrase (eds.) (2008) *Globalisation and the Middle Classes in India: The Social and Cultural Impact of Neoliberalism*. London and New York: Routledge.
Glaeser, E. (2011) *Triumph of the City: How Our Greatest Invention Makes Us Richer, Smarter, Greener, Healthier and Happier*. New York: Penguin.
Gleick, P. H. (2003) 'Water use'. *Annual Review of Environmental Resources*, 28: 275–314.
Gleick, P. H. et al. (2014) *World's Water, Volume 8: Biennial Report on Freshwater Resources*. Washington, DC: Island Press.
Gong, P., S. Liang, E. J. Carlton, Q. J. Wu, L. Wang and J. V. Remais (2012) 'Urbanisation and health in China'. *Lancet*, 379(March 3): 843–852.
Hayes, A. C. (1995) 'On defining the problem in population and environment'. Paper presented at the Annual Meetings of the Population Association of America, San Francisco, 6–8 April.

Hayes, A. C. (2013) 'Population dynamics and sustainable development in Asia and the Pacific'. *Asia-Pacific Population Journal*, 28(1): 57–83.

Hayes, A. C. (2014) 'The mixed blessing of Asia's growing middle class'. *East Asia Forum Quarterly*, October–December: 23–26.

Hayes, A. C. and M.V. Nadkarni (eds.) (2001) *Poverty, Environment and Development: Studies of Four Countries in the Asia Pacific Region*. Bangkok: UNESCO.

Health Effects Institute (HEI) (2004) *Health Effects of Outdoor Air Pollution in Developing Countries of Asia*. Boston MA: HEI.

Hummel, D., S. Adamo, A. de Sherbinin, L. Murphy, R. Aggrawal, L. Zulu, J. Liu and K. Knight (2013) 'Inter- and transdisciplinary approaches to population-environment research for sustainability aims: a review and appraisal'. *Population and Environment*, 34: 481–509.

Hummel, D., A. Lux, A. de Sherbinin and S. B. Adamo (2009) 'Theoretical and methodological issues in the analysis of population dynamics and supply systems'. PERN Background Paper. Available from: www.populationenvironmentresearch.org.

Hunter, L. (2000) *The Environmental Implications of Population Dynamics*. Santa Monica, CA: RAND.

International Energy Agency (IEA) (2014) CO_2 *Emissions from Fuel Combustion: Highlights*. Paris: OECD/IEA.

International Energy Agency (IEA) (2015) *World Energy Trends 2015 Edition*. Paris: OECD/IEA.

Jacobi, P., M. Kjellen, G. McGranahan, J. Songsore and C. Surjadi (2001) *The Citizens at Risk: From Urban Sanitation to Sustainable Cities*. London: Earthscan.

Jones, G. W. and M. Douglass (eds.) (2008) *Mega-urban Regions in Pacific Asia: Urban Dynamics in a Global Era*. Singapore: National University of Singapore Press.

Keyfitz, N. (1991) 'Population and development within the ecosphere: one view of the literature.' *Population Index*, 57(1): 5–22.

Kharas, H. (2010) 'The emerging middle class in developing countries'. Working Paper 285. Paris: OECD Development Centre.

Kjellstrom, T., S. Friel, J. Dixon, C. Corvalan, E. Rehfuess, D. Campbell-Lendrum, F. Gore and J. Bartram (2007) 'Urban environmental health hazards and health equity'. *Journal of Urban Health: Bulletin of the New York Academy of Medicine*, 84(1): 186–197.

Krausmann, F., M. Fischer-Kowalski, H. Schandl and N. Eisenmenger (2008) 'The global socio-ecological transition: past and present metabolic profiles and their future trajectories'. *Journal of Industrial Ecology*, 12(5–6): 637–656.

Lancet (2014) '(Barely) living in smog: China and air pollution' (Editorial). *Lancet*, March 8: 845.

Lange, H. and L. Meier (eds.) (2009) *The New Middle Classes: Globalizing Lifestyles, Consumerism and Environmental Concern*. Dordrecht, Heidelberg, London, New York: Springer.

Levy, A. (1999) 'Urban morphology and the problem of the modern urban fabric: some questions for research'. *Urban Morphology*, 3(2): 79–85.

Li, C. (ed.) (2010) *China's Emerging Middle Class: Beyond Economic Transformation*. Washington, DC: Brookings Institution Press.

Liu, J., T. Dietz, S. R. Carpenter, M. Alberti, C. Folke, E. Moran, A. N. Pell, P. Deadman, T. Kratz, J. Lubchenco, E. Ostrom, Z. Ouyang, W. Provencher, C. L. Redman, S. H. Schneider and W. W. Taylor (2007) 'Complexity of coupled human and natural systems'. *Science*, 317: 1513–1516.

Liu, J., H. Mooney, V. Hull, S. J. Davis, J. Gaskell, T. Hertel, J. Lubchenco, K. C. Seto, P. Gleick, C. Kremen and S. Li (2015) 'Systems integration for global sustainability'. *Science*, 347: 1258832. Available from: http://dx.doi.org/10.1126/science.1258832.

Lutz, W., A. Prskawetz and W. C. Sanderson (eds.) (2002) *Population and Environment: Methods of Analysis*. Supplement to Population and Development Review 28.

Marcotullio, P. J. (2003) 'Globalisation, urban form and environmental conditions in Asia-Pacific Cities'. *Urban Studies*, 40(2): 219–247.

Martine, G., G. McGranahan, M. Montgomery and R. Fernández-Castilla (eds.) (2008) *The New Global Frontier: Urbanization, Poverty and Environment in the 21st Century*. London: Earthscan.

McGranahan, G., D. Balk and B. Anderson (2007) 'The rising tide: assessing the risks of climate change and human settlements in low elevation coastal zones'. *Environment and Urbanization*, 19(1):17–37.

Millennium Ecosystem Assessment (MEA) (2005) *Ecosystems and Human Well-being: Synthesis*. Washington, DC: Island Press.

Myers, N. and J. Kent (2003) 'New consumers: the influence of affluence on the environment'. *PNAS*, 100(8): 4963–4968.

O'Rourke, D. and N. Lollo (2015) 'Transforming consumption: from decoupling, to behavior change, to system changes for sustainable consumption'. *Annual Review of Environment and Resources*, 40: 233–259.
Peattie, K. (2010) 'Green consumption: behavior and norms'. *Annual Review of Environmental Resources*, 35: 195–228.
Pinches, M. (ed.) (1999) *Culture and Privilege in Capitalist Asia*. London and New York: Routledge.
Ravallion, M. (2009) 'The developing world's bulging (but vulnerable) middle class'. *World Development*, 38(4): 445–454.
Robison, R. and D. S. G. Goodman (eds.) (1996) *The New Rich in Asia: Mobile Phones, McDonald's and Middle-class Revolution*. London: Routledge.
Rosenzweig, C., W. D. Solecki, S. A. Hammer and S. Mehrotra (2011) *Climate Change and Cities: First Assessment Report of the Urban Climate Change Research Network*. Cambridge, UK: Cambridge University Press.
Royal Society (2012) *People and the Planet*. London: Royal Society.
Sachs, J. D. (2015) *The Age of Sustainable Development*. New York: Columbia University Press.
Saieg, P. (2013) 'Energy efficiency in the built environment'. In Worldwatch Institute, *State of the World 2013: Is Sustainability Still Possible?* Washington, DC: Worldwatch Institute. Pp. 184–189.
Satterthwaite, D. (ed.) (1999) *The Earthscan Reader in Sustainable Cities*. London: Earthscan.
Shao, M., X. Tang, Y. Zhang and W. Li (2006) 'City clusters in China: air and surface water pollution'. *Frontiers in Ecology and Environment*, 4(7): 353–361.
Smil, V. (2013) *Harvesting the Biosphere: What We Have Taken from Nature*. Cambridge, MA: MIT Press.
Stern, D. I., M. S. Common and E. B. Barbier (1996) 'Economic growth and environmental degradation: the environmental Kuznets curve and sustainable development'. *World Development*, 24(7): 1151–1160.
Stern, N. (2007) *The Economics of Climate Change: The Stern Review*. Cambridge: Cambridge University Press.
United Nations (2015) *Transforming Our World: The 2030 Agenda for Sustainable Development*. New York: UN.
United Nations Economic and Social Commission for Asia and the Pacific (UNESCAP) (1990) *State of the Environment in Asia and the Pacific 1990*. Bangkok: ESCAP.
United Nations Economic and Social Commission for Asia and the Pacific (UNESCAP) (2005) *State of the Environment in Asia and the Pacific 2005*. Bangkok: ESCAP.
United Nations Economic and Social Commission for Asia and the Pacific, and Asian Development Bank (UNESCAP and ADB) (1995) *State of the Environment in Asia and the Pacific 1995*. New York: United Nations.
United Nations Economic and Social Commission for Asia and the Pacific, Asian Development Bank, and United Nations Environment Programme (UNESCAP, ADB and UNEP) (2012) *Green Growth, Resources and Resilience: Environmental Sustainability in Asia and the Pacific*. Bangkok: ESCAP.
United Nations HABITAT (UN-HABITAT) (2003) *Water and Sanitation in the World's Cities*. London: Earthscan.
United Nations Population Division (UNPD) (2014) *World Urbanization Prospects: The 2014 Revision*. New York: United Nations.
World Bank (2015) *East Asia's Changing Urban Landscape: Measuring a Decade of Spatial Growth*. Washington, DC: The World Bank.
Zhao, S., C. Peng, H. Jiang, D. Tian, X. Lei and X. Zhou (2006) 'Land use change in Asia and the ecological consequences'. *Ecological Research*, 21: 890–896.

26
Population, the state and security in Asia

Geoffrey McNicoll

The modern configuration of states in Asia gelled in near its present form with the post-World War II retreat – or defeat – of the colonial powers. Among the few subsequent changes the most significant have been the 1971 creation of Bangladesh out of East Pakistan and the 1991 independence of the Central Asian states in the breakup of the Soviet Union. (Some land and maritime boundaries remain in dispute, in a few cases seriously contested.) States, however, are defined by more than just a territory. They are also characterized by a citizenry, by a government exercising dominant authority within their borders, and by recognition of their independence and sovereignty by others. It is with reference to each of these elements of statehood that the political sphere is influenced by demographic conditions and demographic change – and each is to some degree implicated in the state's influence on population. Those interactions, and their effects on political and human security, are the subject of this chapter.

Asia's diversity makes region-wide generalization difficult. East Asia, South-East Asia and South Asia, however, are widely accepted constructs and this account will be mainly limited to these subregions. This emphasis is supported by sheer demographic scale, but also because Central and West Asia, while they may be needed for formal completeness, are hard to fit into the same strategic narrative. The new Central Asian states, and Iran, are included in South Asia in the UN's grouping, but not in common usage of the term: they are at most touched on here. West Asia – from Iraq and the Gulf states to Israel and Turkey (and for the UN, also Georgia) – is omitted. It presents hugely complex political, demographic and security situations which cannot be treated in short order. (As a subregion, it is also more commonly seen as belonging to a broadened Middle East, linked with North Africa rather than with the rest of Asia.)

The discussion following considers the demographic aspects of security at both the national and international levels. Within countries, what are the effects on governance of the overall size and demographic make-up of the population? Internationally, how does demography affect relationships within Asia's system of states, both in the routine management of formal and informal ties and in periods of tension or actual conflict. Looking to the future, how might the population-security nexus both within and among countries be affected by exogenous trends and events, such as major shifts in environmental conditions or disease regimes? Although necessarily very brief, the chapter aims to review Asia's current and future political demography both within the region and vis-à-vis the rest of the world.

Geoffrey McNicoll

Scale and statehood

Consider first the significance of demographic scale for a country's social organization and governance. There is little theoretical research on this subject, most of it in anthropology and concerned with community structure (e.g. Barth 1978). Investigations of the 'desirable' size of states (e.g. Kohr 1957; Alesina and Spolaore 2003) can suggest scale-relevant features. Benefits of a larger population include scale economies in the provision of public goods and services such as physical infrastructure, legal and financial systems and national defence. Against these can be placed the costs, both economic and political, of dealing with the territorial expanse and cultural diversity that characterize many populous states. But however important it may be, population size is at most weakly controllable: in effect, it is not a decision variable. More relevant insights on the population-governance relationship come from empirical studies of administrative hierarchies and of the varieties of links between central government and local authority – the subject of a large literature in public administration and public finance. It is clear from such work that there are many organizational features of a polity that are not scalable.

At the local level social organization has an inherent logic tied to long-standing patterns of economic activity and modes of collective action. Stability of social organization above the family can be seen in the enduring patterns of village settlement and marketing areas – the spatial ordering of which yields the designs identified by central place theory (see Skinner 1964, 1965a and 1965b on the China case) – and in systems of social stratification. Government administrative structures reach down to and mesh with this local-level social and economic organization, creating routes for policy implementation and, potentially, for upward information flows. Ignorance of local realities is likely to be greater where central authority is far removed, as it necessarily is in populous countries. For example, efforts at administrative reform that seek to override those realities often fail. The history of rural administration in modern China offers a striking illustration. Collectivization efforts in the early 1950s built on and mobilized existing neighbourhood and village solidarities, reinforcing them with village-wide tax and service-funding obligations; the radical attempt late in that decade to establish multi-village communes as the new basic unit of rural society was quickly seen as a failure and abandoned.[1]

In large countries, then, administrative devolution to small population units is inescapable. Formal devolution that is given a constitutional basis in a federal structure is rare in modern Asia. Successful revolutionary or independence movements mostly favoured the unitary state, wary of threatened splits. In China, the Peoples Republic was established in 1949 with six broad administrative regions but had essentially become a unitary state by 1954. In Indonesia, the departing Dutch sought to bequeath a federal system but the new nationalist government flatly rejected that option. Only India and Pakistan among Asia's larger states are constitutionally organized as federations, with designated powers given to their lower-level divisions. But federation or not in formal terms, decentralization in public finance and programme management becomes, eventually at least, a de facto reality. In China, this was acknowledged with the Dengist reforms begun in 1978 and especially since the mid-1980s (Zhao and Zhang 1999); in Indonesia, a radical decentralization measure was adopted in 1999 in the wake of the Asian Financial Crisis and the regime change it precipitated (Crouch 2010).

In the political realm as in the economic, devolution has costs as well as benefits. Relinquishment of central authority may sacrifice administrative expertise and efficiency and block information channels. Vaunted gains in government accountability to citizens may be outweighed by losses in accountability to the state. Debate on such matters is the perennial stuff of domestic politics in all populous countries, rich as well as poor. A separate phenomenon often accompanying decentralization is the multiplication of local administrative units – provinces and districts, or their equivalent (Dickovick 2011). This was seen in post-decentralization Indonesia, for example, and following the market reforms of the 1980s in Vietnam. The resulting weakening of bargaining power at the local level may shift the balance back towards the central authority.

Devolution may not be enough of a response where outright fission can be contemplated. Accidents of history – especially colonial and imperial history – have left few of today's Asian countries ethnically or linguistically homogeneous. Socialist ideology, among its other rationales, was once seen as a means of suppressing any resulting 'splittist' tendencies. More recently the common expectation has been that an expanding and prospering middle class would render those tendencies inconsequential. That expectation is not always borne out, as various European examples such as Scotland and Catalonia attest. In Asia there are numerous cases where conflict rooted in language, ethnicity or religion has security implications for the state, even amounting to serious threats of secession or de facto partition. Pakistan's 1971 East-West split was probably inevitable on geographic and linguistic grounds; ethnic tensions continue to fuel separatist pressures in Balochistan and Sindh. India dealt summarily with the would-be independence of Goa and Sikkim and a short-lived attempt to carve out an independent Sikh state. The Maoist Naxalite insurgency, active in numerous districts, has proven a persistent threat to human security; Hindu-Muslim tensions have periodically erupted in communal violence, as in the anti-Muslim 'Gujarat riots' of 2002. Ethnic conflict is rife in China's sparsely populated western autonomous regions of Tibet and Xinjiang, where native Tibetans and Uyghurs resist Beijing's stern security measures and its vigorous efforts at integration of these regions into the national economy – not least by favouring in-migration by Han settlers. In Indonesia, a decades-long separatist rebellion in Aceh province in Sumatra was ended in 2005 with Jakarta's acceptance of a substantial degree of local autonomy.

Some less populous Asian countries also have ethnic or religious divisions that threaten domestic stability. Tamil separatism in Sri Lanka was finally defeated in 2009 but the societal cleavage remains. Lingering separatist struggles still continue in the Philippines (Moros), Thailand (Pattani Muslims) and Myanmar (Karen and Shan insurgencies). Myanmar has also experienced severe anti-Muslim violence directed against the minority Rohingyas, many of whom are now in refugee camps across the Bangladesh border.

Modern technology can be deployed to lessen some of the governance problems linked to large population size – and, in authoritarian polities, to strengthen the hand of the state vis-à-vis the citizen. Examples of relatively scale-neutral technological advances include some kinds of surveillance capabilities, controls on social media, and digitized identification systems (increasingly designed to incorporate biomarkers). For the last of these, China's and India's registration systems, in place and planned, show what is possible.[2]

Political counterparts of demographic transition

The transition from high mortality and fertility conditions to a modern demographic regime, a process extending over decades, generates distinctive changes in a country's population growth rate and age distribution. The consequences, in outline, are familiar. Falls in mortality and morbidity raise the growth rate – hindering capital deepening – but also improve population health. The concentration of mortality gains at young ages yields enlarged youth cohorts, presenting a challenge for educational systems and for labour absorption. As the transition proceeds, declines in fertility ease child dependency ratios and potentially free up resources for greater investment in physical and human capital. Low fertility also results in fewer close kin and changes the nature of intergenerational ties within the family. Later still, extended survivorship at older ages burdens the economy with an increasing level of public transfers from workers to retirees, though a burden that a stronger economy may be able to support. And typically accompanying the transition in birth and death rates is a major shift in the rural–urban balance of the population.

Demographic transition is usually seen as a counterpart of economic development, tied to it through various paths of mutual causation. Equally significant, however, may be demography's role in political development. The narrative here is far from clear-cut. In its positive form it roughly goes as follows: the youth cohort challenge is met by well-designed labour absorption policies to boost economic output; smaller families and more assured child survival encourage greater public and parental investment in education; an expanding middle class, centred in the fast growing cities, generates pressures for liberalization of the economy and for greater political participation; later in the transition, population ageing steadily increases the political weight of the elderly, but delayed retirement and shifts to funded pensions ease the threat of serious intergenerational tension. A parallel narrative suggests that an older population is less inclined to be aggressive internationally.

Each of these propositions, however, is either dubious or requires extensive qualification. The youth cohort challenge may be unmet, leading to large numbers of disaffected, unemployed young adults. The hoped-for 'dividend' from low child dependency, in the absence of effective institutions to channel private and public savings to productive ends, may fail to materialize, leaving a weakened economy. The slimmer workforce in that economy will be poorly equipped – and perhaps less inclined – to support the expanding numbers of elders. Reliance on traditional family arrangements to cope with an ageing population, a common default position of many Asian governments, may be illusory. Some of the burgeoning cities, far from becoming well-ordered contributors to a modern polity, may remain lawless places challenging state authority (Karachi is often pointed to). And the initial youth bulge may be followed by a fertility 'echo' in the next generation – another bulge, smaller but perhaps sizeable enough to negate any demographically determined expectation of peacefulness.

The potential destabilizing political effects of a youth bulge – concentrated in cities and often loosely identified as students – have long been noted. Keyfitz (1965) recorded the near-doubling of Indonesia's youth cohort size over a few years that came with recovery from the war years of the 1940s; the rising numbers seeking jobs in the country's faltering economy in the mid-1960s was widely seen as contributing to the political turbulence of that period, ushering in the militarized New Order regime. Later and elsewhere, 'youth bulges' became a familiar ingredient of geostrategic scenario-building, not least in scenarios constructed by the US National Intelligence Council in its periodic reports on global trends and predictions. The political significance of a forecast generational-echo fertility upturn is emphasized by Jackson and Howe (2008).

In most of Asia a fertility decline had set in by the 1970s, with fertility roughly halved over the subsequent generation. The economic benefits that could potentially accrue from such a change in child dependency had been estimated for the India case by Coale and Hoover (1958). As it turned out, East Asia offered a far better illustration of the dependency effect, with a significant part of that region's 'economic miracle' seemingly attributable to the deeper human investment allowed by lower fertility (Bloom and Williamson 1998). The fertility link, of course, is not automatic: it is contingent on the behaviour of families, firms and governments, which in turn is influenced by a country's institutional make-up and political circumstances. In India, the beneficial effect only began to be realized when a favourable age structure was combined with the liberalizing reforms of the 1990s; in some other countries (Pakistan, thus far, it is argued) political unrest and ill-chosen policies may offset part or all of youth-dependency-related economic gains.

In major parts of Asia – East and South, though not South-East – the attainment of low fertility has been accompanied by a less welcome demographic feature: a youth cohort that is disproportionately male. Strong and entrenched preferences by families for sons over daughters together with wide availability of prenatal sex determination through ultrasound imaging and ready access to abortion have yielded a strikingly unbalanced sex ratio at birth. Most expectations are that son preference will diminish as development proceeds (as it has in South Korea), although the 'desired sex ratio at birth' calculated from survey-responses suggest this process may be drawn out (see Bongaarts 2013). The adverse social and political consequences of a heavily male youth cohort have been explored by trawling the historical record, yielding suggestive though inconclusive findings.[3] Paradoxically, a relative scarcity of women does not appear to enhance women's status.

The sex-ratio problem aside, economic and social development creates a fast-growing, mostly urban, middle class – in Asia already numbering in the hundreds of millions. Rising proportions of Asia's population are experiencing, for the first time, a relatively high level of human security. Expectations that this will generate a corresponding trend of democratization are widely held. The link is supported on economic grounds by Przeworski et al. (2000) and Acemoglu and Robinson (2006). A specific role for demographic modernization in promoting democracy is argued by Dyson (2013) using historical data for Western countries. The Asian exemplars of democratization are South Korea and Taiwan, with a 'second wave' that includes Indonesia and the Philippines. But Asia also has counter-examples: cases where the political stirrings that accompany growing affluence and widespread education have elicited a renewed authoritarian response on the part of government. In varying degrees, Singapore, Malaysia and Iran might be so characterized. And the rapid expansion of China's middle class shows scant signs thus far of foreshadowing democratic change.

The political outcomes of demographic transition are therefore far from clear. A strong case can be made that demographic modernity and at least moderate economic prosperity are entirely compatible with authoritarian rule – see Jackson and Howe (2008: 134–137). But whether that rule is a way-station on a path to fuller political participation or a more or less stable condition in which greater participation is traded away for security and high consumption is still in question. Part of the reason for this uncertainty is the as-yet unknown effect on political values of the novel and still unfolding demographic situation of extreme population ageing, with societies approaching median ages of 50 or higher. Another part is the similarly unknown degree to which advancing government surveillance capabilities may tilt the balance towards the state.

Relativities and regionalization

In the international arena, the most obvious influence of demography comes from the relative population sizes of states. But important too may be a variety of other relative magnitudes, most deriving from the uneven onset and pace of the demographic transition among countries. Countries at differing stages of transition vary widely in age distributions, mortality and morbidity conditions, rural–urban shares and cross-border migration – each with potential implications for relations among states and for the international security environment.

Formally, international relations do not acknowledge size differences. The doctrine of the sovereign equality of states first gained acceptance in seventeenth century Europe (usually dated to the 1648 Peace of Westphalia), later spreading worldwide, but its full application came only with the dissolution of the colonial empires. Article 2 of the UN Charter asserts the 'principle of the sovereign equality of all its members'. (Sovereign equality was not mentioned in the Covenant of the League of Nations.) The UN's designers in the 1940s would have foreseen the future membership of former colonial territories, if not the later accession of so many micro-states.

State formation is viewed as a once-only process. With rare exceptions, the new states wrought or re-established by decolonization, once recognized, were deemed to be secure within their borders against irredentist claims. Independence movements within them like those mentioned earlier seldom received recognition or support from other states. National minority rights, which had been a pressing issue for the League of Nations, were considered by the United Nations to be an internal matter; in their place was the more generalized, and less politically demanding, endorsement of universal human rights.[4] With assurance of autonomy and non-interference, being small in population thus should not make for vulnerability. In the General Assembly at least, Brunei (0.3 million) is the sovereign equal of China (1.3 billion).

In relations among states, population size counts as only one factor among many ingredients of power and influence.[5] Economic and military capability usually matter more. Residues of history, seen in the make-up of the permanent members of the UN Security Council, also count. And, in the view of many, so does the 'soft power' of cultural values and practices seen as deserving emulation. In any realist assessment of relative power, however, sheer numbers are far from irrelevant. As Hedley Bull (1987: 79) put it: 'A population of 100 million or more today is not sufficient to confer superpower status upon a nation, but it is widely thought to be necessary for this status'. In 2014, seven Asian countries meet that condition: China (1,394 million); India (1,267); Indonesia (253); Pakistan (185); Bangladesh (159); Japan (127); and the Philippines (100). One other is close: Vietnam (93 million). Of course, 100 million is not what it was even 25 years ago. Moreover, for some countries, such as Vietnam, missing the mark could itself be a signal of increasing power, a byproduct of their success in economic and demographic modernization.

Population size matters most when there are large differences within a circumscribed geographical region, where it helps to define a status hierarchy. Asia's distinctiveness in this regard lies in having two demographic giants, China and India, each with some six times the population of the next largest country in their respective 'neighbourhoods' of East (including South-East) Asia and South Asia. The contrast with other major world regions is striking: none of the other regions has a single state with such overwhelming demographic dominance (see Table 26.1).[6]

In influencing the architecture of interstate relations the size of economy may be as or more important than population. In East Asia, since the 1990s, China's GDP in purchasing power parity (PPP) terms has soared past Japan's, though Japan's labour force is still far more productive

Table 26.1 Country population relativities in major world regions, 2014: population size as per cent of population of largest country in region, for the six most populous countries in each region

East Asia		South Asia		Europe		The Americas		Africa	
China	100	India	100	Germany	100	USA	100	Nigeria	100
Indonesia	18	Pakistan	15	France	78	Brazil	63	Ethiopia	54
Japan	9	Bangladesh	13	United Kingdom	76	Mexico	38	Egypt	47
Philippines	7	Afghanistan	2	Italy	74	Colombia	15	Congo	39
Vietnam	7	Nepal	2	Spain	57	Canada	11	South Africa	30
Thailand	5	Sri Lanka	2	Ukraine	55	Venezuela	10	Kenya	26

Source: UN (2013).

and its per capita income is more than three times China's. With China at 100, the relative sizes of the next two largest East Asian economies (as of 2013) are Japan, 30 and Indonesia, 14. (Under market exchange rates, the China-Japan difference is lessened: World Bank estimates put the ratio at 100:53.) In South Asia, India's regional dominance is much the same in the economic realm as in the demographic: in 2013 Pakistan's economy, the region's second largest, was some 13 per cent of India's both in PPP terms and at market rates.[7]

These size hierarchies help to account for significant differences in the character of international relations within the major regions – seen, for example, in the varying strength and scope of emerging regional associations. The rough comparability in scale and technology of the major European powers – a source of their historical rivalries – was an impetus for the demanding project of regional integration after World War II. In East and South Asia, radically unequal sizes and income levels may still allow for trade and investment pacts (like NAFTA in the Americas), but present evident difficulties for a European-style common market. Security alliances are similarly unbalanced.

Sheer population size combined with an economy that has major high-technology sectors well in advance of its neighbours' capabilities give India what is effectively a hegemonic role in South Asia, though one that is rendered fairly benign by India's willingness and ability to provide regional public goods – notably security guarantees – to its smaller neighbours, Pakistan excepted (see Ayoob 1999). Formal regionalization through the South Asian Association for Regional Cooperation (SAARC) has been seen by many as a largely nominal exercise.

In East Asia the security architecture is made more complex by the presence of two great powers, China and Japan, with China in the ascendancy. (The strong East Asian presence and alliance ties of the United States is a further complicating reality.) China's strong trade and investment ties with Japan coexist with fraught political relations. For several decades after its post-war recovery, Japan's economic dominance in East Asia was unquestioned, though wartime memories precluded a security role. China's population size was then more an encumbrance than a claim to status. But China's subsequent rapid economic expansion, combined with Japan's faltering during the 'lost decades' after 1989, brought economics more into line with demography and gave China the ability and will to project its power in the region. Even if economic conditions were to change again – in Japan's favour – the shift in leadership roles is likely permanent.

South-East Asia has sought, with some limited success, to become a coherent subregion of East Asia, separate from the great power tensions and realignments to the north. The Association of South-East Asian Nations (ASEAN) is the institutional embodiment of this aspiration. The population of its ten member countries amounts to over half a billion and its combined economy, nominally larger than India's, has been growing strongly – making it potentially a serious regional actor even in the presence of China. But ASEAN, notwithstanding the range of its activities and the ambition of its rhetoric, has struggled to establish an ASEAN Economic Community, well short of EU-level integration. Free trade declarations encounter resistant non-tariff barriers; comparable obstacles impede market integration in capital and skilled labour.[8]

North-East Asia has no analogous regional entity. A Trilateral Summit programme and a prospective free trade agreement bring together China, Japan and South Korea, but trade is periodically held hostage to tensions in the political sphere. And North Korea presents a continuing unresolved problem for the region.

Strategic links extending outside East Asia are important parts of the regionalization picture. China is centrally involved in the Shanghai Cooperation Organization, an economic and security pact with Russia and the Central Asian states (see Laruelle and Peyrouse 2012; Cabestan 2013). America's involvement includes long-standing security guarantees to Japan, South Korea and Taiwan and a number of bilateral and multilateral trade pacts.[9]

Geoffrey McNicoll

Table 26.2 Population aged 20–40 years in major Asian countries and world regions, estimates and projections (millions), 2010–2050

Country/Region	2010	2025	2050
China	451	398	317
India	390	458	460
Indonesia	79	85	86
Pakistan	54	74	82
Bangladesh	51	60	54
Japan	32	25	21
Philippines	29	39	47
Vietnam	31	31	24
Europe & North America	303	278	272
Sub-Saharan Africa	238	361	646

Source: Estimates and medium variant projections, UN (2013).

The varying paces of declines in death and birth rates across Asia will substantially alter some of the demographic and economic comparisons among countries over the next few decades. Consider, for example, the forecast time-trends in the size of the age group 20–40, the critical young-adult labour force ages. UN medium variant projections of this age group to 2050 for the most populous Asian countries (those near or beyond 100 million total population) are shown in Table 26.2. Some of the figures are striking. China's dropping behind India in total population has long been foreseen; at young ages the crossover is imminent. Falling numbers in Japan are a well-known trend underway for some years. The size and pace of the forecast near-term absolute drop in China's 20–40 population, however, are remarkable – to be followed not long after by a similar drop in Vietnam. Such trends presage labour shortages and rising wages in manufacturing – changes already being experienced in China – and pressures for export industries to shift up the technology ladder or relocate to lower-wage countries. Effects on economic dynamism, and on the geopolitical influence that accompanies it, are more speculative but potentially profound. By 2050, India's numbers in the 20–40 age group, now below China's, are forecast to be 50 per cent larger than China's. The UN fertility assumptions incorporated in these projections are fairly conservative: larger declines are quite possible. Less plausibly, some fertility upturn could occur. (For comparison, Table 26.2 also shows the equivalent population time trends in the West – a modest decline – and sub-Saharan Africa – a dramatic rise of between two- and threefold.)

Population and international conflict

The once commonplace association between population (more precisely, youth cohort size) and military power – seen, for example in France's long unease over Germany's demographic ascendancy in the nineteenth century – steadily eroded in the industrial era, replaced by considerations of comparative economic strength and of technological and organizational capability. Variation across countries in ability or willingness to support a large military further weakens the link with population: only in extreme conflict situations would troop mobilization be constrained by actual cohort numbers. Rankings of military strength among Asian countries, drawing on a range of components, nevertheless echo demography in putting China well ahead, followed by India.[10] Smaller countries punching much above their (demographic) weight include South

Korea and Taiwan. A solid defence alliance with a major power, of course, may achieve a similar force-multiplying effect.

International relations theorists such as Rosecrance (1996), Buzan (1998) and Cooper (2003) have described the more relaxed view of sovereignty they discern in the Western world as the emergence of the 'virtual' or 'postmodern' state. Such a trend is not much in evidence in Asia, where most states retain an overriding concern with territory and resources and with locating production within their borders.[11] 'Westphalian' states are the rule – along with their potential for interstate conflict. The contrast between Asia and the North Atlantic sphere of Western Europe and North America is drawn in these terms by Kissinger (2011: 515). Among the North Atlantic states, Kissinger writes, 'strategic confrontations are not conceivable... Soft power and multilateral diplomacy are the dominant tools of foreign policy'. In Asia, by contrast, 'states consider themselves in potential confrontation with their neighbours... The principles of the Westphalian system prevail, more so than on their continent of origin. The concept of sovereignty is considered paramount'. (The Asian states system has even been called 'Eastphalian'.)

The recent record of strong economic growth in most of Asia has been accompanied in many countries by a build-up of modern conventional armaments. Among existing or plausibly emerging strategic confrontations in Asia, several involve China's efforts to extend its sphere of influence in the Western Pacific. These include, besides the contested status of Taiwan, China's territorial and maritime claims in the East China Sea (the Sea of Japan) and the South China Sea. In each of these areas, any imbalance in population size between the parties is far outweighed in importance by military capabilities and alliance structures. Thus the dispute over the Senkaku/Diaoyu islands, pitting China against Japan, is conditioned more by China's fast-growing naval power and its lingering memories of Japan's 'co-prosperity sphere', and in the background by the strong Japan-US alliance, than by the 11 to 1 ratio of their populations. Conflict in the Korean peninsula, a perennial site of military confrontation in East Asia, is not rendered less likely by the North's having half the South's population.

China is also extending its influence landward – in Mongolia and the neighbouring Central Asian states, in Pakistan and Afghanistan, and in Myanmar – in pursuit of natural resources and, in some cases, access to Indian Ocean ports. The dominant mode here is trade and investment rather than any direct exercise of power – let alone, despite the vast areas and low population densities of some of these states, any echo of 1930s-style *Lebensraum* arguments (see Kaplan 2012).[12]

In South Asia, the major strategic confrontation is the long-running India-Pakistan conflict. Continuing tense relations and unresolved territorial claims have been punctuated by border wars over Kashmir in 1965 and 1999 and by India's decisive intervention on the side of Bangladesh independence in 1971. With US and NATO withdrawal from Afghanistan, that country may become another locus for the conflict. The 7:1 demographic disparity between India and Pakistan is reflected in the sizes of their conventional armed forces but, in Kashmir at least, a rough balance of forces maintains a fragile impasse.

Conventional armaments are not the whole picture: some Asian states have acquired chemical and biological weapons, capabilities in cyber warfare, and, in a few instances, nuclear weapons and their delivery systems. Asia's five nuclear states – China, India, Pakistan, Israel and North Korea – further complicate an already intricate security environment, not least by spurring efforts to redress the perceived power imbalances that result. Several Asian states are considered to have the capability to produce such weapons in a relatively short time-span should they so choose (the condition of 'nuclear latency'): Japan, South Korea and Iran. Possession of nuclear weapons conveys status through membership of an exclusive group of states; it plausibly offers deterrence against aggression. More certainly in an increasingly urbanized world, the targeting of cities by such weapons can negate the value of population size and render 'defence in depth' irrelevant.

Where both sides in a conflict have nuclear arms, as do India and Pakistan, the risk of escalation must be considered. In theory, the doctrine of mutual deterrence should preclude that possibility; in practice, the arms build-up likely continues, along with greater risk of error and miscalculation. In the India-Pakistan case, moreover, there is a danger, some observers believe, of political instability in Pakistan undermining that government's command and control of its weapons (see Ganguly and Kapur 2010; Sharma 2012).

A commonly-made argument is that population ageing will diminish the likelihood of international conflict. 'Geriatric peace' is the term used in Goldstone et al. (2012). The case is set out by Cincotta et al. (2003) – it is analogous, in many respects, to the assertion that democracies do not start wars. Ageing populations, it is said, will become more politically stable and disinclined to violence. Following this line, Sheen (2013) asserts flatly: 'By 2030, Japan, South Korea and China will become too old for military rivalry'. With Russia ageing along with China, any repetition of the Sino-Soviet border conflict of the 1960s might similarly be ruled out. Jackson and Howe (2008) take issue with this proposition, which they call the demographic peace thesis. They concede that ageing makes the civil disorder and violence typically characterized as state failure less likely, but they see no reason to suppose that post-transition authoritarian states are necessarily peaceable. They remark (2008: 135) that 'the nations that engaged in World War II had a higher average age and a lower fertility rate – and thus were situated at a later stage of the demographic transition – than most of today's developing world is projected to have over the next 20 years'. A further reason not to discount possibilities for interstate conflict in a post-transition era is the evolution of military technology. Modern conventional weaponry no longer needs the large troop deployments common in twentieth century wars for it to be vastly destructive. Extreme asymmetry in conflict situations, where demography and territory are essentially irrelevant, is exemplified by major terrorist episodes involving non-state actors.

Whatever the contribution of demography to interstate conflict, it is certain that any actual conflict can have demographic consequences. Post-war baby booms, making up for low wartime fertility, are familiar occurrences, seen in both Japan and other East Asian countries after World War II. Refugees are another byproduct of conflict. A huge though temporary flood of Bengalis entered India at the time of the civil war between East and West Pakistan – one of the triggers for India's entry into that conflict. The North's victory ending the Vietnam War saw a large outflow of refugees to other Asian countries, many eventually finding resettlement in the West. Large numbers of refugees from Afghanistan, generated by the Soviet and later US invasions and the country's long-running civil war, are to be found in Iran and Pakistan; conditions likely to generate further such outflows persist.

'Game-changers'

It is possible to imagine interstate conflict in Asia on a scale large enough to have wide and lasting demographic as well as economic implications. In the period since World War II, however, most conflicts in Asia have been fairly localized. That was certainly true of the Sino-Indian War (1962) or the Sino-Vietnamese War (1979). The Korean War, drawing in China and the United States, and the Second Indochina War (the Vietnam War), spreading from Vietnam to Laos and Cambodia, had wider ramifications – and vastly more casualties – but the effects of these too, receding into history, are hard to discern beyond the immediate territories involved. 'Game-changing' conflict would thus have to be still larger in scope and intensity. The view that such an eventuality nonetheless cannot be ruled out is often defended by the argument that the major twentieth century game-changer, the First World War, was foreseen by none of the belligerent states. The Cold War offers bleak precedents in nearness to catastrophe should the ongoing military build-up in Asia turn into an outright arms race.[13]

What are the other candidates for game-changers? In a review of potentially disruptive events measured in fatalities on a global scale over the next 50 years, the noted geographer Vaclav Smil (2005a and 2005b) put an influenza pandemic in first place (ahead of 'transformational wars'), with a 10 per cent probability of 50 million deaths – perhaps, as in the last such episode (in 1918), mostly prime-age workers – and likely enormous damage to economies worldwide. Comparable demographic effects from major natural catastrophes, in contrast, he sees as at least an order of magnitude less probable.

Climate change presents a broad array of possibilities for radically altered expectations of the future, in Asia as elsewhere. Atmospheric warming at the upper end of the 2–4 degree Celsius range forecast by the Intergovernmental Panel on Climate Change over this century would have major effects on agricultural zones and on the frequency of extreme weather events. Projected rises in sea levels and delta flooding threaten coastal settlement. Further ocean acidification will damage already depleted fisheries. The ranges of crop, livestock and human pathogens would be extended, changing disease regimes. A variety of ecosystem services – pollination, for instance – would likely be degraded. While most such effects are expected to play out over many decades, the possibility for abrupt change also exists (see US National Research Council 2013).

A particular concern is the supply of fresh water for agriculture. The headwaters of the major river systems of South and East Asia lie in the Himalayan glaciers, now in retreat. Depletion of these stores, along with drastic overuse of aquifers, has serious implications for agricultural production in both the Indo-Gangetic Plain and China's irrigated grain belt (Wyman 2013). Food insecurity, seemingly banished from most of Asia over recent decades, could re-emerge. The relative prosperity that has been attained will ensure most Asian countries ready access to world grain markets, although global scarcities tend to elicit trade-limiting protectionist responses by producers.

Rising sea levels are a well-advertised threat to low-lying regions. Major coastal cities – among them Bangkok, Dhaka, Manila, Guangzhou, Ho Chi Minh City, Jakarta, Kolkata, Mumbai and Shanghai – will have to contend with more frequent and severe flooding events (World Bank 2010). Some areas may have to be evacuated: in the Ganges delta, anticipated effects of flooding and salt water intrusion could potentially displace tens of millions of Bangladeshis, with India the most plausible refuge (US National Intelligence Council 2010).

Numerous government and international agency reports have spelled out these possible developments and assessed levels of confidence in forecast trends. But agreement on coordinated international action to mitigate them – chiefly by limiting carbon emissions – has thus far relied only on voluntary compliance. A large stumbling block is allocating emission limits between rich and poor countries, but both groups have been resistant to any control regime seen as likely to slow their economic growth. A favoured policy option of many developing countries is to establish a fixed per capita emission quota for all countries, in effect putting the major burden for compliance on heavy per capita emitters like the United States but relieving heavy total (but low per capita) emitters like China. (Assigning responsibility for pollutant stocks built up in the past would have a similar effect.) Whether future population growth should be penalized, or past achievements in birth control rewarded, are unresolved issues for such a scheme.

Galvanization to act by the international community may have to await the experience of some actual wide-ranging climate-related disasters. That is the view of Michael Mann (2013), who ends his lengthy treatise on social change in modern history with a chapter on climate as a looming uncertainty in the path towards globalization. Yet the desirable outcome on climate change – commitment to long-term mitigation efforts through mutual agreement among states, imposing fair sacrifices on all – is unlikely. What more probably lies ahead, Mann argues, is a breakdown of international comity on the matter, with countries looking to their separate best interests and, in the more powerful countries, with new environmental ideologies emerging 'as varied as other ideologies were earlier in the twentieth century' – 'ideologies comparable to revolutionary socialism, aggressive nationalism, and even fascism' (2013: 397).

Political demography of Asia's century

Asia's share of world population probably exceeded two-thirds over much of human history. It fell appreciably as Europe and America experienced the effects of the industrial revolution but part-recovered as its own demographic transition got underway. Globally, the demographic retreat of the West and the burgeoning population of Africa are the dominant recent trends, leaving Asia's share relatively intact. Within Asia, however, there is a large and widening East-South split in population growth rates and population ageing, reflecting the earlier and faster demographic transitions in the East. The dominant features of the emerging East Asian demographic regime will be falling population numbers and high (and still-rising) median ages. While predictions are hazardous, most informed observers see little sign of any recovery of the region's fertility to near-replacement level: a modal family size nearer one than two may become entrenched. (A skewed sex ratio many would expect to be a more transitory feature.) These conditions may lie in the future of much of the rest of Asia, but delayed by several, and sometimes many, decades.

As intimated above, how such a demographic regime will bear on domestic politics is unclear, though the serious problems it poses for public finance are apparent. Lessons from low-fertility Europe are not directly applicable. There the effects on individual countries are obscured to some extent by the existence of the single market of the EU: in the same way that the countryside empties out in the usual course of urban-industrial development, so whole regions in Eastern or Southern Europe could lose population without threatening the European project itself. Encouraging or tolerating migration from further afield (in a loaded term, 'replacement migration') is a direct possible response to low fertility, one that seems to be more available to Europe than to low-fertility Asia. Europe's major cities seemingly can and do accept the cultural diversity brought by high and climbing proportions of foreign-born (not least, migrants from South Asia), though the many signs of populist reaction signal that their receptiveness is far from limitless.

In the international sphere, a major change already underway is the diminution of US influence in Asia – both as an inevitable result of America's lessening share of the world economy and in response to its succession of failed military interventions. A future can be foreseen in which, for the first time in centuries, the region's relevant great powers will be Asian alone. How might Asia then fare as a society of states, with its huge range of population sizes and disparate stages of development? The many uncertainties in this future as they pertain to demography have been noted in the discussion above. Among outcomes judged as favourable would be one where emerging demographic circumstances moderate China's hegemonic propensities in Pacific Asia and where India and Pakistan find a stable, convergent path to security and prosperity in the subcontinent. Worst case outcomes could echo the rocky paths of the original Westphalian treaty states in the three centuries that followed, but in states now equipped with modern weaponry and facing dire environmental challenges.

Notes

1 For an early account of the reforms and the subsequent retreat from communization, see Schurmann (1968: 490–494).
2 China's National Resident ID card, required for many routine transactions, allows for detailed official monitoring in various spheres and is linked to a government database containing fuller individual-level information. (The separate *hukou* system registers legal place of residence. It was initially aimed at controlling geographic mobility and is used by many cities to regulate access to urban services.) India's Unique Identification system, currently being built up, does not entail an identity card but allows proof of identity by querying a central database.
3 See Hudson and den Boer (2004: 261, 263), who expect the outcome to be 'chronic violence and persistent social disorder and corruption'. For India and China, their 'broad predictions' include slowed democratization in China and a move towards authoritarianism in India, and no resolution of the Kashmir and Taiwan issues.
4 A modification of full state sovereignty has been the recent formulation of a 'responsibility to protect' on the part of the international community, and specifically the UN Security Council, in situations of major violations of human rights, such as genocide or ethnic cleansing.
5 On population size as a contribution to a state's power, see McNicoll (1999).
6 Table 26.1 updates one in McNicoll (2004).
7 World Bank estimates at PPP and market exchange rates for 2013 from http://databank.worldbank.org/data/. For comparative analysis each measure has its defenders: PPP values reflect comparative levels of total consumption; market exchange rates better indicate power in the international economy.
8 A significant ASEAN achievement, however, has been its fostering of the larger discussion forum, ASEAN Plus Three (APT) – the three being China, Japan and South Korea – and the still-wider ASEAN Regional Forum (ARF).
9 Various free-trade initiatives bring together groups of Pacific Rim countries, notably Asia-Pacific Economic Cooperation (APEC), a discussion forum, and the envisaged Trans Pacific Partnership (TPP).
10 One such military ranking is the Global Firepower index (see www.globalfirepower.com). (Cross-national comparative data on size of standing armies, often cited, encounter major problems of definitional consistency.)
11 According to Rosencrance (1996), Japan, South Korea and Singapore have elements of virtuality in this sense; China, notably, does not.
12 China resolved its boundary disputes with its newly independent Central Asian neighbours in the late 1990s (see Laruelle and Peyrouse 2012). Unresolved but dormant territorial disputes with India involve Chinese claims to parts of Kashmir and Arunachal Pradesh.
13 Even 'limited' use of tactical nuclear weapons – in South Asia, for example – could have large and dire demographic consequences through effects on food production. Spelling out such effects was occasionally done in the Cold War era (see Bergstrom et al. 1983) but has largely been dropped as risks seemingly receded. Possibilities of nuclear terrorism offer a new cause for alarm.

References

Acemoglu, D. and J. A. Robinson (2006) *Economic Origins of Dictatorship and Democracy*. Cambridge: Cambridge University Press.
Alesina, A. and E. Spolaore (2003) *The Size of Nations*. Cambridge, MA: MIT Press.
Ayoob, M. (1999) 'From regional system to regional society: exploring key variables in the construction of regional order'. *Australian Journal of International Affairs*, 53(3): 247–260.
Barth, F. (ed.) (1978) *Scale and Social Organization*. Oslo: Universitetsforlaget.
Bergstrom, S., D. Black, N. P. Bochkov, S. Eklund, R. J. H. Kruisinga, A. Leaf, O. Obasanjo, I. Shigematsu, M. Tubiana and G. Whittembury (1983) 'Effects of nuclear war on health and health services'. Report of the International Committee of Experts in Medical Sciences and Public Health, World Health Organization on Thirty-Sixth World Health Assembly in Geneva.
Bloom, D. E. and J. G. Williamson (1998) 'Demographic transitions and economic miracles in emerging Asia'. *World Bank Economic Review*, 12(3): 419–455.
Bongaarts, J. (2013) 'The implementation of preferences for male offspring'. *Population and Development Review*, 39(2): 185–208.

Bull, H. (1987) 'Population and the present world structure'. In William Alonso (ed.) *Population in an Interacting World*. Cambridge, MA: Harvard University Press.

Buzan, B. (1998) 'System versus units in theorizing about the Third World'. In S. G. Neuman (ed.) *International Relations Theory and the Third World*. New York: St Martin's Press.

Cabestan, J. P. (2013) 'The Shanghai Cooperation Organization, Central Asia, and the great powers: an introduction'. *Asian Survey*, 53(3): 423–435.

Cincotta, R. P., R. Engelman and D. Anastasion (2003) *The Security Demographic: Population and Civil Conflict after the Cold War*. Washington, DC: Population Action International.

Coale, A. J. and E. M. Hoover (1958) *Population Growth and Economic Development in Low-Income Countries*. Princeton, NJ: Princeton University Press.

Cooper, R. (2003) *The Breaking of Nations: Order and Chaos in the Twenty-first Century*. London: Atlantic Monthly Press.

Crouch, H. A. (2010) *Political Reform in Indonesia after Soeharto*. Singapore: Institute of Southeast Asian Studies.

Dickovick, J. T. (2011) *Decentralization and Recentralization in the Developing World*. University Park, PA: Pennsylvania State University Press.

Dyson, T. (2013) 'On demographic and democratic transitions'. *Population and Development Review*, 38(suppl.): 83–102.

Ganguly, S. and S. P. Kapur (2010) *India, Pakistan, and the Bomb: Debating Nuclear Stability in South Asia*. New York: Columbia University Press.

Goldstone, J. A., E. P. Kaufmann and M. D. Toft (eds.) (2012) *Political Demography: How Population Changes Are Reshaping International Security and National Politics*. Boulder, CO: Paradigm Publishers.

Hudson, V. M. and A. M. den Boer (2004) *Bare Branches: The Security Implications of Asia's Surplus Male Population*. Cambridge, MA: MIT Press.

Jackson, R. and N. Howe (2008) *The Graying of the Great Powers: Demography and Geopolitics in the 21st Century*. Washington, DC: Center for Strategic and International Studies.

Kaplan, R. D. (2012) *The Revenge of Geography: What the Map Tells Us about Coming Conflicts and the Battle against Fate*. New York: Random House.

Keyfitz, N. (1965) 'Age distribution as a challenge to development'. *American Journal of Sociology*, 70(6): 659–668.

Kissinger, H. (2011) *On China*. New York: Penguin Press.

Kohr, L. (1957) *The Breakdown of Nations*. London: Routledge & Kegan Paul.

Laruelle, M. and S. Peyrouse (2012) *The Chinese Question in Central Asia: Domestic Order, Social Change and the Chinese Factor*. London: Hurst.

Mann, M. (2013) *The Sources of Social Power, Volume 4: Globalizations, 1945–2011*, New Edition. New York: Cambridge University Press.

McNicoll, G. (1999) 'Population weights in the international order'. *Population and Development Review*, 25(2): 411–442.

McNicoll, G. (2004) 'Demographic future of East Asian regional integration'. In T. J. Pempel (ed.) *Remapping East Asia: The Construction of a Region*. Ithaca, NY: Cornell University Press.

Przeworski, A., M. E. Alvarez, J. A. Cheibub and F. Limongi (2000) *Democracy and Development: Political Institutions and Well-being in the World, 1950–1990*. Cambridge: Cambridge University Press.

Rosecrance, R. N. (1996) 'The rise of the virtual state: territory becomes passé'. *Foreign Affairs*, 75(4): 45–61.

Schurmann, H. F. (1968) *Ideology and Organization in Communist China*, Second Edition. Berkeley: University of California Press.

Sharma, A. (2012) 'The enduring conflict and the hidden risk of India-Pakistan war'. *SAIS Review*, 32(1): 129–142.

Sheen, S. (2013) 'Northeast Asia's aging population and regional security: "demographic peace?"'. *Asian Survey*, 53(2): 292–318.

Skinner, G. W. (1964) 'Marketing and social structure in rural China part I'. *Journal of Asian Studies*, 24(1): 3–43.

Skinner, G. W. (1965a) 'Marketing and social structure in rural China part II'. *Journal of Asian Studies*, 24(2): 195–228.

Skinner, G. W. (1965b) 'Marketing and social structure in rural China part III'. *Journal of Asian Studies*, 24(3): 363–399.

Smil, V. (2005a) 'The next 50 years: fatal discontinuities'. *Population and Development Review*, 31(2): 201–236.

Smil, V. (2005b) 'The next 50 years: unfolding trends'. *Population and Development Review*, 31(4): 605–643.

United Nations (2013) *World Population Prospects: The 2012 Revision*. New York: United Nations.

US National Intelligence Council (2010) 'Effects of future climate change on cross-border migration in North Africa and India [excerpt]'. *Population and Development Review*, 36(2): 408–412.

US National Intelligence Council (2012) *Global Trends 2030: Alternative Worlds*. Washington, DC: National Academy Press.

US National Research Council (2013) *Abrupt Impacts of Climate Change: Anticipating Surprises*. Washington, DC: National Academies Press.

World Bank (2010) *Climate Risks and Adaptation in Asian Coastal Megacities: a synthesis report*. Washington, DC: World Bank.

Wyman, R. J. (2013) 'The effects of population on the depletion of fresh water'. *Population and Development Review*, 39(4): 687–704.

Zhao, X. B. and L. Zhang (1999) 'Decentralization reforms and regionalism in China'. *International Regional Science Review*, 22(3): 251–281.

27
The demographic future of Asia

Wolfgang Lutz and Samir KC

This chapter presents a comprehensive assessment of what we can assume today about likely future demographic trends in all Asian countries. We start with some general considerations about the production of assumptions in population projections. Then we look at past population projections for the region and assess their performance. We move on to discussing the substantive basis for assumptions about future fertility, mortality and migration trends in Asia, and conclude with presenting the medium projections and some alternative scenarios for the region as a whole and for individual countries.

Projecting future population size and structure

For many users of population projections the most important piece of information is the future total size of the population. Human populations are not homogeneous, however, and this heterogeneity matters for the dynamics of change over time. Future population growth is a direct function of the age- and sex-structure of the population, and for this reason all modern population projections explicitly incorporate these two sources of population heterogeneity and define their assumptions in the form of age-specific fertility, mortality and migrations rates. Moreover, the age- and sex-composition of a population is also of interest in its own right. Population ageing is considered a highly important socioeconomic issue, which can only be quantitatively addressed if the age-structure of populations is explicitly incorporated in the projection model. This is also relevant for the analysis of the likely social and economic consequences of demographic trends, and even the impacts of environmental change where it has been shown that the vulnerability to environmental change can differ by age and sex.

The same is true for other highly relevant individual characteristics such as level of education and rural/urban place of residence. Both are of dual significance: they are important sources of population heterogeneity, influencing its dynamics, and their changing composition in the population is directly relevant for anticipating a broad range of population related socioeconomic challenges. In this chapter we focus primarily on the population dynamics by age and sex as is conventionally done in demography. But we will also present projection results that explicitly incorporate the population heterogeneity by level of education in addition to age and sex, since

The demographic future of Asia

education directly affects future fertility, mortality and migration trends (see also Chapter 22). We do so by using the techniques of multidimensional population dynamics, after first taking a look back at the performance of historical population projections for Asia.

History of population projections for Asian countries and analysis of past errors

When thinking about future trends it is always useful and instructive to look at past projections and see how they performed in relation to the actual historical development. For Asia, consistent population projections were produced by the United Nations since the 1950s. Fortunately, the experts who produced these early projections not only published their projection results but also documented the specific assumptions made, and in some cases even explicitly wrote about the reasoning behind specific assumptions. This is very useful for a retrospective analysis that tries to understand for what reasons projection errors were made. Only in this way can we learn lessons for our current production of projections.

One of the first projections for the region was published by the UN Economic and Social Committee for Asia and Pacific (ESCAP) in 1958 (United Nations 1958). When the UN experts in collaboration with national and international demographers felt in the late 1950s that it was important to produce population projections for individual countries in South-East Asia, they had at their disposal an increasing empirical database derived from censuses, surveys and to some degree vital statistics. But around 1955, the fertility transition had not yet started in South-East Asia and the total fertility rate (TFR) was in the range of 5.5–7.5 in the countries considered here. Even Singapore, that soon thereafter would see a precipitous fertility decline, still had a TFR above six.

The authors of the population projections published in 1958 speculated about the possibility of a fertility decline in the near future as suggested by demographic transition theory (United Nations 1958). But a comparison with other comparable countries did not seem to justify the assumption of declining fertility, as they stated: 'There are in fact few areas in the world where significant decline from equally high birth rates has, so far, been observed' (Khan and Lutz 2008). As a result they assumed constant high fertility, and even in the alternative projection presented in the main text they only combined a more rapid mortality decline with constant fertility.

For the more recent 1978 and 1982 UN assessments (United Nations 1980, 1985) a more detailed analysis of errors is possible as one can differentiate between baseline errors (incorrect estimates about demographic indicators in the base year of the projections) and projection errors (incorrect assumptions about the future trends in demographic parameters). Khan and Lutz (2008) provide a detailed analysis of these two different kinds of errors for six South-East Asian countries (Table 27.1).

Table 27.1 shows that the total forecasting errors of the 1978 and 1982 revisions, as assessed on the basis of the data given in the UN 2006 revision (2007), display great variation for the TFR across countries, and by the two different sources of error. The base error was particularly strong in Thailand in the 1978 assessment when the current fertility level for the 1975–1980 period was estimated to be 5.53, when it actually had already declined to 3.76 (as assessed by the UN in 2006). For Vietnam on the other hand, the base estimate for 1975–1980 was quite accurate in the 1978 assessment (even better than in the 1982 assessment), but the assumption of future fertility decline was far too small; the 1978 projections assumed that by 1995–2000, the TFR would decline to 4.39 when in fact it declined to 2.50.

The analysis by Khan and Lutz (2008) shows that unlike the 1978 assessment, the 1982 assessment (base year of 1980) was quite accurate in many respects, but it did not anticipate: (i) the

Table 27.1 Baseline errors and projection errors of the 1978 and 1982 UN population projections for six South-East Asian countries.

Country	Projection			2006 revision estimate			Total error	Base error	Change error
	1975–1980	1995–2000	Projected TFR decline	1975–1980	1995–2000	Estimated TFR decline			
	a	b	c = b – a	d	e	f = e – d	g = e – b	h = d – a	i = f – c
1978									
Indonesia	5.13	3.38	–1.75	4.73	2.55	–2.18	–0.83	–0.40	–0.43
Malaysia	4.26	2.7	–1.56	4.16	3.10	–1.06	0.40	–0.10	0.50
Philippines	5.83	3.75	–2.08	5.50	3.72	–1.78	–0.03	–0.33	0.30
Singapore	2.47	2.10	–0.37	1.87	1.57	–0.30	–0.53	–0.60	0.07
Thailand	5.53	3.28	–2.25	3.76	1.90	–1.86	–1.38	–1.77	0.39
Vietnam	5.84	4.39	1.45	5.89	2.50	–3.39	–1.89	0.05	–1.94
1982									
Indonesia	4.81	2.46	–2.35	4.73	2.55	–2.18	0.09	–0.08	0.17
Malaysia	5.03	2.46	–2.57	4.16	3.10	–1.06	0.64	–0.87	1.51
Philippines	4.62	2.87	–1.75	5.50	3.77	–1.78	0.85	0.88	–0.03
Singapore	1.84	1.74	–0.10	1.87	1.57	–0.30	–0.17	0.03	–0.02
Thailand	4.27	2.51	–1.76	3.76	1.90	–1.86	–0.61	–0.51	–0.10
Vietnam	5.48	2.87	–2.61	5.89	2.50	–3.39	–0.37	0.41	–0.78

Source: Adapted from Khan and Lutz (2008: Table 5).

pronatalist policies the Government of Malaysia adopted at about that time, (ii) the continuing influence of the Church and religion on the fertility level in the Philippines, and (iii) the volume of immigration to Singapore between 1980 and 2000. It also underestimated the speed of fertility decline in Thailand and Vietnam and the levels of mortality during the Vietnam War.

Hence the most important lesson learned from this analysis is that culture and politics matter a great deal for the specific paths of fertility and mortality. Similar assumptions made by the UN for the six countries of the region turned out to be much too high for some countries and much too low for others. This is a relevant insight for current discussions about whether projection assumptions should be derived exclusively from a statistical model, as was done in the UN 2012 assessment, or can also be complemented by expert arguments and country-specific knowledge, as discussed below.

Defining the assumptions for projecting twenty-first century population trends in Asia

All population projections crucially depend on three factors: (i) the choice of projection model, (ii) the empirical base line data, and (iii) the assumptions made about future trajectories of the demographic components. In this section, we will focus mostly on the third issue but also briefly touch upon the first two issues, which are often ignored in applied population projections.

In the history of population projections, virtually all projections up until the middle of the twentieth century were based on a simple population growth model, and the only assumptions made concerned the level of the future growth rate of the total population. In this projection model, which today still dominates animal demography (Sibly et al. 2003), any heterogeneity among the individuals that make up the population is simply ignored, but the results can be useful if the composition is fairly stable over time. The rapid fertility declines in Europe and the US during the first decades of the twentieth century and, in particular, the strong fertility and mortality fluctuations associated with the wars, produced a highly irregular age structure, and hence it became necessary to account explicitly for the population heterogeneity by age. Disregarding this evident heterogeneity would have led to serious distortions in the projections. For this reason the so-called cohort component model of population projections (which stratifies the population by age and sex) has become the dominant model since the middle of last century. But this model still disregards other potentially relevant sources of population heterogeneity, such as level of education or urban/rural place of residence.

The methods of multidimensional population dynamics are able to deal with populations that are stratified by further demographic dimensions in addition to age and sex. The International Institute for Applied Systems Analysis (IIASA) – where these methods were originally developed during the 1970s – has recently applied them to produce reconstructions and projections of populations by age, sex and level of educational attainment for most countries in the world (KC et al. 2010; Lutz et al. 2007). Like age and sex, education is viewed as an important source of population heterogeneity, but it is also of interest in its own right. Almost universally more educated people have lower mortality, and more educated women – particularly in countries in demographic transition – have lower fertility; and there is sufficient evidence that this is a real effect and not just owing to selectivity (Lutz and KC 2011). Lutz and Skirbekk (2013) discuss the issue of causality in the effects of education and bring together many studies based on natural experiments, instrumental variable models and other approaches that clearly demonstrate that this almost universal association is not a spurious effect. They coin the notion of 'functional causality' to indicate that – while it is nearly impossible to prove causality for all times and all different cultural settings – there are good reasons to assume that the effect of education on lowering mortality and fertility can indeed be assumed to hold over the projection period covered here. Finally, it needs to be stressed that the indicator of highest educational attainment that is being used here as the indicator of choice for all countries is only a proxy for skills and human capital. It does not include the quality dimension of education (because empirical data on this tend to be limited to rich countries), nor does it cover informal education (which also contributes to human capital, and for which even less reliable statistical information exists).

In general, the availability and reliability of empirical demographic data in Asia today is much better than in the case of the early projections discussed above. Hence we expect only minor baseline errors. But there are still certain important baseline uncertainties for war-torn countries such as Afghanistan, as well as for countries where the level of fertility is a political issue. Much has been written about the uncertainty associated with current fertility levels in China and the projections presented here assume somewhat lower baseline fertility than recent UN projections. With respect to baseline information on education, the data used here are mostly derived from censuses and surveys (for more information, see KC et al. 2013).

The empirical data for Asia show that in virtually all populations – and in particular those that are still in the process of demographic transition – more educated women have lower fertility. These educational differentials can be very significant. For Pakistan, for instance, it is estimated that women without formal education have on average twice as many children (3.8) than women with some post-secondary education (1.9). In the Philippines uneducated women have 4.05 children while those with some post-secondary education have 2.21. Because of these strong associations and the assumed functional causality between female education and mortality and fertility, future changes in the composition of the female population by educational attainment make a big difference to projected overall population sizes. Lutz and KC (2011) have shown that alternative education scenarios alone (assuming identical education-specific fertility and mortality levels) lead to a difference of more than one billion people in the world population sizes projected for 2050.

In terms of defining assumptions about the future trajectories of the demographic components, all national and international agencies producing population projections (including the UN until 2010) have based their assumptions primarily on expert knowledge. There is an extensive literature about the strengths and weaknesses of using different kinds of expert input, and about complementing them with trajectories derived from statistical analyses of past time series (Lutz, Vaupel and Ahlburg 1999; Lutz and Goldstein 2004), that cannot be summarized here. The projections presented here are based on a thorough analysis of all the known problems and biases associated with expert opinion and provide an innovate step forward in two ways: (i) they utilize peer-review-like expert assessments of alternative substantive arguments that bear on future trends, something that experts have been shown to be much better at than simply assuming likely future levels of fertility, mortality and migration (as has been done in conventional expert based projections); and (ii) these country-specific substantive expert-based assessments are blended with forecasts resulting from a purely statistical model (similar to that used by the UN since 2010), which is based on the collective empirical evidence of all other countries without being able to account for country-specific factors and substantive reasons for considering expected discontinuities. Hence the new global population projections produced by the Wittgenstein Centre for Demography and Global Human Capital (which includes IIASA's World Population Program) try to combine the strengths of the statistical and the expert-based approaches while at the same time avoiding their well-known weaknesses (see Lutz, Butz and KC 2014).[1]

The most elaborate part of this analysis and the part that is most relevant for the longer term demographic future of Asia deals with the question of how low fertility is likely to fall in Asia and what are the possible longer term trends in Asian low fertility countries. The long chapter

The demographic future of Asia

Table 27.2 Medium TFR assumptions for China, India and Indonesia according to the 2014 Wittgenstein Centre and the UN 2012 assessment

Country	Source	2010–2015	2020–2025	2030–2035	2040–2045	2050–2055	2075–2080	2095–2100
China	Lutz et al. 2014	1.42	1.40	1.40	1.40	1.40	1.46	1.51
	UN, 2013	1.66	1.72	1.76	1.80	1.82	1.86	1.88
India	Lutz et al. 2014	2.53	2.22	2.03	1.91	1.81	1.69	1.60
	UN, 2013	2.50	2.25	2.08	1.96	1.88	1.83	1.84
Indonesia	Lutz et al. 2014	2.05	1.84	1.68	1.57	1.52	1.56	1.59
	UN, 2013	2.35	2.12	1.98	1.89	1.85	1.84	1.86

Sources: Lutz et al. (2014) and UN (2013).

on 'Future fertility in low fertility countries' in Lutz, Butz and KC (2014) systematically considers all possible forces influencing future fertility, including cultural and social forces (such as fertility intentions, religion, gender preferences and urbanization/living arrangements), employment and socioeconomic factors, family policies, migrant fertility, biomedical factors and the impact of female education. For those Asian countries that still have high fertility, a comparable exercise was carried out and documented in another chapter, where a statistical model based on the recent trends of comparable countries was blended with country-specific substantive expertise. The resulting medium TFR assumptions for China, India and Indonesia are reported in Table 27.2 and compared to the assumptions in United Nations (2013). The comparison shows that for China, the fertility assumptions are consistently lower than in the UN projections, starting with a lower baseline value and then being about 0.4 children lower up into the second half of the century. Due to the great weight of China in Asia this causes visibly lower projections of total population. For India, the difference to the UN projection is smaller, with a somewhat higher TFR in 2010–2015 and then being only around 0.05 children lower. For Indonesia, our fertility assumptions are around 0.3 children lower than the UN projections.

The new Wittgenstein Centre projections are incorporated into another major international scenario building process in the context of climate change analysis. To study the relationships between socioeconomic development and climate change the global modelling community on Integrated Assessment has replaced the older Special Report on Emissions Scenarios (SRES) (Nakicenovic et al. 2000), which only had total population size and total GDP as socioeconomic variables, with a more elaborate framework. The resulting set of 'shared socioeconomic pathways' (SSPs) describes alternative future worlds with respect to social and economic mitigation and adaptation challenges. In addition to several energy and technology related variables and alternative urbanization trajectories, these new scenarios include alternative population projections by age, sex and six levels of education for all countries in the world to 2100. On the basis of these projections alternative GDP scenarios have also been derived that are consistent with the defined population and human capital trends.

Here we present three of the five SSPs. The broader storylines and their operationalization in terms of specific demographic assumptions are described elsewhere (KC and Lutz 2014). Here it suffices to say that the above described medium population assumptions together with the Global Education Trends (GET) scenario – which is considered the most likely – have been set to be identical with SSP2, the 'middle of the road' socioeconomic scenario. This is why Table 27.4 lists SSP2 (on the left side) as the main scenario that can also be directly compared to the UN medium scenario (or to the single scenario projections of the US Census Bureau). On the low end (in terms of future population growth), SSP1 has been set to be the rapid development scenario (also called the 'Sustainability Scenario'), which combines low mortality with low fertility (in non-OECD countries), medium migration and rapid improvements in education. This scenario combines a world of fast social development with high human capital and green economic growth. It is not directly comparable to the UN low fertility scenario, because according to the story line high social development and gender equity result in medium-level fertility in the rich OECD countries. On the high end, the SSP3 scenario refers to a storyline of stalled development combining high mortality and high fertility (except for rich OECD countries where economic stagnation is assumed to result in low fertility), as well as low migration and education. This scenario of fragmentation refers to a future world where current inequalities continue, where there is low human capital combined with only little technological progress, and widespread poverty. The following section summarizes the results of these three scenarios for Asia.[2]

Projection results for all of Asia and individual countries

In discussing the projection results we first focus on total population size for the rest of the century. Table 27.3 presents the projection results for Asia in the global context. Due to the fact that Asia currently is home to almost two-thirds of the world's population the future global trend will be very heavily influenced by developments in Asia. The table shows that the population of Asia is likely to peak around mid-century at a level somewhat above 5 billion people. Mostly as a function of the fertility assumptions described above, it is then likely to decline slowly to about 4.4 billion by the end of the century, which happens to be the same as the estimated level in 2015. Europe is expected to follow a rather similar growth curve with a slightly earlier peak and a fall below current levels by the end of the century. Latin America also reveals this pattern with a somewhat later peak (around 2060) and a still higher population than today by 2100. North America is expected to show a continued moderate increase – mostly due to migration gains – throughout the century, while Africa is expected to see very significant increases by a factor of around 2.5 due to continued high fertility and a strong population momentum.

Figure 27.1 shows the results of the three alternative scenarios mentioned for Asia as a whole. SSP1 (rapid development) gives the lowest population trajectory with the population already peaking around 2040 and then falling to around 3.3 billion by the end of the century. SSP3 (stalled development) on the other hand shows continued population growth throughout the

Table 27.3 Projections of total population size (in millions) for world and major regions to 2100 under the medium scenario, SSP2

	2010	2020	2030	2040	2050	2060	2070	2080	2090	2100
World	6896	7639	8286	8804	9174	9375	9431	9369	9207	8981
Africa	1022	1268	1527	1782	2019	2217	2378	2499	2579	2622
Asia	4164	4557	4855	5049	5135	5111	4999	4826	4611	4380
Europe	738	748	753	755	755	750	741	730	717	703
LAC	590	651	702	738	758	762	754	737	712	684
North America	345	372	400	426	447	470	491	506	516	521
Oceania	37	42	48	53	57	61	64	66	67	67

Note: LAC: Latin America and Caribbean.
Source: Based on data reported in Lutz et al. (2014).

The demographic future of Asia

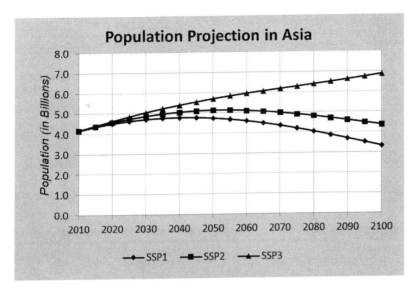

Figure 27.1 Trends in total population size of Asia 2010 to 2100 according to three shared socioeconomic pathways (SSP) scenarios
Source: Adapted from Lutz et al. (2014).

century reaching 6.9 billion in 2100. Viewed together these three scenarios give a range for Asia's future population size of 4.7–5.7 billion in 2050 and 3.3–6.9 billion in 2100.

Figure 27.2 shows the age and education pyramids for 2010 and as projected to 2060 under the medium scenario (SSP2). As discussed earlier, this way of graphical presentation displays the interactions between changes in age and education structures along cohort lines. The cohort of 20–24 year old women in 2010, for example, is to be found in the age group of 70–74 year old women in 2060, not only in terms of its mortality- and migration-adjusted size, but also in terms of its educational attainment distribution shown by the grey shadings.

In Asia today, the population pyramid has already significantly deviated from its traditional triangular shape. This is mostly due to the very strong recent fertility decline in China. As a consequence, currently the largest age group is that of 20–24 year old men and women. And as the shadings indicate, these young adults are already reasonably well educated, with more than three-quarters having received junior secondary or higher education. The figure also shows that women lag behind men in their education, a pattern that is greatly influenced by the Indian situation. By 2060 under the medium scenario (SSP2) depicted in Figure 27.2, the Asian education pyramid is likely to look rather similar to that of Europe today, with the biggest age groups being about 50–54, featuring very high education levels among the working age population.

After this survey of the range of possible future trends in population size and structures for Asia as a whole, we now move to the presentation of results for individual countries. Table 27.4 shows the medium projections (SSP2) and the ranges implied by the assumptions of scenarios SSP1 to SSP3. The range is particularly great for countries that currently still have very high fertility. In Afghanistan, where the TFR is estimated to be currently around 5.0, even the most optimistic SSP1 (rapid development scenario) shows a doubling in population size while the SSP3 (stalled development scenario) results in an increase by a factor of more than seven. In terms of absolute numbers the range is greatest for India, where the difference between SSP1 and SSP3 in 2100 is more than 1.5 billion – much higher than India's population today and three times the

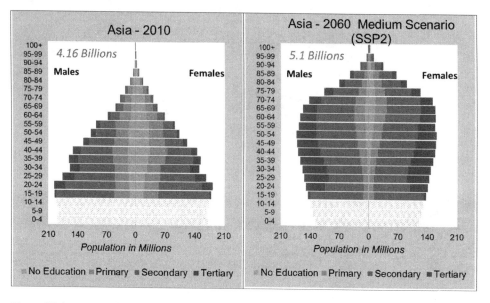

Figure 27.2 Age and education pyramids for the entire Asian continent in 2010 and projected to 2060 under the medium scenario
Notes: The vertical axis refers to Age (in years). For clarity of graphical exposition the education categories have been collapsed into four.
Source: Adapted from Lutz et al. (2014).

current population of the entire European Union. This clearly illustrates how important future education and associated fertility trends are for the future demographic trends in India, but also for all of Asia and the world.

In terms of changing population structures, we will look first at the changing education composition, and then at the changing age composition. The interactions between education and age structures can be shown through the full distribution as given in Figure 27.2. For comparisons it can be convenient to focus on summary indicators such as the mean age of the population, or the mean years of schooling of the adult population. While such indicators summarize information across all age or education groups, they are insensitive, however, to changes in the distribution that do not affect the mean. This limitation can be addressed through summary indicators that simply give the proportions below and above a certain cut-off point in the distribution. For age, such an indicator is the proportion of the population above age 65. For education, the proportion of the female population aged 20–39 that has at least completed junior secondary education has been shown to be a useful indicator; in most countries this implies that girls have been to school at least until the age of 15, and for many behavioural consequences of education this seems to be a critical threshold.

Table 27.5 lists the projected values of this aggregate education indicator for all Asian countries for the SSP1–SSP3 scenarios. For Asia as a whole, currently 63 per cent of all young women have completed junior secondary or higher education. The range goes from 100 per cent in the most developed Asian countries, and in former Soviet republics that for long had compulsory education to that level, to a low of 30 per cent in Pakistan (for Afghanistan we have no good estimates). It is also still very low in India where only 45 per cent of young women have junior secondary or higher education. This compares to 83 per cent in China. Since education

Table 27.4 Trends in total population size (in millions) for individual Asian countries under the most likely medium scenario (SSP2) as well as the rapid development scenario (SSP1) and the stalled development scenario (SSP3)

Country	Medium scenario, SSP2				Rapid development, SSP1				Stalled development, SSP3			
	2010	2030	2050	2100		2030	2050	2100		2030	2050	2100
Total	**4139.9**	**4826.7**	**5105.0**	**4353.7**		**4678.8**	**4725.7**	**3318.7**		**5017.7**	**5680.0**	**6856.3**
Afghanistan	31.4	51.9	75.3	111.7		46.7	59.5	64.1		58.5	100.6	222.9
Armenia	3.1	3.0	2.9	2.3		3.0	2.7	1.8		3.2	3.2	3.3
Azerbaijan	9.2	11.1	11.7	10.3		10.8	10.9	7.7		11.2	12.3	13.8
Bahrain	1.3	2.2	3.0	3.5		2.4	3.1	2.9		2.2	2.8	3.9
Bangladesh	148.7	178.6	190.7	161.6		172.0	174.2	121.5		189.0	219.3	259.6
Bhutan	0.7	1.0	1.2	1.2		1.0	1.1	0.9		1.0	1.3	1.7
Brunei	0.4	0.6	0.7	0.7		0.5	0.6	0.5		0.5	0.7	0.9
Cambodia	14.1	17.1	18.6	16.8		16.5	16.8	12.0		18.2	21.4	26.8
China	1341.3	1377.7	1255.3	754.1		1357.3	1218.8	643.6		1399.6	1309.8	1046.1
Georgia	4.4	3.9	3.3	2.0		3.9	3.2	1.7		4.1	3.8	3.6
Hong Kong	7.1	8.1	8.7	8.0		8.1	8.6	7.0		7.9	8.0	8.3
India	1224.6	1520.6	1714.6	1569.5		1456.6	1543.0	1130.9		1608.0	1982.5	2686.6
Indonesia	239.9	276.4	285.5	225.1		269.5	269.2	181.6		284.6	306.2	292.1
Iran	74.0	90.5	98.1	81.4		87.7	91.6	65.6		94.0	107.7	122.3
Iraq	31.7	50.4	68.3	89.2		47.2	59.0	62.5		55.2	85.1	169.0
Israel	7.4	11.3	15.9	27.6		11.4	16.0	27.6		10.3	12.6	14.9
Japan	126.5	119.9	107.5	74.7		121.9	112.5	84.4		115.1	94.8	45.7
Jordan	6.2	9.8	13.2	16.2		9.4	11.9	12.0		9.9	13.9	21.8
Kazakhstan	16.0	19.0	20.8	19.7		18.5	19.3	15.2		19.3	22.0	25.8
Kuwait	2.7	4.3	5.8	6.5		4.3	5.5	5.1		4.2	5.5	7.6
Kyrgyzstan	5.3	6.3	6.8	5.9		6.1	6.1	4.3		6.8	7.9	9.2
Laos	6.2	7.9	8.8	8.2		7.5	7.9	5.8		8.4	10.2	13.2
Lebanon	4.2	4.9	5.2	4.5		4.8	4.9	3.5		5.0	5.5	6.4
Macao	0.5	0.7	0.9	0.9		0.8	0.9	0.8		0.7	0.8	0.9
Malaysia	28.4	37.6	44.3	46.9		36.3	40.7	36.2		38.8	48.3	68.1

(*continued*)

Table 27.4 (Cont.)

Country	Medium scenario, SSP2				Rapid development, SSP1				Stalled development, SSP3		
	2010	2030	2050	2100	2030	2050	2100		2030	2050	2100
Maldives	0.3	0.4	0.5	0.4	0.4	0.4	0.3		0.4	0.5	0.6
Mongolia	2.8	3.4	3.8	3.6	3.3	3.4	2.6		3.6	4.2	5.3
Myanmar	48.0	51.8	49.8	37.9	50.0	46.0	27.7		54.1	55.3	57.4
Nepal	30.0	41.7	51.4	55.1	39.6	45.5	39.6		45.2	62.5	102.1
North Korea	24.3	25.9	24.9	17.6	25.3	23.6	14.2		26.4	26.2	24.5
Oman	2.8	4.0	4.8	4.0	4.0	4.8	3.5		4.0	5.1	6.1
Pakistan	173.6	237.2	286.3	314.0	223.8	248.6	212.2		255.2	344.1	550.6
Palestine	4.0	6.0	7.5	8.9	5.7	6.6	6.4		6.7	9.8	17.9
Philippines	93.3	122.0	141.4	146.6	116.5	126.6	107.0		131.2	169.7	250.6
Qatar	1.8	3.0	3.9	3.7	3.4	4.6	3.8		3.0	3.6	3.7
Saudi Arabia	27.4	41.8	54.7	65.1	40.5	50.3	49.0		41.9	56.7	90.5
Singapore	5.1	6.6	7.6	7.6	6.7	7.6	6.7		6.4	6.9	7.4
South Korea	48.2	50.0	46.4	30.2	50.6	48.6	34.7		48.3	41.4	18.6
Sri Lanka	20.9	23.4	24.0	20.6	22.6	22.1	15.5		24.4	27.3	34.2
Syria	20.4	28.3	34.5	38.3	26.9	30.7	28.1		29.9	39.7	61.5
Tajikistan	6.9	8.3	8.8	7.9	8.0	7.9	5.8		9.2	11.3	14.6
Thailand	69.1	74.8	72.8	53.8	73.4	69.6	42.7		75.6	75.9	78.5
Timor-Leste	1.1	1.7	2.1	2.5	1.6	1.8	1.7		2.0	3.1	6.1
Turkey	72.8	87.0	93.0	81.2	84.1	86.1	62.6		91.4	104.6	133.5
Turkmenistan	5.0	6.1	6.5	5.6	5.9	6.0	4.2		6.4	7.3	8.0
UAE	7.5	13.1	17.3	17.1	14.2	18.8	16.0		12.7	15.6	17.3
Uzbekistan	27.4	32.8	34.8	29.6	31.5	31.7	22.1		34.8	40.5	49.4
Vietnam	87.8	102.5	105.1	78.1	99.9	99.2	64.0		105.4	112.9	108.5
Yemen	24.1	40.1	56.1	75.7	37.0	47.0	49.1		44.0	69.8	134.7

Notes: For countries in italics, data on education distribution was not available. Regional distribution of education was used as a proxy for the sake of completeness.
Source: Based on data reported in Lutz et al. (2014).

Table 27.5 Percentages of women aged 20–39 with at least lower secondary education for all Asian countries* for which consistent education data were available for the base year

Country	Medium scenario, SSP2			Rapid development, SSP1		Stalled development, SSP3	
	2010	2030	2050	2030	2050	2030	2050
Total	63	76	87	85	93	61	58
Armenia	99	100	100	100	100	99	99
Azerbaijan	92	97	99	98	99	88	89
Bahrain	86	95	97	97	98	89	89
Bangladesh	36	57	70	72	84	46	46
Bhutan	35	72	90	77	94	53	53
Cambodia	24	39	55	54	75	29	29
China	83	91	95	94	97	87	87
Georgia	99	100	100	100	100	98	98
Hong Kong	94	99	100	99	100	96	96
India	45	67	83	80	91	44	44
Indonesia	62	83	93	89	96	73	73
Iran	67	87	95	92	98	72	72
Iraq	47	71	86	81	91	30	30
Israel	88	93	95	96	97	90	90
Japan	99	100	100	100	100	99	99
Jordan	81	94	97	97	99	82	82
Kazakhstan	99	100	100	100	100	99	99
Kuwait	70	93	95	96	97	90	90
Kyrgyzstan	100	100	100	100	100	99	99
Laos	36	54	68	70	84	40	40
Lebanon	83	92	96	95	98	86	86
Macao	90	96	98	98	99	93	93
Malaysia	91	98	99	99	99	90	90
Maldives	54	71	80	80	89	63	63
Mongolia	95	97	98	99	99	93	93
Myanmar	51	64	74	78	87	52	52
Nepal	39	69	88	79	93	37	37
Pakistan	30	52	74	69	85	28	28
Palestine	70	90	97	94	98	70	70
Philippines	76	90	96	93	97	72	72
Qatar	71	82	84	90	92	79	79
Saudi Arabia	78	96	99	97	99	82	82
Singapore	97	100	100	100	100	99	99
South Korea	100	100	100	100	100	100	100
Syria	36	56	72	70	84	33	33
Tajikistan	91	97	99	98	100	91	91
Thailand	71	84	92	91	96	71	71
Timor-Leste	44	79	93	85	96	56	56
Turkey	46	70	86	81	92	42	42
Turkmenistan	100	100	100	100	100	99	99
UAE	82	92	93	95	96	86	86
Vietnam	56	75	82	82	90	70	70

Note: *Some Asian countries are missing in the table due to non-availability of data on education distribution.
Source: Based on data reported in Lutz et al. (2014).

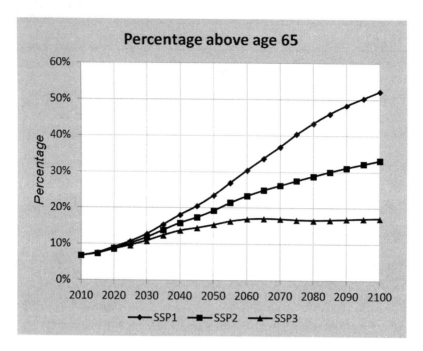

Figure 27.3 Projected changes in the percentages above age 65 under the different SSP scenarios in Asia
Source: Adapted from Lutz et al. (2014).

assumptions are an important constituent part of defining the SSP scenarios, it is not surprising that for all countries the rapid development scenario (SSP1) shows a rapid increase in this indicator, while the stalled development scenario (SSP3) shows a stagnation and in some cases even a decline. Such a decline can result from a situation in which the expansion of the school systems cannot keep pace with rapid population growth. This is more likely to happen in countries that still have high fertility, which illustrates the interesting two-way interaction between fertility and education that is embedded in the model: higher female education leads to lower fertility, but high fertility is an obstacle to the rapid increase of school enrolment rates.

In the final part of this chapter we turn to indicators of population ageing. There is no doubt that Asia is a rapidly ageing region, no matter which ageing indicator is chosen. Currently only 7 per cent of the Asian population is above age 65. This compares to 16 per cent in Europe. But with near certainty, the proportion of elderly (according to this definition) will increase in Asia over the coming decades. As Figure 27.3 shows, even under the stalled development scenario (SSP3) this proportion will more than double to 15 per cent by mid-century and further increase towards the end of the century. Under the rapid development scenario (SSP1), it will increase to 23 per cent by 2050 and to 52 per cent by the end of the century. Under the medium scenario (SSP2), this percentage would increase to one-third by the end of the century.

How can we envisage societies with one-third or more of the population being above the age of 65, and what will be the social and economic consequences of such a development? In order to address this issue under the long time horizon we have to ask also whether a 65-year old person in 2100 is likely to be comparable to 65-year old person today. The answer to this question is clearly no. As life expectancy is assumed to increase over time – here a two-year per decade increase on average is assumed – the general health status of a person is also increasing. There is also strong

The demographic future of Asia

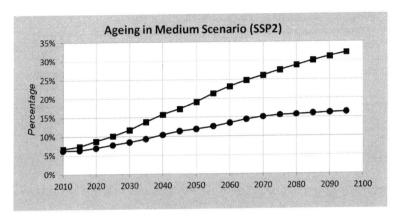

Figure 27.4 Projected trends in the percentage of the population above the age of 65 (squares) and above the age when the remaining life expectancy is less than 15 years (circles) for all of Asia over the twenty-first century
Source: Adapted from Lutz et al. (2014).

evidence that with better education and better physical health, he/she will also be in good mental health longer and able to contribute positively to society and the economy. There have been recent efforts to convert the frequent and well-justified saying '60 is the new 50' (or '70 is the new 60') into new indicators of population age and ageing. Sanderson and Scherbov (2005) and Lutz et al. (2008) have proposed measures of 'prospective age' that take these changes in life expectancy and health status over longer periods into account. One such indicator is the proportion of the population that is above an age where the remaining life expectancy is less than 15 years.

Figure 27.4 shows this new indicator of population ageing in comparison to the conventional percentage above age 65. Currently the percentage above age 65 and the percentage with less than 15 years to live are at the same level for all of Asia (7 and 6 per cent respectively). But over the century the percentage above age 65 increases by about twice the speed as the other prospective indicator of ageing. Under the medium scenario (SSP2), in 2100 the percentage of the population above age 65 will be exactly twice as high (32 per cent) than the percentage of the population that is at an age where the remaining life expectancy is less than 15 years. If we view this latter one as the more relevant ageing indicator (in terms of the likely social and economic consequences of ageing), then indeed the future ageing prospects for Asia are much less dramatic than is usually assumed on the basis of conventional indicators.

Conclusions

This chapter attempts to present a comprehensive overview of what we can see from today's perspective as likely and possible future demographic trends in Asia as a whole and in the region's individual countries. We did so in the context of new three-dimensional population projections by age, sex and level of educational attainment (Lutz, Butz and KC 2014). This effort includes the substantive argumentation and definition of alternative fertility, mortality, migration and education scenarios for all Asian countries through a blend of statistical modelling and country-specific expert-argument-based reasoning involving more than 550 international population experts.

As compared to recent projections published by the UN Population Division (United Nations 2013), the projections are generally slightly lower due to somewhat lower fertility levels assumed

Table 27.6 Projected trends in the percentages of the population above the age of 65, and above the age when the remaining life expectancy is less than 15 years, Asian countries* over the twenty-first century

Country	Proportion aged 65+				Proportion of population with 15 years of remaining life expectancy			
	2010	2030	2050	2100	2013	2033	2053	2098
Total	**7**	**12**	**19**	**33**	**6**	**8**	**12**	**16**
Afghanistan	2	3	4	15	4	4	5	11
Armenia	11	19	24	35	10	12	13	16
Azerbaijan	7	13	18	33	7	11	12	19
Bahrain	2	8	21	38	2	5	10	15
Bangladesh	5	8	16	34	5	7	11	17
Bhutan	5	7	15	35	5	6	8	16
Brunei	4	11	22	42	2	3	7	12
Cambodia	4	7	12	27	5	8	11	16
China	8	17	28	43	8	12	19	22
Georgia	14	23	30	38	13	16	19	19
Hong Kong	13	27	34	43	8	10	16	14
India	5	8	15	31	6	7	9	17
Indonesia	6	10	19	35	6	8	13	19
Iran	5	10	23	41	5	6	10	16
Iraq	3	4	9	29	3	3	5	12
Israel	10	13	15	26	7	7	6	8
Japan	23	31	40	48	12	17	17	17
Jordan	4	5	11	32	4	3	6	13
Kazakhstan	7	11	16	33	8	10	11	16
Kuwait	3	6	18	36	3	4	10	15
Kyrgyzstan	4	8	14	32	5	7	9	16
Laos	4	6	10	26	5	7	10	16
Lebanon	7	12	21	36	7	9	13	17
Macao	7	20	29	43	5	8	14	15
Malaysia	5	11	17	35	5	7	10	15
Maldives	5	9	22	44	4	4	7	16
Mongolia	4	8	14	27	4	7	11	16
Myanmar	5	10	17	27	6	11	17	18
Nepal	4	6	12	32	5	5	7	15
North Korea	10	13	21	38	11	12	16	20
Oman	3	6	19	46	3	4	9	21
Pakistan	4	6	10	25	5	6	8	14
Palestine	3	5	10	30	3	3	5	13
Philippines	4	7	12	30	4	6	8	14
Qatar	1	8	30	46	1	2	11	16
Saudi Arabia	3	7	16	33	3	5	9	14
Singapore	9	20	27	43	6	9	12	14
South Korea	11	24	37	46	7	11	19	19
Sri Lanka	8	15	22	37	6	10	12	16
Syria	4	7	14	34	3	5	7	14
Tajikistan	3	6	11	28	4	5	7	14
Thailand	9	17	24	35	7	12	17	19
Timor-Leste	3	4	5	16	4	5	5	11

Table 27.6 (Cont.)

Country	Proportion aged 65+				Proportion of population with 15 years of remaining life expectancy			
	2010	2030	2050	2100	2013	2033	2053	2098
Turkey	6	11	20	35	6	9	13	17
Turkmenistan	4	8	14	30	5	7	10	16
UAE	0	6	26	43	0	3	11	16
Uzbekistan	4	9	16	33	4	6	10	16
Vietnam	6	13	24	43	5	7	12	18
Yemen	3	3	5	20	3	4	6	12

Notes: For countries in italics, data on education distribution was not available. Regional distribution of education was used as a proxy for the sake of completeness.
Source: Based on data reported in Lutz et al. (2014).

over the long term. While the aggregate level difference in the medium variants is minor by the middle of the century (for all of Asia in 2050: 5.16 billion by the UN as compared to 5.11 in our projections), it becomes more pronounced by the end of the century (for 2100: 4.71 billion by the UN as compared to 4.38 in our projections). The US Census Bureau (which only produces one scenario to 2050) projects the total population of Asia to reach 5.19 in 2050. Table 27.2 which compares our fertility assumptions to those of the UN shows that the most significant difference – with the greatest weight for the total population of Asia – lies in our lower estimate of current fertility in China and assumed lower levels for the coming decades. But since the assumptions in the projections presented here also include many country-specific assumptions based on expert knowledge about the specific cultural and political settings of individual countries, for some countries these projections also turn out higher than the UN projections. Another main difference to the UN projections lies in the fact that their projections are only two-dimensional (by age and sex), and thus do not explicitly address the specific dynamics that result from the significant population heterogeneity by level of education. Yet another difference lies in the way that high and low scenarios are being defined. While the 2012 UN projections define their high and low variants by combining identical mortality and migration assumptions with fertility assumptions that are for all countries 0.5 children higher and lower than the medium assumptions, the different SSP scenarios presented here assume – based on consistent alternative story lines – different trajectories for all four components considered: fertility, mortality, migration and education.

In a nutshell, there is little doubt that Asia as a whole will experience an end to population growth over the course of the twenty-first century. There is also no doubt that Asia's population will be ageing significantly over the coming decades. Finally, there is no doubt that Asia's population in the future will be much better educated than it is today. This is in part already embedded in the fact that in virtually every country the young cohorts are significantly better educated than the older ones and hence the process of 'demographic metabolism' – a notion coined by Norman Ryder on generational replacement – will lead to significant improvements of the human capital of the working age population over time. We also presented new prospective indicators of population ageing that define age through the expected time to death rather than the time since birth, and we showed that this generates a much less dramatic picture of future population ageing. Viewed together, these different expected demographic trends in Asia clearly present major challenges in terms of adjusting the existing institutions and socioeconomic policies of individual countries, but overall they clearly support the view that the twenty-first century will indeed be the Asian Century.

Notes

1 More than 550 population experts from around the world participated in this effort, which included an online questionnaire that assessed in peer review manner the validity of alternative arguments that would impact the future trends of fertility, mortality and migration. In a series of five meta-expert meetings (held on five different continents) the survey findings were evaluated and ultimately translated into numerical assumptions for the actual projections for all countries. The results are documented in Lutz, Butz and KC (2014), written by 26 lead authors and 46 contributing authors; the book provides all the substantive justifications, models and data underlying the projections presented in this chapter.
2 More details can be found under www.wittgensteincentre.org/dataexplorer.

References

Abel, G. J. and N. Sander (2014) 'Quantifying global international migration flows'. *Science*, 343(6178): 1520–1522. Available from: http://dx.doi.org/10.1126/science.1248676.

Barakat, B. F. and R. E. Durham (2013) 'Future education trends'. Interim Report IR-13–014. Laxenburg, Austria: International Institute for Applied Systems Analysis. Available from: http://webarchive.iiasa.ac.at/Admin/PUB/Documents/IR-13–014.pdf.

Basten, S., T. Sobotka and K. Zeman (2013) 'Future fertility in low fertility countries'. VID Working Paper 05/2013. Vienna, Austria: Vienna Institute of Demography. Available from: www.oeaw.ac.at/vid/download/WP2013_5.pdf.

Caselli, G., S. Drefahl, M. Luy and C. Wegner (2013) 'Future mortality in low-mortality countries'. VID Working Paper 06/2013. Vienna, Austria: Vienna Institute of Demography. Available from: www.oeaw.ac.at/vid/download/WP2013_6.pdf.

Fuchs, R. and A. Goujon (2013) 'The future fertility of high fertility countries: a model incorporating expert arguments'. Interim Report IR-13–013. Laxenburg, Austria: International Institute for Applied Systems Analysis. Available from: http://webarchive.iiasa.ac.at/Admin/PUB/Documents/IR-13–013.pdf.

Garbero, A. and E. Pamuk (2013) 'The future mortality of high mortality countries: a model incorporating expert arguments'. Interim Report IR-13–017. Laxenburg, Austria: International Institute for Applied Systems Analysis. Available from: http://webarchive.iiasa.ac.at/Admin/PUB/Documents/IR-13–017.pdf.

KC, S., B. Barakat, A. Goujon, V. Skirbekk, W. C. Sanderson and W. Lutz (2010) 'Projection of populations by level of educational attainment, age and sex for 120 countries for 2005–2050'. *Demographic Research*, 22 (Article 15): 383–472. Available from: http://dx.doi.org/10.4054/DemRes.2010.22.15.

KC, S. and W. Lutz (2014) 'Demographic scenarios by age, sex and education corresponding to the SSP narratives'. *Population and Environment*, 35(3): 243–260. Available from: http://dx.doi.org/10.1007/s11111-014-0205-4.

KC, S., M. Potančoková, R. Bauer, A. Goujon and E. Striessnig (2013) 'Summary of data, assumptions and methods for new Wittgenstein Centre for Demography and Global Human Capital (WIC). Population projections by age, sex and level of education for 195 countries to 2100'. Interim Report IR-13–018. Laxenburg, Austria: International Institute for Applied Systems Analysis. Available from: http://webarchive.iiasa.ac.at/Admin/PUB/Documents/IR-13–018.pdf.

Khan, H. T. A. and W. Lutz (2008) 'How well did past UN population projections anticipate demographic trends in six South-East Asian countries?' *Asian Population Studies*, 4(1): 77–95. Available from: http://dx.doi.org/10.1080/17441730801966964.

Lutz, W., W. P. Butz and Samir KC (eds.) (2014) *World Population and Human Capital in the 21st Century*. Oxford: Oxford University Press.

Lutz, W. and J. Goldstein, Guest Editors (2004) 'How to deal with uncertainty in population forecasting?' Special issue of *International Statistical Review*, 72(1&2): 1–106, 157–208. Reprinted as RR-04-009 by the International Institute for Applied Systems Analysis, Laxenburg, Austria.

Lutz, W., A. Goujon, S. KC and W. C. Sanderson (2007) 'Reconstruction of populations by age, sex and level of educational attainment for 120 countries for 1970–2000'. *Vienna Yearbook of Population Research*, 5: 193–235. Available from: http://dx.doi.org/10.1553/populationyearbook2007s193.

Lutz, W. and S. KC (2011) 'Global human capital: integrating education and population'. *Science*, 333(6042): 587–592. Available from: http://dx.doi.org/10.1126/science.1206964.

Lutz, W., W. Sanderson and S. Scherbov (2008) 'The coming acceleration of global population ageing'. *Nature*, 451(7179): 716–719. Available from: http://dx.doi.org/10.1038/nature06516.

Lutz, W. and V. Skirbekk (2013) 'How education drives demography and knowledge informs projections'. Interim Report IR-13-016. Laxenburg, Austria: International Institute for Applied Systems Analysis. Available from: http://webarchive.iiasa.ac.at/Admin/PUB/Documents/IR-13-016.pdf.

Lutz, W., J. W. Vaupel and D. A. Ahlburg (eds.) (1999) *Frontiers of Population Forecasting*. Supplement to *Population and Development Review*, Vol. 24. New York: Population Council.

Nakicenovic, N., J. Alcamo, A. Grubler, K. Riahi, R. A. Roehrl, H. H. Rogner and N. Victor (2000) *Special Report on Emissions Scenarios: A Special Report of Working Group III of the Intergovernmental Panel on Climate Change*. Cambridge, UK: Cambridge University Press. Available from: www.grida.no/climate/ipcc/emission/index.htm.

Sander, N., G. Abel and F. Riosmena (2013) 'The future of international migration: developing expert-based assumptions for global population projections'. Working Paper 07/2013. Vienna: Vienna Institute of Demography. Available from: www.oeaw.ac.at/vid/download/WP2013_7.pdf.

Sanderson, W. C. and S. Scherbov (2005) 'Average remaining lifetimes can increase as human populations age'. *Nature*, 435(7043): 811–813. Available from: http:dx.doi.org/10.1038/nature03593.

Sibly, R. M., J. Hone and T. H. Clutton-Brock (eds.) (2003) *Wildlife Population Growth Rates*. Cambridge, UK: Cambridge University Press for the Royal Society.

United Nations (1958) 'Report III: The population of South-East Asia (including Ceylon and China: Taiwan) 1950–1980'. New York, NY: United Nations Department of Economic and Social Affairs, Population Division.

United Nations (1980) *Selected Demographic Indicators by Country, 1950–2000: Demographic Estimates and Projections as Assessed in 1978*. New York, NY: United Nations.

United Nations (1985) *World Population Prospects: Estimates and Projections as Assessed in 1982*. New York, NY: United Nations.

United Nations (2007) *World Population Prospects: The 2006 Revision*. New York, NY: United Nations.

United Nations (2013) *World Population Prospects: The 2012 Revision. Key Findings and Advance Tables*. New York, NY: Department of Economic and Social Affairs, Population Division. Available from: http://esa.un.org/unpd/wpp/Documentation/publications.htm.

28
Conclusion

Zhongwei Zhao and Adrian C. Hayes

The main substantive focus of this handbook has been on population change in Asia since the mid-twentieth century, with a few excursions into earlier demographic history and future population projections. In this concluding chapter, we summarize *some* of the main demographic trends and indicate where Asian populations appear to be headed in the near future as a consequence of these trends. We cannot predict the future with certainty but population dynamics exhibit a certain momentum, which makes demographic projections over two or three decades more robust than most economic or political forecasts. Looking ahead to 2050, for example, we already know a lot about the 35-and-over population of Asia – the maximum size of this population, its age structure and level of education – because this population was born before 2016 and is already alive. Major changes in mortality and fertility could severely affect the size and composition of Asia's population in 2050 but the chances of such major changes are relatively small. Accordingly, the demographic backdrop for Asia's social, economic and political development in the next few decades is already largely established. We close the chapter with some reflections on the implications of current demographic trends for development in Asia during the remainder of the first half of the twenty-first century, especially during 2015–2030.

Major demographic trends in Asia in the first half of the twenty-first century

The authors of the previous chapter have presented population projections by age, sex and educational attainment. Changes in the population size indicated by their medium scenario projections are close to the results of the United Nations (UNPD 2015a) medium variant projection for the period before 2050, with the differences increasing thereafter. In this chapter, we use mainly the estimation and projection results published by the UN so as to keep data sources for future population, urbanization and migration changes consistent. This handbook and demographic investigations undertaken elsewhere show that significant population changes have taken place in Asia since 1950, and they have greatly altered the world demographic map. In the early twenty-first century, Asian population changes have displayed several major trends, which are presented below.

Despite their considerable variations, both mortality and fertility are expected to converge to low levels in the next three decades. According to the UN's medium variant projection, Asia's life expectancies at birth will vary between 61.5 years for Afghanistan and 84.5 years for Hong Kong in 2015–2020, and total fertility rates (TFRs) between 1.0 birth per woman for Taiwan and 5.3 births per woman for Timor-Leste.[1] In the next 30 to 35 years, mortality is expected to decline steadily, unless Asia is struck by catastrophic infectious disease, natural disaster or war. The decline will most likely be faster in countries currently having a higher mortality than in those with a lower mortality as identified in Chapter 12. Similarly, a large fertility reduction is unlikely in populations already having very low fertility, and their fertility may even bounce back moderately as observed recently in some North and West European countries (UNPD 2015b). On the other hand, countries and territories currently with high fertility are expected to experience significant fertility decline. Consequently, cross-national gaps in both mortality and fertility are expected to narrow in the next few decades, in line with the UN medium variant projection (UNPD 2015a). By the mid-twenty-first century, the overwhelming majority (if not all) of Asian populations are expected to have completed or have long completed the demographic transition described by Frank Notestein (1945). The demographic regime of high mortality and high fertility will soon become a part of Asian history.

Asian population is projected to keep growing until the mid-twenty-first century, but its speed of increase will decelerate. Asia has made remarkable efforts in curtailing population growth in recent decades and its current TFR is just slightly above replacement. This played a pivotal role in slowing down world population growth. Despite that, the Asian population will grow further, from 4.4 billion in 2015 to its peak of 5.3 billion in 2055, up by 900 million people (which is more than 1.2 times the current European population). This will happen because some Asian countries still have relatively high fertility and are expected to remain so for one or two decades, continuing to offset the population reduction brought about by low fertility in other countries. Furthermore, population increase (or decrease) is not only affected by the level of fertility, mortality and migration, but is also inherent within its existing age structure. The latter shows the effect of 'demographic momentum', which refers to 'the tendency for changes in population growth rates to lag behind changes in childbearing behaviour and mortality conditions' (Feeney 2003: 646–647). This happens because a population with a high proportion of young people can still have a large number of births contributing to population growth even if their fertility has fallen below replacement, or vice versa. The speed of Asian population growth however will decline in the next few decades, from the current rate of about 1.0 per cent per annum. According to the UN medium variant projection, the Asian population will stop growing by approximately the mid-2050s, followed by a long-term reduction.[2] Because of these and population changes in other major regions, the world demographic map will be redrawn in the first half of this century. Proportions of Asian and European populations are projected to decline respectively from 60.6 and 11.9 per cent in 2000 to 54.3 and 7.3 per cent in 2050, while the share of the African population will increase from 13.3 to 25.5 per cent, and the populations of Latin America and the Caribbean, Northern America and Oceania will have a slight reduction or no change. This will contribute to a major reshuffle of world economic and political power as described in Chapter 26.

Significant changes in population age structure will continue and display great cross-national variations. Asian populations have formed a spectrum ranked largely according to their stages of demographic transition and current age profiles (Chapters 5, 12, 21 and 23). At one end of the spectrum, there are Asia's leaders of demographic transition: Armenia, China, Cyprus, Hong Kong, Japan, Macao, Singapore, South Korea and Taiwan. Because of their long-lasting low or very low fertility, they have experienced or will soon experience a notable decline in the proportion of working-age population, and in some cases also a decline in national population. Because of these changes and the remarkable mortality reduction, these countries and territories will continue to witness rapid population ageing. Their proportions of old people will vary between 24.2 to 37.4 per cent in 2050, and will rise further thereafter. Countries positioned at the other end of the spectrum are Afghanistan, Cambodia, India, Indonesia, Kazakhstan, Laos, Pakistan, the Philippines, Tajikistan, Timor-Leste, Turkmenistan, Uzbekistan and Yemen. In the next three decades, these populations are projected to increase by 20 to 130 per cent. Their proportions of young people and child dependency ratios will remain high. The proportions of old people in these countries will rise, but will not be higher than 14.0 per cent by 2050, considerably lower than most other Asian countries. The rest of the Asian populations are spread between these two clusters. In comparison with countries of the first cluster, their demographic transition has either been delayed or prolonged. Changes in their age structure have been less dramatic, and population ageing will occur later and be comparatively moderate. Most of these populations are expected to have relatively low or declining dependency ratios over the next few decades, offering favourable demographic conditions for potential economic growth. Their population ageing, however, will arrive earlier and faster in comparison with countries of the second cluster over the next 20–30 years.

Population density will further increase because of continuing population growth. Rising population density will take place in the next 30 years in all major regions of the world except Europe, where the population size will fall. But this is particularly momentous in Asia, as discussed in Chapter 15. In 2015, Asia's population density already reached 141.6 persons per sq. km, far greater than that for any other major region in the world (all below 40.0 persons per sq. km). In the next three decades, Asia's population density is projected to increase further and reach 169.7 persons per sq. km by 2050. This will be the highest population density ever recorded in Asian history. It will be more than double that for Africa and at least four-fold of that for any other region (UNPD 2015a). For many Asian countries, especially the less developed countries such as Bangladesh, India, Palestine, Pakistan and the Philippines, where population densities are expected to reach 402 to 1,626 persons per sq. km in 2050 (see also Chapter 15), the effect of such an increase on their future development cannot be ignored.

Large scale urbanization will continue, although the speed of urban population growth will be slower than in recent decades. Urbanization is seen as an important 'part of the demographic transition' and no population 'has failed to urbanize' during this process (Dyson 2010: 126). From 2015 to 2050, Asia's urban population is projected to increase from 2.1 billion to 3.3 billion, and its share in the total population from 48.2 to 64.2 per cent (UNPD 2014). The growth of the urban population, which can result from natural population growth, rural–urban migration, and occasionally changes in definition or classification of rural and urban areas, will be faster than that for the total population (Chapter 16). Accompanying these changes, the number of Asian cities, especially large cities, will further grow. According to the UN, 20 out of 30 of the world's largest urban agglomerations – including all top seven – will be in Asia by 2030. These 20 urban agglomerations together are expected to have a population of 415 million. In 1950, 17 out of 30 of the world's largest urban agglomerations were from Europe and Northern America. By 2030, they are expected to be replaced almost entirely by competitors from Asia. Only two American urban agglomerations (New York-Newark and Los Angeles-Long Beach-Santa Ana) are projected to remain in this group (UNPD 2014).

International and internal migration will further increase. Because of the increasing interconnectedness of the world, the rapid expansion of many Asian and world economies, and considerable variations in labour supply among different countries (which is closely related to the stage of their demographic transition), international migration has shown a rapid increase since the start of the twenty-first century (Chapter 17). According to the latest UN report (UNPD 2016),

75 million international migrants lived in Asia, only slightly lower than the 76 million in Europe in 2015.[3] Out of the 20 largest migrant-receiving countries, nine were from Asia. They together hosted about 44 million international migrants. As the world's largest migrant-sending region, Asia also had 11 of the world's top 20 countries with the largest diasporas. The total number of migrants originating from these 11 countries was close to 70 million (UNPD 2016). In the next two to three decades, these trends are expected to continue. A closely related population movement is refugee and forced migration, although it is not usually discussed as a major demographic trend. Asia, with some of the world's largest refugee-sending and receiving countries, has been a major region affected by refugee and forced migration in recent decades (Chapter 18). There is still no sign that this trend will stop soon.

Internal migration is another important demographic process affecting a country's population distribution and urbanization. Yet, the lack of, and inconsistencies in, internal migration data have long prevented detailed studies, especially cross-national comparative studies, from being undertaken (this also explains why such a chapter was not planned for this handbook). Major developments have been made recently. Bell and his colleagues (2015) show that internal migration intensities are still relatively low in many Asian countries, but they are high in South Korea, Israel, Japan and Mongolia. Their analysis also reveals that such migration intensities have moderate to strong correlations with the level of urbanization, GDP per capita, the Human Development Index, mobile phone subscriptions and some other development indicators.[4] Close links are also found between the levels of internal and international migration (Bell et al. 2015). According to these findings and evidence presented in Chapter 16, Asia is very likely to witness a major increase in internal migration in the next 30 years.

Changes in marriage patterns and household formation are expected to continue in the foreseeable future. In the twentieth century, especially the latter half, marked changes took place in people's attitudes to sex, marriage and family, as well as societal acceptance towards these changes. European and North American countries first witnessed an increase in age at marriage, and in the proportion of those not marrying, cohabiting or experiencing divorce.[5] Accompanying these changes, single-person households, single-parent households, step-families and DINK families (double income, no kids) also increased. These and some other changes have been viewed as key components of the 'second demographic transition' (Lesthaeghe 1995, 2010). As shown in Chapters 19 and 20, similar changes have been observed in marriage patterns in some Asian countries in recent decades, but changes in the formation of households and residential patterns have been comparatively slow and moderate. In the next few decades, changes in marriage patterns are expected to continue in many Asian countries. These developments together with sustained low fertility, increasing urbanization and changes in people's residential preferences, will lead to further changes in household formation and residential patterns in Asia.

Human capital measured by educational attainment will further improve in Asia, but it will remain relatively low in comparison with all other regions except Africa. Asia's population has made major progress in improving education in recent decades. According to the three-dimensional (age, sex and level of educational attainment) population projection results reported in Chapter 27 (medium scenario, SSP2), the Asian population in 2030 and 2050 will be better educated than in 2010. For example, the proportion of women aged 20–39 with at least lower secondary education will rise from 63 per cent in 2010 to 76 per cent in 2030 and 87 per cent in 2050, contributing directly to the improvement of productivity of the workforce. This level, however, is expected to be lower than that in Europe, Latin America and the Caribbean, Northern America and Oceania. The level of education in Bangladesh, Cambodia, Myanmar, Pakistan, Syria and Laos is likely to remain notably lower than other Asian countries (Chapters 22 and 27; Lutz, Butz and KC 2014).[6]

Zhongwei Zhao & Adrian C. Hayes

Demographic trends and sustainable development in Asia

What are the implications of these and other demographic trends for the future of development efforts and human well-being in Asia? There is broad international agreement that, in principle, future development efforts around the world need to move towards pathways that not only reduce poverty and increase GDP per capita but in addition are socially and environmentally sustainable. It is helpful, therefore, to reflect on the implications of ongoing demographic trends from the point of view of achieving sustainable development.

There is no universally accepted definition of 'sustainable development', but it is generally agreed that it involves managing sustained economic growth in ways that are both environmentally sustainable and socially equitable. The Programme of Action of the 1994 International Conference on Population and Development (ICPD) states that 'sustainable development as a means to ensure human well-being, equitably shared by all people today and in the future, requires that the interrelationships between population, resources, the environment and development should be fully recognized, properly managed and brought into harmonious, dynamic balance' (UN 1994: principle 6). In 2015, at the UN Sustainable Development Summit in New York, the international community adopted 17 Sustainable Development Goals for member states to reach by 2030 (UN 2015). The manifold details concerning the vision and implementation of sustainable development are a work-in-progress but the three components of sustained economic growth, social equity and environmental protection are regarded as fundamental.

All the demographic trends listed in the first part of this chapter have substantial implications for sustainable development, either directly or indirectly (Hayes 2013). We cannot here analyse this point in depth but we can point to a few examples. The fact that the pace of economic development is affected by population change has been widely researched (Birdsall et al. 2001); Kinugasa, in Chapter 24, discusses in detail how changing population age structure can influence economic growth. As a number of other chapters make clear, changing age structure in turn depends on trends in fertility (Chapters 5 and 6) and mortality (Chapters 10 through 12) and on the overall profile of a country's demographic transition (Chapters 21 and 23). Economic development also relies on human capital: KC and Lutz, in Chapter 22, show how human capital formation is influenced by changing age structure.

Social development and social equity are similarly affected by population change (Khosla 2013). Demographic trends that will need to be addressed if all the countries and territories of Asia are to attain gender equality by 2030 are discussed in Chapter 9 (Das Gupta et al. on son preference), for example, and Chapter 19 (Jones on marriage patterns). Additional human rights issues are touched on in Che and Gu's account of access to contraception and abortion (Chapter 7) and Hull and Hosseini-Chavoshi's discussion of access to other reproductive health services (Chapter 8). Issues of social equity are also inextricably tied up with issues of social integration and social inclusion (Acemoglu and Robinson 2012; Mujahid 2013). Migrants (Chapters 17 and 18), the elderly (Chapter 23), and people affected by HIV/AIDS (Chapter 14) are examples of potentially vulnerable populations for which social safeguards are needed if they are to be fully integrated into society. The effects of population trends on the third component of sustainable development, the sustainable use of environmental resources, are discussed in Chapter 25, and also (with reference to climate change) in Montgomery and Balk's chapter on urbanization (Chapter 16).

Most major demographic trends discussed in the handbook have implications for sustainable development through multiple pathways, and they will affect, and in turn be influenced by, more than one sustainable-development component. Urbanization and migration (both internal and international) are examples: both processes have major implications for economic development and the environment, and both invariably raise challenging issues regarding social equity and integration. Similarly, the security issues discussed by McNicoll in Chapter 26 traverse all three components of sustainable development. Changes in marriage patterns and household formation have multiple implications for sustainable development in the way they relate to fertility, investment in children, women's empowerment, labour force participation and patterns of consumption (Dobbs et al. 2012). Meanwhile a top priority of the UN development agenda for sustainable development (2016–2030) is poverty reduction (UN 2015), which clearly involves all three components of sustainable development. Poverty reduction is not addressed as a specific topic in the handbook but the demographic aspects of poverty and wealth inequality are touched on in several chapters (see also Hayes and Nadkarni 2001).

In short, the demographic trends discussed in this book can facilitate societal transformation towards sustainable development in many ways, and they can also present significant obstacles; some trends can produce both positive and negative impacts simultaneously. This observation is not yet fully appreciated and it points to important areas for future research. The Asian Development Bank (ADB 2011), for example, has examined the conditions and prospects for future economic development in three Asian subregions and describes two possible scenarios for Asia's future growth, the 'Asian Century' and the 'Middle Income Trap' scenarios, respectively.[7] Under the first scenario, if Asia 'continues to grow on its recent trajectory, it could, by 2050, account for more than half of global gross domestic product (GDP), trade and investment, and enjoy widespread affluence.…Asia would regain the dominant global economic position it held some 250 years ago' (ADB 2011: 1). Under the second, 'Asia would follow the pattern of Latin America over the past 30 years', and its contribution to global GDP would be 32 per cent in 2050, and its GDP per capita would be only about half of that under the first scenario (ADB 2011: 30, 119–120). Whether Asia's development actually veers towards the first or the second scenario will depend on a range of conditions outlined in the report; the report includes discussion of a number of population trends but few details are given about how population trends and population policy can help steer Asia towards the first scenario and avoid the second.[8] A comprehensive understanding of the potential contributions of population change to sustainable futures in Asia requires much more in-depth research.

The challenge for policymakers in Asia during the coming decades is to manage policy interventions in ways that enhance the positive benefits of demographic trends and reduce the negative impacts as much as possible (World Bank 2016a, 2016b). Either way, population policy should be seen as playing an essential role in achieving the UN's *Agenda 2030 for Sustainable Development* (UN 2015). This requires recognizing not only that population change and sustainable development are interrelated, but also that demographic trends themselves are interdependent. It requires a holistic approach to population and population policy.

At present, however, research on the interactions between population dynamics and sustainable development is still in its infancy. Our hope is that the *Handbook of Asian Demography* will not only provide an authoritative and comprehensive reference for readers interested in population change in Asia, but that it will also provide a stimulus for further research on the vital role of population dynamics in determining both opportunities and challenges in the countries and territories of Asia as they seek to achieve the goals of sustainable development.

Notes

1 Taiwan has been referred to as other non-specified areas in recent UN population reports.
2 According to the UN medium variant population projection, the Asian population will further decline to 4.9 billion and account for 43.6 per cent of the world population by 2100 (UNPD 2015a).

3 Here, international migrants are defined as people who live outside of the country of their birth (UNPD 2016).
4 Migration intensity is a concept used by Bell and his colleagues in discussing the level of internal migration. They have also developed 'Crude Migration Intensity', 'Standardized Migration Intensity' and other indicators and use them for cross-national comparison of internal migration. For details see Bell et al. (2015).
5 As pointed out by Jones (Chapter 19), divorce rates rose substantially in Western countries between 1960 and 1980. But they have shown little change thereafter and become less meaningful as an indicator of dissolution of long-term relationships because of the rise in cohabitation.
6 Data for some other countries, for example Afghanistan and Yemen, are not available.
7 While the Asian countries included in the ADB report are not the same as those defined by the UN as noted in the first chapter, they include Asia's five largest economies: China, Japan, India, South Korea and Indonesia, which will dominate the Asian economy in the twenty-first century. For details about countries included in the ADB's report and further discussion and assumptions for the two scenarios, see ADB (2011).
8 The UN 2030 Agenda for Sustainable Development (UN 2015) similarly says little about the role of population dynamics in achieving the Sustainable Development Goals.

References

Acemoglu, D. and J. A. Robinson (2012) *Why Nations Fail: The Origins or Power, Prosperity and Poverty.* New York: Crown Publishers.
Asian Development Bank (ADB) (2011) *Asia 2050: Realizing the Asian Century.* Manila: Asian Development Bank.
Bell, M., E. Charles-Edwards, P. Ueffing, J. Stillwell, M. Kupiszewski and D. Kupiszewska (2015) 'Internal migration and development: comparing migration intensities around the world'. *Population and Development Review*, 41(1): 33–58.
Birdsall, N., A. C. Kelley and S. Sinding (eds.) (2001) *Population Matters: Demographic Change, Economic Growth and Poverty in the Developing World.* New York: Oxford University Press.
Dobbs, R., J. Remes, J. Manyika, C. Roxburgh, S. Smit and F. Schaer (2012) *Urban World: Cities and the Rise of Consuming Class.* McKinsey Global Institute. Available from: www.mckinsey.com/global-themes/urbanization/urban-world-cities-and-the-rise-of-the-consuming-class.
Dyson, T. (2010) *Population and Development: The Demographic Transition.* London: Zed Books.
Feeney, G. (2003) 'Momentum of population growth'. In P. Demeny and G. McNicoll (eds.) *Encyclopedia of Population.* New York: MacMillan Reference USA. Pp. 646–649.
Hayes, A. C. (2013) 'Population dynamics and sustainable development in Asia and the Pacific'. *Asia-Pacific Population Journal*, 21(1): 57–83.
Hayes, A. C. and M. V. Nadkarni (eds.) (2001) *Population, Environment and Development: Studies of Four Countries in the Asia Pacific Region.* Bangkok: UNESCO.
Khosla, R. (2013) 'Sexual and reproductive health rights in Asia and the Pacific: the unfinished agenda'. *Asia-Pacific Population Journal*, 21(1): 5–27.
Lesthaeghe, R. (1995) 'The second demographic transition in western countries: an interpretation'. In K. O. Mason and A. M. Mason (eds.) *Gender and Family Change in Industrialized Countries.* New York: Oxford University Press. Pp. 17–62.
Lesthaeghe, R. (2010) 'The unfolding story of the second demographic transition'. *Population and Development Review*, 36(2): 211–251.
Lutz, W., W. P. Butz and S. KC (eds.) (2014) *World Population and Human Capital in the Twenty-First Century.* Oxford: Oxford University Press.
Mujahid, G. (2013) 'Population and social integration policies in Asia and the Pacific'. *Asia-Pacific Population Journal*, 21(1): 29–55.
Notestein, F. (1945) 'Population: the long view'. In T. W. Schultz (ed.) *Food for the World.* Chicago: University of Chicago Press. Pp. 36–57.
United Nations (1994) *Programme of Action Adopted at the International Conference on Population and Development, Cairo, 5–13 September 1994.* New York: United Nations.
United Nations (2015) *Transforming Our World: The 2030 Agenda for Sustainable Development.* New York: United Nations.

United Nations, Department of Economic and Social Affairs, Population Division (UNPD) (2014) *World Urbanization Prospects: The 2014 Revision*, CD-ROM Edition.

United Nations, Department of Economic and Social Affairs, Population Division (UNPD) (2015a) *World Population Prospects: The 2015 Revision*. Available from: https://esa.un.org/unpd/wpp/DataQuery/.

United Nations, Department of Economic and Social Affairs, Population Division (UNPD) (2015b) *World Fertility Patterns 2015 – Data Booklet*. New York: United Nations.

United Nations, Department of Economic and Social Affairs, Population Division (UNPD) (2016) *International Migration Report 2015: Highlights*. New York: United Nations.

World Bank Group (2016a) *Global Monitoring Report 2015/2016: Development Goals in an Era of Demographic Change*. Washington, DC: World Bank.

World Bank Group (2016b) *Live Long and Prosper: Aging in East Asia and Pacific*. Washington, DC: World Bank.

Index

Page numbers in **bold** refer to tables; those in *italics* refer to figures and maps.

abortion: contraception prevalence and 125–126; overview 121–122, 128–129; policies 122–123; post-abortion care 127–128; safe and unsafe 123–125; techniques 126–127
adoption 51, 52
Afghanistan: fertility decline 78–79; forced migration 341; marriage migration 317; population ageing 439; refugees 336, 339, 342–343; security 507
age: forced migration 341; gaps between marriage partners 358; marriage 352, 353–358, 361–363, 382; mortality change and 214–221; mothers *179*
age distribution: capital accumulation and 460–461; demographic dividend and 458; overview 12; projections 521–522, 526–527, 533–534
ageing populations *see* population ageing
agglomerations 276, 287, 292–295, 296, 481, 534
agriculture: fertility and 406; population distribution 270, 277, 281; population dynamics 46–47; sex selection 156; water and 485–486
air pollution 242, 481, 489
alcohol 223–224, 237
Amayesh registration 336
American National Committee of IUSIPP 33
anaemia 237
antenatal clinics (ANCs): child survival 183; HIV testing and 248–249, 250
antiretroviral therapy (ART) 261, **262**, 263
arid regions *302*, 303–304
armaments 507
Armenia: education 418, 420; ethnic composition 401; fertility decline 72, 74; HIV/AIDS 253; pollution 487
arranged marriages 351–353
Asia, definitions of 1–4
Asian Epidemic Model 261–262
Asian Population Association 41–42
Association of South-East Asian Nations (ASEAN) 39, 505
Australian National University (ANU) 34, 39
Azerbaijan: fertility decline 72; HIV/AIDS 253

Bahrain: fertility decline 72–73, 76
balancing equation 27–29
Balfour, M. 36, 88
Bangladesh: abortion 124, 127–128; caesarean deliveries 142; child mortality 171–173, 177, 182–183; demographic dividends 460; education 417–418; family planning 93, 115–118; fertility decline 67, 76–77; flood risk 304–305; HIV/AIDS 250, 255; households 376, 386; life expectancy 194, 214; marriage 353, 355, 358, 361–363; Matlab 38; migration 313, 316; mortality 134, 214, 221, 223, 225; population ageing 448, 450; population distribution 268, 273, 275, 278–279; security 501, 504, 507, 509; sex selection 156–157, 160–161; urbanization 299, 303, 304, 479, 485–486
behavioural surveillance surveys 250
Bhutan: child mortality 171–172; contraceptive prevalence 112; education attainment *416*, 417–418; family planning 100, 112; fertility decline 76–77; HIV/AIDS 253; mortality 134, 214–215, 223, 225
bilateral kinship systems 352, 372, 381
bilateral trade 321–322
birth intervals 169, 178–179, *179*
birth order 156–157, 169, 179–180, *179*
birth size *179*, 180
blood contamination 251
Bogue, Donald 37
Borrie, W.D. 34
brain drain 316–317, 320–321
breast cancer 145
brides: bride price 156; shortages 158–160
British Population Society 33, 34
Brunei Darussalam: fertility decline 72; households 376; migration 315, 320; mortality 172, 190, 210–211; population ageing 447
Buddhist temple records 56
burden of disease 142–148, 237–242, 244–245
business networks 321–322

540

Index

caesarean deliveries 138–142
Cambodia: abortion 128; caesarean deliveries 140; child survival 172; family planning 89, 100, 119; fertility decline 77; HIV/AIDS 249–263, **257**; migration 320; mortality 134–135, 172, 214–215
cancers 144–148, 232
capital accumulation 460–463
car dependency 481
carbon dioxide emissions 489–492, 509
cardiovascular disease 195, 197–198, 223–224
Care for Girls policy 160–161
Catholic Church 76, 97
causes of death *see* death, causes of
cause-specific mortality data 230–231, *232*
censuses 16, 17–21, 56–57
Central Asia: demographic dividends *459*, 460; fertility decline 73, 74; life expectancy 192; mortality decline 220; population ageing 439
cervical cancer 145–147
child mortality: causes 180–182; data sources 169–170; fertility decline 66; under-five mortality 170–174, **184–187**; gender gaps 175–177, **186–187**; neonatal mortality 174–175, **184–185**; overview 168–169; risk factors 178–180; social-economic status and 168–169, 178; successes and challenges 182–184
children: betrothal of 52; HIV/AIDS 261; living with 382–384, **387–391**
China: abortion 128; caesarean deliveries 140; cause-specific mortality data 231; child mortality 171–174, 182–183; family planning 89, *92*, 98, 100, 102, *103*, 373; fertility decline 66, 72–73, 409; HIV/AIDS 249, 251, 256; households 374–376, 382, 384; life expectancy 193; marriage squeeze 158–159; migration 313, 315, 317, 320–323; mortality 408–409; National New-Type Urbanization Plan 286, 300–301; population ageing 436–437; population densities 275; security 505; sex selection 160–161; urbanization 287, 298–301, 303
China, Hong Kong SAR: demographic dividends 459, 464; family planning 89–90, 93–94, 99–100; fertility decline 65–66, 72–73, 81; households 374, 376; marriage 353–355, 364; migration 315, 320, 324; mortality 192–195, 211, 219, 224; population ageing 440, 447
China, Macao SAR: fertility decline 72, 81; households 376; mortality 211, 408; migration 320
China Multi-Generational Panel Dataset (CMGPD) 54–55
cholesterol 197
church and temple records 56
civil registration 21–22, 56, 57, 170
climate and population 275, 281
climate change 276, 301–303, 509–510
Coale, A. J. 34, 41, 88

Coale-Demeny model 209, 210–211
coastal zones 276, 281, 302–305, *302*
cohabitation 359, 364
cohort component projections 27–28
communism 35
commuting 298–299
comparative risk assessment (CRA) for population health 239–242
complexity science 473
Concepcion, Mercedes 38–39
condoms/condom use programs 95, 115, 144, 260–261
conflict: demographic transition 402–403; ethnic or religious 501; fertility decline 77, 78–79; gender 223; life expectancy 194, 195; migration and 345; mortality change and 215, 220–221; population and 506–508
connectedness and commuting 298–299
consanguineous marriage 359–361
consistency checks in data quality 24–25
consumption 475–480
contraception: abortion and 125–126; choice 94–95, 116–117, 120–121; contraceptive prevalence rate (CPR) 89, **90–91**, *92*, *103*, 110–112, *121*; de-medicalization of 94; determinants of use 120–121; discontinuation and switching 117–118; fertility levels and 112–113; methods and patterns of use 93, 113–117; prevalence and trends 110–112; singlehood and 359; unmet needs 118–120
coresidence: background 371–373; data sources 373–374; household perspectives 374–376; individual perspectives 376–384; living alone 378–379; living with a spouse 381–382; living with children 382–384; living with parents 379–381; old-age support 449, 451; overview 370–371, 384–386
crime 158, 160, 201
Cyprus: child survival 171–172; mortality 211

dam construction 345
data and data sources: censuses 17–21, 56–57; child mortality 169–170; church and temple records 56; civil registration 21–22, 57; evaluating data quality 15–16, 24–29; families and households 373–374; family planning 95; forced and refugee migration 335–337; genealogies 53–54; historical demography 53–57; HIV/AIDS 248–250; household registers 54–56; maternal mortality 132–136; migration 310–311; mortality 210–211, 229–231; old-age mortality 201–202; overview 4, 15–17; primary 15, 17–23; secondary 15, 23–24; surveys and surveillance systems 22–23; urban areas 298; used in projections 518
death, causes of: children 180–182; data sources 204, 229–231; female infants 157; overview

541

Index

228–229; projections 242–244; trends in disease and injury 231–236
death registration 57, 229–231
Deccan Plateau 278
decentralization 500–501
decolonization 87–88, 102, 504
deforestation 281
democratic change 503
demographic analysis and census evaluation 18
Demographic and Health Surveys (DHS) 22, 37, 248, 250
demographic dividends: capital accumulation 460–463; demographic transition and 456–457; first in Asia 458–460; human capital and 463; measurement of 467–469; overview 34, 456–457; policy implications 466–467; second in Asia 463–466
demographic forerunners (fertility decline) 68–69, **70**, 72–74
demographic momentum 533
Demographic Training and Research Centre, Mumbai 35, 37
demographic transition: background conditions 401–408; education and 406; ethnicity and 404; examples of 408–409; fertility 399–401, 403–404, 409; income distribution and 407; mortality 395–399, 403–404, 408–409; overview 5, 394–395, 409–410; political counterparts 501–503; population ageing 431–432; public health programs and 407–408; religion and 401–402, 404; stages of 456–457; urbanization 407; war and civil unrest 404–406; women's status and 407
depression 237, 239
desakota 276–277, 298–299
deserts 277, 281, 302, 303–304
development plans 93
development-induced displacement 345–346
devolution 500–501
diarrhoea 180–182, 239
diaspora 321–324
disability, causes of 236–237
Disability Adjusted Life Year (DALY) 229, 236–241, 396–399
disasters 49–50, 346, 487
disease: burden of 237–242; as cause of death 180, 231–236; as cause of disability 236–237; causes of death projections 242–244; data sources 228–229; demographic transition and 396–399; mortality and gender 223; overview 228–229; women and 221–223
divorce 52, 156, 159, 363–365
domestic violence 159
domestic workers 318
dowry systems 156
drug users 251, **252–253**, 255, 256, 258–259, 261
Dublin, Louis 33

early rapid fallers (fertility decline) 68, 72–74
earthquakes 346
Eastern Asia: arranged marriages 352–353; demographic dividends *459*; divorce 364; fertility decline 77; life expectancy 192; population ageing 436–437; population distribution 269
economic conditions/development: age distribution and 458; demographic transition 403, 406; diaspora and 321–322; economic density 281; fertility decline 72; future prospects 537; independent living 376; life expectancy and 201; migration and 312, 319–320; population growth and 88–89; sex selection 158, 161
education: child mortality and 169; demographic dividends 466; demographic transition 403, 406; educational attainment changes 413–416; fertility decline 66, 72, 74; under-five mortality 177; gender differences and 423–425; life expectancy 200, 201; marriage and 355–358; population projections 517–518, 522–525; primary 416–418; role in son preference 160; secondary 418–420; sex selection 160, 161; tertiary/post-secondary 420–423
elder well-being 372–373, 383, 443–446, 449–451
emergency contraception 116
employment of women 73–74, 76, 406–407, 425, 427, 466
energy 487–492
entertainment industry 318
environment: energy 487–492; middle class and 481–485; overview 12, 473–474; population change and consumption 474–478; sustainable development, population change and 492–493; theoretical perspectives 473–474; urbanization and 478–481; water 485–487
errors: in census data 18, 28; in projections 515–517
estimation and data quality 25–27
ethnicity: demographic transition 401–402, 404; forced migration 342–343
Eurasia Project in Population and Family History (EAP) 48
evaluation: of census information 18; of data quality 24–29

families and households: background 47–49, 371–373; data sources 373–374; extended families 48–49; household perspectives 374–376, **387**; individual perspectives 376–384, **387–391**; joint families 371, 372; living alone 378–379, **387–391**; living with a spouse 381–382, **387–391**; living with children 153–155, 382–384, **387–391**; living with parents 379–381, **387–391**; overview 10–11, 370–371, 384–386; population ageing and 443–446, 449–450; projections 535; stem families 48, 371

542

Index

Family Life Education (FLE) 94
family planning: abortion 121–128; in Asia 87–93; associations (FPAs) 93–94; choice and 115; contraception 109–121; evaluating 95–97; fertility and 407; international support for 91–93, 98–99; overview 87, 128–129; policies 73, 77, 78, 99–102; programmes 87, 93–99; quality of care 98; research centres 36; singlehood and 366; trends 102–104; unmet needs 100, **101–102**, *103*, 118–120; voluntarism or coercion 97–98, 114; *see also* contraception
feminization of migration 259, 318
fertility: contraceptive prevalence and *92*, 112–113; control of 51; coresidence and 371; family context and 48, 50–51; global patterns 64–66, *65*; high 78–79; life expectancy and 200–201; low 5, 42, 62, 72–74, 400, 451, 518–520, 533; measures 403–404; projections 533; proximate determinants of 112; replacement and below-replacement level of 5, 64–65, 68, 400, 404; total fertility rate (TFR) 5, 50, 64–66, 82, 87, **88**, 92, *113*, *114*, 120, *125*, 291–292, 395, 399, *400*, *401*, **405**, 515, 533; *see also* fertility decline; reproductive health
fertility decline: in Asia 64–68; child mortality and 168; delayed marriage and 359; demographic forerunners 72–74; demographic transition 399–401, 409; early rapid fallers 72–74; household size and 374–376, 385; laggards 78–79; overview 5–6, 80–81; and population ageing 373, 434–435; preventive checks as cause 46, 50; rapid fallers still in transition 76–78; sex selection 158; slow fallers 74–76; special cases 79–80; transition types 68–72; trends 81, 518–519; urbanization 288–292
flood risk 302–305
forced migration: data sources 335–337; definitions 331–334; demographic characteristics 340–345; drivers of 345–346; levels and trends 337–340; overview 10, 346–347; studies of 334–335
Ford Foundation 34, 35–37, 38–39
forecasting errors 515–517
former Soviet states: fertility decline 73–74; gender 224; mortality 220
fossil fuels 489–493
Freedman, Ronald 36–37
French Institute for Demographic Studies (INED) 34

Ganges Plains 275
gender: care and neglect 157–158; child mortality 175–177, **186–187**; of children 51; education and 423–425; HIV/AIDS 256, **257**, 262; life expectancy 194–198, 221–224; migration 157–158, 340–341; status of women 76, 159, 403, 407, 451; *see also* sex ratios; sex selection
genealogies 53–54

Georgia: education 420; population ageing 440
Gini index of income 403
girls, neglect of 157–158
Glass, David 34
Global Burden of Disease (GBD) 228–229, 230, 237–239
Global Human Settlements Layer (GHSL) 296
Global Report of UNAIDS 249–250
Gobi Desert 277
Gompertz law 209
governance *see* political demography
Gridded Population of the World (GPW) 296
gross domestic product (GDP) 475–478
Gulf countries 223

health: burden of disease 237–238; causes of death 231–236, 242–244; causes of disability and lost health 236–237; data sources 229–231; insurance 409; overview 228–229, 244–245; risk factors 238–242; services 170; *see also* HIV/AIDS; reproductive health
health and demographic surveillance systems (HDSS) 22–23
health transition theory 197–198
hearing loss 237
heart disease 232
hepatitus B virus (HBV) 156
high-density zones 275–277, 279
historical demography: data sources 53–57; Holocene period 269–270; household and family 47–49; marriage 51–52; migration 52–53; mortality 49–50; overview 45–46, 57–58; population dynamics 46–47; reproduction 50–51
HIV/AIDS: affected populations 255–258; controlling the epidemics 260–261; data collection 248–250; emergence in Asia 251; forces shaping the epidemics 258–259; gender gaps 223; hopes and challenges 261–263; origins and background 247–248; patterns and trends 242, 251–255
Holocene period 269–270
Hoover, E. M. 34, 88
hormonal contraceptives 115–116
house prices 372
household registers 54–56, 170
households *see* families and households
housing policies 386
hukou reforms 300–301
human capital: demographic dividends and 463; education at primary level 416–418; education at secondary level 418–420; education at tertiary/post-secondary levels 420–423; educational attainment changes 413–416; educational gender differences 423–425; labour force participation 425–428; life expectancy 201; overview 412–413, 428–429; projections 535; second dividend and 463

543

Index

Human Papilloma Virus (HPV) 147–148
HYDE project 269

immunizations 147–148, 157–158, 170, 183, 407
income 170, 177, 403, 407, 475–478
independent living 378–379
India: abortion 124, 128; caesarean deliveries 142; child mortality 171, 173, *176*, 176–178, 182–183; climate change 302–303; coresidence 378, 382–383; family planning *92*, 96, 97–98, *103*; fertility decline 75–76; HIV/AIDS 250, **257**; labour force participation 425; marriage 352, 353, 355, 360, 362; mortality 214, 221, 233–232; population ageing 438; population distribution 275, 276–277; sex selection 151, 153, *154*, 155–162; urbanization 286, 287–288, 291, 296–297, 298–303, *302*
indirect estimation: data quality and 25–27; of HIV/AIDS 249
individualism and singlehood 365
Indonesia: child mortality 172–173; family planning 37, *92*, 95, *103*; fertility decline 76; HIV/AIDS 251, 255–256, 258–261, 263; labour force participation 427; marriage 351–352, 355, 358–362, **363**, 365; mortality 214, 407; population distribution 275, 276; transmigration programme 278; urbanization *295*, 299, 301
Indonesian Fertility-Mortality Survey 37
industrialization 364, 371, 406, 481
infanticide 51, 151, 157
influenza pandemics 509
inheritance 152–153
injury: burden of disease *236*, 237–242; as cause of death 221, 231–236; causes of death projections 242–244; data sources 228–229; and DALYs 396–399; overview 228–229
Institute of Population Problems, Japan 33
Integrated Public Use Microdata Series International Microdata Series (IPUMS) 21, 373–374, 377
intergenerational coresidence *see* coresidence
internal migration 278, 299
internally displaced persons (IDPs) 10, 336, 337
International Centre for Diarrhoeal Disease Research, Bangladesh (ICDDR,B) 38
International Conference on Population and Development (ICPD) 6, 40, 99–100, 536
International Institute for Population Sciences (IIPS), Mumbai 35, 39, 41
international migration: development and 319–324; diaspora, development and 321–323; feminization of 318; marriage 317; North-South and South-South 316–317; overview 310–311, 326–327; permanent 311–313; policy implications 324–326; projections 534–535; return migration 323–324; South-North 313–314; student 315–316; temporary labour 314–315; undocumented 310, 319

International Planned Parenthood Federation (IPPF) 91
international relations 503–506
International Union for the Scientific Investigation of Population Problems (IUSIPP) 33–34
International Union for the Scientific Study of Population (IUSSP) 91–93
'intimacy at a distance' 386
Inui, Kiyo Sue 32–33
'IPAT' 473
Iran, Islamic Republic of: caesarean deliveries 138, 142; child mortality 172, 176–177; education 416–420, 423, 427; family planning 95; fertility decline 72–73; HIV/AIDS 253; households 379, 384; marriage 355, 358, 360; migration 313, 336, 339, 340–341, 343–347; mortality 134, 221, 223; population density 273–274, 277, 279; refugees 336, 339–340, 343, 345; security 503, 507–508
Iran-Iraq war 223
Iraq: child mortality 172–173; fertility decline 78–79; labour force participation 427; refugees 339–341, 345
Iskander, Nathanael 39
Israel: fertility decline 79, 81; mortality 174, 211, 219; population ageing 449
IUDs 94–95, 115

Jakarta 294–295, 481
Japan: caesarean deliveries 142; child mortality 171, 174, 176, 182–183; family planning 87, 100, 110, 112–119; fertility decline 64, 69, 72, 81, 409; historical population 46, 48–58; households 371–373; HIV/AIDS 251, 259, 263; marriage 353, 355, 357, 358–359; mortality 135–136, 138, 142–143, 192, 194–195, 200–201, 203, 211, 215, 219–220, 224, 230–231; migration 315, 317, 320; population ageing 437; population distribution 268, 272–279; security 505
Java 275, 276–277
Jordan: fertility decline 76–78; and refugees 339

Kaya identity 489–492
Kazakhstan: abortion 123, 125; child mortality *26*, 172; education attainment 416, 420; family planning 112, 116; fertility decline 74; HIV/AIDS 253, 255; mortality 134, 174, 211, 219–220, 224, 408; population aging 439; population density 273, 277, 279
Kerala 275, 276–277, 296–297, 353
kinship systems: bilateral 352, 372, 381; marriage arrangement and 351–353; patrilineal 152–156, 352, 371–373, 380–381
Korea, Democratic People's Republic of (DPRK) (North): child mortality 172–173; family planning 115, 116; fertility decline 79–80; households 376; mortality 174, 193, 195, 215; neonatal mortality 174; security 505, 507–508

Index

Korea, Republic of (South): demographic dividends 457–458, 460, 464–467; education 417–418, 420–428; family planning 36–37, 89, 93–95, 100, 110, 112–116, 119, 126; fertility decline 72, 409; historical population 46, 48–49, 51, 53–56; HIV/AIDS 251; households 372, 374, 381–382; labour force participation 426; marriage 352–360; migration 311, 313, 315, 317, 323; mortality 174, 195, 200, 211, 224; population ageing 440, 446–450; population distribution 274; security 503, 505, 507–508; sex selection 153, 156, 158–161; urbanization 294, 486–489

Korean Institute for Health and Social Affairs (KIHASA) 40

Kuwait: fertility decline 74–76; maternal mortality 135

Kyrgyzstan: caesarean deliveries 142; child mortality 172; contraceptive prevalence 112; demographic transition 440; fertility decline 74; HIV/AIDS 253, 255; mortality 134, 135, 174, 211, 220, 223, 224; population density 273, 277

labour force: human capital and 425–428; women in 73–74, 76, 406–407, 425, 427, 466
labour migration 314–315, 318–319, 325, 346
labour productivity 457, 460–461
laggards (fertility decline) 69, **71**, 78–79
Landry, Adolphe 33–34
Lao People's Democratic Republic: fertility decline 76–77; HIV/AIDS 251, 258, 260–261; mortality 214
Lebanon: fertility decline 72–73; refugees 339; population ageing 439–440
'Life at the Extremes' project 48–49
life expectancy: age patterns of change 197–200, 214–221; capital accumulation and 461–463; demographic dividends 466–467; demographic transition 395–396; gender gaps 194–198, 221–224; old-age future prospects 202; overview 203–204; savings and 461–463; socioeconomic development and 200–202; trends 190–197, 211–214
life-cycle models of savings 461, 464, 466
living arrangements: with children 382–384, **387–391**; living alone 378–379, **387–391**; with parents 379–381, **387–391**; with a spouse 381–382, **387–391**
longitudinal surveys 23
Lorimer, Frank 35
lost health 229, 236–237, 238
low and middle-income countries: climate change 301–303; commuting and 298–299; new research developments 297–301; risk exposure 303–305; scientific comparability 295–297; socioeconomic data 298; trends in 288–292; urban populations 292–295; urbanization 285–286
low-density zones 277–278

malaria 180
Malaysia: education 417, 418, 420; family planning 89, 93–95, 100, 116; fertility decline 72–73; HIV/AIDS 251, 255–256, 259–261; marriage 351–353, 355, 358–362, 365; migration 278, 313, 315, 324; mortality 407; refugees 343
Maldives: caesarean deliveries 138; child mortality 171–172; demographic dividends 460; family planning 119; fertility decline 76–77, 134; migration 320; mortality 134, 214, 221
Malthusian processes 45, 46–48, 49, 56
marriage: age of 51–52, 66, 361–363; arrangement of 52, 351–353; child betrothal 52; consanguineous 359–361; coresidence 378; divorce trends 363–365; historical demography 51–52; migration 159–160, 317; overview 10–11, 365–366; projections 535; sex ratios and 158–160; singlehood and 358–359; trends 353–358
matchmaking 353
maternal mortality: as indicator of reproductive health 131–132; problems of measurement 132–136; skilled birth attendance and 136–137
Matlab 22, 38
media, role in son preference 160
medical abortion 126–127
medical care and gender 157–158
megacities 287, 292–295, 296, 481
men who have sex with men (MSM) 250, 251, 255–256, 262
mental disorders 237
middle class: democratic change and 503; natural resources and 481–485
midwives 94, 136–138
migrant workers and social security 448
migration: corridors 312–313, 332–333; historical demography 52–53; industry 311, 319; net migration 27–28, 291–292; overview 8–10; population ageing and 432; *see also* internal migration, international migration
military power 506–508
Millennium Development Goals (MDGs) 132–134, 169–170, 231, 235–236
mobile populations: HIV prevalence 255–256, 258–259; sex selection 155–156
modernization theory 372–373
Mongolia: cancers 145; child mortality 172; demographic dividends 460; education 418, 420; family planning 115–116, 119; fertility decline 76–77; HIV/AIDS 260; households 379–380, 382, 384; mortality 134, 174, 193, 195, 214, 174; population ageing 437, 447–448; population density 273, 277–279; security 507
morning after pill 116
mortality: age patterns of change 214–221; capital accumulation and 461–463; data and limitations 210–211; decline 7–8, 219–221, 395–399,

545

408–409; historical demography 49–50; measurement 403–404; overview 209–210, 224–225; projections 533; sex differentials 50, 221–224; trends 211–214; *see also* child mortality; maternal mortality; old-age mortality
multigenerational households *see* coresidence
Multiple Indicator Cluster Surveys (MICS) 22
Myanmar: child mortality 173, 184; education 403, 417, 418; demographic dividends 460; family planning 100; fertility decline 80; HIV/AIDS 251, 253, 255–261, 263; marriage 353, 355, 361–362; mortality 134, 214, 232; refugees 340, 341, 343, 345; security 501, 507

National Institute of Family Planning 35
National Institute of Population and Social Security Research 33, 40
National New-Type Urbanization Plan 286, 300–301
national savings rate 461
National Transfer Accounts (NTA) method 463
natural disasters 49–50, 346, 487
natural resources 479–485
needle-syringe exchange program 261
neglect of girls 157–158
neonatal mortality 168, 174–175, 180–182, **185–186**
Nepal: abortion 123–124, 127, 128; child mortality 171–173, 177, 182–183; education 417, 423; family planning 89, 93, 110, 115, 119; fertility decline 76–77; HIV/AIDS 251, 253, 255, 258; households 379, 382, 385; marriage 361, 134, 214, 221, 223; mortality 214, 221, 223; population ageing 447, 448; sex selection 151
neuropsychiatric conditions 237
nomadic groups 277–278
noncommunicable diseases 236, 238–239, 243–244, 396–399
North-South migration 316–317
Notestein, Frank 33–34, 35
nuclear states 507–508
nutrition 223, 242

Office of Population Research (OPR) 33, 34
oil-producing countries 272, 278
old age dependency ratio (OADR) 432–433, 435–436, 441, *443*
old-age mortality: declines in age-specific death rates 197–200, 215, 219; future prospects 202; overview 190, 203–204; socioeconomic development 200–202; trends in life expectancy at age 65 (e_{65}) 190–197
old-age share of dependency (OASD) 433, 434–435, *442*, *443*
old-age support 372–373, 383, 443 446, 449–451
Oman: fertility decline 76, 78
one-child policy 35, 73, 98, 373

outreach in family planning 93, 94
overlapping generations model 461
overweight persons 204, 223

PAC Consortium 127–128
Palestine, State of: education 417–418; fertility decline 78–79; refugees 345
Pakistan: abortion 128; consanguineous marriage 360; family planning 94–95; fertility decline 76–77; forced migration 341; medical care and gender 157
pandemics 247–248, 260–261, 509
Panel on Urban Population Dynamics 291
parents, living with 379–381, **387–391**
parish registers 56
pastoralism 277–278
patrilineal/patrilocal family systems 152–156, 352, 371–373, 380–381
Pearl, Raymond 33
pension coverage 204, 446–449
people who inject drugs (PWID) 251, **252–253**, 255, 256, 258–259, 261
permanent migration 311–313
persons of concern **333**, 337–340
Philippines: abortion 127; child mortality 173–174, 178; demographic dividends 460; education 417–418, 420–421, 423; family planning 89, 93–95, 97, 110, 118; fertility decline 74–76, 81; HIV/AIDS 250, 255, 260; households 153, 384; marriage 352–353, 355, 359, 362; migration 313, 315–318, 320–322, 325–326; mortality 134, 408; population ageing 446–448; population distribution 272–273, 275–276, 278; security 501, 503
pill, the (oral contraceptive) 94–95, 115
pneumonia 180–182
political demography: of Asia's century 510; demographic transition and 501–503; 'game-changers' 508–510; international conflict 506–508; overview 499; political instability 402–403; relativities and regionalization 503–506; scale and statehood 500–501
pollution 479–481, 485–487
population: densities 273–278, 479–481, 534; future trends 520–527, 532–535; historical demography 46–47; size 503–506, 520–521, 533; world **17**
population ageing: conflict and 508; demographic dividends 466, 467; divergence and heterogeneity 440–443; elder well-being 449–450; family and 443–446, 449–450; historical trends 433–436; measurement of 432–433; process of 431–432; projections 526–527; regional variations 436–440; society and 450–452; the state and 446–450
population and environment: energy 487–492; middle class and 481–485; overview 473–474;

population change and consumption 474–478; sustainable development 492–493; theoretical perspectives 473–474; urbanization 478–481; water 485–487
Population Association of America (PAA) 33
Population Council 34, 36, 89
population distribution: across Asia 278–281; Asia's share in the world 268–273; concentration and Lorenz curves 278–279, *280*; densities 273–278; education and *415*; future trends 13; Holocene period 269–270; overview 8–10
population growth and size **3–4**, 34–35, 46–47, 88–89, 109–110, *269*, 269–272, **477**, 489, 514, 529, 533
population health 239, 485, 489, 501
population history *see* historical demography
Population Investigation Committee (PIC) 33, 34
population policies: definition 87; forced migration 343–345; migration 324–326
population projections: assumptions 517–520; causes of death 242–244; history and past errors 515–517; overview 514–515, 527–529; projection results 520–527
population research institutions: Asia from 1980s onwards 39–40; Asia in 1960s and 1970s 36–39; Asia pre-1960s 32–36; Asian Population Association 41–42; China in 1980s 41; the future 41–42; overview 4
post-enumeration surveys (PESs) 18
Preston curve 201
preterm birth complications 180, 182, 239
primary data sources 15, 17–23
primary education 416–418
proactive migration 333
projection models 517–518
pronatalist ideologies 34, 76, 79, 80, 355, 517
prostate cancer 145
public health programs: demographic transition and 407–408; mortality 409

Qatar: fertility decline 72–73; population growth 271–272

rapid fallers still in transition (fertility decline) 69, **70–71**, 76–78
rapid industrializers 68
Ravenholt, Reimert 37
reactive migration 333–334
Red River (Song Hong) Delta region 275
refugees and refugee migration: data sources 335–337; definitions 331–334; demographic characteristics 340–345; drivers of 345–346; levels and trends 337–340; overview 10, 346–347; studies of 334–335
regionalization 505
registration of migrants 336–337
religion 51, 401–402, 404

remarriage 52
remittances 299, 321, 446
reproduction 50–51; *see also* fertility
reproductive health: caesarean deliveries 138–142; Cairo conference and 99–100; cancers 144–148; maternal mortality as indicator 131–136; overview 131; sexually transmitted infections 143–144; skilled birth attendance and 136–137
research institutions: Asia from 1980s onwards 39–40; Asia in 1960s and 1970s 36–39; Asia pre-1960s 32–36; Asian Population Association 41–42; China in 1980s 41; the future 41–42; overview 4
residential care 446
residual methods for evaluating data quality 27–29
respiratory infections 232, 238–239
return migration 317, 323–324
reverse ageing 431, 433, 439
reverse brain drain 323–324
risk: assessment of 238–242; exposure to 303–305; to health 239–242
river basins: maintenance of 487; population 275–276, 281
road accidents 223, 238–239
Rockefeller Foundation 34, 35, 36, 91
rural areas 275, 281
rural–urban regions *see desakota*

Sample Vital Registration with Verbal Autopsy (SAVVY) 23
Sanger, Margaret 32
sanitation 183, 242
Saudi Arabia: child mortality 172; fertility decline 76–78; migration 313; and refugees 345; water 485
savings 447, 461–463, 464–466
scale and statehood 500–501
Scripps, Edward 32
Scripps Foundation for Research in Population Problems 32
sea-level change 302–303, 509
seasonal migrants 255–256, 258–259, 299
second generation surveillance of HIV/AIDS 249
secondary data sources 15, 23–24
secondary education 418–420
security: demographic transition and 501–503; 'game-changers' 508–510; governance and 12–13, 499; international conflict 506–508; relativities and regionalization 503–506; scale and statehood 500–501
sentinel surveillance of HIV/AIDS 248–250
separatist movements 501
sepsis 180, 182
settlement-level data 298
sex industry 258, 318
sex ratio at birth 6, *154*, *155*, 157, 161, 503

Index

sex ratios: in countries of asylum 341; under-five mortality 175–177; marriage migration and 317; mortality change and 221–224; *see also* gender
sex selection: causes of son preference 152–156; consequences of 158–160; evaluation of bans 160–161; factors reducing 160–162; mechanisms and patterns 156–158; overview 151–152; prenatal 157
sex workers 251, **252–253**, 255–256, 258–259, 260–261
sexual behaviour 144, 147, 148, 250
sexually transmitted infections 142–148
Shanghai Cooperation Organization 505
shared socioeconomic pathways (SSPs) 519–520
Sichuan region 275, 277
Simian Immunodeficiency Virus 247–248
Singapore 426, 439
singlehood 353–359, **356**, 378–379
singulate mean age at marriage (SMAM) 353–355, **354**
skilled birth attendance 136–137, 183
skilled migration 314, 315, 316–317, 320–321
slow fallers (fertility decline) 69, **70**, 74–76
smoking 197, 203, 204, 223, 242
social identification 18
social insurance 449
social networks 311, 321–323, 346
social norms 371
social safety nets 449–451
social security 446–450, 464–466
social-ecological systems 473–474
societal change 11–13, 450–452
socioeconomic conditions/development: demographic dividend and 458; HIV/AIDS 256–257; migration and 346; old-age mortality 200–202; population ageing 450–451; second dividend and 464–466
socioeconomic status: child mortality and 168–169, 178; life expectancy 196–197, 204; marriage squeeze 159; mortality 221, 223; sex selection 161
son preference: causes of 152–156, 177; consequences of 158–160; factors reducing 160–162; low fertility and 51, 503; mechanisms and patterns 156–158; population ageing 451
South Asia: demographic dividends 458–460, *459*; fertility decline 74–75, 77; historical population growth 46–47; marriage 353, 355; population ageing 438–439; population distribution 273
South Asian Association for Regional Cooperation (SAARC) 505
South-East Asia: arranged marriages 352–353; demographic dividends *459*, 460; fertility decline 73, 76, 77; historical population growth 47; life expectancy 192, 193–194; mortality transition 407; population ageing 439; teenage marriage 362

South-North migration 313–314
South-South migration 312, 316–317
spouse, living with 381–382, **387–391**
Sri Lanka: caesarean deliveries 142; demographic dividends 460; family planning 93, 100, 110, 115–116; fertility decline 74–75, 80; historical population 51, 55, 57; HIV/AIDS 255; marriage 353, 358, 361; migration 315, 316, 318, 320–321; mortality 197, 230; population aging 439, 447–448; population density 273; security 501
states: demographic scale and 500–501; demographic transition and 501–503; formation of 504; international conflict and 506–508; overview 499; population ageing 446–450; relativities and regionalization 503–506
sterilization: mass campaign 97–98; rates of 114–115, 117
stroke: as cause of death 232; life expectancy 195
student migration 314, 315–316
surveys and surveillance systems 22–23, 248–249
sustainable development 492–493, 536–537
Sustainable Development Goals (SDGs) 131, 169, 183–184, 285–286, 305–306, 492, 535
Suyono, Haryono 37
Syria Arab Republic: fertility decline 76–78; and refugees 339–347

Taiwan, China: demographic dividends 458, 460–464; family planning 88; fertility decline 66, 72–73; historical population 48, 50, 52, 54–55, 57; HIV/AIDS 256, 259–260; household 374, 376; marriage 353–355; migration 315, 317, 322–323; mortality 211, 224; population aging 440, 447, 449–450; population research 36, 37, 38; shortage of brides 159; son preference 161; security 503–507; sex selection 151, 153, **155**, 157, 159, 161
Taiwan Population Studies Center 36
Tajikistan: abortion 125; caesarean deliveries 140, 142; fertility decline 74; HIV/AIDS 253; mortality 134, 174, 211, 219–220, 224
Taklimakan desert 277
Taeuber, Irene 35
teenage marriage 361–363
Teheran Proclamation 91
temple records 56
temporary labour migration 314–315
tertiary/post-secondary education 420–423
tetanus 180
Thailand: caesarean deliveries 142–143; child mortality 172; education 417–418, 420, 423; family planning 89, 93, 94, 100, 110, 115, 116, 260; fertility decline 73; HIV/AIDS 251, 255–256, 258–263; households 372–374, 379–382, 384–385; marriage 352–353, 355, 357, 359–362; migration 315, 317, 318; mortality

548

230; population ageing 439–440, 447–450; refugees 343, 345; urbanization 303
Thompson, Warren 32, 35
Timor-Leste: fertility decline 78–79; family planning 100, 119
Tokugawa Japanese registers 54–55
total dependency ratio (TDR) 433, 458, 466
total primary energy supply (TPES) 487–490
total renewable water resources (TRWR) 485
traditional contraceptive methods 116
trafficking 319
transgender populations 262
transit situations 332
transportation 481
tuberculosis 242
Turkey: caesarean deliveries 138; child mortality 172; family planning 89, *92*, 93, 100, 102, *103*; fertility decline 72–72; mortality 134, 195; population ageing 440; population distribution 274, 278; refugees 339, 341, 345; urbanization 303
Turkmenistan: abortion 125; caesarean deliveries 140, 142; child mortality 172; fertility decline 74; mortality 174, 211, 220, 231–232

under-five mortality 170–174, **184–187**
undocumented migration 310, 319
United Arab Emirates: fertility decline 72–73
United Nations Economic and Social Committee for Asia and Pacific (ESCAP) 515
United Nations High Commissioner for Refugees (UNHCR) 335–337
United Nations Population Fund (formerly United Nations Fund for Population Activities) (UNFPA) 39–40, 89, 91
United Nations Inter-Agency Group for Child Mortality Estimation (IGME) 25, 169–170
United Nations Population Division (UNPD) 33–34
United States Agency for International Development (USAID) 22, 35–37, 39, 98
University of Indonesia 39
University of Tehran 40
University of the Philippines Population Institute 38–39
unskilled workers 315, 318, 319
urban areas: coastal zones and 276; data sources 298; form and design 481; population distribution 281; refugees 343
urbanization: climate change 301–303; commuting and 298–299; definitions and policies 300–301; demographic transition 403, 407; of low- and middle-income countries 285–286; natural resources and 479–481; overview 9; populations 281, 292–295; research developments 297–301; risk exposure 303–305; scientific comparability 295–297; sex selection 161; socioeconomic data 298; trends and projections 288–292, 534
Uzbekistan: caesarean deliveries 142; child mortality 172, 174; family planning 116; fertility decline 74; mortality 174, 211, 219–220; pollution 485; population density 277; water use 485–486

vaccinations 147–148, 157–158, 170, 183, 407
vacuum aspiration 126–127
'variable rate of growth effects' model 461
vasectomies 115
Vietnam: abortion 123, 127; caesarean deliveries 142; education 417–420; family planning 89, 100, 110, 115, 117–118; fertility decline 73; HIV/AIDS 251, 255–256, **257**, 258–261; households 372–374, 384; marriage 352, 355–356, 358–359; migration 313, 315, 317, 320–321; mortality 193, 195, 211, 408; population ageing 439, 446–451; population density 275–276, 278, 281; refugees 343; sex selection 151, 153; urbanization 303, 479
vision loss 237
vital registration 21–22, 56, 57, 170
vitamin supplements 173
voluntarism in FP programmes 97–98
voluntary migration 331–332

war and civil unrest 404–406; *see also* conflict
water: as 'game-changer' 509; population distribution 275–276, 277–278, 281; scarcity 303–304; use and pollution 485–487
wealth 170, 177, 200, 403, 475–478
Western Asia: fertility decline 73, 78; population ageing 439–440; population distribution 269, 270–273
'Westphalian' states 507
Whelpton, Pascal 32
women: in labour force 73–74, 76, 406–407, 425, 427, 466; status of 76, 159, 403, 407, 451; *see also* gender
workers' savings (defined-contribution) schemes 447
World Fertility Survey 37
World Population Conference 32, 91–93, 99
WORLDPOP project 296

Yangtze River 275
years of healthy life lost due to ill-health and disability (YLD) 229, 236–237, 238
years of life lost for deaths (YLL) 229, 235–236, 238
Yellow River Plain 275
Yemen: fertility decline 78; child mortality 171; contraceptive prevalence 110; maternal mortality 134; refugees 339, 345; water 485
'youth bulges' 501–502
youth dependency ratio 461, 502–503

Taylor & Francis eBooks

Helping you to choose the right eBooks for your Library

Add Routledge titles to your library's digital collection today. Taylor and Francis ebooks contains over 50,000 titles in the Humanities, Social Sciences, Behavioural Sciences, Built Environment and Law.

Choose from a range of subject packages or create your own!

Benefits for you

- Free MARC records
- COUNTER-compliant usage statistics
- Flexible purchase and pricing options
- All titles DRM-free.

Benefits for your user

- Off-site, anytime access via Athens or referring URL
- Print or copy pages or chapters
- Full content search
- Bookmark, highlight and annotate text
- Access to thousands of pages of quality research at the click of a button.

REQUEST YOUR FREE INSTITUTIONAL TRIAL TODAY

Free Trials Available
We offer free trials to qualifying academic, corporate and government customers.

eCollections – Choose from over 30 subject eCollections, including:

Archaeology	Language Learning
Architecture	Law
Asian Studies	Literature
Business & Management	Media & Communication
Classical Studies	Middle East Studies
Construction	Music
Creative & Media Arts	Philosophy
Criminology & Criminal Justice	Planning
Economics	Politics
Education	Psychology & Mental Health
Energy	Religion
Engineering	Security
English Language & Linguistics	Social Work
Environment & Sustainability	Sociology
Geography	Sport
Health Studies	Theatre & Performance
History	Tourism, Hospitality & Events

For more information, pricing enquiries or to order a free trial, please contact your local sales team:
www.tandfebooks.com/page/sales

 Routledge Taylor & Francis Group | The home of Routledge books

www.tandfebooks.com